This is the first time that all three volumes of Michael Scott's Irish Folk and Fairy Tales have been collected into one edition. There are 42 stories of myth and legend, peopled by the heroic figures and mythical creatures which make Ireland's tradition of storytelling so fascinating and enduring.

IRISH FOLK
AND
FAIRY TALES
Omnibus Edition

Michael Scott

SPHERE BOOKS LIMITED

SPHERE BOOKS LTD

Published by the Penguin Group
27 Wrights Lane, London W8 5TZ, England
Viking Penguin Inc., 40 West 23rd Street, New York, New York 10010, USA
Penguin Books Australia Ltd, Ringwood, Victoria, Australia
Penguin Books Canada Ltd, 2801 John Street, Markham, Ontario, Canada L3R 1B4
Penguin Books (NZ) Ltd, 182–190 Wairau Road, Auckland 10, New Zealand

Penguin Books Ltd, Registered Offices: Harmondsworth, Middlesex, England

First published in Great Britain by Sphere Books Ltd in three volumes.
Volumes I and II 1983, Volume III 1984.
First published in this omnibus edition 1989.
1 3 5 7 9 10 8 6 4 2

Printed and bound in Great Britain by
Richard Clay Ltd, Bungay, Suffolk

VOLUME I

This book would not have been finished without the help of:

Claire and Harry for their patience, Johanna and Bill for their assistance, Patricia and Tommy for their time and co-operation, Jim White because he asked for it.

And,
Anna, without whom it would not have been finished, with love.

CONTENTS

CONTENTS

CHAPTER 1

THE SONS OF TUREEN
(The First Sorrow Of Irish Storytelling)

Brian loosed his sword in its sheath and called over his shoulder to his brothers. 'Rider coming!'

They edged their horses up beside their elder brother and stared across the flat expanse of the Plain of Muirthemne. A lone rider was racing towards them, his armour and weapons flashing in the early morning sunlight and his crimson cloak streaming behind.

'A Fomor?' wondered Urchar.

'Too tall,' replied his twin Iuchar, drawing his sword.

Brian reined his horse to a halt. 'We wait; let him come to us.'

The rider came closer, his tall white steed galloping effortlessly across the flat plain. He suddenly caught sight of the three mounted warriors and, pulling up short, stood in the saddle to stare across at the sons of Tureen.

Brian slipped a throwing spear from its sling alongside his boot, whilst his brothers drew their swords. In these troubled times, one was always wary of strangers; and even now the three brothers went to join the gathering of the De Danann lords at Tara for the coming war against the deamon Fomorians.

The war arrow had come three days previously. Lugh of the Long Arm - an arrogant trouble maker - had slain a score of the Fomorian tax gatherers; and Balor, the one-eyed king of the northern men, had declared war on Banba.

The three sons of Tureen had gathered their armour and honed their weapons before setting out for the High Court

1

to offer their services to Nuada, king of the Tuathe De Danann.

Already they had been attacked twice on their journey east; once by the great black wolves that men whispered were controlled by the wizards of Balor, and once by bandits. They had slain a score of the wolves and the corpses of the bandits littered the woods.

Suddenly Urchar and Iuchar cried aloud and pointed – the warrior had disappeared!

Brian gripped the spear until his knuckles whitened about the shaft and without a word rode towards the riderless horse. The ground dipped into a slight hollow and in the hollow a herd of swine rooted amongst the gorse and bracken.

'Where did he go?' wondered Iuchar.

'Disappeared,' said Urchar.

Brian pointed down into the hollow with his spear. 'He's there amongst the pigs – and a right fitting place for him. Did you not recognise him?' He turned to his brothers. They shook their heads.

Brian laughed grimly. 'Fine warriors you make; you would have to wait until your enemies were on top of you before you recognise them. That was Cian, father of Lugh.'

'Cian!'

'Aye, Cian, that foul-mouthed black-hearted bitch's cur. The dishonour he and his two brothers, Cu and Ceithne, brought on our sister, has not been resolved. But now we shall have our revenge.'

Iuchar hefted his sword and swung it whistling through the air. 'He had obviously recognised us and assumed the form of a pig.' He turned to his twin. 'Shall we go a-slaughtering, brother.'

Urchar bowed mockingly, his blue-black hair catching highlights from the morning sun. 'Yes, let's butcher a pig.'

'Wait!' Brian snapped.

They turned to their older brother. 'There is no need to slaughter good bacon in search of a lizard. Put up your weapons and I will work an enchantment.'

2

The twins obediently sheathed their swords whilst Brian slipped a short alder wand from his belt. Concentrating intently and calling upon the Dagda and Danu, he passed the wand over his brothers. Their forms seemed to liquify, and tremble as if seen through a heat haze ... and then in their place stood two of the great war hounds of Bamba. With yelps of joy the dogs ran down through the swine which rapidly dispersed in all directions squealing shrilly. But the hounds had one target; for under the enchantment the twins could easily recognise Cian in his true form. Deftly they cut the pig out from the main pack and drove him up the incline towards their waiting brother.

Brian crouched at the top of the hollow, his arm cocked, the throwing spear lying flush against his cheek. As the pig came over the top of the rise Brian threw. The spear caught the pig just below the throat, the force of the blow flipping the animal backwards into the pursuing hounds. Brian slid down the incline, the alder wand already in his hand, muttering a reversal of the shape-changing spell under his breath.

By the time he reached the bottom, his twin brothers had already resumed their human forms. Both had swords in their hands and were prepared to finish off the animal.

'After you,' said Iuchar.

'No, no, I insist, the honour is yours,' replied Urchar.

'He is mine,' said Brian joining them. 'I will avenge our sister's honour.' His sword rasped as it slid from its scabbard. Holding it in both hands he brought it above his head and prepared to cut the pig in twain ... when it spoke, 'No ... no ... you cannot ... cannot slay me ... thus. Upon your mercy ... let me regain the form ... of man so that ... I might die honourably.'

'Does he deserve an honourable death?' wondered Iuchar.

'He is without honour,' said Urchar. 'Slay him now like the animal he is.'

'You are ... men of ... honour. You cannot ... cannot slay me,' gasped Cian.

'Resume your true form,' said Brian wearily.

3

'Perhaps that is his true form,' whispered Iuchar to Urchar.

The pig suddenly grew indistinct, as if it was covered with a thick blanket of gauze ... and then the blanket fell away, revealing the true form of Cian. He was tall, nearly the same height as Brian, his sandy coloured hair now flecked with grey, and his strangely colourless eyes were lined and sunken. But the haughty arrogance that had earned Cian and his brothers their reputation about the Duns and Forts of Banba, the arrogance that he had passed on to his son, Lugh, was still stamped on his proud face. Ignoring the wound which trickled blood from his chest, he attempted to stare down the three sons of Tureen.

'You have made a grave mistake,' he informed them. 'My brothers and son will have your heads for this act.'

Brian struck him a blow which sent him sprawling. 'You presume a lot, my lord. You presume we are about to let you go free. You presume we fear you, your brothers and your son. You presume we are not men of honour. And you presume we will not avenge the dishonour you and your brothers brought upon our sister. But you presume wrongly, my lord. For you are not about to leave this place alive. We will take your death in part payment for that foul deed.'

Cian staggered to his feet.

'I am of the De Danann, steel cannot kill me.'

'My lord,' said Brian coldly, 'I would not stain my blade with your blood; I would rather have the blood of the Fomorians upon it than yours.' He stooped and plucked a stone from the soft earth. 'Let the earth that spawned you slay you.'

Brian threw the stone with all the force of his arm. It struck the De Danann lord high on the shoulder, numbing his arm. The next rock struck him across the head, dazing him. He raised his hand, either to ward off a blow or to beg for mercy, but the third stone struck him full between the eyes and he fell to the ground – dead.

'Thus is vengeance ours,' whispered Brian.

The sons of Tureen dug a shallow trench in the damp

4

ground and buried the body of Cian, covering it with large flat stones. As they stood over the grave, Iuchar said, almost to himself, 'No warrior should die like this.'

'A warrior must have honour,' reminded his twin.

'And Cian was a man without honour,' added Brian.

It was the evening of the third day after the battle. The remnants of Banba's host had returned, and were now gathering about Tara's halls where a great victory feast was in progress. In Maecadre, the main hall, the atmosphere was slightly more subdued, for the princes of the De Danann realised by how close a margin they had beaten the northern deamons; next time they might not be so lucky.

Lugh stood beside Nuada, king of the Tuatha de Danann.

'Our men celebrate victory,' he shouted above the raucous cries that drifted through the thick walls.

'As well they might; they have all felt the Morrigan's breath these last days.' He turned to Lugh, poking him gently in the ribs. 'You fought well. If you keep collecting heads at this rate, soon you'll have to build a separate room for them.'

Lugh spat. 'I do not collect the heads of deamons.'

Nuada gripped the young man by the shoulder. 'You are foolish to mock the Fomorians; they are brave warriors. Aye, their ways are not our ways, and we call them deamons for their swarthy looks and curious mannerisms, but they are many and the days of the De Danann are numbered. Even now our people dwindle, some have already retreated to the lonely places. Some day ... some day ...' he paused and shook his head. 'Enough of this. How fares Cian? I did not see him in battle.'

Lugh spun and faced the king. 'What do you mean, "*you did not see him in battle*?" Surely he fought beside you?'

Nuada shook his head. 'I thought he fought beside you and his brothers.'

Lugh abruptly brushed past the king and pushed his way through the crowded hall searching for Cu and Ceithne. A dark premonition which had haunted him since the eve of battle now returned, a premonition in which he saw the ground seep blood and the stones run red.

He found his uncles in one corner of the room recounting their exploits to a group of wide-eyed youths. Lugh called them aside.

'Have you seen my father? Did you see him during battle?'

'I thought he fought with you,' said Cu.

Ceithne shook his head. 'I have not seen him since he set out six days ago to raise the families of the west.'

'He seems to have disappeared. I fear for him,' said Lugh.

'Let us see if his horse is in the stables,' suggested Cu.

They made their way out of Maecadre, out into the long winding halls and down to the stables at the rear of the palace. The area was bustling with activity, some of the knights only now returning, slack-jawed and bulbous-eyed heads dangling from their saddles.

They searched through the stables, looking for Cian's snow-white steed. Cu grabbed a passing stable boy and questioned him, but he had seen neither the horse nor the lord.

'Something has happened to him,' said Lugh. 'I am going in search of my father.'

And as the moon rose over Tara's halls three riders galloped from the high gates and rode into the west.

They reached the Plain of Muirthemne the following evening. The day had turned cold and a chill ice-laden wind whipped across the flat plain. They had stopped at every Dun and Rath on the road and in every case the story was the same. Cian had passed that way, calling forth the families for the coming battle, but no-one had seen him return.

Lugh and his uncles camped that night in a slight hollow which at least afforded them some protection from the chill wind. Lugh's sleep was troubled. He seemed to hear his father calling on the wind and he was once again troubled with visions of the earth seeping blood. He tossed and turned the whole night unable to find sleep and he arose with the first light of dawn.

He climbed out of the hollow and stood staring into the east where the first crimson tinge of the sunrise was lightening the heavens. He lifted his hand to push back his yellow-gold hair and noticed his hand was stained with red also ... then he realised the wan sunlight had not yet reached him.

He looked closely at his hand in the grey light of dawn. It looked like ...

Blood!

Lugh turned and stared down into the hollow where he and his uncles had passed the night. The rich green earth was dark - stained with a thin covering of blood-red dew. Even as he watched it welled up from between the stones and ran in slow turgid trickles. The hollow was awash with blood - it resembled a battlefield or slaughterhouse.

He raised his bloody hands to his face and screamed aloud.

For he knew. He knew.

Scrambling down, he fell to his knees and began to pull up the stones from the soft earth with his hands, whilst his body shook with an icy fever. Cu and Ceithne awoke and stared in horror at Lugh, his clothes and hair matted with dried blood, tearing at the ground like a madman. And then they looked about at the blood-soaked landscape, the like of which they had never imagined.

They dragged Lugh to his feet, even though he struggled and raved, and kept shouting, 'He's here, he's here.'. Cu struck him unconscious, whilst Ceithne rode to the nearest Rath for help. He arrived back about mid-morning, a band of warriors trailing reluctantly behind. The morning sun had dried the blood and now it crusted the earth in a reeking film. In places the yellowed grass peeped through, giving the hollow the appearance of a gaping, infected wound.

The warriors began to remove the befouled earth, passing

it out of the hollow, digging slowly deeper.

Lugh meanwhile, had awoken and stared morosely at the ground, his eyes flat and expressionless. At last, stirring himself, he pointed to a spot to one side of the hollow.

'Dig there,' he commanded.

The warriors looked at Ceithne for orders. 'You heard. Dig there ... and on your lives take care.'

Shortly thereafter they unearthed the partly decomposed body of Cian.

Cu and Ceithne gently removed the body, whilst the warriors stood nervously about, keeping as far away as possible from the two older men and the wild-eyed youth. Wiping away as much of the grime as possible, they examined the corpse so that they might see how he had been killed. That he had been murdered was plain, for even the earth itself refused to hold the blood of the slain man. He had not been robbed, for his weapons, wand of power, armour and gold were still with him. There was a single wound high in his chest, such as might have been made by a thrown spear, and the bone in his shoulder was splintered and showed through the putrescent flesh. But the major wound - the one that had killed him - was upon his head. Something - possibly a stone - had struck him full between the eyes, crushing the front of his skull like an eggshell.

The brothers stared in horror at the wounds. It was almost inconceivable that a warrior, and a warrior such as Cian, should have been stoned to death, a punishment fitting only for dogs and slaves. Cu attempted to stop Lugh seeing the wounds, but he was pushed roughly aside and the young man went to kneel before the battered corpse of his father.

'Who has done this?' he whispered in anguish. 'Who has done this?' He suddenly screamed, his head thrown back. He fell forward across the mutilated body and sobbed like a child.

As his tears soaked the shattered face, the slack jaw suddenly moved. With a cry of horror, Lugh fell backwards whilst the assembled warriors fingered their weapons,

8

prepared to cut the animated corpse to pieces and burn it.

The jaw moved again, whilst the fingers of one hand convulsed in the earth. Again and again the jaw moved as if it sought to speak.

Lugh crept forward on hands and knees and whispered to the creature, 'Who did this?' He placed his ear close to the cracked and flaking lips. For a moment he could hear nothing and then the jaw moved again. A charnel reek, the stink of decay and offal emanated from the corpse and deep in its dessicated throat Lugh could hear the muted grating rumble of words.

'The ... sons ... of ... Tureen.'

The atmosphere in Maecadre, the Great Hall of Tara was tense and subdued. The kings and lords of Banba in their full armour and finery sat in silence listening to Lugh of the Long Arm finishing his tale of the discovery of his father's corpse. The only part left to tell was the identity of the killers.

'And your father,' Nuada paused, 'your father's corpse, it spoke to you?'

Lugh nodded. 'It is not uncommon for the shade of one foully murdered to linger on in an attempt to communicate the identity of his killers.'

'So you know who killed your father?' persisted Nuada. 'I do.'

'And that is ...?'

'I killed Cian!' said a voice from the back of the hall.

Lugh half rose from his seat of honour and pulled his sword from its sheath. 'Yes, yes, you did, Brian MacTureen, you and your bastard brothers,' he hissed.

Brian shook his head slowly. 'No, my brothers were not involved in the slaying, the actual blow was mine.'

Urchar and Iuchar pushed their way through the crowd and stood beside their brother. 'We are all guilty,' said Iuchar.

'And we freely admit our guilt,' added his twin.

9

'Although I do not think it a crime to slay animals,' said Iuchar into the silence.

With a cry of rage both Cu and Ceithne came to their feet, weapons in their hands, but Lugh only smiled coldly and sheathed his sword. 'Put up your weapons uncles, they do not deserve honourable slaying.'

Lugh rose and walked the length of the wall, 'You deserve death,' he said, 'but I think death is too good for you.'

A murmur of assent rumbled about the hall. And whilst many of the assembled lords had little liking for either Lugh or his kin, they were all in the main honourable men, and the code they lived by was unbreakable. The sons of Tureen had slain and therefore they must be slain or pay whatever fine Lugh might levy.

'We avenged our family honour,' said Brian simply.

'By stoning my father to death?' shouted Lugh.

'It was what he deserved.'

Lugh shook his head slowly. 'No, no, you will not rise me to anger.' He stood by his seat and stared into the shadows which lingered in the corners of the great hall. 'Killing you is too easy.' He gazed at them and added softly, 'Too easy. You are now bound by whatever honour you possess to pay the fine for my father's foul murder.'

Brian nodded. 'Never let it be said that the sons of Tureen were without honour,' he said looking at Cu and Ceithne.

'The fine is in eight parts and each part must be accomplished before your debt is paid in full.' He sat in the high-backed chair and looked closely at the three brothers. 'You understand; all the parts to be completed?'

They nodded.

'You will bring to me three apples, a pigskin, a spear, a chariot and two horses, seven live pigs, a whelp, a cooking spit, and you will complete your fine by shouting three times upon a hill.'

'A curious litany,' said Nuada.

'He places a high price upon his father,' said Iuchar.

'No more than he was worth,' said Urchar.

Brian quietened them with a glare. 'There is more to this I'll wager. Explain your fine.'

Lugh laughed grimly. 'Yes, there is a little more to it. But let me explain that I do not choose these items at random. We will need them in the coming battle against the Fomorians; you can take some pleasure in that, if you wish.

'The three apples,' said Lugh 'are from the Garden of the Hesperides in the Orient. You will recognise them by their colour, for they are warm-gold and the size of a helm. A bite from one of the apples will cure all wounds, however serious.' He looked across the silent table at Brian. 'And they are well guarded, you will not come by them easily.'

'The pigskin,' said Brian softly.

'The skin of the boar is held by Tuas, King of the Land of the Greeks; it has the power to cure all ills; even incurable diseases are not beyond its power.

'The spear,' continued Lugh, 'is from the land of the Persians. It is called the Destroyer. Pezaer, Lord of the Persians guards the spear.

'From Persia you shall go to the Kingdom of Sicily, where you shall find the two horses and chariot of King Doabre, which is capable of travelling on both land and sea.

'Then you shall sail west to the Pillars of the Sun, and capture the seven swine of King Aesal ... The swine are the beasts of the gods - they are immortal, like their masters. They are an inexhaustable supply of food. Even though three or four or five might be slain for the evening meal, there will be seven pigs in the morning. Their flesh is said to heal even the most grieviously wounded.

'The whelp you shall claim from the King of Irouad. It is destined to grow into a beast even the fabled lion will follow and an invincible warhound.' Lugh paused and added, 'Although these are part of the fine, yet are they also weapons to be used in the coming war. But the last part of the fine is payable only to me. You must bring me the cooking spit of the water maidens of Fioncure Island, which is said to lie between Bamba and Alba, but which has yet to be found.'

Iuchar opened his mouth to comment, but Brian gripped his elbow hard, causing his brother to bite his lip in pain.

'And the last part?'

'Ah yes, the last part. Assuming that you have survived thus far – and have found the cooking spit ...'

'And have not died of old age in the meantime,' murmured Urchar.

'You will then,' continued Lugh forcefully, 'make your way to the hill of Midcain in the land of the Fomorians. Midcain and his three sons, Conn, Corc and Aedh, guard that hill and they are under a geas to let no voice be raised in joy nor anger upon its slopes until the New God has come to our land.' He grinned maliciously. 'This then is your task.'

Brian, Iuchar and Urchar bowed and then turned and left the silent hall. Lugh turned to Nuada and grinned boldly. 'Is it a fitting fine my lord?'

The High King nodded solemnly. 'Your father would be proud of you.' He rose to leave and the entire assembly rose with him. 'But though the deed of the sons of Tureen was evil, I'll wager the bards will remember their tale and name more readily than they will remember yours.'

Brian, Iuchar and Urchar stood at the bow of the *Watersprite* watching the waves slip by with ever increasing swiftness.

'This craft chills me,' said Iuchar.

Urchar nodded silently, sharing his brother's discomfort. The *Watersprite* had been lent to them by Lugh, '*to aid then on their way*', he said, and to show that he held '*no ill feelings*'.

It was an elven craft, long and slim, high in the bow and stern, with a single sail set amidships. It was constructed entirely from the white-wood of the forests of Tir fo Thuinn, the Land Beneath the Waves. Its sail was woven of the hair of the Dagda, the Father of gods, and billowed in winds that blew not from this world. At the prow was a figurehead in the shape of a great gape-mouthed, long-fanged serpent, whose eyes burned with an unearthly fire. When one wished to set the craft in any direction, one merely whispered the destination to the figurehead and at once the craft would set forth, skimming the waves.

12

Lugh had come down to the shore as they set out. He had stood on the white sands and silently watched them loading the magical ship with the food and weapons necessary for their journey. Tureen himself had come with his daughter Ethne to see his sons set forth on their quest. Lugh had bowed mockingly to them.

'What honour this will bring to your family,' he remarked.

'What do you know of honour?' spat Ethne. Tureen laid a hand on his daughter's arm and quietened her.

'Say farewell to your brothers,' he commanded. When she had gone and stood by the water's edge, he turned to Lugh. 'Have you come to mock?'

'Mock; no, not I my lord. I have come to see your sons depart safely.'

'They will not shirk their responsibilities. Your fine - which will be remembered as the heaviest laid on mortal man - will be paid in full.'

Lugh nodded silently, and walked towards the shore.

'Why, here is our benefactor come to wave us farewell,' said Iuchar.

'His concern is touching,' added Urchar.

Brian nodded to the De Danann lord solemnly. 'We are grateful for the loan of this craft. Of course, had you not given it, we might not be able to return with your weapons and talismans in time for the coming battle, eh?'

'You understand the workings of the craft?' Lugh asked gruffly.

'We do,' said Brian. He turned and shouted towards the figurehead. 'The Garden of Hesperides in the Orient.' The figurehead's golden eyes blazed, and slowly, silently, the craft wheeled and made its way from the bay.

'It reeks,' said Iuchar, sniffing the rich dark perfume of the island in the distance.

'It is foul,' agreed Urchar, pulling a corner of his cloak across his face to cover his nose.

The *Watersprite* bobbed unmoving just in sight of the

13

shore. It had taken them barely three days to reach it and Brian estimated that they had come almost to the edge of the world. The sun no longer rose in its usual place and even the stars were gone, replaced by strange new configurations. The days here were longer also and the sun burned from a brilliant blue sky, the like of which was rarely seen in Banba. But the nights were as cold as home and sometimes before the dusk fell, great massed clouds would roll in swiftly and then it would rain with incredible ferocity, until it seemed as if the gods themselves wept.

Brian had ordered the craft to halt when it became evident that the shore ahead was its ultimate destination. All that now remained was to claim the three apples.

'We could, I suppose, just ask for them,' suggested Iuchar.

'We could, I suppose, just lose our heads just asking for them,' mocked Urchar.

'This is a barbarous land,' said Brian softly, leaning over the edge of the craft. 'Its manners and customs differ greatly from our own and whilst I have some knowledge of the lands that border and lie to the east and south of Banba, I know very little about this land. Therefore,' he said, taking his short alder wand from his belt, 'we will take refuge in enchantment. We will assume the shapes of hawks and circle over the gardens and spy out the defences. Maybe it will be possible to snatch the apples.'

He shrugged and raising his hand high above his head began to work the enchantment. But the spell seemed to take longer than usual to work. Perhaps, thought Brian, the power of the Dagda and Danu is not so strong in these foreign waters where none worship them. Do the gods live by the faith of men? he wondered.

Slowly, and with a gritty uneasiness, they assumed the shapes of hawks; huge golden winged, razor taloned birds, who took to the air with slow ponderous, powerful beats of their great wings, and headed north towards the lush green land, and the Garden of the Hesperides.

Once they passed beyond the golden sands of the shoreline they were over the rank and impenetrable forests of the interior. They flew over the almost obliterated ruins of cities that had been great before the first invaders had come to Banba.

Huge rivers wound their way through thick forests, rivers which made the Sinann, the longest river in Banba, seem little more than a stream. Away to the north and west loomed great purple mountains, snow-capped even at this late season, and in the east a single great cone belched smoke and fire as if some angry deamons laboured therein. Tiny villages disappeared below, their houses constructed of yellowed grasses, not like the wood and sod dwellings of home. And everywhere there were roads.

In Banba, Nuada was constructing the first of the many roads that would link the country to Tara, but there the roads were rough affairs, indeed little more than tracks, whilst here, huge highways glittering white in the sunlight cut across even the most distant parts of the country. Broad roads also, wide enough to allow two or more of the curious chariots of these people to pass abreast.

The sons of Tureen swooped down towards the largest city they could see, a great sprawling affair that dwarfed Tara. It was surrounded by a large wall of black stone, and its gates were heavily guarded. The buildings were all constructed of pale white stone and some of the domes of the larger buildings were sheathed in gold or a thick black stone, that glittered with shimmering rainbow hues in the sunlight.

As the three hawks flew low over the broad streets, the colourfully clad inhabitants stopped and stared for great birds were not often seen in this part of the world. Guards posted about the city walls noted the growing disturbance and one set out to bring word to the Emperor.

Meanwhile, the sons of Tureen had found the Garden of the Hesperides. It was almost in the centre of the city, attached to a great building of green stone, set with many precious and semi-precious stones. The Garden was surrounded by a barbed-topped wall and guards in laquered armour with hooked pikes patrolled outside the walls. In the

15

centre of the Garden was a single tree. All other vegetation had been cleared away from it and it stood alone on a little knoll. It was tall and thin, its wood a rich dark shade of ochre and its leaves a shimmering emerald.

And growing on the tree were three huge golden apples.

About the base of the tree lolled seven guards, huge men in green-laquered armour, carrying swords and spears. Thick recumbent bows lay on the ground beside full quivers. The guards were engaged in a game which they played on two small chequered boards, moving the tiny ornate pieces from one board to the other.

Without warning the brothers swooped. One of the guards glanced up; his cry brought the others to their feet, their weapons in their hands. A thrown spear hissed by Iuchar, causing him to swerve suddenly in flight, nearly tumbling him from the skies. Two arrows flashed by in quick succession, and the guard was notching a third, when a huge hawk almost tore the top off his head. Iuchar and Urchar followed their brother in the attack – clearly they would not get the apples unless they slew the guards first. One of the guards turned, but not to flee, for attached to a low wall beside the appletree was a short, squat bell. Beside the bell lay an ornamental hammer. The guard had almost reached the hammer, his outstretched fingers brushing its surface, when he was struck a powerful blow on the back of his head. The force of the blow propelled him into the hard unyielding wall with a sodden crunch.

An arrow parted the feathers of Brian's left wing. Abruptly he folded his wings and fell, talons outstretched onto the upraised face of the crouching archer.

Of the three remaining guards, two had decided that they had had enough and turned to flee through the gardens. They had barely gone a hundred paces when Iuchar and Urchar struck like levin bolts, snapping the neck of one with a rotten crack and driving a razor beak into the base of the other's spine.

The remaining guard stood at the foot of the tree. A notched bow was in his hands and driven into the soft earth at his feet were two long lances. He watched the two great bloody hawks lifting from the bodies of his felled companions. These were no ordinary birds. They were twice the size and more of any hawks he had ever seen and the uncanny precision and co-operation they had shown during the attack hinted at only one thing: Sorcery.

And then he paused. Surely there had been three of the large birds? But now there were only two of them before him. Had the third been slain during the brief encounter?

He never even saw the great bird that crashed into his face, driving him backwards into the tree.

Brian, Iuchar and Urchar carefully plucked the apples from the tree and set off for the distant shore, their great wings beating slowly with the unaccustomed weight, and the exertion of battle.

The Emperor regarded the cowering guard through slit eyes. 'Stolen?' His voice rose to a scream. 'Stolen? And you dare to stand before me and tell me that one of the Treasures of my Empire had been lost and you have not died in its defence?'

'Majesty, it was sorcery,' whispered the guard.

'Sorcery,' the Emperor's voice dropped to a hiss.

'These were no ordinary birds sire. They were greater in size and their cunning was preternatural ...' the guard trailed off. The Emperor's eyes had unfocused and he stared intently into the vastness of the presence chamber.

Abruptly the huge crystal doors opened and three slim figures entered and glided to the Dragon Throne.

'Yes father,' they whispered as one.

'Shape-changers have stolen the Apples. They were last seen heading towards the coast; I want them stopped.'

The Emperor's daughters bowed silently and turned and glided from the chamber. As they reached the crystal doors, their forms seemed to shiver and tremble on the scented air. And before the great doors closed the shaking guard could have sworn that three large ospreys had taken flight where the three young maidens had stood.

The brothers rested in the topmost branches of a tree that

would have dwarfed the great world-tree of the northern folk. It rose up for many lengths, bare of both branches and leaves. Its crown, however, spread out in a flat expanse of green. The broad upper branches supported whole colonies of birds and even a small family of tiny men-like creatures covered with fine fur. Several times these creatures had attempted to steal the Apples, but Brian had struck one with his huge pinion, sending the animal tumbling and screaming to the ground far below.

Brian stood and stretched his wings, opening them to the golden ball of the sun. Suddenly he stiffened. Three tiny specks were angling out of the sun. He squinted into the harsh light; these birds moved with unusual determination ...

His cry brought his brothers to their feet. 'Ospreys. Changelings!' He gripped the large Apple in his claws and set off for the shore as quickly as his heavy burden would allow.

The ospreys had recognised their target. Their flat yellow eyes narrowed, and their metallic claws flexed.

It was a race for the shore and the *Watersprite*. The brothers pushed on, but they were exhausted with the weight of the Apples and the battle, whilst the ospreys were fresh and unencumbered. Gradually, length by length, the ospreys gained on the hawks.

As they reached the shore, Brian dropped from the skies, falling downwards in a slow spiral. The larger of the three ospreys broke formation and followed him down, claws outstretched to rend and tear. Abruptly, Brian folded his wings and plummetted, and the osprey, already angling for the kill, overshot, and was now in front and a little above him. The hawk's great wings opened and beat air, once, twice, thrice, and lifted. Its razor bak flashed golden in the sunlight and came away crimson and the osprey crashed to the beach in an untidy tumble of wings. As it struck the golden sands, its shape dissolved and the shattered body of a delicately pretty maid lay broken upon the shore.

The remaining two ospreys had almost caught the hawks,

unaware of their sister's demise. With claws wide they prepared to strike, but suddenly they were buffeted from behind by a powerful pair of wings. Dazed and unco-ordinated they tumbled about whilst getting their bearings ... but in that time, Iuchar and Urchar were upon them and two bloody carcasses fell to the sands below. They too, like their sister, resumed their original shape.

The three brothers hung motionless above the slain maidens on the beach.

'We have paid a high price for these Apples,' said Iuchar sadly.

'Will all the talismans be as expensive?' asked his twin.

'Let us hope not,' whispered Brian softly. 'Let us hope not.'

A day and a half later, the *Watersprite* rested in the sparkling waters of the Aegean, the purple and gold cliffs of Greece shimmering in the early afternoon sunlight.

Brian stood at the bow of the ship staring out across the waters; his brothers joined him.

'We will try a different ploy this time,' he said, 'and perhaps we can avoid bloodshed.'

Iuchar shook his head. 'This quest was founded in blood ...'

'... And in blood it will end,' finished his brother.

'Well then, let us make sure that it is not ours,' finished Brian. He turned to the figurehead. 'Take us into the shore.'

The sons of Tureen took the guise of poets and bards and made their way to the court of Tuas, King of the Greeks. And there they were made welcome, for Tuas was a man of learning and delighted in the tales and sagas of distant lands.

The three brothers waited their turn in the outer chambers whilst the bards and minstrels, poets and harpers of many lands and many colours made their way through the court, each one entertaining the king for one night with their tales of music, poetry or song. If the king found their work acceptable, they were richly rewarded, but even if it did not, he often spent time with the artist correcting errors in his work, a note here, a rhyme there, until both Tuas and the artist were well satisfied.

At last came the brothers' turn. They made their way through the crowded corridors and into the great open inner court. Ambassadors of many lands were there; tall ebon men with flashing eyes and teeth; dwarfed swarthy men, with dull eyes and lowering brows, very much like the Fomorians, blond-haired and blue-eyed giants conversed with hawk-faced, hook-nosed lords whose shining hair and beards lay curled upon their fantastically embroidered robes.

As the brothers made their way through the crowded court, the conversations, held in a score of languages and signs, died as the three proud-featured men passed. The brothers had not the appearance of either bards or poets. Standing as tall or indeed taller than most of the assembly, the bulging muscles of their uncovered arms and legs proclaimed them warriors; their gait - swift and sure, yet almost silent - told of their confidence and their gaze proclaimed them lords.

Tuas leaned across and spoke to his chamberlain. 'These are not poets; where do they hail from, and what are their names?'

'They say they are the sons of Tureen, a lord of the Tuatha De Danann, in the land of Banba, which is the furthest island of this continent. In that country sire, all the poets and lords are warriors. It is a rough and violent land and many of their lays are dirges and their sagas dark and gloomy, full of death and destruction and over it all hangs the dark harpie-like shadow of the Morrigan, the goddess of Death.'

Tuas nodded. 'It will be interesting to see what they bring with them, these warrior-bards of a barbarous land.'

The brothers bowed to the King of Greece, and Brian stepped forward.

'My lord, we have come from the furthest part of this

20

continent, drawn by the reputation of both you and your court. The reputation of Tuas, Scholar-King of Greece has spread even to Banba's misty shores.'

Tuas inclined his head, secretly pleased that his reputation as a scholar had spread so far. 'You bring some examples of your work with you?' he asked.

Brian nodded and began one of the High Sagas of the Tuatha De Danann, which told of an episode in the history of the People of the Goddess and the ancient Fir Bolg. His voice rang out strong and clear in the silent hall and though there were many there that did not understand his tongue, they could appreciate the mastery with which Brian recounted the tale.

Iuchar and Urchar followed him, recounting the tale of the sons of Fearchar who loved the maiden Nerba and who fought and killed each other for her. And though their voices were almost matched, still that slight difference between them, as they sang both parts, made the ancient saga come alive.

And then the three sons of Tureen sang a marching song of the Formorians and sang it with such gusto that some of the assembly joined in the chant.

The sun, which had been at the king's back, had moved across the skies whilst they sang and declaimed and now hung low in the heavens bathing the king in warm amber light. Slowly it sank and the hall drifted into shadow. The sconces were lit, illuminating the corners with wavering light and the pungent odour of herbs.

As the last notes of the march faded into the creeping night, Tuas raised his head. 'Are all the bards and poets of your isle as good as you?' he asked.

'Why lord,' laughed Brian, his voice still strong and clear even after a day's chanting and singing, 'in our land we are accounted poor bards, and our voices lack the clarity and strength of the professional poets.'

Tuas shook his head, his grey-shot hair glittering in the torchlight. 'But you must be rewarded.' He turned to his chamberlain. 'Let three skinfuls of gold be measured and given to the sons of Tureen.' He turned back. 'Go, claim your reward.'

As they left, the assembly stamped their feet, acclaiming their performance. The brothers followed the chamberlain, a tall grey warrior with the scars of many battles upon his arms and face, down a long and straight corridor behind the throne.

At intervals they passed guards, their tall plumed helmets brushing the ceiling, their short swords and tall, broad-bladed spears naked in their hands. At the end of the corridor behind a huge iron-studded door lay the treasury of Tuas. The chamberlain led them through room after room piled high with treasures from all parts of the known world: gold, silver, orchilurum, copper, bronze, iron and a dark blue nameless metal lay piled haphazardly. Gemstones, dia-monds, rubies, sapphires, topaz and a dark green stone which reminded Brian of the fields of Bamba were strewn about the floors. And on the walls were swords and shields, spears and knives, helms and greaves, which the chamber-lain told them contained various magical powers. Shim-mering tapestries hung on the dark walls, the colours shifting and changing in the light of the torches. In the last room was a massive set of scales and pegged to the wall the stretched skin of a pig. The head of the animal had been mounted upon the opposite wall. Its tusks were almost as long as Brian's forearm and as thick as his wrists. The skin was bigger than that of the largest horse.

The chamberlain pointed to the skin. 'Perseus, who slew the gorgon, is said to have slain that beast.'

'By Danu and the Dagda,' exclaimed Iuchar, 'I have never seen anything like it.' He paused and added, 'But it bears a faint resemblance ...'

'To the clan of Cian, Cu and Ceithne,' finished Urchar.

The chamberlain removed the skin from the wall and ordered one of the two guards to fill it with gold. Brian ran his calloused hand down the length of the skin admiring its flawless beauty. Abruptly he grabbed it, pulling it from the guard's grasp. The chamberlain shouted and reached for his sword, but his cry ended abruptly as Iuchar struck him across the head with the flat of his sword.

But the alarm had been raised and the corridor echoed to the pounding of booted feet.

Iuchar and Urchar stood in the door whilst their brother engaged the two guards already in the room. They were taller than Brian, but encumbered by their breastplates and helms, whilst he was clad only in a short-sleeved jerkin and woollen leggings. However, he was also unarmoured. Behind him, metal rang on metal as his brothers engaged more guards.

He tripped the first warrior as he lumbered by, sending him sprawling across the massive scales. The second guard lunged and the point of his blade opened a shallow wound along Brian's forearm.

Brian sidestepped – and then he stumbled on some of the gold that littered the floor. With a roar of satisfaction the Greek held his sword high and prepared to bring it down in a decapitating stroke.

And then he stiffened as Urchar's sword struck him across the base of his neck.

Iuchar and Urchar were bleeding from a score or more of shallow wounds and cuts and Urchar sported a dark, angry bruise on his chin, where the shaft of a thrown spear had struck him. The Greeks had withdrawn to the end of the corridor and seemed to be regrouping.

'I don't like to say this brother,' said Iuchar.

'But we're trapped,' finished his twin.

There was only one way out of the gold room and that was along the corridor, a corridor that was now filled with most of the palace guards. Abruptly the massed warriors at the end of the hall parted and a figure, tiny in comparison with the rest, appeared. It was Tuas the king.

'There is no escape,' he called. 'Come forth now, and at least you will die like warriors and not like trapped animals.'

'He has a point,' murmured Urchar.

'So what do we do brother?' asker Iuchar.

Brian finished folding the pigskin and then tied it about

23

his waist, leaving his hands free. 'You must follow my lead,' he said. 'Sheath your swords so the Greeks can see them. And you Iuchar, fetch me the chamberlain's sword whilst you each take one of the guards' swords. Now hold them flat against the back of your leg . . . and try not to stab yourselves in the shin when you walk,' he added with a grin.

The sons of Tureen walked down the long corridor to join the king and his warriors, their swords visible and in their sheaths, but hidden along the back of their legs were the weapons of the slain guards.

Tuas shook his head as they neared. 'It pains me to order such fine poets and bards slain; but why, why did you attack my chamberlain and guards. Was it gold? You only had to ask and it was yours. Why?'

'It was the pigskin, my lord and we did not think you would grant us that.'

Tuas shook his head. 'It has always bred sorrow. For a magical healing treasure, it has always brought bloodshed with it.' He sighed, and continued, 'But you have broken my laws and thus you must die, but at least you will die by the hand of a king.' He held out his long slim hand – a poet's hand, a dreamer's hand – and a warrior placed his sword in it. 'Come forward.'

Brian bowed and stepped closer to the king. In one fluid movement he brought his sword up and impaled the king upon the point.

For a moment confusion reigned, but that was all the time the sons of Tureen needed. Striking forth left and right they cut a bloody swath through the massed warriors until they reached the throne room. Many of the ambassadors were still present, puzzled at the sounds of battle that echoed from behind the throne, when suddenly three wild-eyed and bloody warriors appeared and fled through the halls like daemons of the pit. Even hardened warriors shrank back from them – for they had the stink of death about them.

The brothers raced down empty corridors, followed by the slow booming of a great bell. The walls were deserted and the gates unguarded; they fled through the dark streets, still hot after the day's sun, but every living soul ran from them, terrified at their appearance. By the time they reached the harbour, the word had spread and the brothers found the wharfs empty save for the huge rats.

Iuchar ordered the craft to put to sea, whilst Brian covered Urchar with the pigskin. The skin glowed with a soft bronze-gold light and Urchar felt a million ants walking over his skin. But it healed his wounds, leaving the flesh unscarred and unmarked. Brian treated Iuchar, and then allowed his brothers to lay the skin over him. He felt it drawing away his fatigue, wiping the wounds clean from his flesh.

But the pigskin could not remove the wounds of his mind and it could never wipe clean the shocked accusation that had burned in Tuas' eyes as Brian killed him; a look of betrayal. It was a look he would never forget.

'It's flat,' said Iuchar, picking up a handful of sand and letting the golden grains trickle through his fingers.

'It's Persia,' said Urchar, 'what do you expect?'

The three brothers tramped up the smooth beach, the fine sand billowing in their wake. It had taken the *Watersprite* two days to reach this lonely bay on the deserted shores of Persia. Two days in which the sea had foamed white before their ship's bow as it sliced through the waves with ever increasing speed; two days in which they had been forced to cling to the mast lest they be swept overboard by the stiffening winds.

'I'm hot,' said Iuchar petulantly.

'And thirsty,' added his twin.

'By Babd and Morrigan!' Brian exploded, 'Will you two shut up.' He swore as he sank into a soft patch of sand.

Iuchar looked at his brother and nodded silently. Brian had been withdrawn and moody since they had stolen the pigskin from Tuas and he seemed to have assumed the burden for the king's death.

The three brothers clambered up the first of the rolling

dunes and stood, staring out over the gently undulating landscape. In the distance a range of low purple mountains shimmered behind a haze, making them seem unreal and artificial. A tiny thread of road, bone-white in the harsh sunlight cut across the dunes towards the speck of a city that nestled amidst a sudden explosion of greenery.

Brian wiped the back of his hand across his forehead and squinted into the impossibly blue sky; there was not a cloud in sight - he wondered if it ever rained in this land. He pointed towards the distant city.

'Our destination.'

The sons of Tureen estimated it would take them three days hard marching to reach the city; six days later they still hadn't reached it. Distances were deceptive and although in the mornings the city walls seemed but a day's journey away; by evening they had always dwindled and seemed as distant as ever. What little food and water they had ran out after three days, but they were warriors and used to marching on little or no rations. And they reckoned they would soon reach the city.

They were wrong.

The heat baked them dry and the sun boiled them. The breeze blowing in from the desert was straight from the pit. Their flesh blistered, their tongues swelled and their lips cracked and by the seventh day, they were close to death. They knew they would not survive another night in the open without food or shelter.

But they were the sons of Tureen, princes of the Tuatha De Danann and warriors of Banba; they would struggle on - to the end.

They spent that last night huddled together in the lee of a dune, shivering in the chill desert air.

And had Brian tears to weep, he would have shed them.

Brian groaned and tried to move his arm. He had lain on it through the night, and it was numb. He winced with the agony of returning circulation. He eased his back from the hard-packed sand - sand that had been so soft and comfortable the night before, but which had now assumed

26

the consistency of rock. He lay there, surprised that he had lived through the night, dreading to open his eyes and look into the merciless sun which the Persians worshipped as a god. And then he suddenly realised there was no sun on his face, although he was facing into the east. Cautiously, he attempted to ease open his tired eyes, but they betrayed him and he blinked. His sudden shout brought both his brothers awake, their weapons in their hands, and their backs to the sand dune.

Before them were a score of mounted warriors.

The two groups faced each other silently. The warriors were clad in loose white robes, although armour glinted underneath, and were mounted upon tall, fine-boned white steeds. Conical metal helmets covered their skulls and a flap of cloth was drawn across the lower halves of their faces. They carried long barbed spears, and short curved swords were thrust into their belts alongside flame-edged daggers.

The sons of Tureen were exhausted and clad in rags and the flesh of their hands was so cracked and blistered that they could barely hold their swords.

One of the riders walked his horse forward until he was almost touching Brian. 'You will ride with us,' he hissed in a flat monotone.

The palace of the Persian king was impressive - far more impressive than the rather simple beauty of the Greek theatre, or the rough stone forts of Banba. Deeply incised reliefs decorated the smooth stone walls, depicting the gods and heroes of the Persian pantheon. Beautifully worked carpets covered the polished floors and woven wall hangings of brilliant and metallic decorated the walls.

The brothers were housed in a suite of rooms overlooking a small enclosed garden. Tiny fountains sprayed perfumed water high into the air where it shimmered in miniature rainbows and the air was heavy with the scents of a thousand colourful blossoms.

27

Once again, they had presented themselves as wandering poets drawn to the Persian court by rumours of the great generosity of the king and his reputation as a patron of the arts.

And now, several days since their rescue from the desert, bathed, well-fed and clad in comfortable robes, they awaited an audience with the king.

Iuchar sat on the balcony, putting an edge on his sword with a whetstone, watching the movement in the courtyard below. The Persians had been reluctant to allow them to keep their weapons, but Brian had pointed out that a man could not truly call himself a warrior unless he was armed and he also hinted that the sword was a powerful religious symbol in their own land.

'There are guards below,' said Iuchar.

Brian nodded. 'They have been gathering since dawn; I think the king must be coming.'

'Or else they are coming for us,' added Urchar. 'Do you think they suspect?' he asked Brian.

'They may. If their court magicians are any good – and I'm told they can work wonders with fire, and that the stars are an open book to them – and if the magicians of the Orient have warned their brethren of the theft of the Apples, or those of Greece of the death of Tuas and the loss of the pigskin, then it is entirely possible that they know.'

'So we might be walking into a trap?'

'We might,' agreed Brian.

'Well, I think it's too late now,' said Iuchar. 'A squad of the palace guard have just mounted the stairs on their way up here.' He stood and slid his sword into its sheath, checked his dagger and slipped them both under his robe.

The door opened and a warrior with the sunwheel crest on his breastplate entered. 'You will accompany me; I am to lead you to his majesty,' he said. And then he added with just the slightest sneer, 'He wishes you to recite for him.'

They were led down into the gardens and through an ornate gate into the private garden of Pezaer, King of the Persians. He was seated on a huge crystal throne before a

28

gilded fountain and surrounded on either side by his concubines and guards.

Brian bowed to the king. 'Sire, we are honoured.'

Pezaer, a huge corpulent man, with signs of dissipation upon his broad fleshy face, looked bored and barely inclined his head. 'You are poets: recite.'

Brian glanced at his brothers, warning them to say nothing and stay alert. Something was wrong. He breathed deeply and began a long epic about the early days of Banba, in the time before man.

The king ignored Brian and continued to whisper with a young boy sitting at his feet. The painted youth giggled and simpered through Brian's performance and watched the De Danann prince through indolent eyes.

'Stop!' Pezaer suddenly screamed. 'Stop this farce. Take them!' He stood and waved at his guards. 'I know what you have come for,' he snarled at Brian, spittle foaming at the corners of his mouth. 'Look!'

A guard handed the king a spear. It was almost as tall as the monarch, with a staff of dull green metal. The head was broad and flat with a hollow point.

Brian slipped his sword from beneath his robe and heard his brother's weapons slide free. The king jabbed at Brian, who blocked the thrust with his sword. But when the head of the spear touched Brian's sword, it exploded in a shower of metal droplets. The head of the spear glowed white-hot and hissed and spat like an angry cat. Brian backed away from the king nursing a numbed arm and shoulder and brushed stinging flecks of metal from his cheeks and forehead.

Pezaer lunged again and the point of the spear, hissing like a serpent, passed over Brian's head, crisping his hair.

The sons of Tureen backed away from the king and his guards. But the latter seemed to be hanging back, letting the king make the kill. Brian looked into the monarch's fevered eyes and drawn lips and he knew the reason why: here was a man who delighted in inflicting pain and killing.

Brian ducked another wild blow and, with a trembling

29

hand, pulled off his cloak and held it loosely in one hand.

Iuchar and Urchar stopped suddenly. Warriors had come in through the small garden gate and were now behind them; they were surrounded.

'You are trapped, barbarians - and you will feed the firespear, the Weapon of Mithra.' Pezaer touched the point of the spear against the branch of an ornamental tree. The spear crackled and the branch abruptly blazed into light grey ash. 'There is no escape.'

The king spun the spear about his head, until the point glowed white-hot and hissed angrily. The very air about the monarch tingled and crackled with suppressed power and the taste was metallic in Brian's mouth. Abruptly, the king lunged. Brian fell to one side, bringing the cloak up and wrapping it about the spearhead. The thick cloth burst into flames which shot upwards and into the king's face. Pezaer screamed as his oiled beard caught fire and enveloped his head in a ball of fire. Dropping the spear, he clawed at his face, his screams of agony rending the peace of the garden.

Brian dived for the spear, catching it well down its length, away from the head which had already crisped and seared the hard earth. A guard pushed the king aside and stabbed at the Banban warrior with his sword. With a desperate effort, Brian threw himself to one side, the edge of the sword scraping down his arm and brought the spear up, impaling the guard in an explosion of bubbling metal and seared flesh.

Iuchar and Urchar attacked the guards, hacking a bloody path through to the gate. The Persians fell back, confused and demoralised at the death of their king and the loss of the Spear of Mithra.

Brian swung the weapon back and forth, weaving an intricate pattern of flaming death. Whatever the spear touched, metal, stone or flesh, it immediately burst into flames or ran in slow bubbling streams.

The sons of Tureen ran down the long leafy walks, leaving a trail of destruction in their wake. Trees and shrubs lay in charred ruins and crisped cinders. They cut down the guards and entered the palace, making their way down the corridors towards the stables. Behind them, doors of beaten gold and worked bronze were rendered into bubbling pits of metal; antique wall-hangings crisped and fell in wreaths of oily smoke and even the very stones glowed red and then white hot with the touch of the spear.

Once they reached the stables utter confusion reigned. Pages ran to and fro trying unsuccessfully to quieten the horses maddened by the stench of burning and the heavy smoke. Iuchar pulled three horses from their stalls and slipped their ornate harnesses over them whilst Brian and Urchar kept watch. They mounted the skittish beasts and trotted through the stables towards the main gate.

As they neared they could see the flurry of activity around the winches that opened and closed the huge gates. As one the brothers dug in their heels and galloped towards the rapidly closing exit. They had barely a few lengths to go before the guards spotted the three madly charging barbarians on the snow-white mounts of the king. One screamed a warning and attempted to pull Iuchar from his saddle as he galloped past. But Brian touched him with the spear, engulfing him in a ball of flame.

Iuchar and Urchar came off their horses at one moment and attempted to pull back the great brass-shod bar that had been rammed home across the closed gates.

'We'll never do it,' Iuchar panted, leaning his full weight against the bar.

'Back off,' ordered Brian, and rammed the Spear of Mithra against the bar. The wood exploded into a hail of firey cinders and the metal bubbled and spat. But the fire was almost immediately extinguished and although the bar was broken through, the door was only badly burned. Brian slid off his mount, tossed the reins to his brothers and ordered them to keep the massing Persians at bay. Then, standing firmly before the huge door, and shielding his eyes as best he could, he rammed the spear again and again against the solid wood.

The weapon hummed and hissed like a living creature

31

with a soul that exulted in destruction. The hardwood - imported from the east - burned with a thunderous roar, sending billows of thick smoke up into the hard metallic sky. Flakes of ash clung to Brian's face and settled on the smouldering remnants of his clothing.

Brian fell back as the heat became unbearable, spitting ash and blood. He dragged himself up onto his mount and called to his brothers, warning them to be ready.

Fire had almost completely enveloped the hardwood gates, climbing crazily from the blackened pit near the centre where Brian had struck it with the spear. The fire swiftly consumed the wood around the massive hinges until even they ran molten down the ruined gates. With a ponderous roar, the great gates collapsed down in a hail of smoke and fire - until it lay, the height of a tall man, across the opening.

'Go!' Brian screamed and kicked his heels in. The crazed beast lunged towards the flaming obstruction, until it seemed as if it were about to crash directly into it. But at the last possible moment, Brian urged it up - up and over. With a powerful surge the animal took flight over the barrier and out into the hot sands. Brian glanced back in time to see his brothers come sailing through the fire and smoke on their wild-eyed steeds.

The sons of Tureen paused as they crested the first of the dunes. A thick pall of smoke hung over the city and they could see countless tongues of fire licking high into the skies.

'It seems death is our gift to the peoples of the world,' whispered Urchar.

'Death and destruction,' agreed his brother.

Brian held the quiescent spear up to the light. 'Are we evil?' he asked, 'Or is it the artifacts we use?' He shrugged and, without waiting for an answer, turned his mount and headed for the shore, and the *Watersprite*.

The grizzled legionnaire eyed the three men standing

before him appreciatively. 'Ah, now here is something a lot better.' He knew professional soldiers when he saw them, having been one himself for almost twenty years before settling down and taking a commission in the army of King Doabre.

'Come to sign up, eh? Well, we can always use good men – all we are getting now are beardless boys and farmers and none of them can hold a sword.' He spat with feeling. 'Mercenaries!' He spat again and sighed. 'Just give your names and countries of origin. Although,' he added with a laugh, 'I doubt if either will be real.'

Brian stepped forward and leaned over the low table until he was face to face with the legionaire. 'We are the sons of Tureen. Brian,' he tapped his chest, 'Iuchar and Urchar,' he indicated each in turn. 'And though we may choose to hire our swords, we are not so free with our honour. Our names are real, as is our homeland. We are men of Banba.'

The legionnaire swallowed hard and nodded at the open-mouthed scribe to record the names and country. 'I cannot promise you much; food and drink and sometimes a dry place to sleep. But I can certainly promise you plenty of fighting. Doabre, the king, wishes to extend his borders – which is going to be difficult considering we're on an island, but before he tries that, he has to secure his own land, especially the mountains which hide bands of rebels. He must hold all Sigar before he looks across the seas.' He shrugged, and then stood and pointed down into the hollow where the camp sprawled. 'There is food down there if you want it, but no strong drink – we fight tomorrow. Get some rest if you can, you're going to need it.'

The sons of Tureen stayed with the mismatched mercenary army of Doabre of Sigar whilst the moon waxed and waned twice. The campaigns in the hills were bloody and sickening, little more than the massacre of unarmed peasants. There was one pitched battle in the foothills in which the sons of Tureen acquitted themselves with honour and held a bridge whilst the army retreated.

And because of that action, their courage in battle and

their proficiency with weapons, they rose through the ranks and quickly became part of Doabre's personal bodyguard.

As the second month drew to a close, Brian drew his brothers aside and suggested that if they discovered nothing about the horses or chariot in the next few days, then they might consider kidnapping the king and 'persuading' him to reveal their location.

Neither the horses nor chariot were kept in the camp, for they had searched it thoroughly, nor was there any mention of the talisman in the king's letters or books.

However, on the last day of the month, Doabre's spies finally succeeded in locating the rebel stronghold. They were camped on a small island off the southern coast of Sigar. The island, which had formerly housed a strange religious order of which nothing now remained save a massive ruin, was connected to the coast by a thin strip of land which was uncovered only at low tide. And even then the way was treacherous with shifting sands and patches that might swallow a man instantly.

For ten days, Doabre laid siege to the island, sending out squad after squad at low tide in an attempt to take the island fortress. But all the attacks failed and none of the mercenaries returned alive. The boats that were sent out were equally unsuccessful, for the currents were fast and unpredictable about the island and the craft were dashed to pieces on the rocks.

In desperation Doabre called his commanders together after the failure of his last attack in which he had lost almost a third of his remaining army. The mercenaries were sullen and dispirited, angry at the king's waste of good men. Some advised starving the rebels out, but Doabre was too impatient for that and, moreover, the island was capable of supporting a small community. A massed sea and land assault was suggested – but it seemed unlikely it would meet with much success. The only other alternative was to wait for the low spring tide – but that was almost half a year away.

'Can no-one here tell me what to do?' Doabre screamed,

his corpulent body quivering with rage, tears of frustration standing in his eyes.

'What we need,' said Brian lightly, yet watching the king all the time, 'is someone who can walk on water.'

The mercenaries laughed – until they saw the king's face. It was the face of a delighted child. 'Of course, of course,' he shouted. 'The chariot; yes we can do it.'

'I don't understand,' said Brian.

'"Someone who can walk on water",' Doabre repeated. 'Or rather, something – something such as a chariot crafted, by the Other Folk and drawn by steeds that are half of this world and half of the Other World: steeds that can pull the chariot as easily across water as they can across land.' He sat back, his small black eyes glowing.

'My lord, do you possess such animals?' asked Brian carefully.

'I do, I do. They were gifts from my father and he had them from his father and so on, back through the generations. They were given to a distant ancestor of mine by one of the early gods.' He rose from the chair suddenly, sending it crashing backwards. 'Come, I will call them.' He almost ran from the tent, followed by a confused and sceptical group of warriors.

Doabre made his way through the scattered camp, down through a crack in the cliffs until he reached the shore. And there in the sheltered cove he raised both hands, palms upwards towards the skies and cried aloud in an alien tongue – and in that moment he no longer seemed a fat old man, but rather a godlike, primeval figure calling upon his subjects.

For a long time nothing happened, and just as the group was beginning to move restlessly, a tiny speck appeared on the horizon. The king pointed. 'Look, it comes.'

The chariot approached with amazing speed, driven by a tall, crimson haired youth, whose skin was bone-white, giving his head a skull-like appearance. But he handled the unnaturally thin and skittish animals with great care, and the utmost ease, bringing them to a gentle stop before the king.

35

Close up, the chariot was a masterpiece of elven art. Carved into the silvered wood were countless tiny pictures and glyphs that seemed to writhe and shiver with every movement of the chariot. The wheels were larger than normal and had only four spokes apiece. A covering of dark metal banded the wheels and set into the hub were slots where knives might be fitted in battle.

'Show them what they can do,' ordered Doabre. 'Bring it back and forth on the beach and into the water.'

Silently the charioteer wheeled the horses and brought the chariot around in a lightning fast turn, sending soft sand showering upwards.

As the chariot manoeuvred up and down the beach and out and over the waves, Brian drew his brothers aside. 'This is probably the only chance we'll have of stealing the chariot – and unfortunately I can think of only one way ...'

'That is?' prompted Iuchar.

'We are going to have to kill the charioteer.'

'Babd and Morrigan,' Urchar spat, 'are we warriors or butchers?'

'Well, if we must kill the charioteer, then we will kill Doabre also – without him, this army will fall apart, the mercenaries will return home and there will be a little less killing.' Iuchar looked at Brian and Urchar. 'Agreed?'

Silently, they both nodded.

The brothers swiftly moved out to a point on the beach where the chariot must pass as it swung in from the sea. They loosened their weapons and waited.

The elven charioteer brought the horses around in a tight circle, until the metal wheels actually cut the surface of the water, sending it showering upwards in a rainbow hued spray and then raced for the shore, demonstrating the speed and stamina of the half-elven mounts.

As the chariot neared, Urchar climbed up the cliff face and clung there out of sight – waiting. When the horses' hooves bit into the soft sand, Brian stepped forward and waved his hands. Swiftly, the chariot slowed, the horses changing from a gallop to a quick trot and then a walk with no apparent effort. Brian could see that they were unlathered and unwinded by their mad dash. The charioteer looked at him enquiringly and Brian pointed to the group standing in the distance.

And Urchar leaped.

He came down with his knee in the charioteer's back. There was a single sickening snap, and the elven youth went limp. Urchar searched the body for signs of life and, finding none, pushed the body from the chariot. Iuchar took the reins and attempted to learn the feel of the horses whilst Brian stood by their high-boned, almost skeletal heads, soothing them – and also to shield them from the king and his commanders further down the beach.

'Let's go,' said Iuchar, confident of the chariot and the horses' responses. Brian jumped aboard and drew his sword, holding it down by his side and Urchar drew his and stood at the other side of the chariot.

Carefully, Iuchar urged the half-elven steeds into a walk, a trot, and then a full gallop.

Doabre didn't realise until it was too late that the chariot careening madly towards him was not driven by its elven master. His eyes, weakened through excesses and old age, could just about make out the fast approaching shape. But as it neared and he squinted against the glare of the sand, he suddenly knew something was wrong ...

And then the chariot was upon him. He saw the glittering edge of a weapon come out of the mists that clouded his sight, and heard the keening blood-cry of a sword, and then ...

The head didn't stop rolling until it reached the waves.

The mercenary commanders fell back, stunned at the sudden assassination of their paymaster. But no-one made any attempt to attack the brothers – theirs were swords for hire, and their contract had just been abruptly terminated. They gathered on the beach, standing above the headless, bleeding body of Doabre, late king of Sigar, and watched the chariot disappear around the island.

*

37

'Hah, that was easy,' Urchar exulted from the bow of the *Watersprite*.

'Killing is never easy,' muttered Brian.

'But by killing the king, we saved greater loss of life,' argued Iuchar.

'And what does that make us? What are we to do then? Are we to wander through these barbarous lands, killing all whom we decide – *we* decide – are causing suffering and death. What are we then, the handmaidens of the Morrigan?'

'But we only had to kill two that time,' said Urchar. 'We killed many more to obtain the other Treasures, and ... Look.' He stood suddenly and pointed. 'The Golden Pillars.'

'I wonder how much we will have to pay for the seven pigs?' murmured Iuchar.

'Whatever we pay, the price will be too high,' added Brian.

Swiftly, the *Watersprite* swept in towards the twin isles of the Golden Pillars. Dusk was falling, but the last rays of the setting sun still touched the tips of the two mountains, striking fire from the gilded shrines to the Elder Gods.

And all along the shores of both isles were tiny points of light – torches. The sons of Tureen were expected and the islanders were gathered and waiting.

Brian ordered the *Watersprite* into the shore and, wearily, he and his brothers gathered up their weapons and prepared for battle.

The elven craft eased its way gently into the natural harbour. The people of the cliffs and beaches were silent, watching the enchanted craft work its way through the treacherous shoals and reefs. With a delicacy that made it seem as if a master helmsman were at the tiller, the craft barely touched the wooden pilings of the dock.

A single figure stepped out of the crowd and walked towards the craft bobbing on the dark oily water. He was a tall, grey-haired and bearded man, leaning on a thick staff. He raised a gnarled hand.

'Aesal of the Golden Pillars gives greeting to the sons of Tureen and honours their quest.'

The brothers' astonishment quickly turned to amazement as seven dusky maidens stepped out of the crowd, each one leading a tiny pig on a silver lead.

'My lord ...' began Brian.

Aesal shook his head. 'Do not thank me, but by the same token, do not think I fear you. I am an old man - death holds no fears for me, but I would not see you rend my tiny kingdom and slay my subjects. Take them, they are yours. We never had cause to use them. And now,' he said, changing the subject, 'you will honour us by breaking your journey and eating with us? We have, you see, prepared for your coming. Indeed, the whole continent is afire with tales of the barbarian princes who seem intent on capturing the elven artifacts of every nation and putting the ruler to the sword.'

'My lord,' Brian protested, 'I know it must seem that way, but that is not the truth. Let me explain ...'

'But not here, not here. Come.'

The sons of Tureen spent the night with the king of the Golden Pillars, feasting and taking their ease for the first time in many months and Brian explained how their quest had come about and the circumstances that had led to the killing of the three princesses of the Orient and the kings of Greece, Persia and Sigar.

Aesal ordered one of his scribes to set down the facts so that the sons of Tureen might be remembered in future ages with honour rather than with fear and loathing.

As the first grey fingers of dawn touched the eastern sky, the king asked Brian where their destination lay and what treasure they now sought.

'We are seeking a pup,' he said, 'but a dog that will grow into a beast that even the lion, the fabled king of all the animals, will obey. And to find this dog, we must journey to the land of ...'

'Of Irouad,' finished the king, staring deep into his goblet.

'You know of it?' Brian asked.

'My only daughter is the wife of Irud, the King of Irouad,' said Aesal sadly. 'But he is a hard-headed and strong-willed man; I doubt he will surrender the dog to you.'

39

'But surely he must, knowing that we will take the animal or die trying – and before we die we will slay many of Irud's warriors, and perhaps even the king himself.'

'He will not surrender the dog, unless ... unless I go and try to reason with him. He might listen to me: you must take me with you.'

Brian nodded. 'We will. We would prefer to be given the animal, but if we must fight for it, then we will do so ...'

Aesal grasped Brian's forearm and held it tightly. 'You must let me try to talk to him. If he will listen to me, then you can avert the bloodshed you detest.'

'If he will listen,' whispered Brian. 'If.'

The *Watersprite* rocked on the gentle swell outside Irouad's harbour. Across the entrance were anchored two huge warships and the cliffs above the harbour were dark with men and machines of war.

The three brothers stood in the bow of their craft and watched the small boat returning with Aesal. The young oarsman was obviously frightened, but trying to put up a brave front before the foreign daemons who slew kings and princes as if they were common beggars.

Aesal climbed aboard wearily and shook his head. 'He will not listen; he does not want to listen. He even admitted that the dog meant nothing to him, but he also said that he would not allow savages to frighten him.' The king shrugged. 'I also think he wants the honour of having been the monarch who slew the sons of Tureen.'

'He will not slay us,' whispered Urchar, gazing far out over the sea, 'we will not be slain by mortal men ...' His voice faded and was lost in the lapping of the waves. Brian and Iuchar shivered, for their brother was fey and sometimes had glimpses of the future, a gift he inherited from his late mother.

'What are you going to do?' Aesal wondered.

'There is little we can do at present,' said Brian. 'The harbour is blocked and the cliffs are manned. Squads of archers and slingers are camping on the beaches and the watchfires have been burning since they first sighted us.' He paused, and squinted into the horizon. 'But I think a storm is brewing and night will soon be coming on. Perhaps we will be able to do something then.'

'I think we'll have to do it quickly then, said Iuchar, pointing off to the starboard side, where tiny specks dotted the horizon. 'Ships: Irud has called upon reinforcements and they will soon have us trapped.'

Brian gazed thoughtfully at the shore. 'Tonight then.'

The storm rolled in late in the afternoon, bringing with it flurries of ice-cold rain, the distant rumble of thunder and sudden flashes of lightning. By late evening, visibility had decreased and the shoreline was only a distant smudge sprinkled with the tiny flickering spots of watchfires.

The *Watersprite* drifted silently towards the shore, running contrary to both the wind and tide, until it rocked gently half a length from the rough beach. The sons of Tureen, clad only in loincloths, their swords wrapped in oiled sheaths, slipped easily into the chill water and swam for the shore.

They made their way past the first two lines of sentries, until they reached the perimeter of the camp. But here there were too many guards and warriors moving about and the light of countless campfires and hissing torches turned the whole area into a rough semblance of day. And here, cunning, rather than stealth, must take them through.

They slew three patrolling guards without a sound and quickly divested them of their clothing and armour. Then, moving quickly and confidently, they made their way through the camp towards Irud's huge and ornate tent in the centre of the camp.

'Halt; state your business with the King of Kings.' The young guard stared insolently at the three warriors clad in crude and ill-fitting garments. His companion grinned and leaned on the haft of his hooked spear.

41

'Well,' said Brian, in a barbarous accent. 'The King of Kings wishes to see us ... I think.'

. The guard laughed crudely and winked at his companion. 'And who might you be, that the Lord Irud wishes to see so badly?' He poked Brian in the chest with the butt of his spear.

'We,' said Brian, slowly and distinctly, all trace of accent now gone, 'are the sons of Tureen!' The guard reeled backwards as Brian struck him across the head and went crashing over into the tent. His companion doubled over as Iuchar kicked him in the pit of his stomach and pushed him on top of the unconscious guard.

Brian, Iuchar and Urchar slashed their way through the rich fabric and into the tent. They found themselves facing a very surprised and dishevelled young man. Behind him, a wide-eyed young woman cowered on the floor, the thick bed furs held tightly against her heaving breasts.

'Who ... What is the meaning of this?' Irud demanded.

'You must be Irud, King of Kings,' said Iuchar.

'And Lord of Irouad,' added Urchar.

'We are the sons of Tureen,' said Brian. 'I think you should get dressed.'

Getting the king out of the camp proved surprisingly easy. With Iuchar walking in front, Urchar behind and Brian by his side with a knife nestling against his ribs, they marched Irud through the rows of tents. Warriors bowed as their lord walked past and looked curiously at the three strange bodyguards, but no one made a move to question or hinder them.

Once they had passed beyond the confines of the tent, Urchar gagged the king to prevent him crying out and then half-carried, half-dragged him towards the shore. Irud's eyes opened wide and a strangled scream escaped as Iuchar and Urchar picked him up and tossed him bodily into the chill sea.

'Swim,' Brian ordered.

*

42

The morning broke bright and clear with a stiff breeze blowing in off the horizon. The craft they had spotted the previous night were much closer now and Brian estimated they would reach the *Watersprite* by mid-morning. He went aft to where Aesal was talking with his son-in-law.

'There is no dishonour in giving these men what they want,' he was insisting. 'I have given them the seven pigs. They have wrested by force the treasures of other kings, even if it meant slaying them. They have captured you and brought you through your camp and yet they might have slain you ... but they did not. Irud, I beg you, give them what they want - give them the pup, I do not want to see my daughter widowed so soon.'

'We must have the dog,' said Brian quietly. 'Do not force us to take it - or your life.'

Irud sat silently, staring towards the shore and then he sighed. 'I do not think you are mortal men. You must be gods, the sons of gods - or daemons - and mortal men, such as I, cannot resist the will of gods.' He turned away.

'You can have the dog. And now,' he turned and looked at Brian, 'what will you do with me?'

'Why, we will put you ashore.'

'I will have the animal sent to you,' he said bitterly. 'And then, go. Go!'

'We will.'

Water dripped in the darkness, but Lugh and his uncles, Cu and Ceithne, ignored it and concentrated on the bowl of ancient silver that lay on the low table before them. The light from the huge fire crackling in the hearth cast a ruddy glow on their faces as they bent over and stared intently at the oily liquid that nestled in the bowl. Gradually, the shadowy figures that had been illuminated in its depths faded and Lugh sat back with a sigh and wiped the sweat from his brow.

'So, they have the pup, the fifth treasure,' he mused.

'I didn't think they would get this far,' said Ceithne.

'They have not finished yet,' said Cu, moving over to the fire and warming his hands before the flames. 'They still have to find the cooking spit and give three shouts on Midcain Hill - and I do not think Midcain and his sons will allow that.'

'Nor I,' agreed Lugh. 'But we need those treasures and we need them now. The Fomorians are massing for another attack - and those treasures might just tip the odds in our favour. We must have them!'

'How?' Cu wondered.

Lugh remained silent for a while and then he stood and paced the hall. He stopped by the fire and stared deep into its depths, tiny fire-images forming and fading before his eyes, smoking shadow-wraiths rising up and vanishing: all part of the fire's magic.

'Sorcery; we must use sorcery.' He turned to his uncles. 'A simple spell, or rather, a double spell. The first part to induce forgetfulness about the cooking spit and the shout and the second part to bring on an intense longing for home.'

'Can you do it yourself,' asked Ceithne, 'or must you bring in a Druid?'

'I can do it myself.'

And a thousand leagues away, off the coast of Irouad, the sons of Tureen directed the *Watersprite* to return home to Banba, joyful that their quest was now complete.

The stone flags of Maecadre, the Great Hall of Tara, rang with the steps of the sons of Tureen. The crowded hall was silent, the atmosphere tense and expectant as Brian, Iuchar and Urchar stood before Nuada, King of the Tuatha De Danann.

'Our quest is complete, we have returned,' said Brian.

'We are pleased to see that you have returned safely; we have heard some whispers of your exploits - you have made

44

the very name of Banba one to be feared across the continent.'

'It was not what we intended.'

'You have the treasures?' asked Lugh, coming up behind the brothers.

'We have,' said Iuchar, turning to face him.

'I have seen some of the treasures outside ... but only some,' said Lugh, and then he added. 'I do not think you have completed your quest.'

'Beware,' whispered Brian in an icy tone, 'lest I stain Maecadre's stones with the blood of a De Danann prince.'

Urchar placed his hand on his older brother's arm. 'We have the three apples from the Garden of the Hesperides, the golden pigskin from the Land of the Greeks, the spear of Mithra from the Land of the Persians, the chariot and half-elven horses from the Isle of Sigar, the seven magical pigs gifted to us by Aesal of the Golden Pillars and the pup, presented to us by Irud, King of Irouad.' He paused, his brow furrowed briefly, but then he smiled. 'That is all, our quest is complete.'

And Lugh laughed, his laughter harsh and mocking.

'No, that is not all! You have forgotten the cooking spit of the women of Fioncure Isle, nor have you shouted thrice upon Midcain Hill. So, you are oath-breakers and liars as well as murderers.'

Nuada's shout silenced the sons of Tureen. 'Tell me,' he said to them, 'did you truly believe that the capture of the dog was the last part of your quest?'

'My Lord, that is so. Although ...' Brian paused, and Urchar continued. 'I felt - indeed, we all felt - that there might be something else, but we did not know what that might be, all we knew that we had to get back to Banba.'

The king nodded. 'I know you to be men of honour, I know you would not break your oath to complete the quest - at least of your own accord.' Abruptly the king stood, and called for Diancecht, his sorcerer-physician.

'Did you not say to me, not two nights past, that you felt sorcery afoot.'

45

The ancient Druid nodded. 'I tasted it on the air, sharp and acrid, with no trace of good in it - only malice.'

'Would it be difficult to cast a spell of forgetfulness coupled with a spell of longing for home?' Nuada wondered.

'No Lord, it is a relatively simple spell.'

'I thought so. Would Lugh be able to cast it?' he asked suddenly.

'He trained with me for a short time during his youth. Yes, he could do it.'

Nuada turned to Lugh. 'Did you cast such a spell, and before you answer, remember that you are in the Hall of Maecadre - do not lie to me.'

Lugh was silent, conscious of the eyes of all the lords of Banba upon him. And then he nodded briefly. 'We need those treasures in the coming battle,' he said defensively.

'You have dishonoured your name and that of your family,' said the king, his voice cold and hard, his eyes blazing. 'Your presence offends me - leave my sight!'

Lugh turned away and as he reached the door, he looked back at the king and the sons of Tureen. 'But they must complete the quest,' he insisted maliciously. 'They must.'

'We will,' said Brian quietly, 'we are not without honour.' He turned and bowed to Nuada and then, followed by his brothers, walked from Tara's Great Hall.

The isle was not listed on any mariner's maps or charts and although they haunted the seaport taverns they could find no-one who had even seen it. Oh, many had heard of the fabled Isle of Women, inhabited by the fairest of all the elven women, all maidens, but nevertheless skilled in all the arts of love.

'It sounds like a sailor's dream,' Iuchar remarked when he heard the story.

His twin nodded. 'A sailor long at sea, imagining fishes to be maids and weed to be monsters. Is it any wonder that he would create an island populated with the most beautiful maids awaiting him - and just beyond the horizon?'

'But it must be there,' Brian snapped, bending over a

cracked and rune-incised chart. 'It must be there.' He tapped the chart again in the space between the irregular mass that was Alba and the oblong that was Banba.

'Could it be confused with Mona?' asked Iuchar, pointing to the isle between the two.

'I've never met any beautiful maids on Mona,' Urchar grinned, 'only dry and bitter Druids.'

'Well then, we'll go to Mona,' said Brian.

'But I've just said that there are only Druids there ...'

'If the isle is inhabited by elven maids and is not listed on any of these charts, then surely only the Druids can help us.'

'But why?' wondered Urchar.

'Because the isle must lie beyond the world of men, in the Shadowland!'

The Druids however, could not help them and the only mention of the isle was in an ancient fragment of verse:

'The Isle of Fioncure
Rests not on Land
Nor on Sea
But in the Place Between'

The moon waxed and waned fully three times whilst the brothers cruised the chill waters between Banba and Alba, searching for the island. And with winter fast approaching, they knew they would soon have to abandon their quest and wait half a year whilst the seasons changed.

But one morning, with the sun pale and wan on the horizon and storm clouds massing in the west, a huge white bird came and settled on the *Watersprite*'s snarling figurehead. The sons of Tureen had never seen anything like it in all their travels. Its wingspan was twice that of even the largest bird and its flat and hard eyes burned with a strange intelligence.

It stayed motionless on the figurehead for most of the morning and then abruptly it took flight, veering away towards the east. Immediately, Brian ordered the *Watersprite* to follow. The bird continued east well into the afternoon, its huge, powerful wings carrying it effortlessly against the stiffening wind. And then towards evening it stopped and waited until the *Watersprite* was almost directly below it. Brian halted their craft. The bird circled overhead for a while and then, with a hoarse squawk, it dived into the sea – and did not reappear.

'I think,' said Brian slowly, 'we may have found the location of the Isle of Fioncure which ...' he paused, and then finished, 'which is between the land and the sea!'

The brothers leaned over the side and stared down into the ebon, foam-lashed depths. 'So who goes down?' asked Urchar.

'I do,' said Brian and then waved his brothers to silence when they protested. 'I have been trained in the arcane arts, whilst only Urchar's foresight has been developed and Iuchar's ghostsight. Neither of you have either the ability or stamina to venture down.'

Reluctantly, the twins agreed and watched in silence as Brian prepared to descend in search of Fioncure.

He stood in the bow of the ship and held both his hands high, as if in prayer or offering and then he cried aloud in the tongue that was ancient before even the Nemedians came to Banba's shores. Hesitant blue tendrils of writhing fox-fire ran along his fingertips and gathered in the palms of his hands. Swiftly, he spun the blue fire together in a crackling web and then pulled his hands apart, stretching it. Deftly, he wove it until it resembled a rough sphere and then he cried aloud and the sphere solidified. It now looked like a rough diamond, cut and faceted, blue-veined and shining, with an open circle at one end.

They then collected long strands of seaweed and wove them into a complicated cross-hatched pattern. Brian stood whilst Iuchar and Urchar wound the weed around his arms and legs and finally set the crystal helmet on his head. With a whispered prayer to the Dagda and Danu, Brian slipped over the side and disappeared in a welter of bubbles into the darkness.

As he fell he spread his arms, feeling the seaweed inflate and help keep him upright. He whispered a word through

48

gritted teeth and touched the helmet. Abruptly, the blue veins in the crystal flared into incandescence, illuminating the blackness all around him. He dropped his arms to his side and continued falling.

Unreal shapes darted before him and once a huge twisting figure slid past with fluid ease, its immensity terrifying him. Shifting tangles of slimy weed clutched at him like the fingers of drowned mariners and he fell through whole shoals of tiny fish, like a god through the world of men.

He had been falling for some time when he became aware of a growing illumination. He touched the crystal helmet and the ghostlight faded, leaving him alone in the growing twilight. He spread his arms and floated, staring down into the depths.

At first, he could see nothing and then gradually, as if seen through shifting smoke, a shape materialised, a shape Brian struggled to make out, until he realised he was looking down onto a mountain.

A mountain and the Isle of Fioncure.

Brian fell into Fioncure's clear morning, descending like a god from the heavens. He was aware when he passed the tip of the mountain that the water pressure and the bone-numbing chill were gone – but still he drifted down ... and down.

The grass beneath his feet was cool and dry. Carefully, he removed the crystal helmet and breathed deeply of the fragrant air, savouring its sweetness. He walked uphill where, hidden by a low copse of trees, a thin thread of smoke spiralled upwards. He paused by one of the trees. It was small and delicate, with a soft spongy bark which yielded to his touch and broad flat leaves which quivered constantly.

The women of Fioncure were waiting for him as he rounded the copse. They were seated on the soft ground in a large open circle, weaving. They spun delicate tendrils of gossamer thread, weaving it into a faery tracery of captured light, but, try as he might, Brian could not see where the finished tapestry went. Certainly it did not gather about their feet as it should, nor was it piled anywhere.

As one, the women turned towards him and smiled. 'Greetings, Brian MacTureen. Welcome to the Isle of Fioncure where the Fate of Man is spun.'

Brian bowed and faced the woman who sat in the centre of the group near a low fire, turning a long spit which held a roasted carcass. 'My Lady, the sons of Tureen send you greeting.' And then he paused and added. 'But I fear my mission will make a mockery of any greeting we may exchange.'

The elven maid raised her long, slim hand. 'You need not continue; we wove your fate long ages past. Your striving, your joys and sorrows, your quest, your coming here, aye, and even your deaths were all foretold here.' She touched a long silken thread and then she stood in one fluid movement. She wrapped a dark cloth about the cooking spit and lifted it off the fire. With a long fork she picked the joint of meat off the spit and then handed the long shaft of metal to Brian.

'Take the spit and, with our blessings, take it as a reward for your endeavour. Now go,' she said suddenly, and resumed her seat, the joint of meat still held on the fork.

As Brian turned to go, she called to him. 'Are you hungry, would you care to join us?'

Slowly Brian shook his head, mindful of the warnings neither to eat nor drink with the elven folk. 'I am not hungry,' he lied.

The maid nodded. 'Perhaps it is just as well,' and then she added, almost wistfully, 'your quest has fed us well,' and sank her delicate, sharp teeth into bubbling flesh.

Brian retched, and then turned and ran from the presence of the women of Fioncure.

'So we are only puppets, playthings of the gods,' Urchar spat.

Brian finished sipping the hot broth Iuchar had prepared for him. 'So it would seem. The maid gave me to understand

50

that our fate had been spun and sealed long ago.'

'Have we no choice then?' argued Urchar. 'Must we now carry out this quest, are we tied to it, like animals to the seasons?'

'We are honour bound,' whispered Brian. 'We have little choice, little choice.'

Midcain Hill overlooked the cold waters of the Northern Seas, deep in the land of the Fomorians. A bleak and barren volcanic rock, pitted with crevasses marking the passing of the great ice flows during the harder winters, it rose, dark and forbidding on the sharp morning air.

And at the foot of the hill was an ancient dolmen and beside the dolmen stood a man.

The brothers rested on the stony beach. They had come armed and armoured, for the Hill of Midcain was said to be guarded by four warriors under a geas to allow no voice to be raised in joy or anger upon its slopes.

Brian loosened his sword in its scabbard and gripped his spear. 'I will talk with him; perhaps if I explain, he might allow us ...' he trailed off, realising how implausible it sounded.

The warrior stirred as Brian approached. He was a giant of a man, standing almost as tall as the dolmen, and topping Brian by a head. He leaned upon a huge double-headed battle-axe and glared at Brian through small dark eyes.

'Come no further,' he growled, his voice harsh and rasping, like an animal's. 'Speak your name, and state your reason for trespassing upon my mountain.'

'I am Brian, son of Tureen; yonder are my brothers, Iuchar and Urchar, and whilst we did not realise that this was your mountain, we have come to fulfil a quest.'

The giant moved, bringing the axe up in one easy movement, as if it weighed no more than a dagger. 'Ah, the sons of Tureen. I have waited for you.' He paused and spat at Brian's feet. 'The killers of my boyhood companion, Cian.' He spun the axe in one hand. 'I am Midcain of the Hill, and my sons and I are under a geas to keep this sacred place silent. But,' and he smiled with yellowed, broken teeth, 'I will gladly break the holy silence with your screams.'

He lunged – and the battle-axe bit deeply into the ground at Brian's feet. Had he not thrown himself back, it would have split him in two. He blocked the next blow with the haft of his spear. The axe swung in low and then Midcain changed direction, striking upwards at Brian's head; the blade skimmed his face, lifting his hair as it passed. Brian jabbed at Midcain's stomach with the butt of his spear, doubling him up, and then reversed the spear and struck him across the nape of his broad neck as he fell. But the blow struck the giant across his mailed shoulders and the haft snapped. Midcain fell to one side, recovered quickly and struck upwards from a crouching position, almost disembowelling Brian.

The son of Tureen fell backwards, coming to his feet in a roll with his sword in his hand and his dagger resting lightly in his left hand. Midcain wove his axe to and fro, the broad blade catching the wan morning sunlight in a glittering, blinding display. The two warriors circled each other, cautiously jabbing, testing each other's strengths and weaknesses. Abruptly, Midcain struck, bringing the axe across in a huge scything sweep. Brian stepped back as the axe whispered past and then leaped inside the blow. His knife found Midcain's throat, whilst his sword sliced at the giant's wrist, almost severing it. Brian's hand was suddenly covered in thick, reeking blood, the knife felt slick in his fingers. Midcain's eyes bulged, he stiffened and then went limp as his life fluid pumped away.

On the hilltop, three figures rose and began to run down, the sunlight catching their armour and weapons.

Iuchar and Urchar joined their brother and Urchar's gaze was troubled. 'Our death approaches,' he whispered.

Brian cleaned his knife on a tuft of rough grass and watched the three sons of Midcain leaping from rock to rock, nearing them. 'Their anger will cloud their judgement and reflexes. They have just lost their father, that will demoralise them, and,' he laughed grimly, 'they have just run down a long hill. We have the advantage, let us make sure we keep it.' He stood as the three dark warriors slid to a halt before him and looked at their father's bloody corpse.

'You have killed him,' one accused Brian.

'In a fair fight.'

'We know you; you are Brian, Iuchar and Urchar, the sons of Tureen of Banba.'

'We are.'

'We are Corc, Conn and Aedh, the sons of Midcain of the Hill,' said the taller of the three warriors. 'You have added the death of our father to your other crimes.' He slid his sword free. 'And you must die.'

The sons of Midcain attacked them with an almost animal-like ferocity. They fought well into the morning and the sun rose over them and began to sink behind the hill in the early afternoon. Both sides had given and received wounds – wounds which would have slain a mortal man. But neither the sons of Tureen nor those of Midcain were truly mortal, for they were of the Tuatha De Danann and thus more akin to gods, and of the Fir Bolg and thus closer to daemons.

But towards the end, Urchar received a long shallow cut across one arm and another, deeper cut in his thigh. He fell back, desperately defending himself from Corc when his foot slipped on the gravel and he crashed onto his back. The son of Midcain straddled the fallen warrior and brought his sword high – and Urchar struck upwards with the last of his strength, disembowelling him in one blow.

Iuchar found himself up against Conn, who wielded a short sword and axe with terrible dexterity; the two weapons flickering and darting like serpents. Iuchar parried the sword on his knife and struck with his sword, but the blade struck ringingly against the axe-head. He twisted his knife and lunged, simultaneously chopping down with the sword. He scored a long flesh wound in Conn's thigh, but received a thrust through his right shoulder in return. They were almost evenly matched and whilst Conn might have the advantage of height and weight, Iuchar's reach was longer and he was stronger. And at last, his strength began to tell and Conn found himself more and more on the defensive. Both warriors were covered in sweat and bleeding profusely from a score of minor wounds.

Conn rallied the last of his strength and attacked. His sudden surge pushed Iuchar back, but realising that his opponent was on his last reserves of strength, Iuchar was content to let him wear himself down. Then he saw an opening. He lunged – and his sword penetrated Conn's throat; he died instantly – but his axe fell, severing Iuchar's ear and biting deep into his neck and shoulder.

Brian's opponent was Aedh, the eldest son of Midcain. Like his father, he stood a head taller than Brian and he was of a heavier build. He fought with a sword almost as tall as himself, a great broad-bladed weapon of some dark, almost stone-like metal, which struck sparks from Brian's rune-inscribed sword.

He found himself almost immediately on the defensive. Aedh's longer reach and the length of his sword effectively kept him at bay. Grinning triumphantly, Aedh played with Brian, as a cat will a mouse, the flickering black sword drawing a thin line across his forehead, cutting one cheek, and then the other, turning Brian's face into a red mask.

Both warriors could hear the cries of their brothers and the clash of metal on metal about them, but beside that, and the scuffle of feet on bare stone, the hill was silent.

Brian could feel his strength going and he knew he must attack soon, or else Aedh would wear him down and kill him slowly. With a desperate ferocity, he attacked. his sword blurred as he beat off Aedh's attack, darting, probing, testing, and then drawing blood along his opponent's forearm and across his chin. But the son of Midcain countered and the black sword seemed to come alive in his hands. He parried a blow and struck – and Brian felt the hot-ice of metal enter his chest high on his right side. He stood transfixed on the weapon, which exited above his collar-bone and for the first time Aedh laughed. 'You are dead, son of Tureen.'

But the laughter died in his throat as Brian, with the last

ragged remnants of his strength, struck the head from Aedh's shoulders.

For a long time after there was silence on the Hill of Midcain. Dark birds gathered and circled on the cold, sharp air, and then, taking courage from the lack of movement, swooped and settled by the blood-spattered bodies.

Suddenly one moved, and the carrion crows took to the air in ungainly flight. The figure, like a spectre of the battlefield, slowly and painfully raised himself on one arm, whilst the other held his chest where bright, thick, red liquid still glistened. Trying to breathe as little as possible, Brian dragged himself over to the body of his brother, Iuchar.

His face and neck were a welter of blood, for the falling axe had cut deeply into his neck and shoulder muscles. But when Brian touched his neck, he could feel the weak and ragged pulse-beat. Gathering what little remained of his strength and an ancient spell, he poured that strength into his brother.

Iuchar's eyes flickered open and he smiled weakly.

Both Brian and Iuchar dragged the stinking body of Corc off Urchar. When one discounted the amount of blood that was Corc's, Urchar seemed to have escaped unscathed. But there was no response when they attempted to rouse him and when Brian felt his pulse, he found it to be almost non-existent. Iuchar examined his brother's wounds more closely and found that the great artery in his thigh had been severed. He had lost a lot of blood and was very close to death.

Once again Brian summoned what little remained of his strength and, with Iuchar holding him, shared it with his brother, willing him to live.

For what seemed like an eternity nothing happened and then Urchar groaned.

Together, the three brothers staggered and crept and crawled up the Hill of Midcain, leaving a slick trail of blood to mark their passage.

The wind pulled and tugged at their stiff blood-soaked garments as they crested the hill. Supporting one another,

55

they turned and faced back the way they had come, looking down the hill.

'We are Brian, Iuchar and Urchar ...'

'The sons of Tureen ...'

'Our quest is complete.'

Three shouts on the hill.

Ethne touched her father's arm, and pointed out to sea. Tureen shaded his eyes with a gnarled hand and stared out across the water. A small craft was rapidly approaching, running against both the tide and wind: the *Watersprite*.

With its sails billowing in no earthly wind, the enchanted craft rode up onto the beach with a tearing and scraping of hardened timbers.

Brian staggered from the craft. He was a terrifying sight, his clothes and hair matted and stiff with dried blood, his face haggard and drawn, and with the bright fire of fever burning in his eyes. He collapsed into his father's arms, whilst Ethne climbed aboard the *Watersprite* and tried to help her dying brothers.

'Father ... our quest is complete,' Brian managed to whisper through cracked and swollen lips. 'Take the cooking spit to Lugh and beg him for Tuas' pigskin ... only it can save us now ...' He sagged and Tureen gently eased his son to the ground, covering him with his cloak. Then, calling upon what he remembered of the Old Magic, he assumed the shape of a great, greying hawk. Clutching the cooking spit in its rough claws, the hawk took to the skies and headed north, for Tara.

Ethne tended to her brothers whilst her father was away, cleansing their wounds and cooling their fevers. But she knew deep in her heart that unless their father returned with the pigskin, her brothers would die.

Towards evening the great bird came winging out of the northern sky and came to rest by the three sleeping brothers. Ethne ran to her father and embraced him and then she drew back, an icy chill enveloping her, as she saw the tears in his old eyes.

'Did he ...?'

Tureen shook his head. 'Lugh refused; he said my sons did not wish to save his father and he does not care to save my sons.' He shook his head and wept openly. 'He laughed as he condemned them to death.'

Brian opened his eyes and smiled through his pain and suffering. 'We were dying anyway - our fate was decided a long time ago. But at least we have completed our quest ... our honour remains unblemished.' He reached out and took his brothers' hands in his. 'Our name will live on ...' he sighed, closed his eyes and the three sons of Tureen died as they had lived - together.

Tureen cried aloud and fell to his knees before the still bodies. Ethne placed her hands on his shoulders and wept also. And then Tureen shuddered and fell forward across the bodies of his sons - dead of a broken heart.

Ethne stared out to sea, the wind catching in the long folds of her gown. The tears had passed and there was nothing left - nothing save a burning anger. She raised her eyes to the darkening skies and whispered to the wind,

'Although my father and brothers may be dead, the legend of the sons of Tureen is only beginning.'

CHAPTER 2

THE CHILDREN OF LIR
(The Second Sorrow Of Irish Storytelling)

The midwife stood before Lir, a cloth-wrapped bundle held in the crook of either arm. The king started awake, blinking in the early morning sunlight, rubbing the sleep from his eyes with a pale, long-fingered webbed hand. He stood stiffly and descended from the huge emerald, rune-carved throne. With infinite care, he pushed back the edge of the cloth that hid the babe's face.

'Twins again?' His voice – strong and booming, like the crash of the surf on the shore – held a trace of wonder.

The old woman's voice trembled as she spoke. 'My Lord, your queen has borne you two lusty male children.' She held one of the boys to the light and Lir could see the sharp elfin features, the slanting eyes and the green tinged skin. The midwife held up a tiny, perfectly formed hand – with webbed fingers.

For Lir was of the Tuatha De Danann and Lord of the Sea.

The king smiled as he took one of the tiny babes into his arms. 'And Eva, my queen, how is she?'

Abruptly, the midwife began to weep. Lir raised her head with one hand and gazed deep into her eyes, reading the truth that lay therein. 'The birth was not an easy one,' she sobbed, 'and the queen was not strong ...'

The king nodded slowly, his face expressionless, his eyes empty. And Eva's death was a reminder that although the De Danann were close to godhood, the Dark Lord could still claim them.

'Leave me,' he commanded, 'tend our ... my children.'

The midwife bowed and shuffled silently from the great hall.

Lir slumped upon the throne, his long thin fingers absently tracing the angular runes etched deep into the stone. He was cold, cold and ... empty.

He stood and went to stand by the high arched window, and stared out over the fields of ripening corn that lay below his hillfort. Tiny ant-like figures moved through the fields, their faint cries drifting up to him, shouts and commands, laughter and screams. They were untouched by his wife's death: life went on.

He suddenly sensed another presence in the hall and, turning with the sun still dazzling his tear-filled eyes, he cried aloud, for his wife stood before him!

'Father ...?'

'Fionuala!' He gathered his daugher into his arms and stroked her white-gold hair whilst she wept. The memory and image of Eva lived on in her only daughter; the high delicate elfin features, wide slanting blue-green eyes, innocent and all-knowing, girl and woman.

Lir and Fionuala stood silently by the window, staring out over the morning. Fionuala touched her father's arm and pointed. 'Look, Aedan is returning.'

A group of youths were running up the long winding path that led to the fort, with one far in the lead, a tall young man with a shock of white-gold hair.

Lir turned to his daughter. 'He does not know yet; will you tell him for me?' He paused and added softly, 'I cannot.'

Fionuala nodded.

'And you have two brothers to look after. See that they are well cared for and find wet-nurses for them: they are your mother's legacy to us.' And as his daughter turned away, the king added, 'Call the larger child, Fiachra, and the smaller, Conn. They were the names your mother had chosen should she bear twin boys.'

Without Eva, Lir found the White Fort cold and deserted.

He found it hard to accept that she was dead and would wander the lonely corridors half expecting to hear her laughter behind him or her light footfall on the stair. And then for him, she began to live again. He saw her in every corner, smelled her scent in every room, heard her voice by his side, felt her presence in his bed. At last he could stand it no longer and, taking his children and servants, set out for the palace of Bove, his father-in-law.

Away from the White Fort, Eva's ghost ceased to haunt him and the children of Lir saw their father begin to smile again.

Although the king had planned only a short stay at Bove's palace on the banks of the Sinann, the months slowly passed and he felt no inclination to leave, for he was loath to return to the White Fort with its memories and ghosts.

And there was Aefe.

She was half-sister to Eva, but whereas his late wife had been a creature of the light and day, Aefe was at one with the night.

He had first met her whilst out hunting with Bove. She had come flitting through the dark wood like one of the Sidhe folk, her long dark hair loose and flying behind and a bloody hunting spear in her hand. Behind her had come her servants carrying the spitted body of a boar.

Her wild dark beauty had first attrracted Lir, her easy laughter and skill with weapons. She often joined him on his forays into the surrounding countryside and she never failed to kill. On more than one occasion Lir remarked on her ability to attract the great wolves or deer, bears or cats to her.

And as the months passed, Lir fell more and more under the spell of this strange woman, more at home in the woods than in the dwellings of the De Danann.

They were wedded on Beltave Eve, when the first of the watch fires burned across the hills.

Lir took Aefe back to the White Fort and life quickly returned to the place. Eva's ghost no longer haunted it, and the only echoes in the corridors now were the happy shouts of his children. Aefe was more than a mother to the four and treated them as if they were her own - for she was fully confident that with the passing years she would bear Lir children and then they would rule, rather than Eva's children.

But the years passed and Aefe remained childless and it was whispered that she had trafficked with deamons in her youth and they had rendered her barren. She took counsel with the Druids, and read the stars and entrails of animals. But there were no children in her future.

She took to watching her husband when he was with his children and the love he bore them rankled within her like a festering sore. She imagined he loved them more than he loved her; her jealousy turned to fear and her fear turned to an all-consuming hatred.

One morning in late autumn, Aefe rose early and crept from the chilly bedchamber. The corridor was deserted, although faint in the distance she could hear the first stirrings of the servants. She stole down the dim corridor until she came to Fionuala's room. She stood outside, listening. There was no sound within, so silently she undid the latch and entered.

Fionuala lay asleep on the furs beneath the window, her childlike features relaxed, her white-gold hair spread like a banner about her head. Looking at her, Aefe was suddenly reminded of her half-sister: this was why Lir loved his children so. They were a constant reminder of his dead wife. She fingered the bronze dagger beneath her cloak. She could strike now - it would be so easy and Lir would be hers.

But Fionuala and her brothers were of the Tuatha De Danann and their blood would cry out for revenge. She could not - must not - slay them. As she stood over the bed, the naked dagger gleaming ruddy in the first shafts of sunlight, a flock of birds rose wheeling and diving from the lake below the fort. In that instant a plan was born. Silently she turned and slipped from the room.

And Fionuala's blue-green eyes snapped open.

*

'Father, must you go?'

Lir kissed his daughter and brushed a strand of hair from her forehead. 'Yes Fionuala, you know I must; this boar must be slain before it kills again. I shouldn't be gone long.

'Father ...' began Fionuala.

Lir paused by his chariot. 'Yes daughter, what is troubling you?'

She glanced over at her stepmother who stood deep in conversation with her ladies-in-waiting. At that moment her three brothers joined her.

'Nothing father. I ...' She gathered her two younger brothers in her arms and Aedan stood by her side. 'We will miss you,' and she added gently. 'We love you.'

As Lir wheeled his chariot out of the high gate, he called one of his young knights, a charioteer named Daire, whose father was of the De Danann but whose mother was of the race of Man.

'My Lord?'

'Daire, you are close to my daughter; how has she been of late?'

'Quiet, my Lord. But if she is troubled she will not admit it.'

'She is proud – like her mother.' He turned and looked back at his four children and then at their stepmother in the background. 'Stay with them Daire, I will feel happier if you do.' He shrugged. 'There was a curious air of finality about our parting. It may be nothing ... but my wife has been acting strangely of late. Stay, be my eyes and ears here whilst I am gone.'

Daire saluted. 'Trust me, my Lord.'

The king smiled. 'I do.'

'Fionuala, where is father going?' asked Conn as the last of the horses and chariots disappeared down the long road.

'He has gone south into the marshes; there is a wild boar there which has killed both men and beasts and destroyed crops. Father must kill it.'

'He will,' said Conn, full of boyish enthusiasm. 'I hope he brings me back the tusks.'

'You got the tusks last time, this lot are mine,' said his twin, Fiachra. He turned and lowered his voice. 'Look, Aefe is calling us.'

The queen stood on the bottom step, below the great bronze doors. Her gown of crimson shimmered in the early morning light, its colour matching that of her lips and long nails. Her raven hair had been piled high atop her head and held in place with a pair of ruby-tipped pins which sparkled like tiny drops of blood. As the four approached, one of her ladies brought the queen her riding cloak and placed it about her shoulders.

'Come children, this day has promise, let us not waste it. I have had provisions prepared; let us ride north and we can break our fast by Derravaragh Lake. What do you say? We have not ridden together for a long time,' she added.

'Mother, I do not think ...' began Fionuala anxiously, but the two younger boys were already running towards the stables. Aedan looked curiously at his sister and then he turned and followed his brothers.

Aefe came and stood beside Fionuala. 'Why do you not like me, child?'

'You are my stepmother, I ... I love you.'

Aefe gripped Fionuala's shoulder with a long nailed hand that brought a gasp of pain from the girl. 'Do not lie to me,' she spat. 'You -and your brothers - you all hate me.' She stared deep into Fionuala's blue-green eyes. 'No, do not try and deny it. You are trying to take Lir away from me.' She tightened her grip on the girl's shoulder. 'But you never will,' she promised. 'Never.' She whirled away in a flurry of crimson, her threat lingering on the suddenly chilled air.

'You are going riding, my Lord?' asked Daire as Aedan saddled his roan.

'Aye, Aefe wants to ride out to Derravaragh; hitch up her chariot, will you? Hurry up,' he called to his brothers, as they struggled to saddle their ponies.

Daire hitched two jet-black geldings into an ornate

chariot, and then for some obscure reason slipped his long knife into his belt.

With Fiachra and Conn astride their shaggy ponies and Aedan mounted upon Nathair, Daire brought the chariot around into the courtyard. Aefe was standing by the gate, waiting for them, a woven wicker basket of provisions on the ground beside her. As they approached, Fionuala ran up, having changed into a riding outfit of leather leggings and jerkin.

'Aedan, where is my horse?'

Her twin frowned. 'I thought you would ride with Ae ... Mother.'

'Of course she will ride with me.' Aefe smiled coldly and, placing a thin hand on Fionuala's shoulder, urged her into the chariot.

They rode down from the high gate along the route that Lir and his warriors had just taken. Aefe led them through the meadows and away from the road, along the banks of the stream that fed into Derravaragh Lake. The queen was in a good mood, singing in her high clear voice, an air that stilled the birds on the trees. Aedan joined in occasionally, but his voice was breaking, and he left it to his brothers to carry the tune in their sweet unbroken voices.

Only Fionuala did not join them.

The queen took the reins from Daire and drove the chariot herself, exulting in the strength and power of the horses, the rush of the wind through her hair as she unbound it and the thrill of impending triumph.

And Daire, standing beside Fionuala, caught the bright glisten of tears in her eyes, as she turned and looked back at the fast disappearing White Fort.

Aefe brought them along the banks of the Derravaragh, the waters cold and dark after the sparkling rainbow colours of the stream. She halted the lathered horses by a large outcropping of rock that stretched out over the lake. The morning sun had burned the mists off the lake and now the waters lay flat and unbroken, almost metallic, to the far distant shore.

Aefe dismounted and went to stand atop the rock overlooking the lake.

Daire helped Fionuala from the chariot, whilst the brothers dismounted and stood by the waters edge.

Aefe pushed a loose stone into the water with her foot. It fell with a dull splash, the ripples growing into the distance. 'Children, would you not like to swim?'

Conn shivered. 'Too cold.'

'Nonsense,' chided the queen. 'Why, if you wish to ride with your father's warriors, you must be able to endure far colder water than this.' She turned to Daire. 'Is that not so, charioteer?'

'We are often forced to bathe in freezing water,' he agreed cautiously. 'But we prefer running water,' he added. 'It is purer and cleaner.'

Conn clambered up the hanging rock and standing by the edge, stared down onto the lake. 'It looks evil,' he whispered, 'who knows that serpents may live in it.' He wandered closer to the edge. 'It shines like mouldy copper.'

'Be careful Conn,' Fionuala called.

Aefe stepped forward, her hand outstretched to grab the boy, but her foot slipped on a patch of weed and she fell heavily against him. With a shrill scream, Conn toppled into the dark water.

Aedan launched himself from the shore, striking out strongly for the thrashing boy, Fionuala immediately following him.

The shock of the chill water was like a blow, instantly robbing her hands and feet of all sensation. The water stung her fair skin and tasted acrid in her throat. Her body responded automatically; the tiny gill-like slits behind her ears opening, extracting the oxygen from the water, and the inner eyelid sliding down protecting her eyes. Deftly she unhooked her cloak and kicked off her boots, and then, with her arms by her side, slid through the water like an eel. She could hear the frantic booming of her younger brother as he struggled before her, and the steadier beat of Aedan approaching. She opened her eyes wide, but the water was

65

dark with silt and peat and she could only grope in the darkness for her brother. Her questing fingers closed on sodden cloth ...

Abruptly the water boiled and exploded and a weight struck her across the back, pushing her down ... down ... down.

Blind panic made her strike out; her fists struck something soft and yielding. She grasped it convulsively and pushed upwards for the surface. And when she had brushed the water from her eyes and the inner eyelid had retracted, she found she was holding her brother Fiachra.

'She pushed me,' he gasped.

Aefe capered on the rock above them like a wild thing. Her long black hair and crimson riding cloak streamed out behind her in a breeze that did not ruffle the water.

'Sorcery,' shouted Aedan, as he attempted to keep Conn's head above water.

The queen raised both hands above her head. She was clutching a stave ... a stave the children of Lir suddenly recognised as their father's Rod of Power.

It was a short length of silver wood, cut from the forests of Tir fo Thuinn, the Land Beneath the Waves. Ogham runes were incised along its length, angular, gold-filled lines set with tiny stones. Thin tendrils of fox-fire writhed along the wand, striking sparks from the stones, turning the gold molten. Blue fire throbbed and pulsed as she waved it to and fro and the ogham runes seemed to hang trembling on the suddenly darkened sky.

Aefe began to chant in the Old Tongue, a language that predated the Tuatha De Danann, or the Fomorians, and was even older than the Nemedians; the tongue of the Partholonians. She screamed aloud, but her voice was lost, torn and shredded on the ghostwind. But her words had effect.

The water suddenly blazed about the children of Lir, a chilling blue-white fire which blinded without burning. Fionuala lost sight of Aedan and Conn and even Fiachra seemed thin and insubstantial in her arms. The light dazzled her eyes, bringing tears and causing red-black spots to dance wildly on her retina. Sensation returned to her limbs in a rush and she almost screamed in agony, and then almost as quickly it went again, until she lost all sensation. The world lurched; the dark sky and burning water losing definition and depth whilst the colours shook and vibrated.

And above it all the voice of Aefe chanted in the Old Tongue, calling forth her familiars to bear witness and carry word to their masters of the sacrifice she was sending them. Dark shapes gathered behind her, bestial and hideous, but with frighteningly human eyes. With a final flourish, Aefe completed her incantation and reverted to the tongue of the People of the Goddess.

'And Earth shall not hold thee,
Fire shall ye fear,
Water be thy element,
And that of Air.'

And as the blinding light died off the lake, Daire, cowering in the reeds on the bank, saw that the four children were gone ... and in their place floated four snow-white swans!

'This is your punishment,' Aefe screamed. 'You tried to take Lir from me, but now I have taken you from yourselves.'

And the largest of the swans replied. 'No, queen; you may take our forms, but you cannot take our spirits and whilst that remains, we remain.' The voice was Fionuaia's.

'How long must we remain in this form?' she asked then.

Aefe etched a glowing rune into the silent air with the tip of the wand. 'I have set the spell for thrice three hundred years,' she gloated. 'You will spend the first three hundred here upon Derravaragh, the second in the Straits of Moyle which lies between Banba and Alba, and the final three hundred in the wild seas about Inish Glora, in the Western Ocean.'

'Father will save us,' shouted one of the smaller swans, Fiachra.

Aefe boiled the water about the swans, sending them fluttering on untried wings into the air. Exhausted they fell back. 'Your father has not the power,' she laughed. 'He will need this wand to undo the spell, none other will suffice, and if he is without the wand ...?' With a shrill cry Aefe tossed the Rod of Power high into the air.

There was a stench of something rotten, of death and decay and a monstrous shadow passed over the dark waters of the lake. A giant black raven hovered over the queen for a moment and then it turned and disappeared south, the wand clutched in its talons.

'Is there no escape?' whispered Conn.

'Not until the day when the bell of the New God rings across the waters of evening and the man of the north shall take in marriage the woman of the south. Only then will the spell have run its course, only then will the enchantment be lifted.'

'I pity you,' said Aedan suddenly, 'for you have yet to face our father's wrath.'

Aefe gathered her cloak about her. 'Your father will have no-one left, he will not harm me, for he needs me: I am all he has.' And then she added. 'He will never know anyway; you were swimming in the lake, and you drowned,' she shrugged.

Fionuala laughed gently. 'We are the children of Lir, the Lord of the Sea; we cannot drown.'

Aefe frowned. 'I will think of something.' And then she turned and leaped down from the rock, heading back towards the chariot. She paused by the horses, looking for Daire. Abruptly she laughed and said softly, almost to herself. 'No mortal man could have witnessed the transformation and retained his sanity.' The queen climbed into the chariot and pulled them about, heading back for the White Fort.

Daire had remained hiding in the reeds until Aefe had disappeared over the brow of the hill. When he rose and stood knee deep in the chill water, the four swans drifted over to him and the largest laid its head on his arm.

And though the body was that of a swan's, the eyes and voice were those of Fionuala.

'Daire, you stayed.' There was surprise and affection in her voice.

'Your father asked me to keep an eye on you,' he said gruffly, 'much good I did.'

'No Daire, there was nothing you could do; why you are lucky to be still sane. The spell should have blasted the mind of any mortal man.'

'I am partly of the People of the Goddess,' said the charioteer. 'That saved me.' He looked at Fionuala. 'What must I do now?'

'You must reach our father, for you are our only link with him. And Daire ... be careful.'

'Aefe thinks me mad and running wild through the woods,' he said. 'She will do nothing against me.'

'She might accuse you of killing us,' said Aedan, drifting close to his sister.

The charioteer nodded. 'She might; and if I were to be found later, hopelessly insane, then no-one could doubt her story that I killed you. I will be careful. I'll ride directly south and attempt to overtake your father before he goes into the marshes and then I'll bring him directly here where he will have the evidence of his own eyes.'

'Take my horse,' suggested Aedan, 'he will find the king, and remember, avoid the White Fort at all costs.'

Daire agreed, his voice curiously muffled and then he turned away and ran stumbling from the lakeside, before they could see the tears that ran from his eyes.

The charioteer rode south as fast as the roan would carry him. He gave the White Fort a wide berth, but even from a distance he could see it was the scene of great activity. Armed men patrolled the heavily wooded countryside and guarded all the wells and pools of fresh water. It was then Daire discovered how the horse had earned its name, Nathair - Serpent - for it slid through the thickest undergrowth and even the most impenetrable woodland to avoid the patrols. The charioteer spent much of his time lying flat across the animal's back, lest he be torn from the saddle by branches.

It was late in the afternoon, four days after the transformation of the children, when Daire came upon Lir's camp.

It was situated on a small knoll in a clearing in the forest. Beyond the camp, the first sodden outcrops of the marsh trickled off into one of the countless streams that ran through the trees. A great fire blazed in the centre of the camp and Daire could see Lir's tall form stride in and out of the firelight, appearing and disappearing like a woodsprite. A snatch of song drifted across the clearing to the charioteer and the smell of roasting meat hung upon the heavy air.

He had ridden halfway across the clearing towards the camp when a sentry stepped out from the undergrowth and placed the tip of a spear in his back.

'No further. Your name and business.'

Daire turned in the saddle. 'Conal, it's me. I must see the king.'

The sentry relaxed his guard. 'You're a long way from home, is something wrong ...' he paused and stepped closer to the horse. 'Isn't that Nathair, Aedan's mount?' he asked suspiciously.

Daire nodded. 'I must see the king,' he repeated, his voice trembling with exhaustion.

'Go then; Lir is by the fire. Call out to Starn and Gamal by the stream and they'll let you pass. What's wrong?' he asked as the charioteer spurred his mount away. But he received no answer.

Lir knew something was terribly wrong as soon as he saw the foam-flecked horse bearing the slumped rider push its way towards the firelight. A sudden silence fell on the assembled warriors.

'My Lord,' gasped Daire, rising from the saddle, 'treachery ... sorcery ...' and he fell from the roan in a dead faint.

When he came to some time later, Lir was bending over him, pressing a flask of bitter-sweet liquid to his chapped lips. He coughed and struggled to rise, but the king pushed him back with surprising strength. Lir's large colourless eyes glittered strangely and his inner eyelid flickered once or twice across his retina, like a snake's. The dancing firelight lent his skin an even deeper greenish hue and gave his high, thin, elfin features a sinister, evil cast.

'Speak,' he commanded. 'What has happened?'

'My Lord,' began Daire slowly, 'your queen has, by foul sorcery and by calling upon the Elder Gods, changed your children into the likeness of swans upon Lake Derravaragh,' he finished in a rush.

Lir moaned as if in pain. His warriors drew back in horror, some making the sign of the fist or horns, whilst others clutched talismen or amulets. For sorcery could only be fought by a darker sorcery and whereas they would gladly give their lives in combat, the very whisper of sorcery filled them with a mind-numbing fear.

'But how?' wondered the king, 'she has not the power.'

'She used your wand,' said Daire, 'and then, when she had set the spell, she tossed the wand high into the air and a raven of enormous proportions and carrying with it the stink of death, carried it off.'

'One of the Morrigan's pets,' Lir murmured. He stood abruptly, towering over his men. 'Break camp, we ride at once for Derravaragh.'

The camp immediately dissolved into a whirling chaos of shouting men and skittish animals. Chariots were hitched, horses saddled and tents struck – and all within the length of time it took Daire to snatch a hurried meal and quench his thirst. The sky was ablaze with stars when they moved out. They galloped all through the night and rested briefly with the coming of the morn. By noon they had set out again.

The chariots thundered down the High Roads, flanked on either side by horsemen and those they passed on the road kept to their homes and bolted the doors, making ready their weapons, for they feared that the Fomorians had come south again and Lir went to do battle with them.

A day later, as the sun rose over the dark waters of the lake, Lir and his company reached Derravaragh. The king waved his men back and went alone to the lakeside where, far off in the distance, four snow-white swans could be seen making their way swiftly towards the shore. As they neared it, they uttered strangely human cries of joy and sorrow which Lir recognised as the voices of his children. The four swans crowded about the weeping king, pressing their long slim heads against his rough hands, and they too wept.

Lir spoke with his children there by the lakeside on that cold, bright winter morning and when he did rejoin his men about midday, he seemed resigned to their fate. Leaving half his men by the lakeside to tend to their needs and protect them, he rode for the White Fort - and vengeance.

Bove had arrived at the White Fort in Lir's absence. He had been met by his daughter, her face ashen, her eyes swollen with tears. She had told him that whilst Lir hunted boar in the marshes, the four children had gone missing, kidnapped and presumably slain by a charioteer named Daire.

And as the Lord of the Sea rode through the main gate, Bove was making ready to ride out in search of Lir, the children and the missing charioteer. A sudden silence fell on the courtyard as the king dismounted. He had lost weight, his eyes were sunken, lost in his haggard face.

Aefe, standing by her father's side, suddenly caught sight of Daire. 'There he is.' She pointed accusingly. 'He has kidnapped our children.'

She went to Lir and embraced him. 'You have captured him, my husband; but how? How did you know?' she wondered.

With a sudden savage moment, Lir struck her and she fell sprawling at the feet of the Red King. 'Witch,' he spat. 'I have spoken with my children: the children you so treacherously changed into the likeness of swans. You have betrayed me.' He slowly drew his rune-inscribed sword from its sheath.

Bove stepped between the king and Aefe. A stray shaft of

72

afternoon sunlight touched his fiery red hair and beard, touching it with gold. 'Wait Lir, I must hear more of this tale before you strike. I was told your children had been kidnapped by a charioteer named Daire, who was now running wild through the woods. We were about to ride in search of him.' He gestured at Daire. 'Yet here he is with you and clearly he is not a prisoner, but you accuse my daughter of sorcery against your children, my grand-children ...'

'He lies,' screamed Aefe, scrambling to her feet, one hand pressed against her split lip, which leaked a pale ichor.

Lir shook his head sadly. 'I do not lie.'

'I wouldn't have the power to do as you have said.' She grinned in triumph. 'You have been caught in your own lies!'

The king shrugged and then he presented his sword to Bove. 'Test her on my blade.'

The Red King took the proffered weapon and held it up. Silver light suddenly blazed upon the length of the blade, sharp and bright.

'Place your hand upon the sword,' he commanded Aefe. Silently she shook her head. 'Do it!' he snapped.

Reluctantly the queen touched the shining blade.

'Now,' began Bove, 'you are oath-bound to answer me truthfully; lie and the blade will show it.' He paused and looked deep into his daughter's eyes, but he found no comfort there. 'Do not lie,' he whispered softly. And then, raising his voice so that all might hear, he asked, 'Have you used sorcery against the children of Lir? Have you changed them into the likeness of swans?'

The silence hung heavily over the courtyard. Aefe remained silent, her eyes fastened on the blade, her fingers stuck to the shining metal.

'Answer!'

She started at the sound of her father's voice, and slowly she shook her head. 'No ... No, I have not.'

Instantly a crimson stain spread down the shining silver length of the sword, until its radiance was lost beneath a

73

blood-red covering. An angry murmur ran about the courtyard, quickly swelling to a roar.

'She lies!'

Bove sighed resignedly, as if the answer did not surprise him. 'You have betrayed your husband, you have betrayed your adopted children ... and you have betrayed me. Why?' he asked, his voice heavy with confusion and pain.

'Because I loved him,' said Aefe. 'Because I loved him so much I did not want him to share that love with anyone, and because he loved his children more than he loved me.'

'No, no it was never like that. They were my children – but you, you were my wife.'

'Well now, you do not have to share your love,' Aefe sneered. 'I am all you have left.'

Lir shook his head. 'No; you are nothing to me now.' He turned away, and stared into the evening sky.

Bove lowered the sword. 'The High Law will permit only one sentence.'

'But you cannot slay me,' cried Aefe triumphantly. 'I am of the De Danann!'

Her father nodded. 'That is true, we cannot slay you. But we can do to you what you have done to the four children: rob you of your natural form, and then cast you out.'

Aefe shrank back as Bove handed Lir his sword and then called for his Rod of Power. The king turned suddenly and touched his wife with the tip of his sword. 'You are still, oath-bound; what form would you fear most, what form would you deem fitting punishment for yourself?'

Aefe clasped her hands across her mouth, trying to prevent herself from answering, trying to prevent pronouncing her own judgement. Her throat worked, and the answer was torn from her mouth. 'A deamon of the air.'

Lir sheathed his sword. 'Thus shall it be.'

Bove agreed and, raising his wand high in the air, called aloud for the Old Gods. The hushed courtyard felt the eerie trickle of power from the wand. Abruptly it blazed with a brilliant blue-white fire that shed light but gave off no heat. A globe of pulsating foxfire gathered at the tip of the wand,

74

growing larger and larger, until it waxed like a full harvest moon. Slowly it detached itself from the wand and drifted down over the queen. The globe of light shivered and darkened and then swiftly dispersed in a shower of glittering dust motes.

And where once a young woman had crouched, now a hideous winged serpent clawed the earth with hooked talons. But its eyes were those of Aefe. With a terrifying screech, the deamon took to the air and disappeared south in a rush of leathery wings.

The years passed. Lir moved his household and court to the banks of the Derravaragh to be close to his children. He sought Druids and Mages from all parts of the known world and offered them vast rewards should they succeed in lifting the spell – but every attempt failed and at last Lir grew resigned to his children's fate. He had bards and minstrels, sages and teachers from the length and breath of Banba brought to instruct the four and the new court at Derravaragh quickly established itself as a centre of learning and culture. The other De Danann lords came to the lakeside also, but they came for a different reason: to hear the children of Lir sing.

Their music was not of this world, it was hauntingly eldritch. It could soothe the most violent warriors and calm the crazed beasts, it could lighten the heaviest hearts or break the hardest. And in the evenings, as the sun dipped behind the far distant mountains and shed its last light across the dark waters of the lake, the children would sing. And the crowded lakeside would grow silent, listening to the ancient lays and ballads of the De Danann, or the softer, sadder songs composed by the four.

And their fame spread.

But the years passed.

One morning late in the year, with the bite of winter already

75

in the air, Fionuala awoke from a troubled sleep and called her brothers together.

'The first part of our sentence is done; we have spent three hundred years upon this lake and now we must make our way to the Straits of Moyle.'

They made their way out of the mists which still clung to the waters for the shore, where they knew their father would be waiting – as he had waited every morning since he had first come to the lake. He was standing on the banks of the lake in full armour, the burnished metal mirroring the waters and the distorted shapes of the swans.

Fionuala looked at him, her eyes heavy with unshed tears, conscious that she would never see him again. Although the children had not aged and Lir was of the Tuatha De Danann – and thus more akin to god than man – Fionuala noticed for the first time the lines about his eyes and the silver in his hair. He embraced each of his children in turn, his hands trembling and his jaw clenched, but he couldn't hide the tears in his eyes.

They parted swiftly and the swans took to the air, their large wings ruffling the waters of the lake, sending tendrils of mist darting and writhing like serpents. They circled once over the palace and the lonely figure standing on the shore, and then they turned and set out for the north and the Straits of Moyle.

The Straits of Moyle was a long open stretch of sea between Banba and Alba. It was a chill, desolate place, with the dark cliffs of Banba on one side and the distant blur of Alba's many islands on the horizon. Often small iceflows from the northern seas would make their ways south into the Strait and even in the height of summer, the water was always chill.

In winter it was bitter.

Storms were frequent upon the wild waters and few ships braved the Strait. In winter even the hardy seabirds were forced to move to a less inhospitable spot.

The children of Lir arrived in time for one of the worst

storms in recorded history upon the sea of Moyle.

The day had dawned dull and overcast with a chill wind sweeping in from the north. Low dark clouds had massed on the horizon and frequently a flash of lightning would ripple through the skies, touching the crests of the heaving waves with silver. By noon it was almost pitch black and the four swans could barely make out each other. Above the howling of the wind, Fionuala ordered them to keep together if possible, but if they were separated, then they were to make their way to Carricknarone - the tiny chunk of windswept rock they had landed on the day before.

The storm rolled in swiftly and the sea rose in welcome. Towering waves crashed and rose again, huge fists hammering at the shivering birds. Ice-flecked gales tore across the turbulent waves, stinging and blinding. Levin bolts ripped through the roiling heavens, their bone-white light etching the swans in stark relief onto the blackness of the storm tossed seas.

Time lost all meaning, day drifted imperceptibly into night and back into day again. The storm lasted three days and soon the Strait was littered with lumps of ice washed down from the northern iceflows, trees and parts of buildings ripped from the land, and bodies ... many torn and shattered bodies, some still clad in the tattered tartans of Alba.

The four swans were separated early in the storm, for it was impossible to keep together in the wild seas.

The sun rose in a clear sky and the sea was calm and gentle when Fionuala reached Carricknarone Rock. She was bitterly cold and badly bruised from the battering she had received from the waves. She struggled up onto the rock and slumped there - waiting. But as the morning drew on and there was still no sign of her brothers, she began to fear that they had been slain and she mourned their passing, singing a piteous lament that carried across the chill waves. And the morning grew very quiet.

And then, from her position high atop the rock, she saw a tiny white speck far out over the waves. A new note entered her song, one of joy, one of welcome, drawing the swan on. It was Fiachra. He struggled up battered and bruised, his slim head drooping in weariness.

'Fionuala,' he gasped, 'it was your singing that led me here. I feared you lost ... I thought ... I thought I was alone.'

Fionuala embraced her brother and, nestling close to him, covered him with her wing. Fiachra, trembling and weary, soon fell into a fitful doze and his last conscious memory was of his sister's voice ringing out sharp and clear on the late morning air.

When he awoke, he found that Aedan, his elder brother had arrived, also drawn by Fionuala's song.

But of Conn, the youngest, there was no sign.

They spent a cold and anxious night upon the rock awaiting their brother. Fionuala, her voice hoarse and raw, could sing no more and she stared desperately at the surrounding waves, willing her brother to appear. Aedan and Fiachra sang together, both for their own comfort and in an effort to call Conn - if he still lived - to the rock.

The following morning dawned bright and cold, with low clouds whipping across the distant horizon and the morning so clear they could see the far shores of Bamba. Fionuala awoke abruptly, stiff and aching and scanned the seas about her. Her shrill cry brought her brothers suddenly awake.

For in the distance, weaving slowly towards them, was their brother, Conn.

Aedan and Fiachra swam out to the small figure and helped him back to the rock. The storm had tossed him far and he was cut and bruised after being dashed against the cliffs of Banba and his left wing was twisted and broken. Fionuala wept when she saw his injuries, but with Aedan's help, she cleansed the wounds as best she could and set the wing.

And then they slept in peace, united at last; Aedan beneath Fionuala's right wing, Fiachra beneath her left, and Conn tucked under her breast.

The years they spent upon the Straits of Moyle were the

hardest they had to endure whilst under enchantment. Often it was so cold that the flesh of their feet stuck to the cruel rock; they were often hungry and always cold.

But the long cold years passed and one day, as the first of the autumnal storms gathered, Fionuala called her brothers together. 'Our time here has ended and now we enter the last part of our sentence. We must fly west and a little south to the Western Ocean and Inish Glora.'

The four swans took to the air, their powerful wings lifting them higher and higher, until they could see both the shores of Banba and Alba and in the far off distance the shadow that was the Isle of Mona. They flew westwards across the green and wooded fields of Banba, which a later race would call Eriu.

It seemed little changed in the three hundred years since they had left it. There were new roads and new forts, but these were insignificant when compared with the vast forests and lush pasturelands. Suddenly Conn, who was flying a little below the others called, 'I want to see home.' He wheeled south in a long slow arc, ignoring Fionuala's frantic cries. They were forced to follow him down, skimming low over the land and here the differences were more apparent. The open fields were now fenced and many of the great trees had been felled and used for kindling. Huge open pits were cut into the soft earth and vast quantities of stone had been removed to build the small, but growing, towns. And when they reached the spot where their home should be, they found nothing but a grass-covered mound and even Lake Derravaragh seemed somehow smaller and not the vast expanse of water they had known.

For the Age of Gods and Heroes had passed and that of Man was at hand and the children of Lir had lived beyond their time.

In many respects the seas about Inish Glora - a barren windswept island - were much like those of the Straits of Moyle. The wind sweeping in from the grey Western Ocean was always chill, bringing with it sleet and snow and they spent many nights flapping their wings in an attempt to stop freezing to death. And death began to have a strange attraction. It would have been easy, so easy, to surrender to the sea and the cold and sink down into its warm embrace, thereby gaining release.

But they could not – for they were the last of the Tuatha De Danann and proud.

One day, whilst flying over the island, Fiachra spotted a tiny inshore lake. It was sheltered somewhat from the wild seas, but was still part of the Western Ocean and thus it did not break their geas to move there.

In the evenings, as the sun was setting in a bloody death across the waves, shedding its baleful light across the heavens, they would sing. Their voices were high and pure, untainted and unbroken by their great age and flocks of birds flying homewards would often swoop down to listen to them, settling upon the still waters of the little lake, or upon the stunted trees and bushes that bordered the banks.

In time the island became known as the Bird Isle.

Now, towards the end of their enchantment, an old man came to the deserted isle. He was small and dark and his hair and beard were long and silver, but he walked without a stoop or the aid of a stick. The children recognised his type, for even in their youth, there had been hermits, men so devoted to their gods that they would cut themselves off from all others, spending their time in prayer and contemplation. And the children of Lir wondered what gods this hermit worshipped; surely not the Dagda and Danu, the gods of their people.

The hermit set about building a rude hut by the lakeside, a makeshift affair of reeds and mud and upon the hut he erected a tall length of wood, with a shorter crosspiece halfway up it.

He spent many days in prayer and fasting either outside the hut facing the curious crosslike affair or else by the lakeside. He took an almost childlike delight in the presence of the swans and he spoke to them, as a man will when he is alone, talking of his plans to build a monastery upon the island, a place of peace and solitude. When he had it, he gave them bread, although he could ill afford it for his diet consisted of roots and boiled fish.

As the year turned, men came to the island, bringing with them many slabs of dressed stone and polished wood, and in a relatively short space of time they had constructed a sturdy beehive-shaped hut and now the device they raised over the roof was of metal and not wood. They also built a smaller stand outside the hut, its roof slanting to either side covering a small upended cup.

When the builders left, the peace on the island seemed even more profound. But that evening the terrified children of Lir heard for the first time the liquid notes of a bell drifting across the still waters of the lake.

Fionuala suddenly remembered her stepmother's mocking words, uttered so long ago on the day she had set the spell. ' "... the day when the bell of the New God rings across the waters of evening ...".'

That night, as the moon cut a silver swathe across the black waters, the hermit stood by the lakeside, gazing serenely into its ebon depths. A tiny splash disturbed the silence of the night. He looked up as the four snow-white swans appeared from the rushes that bordered the lake. He smiled and raised a hand in welcome. He had once thought it strange that such beautiful creatures should want to live in such a desolate place, but when he sometimes despaired, he thought of the swans and took comfort from their presence – it was as if they were a sign, a sign telling him to continue, to carry on.

'Greetings hermit.'

The old man reeled back in shock, one hand clutching for an amulet that hung about his scrawny neck. He stared at the four ghost-like birds in horror. One of them had spoken!

'I am sorry, I did not mean to startle you.' The voice was soft and gentle, that of a young woman. And it came from the largest of the swans.

The hermit swallowed hard and squeezed his eyes shut.

Perhaps he was going mad ... lack of proper food ... little sleep ...

'No,' said one of the smaller swans, this time with the voice of a young man, 'you do not imagine us, we are real.'

The hermit took hold of himself and, straightening up, raised his hand and etched a strange symbol in the air before him. 'In the Name of God the Father and of His Son, that is of the One and of the Ghost, that is also of the One, if ye be spirits of evil or deamons of the pit, I command ye depart.' He paused, but the swans remained.

'What ... Who are you?' he ventured at last.

The large swan with the voice of a young girl, but with the eyes of an old, old woman, answered. 'We are the children of Lir, condemned by a jealous stepmother to spend a thrice-three hundred year enchantment upon the cruel seas about Banba's shores.'

'The children ... the children of Lir,' began the hermit in excitement. 'Yes, I have heard of you, the legends speak of the swan-children.' He fell to his knees by the lakeside and stretched out his gnarled hands to the swans. And one by one they came and placed their heads in his palms and as they did so they introduced themselves:

'I am Fionuala ...'

'... and Aedan, her brother and twin ...'

'My name is Fiachra, and this is my twin ...'

'Conn ...'

'And I am called Kemoch, sometimes called the hermit, but usually called mad.'

'We heard your bell,' said Fionuala, 'and we came, for it was prophesied that the sound of the bell of the New God would mark the nearing of the end of our sentence.'

'Teach us of this New God,' said Aedan.

And there by the lakeside, Kemoch the Hermit, taught the children of Lir, of the New God, of the One called the Christ, and of His followers, and of Patrick, who had brought the faith to Banba, which men now called Erin.

*

About a year later, Decca, a princess of Munster in the south was bethrothed to Lairgen, the king of Connaught, and he, wishing to impress her, said that she might have anything she so desired.

'I have heard,' she said, 'of a lake which lies within your domain . . .' and she paused, for Lairgen had raised his hand.

'No, I know what you are about to ask me, but I beg you, do not request that; do not bring the ancient taint of sorcery into our marriage . . . see what it did to the marriage of Lir and Aefe.'

'What,' cried Decca, her dark eyes flashing in amusement, 'is this fear I see in bold Lairgen's face. What do you fear, my brave warrior,' she asked mockingly, 'an old man and four swans?'

'Someday,' promised the king, 'someday, you will go too far in your demands. Yes, I will get you the swans, though I think you will get little pleasure from the poor creatures.'

The morning was cold and bright with a stiff breeze blowing in off the Western Ocean, when Lairgen at the head of a small company of mounted warriors rode out to Kemoch's little cell and chapel.

The hermit was nowhere to be seen, but from within the tiny chapel came the sound of the most beautiful singing the king had heard. The music itself had life, it was vibrant and pure, etherial. But when Lairgen strode into the building, his armour and weapons jingling and flashing in the sharp sunlight, there was no-one there except the old hermit . . . and the four swans.

'So, the legends are true,' snapped the king. 'The children in swan-shape do exist.' He had only half-believed it. He felt the chill breath of ancient magic blow across the nape of his neck. He wanted nothing to do with this. But . . . but he was committed and if he did not return with the swans, what would Decca say?

Kemoch had arisen and now stood before the king. 'You are in the House of God, sir; remove your helmet and arms,' he cried angrily.

Lairgen pushed the old man roughly aside, and he fell

sprawling on the cruel stones. 'I have come for the swans, hermit, do not stand in my way.' He commanded four of his men to take the birds outside where they had nets ready for them.

The children did not struggle, but once beyond the confines of the church, the warriors stumbled as if beneath a great weight and then were thrown backwards by an invisible hand.

Time stood still.

'"... and the man of the north shall take in marriage the woman of the south ...".'

The air suddenly chilled and rime formed on the feathers of the birds, turning them silver. The silver flowed and ran with a myriad of rainbow colours and the bright sun shattered upon it blindingly, making it impossible to make out the forms of the birds. The warriors covered their eyes, some making the Sign of the Cross, or the older Fist of Thor, or the Horned Sign of Cernounoss; some cried aloud, for there was no shame in fearing sorcery.

The colours froze and the four birds were now enclosed within a glowing silver sphere that dazzled and burned the eyes; a wind howled about the ball, but it was the wind of the Other World, for it did not even ruffle the waters of the lake. Voices cried on the wind, the howling of the damned, the lost and the air was heavy with the pungent odour of cloves and salt.

And abruptly it was gone.

The wind died; the sphere contracted and disappeared. The children were gone and the swans were gone ... but in their place stood four incredibly ancient creatures. They stood taller than the warriors, although their backs were now bent and some of the majestic beauty of the De Danann could still be seen in their skull-like faces. One was barely recognisable as female, whilst the other three were male. The female turned to Lairgen and Kemoch and spoke and her voice was that of a young girl, made all the more obscene coming from those withered lips and toothless gums.

'Behold the children of Lir.'

84

Lairgen suddenly broke from the spell that had held him rooted to the spot and ran for his horse, his warriors stumbling and falling in an effort to mount up.

The four ancients and Kemoch watched them flee. 'We really should thank them,' said one, which the hermit knew was Fiachra, from his voice.

'They have freed us,' agreed Fionuala. 'A woman's greed, and a man's lust.' And then she turned to Kemoch. 'Our time grows short. You have taught us of the Christ and His works and now we wish you to baptise us into the Faith before we die - for our gods are long since dead and no man should go godless to his death. And when we die, I wish you to bury us in the old way, that is, standing up. And you will put Aedan on my right side, Fiachra on my left and place Conn before me, for that is how I sheltered them upon the sea of Moyle and off Glora.'

Kemoch nodded silently, not trusting himself to speak.

And he buried them there by the Lake of Birds in the manner that Fionuala had requested and he placed a stone above their grave. Upon it were the words:

'The Children of Lir: Betrayed; Enchanted; Saved.'

CHAPTER 3

DEIRDRE AND THE SONS OF USNACH
(The Third Sorrow Of Irish Storytelling)

Deirdre and Naise stood on the cliffs, listening to the crash of the waves on the shore and the mewling cries of the sea birds. A stiff breeze was whipping in off the chill Western Ocean, bringing with it the promise of rain. Deirdre snuggled closer to Naise, shivering slightly. Gently, he caressed her red-gold hair and kissed the top of her head.

'Are you cold, my love?'

She shook her head. 'A ... feeling.' She pointed out over the foam-topped waves, to where three lone birds winged westwards into the sinking sun. 'I had a dream last night. A dream about three birds.' She turned and faced Naise, looking up at him from wide green eyes that glistened with unshed tears. 'Naise, I'm frightened.'

Naise kissed her lightly. 'There is no need to be; nothing can happen to you - not whilst Ardan, Anle and myself still live.'

Deirdre ran her long fingers through his blue-black hair, feeling it flow like raw silk in her hands. 'I do not fear for myself. The three birds I dreamt of last night - they were three great ravens and although they had the touch of death about them, they were not Morrigan's pets.' She closed her eyes and her voice became distant and sad. 'They came out of the south and west and alighted on the palisade of our fort.'

Unconsciously, Naise glanced back along the cliffs to the ruined fort which clung to its edges.

'And then, one of our men offered the ravens a piece of meat from a golden platter. The birds would not touch it, but only opened their beaks and left three glistening drops of amber honey on the plate. And then blood seemed to seep from the meat and soil the honey and the ravens each took a sip of the bright blood and took flight ...' her voice faded and was lost on the breeze.

Naise shivered suddenly and then forced a laugh. 'It is probably nothing. You are tired, exhausted. We have been running for a long time – but now we can rest.'

'But can we?' she whispered.

He pointed to the fort. 'Ardan and Anle are supervising the rebuilding of the main section and the outer wall. Once that's fortified, no-one, neither Banban king nor Alban warlord will be able to take you from me.'

Deirdre sighed. 'I wish that could be so ... but I cannot believe it. You know Conor wants me; has wanted me, since the day – the very hour – of my birth.'

Naise laughed. 'Ever since the Druid prophesied that you would be the most beautiful woman in all Banba.'

'He also prophesied that I would cause the downfall of kings and the death of princes,' she added bitterly. 'Some of the other lords present wanted me slain then and I sometimes think it might have been for the best.'

Naise held her tightly. 'No, never say that.'

'But because of me, Conor has exiled you from Banba and put a price on your head; because of me you are now a mercenary; because of me, you and your brothers have been forced to sell your swords to a succession of petty Alban warlords – and because of me, we have had to flee each time.' She raised a tear-streaked face to the skies. 'Why could I not have been born ugly?' she cried.

'But you were not. You were born beautiful and I love you.'

'Do you?' she asked gently.

'With all my heart,' he smiled. 'I've loved you since I first set eyes on you outside that woodsman's hut where Conor had hidden you away.'

Deirdre smiled fondly. 'I remember. My guardian had brought in a hart he had slain and it was beautiful, even in

87

death. Some of its blood had stained the snow beneath its breast and there was a night-black raven perched on the hard ground beside its head. I remember turning to Lavarcham, my teacher and guardian, and telling her I would wed no man but the one with the colour of the hart's blood in his cheeks, the colour of the snow in his skin, and,' Deirdre touched Naise's hair, 'the colour of the raven in his hair.' She laughed gently. 'And she brought me you, Naise MacUsnach, and I brought you only trouble.'

'No, no,' Naise corrected her. 'You brought me love,' and he kissed her with a passion that matched the foaming of the waves against the wild, windswept cliffs of Western Alba.

The sun sank into the sea in a welter of crimson and gold. Dark storm clouds were massing in the north and the breeze had stiffened and moaned about the draughty hall. A huge fire roared and spat in the rebuilt hearth, bathing the large room in a gently wavering light.

Deirdre and Naise sat huddled together by the fire, basking in its heat and light, whilst Ardan and Anle sat hunched over a chessboard. In the shadows, a harper gently strummed his instrument, matching its haunting melody to the rising and falling of the wind. The few servants who had accompanied Deirdre and the sons of Usnach into exile moved about quietly, removing the remains of the spartan evening meal.

The door scraped open roughly and the captain of the guard crossed the worn flags, his boot heels clicking ominously in the sudden silence.

He stopped before Deirdre and Naise and bowed. 'My lord, my lady. There is a craft approaching the loch, running contrary to both tide and wind, coming from the direction of Banba. It's hard to tell in this light, but there seems to be at least three men in it.' He paused and added, 'But no crew.'

*

The three sons of Usnach stood on the cliffs above the inlet and watched the small craft slip in almost silently towards the shore. The sail had dropped and no sound of oars disturbed the water, but still the craft came on. Anle pointed to the thin lines of blue fire that hovered about the figurehead.

'Sorcery,' he spat, with a warrior's disdain of magic.

Ardan touched his older brother on the elbow. 'Our men are in position. We can sink that craft now – and all in it.'

Naise was about to agree and then something ... something stayed his hand and he held off giving the order. Deirdre joined them on the windswept cliffs and watched the craft beach itself with a scrape of hardened timbers.

In the twilight, they could see a single figure disembark and move up the deserted beach. Abruptly, a single flame shot upwards, illuminating the warrior and the craft in a brilliant circle of light. A battle cry echoed off the cliffs above the pounding of the waves.

'Banban!' Ardan and Anle said together, recognising the shout.

'No, I think it's Alban,' corrected Deirdre.

The shout came again.

'It's Banban,' Ardan insisted.

'No, no, it's Alban,' Deirdre repeated, with a touch of desperation in her voice.

The flame on the beach suddenly roared higher and the cry came again, only this time, sharper and clearer.

Naise took Deirdre in his arms. 'That's the cry of Fergus, son of Roy, one of Conor's Champions,' he said gently.

Silently, Deirdre began to weep.

Naise said quietly to Ardan. 'Have him escorted to the fort.'

Fergus MacRoy was standing with his back to the fire when Naise and Deirdre finally entered the hall. The flame-haired warrior bowed mockingly, his wide eyes glinting in amusement.

'My lady, you are as beautiful as rumour paints you.'

Deirdre bowed. 'Your reputation goes before you, Fergus MacRoy,' she said coldly, and took a seat away from the fire, in the shadows.

Fergus indicated the two younger men standing to his left. 'My son's,' he said proudly. 'Illan, called the Fair, because he takes after his mother, and Buinne the Red, sometimes called the Ruthless Red – because he takes after me,' he winked.

'Fergus, why have you come here?' Naise asked suddenly, seating himself by the chessboard and absently toying with a knight.

Fergus hooked his foot around a stool and pulled it over to the fire. He shivered. 'The night is cold and the chill of sorcery is still in my bones.' He nodded in the direction of the shore. 'Catbad, the Druid, called forth some wind elementals to propel our craft across the waves; we could hear the lost souls whispering and chanting all about us. Sometimes the voices became almost distinguishable and we would hear names, always names on the wind, as if the elementals sought to retain their identity.' He downed a goblet of local ale. 'Ah, doesn't compare with the home-brewed stuff. But now ...' he set his goblet aside and leaned forward, his elbows on his knees, and stared intently at Naise and Deirdre.

'Conor wants you back!'

'And has done for a long time,' said Naise.

'But now he is prepared to pardon you!'

For a few moments the hall was so silent they could hear the flames eating away at the dried wood and then Deirdre snapped, 'It's a trick.'

'No trick, my lady, you have the word of Fergus MacRoy on that,' he tapped his chest.

'Why the sudden change of mind?' Naise wondered, toppling the black knight.

Fergus shrugged. 'Who can say? Conor is an old man now, Deirdre no longer seems so important and ...' he smiled apologetically at the shadowy figure in the background, '... he has other mistresses.' His voice changed then and he added, 'And he cannot afford to deplete the fighting force of

90

Banba at the present. Next to the Three Champions, Conall the Victorious, Cucuhulain the Hound and myself, there are no greater warriors in Bamba than the sons of Usnach.'

Ardan stepped out of the shadows, the firelight painting his thin features in sharp angles and planes. 'Can we trust Conor though?' He caught the glint in Fergus' eye, and added hastily, 'It's not that I do not trust you; the word of Fergus MacRoy is legendary, but I would trust Conor only as far as I could spit in a strong wind.'

Fergus nodded. 'I am sorry to say that I must agree with you - but he has given me assurances that you will not be harmed, and,' he added slowly, 'you have *my* assurances that you will not be harmed.'

'That is good enough for me,' said Ardan, looking at Naise.

'And me,' said Anle.

Naise toyed with a white queen, looking intently at its finely carved features. 'Fergus, Conor had pursued us the length and breadth of Banba and had even sent raiding parties into Alba after us. He hired local chiefs to attack us on the roads and sent spies to Lurgan, the High King, telling him of Deirdre's beauty, inflaming his passions, until we were forced to cut our way to freedom through his warriors - warriors who had only that day been our comrades in arms.'

'I can understand your distrust,' said Fergus. 'But he has changed,' he added earnestly, 'he wants you back. Trust me.'

Naise turned to his brothers. 'What do we do?'

'Let us go home,' said Ardan.

'I agree,' said Anle.

'It would be nice to see the green fields of Banba once more,' mused Naise. Turning to Deirdre, he asked. 'What would you have us do, my love?'

'If you return to Banba, you are going to your deaths,' she said ominously. 'Remember my dream? The three drops of honey brought by the ravens are the promises Fergus brings you now - and the three drops of blood signify your deaths. There is nothing for you in Banba except betrayal, treachery and death.'

Fergus surged to his feet, sending the stool crashing

backwards into the fire; Illan and Buinne were at his side immediately. The sons of Usnach closed protectively around Deirdre.

'My lady, you insult me!'

'If I have offended you, then I apologise,' she said. 'I meant to cast no slur upon your honour – but I do not trust Conor and you are a fool if you do. You may be one of his Champions, but he is not above lying to you when the need arises.'

'He would not,' Fergus said immediately, but his voice held a trace of doubt. Abruptly, he pulled his sword free from its sheath, the firelight running like amber liquid down its length. He held the sword out from him, the point tilting up towards the age-blackened rafters. He quietly commanded his sons to place their hands upon the shining blade.

'I swear by this sword, my lady, to protect you from all harm. It will strike in your defence and shield you from all blows. If any man passes insult on you, it will be taken as an insult to me – and avenged, for your enemies are now my enemies ... and my sons'.'

Deirdre stepped from the shadows into the light. The effect was startling; it was as if the goddess Danu had taken corporal form and life. She smiled at Fergus and his sons. 'My lord, I could ask for nothing more; you have calmed my doubts and fears and if Naise wishes to return to Banba, I will gladly accompany him.'

The mists hung low over the chill waters of Loch Etive as Deirdre and the sons of Usnach set out with Fergus and his sons for Banba. The craft was still under enchantment and steered itself at Fergus' command, slipping silently from the mouth of the loch and into the Firth of Lorne. As they passed out into the chill waters of the Western Ocean, the sun burst through the mists, turning the sea into a blinding metallic bowl.

Naise made his way back through the swaying boat to

where Deirdre sat in the stern, staring back at the rapidly disappearing shore of Alba.

'What troubles you, my love?'

She turned and looked at him and Naise was shocked to find her eyes full of tears. He gathered her into his arms and held her gently until her sobs subsided and she lay still.

At last she stirred and looked back at the sinking cliffs, her eyes full of longing. 'We will return some day,' said Naise.

'No. No, we are going to our deaths,' she said, with a note of resignation in her voice.

The morning wore on and presently the misty outline of the cliffs of Banba appeared on the horizon. Naise led Deirdre to the bow and pointed across the waves, and began to speak. But she laid her hand across his arm, her long nails digging into the hard flesh. 'Listen,' she whispered.

'I hear nothing ...' he said after a moment.

And then they all heard it. The haunting, melodious cries echoed across the oily waves, cutting through the air like a knife through flesh. The sound was heavy with pain and anguish – and an incredible loneliness.

It was the song of the cursed children of Lir, as they endured their second term of banishment upon the Sea of Moyle.

'It is a portent of death,' said Deirdre.

It was close to midday when the craft beached on the rough sands of the northern coast. The sun had burned away the last vestiges of the morning mist and the air was heavy and warm, thick with the smell of the sea and the mewling cries of the gulls.

Ardan leaped ashore and breathed deeply of the heady air. 'You can almost taste it,' he shouted.

Naise helped Deirdre ashore, carrying her through the foaming shallows to the drier upper reaches of the rocky beach.

'We're home,' he said simply.

93

And a party of horsemen moved out of a cave in the cliff.

Naise shouted a warning, his sword rasping from its sheath. Ardan and Anle raced across the beach to their brother, followed by Fergus and his sons.

The horses moved skittishly in the shadows, their metal shod hooves ringing hollowly against the cliff-face.

'Come forth and face us,' Fergus called, hefting his huge broadsword.

A single rider broke from the group and urged his horse forward, letting it pick its way through the boulders down onto the beach.

He reined his mount to a halt before Fergus. 'Identify yourselves,' he called, his voice harsh and cold – and knowing.

Fergus stepped forward. 'I am Fergus, son of Roy, one of the Three Champions of Conor and this party is under my personal protection.'

The rider leaned forward over his horses' head. 'Identify them.'

'Your manners leave much to be desired,' Fergus said softly. 'Take care, lest I teach you some. These are my sons, Illan and Buinne,' he continued. 'And this is Naise, Ardan and Anle ...'

'The sons of Usnach,' finished the rider, 'and this,' he said, looking intently at Deirdre, 'must be the beauteous and treacherous Deirdre, daughter of Fedlimid, the Bard.' The rider spat at Deirdre's feet. 'Whore!'

Before anyone had time to react, Fergus struck the horse across the throat, causing it to rear up, throwing its rider onto the stones. Dragging him to his feet, Fergus struck him savagely across the face with the hilt of his sword, opening a long gash from temple to chin. The warrior moaned and went limp. Fergus hefted the body and hurled it before the rapidly advancing horsemen. A horse reared as the body tumbled in its path, crashing sidelong into another, sending them both screaming to the ground.

And then Fergus was amongst them, swinging the huge sword as if it weighed no more than a dagger. With brutal precision, he butchered the warriors, slew two wounded animals and gathered together the six remaining horses. When his bloody work was complete, he leaned upon his sword and grinned crookedly at Deirdre. 'Thus end all who insult you. You see, I keep my word.'

Deirdre bowed and smiled thinly. 'It is a deed that Cucuhulain himself would have been proud of.'

Buinne the Red moved amongst the butchered bodies. Nothing moved save the wind idly plucking at scraps of torn cloth. Some had been shorn almost in two by Fergus' longsword, whilst others lacked heads or limbs.

'Do you want the heads, father?' Buinne called.

Fergus, collecting the reins of the horses, spat in the direction of the corpses. 'I would rather collect the heads of wolves than such scum.'

They had ridden the stolen mounts up the rocky beach and had almost reached the gap in the cliffs, when more riders came pouring out of the caves.

'It's a trap,' Anle shouted, dragging his sword free, but Ardan grabbed his arm and held it. 'Wait,' he cautioned.

The warriors quickly surrounded them, the sunlight turning the armour gold and bronze and striking fire from their shields. Their swords were sheathed and their spears held upright. An older man rode forward and saluted Fergus.

'I am Borrack, sent by Conor to greet you on your return to our land and to extend the hospitality of my Fort to you.'

Fergus bowed. 'I thank you, Borrack, for your invitation, but I fear we must refuse, we cannot delay ...'

'What! You are refusing my hospitality; I did not think that was possible for you.' Borrack leaned forward in the saddle and smiled slyly.

Fergus ignored him and rode back to Deirdre and Naise. 'You heard? He has invited us to his Fort – it would mean losing a night and possibly a morning. We cannot afford the time.' He jerked his head back in the direction of the still-steaming bodies. 'You saw what our reception is likely to be. The price upon your heads is too high and too tempting for most people.'

'I think we'd better hurry on,' Naise said softly. 'At least when Conor acknowledges our presence and takes the price off our heads, we'll not be subject to such abuse and I'll breathe a lot easier.'

'Can we not just refuse Borrack's invitation?' asked Deirdre.

'My lady, in my youth I refused a traveller hospitality; but he was a Druid and in return he placed a geas upon me never to refuse the hospitality of another. I must accept.'

'I see Conor's hand in this,' Deirdre murmured.

Fergus looked uncomfortable. 'It's possible, it's possible; he could be attempting to divide the party. Look,' he said, reaching a decision. 'I will go with Borrack – I have to – but Illan and Buinne will stay with you. And you must ride with all speed for Emain Macha. Once there, Conor would not dare harm you.'

'But until we get there?'

'Until you get there ...' Fergus paused and added ruefully, 'You are fair game for any wandering mercenaries, outlaws or even slaves, tempted by the huge reward.'

'Is there nothing we can do?' asked Deirdre.

'Nothing, except run for Emain Macha, Conor's capital.'

Borrack led the small group surrounded by his guards up through a sharp cleft in the cliffs, their horses' hooves echoing off the dark stone. Once they were up off the beach, the ground levelled out into a broad plain dotted with a few stands of stunted trees and in the distance the rising walls of Dun Borrack crowned with a thin spiral of smoke. They followed a worn beaten track that led from the shore in the direction of the Dun until they came to a slow meandering stream.

'We must part company here,' said Naise suddenly, as the company milled about the small ford.

'You are very welcome,' said Borrack, but without much enthusiasm.

'No ... No, I do not think so; we must go on.' Naise wheeled his mount and, followed by Deirdre, his brothers and the sons of Fergus, set out for Emain Macha in the south and west.

'I'll follow on as soon as I can,' Fergus called and then he turned to Borrack and lowered his voice. 'If I find that you are holding me here on Conor's orders so that he can try and slay them . . .' He let the threat hang for a moment, and then added, 'I will add your head to my collection.'

Borrack looked after the sons of Usnach and Fergus, with the slight figure of Deirdre in their midst and smiled weakly.

They camped late in the afternoon by a stream in a forest glade. The day had turned chill and overcast and there was rain on the wind. They sat in silence around a small smokeless camp fire, listening to the wind rustle the leaves and moan through the branches.

'You do not have to stay with us,' Deirdre said suddenly to the sons of Fergus.

Illan smiled briefly. 'My lady, we do – our father bound us to you.'

'You are likely riding to your deaths, do you know that?'

'It will be an honourable death, at least,' smiled the fair-haired youth.

'And our father will avenge us,' added Buinne.

'Why was your father chosen from the Champions to come for us?' asked Ardan.

Illan broke a twig across his knee and tossed it on the fire. 'Conor called together the Three Champions and told them of his decision to pardon you. And then he asked them – a rhetorical question, he said – what would they do if you were . . . slain?' The youth paused.

'And?' Ardan prompted.

'So, Conall said he would slay anyone who laid a hand on you, be they beggar or king. Cucuhulain said he would slay even Conor himself, should he attempt to break his word and slay you. But our father said that he would slay anyone who so much as offered you insult – except the king, to whom he owed his first loyalty.'

'Do you think Conor will betray us?' asked Anle.

Buinne grinned broadly. 'He will undoubtedly try – and we will probably have to kill a score or so of his men to discourage them. It promises to be great sport.'

'Killing is not sport,' said Deirdre coldly. 'Men are not animals.'

'When men are without honour, my lady, then they are little better than animals.'

And in the silence that followed they heard the baying of war hounds in the distance.

They fled into the gathering night, the harsh cries of the dogs spurring them on. As they rode out of the forest they could see the golden spots of torchlight moving through the trees in the distance. They crested a rise and halted their lathered mounts. The forest was behind them and in almost total darkness, save for the torches and one spot, where the last rays of the sinking sun brought a stand of trees to vibrant life. And through this band of light rode a large body of mounted warriors, their armour and weapons molten, and, running before them, a pack of huge wolfhounds.

Naise stood in the saddle and stared at the war-party. 'I don't recognise them – they are carrying no standard or totem. They could be bandits, mercenaries ...'

'Or Conor's men,' said Buinne, joining him. 'Probably mercenaries in his employ. He has hired some companies of Alban and Monan fighting men and even some from across the seas; tall, blond haired, cold-eyed giants.'

'Do we fight or run?' Naise wondered aloud.

'We run and choose our own battleground.'

The warhounds pursued them through the night, gaining relentlessly. Naise ordered them to pace their mounts, walking them as much as possible, but towards morning it was obvious that they could not continue. And even Deirdre, accustomed as she was to hard riding, was reeling in the saddle, her face pale and drawn with exhaustion. As the first grey tinge of the approaching dawn lightened the eastern sky, Naise called a halt.

'We can't go on like this much longer. The dogs will have caught up with us by sunrise and even if we push our mounts to the limit, we wouldn't reach Emain Macha until noon. We'll have to stand and fight.'

'But not here,' said Buinne. He pointed south and east. 'There is an old fort there; if we reach it before the hounds get us, we'll have something at our backs.'

They reached the tumbled ruins just as the first of the massive hounds caught up with them. A huge wolfhound leaped at Anle's throat, sending him crashing from his exhausted mount. He felt its warm breath against his face and the scalding splash of saliva across his throat. He frantically scrabbled for his knife, but his arm lay trapped beneath him and his other shoulder was numb and useless from the fall. The beast growled deep in its throat and opened its mouth.

He closed his eyes.

Abruptly, the weight was gone and he opened his eyes in time to see Buinne lift the hound above his head and dash it against the stones - the sudden snap sounding sharp and clear on the morning air. Buinne reached down for Anle and then his dark eyes widened in shock and horror as the son of Usnach stabbed at him with his sword. The glittering steel slipped under his arm, almost brushing his ribs and Buinne heard a liquid grunt behind him. A weight fell against his back and a long dagger fell from a mercenary's lifeless fingers.

Naise pushed Deirdre into one of the small rooms which had withstood the ravages of time and weather and then stood in the doorway, beating off the slavering hounds and savage mercenaries, until they piled before him in a gory wall. Ardan and Illan led the mounted warriors through the ruins, splitting them up, and then attacking, until the worn stones echoed to the savage screams and childlike cries of men and beasts.

Illan was struck to the ground and Ardan stood over him, until Buinne and Anle joined him. The shattered corpses of a score of warriors and the hewn remains of an equal number of hounds told of his battle.

A single blast of a hunting horn broke through the sounds

of the battle. The mercenaries retreated, picking their way through the ruins, harried by the sons of Usnach and Fergus, leaving their dead and wounded on the bloody stones and with the few remaining hounds limping in their wake.

Ardan held Illan as he stumbled. The youth was dazed and a thin trickle of blood ran down his face from a shallow wound in his scalp.

Naise and Deirdre joined them and she, with a strip of cloth torn from the hem of her dress and water from a canteen, cleansed and dressed Illan's wound.

Naise and Buinne meanwhile, moved through the dead, seeking a token or banner – anything that might show their allegiance. They found a wounded mercenary, one of the northern folk, with corn-yellow hair and ice-blue eyes, lying apart from the others. He had been wounded high in the chest on the left side, the blow having sheared through the thick leather and metal rings to bite deep into his flesh.

Buinne turned him over with his foot. 'Now here's one that still lives – but not for long, by the looks of him.'

Naise squatted down beside the northerner. 'Who hired you?'

The mercenary grinned, his lips pulling back over his teeth in a ghastly shadow of a smile. 'I knew we couldn't take you, not even with the dogs,' he gasped. 'He has betrayed you ...'

'Who?' Naise asked. 'Who?' he cried – although he already knew the answer.

Buinne touched his shoulder. 'Leave him, he has gone to his gods.'

Naise's face was cold and hard when he rejoined the others and Deirdre shivered at the brooding fire in his dark eyes.

'Where to?' Illan adjusted the rough bandage on his head. 'Do we go to Cucuhulain?'

Naise shook his head. 'We ride for Emain Macha with all speed. Once there, Conor must acknowledge us pardoned and then he dare not move against us.'

*

It was late in the evening when they crested the rise above Conor's capital and found themselves looking down on the stone walls of Emain Macha. The sun was sinking behind the rough walls, touching them with crimson and gold – it looked as if blood had been spilt on bronze, and Naise recalled with a shiver Deirdre's dream of the ravens with their gift of honey and blood.

As they neared Emain Macha, they could see the sudden flurry of activity and the flash of sunlight on weapons and then the huge gates opened and a long line of warriors marched out.

Anle squinted against the sinking sun. 'They are the Knights of the Red Branch, the élite.'

Naise grinned bleakly. 'We have little to fear from them, they are honourable men. I doubt they would attack us even if Conor himself ordered it.'

The warriors lined up along both sides of the dusty road and some touched their hearts and bowed as Naise and the veiled Deirdre passed.

Once inside the gate, the great doors swung shut and were barred for the night. The courtyard came alive with torches, banishing the dusk. Fiacha, Conor's son stepped into the light. 'My father bids you welcome and has set aside the Hall of the Red Branch for your personal use. There is food and drink prepared and he bids you break your fast, rest and refresh yourselves – he will attend you then.'

Deirdre laid her hand on Naise's arm and whispered urgently. 'Let us leave now, because once we enter the Hall, we will not come out alive.'

Naise gripped her hand and squeezed tightly. 'He dare not touch us now.'

Conor flung the goblet into the raging fire. The volatile liquor exploded into blue-green flames. 'I will have her,' he screamed, his eyes bulging and the cords in his neck standing out. 'She is mine by right and I will have her.'

'You cannot father, you have promised them your pardon,' Fiacha protested.

Conor looked at his son with contempt. 'If you intend to rule this land when I am gone, you must learn to abide by no other laws save your own – and a king makes his own laws, changing them when it suits his purpose. Tell me what she looked like,' he asked suddenly, changing the subject.

'She ... I do not know, she went veiled and cloaked.'

'Her voice then, describe it.'

'She spoke only once and then it was in a whisper to Naise.'

'I must know whether she still retains her beauty,' the king muttered.

'And if she does not?' Fiacha wondered.

'Then Naise can keep her,' Conor snapped. 'But if not ...' his voice chilled and his laugh was ugly.

Fiacha shivered.

Conor poured himself another drink, a quiet smile playing at the corner of his lips. He turned to his son. 'Find me Lavarcham, Deirdre's old teacher and nurse; perhaps she can help us.'

Naise moved his queen. 'Check,' he said quietly.

Deirdre smiled and moved her king, the light from the large fire turning the crystal pieces to amber. Ardan and Illan walked out of the shadows at the back of the huge hall murmuring softly together. Anle sat before the fire honing his sword with slow persistance, whilst Buivva hovered about the barred door. The food and drink which had been prepared for them lay untouched and although they were almost exhausted they were too excited to attempt sleep.

Suddenly Buivva spoke from beside the door. 'Someone approaches.'

Deirdre was abruptly aware that everything seemed to be coming together – it was almost as if she were part of a play,

102

a drama which had been prepared a long time ago. 'Lavarcham,' she whispered softly to herself, as Buivva opened the door and admitted a cloaked and hooded figure.'

'It's Lavarcham,' he said.

Deirdre embraced her old teacher and nurse, tears flowing down her face. The old woman stroked her wild red hair, soothing her as if she were a child.

'I'm frightened,' she whispered softly, 'not for myself, but for the sons of Usnach and Fergus.'

Lavarcham eased herself into a chair by the fire. She was frail and birdlike, her hair snow-white, almost feather-like in its texture. But there was nothing soft about her eyes; they were hard and sharp and glittered with almost eight decades of experience. 'You must listen to me carefully,' she said, and like her eyes, her voice was vibrant and alive. 'Conor wants Deirdre and he is prepared to break every oath and principle of kingship to get her. And if he takes her by force, he will plunge this land into almost three hundred years of warfare and strife. But he only wants Deirdre if she still retains her beauty,' and the old woman smiled, 'which she does.'

'Is that why he sent you here?' asked Illan.

'I was sent to see if Deirdre was still as beautiful as she was when he last saw her. I will go back and tell the king that she does not, but I don't think that will be enough, I'm sure he will want to see for himself. So, you must bar the windows and guard the door - at least until the morning. Cucuhulain is on his way and Fergus is approaching also, they should be here by then and they will not let Conor refuse to fulfil his promise.' She stood suddenly. 'I must go, but remember, be on your guard, Conor is treacherous.'

The king raged when he heard that Deirdre's incredible beauty was lost and that she was now haggard and drawn, wasted by the years of rough living, fleeing Conor's wrath. But there was something about Lavarcham's story, something intangible, some note which rang false - or perhaps the king just did not want to believe it. But he sent one of his personal bodyguards to the hall of the Red Branch with instructions to check the old woman's story. The guard found the long wooden building in almost total darkness; chinks of flickering light showed through the cracks in the shutters and all the doors were barred. He pressed his ear against the smooth wood, but he could hear no sound from within. He walked around the building. There was a tiny open window set high up in the south wall and so, taking off his boots, he began to climb the polished timbers.

Within, Deirdre and Naise sat side by side crouched over the chessboard, vainly attempting to while away the few remaining hours to morning. Anle and Ardan and the sons of Fergus prowled restlessly about the hall, awaiting the attack which they knew would almost certainly come.

The guard gripped the sill and pulled himself up level with the window. He found he was looking down into the hall almost on top of Deirdre and Naise.

And his breath caught in his throat as Deirdre moved into the light.

He had always imagined that the stories of her beauty were greatly exaggerated, mere poet's fancies and bard's tales, but she was even more beautiful than they painted her. She turned to say something to someone out of his range of vision and the flickering light touched her face, bathing it in gold, turning her eyes to points of amber light. She stood and as he moved to follow her, the hilt of his dagger clinked against the edge of the windowsill. He saw Naise's lined and weary face look and the cold dark flash of his eyes. He saw him pluck a chessman from the board before him and throw ...

The queen struck the guard in the eye. With a hideous scream, he clawed at his face and fell backwards onto the ground with a sickening crunch. He lay screaming on the rough stones, his legs twisted at an unnatural angle, blood trickling from his lips.

A score of guards ran up and one knelt by his side. 'Tell ... tell the king ... that she ... she is beautiful,' he gasped and then he pleaded, 'kill me.'

*

Conor's anger when he heard of Lavarcham's treachery was awesome to behold, but the old woman was gone, having fled back to the mountains of her birth. And the flame of his anger raged higher when the Knights of the Red Branch refused to surround the Hall, for they were honourable men and wanted no part of the king's proposed treachery and betrayal. And, in the end, Conor was forced to use his mercenaries to surround the hall.

Buivva's sword rasped as it slid from its sheath, the sound shockingly loud in the silence. 'They are coming.'

Deirdre, with the sons of Usnach and Fergus, peered from the slits in the shutters, watching the armed and armoured warriors quietly taking up position around the hall. At last Conor appeared. He stood before the main door and folded his arms across his broad chest. 'I will receive you now, you may come forth.'

'Let us wait until morning, king; the morning sun will bring many things,' Naise called.

'Obey me; come forth now!'

'Dawn is fast approaching,' said Ardan. 'We can afford to wait.'

'But Conor will not,' said Buivva. 'I will go out and engage his men in single combat, they are honour bound to stand before me singly and perhaps Cucuhulain or my father will arrive early.' He slid the bar across the door and slipped out into what remained of the night. Illan quickly dropped the bar back into place.

Buivva faced Conor and his warriors outside the door. The king smiled, but only with his lips – his eyes remained hard and chill. 'So, you have come to join us; someone knows where his duty lies.'

Buivva shook his head. 'You are mistaken, lord, I have come out to challenge your warriors to single combat.'

'Fool!' Conor spat at Buivva's feet. 'Why not fall on your sword now and have done with it. What are you about to die for? What are the sons of Usnach to you? Does Deirdre mean anything to you?'

105

'I am honour bound to protect them,' he said simply.

'Have they honour? Had the sons of Usnach honour when they stole my bride and then fled my court? Naise, Ardan and Anle had sworn oaths of fealty to me, they were Knights of the Red Branch and honour bound to protect their king and their country. And what did they do? They abandoned one and deserted the other.

'How can you protect them knowing of their crimes? By doing so it makes you worse than them. It makes you a traitor, it makes you dishonourable, it makes you a coward ...'

Buivva's face burned red in the flickering light of the torches and when he spoke his voice was low and trembling. 'Your kingship protects you Conor, but have a care lest I forget that kingship ...'

'And what will you do?' Conor sneered. 'Kill me? You can try, but at least these men –' he gestured at the shadowy figures surrounding the hall, '– at least they are men of honour; they have sworn to protect me and they will not desert me.' He paused and added, 'As you did.'

'Never!'

The king looked surprised. 'Then what are you doing now, eh? You are protecting traitors, killers, thieves – so what does that make you?' Conor shrugged and turned away.

'Wait.' Buivva let his sword fall to his side. 'Tell me what to do,' he pleaded. 'My father has ordered me to protect them with my life and you ordered him to bring them home – and yet, now you tell me it is dishonourable to protect them. What is right?' he cried.

Conor smiled indulgently. 'Your first duty is to your father, of course, but his first duty is to me and even he, Buivva, cannot always be right. And I fear he has been sadly misled by the sons of Usnach.'

'I am uncertain ...'

'You honour your father,' Connor persisted, 'and he honours me – am I not then like your father? And answer me this: where does your duty lie – with the traitorous sons of Usnach or towards your king?'

'Towards my king,' Buivva said slowly. Sheathing his sword, he walked the short distance across the pool of light into the shadows by Conor's side.

'You will be well rewarded,' assured the king.

'I do not want your reward - only spare my brother.'

'I will do what I can.'

Inside the hall, Illan hung his head in shame and wept bitterly. Deirdre laid her hand on his arm. 'Do not curse or grieve for him; he has been tricked by Conor. He is not the first, nor will he be the last.'

But Illan refused to be comforted and, taking his sword and gear, went out to do battle with Conor's mercenaries. 'I will not listen to you,' he shouted as he came out the door, 'so do not waste your time trying to beguile me with your lying tongue - but come closer lord and I will cut it out for you.

The king shrugged resignedly and, breaking all the codes of honour, sent three of his men against the single warrior. With almost mechanical ease Illan cut them down, parrying their blows with his spear and thrusting with his sword. Conor ordered another trio of warriors against the son of Fergus. But Illan had been trained by one of the greatest warriors in Banba - his own father - and could not be taken by common mercenaries.

Conor called his son to him. Fiacha was taller than his father, though with the same small mouth and tiny eyes. He was well built and his long reach and dazzling skill made him an almost unbeatable swordsman. The king armed him with his own weapons - a long, double-edged sword forged from starstone and a large circular shield which wailed with the voice of a banshee when its bearer was in danger of death.

Fiacha strode confidently into the circle of light cast by the torches, his arms and armour glittering golden in the warm light. Illan watched him carefully. The prince felt certain of victory, both his long reach and now the unusual length of the sword assured him of victory. But the weapons were new to him and the shield weighed heavily on his arm,

107

whereas Illan was fighting with his own weapons and unencumbered by a shield.

Fiacha attacked suddenly, without the courtesy of a challenge. His sword darted out, feinted to the right and then came back in a long slash, which would have opened Illan from side to side had it connected. But the prince's eyes had betrayed him; Illan stepped back from the blow, caught Fiacha's sword on his spear and beat it to the ground.

Illan attacked, the point of his sword scoring a long wound along Fiacha's forearm and another below his neck – but although both were painful, neither were serious. The prince was more wary now, he brought the shield across his body and waited. Illan probed with the point of his spear, testing the metal of the shield. It rang with a dull, heavy clang and the surface of the metal was unmarked.

Fiacha suddenly brought his sword up and over his body, driving it downwards in a vicious arc, whilst at the same time pushing forward with his shield. The heavy metal hit Illan on the left side, numbing his shoulder and arm and his sword dropped from nerveless fingers. He barely deflected the sword with his spear, batting it to one side. He continued the spear's circular motion, striking Fiacha across the side of his head with the butt. The prince stumbled back, dazed and sick with the pain. Illan brought the spear in low, cracking it across his shins and then bringing the butt up again, striking Fiacha under the chin. The prince's jaw closed with an audible snap and his eyes rolled in his head as he slumped to the ground. Illan brought the spear around for the killing stroke ...

And the shield moaned.

It was a long strident tone that plucked at the nerves and set the teeth on edge. It hung trembling on the cool pre-dawn air – a terrifying otherworldly death knell.

And then out of the shadows came a warrior, the torchlight running like blood along his drawn sword and gleaming armour. It touched his broad face with amber and shaded his red beard and his long trailing red plait to rust. He was Conall, called the Victorious, one of the Three

Champions of Conor. He had been drinking in his rooms in the main building, his thoughts dark and angry, a slow hatred of Conor building, when he heard the moaning of the warning shield.

His king was in danger.

The discontented thoughts disappeared as almost three decades of unwavering loyalty to the monarch took over. Grabbing his sword, he raced for the Hall of the Red Branch. He pushed his way through the mercenaries. The moaning grew louder, more urgent, bone-chilling, mind-numbing.

Bursting into the circle of light, he saw a figure standing over a fallen warrior. The man on the ground wore the royal insignia, and Conall recognised the long black sword. The warrior standing above the fallen king raised his spear and prepared to strike ...

Conall lunged – his sword passed through Illan's body and emerged from his chest. He stood swaying, the sword still protruding from just above his heart as Fiacha pushed himself to his feet, a broad grin on his face.

Conall staggered back aghast and then Conor stepped out of the shadows. 'You have done well, my Champion, now slay him.'

Conall turned and looked at Illan. All traces of pain and fatigue had faded from the youth's face, as if the cares of this world were fading as quickly as his life.

'You have tricked me,' Conall screamed. 'This was my friend.' He held Illan as his legs began to buckle.

'He was a traitor,' said Fiacha casually. He struck at the dying warrior with his sword, but Conall caught the blade in his mailed fist and wrenched it from the prince's grasp. The Champion deftly flipped the weapon and, with a single blow, struck Fiacha's head from his body. He spat on the decapitated body.

Illan sank slowly to the ground, despite Conall's supporting arm. 'Find ... Cucuhulain or ... my father ... tell ... tell him,' he gasped. 'And ... beware Conor's treachery.'

And Conall wept as Illan, his life-long friend died in his

arms. He gathered up the body and walked away from the Hall of the Red Branch. Conor stared after him, fingering his sword, refusing to look at the headless thing on the blood-clotted ground. And abruptly, he remembered Old Catbad the Druid's warning the day the child Deirdre had been born: 'She will bring with her death and destruction. She will divide the kingdom, and set brother against brother, she will cause the downfall of kings and the death of princes.' And Conor shivered.

Thrice, during what little remained of the night, the king's mercenaries attempted to fire the building. But its builders had constructed well and the hardwood only scorched and refused to burn. The fire arrows sputtered out harmlessly against the sloping roof and the thrown spears snapped against the walls. Conor refused to let the mercenaries storm the building. There was too little time left and he could not allow the sons of Usnach to be slaughtered within the Hall of the Red Branch, lest the Knights themselves turn on him.

The first grey tinge of dawn touched the eastern sky and the king knew that either Cucuhulain or Fergus would arrive soon. And in desperation he sent for Catbad, the Druid.

Within the hall, Deirdre and the sons of Usnach awaited the coming dawn. Conor could not afford to anger all three of his Champions, not now, not whilst Maeve was gathering her armies in Connaught. As it was, his reputation was tarnished almost beyond redemption. He had lost Conall and surely he had lost Fergus now as well, and Cucuhulain, who placed honour above all other things would leave him also. All that was left for the king now was the capture of sons of Usnach and the taking of Deirdre.

'You will work an enchantment - drive them out,' said Conor to the aged Druid when he arrived.

'I will not.'

'You will do as I say old man, or ...' Conor let the threat hang.

The Druid laughed gently. 'You will what? For all your

blustering, you are nothing more than a coward and a dishonourable coward, at that. I will work no enchantment to drive them out.' Catbad gathered his long robes about him and left. When he was gone, a young man in the pale blue robes of a student approached the king.

'My lord, I could not help but overhear what you were discussing with my master.'

The king eyed the young man disdainfully. 'Yes, and what can you do?'

'I am not unaccomplished in the arcane arts ...'

Conor nodded slowly. 'I see. Can you drive them out?' He nodded in the direction of the hall.

'It would be a little difficult, but it could be done,' the young man hesitated, and the king recognised the look in his eyes.

'You would not find me ungenerous,' he said. 'Catbad is an old man now and today he has refused my command; I will soon need a new court Druid.'

The young man nodded and smiled quietly. He stepped away from king and raised his long alder wand high. The first rays of the sun touched its tip with fire as he chanted aloud in the Old Tongue – a tongue which men said was older than the land itself.

In the hall it was still dark. Naise and Deirdre huddled together by the dying embers of the fire, whilst Ardan and Anle stood by the shuttered windows, staring out from the cracks into the morning.

'There is a Druid outside,' said Anle.

And fire blossomed in the hall.

It hung in the centre of the long room, a glowing, pulsating ball of intense white light. Naise grabbed a pitcher of water and threw it at the fireball. The clay pitcher exploded with the heat and the water steamed furiously as it touched the outer fringes of the fireball. The heat was incredible. The wooden table and chairs began to smoulder and char and Ardan yelped as the metal of his breastplate grew too hot to touch.

And slowly the ball began to grow.

'We must get out,' said Ardan, 'before we bake.'

The sons of Usnach doused themselves and Deirdre with water and stood by the door. They formed a fighting wedge, Ardan to the left, Anle to the right, Naise leading and Deirdre behind him and between the brothers. As quietly as possible, Naise lifted the bar from the door. But before they went out into the morning, Naise looked back at the rapidly expanding ball of fire and spoke the Name of the Dagda, the Father of All.

The fireball suddenly shrank in upon itself with an icy blast and as they erupted from the hall, their weapons ready, the first thing they saw was the Druid wrapped in writhing blue flames which consumed him before their eyes.

Conor ordered his mercenaries against the trio. But the sons of Usnach beat them off, taking only minor cuts themselves. The king retreated deeper and deeper into the body of his men as the three warriors cut a bloody path through his guard. But then the archers appeared.

The sons of Usnach gathered shields from their fallen foes and sheltered behind them as the arrows rained about them. And still they advanced.

A runner approached the king, one of the guards from the battlements. He had seen a cloud of dust in the west – Cucuhulain was approaching.

Conor stepped out from his men and ordered the archers to cease firing and called the others off. He held out both hands to Deirdre and the sons of Usnach. 'I offer you peace,' he said.

Naise laughed. 'Peace; you call this peace?'

'It was an impulsive act; anger momentarily clouded my judgement.'

'You are a liar,' said Naise. 'A traitorous, cowardly liar.'

Conor smiled, showing his teeth like a cornered animal. 'Can we not settle our differences?'

Naise looked around him at the dead and dying. 'I doubt if our differences can ever be settled – except in blood.'

'And there has been enough shed this day,' said the king piously. 'Let there be an end to it.'

112

Naise nodded his head. 'Aye, let there be an end to it. I grow weary of this fighting, the stench of blood disgusts me.' He looked over his shoulder at his brothers and Deirdre. 'Do we trust him?'

Ardan and Anle laughed. 'Trust him; never.'

'But in this case,' Naise persisted, 'can we trust him now?'

'I think he has little choice,' said Anle.

'Do not trust him,' said Deirdre quietly. 'There is treachery in his eyes.'

'Come, come, let us be friends – or if not friends, then let us not be enemies,' Conor amended.

'That is impossible,' said Naise sadly. 'There are too many years, too many bodies, too much blood between us.' He raised his head and looked into the morning sunrise.

'Look, a new day is dawning, let it mark a new beginning between us also.' He sheathed his sword with a snap.

Reluctantly his brothers followed suit and Deirdre's murmured protest went unnoticed.

Conor came forward, his arms outstretched, his face creased in a smile. He held Naise by the arms. 'I have waited a long time for this moment,' he said gently. 'SEIZE THEM!'

Thus were the sons of Usnach taken through treachery.

'Who will slay these traitors for me?' the king called. No-one moved. To slay bound warriors was the act of a coward.

'Is there no-one man enough to slay them – or must I do it myself?'

'You know you cannot do it yourself,' said Naise, still standing tall and straight despite the bonds which cut into his wrists. 'You know that if you kill us, either Cucuhulain or Fergus will have your head.'

A tall, blond-haired, blue-eyed youth came out of the crowd. 'Let me kill them; I do not fear your Champions, king.'

'Then you are a fool,' laughed Ardan.

The youth pulled his sword from its sheath. 'Which one shall I kill first?' he asked Conor.

113

'You must kill me first,' said Naise.

'No, me,' said Ardan and Anle together.

'If you slay them, then you must slay me also,' screamed Deirdre, held in the grip of two warriors.

'One of you must die first,' said Conor reasonably. 'Come, who is man enough to die first?'

'I have never been called a coward,' said Naise. 'I have fought deamons and beasts and men, without flinching – but I cannot bear to see my brothers slain, or to see Deirdre's face broken in sorrow.'

The youth raised his sword and prepared to strike Naise.

'No, you cannot,' said Ardan. 'We were always one in life, let us die together.'

'That is impossible.'

'Take our sword, "The Retaliator",' said Naise. 'It was a gift to us from the Lord of the Sea, but we have never had cause to use it.'

The sword was found amongst their belongings in the hall, a long, single-edged weapon, almost three times the length of a normal sword. It glittered blue-green in the morning sunlight.

Naise, Ardan and Anle knelt on the ground together. Their executioner raised the overlong sword and Naise looked across at the weeping figure of Deirdre. 'I love you,' he whispered.

The sword fell.

Thus ends the tale of the sons of Usnach. But for Conor, it was only the beginning of the end of his kingdom. When Fergus returned and found one of his sons slain and the other's treachery, and learning of Conor's own treachery, he gathered together his men and marched south and west for Connaught and took service with Maeve. Some time later, Connaught attacked Ulster, and it was Cucuhulain the Hound who held the army of Maeve, commanded by Fergus, at bay, but when he fell, Ulster was overrun, and Emain Macha was no more.

But beyond the hill that was once the capital of the north there is a little grove of trees surrounding a sparkling pool. And it is said that the pool sprung from the tears shed by Deirdre for Naise and his brothers. The trees are said to grow from the spot where the three sons of Usnach are buried and across the pool is a single tree, a willow, its branches drooping in sorrow into the pool - and it grows from the spot where they buried Deirdre, for she slew herself before Conor could claim her.

CHAPTER 4

MIDIR AND ETAIN

'The harlot has stolen Midir away from me,' said Fuanach, Queen of the De Danann, the People of the Goddess.

'His heart is certainly hers,' agreed the Druid cautiously, 'but what do you want me to do about it?'

Fuanach paced the stone cell impatiently, measuring its length and breadth in angry steps. Dusk was falling and the tiny fire in the rough grate bathed the little chamber in wan amber light; smoke coiled about the blackened stones, stinging the queen's hard eyes and burning her throat.

'You must kill her!'

Tarlaim the Druid shook his head. 'You know that is impossible, she is of the De Danann, I have neither the ability nor the power to kill her.' He stirred the coals of the mean fire with his brass shod staff. 'However,' he added, 'we could dispose of her ...'

Fuanach gripped the Druid's thin shoulders and gazed into his sightless eyes. 'How?'

Tarlaim ran a calloused hand down the queen's raven hair, seemingly lost in thought. Abruptly he gripped it and pulled hard; tears started into her eyes, but she bit her lip and made no sound. 'By turning her into what she is not ...'

'A transformation?' asked Fuanach between clenched teeth

'A transformation,' agreed the Druid. 'And what would you have her: bird ... beast ... insect ...?'

Fuanach pulled away and knelt, staring into the glowing embers. 'Can she be killed in her new shape?' she wondered.

'Certainly, but not by any deliberate action of yours. But

were she to succumb to hunger, thirst or exhaustion – then she would die.'

The queen nodded silently, her ice-grey eyes glittering strangely and then she laughed. And Tarlaim – who had traded his eyes with the deamons of the pit in return for arcane knowledge – shivered with the sound of that pitiless laughter.

'Then turn her into a butterfly, Druid: it should suit her character, something beautiful, but shallow and fragile – something easily broken. Then call up a wind, the like of which has never before blown across Banba's shores, and let it carry Etain to the ends of the land.'

'That can be done,' agreed the Druid.

'Why do you wait?' asked Fuanach, when he made no move to set the spell. 'Do it now!'

'And payment?' wondered Tarlaim mildly.

Slowly Fuanach rose from before the fire and, taking the Druid's hard hands, placed them on the gold clasp high upon her shoulder. His breathing quickened as he fumbled with the pin, and then it was undone and her heavy gown fell in shimmering folds about her feet. Savagely Fuanach kissed him ...

Night crept slowly over Bre Leth, the fort of Midir, King of the De Danann. But the stars that shone over the sidhe were not those that glittered in the heavens above the world of Man. And whilst the De Danann might inhabit the world of Man, they were still separated from it, living in a realm of their own, a Shadowland, where death held no domain and sickness was unheard of.

The tiny sliver of the new moon rose low in the sky, touching the few clouds with silver, whilst overhead, the alien stars trembled hard and sharp on the thick velvet cloth of heaven.

Midir and Etain stood on the battlements and watched the skies. The king encircled Etain's shoulders with one arm whilst pointing out constellations with his free hand.

117

'See, there is the Evenstar and there below is her maid-servant, Etive, and that triple cluster to the right are her bodyguards, Conn, Corann and Conan.'

'And that one, my lord?' asked Etain, nestling close to her lover and pointing to a group of stars.

'That is the Cup of Heaven; see there is the bowl, the stem, there the base. It is a horn of plenty, or riches and ...' he bent and kissed the top of Etain's corn-yellow hair, '...of love.'

They stood awhile longer, staring silently into the night, content in each other's company. Suddenly Etain shivered. 'It has grown chill.'

Midir slipped the cloak from his shoulders and drew it about Etain. 'Let us retire now, my love,' he said.

Shivering, she agreed.

By the time they reached Etain's bedchamber, she was shaking so badly she could hardly stand. Midir placed his hand on her brow, but she was not feverish. Lifting her in his strong arms, the king carried his mistress to her bed, and wrapped the thick furs about her.

'I will fetch a physician, this is not natural,' he said.

As soon as Midir left her, the shivering stopped. And suddenly the room was like a furnace. Scrambling from the smothering furs, Etain went and stood in the window, her face turned to the light breeze trickling through. But she still burned and her light garments weighed upon her like a warrior's mail. He hands trembled and her fingers were numb and unresponsive as they struggled to undo the straps and pins. A pin pierced her thumb as she frantically pushed her gown and shift to the floor. She felt the cool breeze flow across her hot skin like balm. Throwing her head back, she closed her eyes and luxuriated in its cool embrace.

Gradually she became aware of a tingling in her hands and feet, a tingling that spread rapidly until it engulfed her as if she were sinking into a pit of sand.

She opened her eyes, but the room swayed and lurched as if she were standing on the deck of a storm tossed ship. Tiny points of coloured light exploded before her eyes, leaving

118

trembling afterimages of blackness. The room vanished behind a coloured gauze curtain of shifting light. She was blind.

Etain opened her mouth to scream, but she could make no sound – her body was no longer hers, it was separate, unreal, a stranger's. She became aware of a dull pounding, like that of the surf on the shore, a pounding that embraced and then engulfed her, until she felt as if her entire being might shatter.

Abruptly, it ceased.

Sight had returned, but only a flat, two-dimensional, colourless vision. Hearing had also returned, but now she heard with her entire body.

Body?

Sorcery!

The truth hit her with an almost physical blow. A shape-change; someone had wrought a transformation upon her. And she did not even have to wonder whom: Fuanach. But what shape had her body been warped into? Clumsily, she directed her body to a pitcher of water which lay beside her bed. The room glided past underneath – *underneath?* – and curved off at the edges, making progress erratic and difficult. Reaching the pitcher of water, she forced herself to stop – although she was constantly pulled and tugged in countless directions by intangible, but irresistible forces. Etain directed her gaze downward.

And had she a mouth to scream, she would have done so. For reflected in the water was the image of a butterfly.

Midir raced down the corridor followed by his physician and two warriors. He was conscious of a heavy foreboding nestling at the base of his skull. Etain's sudden sickness reeked of sorcery – but who would wish to harm such a beautiful and innocent maid?

Fuanach!

If she were behind this, the king swore, he would have her head and the heads of those who had helped her. Reaching

119

the door of Etain's bed-chamber, he paused. There were noises within. Drawing his sword he pushed the old physician back and called his warriors forward. Weapons at the ready they pushed open the door and launched themselves into the room ...

... Into chaos ...

It was as if they had stepped out into a winter gale. An icy wind tore at them, buffeting them in all directions, threatening to strip the flesh from their bones, numbing and burning at the one time. The bed furs flapped like angry birds, and the window coverings of heavy cloth were ripped off and flung in their faces.

Midir braced himself against the doorframe and pushed himself into the centre of the room, seeking Etain. The low bed had been stripped bare, and nothing but the leather straps and polished wooden frame remained. As he fought his way to it, the entire frame slowly overturned and came tumbling towards him. He felt someone grip his leg and jerk him forward, and he crashed to the floor beside his warriors. The heavy frame rose on the gale and shattered against the wall over their heads, showering them with thick splinters.

Jars and small bowls flew about the room like angry wasps, breaking against the walls, smearing the stones with expensive oils and ungents. One of Etain's bone combs raked against the king's face, drawing blood and narrowly missing his eye.

Midir scrambled backwards out of the room, his warriors crowding him in their eagerness to quit the enchanted place. Behind them the room dissolved into a maelstrom of destruction.

'Sorcery,' screamed Midir. 'Sorcery. Seal the fort, let no-one leave.' He pushed away the physician, who was dabbing at the cut on his face with a cloth. 'Leave it; you will have blood soon enough to wipe.' He turned to his guards. 'Bring Fuanach to the main hall and all her servants and slaves, aye, and her pet Druid also. Heat the irons and have chains prepared – I will have the truth; I will have my Etain!'

*

The gale gripped Etain in a constricting fist, tightening and squeezing, battering her with incredible force. She could not resist it, she could only allow herself to be propelled at the will of the storm. And as she was flung into the night, her last thoughts were of Midir, her love.

For seven years the gale that had torn through Bre Leth whipped across the fields of Banba, sometimes at such a great height that the only evidence of its passing were the rapidly shifting clouds. But often the gale would tear along at ground level, destroying entire forests in its fury, flattening crops, laying waste entire communities and devastating the hill forts where they were exposed to the full fury of the sorcerous wind. Many died in the Land of Men, and even the People of the Goddess, the De Danann, were hard put to defend themselves from the elemental fury of the storm. They could not reverse the spell, for they did not know how it had been set – and Tarlaim could not tell them, for Midir's guards had found him with his throat slit.

Midir had taken Fuanach and had her questioned under torture, but she had revealed nothing and because she was of the De Danann, he could not order her slain.

The king called together the greatest of the Druids from Alba and Mona and from the Land Across the Water, where men went daubed in blue and the Druids there worshipped in great stone circles and ancient places of power. But even these were unable to wrest from the queen the location of Etain. And in desperation they tried to raise the shade of Tarlaim, but he had been damned and thrice damned in life and now paid the price in death and his shade wandered beyond the Fields of Life, in that place it is not wise to visit.

And in revenge, Midir ordered the assembled Druids to work an enchantment upon the queen and turn her into a lizard and then they cast her out into the Fields of Man, where she wandered for a thousand years until the coming of the New God and of the Truth-Bringer, the one men would call Patrick.

But Fuanach cursed Midir, saying that 'though he would find Etain after thrice seven years of searching, he would lose her again, after thrice seven days, and their second parting would be the hardest to bear, for it would be Midir himself who would cast her out'.

And then Midir set a regent to rule his land in his stead and taking his harp and chessboard, sword and spear, set out for the Fields of Man to search for his lost love.

Etain wandered for seven years over the fields of Bamba knowing little rest and no ease. Hunger and thirst were with her always and her delicate body always ached. Her greatest fear was that her gauzy wings might break beneath the onslaught of the gale and leave her helpless and broken on the ground below.

One morning as she rested on a stone by a tiny glittering stream, she saw a youth approaching and because she was of the De Danann and able to see beyond the surface of things, she recognised him as Angus, the god of Love and Lord of the Birds.

He stood taller than a mortal man and his hair was of the palest gold, as were his eyebrows and lashes. His tunic was of pure white wool and about his wrists were bracelets of rune-inscribed gold.

Etain took flight and fluttered before the god, wary of the four birds that circled above his head. The god raised his hand and the huge butterfly settled gracefully down onto it, her large wings pulsating gently. Angus looked upon her and, with his sight that saw beyond the corporeal, he made out the form of the maid beneath the enchantment.

And the god recognised her, for the tale of Fuanach's jealousy and revenge had quickly spread.

'You are Etain.' The god's voice was sweet and pure with a strangely bell-like quality. With infinite care he stroked her beautiful wings. 'Come with me,' he whispered, 'perhaps I can help you.' And so he took her to his palace beyond the Shadowland, in the place where time stands still.

The god attempted to remove the enchantment, but even he was unable to reverse the spell totally. However, with the

122

aid of the Goddess Danu, he could lift the enchantment from dusk to dawn, but not fully. For, during the hours of shadow and night, Etain regained the form of a maid, but she still retained the great gauzy wings of the butterfly.

Etain stayed with Angus for some years - although it was impossible to measure the length of time she spent in the god's domain. It seemed distant and dream-like, and although she was physically present, her thoughts were always with Midir.

The god had set apart a small grove in a secluded corner of his kingdom for the maid and had his curious servants furnish it with all manner of comforts and trappings, and ordered them to tend to her needs. And he had a tiny jewelled casket fashioned of the pure white gold from the eastern hills of Banba and had it inlaid with crystal from the south, green stone from the west and set on a plinth of red stone from the north and there Etain stayed during the days whilst she was trapped in the form of a butterfly.

But her enforced captivity began to tell upon her and she begged Angus to let her go free during the day and stretch her wings flying over the god's vast kingdom. But he refused, for he feared Etain would leave him - and the God of Love had been smitten by his own gift: he had fallen in love with the maid.

One night, just before dawn broke over the god's kingdom, Etain rose from his bed and went to the tiny casket, and with a pin, she undid the clasp so that it would not lock properly, and then, folding her wings back, she returned to Angus' side.

When the god awoke, he found that Etain had undergone her transformation as usual and where once a fair maid had lain, now only a large golden butterfly lay upon the pillow. Gently, he took the creature upon his finger and placed her within the casket, never noticing that it did not lock fully.

When the god returned about mid-morn, he found the tiny gate of the casket open and the butterfly gone. Angus raged and the very heavens trembled with his wrath. He called together his servants and followers and sent them out in search of the butterfly and then he gathered the legions of the skies – for he was Lord of the Birds – and commanded them to find and return his love to him.

But as the months passed they all trickled back with the same tale: Etain was no more, she must be dead.

And Angus, God of Love grieved, for he felt she was dead and surely if she still lived, one of his winged scouts would have found her? The god walked no more over the Fields of Man, and love ceased to exist in Banba. Husbands quarrelled with wives, parents with children, and brother with brother. And at last the goddess Danu was forced to call upon all her powers to heal her son, but it was said that Angus never fully recovered from his loss, and thus love is one of the most fragile of emotions, beautiful and terrible, life-giving ... and deadly.

Etain wandered far in the guise of the butterfly when she stole from the god's palace. She knew Angus would pursue her and so she fled east, ever eastwards into the dawn, without resting or taking food or drink. It was three days after she had fled the god's realm and returned to the Fields of Man before she saw a building in the distance. It was a large hill fort, built on a knoll overlooking a wide, meandering river. Night was falling and the palace was a blaze of lights and on the still air came the sound of harps and pipes and the voices of many making merry.

Etain flew in through a high window and perched on a smoke-blackened beam overlooking the main banqueting hall.

The noise, the heat and the stench were almost overpowering. The hall was filled to capacity with the nobility of Banba in all their barbaric finery. Almost directly below the trembling butterfly were the two guests of honour and their clothing and ornaments proclaimed them king and queen. They sat close together and whispered often and Etain guessed that this must be their wedding feast.

Suddenly the main doors were thrown open to admit the cook and his retinue bearing a whole roasted ox. But the sudden gust of wind upset Etain and she tumbled from her perch. She fell - straight into the upraised goblet of the queen ...

The queen toasted the ox and then, as custom dictated, downed the heady ale in one swallow.

Nine months later, a girl-child was delivered to the queen of Leinster. And she and her husband rejoiced to have been blessed with a child so soon after their marriage. And they named the child Etain, after the mythical De Danann princess.

Now the years passed, and the child Etain grew into womanhood. She was remarkably beautiful and many observed that she resembled neither her father's dark swarthy looks nor her mother's fiery red complexion and hair.

Etain's hair was corn-yellow, soft and fine; it was a halo in the sunlight. Her eyes were wide and tilted and of the purest green - what the country-folk call elven eyes. She stood taller than most of the youths in the palace and her carriage was always regal and proud.

But of her previous life as Etain of the Tuatha De Danann, Etain the maid knew nothing.

Now Eochaid had recently come to the throne at Tara, and had been proclaimed Ard Ri - High King - before a Council of Kings, and to celebrate, he had announced a great feast to be held in Tara's halls and called for the kings and queens of Banba to attend.

But one by one his messengers returned and all bore the same reply: it went against custom to be guested by a man only and thus they would not - could not - attend until Eochaid had found himself a wife. The High King raged and swore he would rule alone at Tara until such time as he chose - and he would not be hurried or pushed into finding himself a wife.

And one day in late summer, when the high king rode in search of the great wolves that still roamed Banba in those times, he ventured east and south into Leinster's domain. He spent the night with the king, feasting and making merry. And there he met Etain, daughter of the king. She was by then a maid of eighteen summers and well past the age of betrothal and the very night Eochaid asked for her hand.

They were married on Samhain Eve.

Midir wandered the length and breadth of Banba searching for Etain. In the guise of a harper or healer, sage or seer, he went from fort to fort, hall to hall, seeking any clue that might lead him to his love.

And at last he began to hear rumours of Eochaid's recent marriage and the incredible beauty of his bride, a bride that bore the name Etain in memory of the legendary De Danann princess – and who bore a startling resemblance to her namesake. Midir made his way to Tara, stopping off in Leinster to confirm the rumours. He heard the tales the country-folk told of Etain's elven beauty and how the birds and beasts flocked about her; and one wise woman even whispered that she thought the princess a goddess reborn in the guise of Man.

And so Midir came to Tara in the guise of a harper. In the evenings and long into the nights he sang the old lays and recounted the tales of gods and men; he sang of the Dagda and Danu, of the Babd: Macha, Neman and Morrigan; he told of the conquests of Banba by the Partholonians, the Fomorians, the Nemedians, the Fir Bolg and the Tuatha De Danann. The great hall would grow silent whilst he sang and if men closed their eyes they could almost see the invaders come and go, the cries of battle, the shouts of victory and screams of death and the rise and fall of kings and heroes. There was magic in his voice and enchantment in his music.

But the harper troubled Etain. When he sang of the

126

Tuatha De Danann, his words seemed to linger and echo in her head, sending disturbing ripples deep into her unconscious. She found she could put names to faces, she could visualise the locations and the antique architecture of the elder race. For her, his stories lived.

Her dreams were troubled; strange lands and even stranger peoples wandered through her nightmares ... and they were all so achingly familiar.

She would awake suddenly from sleep, her screams still echoing about the bedchamber and find Eochaid awake and staring at her with a troubled gaze. But when he questioned his wife, she would tell him nothing save that she had dreamt, and even when he pushed her to describe her dream, a strange reluctance stopped her and she protested she did not truly know.

The High King sent for his physicians, but when they examined the queen they found her to be healthy, although exhausted. Eochaid then summoned his Druids and they laid spells and incantations about the chamber and placed runes and amulets on the queen's bed designed to protect her against sorcery or witchcraft.

But the dreams still persisted and daily Etain grew more wan and pale. Her clear eyes unfocused and gazed into the distance - a distance unfathomable by mortal man. She heard the harper's songs always now, they haunted her, and they drew her - but where?

For Etain had been too long in the Fields of Men, and her previous life was all but lost to her - except in dreams.

'I am beginning to despair, harper,' said Eochaid, leaning over and filling Midir's cup. 'I am losing her.'

Midir nodded and sipped at the strong ale.

The High King and his harper sat alone at the top table. Around them the company sprawled in drunken abandon amidst the dogs and scattered debris of their feast. A single sconce remained alight above them, bathing them in wavering amber light, whilst the rest of the hall drifted off into shadow. Silence reigned over Tara and only the muted footfalls of the distant sentries disturbed the night.

'It is a bad business,' agreed the harper.

The High King downed his drink and quickly refilled the goblet with a trembling hand. 'It is; it is almost as if she were living in another world. But she is mortal!' he suddenly shouted. 'I know her parents, and whilst it is true that she resembles neither of them, she is their child, born of her mother's womb. And I know that she cannot be a changeling, for she was born with that hair and eye colouring.' The High King buried his head in his hands. 'I don't know what to do.'

'There is little you can do – save wait. Perhaps it will wear off, perhaps the Druids' spells will work.'

'But they say that there are no spells or enchantments laid on her. What she sees is all within her own head, she dreams, she dreams.' Eochaid drank again quickly.

'But she is being drawn into that dream,' said Midir, 'and there is nothing you can do about it.'

'I know,' the king whispered, 'I know.' He shrugged. 'Perhaps her mood will change, perhaps she will return to me. We can only wait.'

Midir picked up his harp. 'Will I play for you, my lord?'

'No; I fear I would find little cheer in your music – it allows one time to think and dream and I wish to do neither at the moment. But I will get a servant to bring my chessmen; we will play together.' He paused. 'Ah, I cannot. The board and pieces are in Etain's chamber and tonight she sleeps peacefully and does not toss and turn; I don't wish to disturb her.'

'We will use my board then,' said Midir. 'Clear a space whilst I fetch it.'

Eochaid swept the table clear, knocking the goblets and platters onto the floor and keeping only a flagon of ale and two drinking horns by his side.

The harper returned almost immediately, a large cloth-wrapped bundle tucked under one arm. Placing it down before the king, he carefully unwrapped it. Eochaid gasped in surprise, for Midir's chessboard was carved from a single piece of pure quartz as thick as his thumb. Intricate runes were incised into the margins of the board and a representation of each of the four prime elements were cut into the four corners of the board. Every second square cut into the quartz was sheathed in a thin foil of gold. The chessmen were individually wrapped in velvet and carved from flawless black and white marble. They were worked in marvellously intricate detail, even down to the expressions on the pawn's faces.

'Elven craft,' Midir explained, setting up the pieces.

Eochaid nodded. He had always thought his own board of silver and pale gold the most beautiful in Banba, but this . . . this was beautiful almost beyond imagining.

'Shall we set a wager, lord?' the harper asked. 'I will perform a single task for you if you win.'

'And I will grant you a single wish if you win,' Eochaid replied.

They played. The dawn broke over Tara and the palace blazed with morning gold, a gold which hardened as noon drew on and then softened to russet as evening came. At last night returned.

Eochaid moved his queen and said, 'Your king is almost lost.'

Midir nodded and toppled his king, the sound of marble on gold hard and sharp in the silence and conceded the game.

'I have never met a player like you,' said the High King. 'You are not what you seem,' he added.

But the harper only smiled enigmatically and began to reset the pieces. Eochaid rose and went to the window and stood staring down over his fields. Midir joined him.

'And now your forfeit,' he pointed down into the shadows. 'My slaves struggle to till that land, but the ground is hard and even with oxen they make little headway. There must be an easier way, a simpler way.' He smiled slowly. 'Tell me how they might till the land more easily.'

Midir laughed gently. 'Why lord, that is easily done.

129

Instruct your slaves to place the yoke and harness about the oxen's shoulders rather than on its brow. It can then pull with its full weight, rather than with its head only and you will have fewer blinded or crippled beasts also.'

Eochaid nodded slowly. 'I see how it might be done; it is sound advice - you have paid your forfeit. Now go and rest yourself, we will play again at dawn.'

And Eochaid and Midir played again as the first glimmerings of dawn touched the eastern sky and the game lasted all through the day and into the night, only finishing in the late afternoon of the following day.

Once again, the High King won.

And again Eochaid took Midir to the window. The sun was sinking in the west and the High King could almost imagine it dying a bloody death in the vast Western Ocean. Night was drawing in from the east and Tara seemed caught between night and day.

The High King pointed down and then out to the fields beyond Tara. 'It has always been my wish to build a road to the west through there,' he said. 'That is your forfeit: build me that road!'

Midir bowed and left silently; and Eochaid, rising with the dawn the following morning, went and stared out from his window. In the wan light of morning, a road, broad enough for two chariots to pass abreast, cut into the distance. Several hundred years would have to pass before another road like it would be built across the water in Britain by the southern invaders in their strange metal armour.

And so Eochaid and Midir played together a third - and final - time. But before the game commenced, the harper said; 'Let us change the wager this time; I will stake my most valuable possession: this chessboard. What will you wager?'

The High King laughed. 'My most valuable possession is my wife Etain; I will not stake her.'

'A kiss then,' said Midir slowly. 'If I win let me claim a single kiss from your wife.'

And Eochaid reluctantly agreed, although having won

130

two games, he felt confident he would win the third.

They began to play at noon and by evening Eochaid had lost. He stared in amazement as his checkmated king. 'You allowed me to win previously,' he accused the harper.

Midir bowed slightly. 'My lord,' he said ironically, 'you lack my experience.'

And then he stood. 'I claim my prize: a single kiss from your wife.'

'No!'

Midir rounded on the High King. 'What, you are refusing to honour a wager? Would you wish men to remember you as Eochaid Oath-Breaker?'

The High King gripped his goblet of ale and downed it in one swallow and then he squeezed until the metal buckled and crumpled in his fist. 'You must give me time to prepare my wife,' he gasped. 'Return to me when the moon is full – you may claim your prize then.'

Midir nodded and, gathering together his chessmen and board, took his leave with the promise that he would return in one month.

Eochaid stood by the window and watched the harper ride away on his snow-white horse along the new road and he swore the strange harper would never claim that kiss.

The month flew by and each night the moon, waxing now towards fullness, mocked him with its harsh bone-white light. Eochaid ordered the defences about Tara doubled, and then re-doubled, although he could not say what he truly feared. But the very thought of the harper kissing his wife chilled him.

He was certain the harper was not of the race of Man, but was he one of the sidhe folk? It was true that he carried their handicraft, but the elven race often gifted mortals, so that was no indication. The harper could have elven blood; his height and fair colouring, his curiously delicate fingers and slanting eyes were all features of the old race. But there were many who carried a touch of the old blood and with the blond foreigners coming from the east and the swarthy traders from the south, it was by now almost impossible to tell a man's lineage from his looks.

But why had he chosen such a strange prize – and why did Eochaid fear that single kiss? The High King walked the battlements with Firgoil, his Druid, on the eve of the harper's return.

'Why does he frighten me, Firgoil?'

The tall Druid ran his acid-scarred hands through rapidly greying hair. 'Some men have the ability to induce fear in others, just as others have the ability to inspire respect. But I think you fear the harper on a deeper level; I think you fear him because he threatens that which you love most: your wife.'

'But how?' Eochaid wondered. 'How?'

'Then let me ask you this, lord: When did your lady wife begin to fade; when did the nightmares start?'

'A little more than a month ago.'

'And when did the harper first come to your court?'

'Why, a little more than ...' Comprehension dawned in Eochaid's hard grey eyes. 'A little more than a month ago!'

'It is perhaps a little too much to be a coincidence,' said the Druid.

'Do you think he plans to take Etain from me?'

Firgoil leaned on the rough stone battlements and stared out over the fields, now silent and mysterious with the coming of night. 'Lord, do you know the tale of Midir and Etain; it is sometimes sung by the bards and harpers?'

'It is familiar, vaguely so,' said Eochaid.

'Much of it is unimportant here, but this much is significant. Etain the elven - the De Danann - princess is stolen from her lover's fort - and he goes in search of her. Both disappear and are never heard of again ... at least thus far.'

'Druid,' said Eochaid, 'I do not like what you are hinting at.'

'Midir, the De Danann prince,' continued Firgoil, 'was an accomplished harpist ... and an unsurpassed chessplayer,

132

his board and men having been crafted by the greatest of the De Danann smiths.'

'The harper,' groaned Eochaid, 'is Midir. He has come to claim Etain.' He struck the stones with his fist. 'But he is wrong. Etain – my Etain – is human, she is not the lost De Danann princess.'

The Druid shrugged. 'She was born of woman it is true; but the gods are often born of mortal man.'

There was silence on the battlements then, the only sound the chill wind whipping in from the west and when the High King spoke again, the Druid had to struggle to catch his words.

'But he shall not have her; he shall not have her.'

Eochaid put his armies on full alert and had them camp in the fields about the palace. His captains grumbled at what in their opinion was a stupid display – and dangerous also, for some of the lesser kings might construe the gathering as a threat. And the High King ordered his captains to set pickets; they were to let no-one approach Tara without his permission, and no-one, absolutely no-one was to leave until dawn.

In the main hall, Eochaid gathered his personal guard and explained to them that an attempt might be made to abduct his wife. The doors were locked and the high windows covered with heavy cloths; a huge fire roared in the hearth in the centre of the floor, sending sparks spiralling up to the circular opening in the soot-blackened ceiling. The flickering firelight burnished the weapons and armour in warm hues of bronze and gold.

Etain sat before the fire, a heavy woollen cloak thrown over her shoulders. Eochaid sat beside his wife, her thin pale hand clutched in his. Firgoil stood behind the High King nervously tapping his metal-shod staff against the cold flags. Tonight, Etain seemed even more distant than usual, her eyes were half-closed, with only the whites showing and

133

occasionally she would hold a broken conversation with someone only she could see.

The Druid had blessed her with alder, willow and oak, and hung a wreath of apple-blossom around her neck. He had also scratched runes in charcoal over the door and touched the walls with his staff, drawing a protective barrier around the room. And they now sat still and silent awaiting the coming of the dawn, for if Midir had not claimed her by sunrise, then the wager would be forfeit and Etain would be Eochaid's - always!

The night wore on and the sconces burned low throwing the hall into shadow and one by one Eochaid's guards fell asleep, until only the High King and the Druid remained awake with the semi-conscious Etain between them.

'Dawn is almost upon us, lord.'

Eochaid nodded. 'I think we have defeated him.'

'I am not that easily cheated, my lord.'

Eochaid spun around and roared a challenge, his sword in his hand. Firgoil hissed a spell and pointed his staff at the De Danann prince as the first of the guards stumbled sleepily to their feet.

The High King lunged - and Midir was gone. The Druid's staff sparked green fire which hung trembling in the air where the De Danann lord had stood a moment before. He reappeared in the midst of Eochiad's warriors, striking out with two short silver swords, cleaving through armour and flesh without apparent effort. Again Firgoil launched a bolt of green fire - and once again Midir disappeared ... and reappeared by Etain's side.

He kissed her.

Abruptly, her eyes snapped open. For a single moment confusion reigned in their clear depths and then her gaze alighted on the prince.

'Midir!'

And her cry broke Eochaid's heart.

'Etain, my love.' The De Danann prince gripped her about the waist and as one they began to ascend. A warrior raised a spear and brought his arm back, but Eochaid knocked it aside in case he hit Etain and he could only watch helplessly as they passed gracefully through the high window.

Eochaid and Firgoil, followed by the guards raced outside, but all they could see in the still morning air were two snow-white swans which circled once over Tara's proud halls before winging south.

Midir had found and claimed his lost love.

But the tale does not end here, for Fuanach's curse had still to take effect. Eochaid led his army south in the direction the two swans had taken and, led by the Druid, Firgoil, passed beyond the Fields of Men and into the realm of the Tuatha De Danann.

There they laid siege to Bre Leth, and whilst a squad of warriors dug out the foundations of Midir's palace, others roamed the faery countryside, laying waste to all they found.

Death had come to the elven lands.

And Midir, high in his tower, could see only the smoke and flames as the forests burned and hear the screams of the wounded and dying.

Etain came to him and begged the prince to return her to the High King. She loved Midir, but she could not bear to see the land of the goddess devastated in this manner, nor could she allow Midir to blame himself for what was happening. At first the De Danann prince refused, but at last he could bear it no longer and consented, on one condition: that he might be allowed to cast a spell of forgetfulness upon Etain before she returned to Eochaid.

And so Etain returned to the High King, with no memory of her previous life, of her short return to the Lands of Faery, or of her lover, Midir. It was lost to her forever, even in dreams. And although time holds no sway in the Shadowland, once Etain returned to the Land of Men, she was once again made mortal.

And in time she bore Eochaid one child – a daughter – and she too was named Etain. Although she bore her mother's otherworldly beauty, she had her father's wide grey eyes. Etain Once-Elven died at a great age, an old, old woman - but still as beautiful as she had been in her youth when gods and men had vied for her.

CHAPTER 5

CONLA AND THE FAERY MAID

Conn awoke suddenly and lay staring up at the dark bulk of the tree above his head. The sky was lightening towards dawn, but the sun had not yet risen and a misty twilight still lingered. Conn lay wrapped in his sleeping furs, listening to the muted whispers of the nearby guards, wondering what had awakened him.

Perhaps it was the dream. He had dreamt of a voice talking to him out of the shadows, calling him, urging him ... He sat bolt upright; there it was again – and this time he was not dreaming.

It was a woman's voice, sharp and clear on the still morning air.

He rose in one fluid movement, one hand reaching for the broadsword that lay naked by his side. A guard hurried over to him. 'What is it?'

The guard bowed briefly. 'We have been hearing snatches of conversation since first light; yonder.' He pointed through the trees in the direction of the beach. 'But there is no-one there,' he continued, 'no-one except your son Conla, speaking to himself.' The guard paused. 'But a voice replies, lord; there is someone there – and a young woman too, by the sound of her voice.'

By now the entire camp was awake, standing silently, listening. Aodh, the king's champion, joined him, slipping a bone amulet over his head. 'I don't like it.' He jerked his head in the direction of the shore. 'This reeks of sorcery.'

The king agreed and then a stray gust of wind carried

voices on the air. '... And you shall rule in the Land of the Ever Young ...'

They could not make out the young prince's muttered reply, but the soft, gentle voice continued.

'But why content yourself with a petty kingship in this miserable land? And unless you have a mind to slay your father – and I doubt that you could – you must be content to wait many years before assuming the mantle of kingship.'

Conn gripped Aodh's arm and pulled him forward. They moved through the fringes of the forest as silently as possible and down towards the beach. The sound of the sea was clearer now and the woman's lyrical voice rose and fell with the susurration of the waves.

'And what would you rule? A kingdom of savages, where violence is ever-present, and death always threatens, and hunger is your constant companion; is that what you want?'

Conn and Aodh peered through the undergrowth onto the beach. The sun rose like a ball of crimson fire out of the sea, turning the waves to blood and the beach to bronze. It touched the youth standing on the shore, etching him like a sun god. Conla was standing in the shallows, squinting into the sunrise, the wind whipping his cloak across his face. Impatiently he pulled it away, and spoke – seemingly into thin air.

'And you. What of you?'

The voice came from almost directly in front of Conla. 'I will be your wife in the Land of Youth, and we shall rule together ... forever.'

'I am tempted,' whispered the youth. 'I have never before seen one so fair.' His hand rose and touched something. 'You are beautiful.'

Conn whispered urgently to Aodh. 'Return to camp and get Kernann, the Druid. There is sorcery here and that we cannot combat.'

Aodh nodded and slipped back through the undergrowth towards the camp.

'Let me tell you of the Land, that place men call Tir na nOg.' The woman's voice was softer now, more insistent,

138

alluring, compelling, commanding. 'It exists beyond this world, beyond the Shadowland, in a place which is set apart. A different sun shines on the Land, a great amber ball that bathes the Isle in golden light – and it is ever summer there.' The voice faded, as if lost in memory and even Conn could feel deep within himself, the need, the yearning to visit the Land of the Ever Young.

'There is no evil in the Land, nor is there death,' continued the alluring voice. 'There is no sickness, nor is there birth.'

The undergrowth rustled as Aodh led Kernann, the aged Druid forward.

'And the Land is inhabited by a happy people, the elven folk, the last of the Tuatha De Danann, who once ruled this land when it was young. But there are many heroes of this world there also, taken there by the elven folk either as reward for some great service or else . . .' The voice faltered and then continued, softer than before. 'Or else because one of the elven folk loved one of the sons of Man.'

'Stop her,' insisted Conn. 'She seeks to lure my son away.'

The Druid nodded. 'I will do what I can. She is one of the Sidhe-folk, the elven race,' he explained. 'If Conla goes with her, you will never see him again.' He took a short alder wand from his belt and plunged it into the damp soil, drawing power from the earth. The wand pulsed and throbbed and the soil began to flow and twine in arcane patterns.

Conla stretched out his hands, and took a step forward.

Kernann stood suddenly, the wand held high above his head. The alder pulsed with a warm green light, a light reminiscent of life and growth. The Druid sketched a symbol in the damp salty air, a symbol which lingered in a ghostly afterimage. And then Kernann called out in a strange guttural tongue, more animal than human.

Conla stopped abruptly. He raised his hands imploringly and they were immediately touched with thin tendrils of green fire.

Once again Kernann called out and this time a wavering wall of green mist coalesced before the youth, cutting him off from whatever he alone saw. Conla turned and looked at the Druid, Aodh, and his father. His eyes glistened in the morning sunlight. 'Why?' he implored. 'Why?'

And then he turned back and looked out to sea, as if his name had been called, and he raised his hand as if to catch something and then he fell on his knees in the sand and wept.

The Beltane feast came and went as the year moved swiftly towards summer and the moon completed its cycle across the heavens. In all that time, Conla neither ate nor drank.

'I think he has been given one of the elven fruits,' said Kernann, when Conn questioned him. 'If so, then he is already living partly beyond this world, in the Fields of Faery, for as you know, one must never eat nor drink the elven food.'

Conn stalked about his chamber. He felt so impotent; he was losing his son and he could not stop it happening. He could not battle sorcery. Although he was not a coward, he was frightened now. He had fought in many battles and skirmishes – in those days Eriu was threatened from both without and within – and in one day alone, he had defeated fully one hundred warriors in single combat, thus giving him his name, Conn of the One Hundred, but this, this he could not fight. He was forced to sit at his table day after day and watch his son refuse all food, merely staring into the distance with a secret smile upon his lips, as if he alone saw and heard sights and sounds beyond the ken of mortal man.

'Your son is already lost,' said the Druid gently. 'It might be better to let him go to the Land of the Young.'

'Never!' Conn felt the rage building up inside, a battle fury that threatened to overwhelm him. 'He is my son, I will not lose him to some banshee.'

Kernann bowed. 'I will do what I can, my lord; I will do what I can.'

The white-capped waves rolled in and broke lazily, hissing

upon the dark sands like serpents and then broke into a creamy froth that disappeared beneath the sands. Tiny crabs scuttled through the shallows and tiny darting creatures were trapped in sand-locked pools. It was the hour after sunrise, when all colours still seemed wan and undefined and the sea was a blinding mirror of reflected light.

Conla walked down the deserted beach, his head sunk upon his chest, lost in thought. He shook his head to clear it – but the mists and drifting fragments of dreams that were utterly alien to him persisted. On one level, he knew it was because he had eaten the apple the elven princess had thrown him that first time he had met her. He pulled the fruit out of the pouch by his side and held it up to the light. Its skin was warm and sensuous to the touch and it held the light like satin.

He remembered eating it that first evening. Its flesh was moist and succulent and it had numbed his mouth and throat with a thousand tiny needles of fire, but he had finished it. And when he awoke the next morning after a troubled dream-haunted sleep, the apple was whole again. Every morning it was the same: the apple whole and uneaten where the core had lain the night before. He neither hungered nor thirsted after eating the fruit, but he always felt immeasurably distant afterwards. His thoughts were clouded as if he wandered through a dream – and at nights he dreamt of strange and distant lands, of curiously-hued peoples and equally curious beasts. But the dreams were becoming more and more tangible ...

'Conla ... Conla ... Conla ...'

The youth started. She was back. He felt the burden that had rested against the base of his spine since their last meeting leave him – and for the first time in a month he felt complete.

'My Lady ... you have returned.'

She smiled gently, her full red lips parting over startlingly white teeth. Her hair was white-gold, the colour of the sun-touched spray and her skin was as soft as smooth water. She was tall – almost as tall as Conla and her strange head-dress made her seem taller. Her garments shimmered and reflected like metal, always changing, always in motion.

'Come with me, Conla.' She stretched out her hands, the fingers long and incredibly delicate. 'Come with me.'

The youth could feel the decision forming within himself when, from the forest that bordered the beach, his father and Kernann the Druid appeared.

'Conla, my son ...'

The Druid called aloud in the tongue of the Elder Race and the green fire leaped and darted from his wand.

But the elven maid merely laughed. 'Your pretty magics cannot harm me now – for he is almost mine.' She stretched out her hands again and Conla reached for them. On the beach Conn and the Druid could only see him reaching into thin air.

Tiny spots of green fire darted before the youth's eyes and flickered in long traceries of light across the space that separated him from the banshee.

'Your power is spent, Druid,' she called. 'You are a dying breed; soon a new race of magicians will challenge your power and they will cast you and your elemental gods back into the Abyss whence they came.' And the maid gestured, shattering the green fire like so many pieces of broken glass.

'Come Conla.'

And out of the waves rose a longship of white crystal, without sail or oars and its name was cut into the side in red gold.

'Come Conla, we will rule in Tir na nOg for all eternity.'

The youth paused on the beach and then he turned and looked back at his father and the aged Druid, his brow furrowed as if he sought to remember something very important.

'Come Conla,' she persisted, 'your people await.'

Slowly shaking his head, Conla turned back to the sea and climbed into the crystal boat – and he never looked back as it set out for the horizon, rapidly disappearing into the morning sun.

On the beach Conn of the One Hundred wept.

CHAPTER 6

BIRTH OF THE SHANNON

Sinann crouched behind the hedge of wild holly watching the Arch-Mage complete the incantation and put the final touches to the runes incised into the crystal fountain. The Druids stepped back and the Arch-Mage touched the base of the fountain with his long alder wand. Immediately water rose and fell in a graceful arc, fracturing into a million tiny diamonds in the first slanting rays of the morning sun. He then touched each of the seven hazel trees that surrounded the fountain, linking them to it in a protective circle. The leaves on the trees began to tremble violently, the berries pulsed and throbbed with slow persistence and almost before their eyes, the hazelnuts swelled and hardened.

The Arch-Mage bowed reverently. 'Behold the Fruit of Knowledge.' The Druids murmured a refrain as the old man went from tree to tree inspecting the fruit.

'They are all perfect; our task is complete.' He leaned upon his long staff and his hard grey eyes softened as they stared into the morning sun. 'It is the beginning of the end.' With the sun at his back, he turned and walked away from the small grove surrounding the crystal fountain.

'How long will it last?' asked one of the younger men.

'Until man gains the knowledge to breach its defences.' He gestured back towards the grove. 'We have gathered together the entire knowledge of the Tuatha De Danann in those seven trees and in the fruit they bear – we cannot allow it to fall into the wrong hands ...' The voices faded as they passed beyond the maid and disappeared amongst the trees.

Sinann waited until she was sure they had gone before

coming out from behind the bushes. The wan sunlight sparkled off her dark hair and highlighted the green tinge to her pale skin. She raised a web-fingered hand and shielded her oddly slanting eyes.

For Sinann was kin to Lir, the Lord of the Sea.

Slowly she walked towards the grove. Even from a distance it radiated an aura of power; of strength held tightly under control. And the crystal fountain was at the centre of the power; it was the protective talisman which linked the seven artificially mutated trees in an unbreakable bond.

The trees were more delicate than normal hazels, their branches longer and the colours of their leaves more vibrant - only the fruit seemed the same. But the fruit of the trees contained the Seven Branches of Learning - the entire knowledge of the People of the Goddess.

And it was hers for the taking.

Sinann smiled, her sharp teeth glinting yellow in the light. With the knowledge she gained, she could vanquish the remnants of the Tuatha and rule the younger, stronger race of Man. And she would be immortal.

She stood beside the fountain touching the blocks.

The crystal was surprisingly warm to her touch and soft, rather like skin, yet the water itself was cold, ice-cold.

The Druids would not leave the grove here; she knew they intended to shift it beyond this world to a Shadowland, a Place Apart, where it would be accessible only to someone with great knowledge and arcane power.

She trailed her hand through the chill water, revelling in the tingling sensation that engulfed her hand and forearm. She could feel the power of the place crawl over her body and raise the short hairs on the back of her neck. With a shiver, she stretched out her hand to pluck one of the hazelnuts ... and her world exploded.

The fountain seemed to erupt in all directions. An icy hand gripped the maid and dashed her against the ground again and again. She retched as foul water forced its way into her lungs, choking her, drowning her. But she couldn't

144

drown, it was inconceivable – she was a water maiden. Sinann attempted to breathe the water and extract the life-giving oxygen – and failed.

The maid panicked, her arms thrashed wildly and her legs scrabbled for purchase. But the grove was gone; the fountain was gone; there was nothing except a world of ice-cold water, which paradoxically burned her throat and eyes like fire. She was lifted higher and higher. She attempted to scream, but there was no sound, she was deaf. The water continued to rise, and rise ...

Abruptly, it fell.

The huge wave carried the shattered lifeless body of the maid south and west, cutting a deep and wide swath through the lush countryside, until it reached the Western Ocean. It was a magnificent river and one later generations would call the Shannon, in memory of the maid.

CHAPTER 7

THE GARDEN OF THE TUATHA
DE DANANN

Cathan the Mage raised his alder wand high and cried aloud in the Old Tongue. The wand erupted into writhing eldritch flames, bathing the Mage in emerald light and turning the night into an eerie semblance of day. A ghostwind sprang up, whipping out of the darkness, bringing with it the scent of cloves mingled with the heavy tang of salt, as if it had blown across the seas from distant lands. But he was many leagues from the sea.

Cathan whirled the wand and then struck it against the ground. A single levin bolt exploded from the starlit sky and struck the ground almost directly in front of the Mage. The harsh bone white light lent his thin features a ghastly appearance, like one long dead.

But where the levin bolt had struck, the ground glowed and shimmered in the emerald wand-light, and long tendrils of fog rose from the earth. The fog twisted and coiled in the ghostwind, coalescing into a shifting fogbank.

Cathan spoke again, his words trembling on the sharp night air.

The green light paled and shrank back into the smouldering wand – and out of the fog came a glowing milk-white light, softer than sunlight, sharper than moonlight. Cathan shut his eyes, knowing that to look now would be to destroy his sight forever, for the mind could not comprehend the opening of the Door Between the Worlds.

He waited until the light dimmed against his eyelids, and the warm clove-and-salt scented breeze was blowing

146

steadily against his face, ruffling his long dark hair and then he opened his eyes ... and looked into another world; into the Garden of the Tuatha De Danann.

Cathan stepped forward and looked through the shifting oval of white fog hanging on the night air. The Garden was smaller than he had expected. He could see a small crystal fountain set in the centre of seven small, delicate hazel trees, whose leaves burned with harsh vibrant colours. No insect or bird flew about the trees and nothing crawled about their roots.

It was a dead world.

Cathan stepped into the Shadowland. The shock ripped through his body, leaving him pain-wracked and gasping on the sickly, pale sward of the Place Apart. Almost immediately he became aware of the delicate music of the crystal fountain. The water rose and fell in a graceful arc, each drop of water sharp and distinct on the silent air - for there was no other sound. The noise of the water grew, and grew, until each drop seemed to shatter in the innermost recesses of his mind.

With a groan he lurched to his feet and stood whilst the landscape swayed before his eyes. He pressed his hands against his ears, but he could still hear the falling water. He took a step forward and fell. Slowly he began to crawl towards the crystal fountain, gritting his teeth against the tearing cry of the water. Dark waves rippled across his tortured eyes and his head pounded in unison. With an agonising effort he stretched to his fullest and the tips of his fingers touched the jewel-like water. Bringing his wet fingers back to his lips, he drank. The liquid flowed down his throat like ice with a delicate, almost perfumed taste.

Abruptly he realised the pain was gone - or else he was no longer aware of it. Carefully, he pulled himself to his feet and staggered across to the fountain. The crystal was cool and sensuous beneath his fingers, with a texture that resembled human skin. He dipped a hand in the sparkling water and drank from his cupped palm, savouring the sweetness and delicacy of the liquid. He stared deeply into

147

the diamond studded depths and found himself wondering what he had come here for!

The Mage experienced a brief moment of panic. He could recall neither his name nor his mission. And then he turned and looked back at the way he had come. The milky opalescent wall that surrounded the Garden was rent and torn and through the gaping hold he could make out the tiny points of distant starlight from another world.

Memory returned.

He was Cathan, a Mage, come in search of the fabled Fruit of Knowledge in the mythical Garden of the Tuatha De Danann. And he had found it.

He walked around the fountain and inspected the trees. He could only admire the ancient Druids of the People of the Goddess who had moved this entire grove from their world to this Shadowland, where it would be safe from the curiosity of man. And only when the New Race had gained enough knowledge to breach the defences would the knowledge of the demi-gods be released.

Only once, in the first days of its creation, had the Garden been disturbed and then the waters of the fountain had risen and swept the intruder away.

Cathan gathered the hazelnuts from the seven trees. They were hard and smooth and deep down a slow pulse seemed to beat. He cracked one and bit down hard on the kernel, wincing at the acrid bitter taste. He began to chew methodically ...

When he finished, he sat down with his back to the crystal fountain, the trickle of water now pleasant and lulling. The bitter taste of the nut had faded and his mouth and tongue now tingled as if he had eaten a fresh apple.

He breathed deeply. Strange thoughts flashed across his mind's eye; warriors with flashing swords and clad in gilded armour fought beastmen; sorcerer-Druids fought with fire and lightning from hilltop to hilltop; great armies clashed across sodden marshes; their blood staining the dark earth an even deeper hue; high-prowed ships appeared over the horizon, promising death and destruction. Faces flickered before the Mage's eyes; high-boned, slant-eyed, arrogant faces, with hair as fine as silk and eyes harder than jewels. There were women of incredible beauty wielding swords and spears with the skill of warriors and warriors laboriously working with precious metals and rare gems to create artifacts of delicate beauty.

The Tuatha De Danann.

The Mage shook his head, attempting to clear his head. Gradually, the alien images faded and settled back into his mind, to be called upon if needed. All the images but one ...

A face drifted before his eyes, the face of an old, old man. The face solidified, until Cathan could see the iron-grey hair still streaked with black and the curious innocence in the pale, almost colourless eyes.

'Speak ...'

The voice rang hollowly in the Mage's head and, although the image had not moved its lips, he knew it had spoken.

'I ... I have a question ...' he began hesitantly.

'Then ask it.' The image seemed to regard him with some amusement.

'Is ... is there a meaning to this existence?'

The image laughed, a long mellow laugh, that reminded Cathan of a god's. 'Herein are gathered the Seven Branches of Learning of the Tuatha De Danann, the People of the Goddess. Herein is knowledge, and knowledge is power; used correctly it could make you the ruler of your world, or its destroyer. But in all that accumulated knowledge you will find no answer to your question.' The image paused and began to fade. An icy wind blew across the mage and when the voice came again, it echoed from a great distance. 'For there is no meaning.'

And the fountain erupted in all its fury.

CHAPTER 8

FIONN AND THE RED MAN

'And I'll tell you, I'll have a bridge across there if it kills me!' Fionn ripped the side off a nearby mountain, scraped off bushes, small trees and loose earth and pounded it into a rough oblong. 'And we're going to call it Fionn's Causeway.' He pushed the huge rock into the soft earth and pounded it in deeply with his fists.

His cousin Niall shrugged and plucked a nesting eagle out of his beard. 'Whatever you say; only we,' he indicated the rest of the giants with his huge fist, 'want it to be called the Giant's Causeway.'

'Fionn's Causeway!'

'Giant's Causeway!'

The two giants glared at one another across the partly completed causeway of black basalt.

'It was my idea,' snapped Fionn petulantly.

'You only suggested it because you didn't want to get your feet wet every time you crossed to Alba to steal a few cows.'

'I don't like wet cows.' Fionn pounded a large boulder to sand. 'I'm going home,' he said. 'I need the rest.'

Niall turned away in disgust. 'Well good luck to you; and mind you watch out for the Red Man.'

Fionn snatched at a firtree and began to tear off the branches, muttering, 'Red Man, Red Man; do they think I'm afraid of the Red Man?' He stamped his bare foot into the side of a mountain, leaving one large cave with four smaller ones in the solid rock.

But the morning was bright and Fionn soon forgot his

bad humour and set off whistling for Knockmany and his wife Una. He swung the stripped firtree through low copses of trees, beheading them like so many flowers and playfully hefted a rock and batted it from one end of Banba to the other with a single blow.

He stopped only once and that was when a lone figure darted across the horizon. Fionn squinted into the sunlight and thought he could see fiery red hair and beard. He squatted down and contented himself with diverting a stream, and no, he wasn't hiding himself from the Red Man, he told himself; the stream needed diverting ... didn't it?

When he looked up, the figure was gone, lost in the mist which still clung to the west and Fionn hurried on, looking right and left, alert for any sign of movement.

No-one knew who the Red Man was. Some said he was the son of a Banban Giant and an Alban Giantess. Fionn said he was the son of a Banban bull and an Alban Mountain.

He was bigger than most giants and had made it his mission to challenge all the Banban Giants – and had won.

All that is except Fionn.

And if any doubted the Red Man's great strength, he would remove a round disc with jagged edges from his pocket and loudly proclaimed that it was a passing thunder bolt he had flattened as it whipped by his head.

He was looking for Fionn.

It was close to midmorning when Fionn finally reached his fort on Knockmany Hill. The sun beat down strongly turning the rough black stones of the crude fort into a blinding mirror.

'I must do something about that glare,' Fionn muttered shielding his eyes. He snapped a small oak tree in half and rubbed its thick sap experimentally against the wall. He had stepped back to admire his work, when a huge voice roared behind his ear.

'FIONN!'

The giant leaped straight up into the air, to almost three times his own height – which was considerable – and when

151

he came down, the resultant shock waves sent ripples as far as the lonely western islands.

· Fionn climbed out of the hole he had made and found himself staring into the broad peasant face of his wife.

'Oh,' he said weakly, 'it's yourself Una.' His wife nudged a pile of earth back into the hole with a flat foot.

'Now, this is a pleasant surprise,' she said, kissing him soundly on both cheeks.

Across the seas the first of the race of men heard the smacking sounds and prepared for a summer thunder storm.

'You nearly killed me with the fright,' Fionn complained.

'My, and aren't we very jumpy.'

'Ah, but it's good to be home,' he said, quickly changing the subject.

'It's good to have you home. Come on in, and I'll get you something to eat; I've a few cows out in the pen, will they do you?'

Whilst Una prepared the cows, Fionn brought out his collection of weapons and using a boulder sized whetstone began to sharpen his long spear.

Una laid a couple of boiled cows down on the plate and topped it with a small field of corn. She looked at him curiously. 'What are you doing?'

Fionn shrugged and attempted to look nonchalant. 'Oh nothing, just giving the old spear a good cleaning; a warrior should always have respect for his weapons,' he added sagely.

Una looked suitably disbelieving and went and stood by the window as Fionn tucked into a haunch of cow. She glanced over her shoulder at him once, judging her moment. And then she grinned maliciously.

'There is a tall chap with red hair coming up the hill,' she said casually.

Fionn sputtered and choked, spraying half-chewed cow across the room. He tripped over his own feet as he fell, pulling the table and chair down with him. With one blow of his fist he turned the oak table into matchwood and was half way out the back door, before he realised Una was laughing at him.

'Ah, you can't fool me, my boy; it's the Red Man has you terrified.'

Fionn shook his head. 'No, no, I just remembered I've got to see a man about ...' He trailed off, looking sheepish, and then he nodded. 'You're right, it's the Red Man, and frankly, he frightens the wits out of me.'

'Not that there's many to frighten,' Una muttered. 'Where is he now?' she asked.

Fionn stuck his thumb in his mouth and concentrated. Like many of the giants, Fionn's fingers were gifted with various magical powers; and Fionn's thumb had the gift of prophecy.

'I see him,' he said. 'He's ... he's just leaving the Dun of Gann - what's left of it.'

'And where's he going?' asked Una.

'He's ... he's headed in this direction,' he said with a yelp. 'I'm off.'

Una laid a hand the size of a small house on his shoulders and pushed him down. 'What time will he be here?'

Fionn sucked on his thumb until he grew red in the face. 'The second hour passed midday tomorrow,' he gasped.

'Well now, that gives us plenty of time. Be off with you now and fetch me a score or two of salmon for supper, I'll figure out what to do with the Red Man.'

When Fionn had gone, his fishing rod over his shoulder whistling up a storm, a small gale and a cloudburst, Una took nine multicoloured threads from her pocket and murmuring in the language of the gods, wove the nine strands into three cords of Endeavour, Invention and Success, and tied one around her right arm, another about her breast and the third about her right ankle.

When Fiona returned that night, two score salmon dangling over his shoulder and a small cow in his pocket, Una had a tableful of small round loaves.

'Just what I need,' said Fionn, juggling a hot loaf in his hands.

'PUT THAT DOWN!'

'Put what down?' he asked, trying to look innocent.

Una staggered in from the kitchen, her arms full of a second batch of loaves. 'If you had taken a bite from that, you wouldn't have a tooth left in your head,' she said. 'Here,' she tossed him a loaf from the tray she had just brought in.

Fionn, eyed it carefully. 'What have you done with it?'

'Oh, this tray is right enough, but that,' she pointed at the table, 'has iron griddle baked into it.' Fionn tapped one of the loaves off the wall, and it rang with a dull metallic clang.

'Well have you got anything to drink,' he asked, 'I'm parched.'

Una shook her head. 'I've turned all the milk in the house into curds and whey, you'll have to do with water.'

'Water? Water! Me, the foremost giant in all Banba, having to drink water. Ooh, the shame of it.'

'Well it's either drink water tonight or blood – your own – on the morrow.'

Fionn drank water.

Fionn grumbled at the indignity of having to masquerade as his own child. Una merely ignored him and pulled the bonnet tighter under his chin, felt his cheeks to see if he needed a shave and tucked him into the cradle.

'God save all here,' said a voice with an accent so thick, it could be sliced with a blunt knife. A figure moved through the open door. 'I'm looking for Fionn and I'm told he might be here.'

Una eyed the giant with the wild red hair and a flowing beard to match with some concern. Why, her own Fionn, for all his great strength and prowess was only a boy compared to this monster. 'Well sir, I'm sorry to say he's out at the moment; he's gone off chasing some poor lad . . . the Red Man . . . or something.' She sighed. 'Oh, I pity the lad when Fionn gets his hands on him, he was in a fierce temper.'

The Red Man raised his bushy eyebrows until they disappeared into his hair. 'Why, sure I am the very same

Red Man and hasn't Fionn been avoiding me for the past twelve months.'

'Sure, and wasn't that only for your own good; he didn't want to hurt you. But come on in, sit and have a bite to eat; you can wait for him and you can settle your differences when he comes.'

'Now that's very kind of you, I will.' The Red Man sat by the fire and eyed the piled loaves of bread longingly. His stomach rumbled like a winter thunderstorm.

Una suddenly shivered and pulled her shawl tighter about her shoulders. 'Ah now, will you look at that? The wind has shifted and isn't it blowing straight through the door.' She turned to the Red Man. 'Would you be so good sir, as to turn the fort for me; Fionn always does it first thing in the morning, but he went off in such a temper this morning that he forgot. We like to have the sun in the morning *and* in the evening,' she explained, 'and so he turns the fort to face the sunrise and sunset.'

The Red Man nodded doubtfully, went outside and walked around the house. In one corner he found a crack where, he supposed, Fionn must turn the house. He flexed his right hand and then spat upon the middle finger, the source of his strength. He squatted down and using the incredible strength imbued in his hand lifted the entire fort and turned it almost completely around.

He heard a sound inside the house which could have been a yelped 'help,' but it could equally have been the stones settling.

Una came out and joined him. 'That's a grand job you've done. Now there's one other thing.' She pointed down the hill to a flat rocky plain. 'I've barely a drop of water in the house, but Fionn says there's a fine drop well under all that rock ... and if you wouldn't mind ...'

The Red Man stamped down the hill, tapping his right middle finger against his belt. The more he heard of this Fionn the less he liked the sound of him.

The ground was solid rock, without a crack or cleft in it. The Red Man tapped it, kicked it, jumped up and down on it and cursed. When the avalanches and rockfalls had ceased and the air had cleared somewhat, he found that he had opened a tiny crack in the rock. With a sigh of relief, he got down on his hands and knees, and stuck his finger into the crack and pulled.

The ground moaned, and ripped in a long jagged tear, over a quarter of a mile long and nearly five hundred feet deep, which later generations would call Lumford's Gap.

Out spurted the spring of crystal clear, ice-cold water.

The Red Man trudged back up the Knockmany Hill. 'How is that?' he asked proudly.

'Oh, it's fair enough,' said Una casually, 'fair enough.'

She brought the giant in and set him down by the table, telling him to help himself, but to be as quiet as possible, for she had just got the child to sleep. The Red Man nodded and reached for one of the larger loaves. It was pleasantly soft and warm, and his mouth watered. He bit into it.

The scream brought most of the sons of Man in the Western World awake and preparing to meet their gods and the following day, scores of birds were found scattered about the fields of Banba, killed with the shock.

The Red Man nursed a bloody mouth, whilst on the plate before him lay two shattered white stone-like objects; his teeth.

'Me feet ... me feet,' he moaned.

'What's wrong with your feet?' asked Una innocently.

The Red Man spat blood into the fire. 'Me teeth; I've just shattered two of my good teeth on your bread.'

'What this?' Una picked up two loaves and handed one to the Red Man. 'This is Fionn's bread, on a good day, after a day's lake building or mountain sculpturing, he'll scoff a table full of these. Here, try again.'

The Red Man stuck one in the corner of his mouth and bit ... It sounded like two mill stones grinding together. The Red Man spat two more teeth onto the table.

Una shook her head in astonishment. 'Well I don't know. Why, even the child eats it.' She shook baby Fionn 'awake' and handed him a loaf of bread – this time, one without an iron griddle in it. The Red Man watched in amazement as the child consumed it with relish and asked for more.

'Look,' said Una to the 'child', 'this here's the Red Man; he's come to fight with your father.'

'Baby Fionn' looked the giant over with wide eyes, whilst the Red Man in turn, eyed the enormous 'child' with something approaching fear. If this was only the child, what must the father be like...?

'Here,' said Una, tossing the Red Man a stone and Fionn a ball of curds, disguised to look like a stone. 'Will you play with him for a while?'

'I don't want to,' said Fionn petulantly and squeezed the ball of curds until the whey ran out of it like water. 'Can you do that,' he asked the giant innocently.'

The Red Man grinned weakly and squeezed the rock, but unfortunately he couldn't find the proper leverage for his strength-finger and was unable to crush the stone.

Fionn watched with childlike glee, cheerfully munching on another loaf of bread.

The Red Man dropped the stone. 'It's no use; it's clear I'm no match for Fionn; will you tell him I was here and that I'll trouble him no more.' He watched the child chewing contentedly. Absently he nursed his aching jaw.

'Would you mind if I had a look at your child's teeth,' he asked. 'They must be a powerful set to chew that bread of yours.'

'Ah, they're something any mother would be proud of. Look.' She took the Red Man's right middle finger and stuck it into Fionn's mouth, as far back as it would go. Immediately Fionn bit down with all his strength, shearing off the finger just above the knuckle. The giant swayed on his feet, feeling waves of weakness lapping outwards from his shattered hand. He looked at the child in amazement - and then shouted aloud when the child leaped from the cradle ...

When Fionn was finished, he scraped what was left of the Red Man into a small jar and sent it home to Alba.

CHAPTER 9

THE LEPRECHAUN'S TALE

'Here, hold your whist now and let me tell you about the only time one of the Big Folk ever laid his hand on me.' Sheámus Ban the old Leprechaun adjusted the tiny spectacles on his nose and looked solemnly at the Cluricaune and Fir Darrig gathered about the blazing fire.

Carefully Sheámus straightened his legs, the joints cracking and popping like dried wood. 'Aaah,' he sighed, 'It's pure murder sitting with the old legs folded under you all day – and me with the rheumatics something terrible.'

One of the Fir Darrig pushed his red cap back onto his head and opened his mouth to reply, but then, catching the glint in the old Leprechaun's eye, shut up and said nothing.

'I must have been just a slip of a lad, but even then I was the best cobbler in all of Ireland. Look,' and he lifted up one foot. 'I made these myself about that time.'

Dutifully the Cluricaune and Fir Darrig admired the tiny black boots with their huge silver buckles.

'It was early morning,' he continued, 'and I was sitting under the oak tree down by the stream that runs through Dillon's Farm. I had a fine pair of brogues that needed heels and I was tapping away, at peace with myself and at home with the world.' He stopped and filled a long briar pipe with pungent tobacco. 'Now ...' He puffed vigorously until the bowl glowed cherry-red. 'Now, there I was and not a soul about – or so I thought – and not a sound on the air save the chirping of the birds and the ringing of my hammer. It was a morning to bring a smile to your lips and a song to your heart.' He paused for effect. 'Suddenly, I was pounced upon and held by one of the Big Folk.' He paused again and his audience murmured appreciatively.

'And weren't you afraid?' asked a Cluricaune, sipping some of the clear whisky.

'Ah no, sure don't we all know that the Big Folk are just plain stupid?'

Several heads were nodded wisely and one nodded so vigorously that he banged his head against the wall of the ruined barn where they were meeting and fell down stunned.

'He was a giant of a man,' continued Sheámus. 'He was easily three times my height and with arms on him that could strangle an ox. He was dressed in drab and colourless garments,' - unconsciously the Leprechaun touched his own gold embroidered red waistcoat - 'and over his shoulder hung a basket.'

'A poacher?' asked a Cluricaune.

'Aye, that's what he was sure enough. There was a brace of rabbits and a line of fish in that basket I shouldn't wonder.

'Well, he had me, fair and square and with a greedy look in his eye he asks, "your pot of gold, where is it little man? No tricks now, or I'll use you as fish bait." '

'Of course I pretended ignorance - but he wouldn't be put off, and at last I was forced to relent; but only after he had held me out over the river and promised to drop me in tied to a stone.' The Leprechaun nodded gravely at the frightened whispers that ran around the assembly.

'And it's true, and not a word of a lie in it.'

'What did you do?'

'Well, I'd very little choice, for he didn't take his eyes off me for an instant and so I led him over the bridge and up towards the quarries. I'll tell you - it was a merry dance I led him for most of the morning. By midday he was sweating like a horse - and smelling like a pig.' The Leprechaun paused to relight his pipe.

'But in the end there was nothing for it and I had to bring him to the far end of the quarry. "It's there," I said, and pointed to a flat stone. Well he lifted and tugged and pulled

159

until he was fit to burst, but he couldn't move the stone, and at last declared that he needed a pick and shovel. "And what about me?" I asked. "There's not much I can do for you now."

"Oh, be off with you," sez he. Well as soon as I disappeared, he starts looking round for something to mark the stone with, for if you recall, that end of the quarry is floored with a good many flat stones. And at last he takes up a piece of flint and cuts a cross into the rock. And off he goes in search of a pick and shovel.' Sheámus Ban tapped the ashes out of his pipe and finished the dregs of whisky in his glass and then stood up and made ready to go.

'And what happened?'

'Did he get your treasure?'

'Where are going?'

The old Leprechaun looked disgusted. 'Of course he didn't get my treasure – all he got was trouble. Sure as soon as he was gone, I crept back and cut a cross into all the stones at that end of the quarry!'

CHAPTER 10

THE UNCOVERED LAND

Shea watched the tide slowly receding down Dingle Bay, uncovering the soft wet ground beneath to the early morning sunlight. He stood in the saddle until the waters passed the low watermark and beyond. It had been seven years since he had last witnessed this event – seven years since he had first heard the legend of the Uncovered Land.

Legend had it that the bay had once been part of the land, a broad plain stretching from what was now the Great Blasket Island to Valencia to the south. But when the remnants of the Tuatha De Danann had returned to the land, their magicians had caused the Great Western Ocean to roll across the green and fertile land, whilst they remained safe in their enchanted kingdom of Tir fo Thuinn, the Land Beneath the Waves.

However, every seven years the sea receded almost to the horizon and exposed the elven land to the light of the life-giving sun. And then the descendants of the People of the Goddess would come forth and sing and dance for a short while on the dry land until the tide turned and the magical land was covered for another seven years.

The faery folk laid a cloak upon the ground, a cloak woven of the mists of morning and the spray of a storm-tossed sea and it was this talisman that controlled the sea. And it was whispered that whomever held the cloak could command the waters to stay beyond the horizon, thus gaining lordship over the Uncovered Land.

The sun rose higher in the heavens, shortening Shea's shadow on the ground before him as he waited. The ground

161

steamed in the warm sunlight, wreathing the plain in a heavy mist, through which the silent watcher thought he could hear the faint and distant sounds of music. Shadows moved in the distance and through the thinning coils of mist a figure might suddenly appear, moving in a fluid, graceful dance with an unseen partner.

About mid-morning, as the sun was almost overhead and burning fiercely, the sounds of music and song faded and even the calls of the birds were stilled. Shea, who had been nodding in the saddle, abruptly jerked awake. He leaned forward over his horse's head and stared down into the bay . . .

. . . Into a faeryland.

The mists were gone, revealing a wide, gently sloping plain covered with a grass of emerald green, dotted with large circles of lighter coloured grass studded with jewel-like spots of shimmering colour.

And in the centre of one of the larger circles, Shea could see the small man-like figures lying as if asleep or intoxicated and just outside the circle, lying flat on the ground, was a large square of grey-white cloth: the faery cloak of the sea.

As quietly as possible, Shea urged his mount down the slope and onto the soft moss-like grass of the Uncovered Land. The ground moved beneath his horse's hooves, but it was perfectly dry and it was unimaginable that only that morning it had been covered by the waves.

It took him longer than he had expected to reach the place where the faery folk slumbered within their magical circle and he was surprised when he glanced back to see how far he had come.

Shea dismounted and crept forward. He could see the faery folk quite clearly now. They were taller than he had imagined and their limbs, although long and thin, did not look frail or fragile. Their features were sharp and pointed and their eyes slanted upwards. And he noticed that there seemed to be a thin web of skin between their fingers and toes. There must have been twenty or more asleep in the circle, their faces turned towards the sun like flowers, the harsh light catching tiny sparkles of green and blue in their long fine jet-black hair.

Shea eased nearer the cloak, and 'though there was no wind that morning, the cloak rippled and twitched in a slow regular beat that reminded him of the beat of the sea. Holding his breath, his heart pounding in his chest, he gently lifted the pulsating cloak from the ground and wrapped it about his shoulders. It felt cool and airy, heavy with the tang of salt and its power tingled through his spine. Turning, he ran for his horse.

The horse whinnied as Shea mounted her in one leap – and the cry brought the faery folk instantly awake. He could hear their high, thin, almost musical voices, raised in anger behind him. He fought down the desire to look behind and only dug his heels in, chillingly aware of the need to reach the shore.

He was almost halfway there when he became aware of the low rumble. He felt it coming up through the horse's hooves, vibrating into his stomach and then up into his head until he felt as if his skull was about to burst.

Looking over his shoulder he saw the gathering Tonn Toime, the Faery Wave.

The elven folk had launched their only defence against the thief and the Uncovered Land was rapidly being reclaimed by the sea. The water mounted in a massive wave, gathering strength and height as it came, until it seemed as if a giant grey-white-green mountain was bearing down on the lone rider. The noise was incredible; Shea screamed aloud at the thought of that massive wall falling down on him, but his cry was lost in the roar. He felt a wetness in his ears and across his lips and realised that both his ears and nose must be bleeding. The vibration was almost shaking him out of the saddle and the horse was crazed with terror. But it was that very terror which might save him, for the crazed animal fairly flew towards the nearing shore. Already they had passed the low watermark and he could see the high tide mark clearly. If only he could reach it before the mountainous wave fell ...

And then the sound behind him changed in tone. The

rumble disappeared and was replaced with a sound like glass shattering – but magnified a thousand times. The Tonn Toime was falling! Shea shouted aloud … and was engulfed in a wall of water.

It hit him like a blow, sweeping him off his horse, battering him against the ground. He felt pain lance through his left leg and wrist; his head felt as if it were being squeezed between two stones and the pressure in his chest was almost unbearable. But the forward motion of the wave carried him far up onto the beach, and 'though it clawed at him with almost tangible fingers, Shea had cheated the faery folk and the Tonn Toime.

He pulled himself along the beach, dragging his left leg and wincing every time his left wrist touched the soft sand. Every time he breathed, pain stabbed into his side and when he coughed, blood spattered the golden sand before his face.

There was no sign of his mount and he felt curiously angry that the elven folk should have claimed even her; she had been a brave animal and had made a gallant effort to reach the beach – and had almost made it.

But he had won, he had the magic cloak and the sea was his to command. Trying to move as little as possible, he reached around to lift the cloak off his back … and his fingers touched nothing. It was gone. The faery folk had won and it had all been in vain.

Shea lay on the golden sands, a broken man, and wept.

CHAPTER 11

THE SEA MAID

Brendan wandered along the shore the morning after the storm. Long strands of weed splayed like fingers even on the upper reaches of the cliffs, testament to the storm's fury. Driftwood piled against the rocks, rotted and thick with barnacles. Brendan rooted amongst the wood, seeking the firmer, fresher pieces and dropping them into the lobster pot slung over his shoulder.

The waves still shattered against the rocks in the bay, but their fury was gone and this was only the persistent heartbeat of the sea. The foaming white water ran hissing up the rough beach almost to his bare feet as he made his way down the shore to the sand spit where he knew he would find sea wrack.

As he walked out onto the spit, a flash of iridescent green caught his eye. He stopped and squinted into the blinding mirror of the sea. There was a shimmering green shape moving through the water towards him. Dropping to his knees in the wet sand, he threw off the lobster pot and pulled a long knife from his belt.

Perhaps it was a seal ...

The water foamed briefly and a shape slid gracefully from the waves. Brendan almost cried aloud and the knife dropped from suddenly lifeless fingers – for a young woman had risen from the sea. Pressing himself down into the soft sand, he watched and waited.

The maid rose and stretched languorously, running her fingers through a mane of long luxurious black hair glittering with emerald highlights. She was tall and almost painfully thin and clad only in a long cloak of silver-shot green. With long, slim, slightly webbed fingers she unclasped the cloak and laid it down on the sand. She stood and raised her hands to the skies, as if she exulted in the caress of the wind on her naked body and then slowly she sank onto the sand, her face towards the sun.

Brendan squeezed his eyes shut until tears came, but when he looked the maid was still there – he could just make out the dark mane of her hair and the swell of her breasts against the sand. For a moment he had imagined her to be the product of hunger induced delirium.

But she was real.

Brendan struggled to recall what little he knew of the water maids. They were said to be the subjects of Lir, Lord of the Sea, and hail from Tir fo Thuinn, the Land Beneath the Waves, but they were equally at home on land as in water. They could travel from one realm to the next with the aid of a water cloak, a talisman woven of the essence of the sea and the elements of the air, mixed with the spirit of the land. It encased the wearer in an invisible protective sheath.

As the sun moved on towards mid-morning, the wind died, the sea grew calm and a deep, heavy silence fell over the beach. Brendan started awake convinced he had dreamt it all, but the maid was still there, her head thrown to one side, her breasts rising and falling regularly in sleep.

Slowly, carefully, Brendan began to crawl along the sand spit towards the water maid. His questing fingers touched the hem of the cloak; it felt ice-cold and wet to his touch and yet it had lain in the sun for hours. Holding his breath, he began to pull it back towards himself, his eyes on the still-sleeping maid. He almost had the cloak when the maid stirred. He froze. Her eyes snapped open, emerald-green in the harsh sunlight. Slowly her head turned ...

Brendan leaped up, grabbed the cloak and ran.

With a shrill inhuman cry, the maid followed. Brendan ran for the shore, his bare feet sending up spumes of sand and water. The maid's shouts were almost distinguishable and he occasionally caught a word he almost recognised. He glanced back - and fell headlong in the sand. He rolled and pushed himself to his feet - but the maid was closer now and he could hear her rasping breath and smell the heavy tang of the sea. Her long nails scored deep furrows down his bare back. But Brendan had now reached the foot of the cliffs where the going was rougher and the soft sand, which favoured the maid's webbed feet, was gone. Here, there were only hard stones and jagged rocks, and the sea maid soon limped on bruised and bleeding feet. By the time Brendan reached his cottage tucked away in the lee of the cliffs, the maid was far behind.

He was leaning on the half-door when the maid staggered up. Wordlessly she stretched out her hand; silently he shook his head. Again she reached out. Again he shook his head, saying clearly and distinctly, 'No.'

'Why?'

Her question surprised him; he had not known she understood Irish. She spoke it with just a trace of accent and used an archaic variant of the tongue.

Brendan shrugged and shook his head. 'I don't know,' he confessed. And then he added shyly, 'I've never seen anyone quite as beautiful as you.'

The maid coloured, and then, abruptly realising she was naked, attempted to cover herself with her hands. Brendan turned away in deference to her modesty.

'Please give me back the cloak,' she said, 'otherwise I am bound to you.'

'I know,' he said quietly. 'I know.'

The years passed and Murgaine the sea maid stayed with Brendan and in time she bore him a son and two daughters. The boy resembled his father but the girls had their mother's elfin looks and colouring.

As the children grew up and became more and more inquisitive, Brendan was forced to move the cloak from hiding place to hiding place for fear they should accidentally stumble across it. But he could never leave it alone for long and would often start awake from a nightmare in which his wife found the cloak and, taking the children with her, would disappear beneath the waves.

In the long hot days of late summer, Brendan set about thatching the cottage in preparation for the coming winter. He was laying the first layer of thatch when the idea came to him: he would hide the cloak under the reeds, away from both his wife and children and there they would never find it.

The following morning he set off for the shore, the lobster pot over his shoulder, for he still went hunting along the beach for sea wrack and driftwood. Murgaine followed him as far as the shore and stood gazing longingly at the receding tide. With tears in her eyes, she turned her back on the sea and wearily made her way up the rough track. When she reached the cottage she found her young son struggling to raise the short ladder against the wall.

'Brian, what are you doing?'

'I want to look,' he said, his voice carrying a trace of Murgaine's eldritch accent.

She knelt by her son, and stared deep into his emerald flecked colourless eyes. 'What do you want to look at?' she asked gently.

'Why mother, did you not see father laying a shining cloth under the reeds when he was thatching?'

Murgaine felt her world tremble and dissolve before her eyes; her breath caught in her throat in a sob and the sudden pounding of her heart frightened her. With trembling hands she placed the ladder against the wall and climbed up to the low roof. Carefully she parted the bundles of thatch . . . and there was her cloak.

Climbing down, she took her son in her arms. 'It is only an old oil-cloth, perhaps it was the way the light caught it made it shine; it is nothing.' The child looked at her from big solemn eyes and nodded slowly.

When Brendan returned later that evening, he noticed his wife's air of suppressed excitement. She dropped plates, burned herself on the hob and almost ruined the dinner. He smiled inwardly; before she had told him she was expecting their first child, she had been this way.

Murgaine set a large meal down before him and then went outside to draw some water. And Brendan was almost finished when he realised she had not returned.

Outside the ladder and tufts of straw and rushes from the roof gave mute testimony to what had occurred.

He set off for the beach at a run, terrifyingly aware that he had not heard the children playing about the cottage. His heavy meal weighed uncomfortably in the pit of his stomach as he leaped over the broken ground and down onto the beach. He sank, cursing into the soft sand as blind instinct directed him towards the sand spit. He fell, and lurched to his feet, only to fall again. He lay, the sand rough against his face, quelling the urge to vomit and then with a groan, pushed himself to his feet. But when he rounded the bend in the cliffs, his heart lurched and almost stopped.

The sea maid stood by the edge of the waves, the long silver-shot emerald cloak fluttering about her bare shoulders and with her two daughters in her arms. Brian sat on the wet sand beside her, struggling with the laces on his boots.

Brendan screamed and the gulls rose and mocked him with their cries. He ran down the long spit swaying from side to side like a drunkard, his hands outstretched, his fingers hooked into claws.

The maid turned slowly and looked back, the ghost of a smile playing about her lips. She stooped and said something to the boy and he renewed his efforts to pull off his boots.

Brendan was nearer now; he could see the abrupt flicker of fear in his wife's eyes and his son's look of intense concentration as he unpicked the tightly knotted laces. And even as the fear of losing his family ate into him like acid, he could still admire the otherwordly elfin beauty of Murgaine. Almost six years of hard living and bearing three children had not abraded her beauty. She was still as slim hipped and high breasted as the first time she had risen from the sea and her hair, which she had groomed carefully every night and morning, shone with the same metallic green-black sheen. She was beautiful.

He was almost on top of them now – and with a look compounded of both terror and triumph, the sea maid leaped into the waves with her two daughters in her arms.

The boy stood and would have followed had Brendan not thrown himself on top of him and buried his face in the sand so that he might not see the thrashings of his sisters as they drowned.

And the look of horror and loathing on Murgaine's face would haunt him always.

170

CHAPTER 12

THE FAERY HOST

The silence of the night was broken by the sharp ringing steps of a late traveller on the frost-rimmed road. The young man tucked his head down deeper into his collar and pushed his hands into his pockets, feeling the chill bite through the thin cloth. It was a bitter night and a full moon sparkled on the road, etching it in silver, the harsh light adding to the chill.

He stopped and pulled a hip-flask from his back pocket. The locally-brewed liquor burned its way down his throat and settled in his stomach like hot coals, and the fumes made him pleasantly unaware of the lateness of the hour or the lonely road he travelled.

He had been humming the refrain of an air the piper had played back in the town for some time, when he became aware that his voice was not the only one on the road that night. He stopped and listened. And there, sharp and clear in the distance, he could hear voices raised in laughter and song, with the thin skirl of the pipes and the delicate tracery of a harp hanging on the air.

The young man leaned on the hedge that bordered the road and stared across the fields, but he could see nothing and the night was so clear that the sounds could have travelled some distance. But his curiosity had been aroused and, ignoring all the tales the country-folk told of this part of the west and the warnings never to leave the road, especially at the full of moon, he vaulted the hedge and set out across the frozen fields towards the sounds.

The fields, he knew, were part of the estate of the O'Donnell, the local landlord, an evil man with a dark reputation. A man of whom it was said, bore an uncanny resemblance to both his father and grandfather.

The young man stumbled and fell on the hard earth. He groaned aloud and then screamed as a hand came out of the night and helped him to his feet. He cowered back and stared up at the stranger ... no, not a stranger, someone familiar. He shook his head, trying to clear the fumes and dizziness that made his senses swim.

'You are Colum MacMahon,' stated the stranger.

The young man nodded dumbly, and then recognition dawned. 'You are the O'Donnell,' he whispered, and unconsciously crossed himself.

'Why are you trespassing on my land?'

'I heard the music and singing sir and I just followed it ...'

The O'Donnell smiled and Colum shivered, for it gave his face a skull-like appearance in the bleached moonlight. He recalled the stories whispered about this man and especially the one which said that he had traded his soul and humanity for communication with the Elder Gods and spirits that once walked the land.

'Why then,' the O'Donnell said, 'let us find the source of this merriment.'

He gripped Colum by the hand, and the young man winced and would have pulled away if he could, for although the night was chill, the man's hand was even colder.

The O'Donnell hurried across the fields, his footing sure and certain, never stumbling nor falling, dragging Colum behind him. And if he had not been gripped so tightly, the young man would have believed he followed a wraith, for the man made no more sound than blown smoke and was almost as visible. He was clad all in black, from his high-collared jacket to his black hose, and save for the silver buckles on his shoes and the silver buttons that glittered like tiny stars on his jacket, he would have been invisible.

They marched across field after field, pushing through frozen hedgerows and ice sheathed rivers and streams.

Several times, Colum tried to strike up a conversation with the dark figure before him, but his words hung, forced and empty, on the cold air and the O'Donnell did not deign to reply.

Eventually, they topped a rise and found themselves looking down into a hollow. The depression must have been almost a half mile across, topped on three sides by trees and low bushes. The silver thread of a stream cut across from the left and vanished into the night. And although it was dark in the hollow, Colum could see vague forms moving to and fro.

The O'Donnell pointed down. 'There is the source of your music and laughter. They dance within.'

Colum strained, but the sounds were still as distant as ever ... and who were 'they'? He turned back to the older man, but he was gone, vanished into the night whence he came. The young man backed away from the hollow fully intending to turn and run when he could bear to have the sounds at his back. But suddenly there was movement in the hollow and two figures loomed up out of the shadows.

They were smaller than he and clad in sombre colours of a peculiar cloth which reflected the moonlight like oiled silk. Their features were thin and pointed, their eyes slanted upwards and seemed split-pupiled like a cats'. Their hands, when they reached for him, were long and thin, with delicate, graceful fingers and over-long nails.

Taking him by the hands, they drew the young man down into the hollow. It was as if he were walking under water; all sounds ceased and were replaced with a muffled pounding like the surf on the sands – and which he abruptly realised was the pounding of his own heart. Familiar objects – even the trees – took on grotesque and fantastic shapes; tiny faces seemed to leer at him from their boles, and feral eyes gleamed in the depths of the bushes. Tendrils of white mist – which he had not seen from above – now drifted past his face, carrying the acrid odour of crushed herbs and unfamiliar spices.

Colum tried to talk to the two creatures who were leading

him into an unfamiliar world, but although he could form the words, they came out strange and garbled.

The fear and terror he had felt was fading now and the urgency to be away from this place seemed unimaginably distant and unimportant. He felt himself slipping into an easy acceptance of the unreal situation, it was as if he were wandering through a dream – but at some deep, almost unconscious level, he realised that this was no dream. The fog thickened as they moved down into the hollow – and then it abruptly disappeared. Colum looked around in dull confusion. The hollow seemed larger than he had first imagined it to be – it now stretched away to a misty horizon. Buildings shimmered in the distance and the pale silver ball of the moon overhead, now glowed with a wan golden light, like a morning sun.

And the Faery Host had gathered.

They thronged the hollow in a colourful, murmuring mass, like a great swarm of insects. Many were like the two leading Colum; thin, high-featured, elven creatures, dressed in shimmering garments which whispered together when they moved. There were others: small, gnarled, crooked creatures, that seemed neither man nor beast; tiny creatures no longer than his hand who flew on huge butterfly wings, and there were small – but perfectly formed – men, clad in rough clothes of red, green and brown. Some bowed mockingly to the young man as he was led through the mass, whilst others either ignored him, or looked pityingly on him. The low susurration of voices stilled as he passed and the throng backed away on either side, leaving an avenue down which he must pass.

Facing him at the end, seated upon a cloth-draped treestump was a man, crowned like a king and clad in a lord's finery.

Colum stood before the elven lord and stared deep into his colourless eyes; he felt he could drown in them, they were so empty. The king rose – and he was a head taller than the young man – and placed a long-fingered hand on his trembling shoulder. 'I am Illan, Lord of the Elven Folk.'

174

The company murmured their lord's name, as if in benediction.

'You are welcome to this gathering, son of Man,' he gestured about with his right hand. 'Enjoy,' he commanded, and resumed his seat.

The young man was grabbed by two of the elven maids and dragged into the whirling crowd. The faery music began again: two harpers, their instruments the most beautiful and delicate Colum had ever seen, and a piper caressing an instrument which looked impossibly old. The music inflamed him – it was so wild and free, almost alive, not like the poor shadow of sound that passed for music in ... in ... where?

The faint echo of an air haunted the dim recesses of his mind. He groped for it with blind fingers, suddenly realising that it was of immeasurable importance to him.

One of the elven maids pressed a goblet of purest silver into his hands and urged him to drink. He raised it to his lips and the potent vapours made his head swim, but some primal warning urged him not to drink ... no, nor eat the food of faery.

He worked his throat, but handed the maid back the goblet untasted. He refused all food, pretending to be chewing when someone offered him a delicacy.

He danced with many of the elven maids, whirling around and around in a mad swirling that left him dizzy and gasping. Many of the faery folk seemed to want to touch him, as if he were some token or charm and one, an old, old woman, no taller than his waist, wept as she kissed his hand.

The night – if night it was – passed swiftly and as the dawn tinged the eastern sky with pale light, the tiny lanterns were extinguished and, one by one, the faery folk disappeared back into whatever time or place they inhabited. And as they did, the golden moon-sun faded from the skies and sank into the west, the trees and stones ceased to stare and the sounds and smells of faery faded, leaving only the mundane behind.

Colum started suddenly. He had been staring into the eastern sky, welcoming and yet regretting the coming dawn, when someone touched his shoulder. It was Illan, the elven lord.

'You have cheated us, son of Man.'

'I don't understand.'

Illan gestured into the east. 'The dawn is almost upon us; the faery folk are gone and by rights you should have gone with them.'

'But why?' wondered Colum.

'Why? Because you were part of a tribute paid to us by the one you know of as the O'Donnell.'

'What tribute?'

'The soul of a baptised follower of the New God, the One you call the Christ. In return we extend the life of the O'Donnell.'

'How old is he?' Colum asked suddenly.

'As we reckon time, four nights – you were to pay for that fourth night, but you cheated us, for you neither ate our food, nor drank our wines and thus we have no claim on you.'

'Four nights is not a long time,' said Colum.

'Time, as we measure it,' said the elven lord, 'differs greatly from your measurement of it. Look,' he pointed into the east. 'The sun arises, I must depart. I wish you well – although I pity you and soon you will wish you had followed us beyond this world, into the Shadowland, the realm of faery. Farewell.' Illan, the lord of the elven folk, moved across the hollow towards the west and as he did so a shadowy figure stepped from behind a tree and joined him. And Colum could have sworn that it was the O'Donnell.

Then they were gone.

The road back to the village was *wrong*. It was not something he could describe, more an overall impression. He had travelled that road for as long as he could remember, he knew every stone and crack in its rough surface, every tree and bush that lined the winding way, and every lichened-covered wall.

But now they were different.

Perhaps the road seemed wider, the bushes and trees just a little bigger, a little more unkempt than he remembered them. He noticed new bushes and young trees which, he felt sure, had not been there the night before; and there were also gaps where he knew there ought to be a certain bush or a low wall.

He began to run.

The sun came up and his dew-soaked clothes steamed in the hot summer air. *Hot ... summer ... air ...*

But it had been the depths of winter only last ... night.

Filled with a mind-numbing fear, Colum fled towards the village. Everything on the road was so familiar - and yet so strange; so old and yet so new.

The village was much as he remembered it; perhaps the buildings a little more dilapidated and the church slightly more decrepit - but that gilt cross on the steeple was new, it had not been there last night.

The inn was almost unchanged, save that the roof had been recently thatched. All conversation ceased as he entered its familiar dark, low-ceilinged interior, redolent with the heavy odours of strong spirits, stale beer and sweat. Colum nodded to a score of faces he knew - or thought he knew, but they merely looked puzzled and were slow to return his greeting. He ordered a glass of dark beer and lounged back against the smooth wood of the bar.

The locals, their scrutiny of the stranger finished and apparently satisfied that he was one of themselves, turned their attention back to the old man in the corner by the turf fire. His voice was rough, for it had been a long night's storytelling and it was only now coming to an end. He sipped from a heavy mug and resumed.

'From this very spot it was, and sure wasn't it my father - God rest him - who saw him. Out he went and with a few jars inside him, for it was a bitter night and cold enough to crack the stones. And he took the old straight road home.'

177

The storyteller paused and sipped his drink.

'But he never reached it. Oh, there was a search made of course, but sure, he was gone and there was little to be done about it. But,' and the old man paused for effect, 'they found a scrap of cloth torn from his coat just above the faery dell in the O'Donnell's lands. The faeries got him.'

'And who was he and how long ago was this?' Colum asked into the silence.

'Sure, and wasn't he a local lad, Colum MacMahon, and it's nigh on a hundred years since he went with the faery host!'

CHAPTER 13

SAMHAIN EVE

Brian and Mary huddled in the porch of the ancient church watching the rain turn the earth to mud. Thunder rumbled out over the ocean, and lightning flared above the jagged rocks at the mouth of the bay. The angry sea foamed and boiled at the foot of the cliffs far, far below them, sending foaming tendrils of spray high into the salty air, soaking the young lovers. A warm breeze blew in off the ocean and rustled through the bare trees with the sound of muted whispers. Stray leaves whipped through the leaning headstones of the clifftop graveyard.

'I'm frightened, Brian,' whispered the young woman, clutching the shawl tighter about her head. 'Can't we go now?'

'Soon, soon, it's almost time; we'll wait 'til then.'

Mary nodded and shivered in her thin coat, nestling against Brian for warmth. 'What time is it?' she whispered.

Brian glanced up at the heavens, where a full moon was obscured by racing clouds. 'Midnight,' he said, the tension showing in his voice.

They waited, whilst overhead the heavens quickly cleared, the summer storm dying as quickly as it had blown up, leaving the full moon shining sharp and clear in an empty sky. The silence began to grow; the wind died, the rustlings of the night creatures disappeared and even the booming of the waves far below seemed muted. A deathly silence fell over the churchyard and the very night itself seemed to be waiting.

Abruptly Brian stiffened and Mary stifled a scream. A

couple climbed the long cliff-face stairway and moved through the silent tombstones and falling behind that another shadow-couple and then a long line winding through the tombs towards the porch. The moonlight glittered on their pale forms, dusting them with silver.

Brian and Mary cowered back as the first of the figures approached. It was the image of a young couple, youths they both recognised as coming from the nearby town. Behind them came the shadow-figures of a young man and woman from the same town. Both shadow couples passed through the heavy wooden door of the church and faded.

'That's Eileen NicMorichue, and Dermot MacBrien,' grinned Brian, 'so they are to be married.' The shadows drifted slowly towards the church and they seemed thinner, more etherial than the rest – or perhaps it was just the brightening skies paling them. As they neared the church Brian gripped Mary's hand tightly and smiled broadly in triumph.

For the shadows were of themselves.

'See, I told you we would be wed this coming year.' He kissed her gently and taking Mary's hand in his set out for the long road home.

The seasons had changed and winter was fast approaching. Once again Mary and Brian climbed the dangerous winding stairway to the ancient church which clung precariously to the clifftop. Every year the sea claimed a little more of the land and often after a storm, shattered headstones and yellow splintered bones would be found on the beach far below.

It was Samhain Eve, one of the great Old Feasts, when the spirits of the dead walked and the borders between this and the Shadowland blurred and time itself rippled and flowed. The country folk avoided the Old Places, the ancient mounds and rugged dolmens, the cairns and faery rings. Most kept to their cottages and only ventured out if it was unavoidable.

Mary was shivering as they made their way through the silent graveyard that was attached to the old church.

'Brian,' she whispered, her voice so low as to be almost inaudible, 'must we?'

Brian squeezed her hand tightly. 'Remember what we saw on Beltine Eve? Who knows what we might see this night.'

'This is an evil night,' she whispered and clutched the small oaken crucifix about her throat. 'Only evil is abroad this night.'

'I'll protect you,' Brian said, with a confidence he did not feel.

They stood in the porch of the church and listened to the night move about them. Tiny rustlings and cracklings seemed unnaturally loud in the silence. Once a barn owl hooted nearby, causing Mary to stifle a scream.

The night was mild and dry; surprising for so late in the year and indeed the summer had been hot and dry and the streams in the district ran low and turgid.

It was after midnight when the lovers became aware of the growing silence. All the tiny noises of the night had faded, leaving only a thick silence. They could feel the tension growing, as if a thunderstorm were brewing – but the sky was clear and the full moon bathed the churchyard in a harsh bone light that contrasted sharply with the ebon shadows. They could feel the pounding of each other's hearts and imagined they must be beating out into the countryside like drums. Abruptly the first of the shadows approached.

This time they came singly and whereas the Beltine shadows were images of people in the full of their health, some of these were thin and wasted, whilst others bore the evidence of wounds, as if they had died by violence.

For these were the shadows of those who would die during the coming year.

The procession was longer than the one at Beltine. Many of the folk, Mary and Brian recognised; some were from their own towns. They passed in a ghostly silent procession and filed through the thick oaken door and into the church.

181

The moon was low in the sky when the procession came to an end.

The last shadows were of a couple. They glided silently through the grave stones and the moonlight turned the milky opalescence of their shadows to silver. As they neared the porch, the young lovers suddenly realised that there was something terribly familiar about the pair ...

As the shades passed, they turned and looked at Mary and Brian ... And they found that they were looking at the shattered images of themselves!

The shade of Brian reached out for Mary, whilst the shadow of Mary reached out as if to embrace the living Brian.

Mary screamed - a long terrified, almost animal-like cry and Brian struck at the outstretched hand of his shade. It was cold - so cold that it burned like scalding steam; he cried aloud in pain, and the image seemed to smile through broken lips.

The lovers fled terrified from the church, stumbling blindly through the headstones which loomed suddenly out of the night and seemed to deliberately impede their progress. Once, Mary fell, pulling Brian down with her and when he glanced back, he could see the ghastly bone-white shades following, their arms outstretched. He dragged Mary to her feet and pushed her out of the graveyard onto the first of the steps. They ran down the rough steps, keeping as close to the cliff-face as possible. Loose stones and pebbles clattered out into space to fall the hundreds of feet to the jagged rocks below.

And then suddenly, Mary stopped and went rigid as a shadow appeared before her. Brian crashed into her and then screamed as a burning cold hand touched his face. He took a step backwards ...

Into space ...

CHAPTER 14

THE BLACK CROSS

The spade hit the wood of the coffin with a solid thud that echoed about the deserted graveyard. Nuala froze, listening. But, save for the slight soughing of the wind through the leaves there was no sound and even the drone of the late-night insects had died off. The young woman glanced up into the skies, watching the dark clouds that threatened to obscure the full moon that rode like a silver coin across a purple cloth.

She hadn't much time.

Nuala dropped down into the freshly dug grave and scraped the earth off the polished wood of the coffin. She pulled a long metal bar from the bag on her back and inserted it into a crack in the thin wood. She leaned on the bar, pressing down with all her stength, and the wood creaked - an almost human scream that set her heart pounding - and then it snapped with a pistol-shot crack.

She looked up out of the grave. The clouds had neared and would soon hide the light of the moon. She must hurry.

Working as quickly and as silently as possible, she levered off the coffin lid and, laying it to one side, grabbed the stiff corpse under both arms and dragged it out of the grave.

Nuala laid out the body by the gaping hole. The moon-light touched its face with shadow lending it character, giving it life. It was the corpse of a young man, not yet into his twenties, who had been buried that morning after a long, lingering illness.

With a short knife, Nuala sliced the threadbare suit from his wasted limbs. Critically, she examined the body.

Although it was pitifully thin, the skin was whole and unblemished - it was perfect. She pulled a tiny knife from her bag and held it up, allowing its razor-sharp and almost hair-thin blade to catch the light. She rolled the corpse over onto its face and, pushing back the lank hair, proceeded to cut a strip of flesh about an inch wide from the back of his neck down to his heel. Calmly, she held the flesh up to the pale moonlight, examining it carefully for flaws or imperfections and, finding none, rolled the defiled corpse back into the shattered coffin, kicked the shredded clothes in after and started to fill the hole.

Her eyes glittered strangely in the silver light; they were hard, cold and metallic. They were inhuman.

Abruptly, the moon was obscured, plunging the grave yard into almost total darkness, and only the sound of falling clay was audible in the night.

Nuala returned to her cottage by the shore as the sun was rising, the wan light touching the waves with pale gold and salmon. In the morning light, her face looked drawn and haggard and there were dark rings under her eyes, but she moved with an almost childlike eagerness, her eyes burning with a frenzied fever.

She treated the skin carefully, washing it in warm water and then drying it inch by inch before the turf fire, allowing the rich smoke to dust the pink flesh a light tan. It was a lengthy process and night was already falling as she completed her preparations.

With infinite precision, she laid the strip of skin out on the cleared floor of her cottage in an intricate pattern that resembled the figure eight. She piled twigs from seven trees and berries from three more in one loop of the figure and then took her place in the other.

A great stillness came over her as she awaited the time to begin the final part of the spell. And while she waited, the tiny question that plagued her during the past few days rose again from the inner recesses of her mind, and this time she could not banish it. The question remained. Was it worth it?

Was it worth destroying her immortal soul in return for earthly pleasures? A tiny voice said no, but another stronger voice answered yes. Soon, soon he would be hers. Soon, she would feel his strong arms about her, soon, she would feel his hot breath on her lips, soon. Nuala shivered in anticipation. Soon.

The spell was old and it was said to go back to the days when the first invaders came to Ireland, when the ice-sheets had retreated leaving behind a blasted landscape and men that were little more than beasts. There were several variations on the basic spell, but one thing remained constant: the flesh of the newly dead.

A strip of skin - in some cases from about the arm, the brow, the groin and breasts or from the head to the heel - was taken from a fresh corpse. If a woman desired the love of a man, then the flesh was taken from a man, and if a man lusted after a woman, he used the skin of a woman. This was then dried and treated and at a certain hour one called upon the Evil One and swore upon the flesh of the dead and the immortal soul, to pay homage to the Powers of Darkness, if one's wishes were granted. And then the strip of flesh was placed about the body of one's loved one whilst they slept. When they awoke, they were lost, captured in an evil web that could not be broken.

Nuala felt the silence of the night deepen and even the lapping of the waves grew distant. She saw the moon move across the cottage's only window. Midnight was approaching.

With trembling fingers, she lit the twigs and berries. They sparked and caught, suffusing the room with a bitter, pungent odour that tugged at the throat and stung the eyes. Nuala began to chant aloud in the Old Tongue, calling upon the powers of Shadow and Darkness, calling forth the Lord of the Night.

Her voice rose in power and strength, taking on a note of authority and command. Thunder rumbled close by, the sound of the gathering storm matching the voice exactly.

Lightning flashed, etching the room into deeper night, leaving seared images behind.

And then silence.

The birdcalls awoke Nuala. She opened her gritty eyes, feeling the rough floor beneath her cheek – and the events of the night flooded back like a polluted tide. She sat up, the effort making her head swim and pound, bringing bile to her throat. She looked at the floor and suddenly her discomfort was forgotten. For the strip of flesh, which had been wound into a figure eight had shifted and now resembled a horse-shoe.

The young woman wore the obscene belt beneath her clothing next to her skin for two nights and a day, suffusing it with her essence and aura. And on the morning of the second day, with the belt in her bag, set out for the market-town of Swords – and Donal.

Her excitement mounted as she neared the town overlooked by its round tower and high belfry. It was Wednesday, market day, and a long stream of carts and wagons were making their way through the town, some having come from as far away as Dublin to attend. Cattle ambled through the crowd, ignoring the screaming children who chased them with sticks; dogs herded thin sheep down the main street and the air was heavy with the mingled odours of animal dung and sweat.

Nuala wandered about the small town looking for Donal, eventually finding him in the inn, slightly drunk, with a girl on his arm.

She felt her temper rise, but bit back her anger, nodded pleasantly to Donal and his companion and sat down beside them. The young man squinted through the dim smoky atmosphere.

'Nuala! Nuala, where've you been?' He had to shout to make himself heard above the din. 'I've not seen you for ... for ...'

'A month,' she said sweetly.

'Aye, a month. What'll you have?' Without waiting for an answer, he turned and shouted for the harried barman.

'Porter, a bottle of porter for my friend.'

The barman brought Nuala a bottle of the thick black liquid and refilled Donal's glass.

'Are you not going to introduce me?' Nuala smiled, but only with her lips.

'Of course, of course, forgetting my manners.' He slipped his arm through his companion's. 'This is Mary, a very good friend of mine, and this,' he patted Nuala on the arm, 'is Nuala, our local wild-woman.'

Mary smiled politely, and then turned away and ignored Nuala. The young girl ran her fingers through Donal's unruly black locks and leaned close to whisper in his ear. As she did so, Nuala emptied a small packet of rock-salt into the young girl's drink.

Donal grinned, and then laughed aloud. 'It's a grand idea, let's drink to it.' He raised his glass and emptied half of it in one swallow. Mary drank.

Nuala engaged Donal in small talk for a few moments, watching Mary closely all the time. Abruptly her hand flew to her mouth, and she stumbled through the crowd towards the door, but before she reached it she was violently sick.

Donal suddenly looked disgusted. 'Christ! She can't hold her drink.' He looked away and ignored her. Nuala laid her hand on his, the long nails scratching the weather beaten flesh in a slow rhythm. 'Come outside,' she whispered, her mouth close to his ear.

They pushed their way through the crowd, circling around Mary as if she was not there. Nuala led Donal down through the town and out into the fields beyond. He felt curiously detached, as if the drink had numbed his body, leaving only his mind alert. He knew what was happening even though he had no power to stop it. He knew Nuala was going to make love to him even before she kissed him with a fierce longing. And he knew he would respond.

And when she laid her underskirt on the damp ground

behind the high hedge and slowly unbuttoned her bodice, he knew he was lost.

And he awoke in the morning with a curious belt wound around his waist.

Their's was not a happy marriage. It was dogged by ill-luck and death. They were shunned by their neighbours and their children hated because of their looks. For, nine months from the night when Nuala lay with Donal in the field, she gave birth to triplets. And each one bore a long black mark down his back, from his head to heel and another about his waist – the shape of the black cross.

The mark of Satan.

CHAPTER 15

I: THE MAGIC LINGERS ON ...

'Father, is she dying?' Niall's voice broke and he clutched the old priest's arm and wept.

Father O'Dwyre looked down at the tiny, wizened creature in the bed and shook his head slowly. 'I don't know, my son; I've never seen anything like it and I know of no sickness that would age and change a person so quickly, so thoroughly.' He eased the young man from the bedroom and into the cottage's only other room. Niall went and knelt by the fire and began to feed it rough chunks of still wet turf.

He turned to look at the priest. 'Father, what has happened to her?'

The old priest stood by the half-door, staring out into the misty morning air, whilst behind him Niall wept for the wife he did not know, for the wife he had lost.

Father O'Dwyre couldn't answer it. Barely a month ago he had married young Eileen and Niall and then she had been a bright innocent young girl, just turned eighteen, with a wide-eyed fresh beauty. And yet in one short month she had turned into ... He glanced back at the closed door of the bedroom and he wondered, what had she turned into?

Her clear, unblemished skin had turned leathery, scored with countless wrinkles and it glistened unpleasantly when the light struck it - which was not often, for the creature in the bed detested the light, claiming it hurt her eyes.

Her eyes.

The eyes of the maid Father O'Dwyre remembered had been bright and clear, still full of the wonder of youth - but

189

now those eyes had aged and hardened, glittering with cunning and experience.

It was almost as if ...

Abruptly the priest turned from the door. Niall was still crouched by the fire, staring unseeing at the guttering flame. He started when the priest called his name.

'Niall, I have done all in my power to help you, I can do no more ... except perhaps to make a suggestion which you might find strange.' The priest paused and smiled grimly. 'I am an old man now and have spent over sixty years in the service of God and if there is one thing I have learned in all that time, it is not to take what we call the supernatural, lightly.' The priest lowered himself heavily into the room's only chair.

'I spent many years in the missions abroad,' he continued. 'In India, I saw men do the impossible and in Africa I witnessed the power of the shaman, the Witch Doctors, but it was not until I returned to Ireland that I discovered that the borders between our world and the Other World are not as substantial as they seem. There is something about this land, something we do not feel because we are so close to it and bound so strongly to it. The strangers and visitors here feel it, on the air and in the wind; it is as if the magic still lingers.' The priest laughed quietly. 'You must forgive an old fool, Niall. Here you are heartbroken and me running on like an old woman outside church.' He leaned forward, resting his elbows on his knees. 'Look, you know Nano Hayes in the village?'

The young man nodded. 'They say she is a witch.'

The priest shook his head. 'She is no more witch than I am – and I think I might be able to work more magic than she ever could. But go to her, she is wise in country lore, perhaps she will be able to help. And here,' he took a small bottle from his pocket, 'it is blessed water – just in case you need it.'

Nano Hayes moved slowly around the bed, looking at the woman from every angle. It was just after noon and the

190

summer sun burned from a cloudless sky, but in the room it was dark and close, for Eileen – if it truly was Eileen – could bear no light.

'Well, it's plain enough,' said Nano Hayes, startling Niall, her voice surprisingly youthful for such an old and frail woman. 'Come outside, and I'll get what I need.'

In the other room she ordered Niall to boil a kettle of water and fetch his sharpest knife. But when he asked her what she was doing, the old woman would only smile secretly and shake her head.

When the kettle began to boil, she instructed him to heat the blade of his knife in the flame until it glowed red, whilst she soaked several rags in the scalding water.

And when her preparations were complete, she entered the bedroom. She stood by the foot of the bed, staring down at the wasted creature. 'You know,' she said wistfully, 'I am thinking you're no ordinary maid – I think you're one of the elven folk.' She glanced down at the woman. 'Ah, but sure you're not likely to tell me of your own accord, eh?'

The woman in the bed remained silent, staring at Nano Hayes through slitted eyes.

'Who, no, *what* are you?' asked the old witch – and dropped one of the steaming cloths onto the bed.

The creature in the bed screamed and hissed like a cat, her hard yellow eyes wide in terror and pain.

Nano Hayes reached across and took the heated knife from Niall's lax grip. 'Now if you're not going to tell me,' she began, and waved the heated blade before the creature's eyes, so that she could feel the heat radiating from the knife.

'Stop,' grated a harsh voice, totally unlike Eileen's.

'Who are you,' repeated Nano, 'and what have you done with this man's wife?'

'You may threaten and torture me, but you will never learn the truth.' The creature's eyes blazed with malice.

'Niall,' said Nano Hayes mildly, 'would you open the curtains.'

'No, stop,' the creature shrieked and curled up in a ball in the bed.

'She is a creature of the barrows and of the night, the light

191

of day would surely have shrivelled her,' explained the old woman to the thoroughly bewildered youth.

'I am Fethlin, a banshee, a woman of the Sidhe,' grated the muffled voice of the creature.

'The elven folk,' nodded Nano Hayes. 'And why have you taken the place of this man's wife?'

'Because my lord desired her – I had no choice,' said the banshee bitterly.

'So the faeries have Eileen,' said Niall, in a daze. He shook his head slowly and then looked at the old woman with innocent lost eyes. 'Is she gone forever then, have I lost her?'

But it was the banshee who answered him. 'They ride out of the fort each evening at dusk and your wife is with them ...' And the creature looked at the young man with a smile. 'You could try and take her then – but she is well guarded, for part of the faery host ride with her.' And then the banshee laughed, a hideous cackle, more animal than human. 'And you will never take her from the host – she is lost, gone forever.'

But Nano Hayes patted the young man's hand and said softly, 'Perhaps there is a way, perhaps there is.'

Niall reached the faery mound late in the evening. The sun was sinking and the trees cast long shadows over the hard earth, bathing one side of the fort in warm amber light, whilst the other drifted into dusk. Niall walked around the mound several times, carefully searching the ground for any sign that might tell him in which direction the faery host rode.

But the grass was unmarked and the mound itself showed no sign of a door or opening.

Wearily Niall climbed to the crown of the mound and looked down into the fields ... He saw it almost immediately: on the east side of the mound was a long thin swath of discoloured grass disappearing into the shadows. Niall slid down the side of the fort and made his way to a gap in the hedge through which the host must ride. On one side of the hedge he traced a circle on the grass with holy water and then, slipping the black-hafted silver bladed knife from his belt, knelt behind the hedge and waited.

The sun was slow in sinking for it was close to midsummer, and although the sky deepened to purple in the east and the nightstars began to glimmer dimly, yet the western sky still burned salmon and rose. A few nightbirds attempted a half-hearted song and once a barn owl hooted plaintively. Otherwise the night was still and silent – waiting.

Dusk gradually deepened, softening the harsh outlines of trees and bush, lending a mysterious air to the hedgerows and turning the faery mound to a place of shadowed mystery rather than just a grass covered mound. Niall, glancing out from behind the hedge, shuddered, for he felt he had been transported back a thousand years into Ireland's past.

And then the mound opened.

There was no rumble of earth or grinding of stone, rather it was as if the earth itself had shifted and dissolved. Tiny coloured lights winked far down in the depths of the mound and faint and sharp on the night air came the sound of elven horns. The clear and unmistakable ring of horses' hooves on stone coupled with the jingle of harness.

The faery host rode out.

Niall's first impression of the Sidhe folk was of height, for they seemed to tower above the ground. Their steeds were tall and incredibly thin, with wild darting eyes and long flowing manes, that burned snow-white in the dusk. They were richly adorned and the bits and harness were of silver.

The riders were tall thin creatures from man's past, in silver armour and carrying swords and spears. Their features beneath their crested helms were thin and pointed, with high slanting eyes, pointed ears and flowing hair. Their eyes burned with a strange fire and seemed lost – as if they stared into a dream.

And in their midst came Eileen.

Niall caught his breath and for a moment doubted that he was seeing his wife. She was riding one of the eldritch steeds and clad in a long shimmering robe that trailed on the night air and rippied in a breeze not of this world. Her hair had been coiffeured and flowed down her back in long silken waves. About her brow glittered a diadem of twisted silver wire and a matching necklace nestled against her throat. But it was her eyes her husband noticed, for they were flat and expressionless and seemed to stare into another world.

The faery host trotted across the fields towards the gap in the hedge and Niall suddenly realised with a chill that the horses' silver hooves barely touched the dew-glittered grass.

The first of the riders scraped through the hedge, not six inches from the terrified young man. And then another and another of the elven riders followed, bringing with them the chill of the Other World and the sweet, faintly repellent perfume of the barrow.

The next rider was Eileen. Niall waited until she was almost through the hedge and then he leaped for the reins. The horse reared and nipped at him with a click of huge teeth. But he struck the animal with his knife, drawing a thin line of pale liquid from its neck and then he had sliced through the saddle girth. He caught Eileen as she fell and almost threw her into the protective circle he had drawn earlier. And then he prayed.

The faery host attacked with a battle cry that shattered the stillness of the night like breaking glass. But thrown spears shattered about the pair as if they had struck an invisible wall and swords rang above their heads with high musical notes. But the circle held.

Within the circle Eileen stirred and her eyes cleared. 'Elfrann? ... Niall? ... *Niall*!' She buried her head in her husband's shoulder and wept. 'Oh Niall I dreamt ... I dreamt.' Niall smoothed her hair and whispered gently to her, but his eyes never left those of one of the elven warriors, one who remained apart from the rest.

'Your god protects you,' said the elven warrior suddenly, his high musical voice ringing in Niall's head. He came forward and stood beyond the circle. 'It is good to have gods; the gods of the Old Race have long since died – as we should have. But we are tied to this land and whilst it survives, so will we.' With a word the elven prince called off his warriors. The host withdrew and stood staring at the couple huddled within the invulnerable circle on the grass. The elven prince came and crouched just beyond the ring.

'I . . . I cannot say I regret taking her . . . but you love her – you must know how I felt . . .' He looked away and when he spoke again his voice was heavy with emotion and his strange colourless eyes were moist. 'I love her, son of Man,' and then he added in a rush, 'and I need her, for our race is dying. We need new blood. In the elder days the sons and daughters of Man were honoured to join the elven race; they gave us their seed and our children grew strong and the race was preserved. Some stayed with us, but the few that returned to the mortal world where gifted with foresight, the ability to see beyond the veil of their own world or the gift of healing. But it has been a long time since one of the sons of Man bedded one of the elven maids, or one of the daughters of Eve lay with a man beyond the Fields of Man.'

'I have met one of your elven maids,' said Niall bitterly. 'I would not be tempted to bed one.'

'Oh, they are not all ugly and wizened; it is only when they reside in this world for a while that they lose their looks and begin to age rapidly.' And then he laughed gently. 'But if you were to cross the borders into the Other World, then time would not touch you; the years would slip by like days – you would be close to being immortal.' His voice softened. 'I can promise Eileen this, if only you will let her go.'

Niall shook his head. 'I will never let her go – and I would kill her rather than see her go with you.' His voice rose with anger. 'You stole my wife, bewitched her and held her in thrall. You say that you love her – but does she love you? Can you not see that taking a girl just to bear you children is wrong; can you not see that once your spell has worn off, she will do nothing but fear and hate you always? That is not the way.'

The elven lord reached out his hand, as if he sought to touch Eileen, but he withdrew it abruptly with a gasp as if his fingers had been burned. 'She is so beautiful,' he whispered.

Niall laughed gently. 'She is, I'll grant you that; but there are many even more beautiful. But beauty is not everything,' he added.

'In the elven lands, beauty is everything,' said the elven prince.

'Perhaps if you were to woo a maid and she in turn, loved you, then she would willingly go with you into the elven kingdoms and gladly bear your children.'

'Perhaps,' said the elven lord wistfully. 'I think I recall now why the sons of Man gained supremacy over the Elder Folk.' He sighed and his eyes looked back into another age. 'In the end, we grew selfish and we had the power to take what we wanted – and what we wanted we took.' He smiled at the young couple. 'Remember that.' And then he glanced at the lightening sky. 'The night is almost done and we must be gone, but I think we have both gained something this night: you, your bride, and I ... and I, wisdom.' He mounted his wild-eyed steed, and as he led the faery host back into the mound, he turned and called, sharp and clear on the morning air. 'I will take your advice.'

The mound closed as the first rays of the morning sun touched it with bronze and gold.

Niall stood with Eileen in the crook of his arm, staring into the sunrise. 'You know,' he said suddenly, 'the old priest was right: the magic lingers on.'

CHAPTER 16

II: ... INTO THE SHADOWLAND ...

Brigid sat on the banks of the stream, dangling her legs in the cool water - waiting. The sun was sinking behind the low mountains to the west and dusk, the forerunner of the night was rapidly creeping across the fields. But the warmth of the day still lingered and the young girl was content to sit cooling her feet in the stream and listen.

And then as the last of the sun's rays faded and the bird calls died, the music came. It was thin and high and occasionally faded as if it passed beyond the range of human hearing - and it was incredibly beautiful. Brigid listened entranced as she had for the past three nights. She was unable to decide what instrument was playing, whether it was the pipes or a harp. The music had all the delicacy of the harp, but it flowed with that breathless quality peculiar to the pipes. And then Brigid realised that tonight the music was clearer and sharper ... and nearer. Abruptly she stood and ran lightly across the shadowed fields towards the forest and the strange otherworldly music.

It spun a delicate web on the night air, calling, insisting, luring her on, deeper and deeper into the forest that bordered the fields. She paused at the edge of the trees and stood, undecided - the local people told stories about the place, and connected it with the faery mound that rose just beyond the village.

But the music had her firmly under its spell and throwing caution to the winds she pushed on. As she moved deeper into the forest, the music grew louder until it was all about her ... holding her ... pulling her ... pushing ... whirling her around ... and around ... and around ...

She felt the forest spinning ... spinning ... spinning, and she fell.

When she awoke, she was lying by the tiny pool that lay almost in the centre of the forest. The night was far advanced and the heavens sparkled with stars. Brigid sat up suddenly. The time, what time was it? How long had she lain here – and how did she get here? Something moved at the corner of her eye and she stifled a scream.

'You have no need to fear me.' The voice was that of a man, thin and high like the music and it seemed to echo within her head.

'Who ... who are you?' she whispered, her voice cracking with the strain.

The shadow moved closer, until she could make out the outline of a tall thin man. He smiled, his sharp teeth startlingly white in the shadows and pushed back the hood of a long cape. His hair was long and pale and seemed incredibly fine.

'I am Elfrann,' he said. Again the voice seemed to ring in her head and she struggled to make out the accent. It was unlike her own, nor was it like that of the schoolmaster whose accent was harsh and flat, nor was it like Mr Cunningham's, who owned the big house on the hill, but who lived across the water for most of the year. And yet it was familiar – hauntingly familiar. It was soft and flowing and liquid, like ... like the music she had heard.

The music.

'I heard music,' she murmured, 'I followed ...'

The stranger held out a hand harp. 'I often play as the night draws on,' he smiled.

Brigid looked at the harp in wonder. It was carved from a shimmering white wood that seemed to burn on the night air and long wavering lines like script had been cut along its length. Its strings sparkled like silver wire and moaned slightly as Elfrann moved the harp to and fro.

'I have never seen anything like it,' she whispered and stretched out a hand to touch. But Elfrann moved the harp away.

'You cannot,' he said gently, 'it would ... it would burn you,' he explained. And then he added, 'It has been in my family for many years - it is very old.' He glanced at the sky, his eyes burning briefly amber, like an animal's.

'I must be going,' he said and his voice held a trace of regret. 'Will I see you again?'

Brigid nodded dumbly.

Elfrann stood and gathered his cloak about him. 'But I do not even know your name, pretty maid.'

'Brigid,' she murmured.

'Brigid,' he repeated, his strange accent making it sound alien and exotic.

And as he turned to go, he looked her full in the face and his strange eyes caught and held hers. 'But not a word of this to your father or sister - do not tell them about me.'

And then he turned and was gone before she realised she had not told him of her father or her sister.

She met Elfrann the following night in the same place just after dusk. When she came upon him he was playing the harp, the delicate liquid notes hanging trembling on the still night air. And even when he laid aside the harp, the music seemed to linger. He kissed her gently as he greeted her and she felt the blood rush to her face, but the touch of his lips tingled pleasantly on hers and she felt lightheaded and giddy.

Elfrann walked with her through the moonlit woods and although he talked little of himself, she felt she knew him.

And once again he left before sunrise, but not before making her promise not to tell her father or sister.

They met every night after that and the long hot days of summer drifted slowly into autumn and although Brigid spent most of the night with Elfrann, she never felt tired or exhausted the following morning - it was as if she had dreamt it all.

The lingering golden days of September gradually gave way to the colder, wetter weather of October, but Brigid was almost unconscious of the changing days, she lived only for the nights and her lover, Elfrann. She became wan and pale and her eyes grew shadowed and seemed to look into another place or time.

Deep down she knew Elfrann was not human, but he was neither deamon nor devil and she only suspected he was of the Elder Folk, the Faeries.

October passed.

And then on the last night of the month, Elfrann took Brigid to the Faery Fort, the mound that stood beyond the village, and together they climbed to the top and stood staring into the east, where the sky was already brightening in anticipation of sunrise. Elfrann took Brigid's hand in his and looked down into her gentle eyes.

'Tonight,' he whispered, 'is perhaps the last night I will see you . . .' he raised his hand and pressed his finger to his lips, stilling her reply.

'No, you must listen to me. Tonight is Samhain Eve, it is my last in your world. I must return.'

'Return?' Brigid frowned and then her eyes opened wide in understanding. 'You *are* of the Sidhe!'

Elfrann bowed. 'I am Elfrann, Lord of the Elven Folk, descendent of the Tuatha De Danann.' He paused and looked down at the mound below his feet. 'And tonight I must return to my kingdom.'

'Take me with you,' she said quickly.

He hesitated.

'Please,' she whispered, 'I love you.'

Elfrann held her tightly, stroking her long red hair. 'Truly? Do you truly love me?'

She nodded dumbly.

'But you know what I am. I am one of the elven folk – I am not human, at least not by your standards.'

'I love you,' she repeated.

She felt him shudder and when she looked up at the elven lord, she was shocked to find tears on his face.

Gently she brushed them away. 'Why do you weep, my love?'

'I weep because once I thought that love was little more than another name for longing. I weep because once I took a woman of your world. I thought I loved her, but her husband taught me what love really was when he challenged the faery host for her – and won. He taught me a lesson.' The elven lord kissed her. 'He taught me that love must grow of its own accord, it cannot be taken or made.'

'Do you love me, my lord?' she asked.

'I love you,' he replied simply.

Together they walked down the mound and stood at its foot. Brigid could feel the air tremble with suppressed power. Abruptly Elfrann laughed.

'What is it, my lord?'

'That man of your world told me that someday I would find a woman willing to wed me, willing to go beyond the veil into the Shadowland, the Realms of Faery.'

The feeling of suppressed power grew and intensified, until the young girl could almost taste it. Lightning flickered across the clear morning sky and her hair rose in long static streamers. The side of the fort trembled and shimmered and then abruptly it was gone and a great door stood in the side of the fort. Silently it swung open revealing a long passage leading down, deep into the depths of the Shadowland. Tiny lights winked and pulsed and on the air came the haunting melody of Faery, a melody similar to the one which had drawn Brigid to Elfrann.

'You know if you come with me there can be no return?'

She held his arm tightly. 'I would not want to return without you.'

'So be it.'

And together they walked from this world into the Realm of Faery.

The pale November sun burned through the thin grey clouds, giving the mound a bleached dusky appearance. Slowly it crept down the side of the fort ... until it touched the stiff body of a young girl.

CHAPTER 17

III: ... INTO ETERNITY

Nano Hayes sat by the smoking fire, staring deep into the shallow bowl she held cupped in the palms of her hands. She glanced up at the white-faced young woman sitting across from her. The wavering firelight turned the old woman's skin parchment yellow and turned her eyes to points of amber light. With a sigh she tossed the contents of the bowl into the fire, which abruptly blazed blue-green flames. The young woman stifled a scream.

'Now there's no need to be frightened child,' the old woman chuckled. 'I did the same for your mother and your two sisters and haven't they all made a fine match?'

Eithne nodded nervously, clasping her hands tightly together in her lap. She was frightened; the villagers told strange stories of the old woman, some whispered she was a witch and consorted with deamons. But her mother had laughed at the stories and insisted that she see Nano, especially now since she had turned eight and ten years and still with no sign of a husband.

The young girl cleared her throat, but when she spoke her voice was little more than a whisper. She coughed and tried again. 'Who ... Who did you see?' She nodded at the empty copper bowl.

'Why, I saw your husband, dear. And a fine match he will make.'

'Who is he?' Eithne asked, interested now in spite of herself.

'It's Seámus MacMahon - he lives down beyond the stream,' grinned Nano Hayes.

'Isn't he the brother of Niall who married Eileen Ni Sullibhan, who was taken very bad last year?'

'The same.'

Eithne stared deep into the fire, a tiny smile playing about her lips. She looked sidelong at the old woman. 'I've always liked Seámus.'

Nano nodded. 'There now, so you're getting a man you like – aren't you the lucky one? There's some now that have a match made for them and they not knowing the man until they meet him at the altar.'

'I like him,' said Eithne slowly, 'but I'm not sure whether I love him, or whether he loves me.'

The old woman laughed, a dry cackle that sent a shiver down the young girl's back. 'Liking him is good enough for a start, you can learn to love him later.' She glanced at Eithne. 'Do you not believe me? But you wait, love will come.'

'I always imagined it would be different,' she whispered.

Nano smiled at the young girl's romantic fancies. 'I tell you what, I'll give you this.' She handed Eithne a small linen packet of dried and crushed herbs. 'It's a love charm: slip it in his drink the first chance you get, and you can be sure he'll love you and none other.'

Eithne slipped the packet into her bodice. 'What's in it?' she asked.

'It's ten leaves of hemlock I picked on All Hallows Eve from the churchyard; oh, don't look so shocked child, I picked them in the name of the Blessed Trinity – they can only do good. Now if I had picked them in the name of the Evil One, then they could cause only harm and even death.' She stood and reached above the fire, taking down a mortar and pestle. 'I crushed the leaves here, and look ...' She tilted the bowl towards the fire, and Eithne could see strange flowing letters cut into the hardened clay.

'What do they say?' she whispered.

'It's Greek,' explained Nano. '"*Panta men kathara tois katharois*" – all things are pure to the pure.' She laughed and replaced the ancient objects above the fire. 'Oh, I know I'm called a witch in the village – not that that stops them when they need a cure of some healing herbs – but I've always honoured the True Gods.' She stood and pressed her hands against her back. 'Aaah, but it's old I'm getting.'

Eithne stood and handed the old woman a copper coin. 'It's all I can afford ...'

Nano Hayes took the girl's hand and pressed the coin back into it. 'There is no charge, child; I'll be fully paid when I see you happily wed.' She moved to the cottage's only door and pulled it open with a scrape of warped timbers.

Night had fallen and they both shivered in the sudden chill. 'One last thing,' said Nano. 'When you give Seámus the potion, make sure you say the following, three times:

> You for me
> And I for thee,
> And for none else,
> Your face to mine
> And your head turned away
> From all others.' "

Eithne repeated the charm, and then pulled her shawl up around her head and shoulders. Stooping suddenly she kissed the old woman on the cheek and then set off at a run down the deserted street, her bare feet making no sound on the sunbaked earth.

Nano Hayes stood in the door watching the slight figure disappear into the night, and smiled gently.

It was close to midnight when the old woman heard the muffled hoofbeats and the clatter of wheels coming down the long street. The fire had sunk to a dull bed of embers, barely lighting the single-roomed cottage. She leaned over and stirred the coals. Shadows danced and flickered on the damp streaked walls, and tiny sparks rose spiralling upwards.

A chill wind whipped through the room, fanning the flames, as the door suddenly opened. A tall dark figure stood in the doorway, outlined in stark relief against the yellow harvest moon hanging low over the thatched roofs. And Nano Hayes shrank back, her breath catching in her throat.

For the stranger cast no shadow.

She could feel her heart pounding her chest, frighteningly loud. Blood rushed to her head and she swayed and had to clutch the back of a chair for support. She squeezed her eyes shut, her lips moving in a silent prayer – and when she looked again, she could see the stranger's shadow stretch into the room almost to her feet.

'You are Nano Hayes.' It was a statement more than a question. The voice was male, but was thin and high – almost like a child's – and it seemed to come from a great distance.

'I am,' the old woman nodded. It gave her some satisfaction that her voice was firm and unquavering.

The stranger stepped into the room, the moonlight catching him in profile, painting one half of his high, thin slant-eyed face in wan yellow light, and leaving the other in shadow. His eyes glittered like points of metal.

'I am surprised to find you still up.' His voice rang off the damp walls as if they were metal. 'You were expecting me, perhaps?'

'I was expecting someone,' Nano said carefully. 'I felt someone would come tonight ...' she shrugged. 'But now you're here, what do you want with me?'

'My wife is close to childbirth and she wished to have a ... to have someone with her. I have a carriage without, will you come with me?'

Nano hesitated. Something about this tall stranger chilled her – and although she was close to seventy summers her eyes were still as sharp as a cat's and yet she could not make out his features. And his voice; the more she heard it, the more convinced she became that it rang within her head.

'I will pay you well,' he said, as Nano remained silent.

The old woman dismissed the matter of payment with a wave of her hand and piled some of the things she knew she would need into a woven wicker basket and then followed the stranger outside. He was standing by the open door of a small closed carriage, staring intently into the eastern sky. As he helped the old woman into the carriage, he said brusquely, 'We must hurry, dawn will be early.'

'Where are we going?'

'To my home,' he said and slammed the door. Inside it was warm and dark, the rich odour of polished leather and wood hanging heavy on the air. There were no windows in the coach and when, on an impulse, she tried the door, she found it was locked. She sat on what seemed like velvet, her basket on her knees, clutching it tightly. She knew everyone in the village and many of those surrounding villages along the coast and she knew of no pregnant girl, especially one near childbirth. Unless of course, the child was illegitimate and the parents and families had managed to keep it a secret all these months; but she didn't believe that was possible in such a small close-knit community.

The carriage lurched and moved down the street, the hooves of the strange horses she had only half-glimpsed, sounding muffled and distant.

There was another possibility - a distasteful one. Many years ago she had been called out in the dead of night to attend a birth - or so she had been told. But it had turned out to be nothing of the sort. A young girl of a good family - who had all since emigrated - had found herself to be with child. Her parents would have killed her and the disgrace would have ruined the family, had the father of the child not hit upon a plan. He had brought Nano Hayes to a deserted cottage down by the shore and, believing her to be a godless woman, had told her to get rid of the unborn child. Nano had refused and the couple had grown pleading and threatening in turn, but she had remained firm, despite the threats to denounce her as a witch. The girl never did have the child, although Biddy Early, up in Clare, told her some time later that the couple approached her for a potion to destroy the babe - and she too had refused. Nano Hayes shook her head, someone, somewhere had taken that little life ...

The sounds of the carriage's wheels suddenly changed - it

was now running across grass rather than hard earth. Gradually the ground began to rise and then abruptly slope downwards. The horses' hooves now echoed sharp and clear, ringing on dressed stone and off nearby walls. Nano strained and fancied she could hear music and the sounds of merriment growing louder. They must have entered a courtyard she decided, near a large house.

The carriage stopped.

Nano could hear muttered voices outside the carriage and then another voice raised in either anger or command. But the language was strange, although parts of it seemed familiar and she couldn't make out what was being said. Abruptly the carriage door was thrown open. The old woman squinted into the harsh burning light which streamed in, making her eyes water and fill with tears. Someone reached in and gently helped her down, whilst another took her bag. She could see nothing through her tears save a shimmering kaleidoscope of colours and the misty shapes of people as they passed by. An incredibly delicate girl's voice warned her of steps just before they began to climb. Nano paused and wiped her sleeve across her eyes, but they continued to fill with tears and render her almost blind. She heard a lock click, a section of the wall before her swung open and she was gently pushed into a large warm room.

Nano squeezed her eyes shut and blinked and as abruptly as they had started, the tears ceased. She was standing in a large bedroom; to one end of the room was a huge blazing fire, whilst at the other end was a marvellously ornate bed. The high walls were hung with delicately woven tapestries, depicting curiously elfin creatures and strange mythological beasts, whilst the floor was covered with a thick brown-and-ochre carpet, which exuded a musky fragrance with every step she took. There was only one door – the one through which she had come and no windows.

A low moan attracted her attention. There was a young girl in the bed, her face pale and drawn and her eyes tight with labour pains. Nano Hayes frowned; there was something terribly familiar about the girl.

'Hello, Nano.'

And suddenly she knew – the girl in the bed was Brigid Farrell! The old woman felt her blood run cold, for the body of young Brigid had been found at the foot of the Faery Fort outside the village almost a year ago!

The girl smiled weakly. 'Yes, it's me. There's no need to fear – no-one will harm you here.'

'Where are we?' wondered Nano.

'You have passed beyond the Fields of Man into the Realm of Faery; you are one of the few Daughters of Eve ever to have done so and still retained your mortal form. When I came through almost a year ago, I had to leave my body behind.'

'But you are real.' Nano reached out and touched the girl's fevered brow.

'I am real,' she insisted. 'What I left behind was only a husk – a shell of mortal fears and worries, of mundane passions and desires. This is the real me ...' and then she caught her breath and bit back a scream.

Nano Hayes suddenly forgot her questions – she had a young girl in labour to attend to.

'If there is ... anything ... anything you ... need,' gasped Brigid, 'call ...'

Nano looked around, but there was neither hot water nor clean linen. She ran lightly across the thick carpet, the thin odour of musk cloying and catching in her throat. But the moment she opened the door, her eyes filled with tears and once again she was looking through a watery veil.

'I need boiling water and some fresh linen,' she called and slammed the door, lying back against it, blinking her eyes until they cleared.

Almost immediately the door opened and a young maid entered. She was tiny, almost child-like, but perfectly formed, but her eyes betrayed her true age, for they were old and wise with experience. She carried a huge pitcher of steaming water to the small bedside table and laid it down and placed a small bundle of clean white linen beside it. Without a word she turned and left.

Brigid tensed as another spasm shot through her and then another and another. She screamed ...

Nano Hayes washed the child carefully in the still tepid water, wrapped him in a linen sheet and placed him in his mother's arms. Brigid held him as if he were made of glass and looked into his huge black eyes. Tears of joy replaced those of pain which had recently flooded her eyes.

'He is perfect in every way,' said Nano softly.

Brigid pushed the cloth back from the babe's head. His tiny ears were pointed and upward sweeping and both his chin and nose seemed unnaturally sharp.

'He is a child of both worlds,' she said. 'He is beautiful.' And then she looked at Nano Hayes, at the lines of fatigue etched about her eyes and mouth. 'You are tired.' She seemed surprised. 'But I forgot; fatigue is almost unknown here. And you are probably hungry too. But listen to me carefully now. If they offer you food or drink, refuse it unless they can offer you salt with it. If you eat the food of Faery, you will be trapped here for all eternity. You must also refuse if they offer you gold or silver – take nothing above your normal fee; you must take away from Faery only what is yours and yours by right.'

'And what about you?'

Brigid gently kissed her young son's head. 'I am happy here – I came here of my own accord and although I little knew what I was doing, I loved Elfrann, I would have followed him anywhere. But this is my home; my husband is here ... and now my son is here. I cannot leave.'

'But are you happy?' wondered the old woman.

Brigid shrugged. 'Oh, I'm happy ... I suppose. Some of the elven folk despise me,' she added, 'but the birth of my son will silence them. Some said he would be born deformed – that the Elder Race and the newer race of Man could not interbreed and others said he would be stillborn. But this is the first birth in this land for almost a thousand years of your time. My son is the first of a new line of elven lords – he will carry the race on and into eternity.' She ran her fingers across the babe's finely downed head.

The door opened and the stranger who had brought Nano through into the Shadowland entered. He crossed to the bed in long strides and went on his knees beside it. Brigid lifted the child and held it out to him. 'Elfrann, behold our son.'

The elven lord took the boy in his long delicate hands and kissed his wrinkled forehead gently. And then he laughed and held the child aloft as if in offering. 'My son,' he cried and handed the boy back to Brigid, 'Our son,' he corrected himself.

'The race will survive,' she said.

Elfrann shook his head slowly. 'He is the last of the Tuatha De Danann.' He stood and turned to Nano, handing her a silken purse. 'This is but a token – all my treasure could not pay you for bringing this child safely into the world. Now come, you must be famished: there is food and drink prepared.'

Nano shook her head. 'I thank you – but I cannot take this.' She opened the purse and extracted one silver coin.

She smiled thinly. 'Render unto Caesar only what is Caesar's,' she quoted, and handed him back the purse.

The elven lord laughed. 'I did not think you would pay homage to the New God.'

'The New God survives and thrives,' she said, 'and where are the Old Gods of your people now?'

'They are but dim memories,' whispered Elfrann.

Nano gathered up the damp cloths and piled them by the side of the bed. The door opened and the creature with the child's body and the woman's eyes entered and silently removed them. And the old woman noticed how her strange eyes lingered on the babe and seemed to suddenly fill with tears.

Elfrann weighed the purse in his hand. 'I'll wager you will not eat with us,' he smiled.

Nano returned his smile. 'I like my food well salted.'

The elven lord nodded gravely. 'I understand. But before you go, know that you have my thanks and you may be sure I

210

will tell my son of the woman who aided him into the world. And if there is anything I – or indeed he in time – can do for you, then you will need only call.'

Nano thanked him and, taking her wicker basket, stood by the door, whilst Elfrann and Brigid whispered together over their son.

The elven lord led her back through the corridors and rooms of the fort. He had covered her eyes with a silken cloth and he clutched her wrinkled, veined hand in his. As they began to descend the stairs, he stopped and spoke with someone in the strange lilting, musical tongue of the People of the Goddess. He broke off and she could hear the alarm in his voice. 'We must hurry, dawn is almost upon us.' Abruptly, he swept her up in his arms and raced down the stairs, the sudden descent making her thankful for the cloth that covered her eyes. And if she hadn't heard the sound of his bootheels clicking off the echoing stones she could have sworn she was flying.

The sound changed and they were now out into what she assumed was a courtyard. The elven music had stopped and the sounds of merriment had long since ceased.

Elfrann ran on, climbing uphill now, his breath coming in laboured gasps and every now and again he staggered under his burden. At last he skidded to a halt. He called aloud in the Old Tongue and Nano could feel the very air tingle, as if a thunder storm were brewing. A chill wind suddenly whistled past her head and then it was gone and she could feel the fresh morning breeze on her face and taste the damp air.

'I must leave you here,' Elfrann said. 'You have my thanks, now and always.' And he was gone.

She stood listening for a moment, but the morning was silent save for the first tentative calls of the dawn chorus. Stiffly she removed the blindfold and stared into the east, awaiting the sunrise. She looked around, and was not surprised to find herself at the foot of the Faery Fort and almost at the same spot where the body of Brigid had been found. She picked up her wicker basket. Lying on top was a silken purse. She picked it up carefully, feeling the hard shapes of coin through the cloth.

Legend went that whomever was given gold by the faery folk usually ended up with nothing more than lumps of earth or stone. Almost unconsciously her fingers found the draw string and pulled - and a stream of bright golden coins fell onto the dew-damp grass.

Nano Hayes knelt and replaced the coins in the purse. It was the beginning of a new day, a new month and a new season; and a new age for the elven folk, the last of the Tuatha De Danann.

For they had a new lord, a child of both worlds, one who would lead them on ... on and into eternity.

VOLUME II

For Derek and Jacqui whom I missed the first time around. Willie and Maeve, Catherine, Sara-Jane for various reasons. And Anna, for one very good reason.

CONTENTS

CONTENTS

CHAPTER 1

THE DAWN

The dark bulk of the island suddenly appeared out of the mists, rising from the flat ocean like the back of some great sea creature. The shouted warnings came too late, and the longship shuddered and screamed as it ran up onto the beach. It tilted once, righted itself, and then tilted again, its port side almost touching the sands. A small olive-skinned man, clad in rough animal skins and worn leathers climbed slowly from the wrecked craft and walked shakily down the beach. The muscles in his legs bunched and knotted, and he had to resist the temptation to roll as he walked. It felt strange to be back on dry land again after being so long at sea.

He climbed the dunes and stood on the grassy crest, staring down into the shallow bowl of land that rolled away into the distance. There were three lakes situated at one end of the depression and he counted nine small, swiftly-flowing rivers, some feeding into the lakes and then flowing out into the sea. He breathed deeply, savouring the fresh moist air, redolent with the tang of salt and growth. He ran his thick, gnarled fingers through his long coarse hair, and felt the peace of the new land sink into him. The swarthy southerner nodded decisively and made his way back down onto the beach.

The dull sound of hammering broke the silence of the quiet land as the crew attempted to secure the longship to the beach with thick hempen ropes tied to stakes driven into the harder high ground.

'Well?' His son lifted the heavy mallet and looked up, squinting into the morning sunlight which haloed his father's head.

1

Partholon nodded. 'It is the Land.' He clapped his son on the shoulder, 'Let's tell them.'

Brechan pushed himself to his feet and brushed his hands against his woollen jerkin. He stood a head taller than his father and had his mother's pale eyes and light coloured hair. 'How far does the land extend?' he asked.

'Far enough. There are rivers and lakes and a broad fertile plain over the lips of that rise.'

'Mountains? Hills?' Brechan stopped and looked up and down the beach. 'Cliffs?'

'I have told you all that there is,' Partholon said quietly.

'That's all? There must be more; there has to be more. Father, there are twenty-four families aboard that ship – there is no room for them all. We must move on.'

Partholon smiled grimly. 'We will stay,' he snapped, and added, 'we have no choice.'

His son opened his mouth to protest, but the older man raised his hand, the smile slipping from his face. 'Watch!' he commanded.

He knelt on the rough beach and plunged his hands deep into the coarse sands. He closed his eyes and his brow furrowed in concentration, beads of sweat starting out just beneath his hairline.

Brechan sat back on his haunches and watched his father with concern. The old face suddenly relaxed and then assumed a stiff, mask-like appearance, and under the dark tan it grew pale. The thin lips peeled back from startlingly white teeth, and his eyes rolled in his head. Brechan could feel the tension growing, could sense the gathering power, felt its static ripple along his arms, flowing through his fingers, sparking from his hands. He knew his father had access to a Power, a raw elemental Power that had been created with this world, a power which he, even though he was but a generation removed from it, could sense only dimly, and grope for blindly.

Suddenly Partholon began to mutter in a liquid, flowing tongue, totally unlike the guttural language of his own race. And slowly, the grains of coarse sand about his hands began to twist and twirl, shaping themselves in strange and arcane

2

patterns, spirals, ovals and complete circles.

Partholon's eyes snapped open. He regarded his son's fear and awe with amusement. 'You see; there is Power in this land, Power beyond measure. It was one of the last to be created and the gods spent themselves in its making. The magic is strong here.' He stood and smiled mirthlessly.

'We are now tied to the land, we are now a people of the land, and as we grow, so shall the land. The eternal sea will wash back, relinquishing the land to us so that each man might have space enough to expand.' He held out his hand and let the golden grains fall like liquid onto the beach. 'Is that enough for you?'

Brechan nodded. 'It is enough. I will tell the others.'

Partholon nodded, dismissing his son and then turned away and climbed the dunes again. He stood there, staring down into the green bowl. The sun had not long risen and the pastures gleamed in the warm golden light and the waters of the lakes and rivers flowed like metal. It was not the harsh burning sunlight of his own homeland, but a rarer, finer light; it would give life and heat without slaying, give light without searing. It was indeed a fine land.

The southerner took the first steps down onto the broad plain, his shadow dancing on the grass before him. A tiny cloud obscured the sun, abruptly chilling him. He shivered as icy fingers touched the base of his spine and for a single moment he felt the cold hand of Death touch his brow and he was suddenly reminded that this day was sacred to Bile, the God of Death: Beltaine.

That night, the shipwrecked crew of the longship and their passengers gathered in a huge tent of wood and hide on the edge of the plain. The atmosphere was light and bantering, but the laughter was forced and overloud and Partholon could almost taste the undercurrent of fear. Brechan and his brothers moved quietly through the crowd, filling goblets with the last of the stored wine, making some pretence at celebration.

Partholon sat at one end of the tent, well back from the

rushlights, in the shadows. His dark eyes darted about the crowd, noting the allegiances and cliques forming and re-forming; his agile mind singling out those likely to 'cause trouble. There were two, he knew, he had most cause to fear: Aeolas the sorcerer, a wild-eyed sun-worshipper from the Isle of Samothrace, and Mercan, the proud young general who had covered his retreat from the gutted remains of the palace. He sliced into a fruit with his knife, the rushlight dancing along the blade and abruptly, the Scythian saw the knife in his hand rising and falling, rising again, streaked with red, and the body of his father falling across his mother's . . .

He had been close; so close.

The crown of Scythia had been almost in his hands. And then it had blown away like wind-strewn ashes. The guard had remained loyal to Bescosmis, his brother, and had turned on the renegade prince and his forces.

Not many had survived the massacre that followed. The loyalists had pursued Partholon and his followers to the harbour where a score of ships waited as a last line of retreat. There the fighting had been fiercest and the waters of the Mid-Sea had run with red. And only two ships had sailed from the small harbour; and one of those had been lost between the Pillars of Hercules.

And now here he was, a murderer, and worse, guilty of both parricide and regicide, hated and feared by his men, mocked by his sons and loathed and despised by his wife. His generals were plotting against him and there was some talk amongst the families – especially the Tocket and Detchu – of returning to Scythia and throwing themselves on the mercy of the court.

But no, they would never do that, not while he still lived. He surged to his feet and moved out of the shadows, calling loudly for silence. When he had their attention, he began.

'My lords ... ' he acknowledged them with a short nod, 'there are some decisions we must make now. This is a fine land, a young land, still steeped in the Elder Magic. It is admirably suited to our needs, but like all new things, it must be explored carefully, with every aspect considered ... '

4

'But there is nothing here,' Aeolas the sorcerer interrupted. 'I have stood on the lip of the world and looked across the plain. You speak as if we are staying here, but save for a few rivers and lakes, there is nothing here.'

Partholon raised his hand, his dark eyes flashing dangerously. 'You are a mage, a sorcerer, surely you can feel the Power in this land?' he snapped. 'There is enough Power here to fashion whatever one needs; to bring forth mountains if one wishes, call up forests if that pleases one. What more do we want; what more do we need?' he demanded.

'We need room. There is hardly enough space here for us now; what will happen in a little while when there are sons to stake their claim to the family holdings?' The voice was smooth and slightly rasping, cultured and deadly.

Partholon rounded on the speaker. He was a young man, a head and more taller than the prince. His hair and carefully curled beard were golden, and the torchlight burnished them with crimson highlights. His eyes were large and innocent – the eyes of a child, and with all the capacity for the vicious cruelty of a child.

'Mercan,' Partholon said quietly, 'there is nowhere left to go. We have reached the edge of the world.'

The young general waved his hand at the sorcerer. 'Aeolas claims that there is land to the west ... '

'I have never heard of it,' the prince snapped.

'It is true,' the Samotharcian said quickly. 'Beyond the horizon there is a land the like of which you have never seen before. The gods created it for their own use, and then abandoned it in favour of their sport with mortal man and the Demon-Wars. But it is there,' he added.

'And how many days sailing is it?'

The sorcerer's voice faltered. 'I do not know lord, but it would be many moons.'

Partholon laughed in disbelief. 'Many moons! And where will we find a craft that will take us to this land of yours? You know the condition of our own ship. Even if we had the proper tools and equipment there is several moons repair work to be carried out on it. And we'll have to strip parts of

5

the ship for timbers for a new hull, which will leave us with no storage space, no crew quarters. Where would we store the provisions for such a lengthy journey, where would we shelter at night?' He spat at Mercan's feet. 'Am I surrounded by fools? You!' He jabbed a finger in the general's face. 'If you wish to undertake this fool's errand, then go, and do not let us detain you. I release you from your service!'

The assembly went suddenly silent and the thin keening of the wind across the flat plain suddenly seemed magnified.

The young man smiled coldly, thin lips drawing back from mis-shapen teeth. 'But I do not release you from your debt, Partholon. You owe me your life. If my forces had not been there to carry you to safety, you would have been torn to pieces by the people. To slay one's father is a terrible crime, but to slay one's mother also so that there could be no further claimant to the throne is surely abominable.' The words were cold and precise, delivered with a malicious delight.

'And if I had taken the throne, general, you would have been one of the ones to gain the most. We both gambled, soldier – and we both lost.'

The tension between the two intensified. Mercan fingered his flame-edged dagger uneasily. The older man was unarmed, but there was a strange, gloating look in his hard dark eyes, almost ... almost as if he wished the general could try and kill him.

The assembly were silent, but Mercan recognised the bright glitter in their eyes; he had seen it far too often during his campaigns in the islands and on the mainland; it was the look of a mob expecting blood. He swallowed his anger and forced a smile to his lips. 'Come now,' he protested, holding out his hands to Partholon, 'surely we must not sully our first night in this new land with harsh words and recriminations. We have yet to see this land in the harsh light of noon – because I, for one, was too busy hauling everything off the ship today to see anything. Let us wait until the morrow – we can pass judgement then.'

The Scythian nodded gratefully and returned Mercan's

smile. 'The night is far gone and we have travelled long and hard; we are all overtired. Let us retire for the night, the morning will bring many things.'

There was a general murmur of assent, and then a voice asked from the back of the tent, 'What should we call this land?'

Partholon gazed into the last flickers of flame still clinging to one of the torches and when he spoke, his voice was soft and gentle. 'This land will have many names, some fine and fitting, some shameful – let us not name it yet, for the land is not truly ours ... ' He blinked as the flame flickered and died. 'One names a possession – we do not possess this land.'

'Yet!' Mercan added as Partholon turned to leave.

The following morning the Partholonians awoke to find their sentries slain and their damaged craft reduced to tinder wood. It seemed they were not alone on the island.

Delgrade stood by the entrance to the tent watching her husband making his way slowly down the beach towards the remains of their craft. Her long blonde hair was unbound and fell in gentle ripples down her flawless back. She was wearing a long gown that had been fashionable at court over a year ago. It was low cut and gossamer thin, and she could feel the chill wind bite through the thin material and caress her smooth skin with icy talons.

She felt eyes on her, a dull tingling at the base of her neck, and turning suddenly, she caught one of the slaves staring at her, his eyes eagerly probing through the gown. Delgrade read the lust in his eyes and moved slightly, allowing the gown to fall open, exposing more of her body to him. She waited a moment and then said softly, 'My husband will have you flayed alive for what you have done.'

The wide-eyed youth started, blood rushing to his face. 'I ... I ... ' he stammered.

'Do not attempt to lie to me,' Delgrade said softly. 'Come here.'

7

The princess examined the youth critically. He was not above middle height and of slight build. His hair was dark and shining and the first touches of a beard were upon his cheeks. She took one of his hands and ran her nails along the palm, making him twitch. It was hard and calloused, the nails short and broken, encrusted with grime. She dropped the hand in disgust.

'Who are you?' She caught and held his dark eyes with her direct gaze.

'I am Togha,' he stammered.

'And your tasks, slave?'

'On board the ship, I scrubbed the decks, cleaned ... whatever was needed. But now ... ' he shrugged, 'I have no assigned tasks.'

Delgrade looked past the slave, down onto the beach, where a small figure made his way slowly through the wreckage. A strange gleam came into her light eyes and a curious smile played about her lips. She turned back to the youth and stroked his thin face with her long, pointed nails. She relished the fear that started into his eyes, but she caught the sudden increase of the pulse in his throat, and felt his breathing quicken. 'I want you,' she whispered, 'to attend me as my servant ... '

Togha blushed and his voice trembled. 'My lady, I know nothing of such ... there are others ... you have slaves to attend you ... '

The princess caught his jaw in her hand and squeezed. Her eyes widened and there was a glint of madness in them. 'I have slaves to attend me,' she agreed, 'and you too will attend me. You will attend me in all things.' And her laughter hung on the still morning air like a curse.

Mercan stooped and lifted a jagged spar of wood from the sands and handed it to Partholon. 'Look at this. See how this wood has been shorn through as if struck by a blade, but this,' – he held up another piece of wood – 'has been shattered by a blow.'

Partholon examined the wood, his dark eyes troubled.

8

'There was no storm last night and the tide was not running high ... ' he reasoned.

'The ship was attacked,' Mercan stated flatly, 'and you said this island was uninhabited.'

'I know, I know,' the Scythian said coldly, 'but it seems I was wrong.'

'It was a costly mistake,' Mercan said, kicking sand over a dried bloodstain. 'Eight men dead and our craft destroyed. We are now trapped on this cursed isle, and speaking frankly Partholon, it is indefensible. There are no mountains, no forests, no caves ... '

The prince silenced him with a wave of his hand. 'You will have your mountains, rivers and streams,' he snapped. And then his voice changed and took on a curious note, one almost of fear. 'This is a magical land, but it has tasted blood too soon and I fear its history will be steeped in bloodshed.'

Mercan snapped a piece of wood in half and tossed it into the sea. 'I care little for your fears for the future. My fears are for now; and I fear you have brought us to our deaths,' he said quietly.

'Perhaps.'

The last rays of the setting sun burned across the plain, touching the small rounded hillocks with shadow, gilding the beach in ochre and bronze. A thin, cold breeze whistled in from the sea, dispersing the smoke rising from the fire built in a small circle of stones near the dunes. Four figures stood on the beach about the wildly flickering fire, their hands raised to the darkening skies.

Partholon glanced anxiously into the west. The light was almost gone and the incantation must end with the death of the day so that the forces of night might gather and work their will in the darkness. He watched Aeolas, supported by his fellow sorcerers, Fos the northerner and Faud, the stout magician from the land to the east of Scythia, lower his arms and prepare for the final incantation. The Samotharcian's face was lined with fatigue, his crazed eyes glazed, and he could barely stand upright. Fos and Faud stood beside him, lending him their support and strength, allowing him to draw from their reserves – but they too, were rapidly weakening.

Aeolas made one final effort, raising his hands and calling forth into the gathering night, but the strain was too much and he staggered back as if he had been struck and fell to the ground. Partholon grabbed him, pulling him upright. 'Finish it,' he hissed, his voice harsh and chill.

'I cannot,' the sorcerer gasped.

'Too late,' screamed Faud, and even as he spoke, the ravening elemental forces gathered.

Lightning flared from the evening sky, coming to earth on the beach, fusing the sands into solid globules of glass. The air stinking of ozone and raw power, trembled and vibrated, awaiting the unleashing of the destructive elements that would utterly annihilate the puny forces that had dared to tamper with it.

The prince caught the sorcerer's head in both his hard hands and twisted it savagely. His dark eyes, as hard as pebbles, bored into the Samotharcian's. Aeolas felt the abrupt transfer of strength flow from the prince into his own exhausted body. He saw Partholon's eyes widen and then suddenly shrink to tiny pinpoints, and then he felt the pain lance through his eyes, rip through his head and erupt from his mouth in a long agonised scream.

He rose jerkily to his feet, moving like one possessed. And with his new found strength, he found that the forces gathered about him were almost visible, almost tangible. Shadows gibbered at the corners of his vision and he could sense the raw chaos lurking beyond them.

He cried aloud the final incantation and heard it shout from his throat in a strange commanding voice, totally unlike his own. And from behind him, he heard Partholon cry aloud, 'Fathers, aid us.'

Thunder and lightning detonated all about them, encircling them in a wall of light and sound. Low clouds rolled swiftly in from the west and north. Icy blasts of wind whipped in across the suddenly turbulent seas, carrying sleet and snow and howling like the damned souls of Hades.

A driving rain hissed across the beach, extinguishing the small fire, washing away the blood of the sacrificed fowl.

And then the earth moved.

Partholon grabbed Faud and screamed into his ear, 'Take Fos, I'll carry Aeolas; we must begone, even now the sea rises.' And, half-carrying, half-dragging the semi-conscious magicians, Faud and Partholon staggered across the still smouldering and hardened sands.

Partholon and his followers kept to their tent that night. The prince had surrounded it with a magical ring, and although he had promised them it was completely safe, they still murmured prayers to their gods and huddled together in fear.

Beyond the circle, the elemental forces of Chaos and Night raged and worked their will upon the land. The seas about the island rose, swamping most of it, and then swiftly retreated, leaving vast tracts of steaming land uncovered. The earth buckled and heaved, throwing up formidable mountains that crumbled and formed and then re-formed. The earth shuddered and split with rivers which quickly vanished only to reappear as lakes, only to disappear into the bowels of the earth again. Valleys were carved out and cliffs formed; parts of the island were cut off and surrounded by the sea, forming other, smaller islands.

And through it all, in the tent ringed about by the magical circle, the Partholonians remained safe whilst the land rose and fell about them.

And generations later, the savage northern Vikings would discover the small, almost circular valley surrounded by the mountains on the east coast of the fresh green land they sought to conquer, and there they would build the city they would call Dubh Linn.

Partholon led Mercan along the beach the following morning. The general had been silent ever since he had stepped from the tent and seen the low mountains rising to the south where none had risen the day before.

The prince stopped and pointed out across the waves.

11

Mercan squinted into the heavy morning mist that still clung despite the height of the sun. He shaded his eyes, unsure of what he saw. And then he gasped. 'It is an island!'

Partholon nodded. 'It is an island,' he agreed. 'And there are islands all about the coast now. The land itself is three times bigger than it was yesterday. There are mountain ranges all along the eastern and south-western, the northern and north-eastern coasts. Overnight nine new rivers have sprung up and there are seven new lakes ...'

The general shrank back from Partholon. 'How do you know all this?' he asked quietly, but with a tremor in his voice.

But the prince just smiled. 'I know,' he said, 'I know.'

'What else do you know?' Mercan demanded, his fear turning to sudden anger.

Partholon laughed gently, his laughter only serving to infuriate the general. 'I know,' he said, 'that there is an island to the north of this, an island called Taure. And there is a crystal tower upon this island, and about the tower are curious dwellings of creatures neither beast nor man, but something caught in between; the obscene fruits of the union between a demon in man's form and a woman once of this world.'

'What are they?'

'I do not know. They are creatures, intelligent creatures of sorts,' Partholon said. 'However, I do know that their lord is called Cichal One-Foot.'

'Are they dangerous? Will they attack?' Mercan asked quietly, for this was something he could understand; the clash of weapons and the screams of the wounded and dying were tangible and real, they were something he could deal with.

'They are already spying on us – and have been since we first landed. They fear us now – the enchantment last night slew many of them and the remainder have fled northwards for the present. But soon their fear will turn to hate – and then they will attack.'

'And until then?'

'Until then this land is almost ours; we can only strive to

12

make it wholly ours, build our forts and roads and prepare for that not too distant day.' He turned and gestured inland. 'There is ample room for all of us now. You have your mountains and valleys, rivers and streams: make of them what you can.' Partholon turned away and walked slowly down the beach, wisps of fog parting before him and swirling in behind, until it seemed as if he were swiftly fading from this world.

Mercan watched the prince until he was lost in the mist and then turned and continued up the beach. What Partholon had told him was disturbing – almost frightening – but the general relished the icy tingle of fear. To conduct a defence . . . no, not a defence he decided, an attack! He would not sit back and allow the creatures in the crystal tower to come to him on their terms; he would attack them on his terms, in his time, with his weapons. But before he could do that he knew he would need a map of this new land.

Delgrade sank back into the large crystal bath, allowing the warm water to lap about her midriff, feeling it caress her thighs with smooth intimacy. She ran a long polished nail along the edge of the bath tracing the outline of a naked faun pursued by a horned and tailed creature with an enormous phallus. The bath was decorated with thousands of such carvings drawn from the already ancient mythology of her people. The bath itself had been taken by her husband in an expedition to the continent across the sea to the south of Scythia, where the dark-skinned ones came from. It was, he claimed, the largest piece of crystal in the world, and though it was not a diamond, it was very close to one. Partholon had found it on the dried up bed of what had once been a huge inland sea. It had once been a perfect sphere, and there had been broken pieces of glass scattered all about it, but now little more than half remained. Bringing it back to Scythia, he had ordered the foremost artisans of the day to carve and decorate it according to Delgrade's instructions. The subject, the style and even the placing and manner of the carvings he had left entirely in her hands and although

13

he had not been pleased when he had seen the finished result, there was little he could do, for the glass was preternaturally hard and had blunted even the sharpest tools and implements.

Delgrade opened her startlingly blue eyes, a slight frown creasing her forehead. 'Togha,' she called, 'where are you?'

The flap of the large tent opened and the youth entered, struggling with a heavy bucket filled with steaming water. 'My lady, the water ... ' he began.

'This water cools,' she said softly, a seductive note honeying her sharp voice, 'add some more – and slowly,' she warned.

Togha knelt beside the crystal bath and, taking a silver bowl from beside it, began to add the steaming water slowly, keeping his eyes low and concentrating intently on his work.

'Togha,' Delgrade said softly, 'look at me.'

The slave raised his head and stared defiantly into her wide eyes.

'Do you desire me?' she asked him almost in a whisper.

Togha shook his head. 'No my lady, I do not desire you.' His voice trembled, but he held her gaze.

'But surely you have some feelings for me?' she persisted.

'I fear you,' he said simply.

Delgrade's eyes narrowed slightly. 'You have nothing to fear from me,' she said reasonably, 'surely you have ... other feelings for me?' She reached out and, taking his hand, placed it on her breast.

'What do you feel?' she murmured, her cold eyes sliding over his body.

The youth shivered suddenly, and then, almost un-willingly his rigid fingers relaxed and he cupped her breast.

'Join me,' Delgrade commanded.

Trembling violently, Togha pulled his jerkin over his shoulders and ripped the loin-cloth from about his body. Smiling triumphantly, Delgrade spread her arms and pulled the youth into the warm water beside her.

*

Partholon sat on a smooth lump of stone on the beach and watched the waves wash up thousands of tiny silver fish, leaving them stranded to die. Mercan stood by his side, a tightly rolled chart in his hand, seemingly absorbed in the relentless action of the tide and the death of the fish.

The prince pointed out across the beach and said softly, 'We are like those silver fish. We have been cast up on a strange beach, where we will flap briefly and then die. In the morning we will be swept away again.'

Mercan shrugged. 'Such is life. We know nothing and we have no control over what we do know. We are playthings at the will of the gods.'

Partholon agreed, and then he added, 'Perhaps one day we will have control over our own destinies.'

The general smiled down at him. 'Perhaps. But neither you nor I will see it.'

'Agreed.'

Partholon moved aside and made room for the general to sit beside him. In the month since they had landed on the strange island, their previous animosity had changed to something akin to friendship, but with each fearing and distrusting the other. However, they each in their own fashion respected each other.

'Well, what have your spies discovered?' Partholon asked, tossing a pebble out into the sea.

The general smiled. 'Is nothing secret from you?' He shrugged and continued. 'My spies are in effect, cartographers; they have been engaged in mapping this isle. And this,' he held up the chart, 'is the result of the past month's work.' He spread the animal skin out on the sand, using heavy stones to hold down the curling corners. With a twig he began to point out various features.

'The island is roughly oblong – and by the way,' he smiled wanly, 'one of my men, Kullarn, has coined a name for this land: *Inis Alga* ... '

'*Noble Isle*,' Partholon mused, 'it's as good as any, I suppose.'

'It will do,' Mercan said and continued. 'There are mountain ranges all along the coasts; the highest in the

15

south-and-west and the north-and-east. There are several lakes of respectable size, but the largest seems to be in the north – here. There are rivers everywhere, although none of any great size or width.' Mercan pointed with the twig to the west coast. 'There are islands here, but not many and it seems likely that they will in time return to the mainland as the sea retreats . . .'

'I think not,' Partholon interrupted, 'but continue.'

The general pointed north. 'There is something here – and I'm not sure what. My man did not return . . . '

'Where are we on this chart?' the prince asked.

Mercan pointed. 'Here. It has been named *Sen Mag*, the Old Plain.'

'Therefore, if whatever lurks in the north mounts an attack, they will have to march almost half the length of the country.'

The general nodded. 'That is so. But we must have further information. I propose to send a small force northwards to spy out these creatures and their defences. Perhaps it is feasible to attack them first and wipe them out completely.'

Partholon shook his head. 'We cannot afford to send any more men out. Our forces are sadly depleted as it is and we must consolidate our position. Let them come to us, let them exhaust themselves doing so.'

'But we don't even know what they look like, we don't even know what weapons they use. Remember our ship,' he gestured wildly down the beach to where a few spars still rose from the sands like the skeletal remains of a whale, 'remember how that was attacked and destroyed. You remember the damage – we need to know how that was caused. We need information!'

Partholon nodded and sighed wearily. 'You are right of course,' he said, 'but I cannot spare you any men.'

'Give me slaves then – anyone, and if you do not,' he warned, 'then I must go alone.'

'I will see what I can do.' He rose stiffly, shivering slightly in the damp chill. 'Walk back with me,' he suggested.

They had almost reached the prince's tent when they heard the soft cries and moans coming from within.

16

Partholon looked at Mercan in alarm, but the general waved him to silence and, slipping a knife from its sheath, crept to the tent. Silently, he slit the leather ties that held the flaps shut and eased them aside.

Togha looked up from the supine body of the princess as a blast of cold air dried the sweat on his body. He saw the shadow in the door and attempted to pull away from her, but Delgrade clasped her legs about his waist and held him all the tighter.

They lay on the rug-strewn floor before a small brazier burning spices and scented coals. The warm light bronzed their bodies, gilding the sweat on their skins, the flames dancing in their eyes. Delgrade, looking over Togha's tousled head, saw the stooped figure of her husband in the light and smiled secretly. She moaned loudly and dug her nails into the young slave's back, pulling him even closer to her. Togha struggled to free himself – and then he was torn from the princess's arms and tossed across the tent. Mercan advanced on him, a feral smile glinting in his hard eyes, his knife slowly weaving to and fro. Partholon stopped him with a word.

The prince stood over his wife looking down at her naked body still flushed with lust. He smiled contemptuously. 'So this is how you amuse yourself: with slaves.'

'He is more a man than you will ever be,' Delgrade taunted.

'It is a change from dogs and rams,' Partholon said, turning away.

Delgrade screamed and spat. '*Sumer*: kill!'

A huge hound leapt up from the corner where it had lain and launched itself across the tent at Partholon's throat. The Scythian threw up a hand and the hound's jaws closed on the bronze wristlet he wore. The prince's left hand scrabbled for the dagger in his belt, but his wife suddenly gripped his hand and sank her teeth into it. Partholon grunted in pain and the momentary distraction was enough for the heavy dog to bear him to the ground. Scalding saliva dripped onto his face as the massive jaws came closer to his throat.

17

Mercan turned back to help his prince, but Togha, his eyes wide in terror, leaped onto the warrior's back. The general brought his elbow back and up, driving it into the slave's midriff; he slid off onto the ground and doubled up gasping for breath – and the general's knee came up and caught him under the jaw. His teeth clicked shut and his eyes rolled in his head. Mercan pulled Delgrade off Partholon by the hair and tossed her almost casually to one side. He kicked the dog once, with brutal precision, beneath the ribs, and the beast fell back howling. Partholon struggled to his feet as the dog rolled to one side. And then the animal was on its feet again, its belly low to the ground, its gleaming fangs wet and dripping. Mercan took a step towards the dog, and then Delgrade threw herself upon him, her clawed fingers tearing at his eyes. Sumer leapt at Partholon, its jaws wide, its eyes wild.

The general swore and then struck the princess with the back of his hand, sending her sprawling. He threw his dagger underhand, but missed the dog by a fraction, and the knife buried itself in the tent pole. Delgrade went for the knife, snarling like an animal – Mercan's fist caught her on the point of the jaw, knocking her backwards onto her groaning slave.

Partholon stepped to one side and caught the dog in his hard hands. He held it tightly at neck and crotch and hefted it above his head. The beast choked and kicked – and then the prince brought it down onto his upraised knee. There was a loud snap, Sumer shuddered and twitched and then lay still, and the tent was silent save for the angry sobbing of Delgrade.

Mercan dug his dagger out of the tent pole and turned to Partholon. 'I heard rumours of your wife's harlot ways back in Scythia, and aboard ship there were certain whispers . . . But now – here is the evidence of her infidelity; she has betrayed your trust and sullied your name. Let me slay her now.'

The prince shook his head wearily. 'No. Killing her would be too . . . easy.' He glanced at the groaning youth. 'She has chosen her road, let her follow it now.' He looked back to his wife, his eyes hardening. 'You will be gone by morning – and take him also. If I find you still here when the sun rises I will kill you both.' He turned away and pushed through the torn flap.

Mercan paused before leaving. 'And I will ensure he kills you slowly,' he added.

The firelight ran liquid in the small round chamber. The crystal walls reflected back the light with blinding intensity and the very air seethed with the amber radiance.

Loat sat before the fire staring into the wavering flames, her brow furrowed in concentration, trying to absorb and make some sense of the strange shapes therein.

A shape moved behind her, casting long towering shadows on the crystal walls, and a hooked talon sank into the hard flesh of her shoulder. 'Tell me what you see,' Cichal One-Foot hissed.

'Quiet my son,' Loat murmured, wrapping her gnarled fingers about a long bone and poking the fire, sending sparks spiralling up towards the hard translucent ceiling.

The Lord of the Fomors hissed angrily and moved about the chamber. He stopped by one of the circular windows and peered out into the misty morn. His talons gripped the scarred edges of the window and his single, red-rimmed eye glared out across his domain. To the north, west and east there was nothing but sea, disappearing flat and grey into the distance. It was true that in the east, on a good day, it was possible to see the distant shoreline of a land, but today, with the weather closing in he could see nothing but grey cloud. But to the south ... Aaah, that was a different matter. For there was a sweet land, a young land, a land ripe for the plucking.

And it would be his.

Cichal One-Foot ground his fist into the window-ledge. It would be his. He turned back to Loat, his mother. 'What do you see?' he demanded.

The old woman turned and smiled fondly at her son. Time had made her blind to his deformities: his single foot with its hooked talons, his barbed tail, the barrel chest and the long simian-like arms which glistened with armoured scales; the huge head, with neither nose nor ears, the long curved fangs and the huge slit-pupilled eye set in the centre of his massive ridged forehead.

He was the product of her youth, oh, so long ago, in a time when the gods themselves walked their newly created world, and dallied with their creations. And Man, the last of the gods' creations, found favour with their parents, and in time there came forth upon the new world creatures that were neither men nor god, but something of both. And in some the best of both god and man mingled to form what later generations would call the Tuatha De Danann, the People of the Goddess Danu; but in others, what was abhorrent to both the gods and men was brought forth from where it lurked deep within them both. And so the Fomors were birthed, abominations shunned by both men and beasts and despised by the gods.

Cichal was a Fomor, a single-footed, clawed, tailed, single-eyed monster, and Loat loved him.

'Mother; what do you see?' he demanded once again.

Loat smiled, her toothless gums drooling saliva onto her stained shawl. 'I see the new race gathering, preparing for war, preparing to attack, preparing to destroy you.' She giggled and then lapsed back into silence.

Cichal howled like a dog. 'Impossible!' He leaped past the woman and scattered the flaming sticks with a sweep of his tail. 'Impossible. They are puny, soft-skinned humans.'

Loat nodded. 'That may be so. But remember the magic they worked soon after their arrival to change the very land to suit themselves. You are a fool if you think they are weak and defenceless.' She stood and stared up at her son. 'And remember, I too am a human, and you can judge for yourself whether I am defenceless.'

Cichal stepped back and bowed. 'You are different, mother,' he protested. 'You are not human now,' and then he added quickly seeing the fury rising in her mild eyes, 'you are more than human, you have transcended all human bonds, you are godlike.'

The old woman simpered and smiled. 'It is true,' she acknowledged.

'What would you have me do?' he asked.

'Attack – and attack now; strike before their preparations are fully complete.'

The Fomor nodded thoughtfully. 'It will take a little time, but it will be done as you say.'

Mercan knelt over the beast he had just slain. He cursed, examining his blunted dagger: the creature's skin was as hard as stone and its blood like acid. He looked over his shoulder at the crystal tower rising in the distance and then back down to the creature.

It had attacked the general and his young servant as they lay in the long grass watching the activity about the base of the gleaming tower rising out of the grey sea. Before Mercan could draw his dagger, the beast had shorn young Fea in two with a single blow of its sickle-like tail. The general had thrown himself onto its back, the armour on his forearms and wrist scraping metallically as it brushed against the beast's scaled torso. He struck at its throat – but it was like striking stone, and his fingers and wrist tingled numbly. He retched with the vile odour of the beast. And then its tail came up and flicked him across the back, sending him crashing to the ground. The creature swung around and Mercan could almost hear its long talons click into place like a cat's. It opened its mouth and hissed like a snake, its yellow fangs gleaming with saliva. The general came slowly to his feet, knowing that if this creature even got close to him ...

His left hand dug dirt from the soft earth and flung it in the beast's face and at the same time his right hand flicked out – and his dagger buried itself to the hilt in the creature's single eye. It screamed – a high-pitched cry that grated along the nerves and set the teeth on edge – and clawed at its ruined orb. Scalding juices ran down its snout, leaving long smouldering tracks in its skin, crisping the earth where it fell. The creature stumbled towards Mercan and then fell and lay twitching at his feet.

The general turned it over with his foot and, careful not to touch the reeking ichor that still gouted from the centre of its forehead, plucked the dagger out. The bronze blade was pitted and scored where the blood had eaten into it.

A curious shivering sound in the chill air brought him back to his senses. It was coming from the crystal tower, a hollow tolling that pulsed in time to the tower's sudden changes in colour. Now the tall cylinder pulsed red and blue in long ripples and the plain before the tower was swarming with hopping creatures.

Mercan wrapped the ruined body of his companion in his cloak and ran for his horse ...

'A demon,' Mercan stated flatly.

'A demon,' Partholon repeated. The prince bent and scooped up a handful of pebbles. He tossed one into the oncoming waves. 'You're sure?'

Mercan swore. 'By all the gods – of course I'm sure! It was closer to me than you are now. It sliced Fea in two ... well you've seen for yourself, and that was with its tail.'

Partholon walked down to the water's edge, gravel and wet sand crunching under his feet. 'Describe it,' he said quietly.

Mercan breathed deeply, calming his ragged nerves. 'A round head, no ears, no nose. A single eye set in the centre of its forehead surrounded by a ridge of bone. Its mouth a slit, its fangs enormous and pointed, and they seemed to lock into one another. Huge chest, long arms. Its skin was scaled like a serpent's. It had one leg and a claw like that of a hunting bird's, with talons to the front and one behind. It also had a long barbed tail. Demons,' he said quietly.

'They sound like cousins to the harpies,' Partholon said, throwing a fistful of stones into the water, watching the white flecks disturb the oily swells.

The general laughed. 'They make harpies look pretty.' He looked curiously at the prince. 'You do believe me?'

Partholon nodded and sighed. 'Oh, I believe you – I have no reason to doubt you.' He shivered suddenly and drew his heavy woollen cloak across his shoulders. 'Before she left Delgrade prophesied that I would be slain by a one-footed man ... ' He shrugged and turned back up the beach. 'Come, I set our three magicians a task: to discover the identity of our enemies and also, one of your men brought in some bones in your absence ... '

'Human bones?'

'Aye, human. I am curious to find out who landed on this isle before us, and I'm sure either Fos or Faud will be able to tell us.'

The small tent reeked of spices and herbs and the choking tang of sulphur cut at both throat and eyes. As Mercan and Partholon entered, sparks ran along the general's sword and wristlets and danced from the prince's headband.

The three magicians were seated in a circle about a large shallow bowl in which oil swirled lazily. Tiny coloured motes drifted across the surface leaving long traces in their wake and, now and then, the oil would crack and snap with flashes of blue fire. The tent seemed full of whispers, sibilant susurations that lurked just beyond audibility, and the general found the hair at the nape of his neck rising.

The prince sank slowly to the ground before the three magicians and stared intently into the bowl; Mercan knelt by his side.

Aeolas passed his hand over the surface of the bowl and the liquid ignited with a sudden hiss. It burned furiously for a few moments and the whispers rose to hissing screams that reminded the general of the creature's death cry. The Samotharcian looked up at the prince, his eyes sunken and red-rimmed.

'Well, what have you found?' Partholon demanded.

'What do you wish to know?' Aeolas asked gently, mockingly.

The prince's eyes darkened and then he bared his teeth in a smile. 'The time for such games is past. Tell me what you have discovered,' he grated.

'They are called the Fomors,' Faud said quietly, looking quickly at Aeolas and then back to the prince. The stout easterner leaned back on a pillow and continued. 'They are what we would call demons – the result of breeding between gods and men. They embody the worst of both. Each one differs slightly, but in the main, they are as you described them. They are commanded by the one called Cichal One-Foot, and he in turn is controlled by his mother, a human called Loat the Active – or she was in her youth anyway,' he added with a grin. 'She is the more dangerous of the two. Cichal wants nothing more than to destroy, but that is not for her, she wishes to rule. Slay her and ... ' he shrugged expressively.

'Can it be done by sorcery?'

'She is an accomplished sorceress. And although her arts differ from ours, she has the ability to protect herself from anything we might send against her.'

'And that is all?'

'On that, yes. On the other matter however ... ' Faud sat forward and picked up one of the gleaming white bones that one of Mercan's cartographers had found on a beach in the far south. In the dim light the bone, polished by the elements, resembled marble. 'It is the thigh bone of an Aegypthian woman from the Isle of Meroe in the Nile. She was named Banba Caesir, the daughter of Bith, and she fled her native land some three hundred years ago.'

'Where are her descendants?' Mercan asked.

'She left no descendants. There were fifty women and three men in the craft that wrecked itself on these placid shores – and internal strife and plague destroyed them all.'

'So, it's just the Fomors we're up against,' Partholon mused.

'You will never destroy them,' Fos, the pale northerner said quietly in his guttural accent. His ice-blue eyes bored into the prince's, and his gaze was curiously vacant as if he stared into another, different time. 'You may succeed in wiping out this colony of the demon-race, but you will never destroy them entirely. For their fate is inextricably entwined with man's; they are man's darker shadow, a reminder of what he might have been – or what he might yet become.' The small magician smiled grimly, showing rough filed teeth, and his cold eyes were hard and sharp.

'You are fighting a battle in an ancient war, a war without beginning, a war without end.' He leaned back into the shadows and the firelight ran off his face like water, lingering briefly at his glazed eyes. 'It is a war you can never hope to win.'

The Partholonians set about colonising the land, settling along the banks of the rivers which had sprung up when their prince and his magicians had worked that first great magic: the Buas, Bonna, Leio, Bearbh, Saimer, Sligo, Mudhour, Maudh and Liffee. They built their forts and towns on the shores of the lakes that had come forth with the rivers: Loch Cam, Measg, Direchaiodh, Laighline, Eochtra, Rughraidhe and Luan. They built roads and bridges, cleared forests and reclaimed more land from the sea with the aid of their magic. Their merchants began trading further and further afield, and in turn, traders from the southern lands and islands ventured north and west to Banba or Caesir, as some of the settlers now styled it, bringing with them the exotic fruits and spices, metals and cloths which they had been accustomed to in Scythia.

But in everything they did there was the threat of the demon Fomors hanging over their heads, but it was not until seven years after their landing that the first great battle was fought.

Of course, over the years scores of bloody skirmishes had been fought and occasionally a band of Fomors would raid an isolated farm or village, and in retaliation either Mercan, Creachar or Eaocha would ride north and fire one of the demon encampments. But in all that time the Fomorians had been merely testing the humans' weaknesses and strengths, probing and probing again, seeking a weakness, biding their time and readying themselves for the ultimate battle.

It had been a mild winter and now the days were beginning to stretch and the year had almost turned back into spring.

The snows thawed in the mountains and the streams ran with renewed vigour, washing down the mountain debris onto the plains. The Partholonians rejoiced and Áeolas offered sacrifices to his sun-god, welcoming his return and asking his favour in the coming year. The new season started well, bringing with it clear days and a warm southerly breeze that augured well for the growing season.

It also brought the Fomorians.

They poured down from the hills in droves, slowly cutting off and destroying the Partholonian strongholds by sheer force of numbers. They cared little for their own lives and launched themselves in wave after wave of suicidal attacks on the walls of the forts. In that long cool spring and on into the summer the Fomorians, using surprise and absolute ferocity in their attacks, beat back the humans. But as winter rolled in, and the forces of Night and Darkness grew stronger, Aeolas by his arcane arts, discovered one of the demons' strongholds in the mountains of the west. With the aid of Fos and Faud and under the direction of Partholon they called forth the wild elemental magic of the land and tumbled the mountains in upon the Fomors. None of them escaped the mountain's shifting; none that is, except Cichal One-Foot, his mother Loat and a small band of demons who had already departed for the crystal tower.

Following the defeat of the Fomorians, the Partholonians renewed their attempts to colonise the land, venturing further and further afield, settling in even the most desolate spots, and the original colony at Sen Mag grew smaller and smaller as the years passed and the people drifted away. Partholon remained, seemingly ageless, still as agile and alert as before, although those who knew him personally could see the years beginning to lean heavily upon him. He spent many hours on the beach, watching the eternal waves washing the pebbled shore, listening to the rattle and hiss as the waters foamed back and forward. Occasionally, when he had drunk a little too much, he would walk on the beach with Mercan – who had become almost his constant companion – and he would speak of his wife.

During the First Fomor War, the prince had sent out scouts to try and find Delgrade and bring her into the safety of Sen Mag – for somewhere, deep in his heart, he still loved her very deeply. But the scouts had returned with no news of the golden haired princess nor of her slave, and Partholon sorrowed, for he feared she had been taken by the demons.

Little was heard of the Fomor now. The odd report of a wandering demon was carried back to Sen Mag, but these were usually unsubstantiated and were generally ignored. The crystal tower on Taure Isle was unapproachable – an old spell of the demons' still held and anyone who approached too closely to its gleaming walls was seized with agonising cramps and blinding headaches; even Aeolas couldn't break through the barrier, for it was constructed of an alien magic fashioned by an alien mind.

The Partholonians prospered and grew ... and so did the land, for it was, as Partholon had promised, linked to the people. The Partholonians settled its four corners, and there were even some who moved north and lived in sight of the crystal tower, and it was from these that the first rumours of a Fomorian presence came. They saw lights in the tower and occasionally strange cloud formations would gather above it and jagged streaks of lightning would dance along the crystalline walls. And slowly, the vegetation which in past years had crept closer and closer to the tower, began to die.

The Final Battle with the Fomorians took place on the Plain of Ith on that day sacred to Bile, the God of Death – the same day the Partholonians had first come to Banba.

The demon hoard had been massing in the northern and western hills all through the winter, which this year had been unusually severe. As the winter slowly and reluctantly drifted into spring, a thick white wall of seething mist had gradually swept southwards from Taure Isle, and the Partholonians had fled before it. Those who remained, or spies sent north by Mercan, returned – if return they did –

with tales of creatures that were neither Fomor nor beasts, but something akin to both, moving within the shifting walls. A stench began to pervade the fresh countryside – the stench of offal and blood, of roasting meat and putrefaction. The rivers and lakes in the northern half of the country were rapidly befouled and a thick scum sat upon the water, and the rivers washed the foul slime into the coastal waters. Soon the beaches stank with rotting fish and sea birds struggled helplessly in the thick muck. It snowed often that winter, and the pure white snow was tinted with a thick grey effluence that clung and hardened when the snow melted, leaving a scabrous coating in its wake. The rainwater was tainted and ate like acid into metal and rotted wood, and even stone seemed scarred by its corrosive effect.

The Partholonians were forced to abandon their newly colonised lands and retreat to Sen Mag on the shores of the eastern sea and there await the coming of the Fomorians.

Mercan leaned across the polished table and pointed with the tip of his dagger to the curve of a river on the painted chart. 'And here Eaocha?'

The grey-haired commander shook his head. 'I lost a troop of men trying to hold that fort,' he said softly. 'The mist rolled in and we suddenly found ourselves fighting in semi-darkness. Even the torches were doused by it, and the stench was unbearable. We stood no chance ...'

The general tapped the chart with the hilt of his dagger. 'So we only hold Sen Mag,' he mused.

'Aye, but for how long?' Creacher asked. He leaned across the table and pointed. 'My troops hold the four roads about Sen Mag, but we cannot keep those positions if we have to fight in darkness and a poisonous fog.' His fist crashed down on the table. 'We have to do something – we just can't sit here and let them come for us!'

'I'm open to suggestions,' Mercan said quietly.

'Well then, we attack them – before they attack us.'

'Tell me how,' Mercan said, 'and you can command this army in my place.' He straightened and slipped the dagger

28

back into its sheath. 'If you think you can do a better job of it than I can then you are welcome – more than welcome to it.' He smiled thinly. 'Well?'

The commander's shoulders slumped. 'No-one is trying to dispute your position,' he said wearily. 'I don't know what we can do ...'

'This gets us nowhere,' a thin voice said from the shadows at the back of the tent. A chair creaked and then Partholon came forward into the light, the torch flames giving his face a yellowish cast. He looked around the assembled warriors seated at the table, and he recalled with vivid clarity the first time he had seen very much the same group gathered together. It had been that night so long ago, when they had first come to these foreign shores; they had all been distrustful then, fearing each other, hating him, but drawn together because they had backed the wrong side and lost. And now they were gathered together again, dependent on one another, bound by a common enemy and the fear of death.

'My friends,' he began, his voice betraying his age and weariness, 'we have grown old together in this land; we struggled to make it ours – and we will not let these foul demons take it from us! We defeated them once before – and we will do so again; but we were united then – and we must remain so. We cannot allow petty bickering to divide us. Now ...' His blunt fingers touched the thick parchment chart and swivelled it about. Those seated about the table gathered closer. Partholon pointed. 'We are here ...' His fingers moved north and west. 'The Fomor are here, camped on the Plain of Ith.'

'How do you know?' Mercan asked.

'Aeolas informed me,' the prince said quietly. 'The demons are still surrounded by the mist ...'

'Then we cannot attack them,' the general said.

'Let me finish!' Partholon snapped, his eyes blazing, and for a moment he seemed a younger man, the man who had led them out of defeat in Scythia and into a new beginning in Banba. 'Aeolas, Fos and Faud are, even now, calling upon their Art to conjure up a wind that will shred the fog; and to re-inforce the effects of the wind, the Samotharcian has sworn that his god will shine tomorrow. We must be prepared to attack them. The wind will whip away the fog and the sun will shrivel some of the demons of the night, but there will be others used to the light of day – although the pure white light of the sun will undoubtedly hurt them.'

'Who commands the Fomor now?' Creachar asked.

'Our old enemy: Cichal One-Foot.'

In the first slanting rays of the morning sunlight, the fog wall seemed both insubstantial and beautiful. The crimson rays writhed along the shifting surface and sparkled with myriad rainbow hues, occasionally glinting off metal as they touched the creatures within. Shadows moved within the fog safe behind the undulating wall, and the Plain of Ith echoed with shouts and cries, animal grunts and chilling laughter.

Partholon stood with Aeolas and Mercan on a low hill at the edge of the plain. Behind them, the huge Partholonian army was gathered, standing silently, awaiting the order to attack.

The prince looked into the east, to where the sun had already risen above the horizon, and then he nodded at the Samotharcian sorcerer.

Aeolas raised his hands and faced his god. Crimson sunlight burned across his face, turning his eyes to hard points of light. He opened his hands and greeted the new day with an invocation that was older than man. The air, which had been cold and damp, began to move as a slight breeze blew warmly across the plain from the east, and almost immediately the day began to grow warm.

Below the magician, Fos and Faud worked over their smoking braziers, calling forth the myriad wind elementals and sprites.

And the Fomor began to move. The huge unbroken fog banks rolled nearer and now creatures darted out from its protective cover and raced for the foothills, their long bounding gait sending them flying across the smooth ground. Mercan called up slingers and archers to the brow of the low hill, and their specially-treated slingshot and arrows took a terrible toll of the Fomor scouts.

And then the sun came up in a blast of sudden heat that seared the morning air. Parts of the fog wall instantly dispersed and left demons writhing on the churned ground as the sunlight touched them.

But the central core of the wall held.

And then the braziers of Fos and Faud erupted blue flames that died in a rush, leaving a thin tendril of blue smoke drifting slowly skywards – a tendril of smoke that was suddenly torn and shredded by a hot gust of wind that whipped in off the sea and howled across the flat plain. What remained of the fog wall dissolved before the hot wind exposing the Fomor cowering beneath the pitiless white-hot orb of the sun. Some fell, immediately crisping into charred lumps of hard flesh, whilst others wandered blindly, ichor leaking from their faces where the sun had seared their sight.

And whilst the confusion reigned the Partholonians attacked.

Lines of archers and slingers rose above the brow of the hills encircling the plain and sent wave after wave of arrows and slingshot into the massed ranks of the demons. The metal shot and arrow heads – dipped in a concoction brewed by the sorcerers – hissed as they flew through the air and ignited into a blinding white-hot point of heat. The flaming missiles tore through the thick hides of the demons leaving gaping wounds. Scores of small fires started and soon the stench of burning flesh drifted across the field. The flames were fanned by the breeze and entire sections of the hoard were cut off by the fire and destroyed by the Partholonians. Lines of footsoldiers advanced slowly down onto the plain, their long pikes extended before them, presenting a solid wall of pointed death. The Fomor attacked in suicidal waves, impaling themselves on the spear-points so that their companions might use their twitching bodies to climb over the spear wall and throw themselves into the midst of the spearmen.

But the spear wall held and advanced inexorably into the heart of the demon horde.

Cichal screamed and raged as he watched his army being broken by the remorseless Partholonians. He shook a fist defiantly at the sun and attempted to call upon his magic to enshroud it with clouds – but the Partholonian sorcerers had command of the wind elements and he couldn't wrest control of them from the humans – not now in the midst of battle. He glanced at the sun again – it had barely risen out of the sea, but was hotter than a noon day, and already his army had been destroyed. He screamed in rage as another hail of burning meteor-like missiles tore into his ranks leaving almost two-score smouldering dead and another score screaming in agony as the molten metal ate through their flesh. He shook with an icy fever and a red mist floated before his single eye. His only thought was to kill ... and kill ... and kill ... He spun around as something touched his shoulder and his huge fist rose as he saw the hateful shape of a human beside him. His fist prepared to crush the fragile skull of the human ... and then a chill voice spoke inside his head.

'Cichal!'

He staggered as if he had been struck and the single word wiped away his killing lust. 'Mother ...'

Loat pulled her son back from the ranks and pointed up towards the foothills with a long-nailed hand. 'Look Cichal, look! There is your enemy, the small man; he is Partholon. Destroy him and you destroy the army's morale. And beside him is Mercan, commander of this rabble, destroy him and they will run about like a headless fowl.' She squeezed his scaled bicep. 'Destroy them my son. Destroy them.'

Cichal grunted and began to move back through the ranks, picking out individual demons, forming an attack force. With a decade of monstrosities by his side he broke away from the body of the horde and raced for the foothills, making for Partholon and Mercan. Some fell before they even reached the slopes and most of the others died as they fought their way up the low hill.

Partholon caught Aeolas and pushed him down behind him and then, dragging his sword free, he awaited the Demon-Lord. Cichal and a monster called Caoinh reached the brow of the hill. Caoinh leapt upon Mercan, hooked talons reaching for his heart. The general threw himself to one side and his sword sliced through the demon's chest, bringing it down. Mercan pulled his sword free as the demon fell and neatly decapitated it before it hit the ground.

Cichal attacked Partholon. One long bound took him up and over the prince, his barbed tail lashing out, almost tearing the Scythian's head from his shoulders. Partholon's sword licked out and caught the edge of its tail, opening a long shallow wound. The demon screamed as it landed, more in anger than pain, spun and launched another attack. The prince turned aside the flailing claws with the edge of his sword and pressed home his attack driving Cichal back down the slope. And then the demon's tail came up and around and struck him across the back of his head; he staggered and fell, black stars dancing before his eyes. Cichal shouted in triumph and leapt upon Partholon – and was spitted upon his upthrust sword! The demon's eye opened wide in astonishment and pain and then snapped shut in anger; and as it died, its long filthy talons plunged deeply into the prince's chest.

Mercan dragged the demon off Partholon and knelt by his friend's side. 'Lift me,' the prince whispered, 'let my men see me ...' he coughed blood and spat. 'And get this thing hoisted up on spears so the Fomor can see it,' he coughed again and Mercan held him while he shuddered.

The general lifted the wounded prince to his feet and half-carried him to the edge of the low hill so he could look down upon the battle. A loud cheer went up as the slim, stooped figure appeared at the crest of the hill bathed in the crimson morning sunlight – and only those closest to him could see that it was not just the slanting rays of the sun that ran crimson. Mercan raised his sword high and the morning sunlight coloured the stained metal a deeper hue.

And then the obscene corpse of Cichal was lifted high, its

mis-shapen limbs flopping ungainly, its head lolling to one side. The Fomorians moaned and almost immediately began to fall back, some even turning and fleeing across the battle scarred plain – only to be cut down by the archers. The remainder of the demon horde continued fighting, but their morale was broken and their defeat inevitable.

Loat stared in anguish at the corpse of her son dangling like the carcass of a beast from the Partholonian spears. She screamed aloud, her curse suddenly stilling the noise of battle, calling upon her demonic lord to aid her now and lend her his strength. A monstrous shadow appeared behind her left shoulder, but it was thin and misty and writhed in the pure light of the sun. Loat screamed as her familiar drifted back into its infernal region, leaving her alone and unprotected. But a shadow of its strength had touched her and, plucking a sword from a fallen Partholonian, she raced across the plain towards Partholon and the general.

Mercan lifted his sword and awaited the long-haired, wild-eyed woman. A spear flashed by her and a sling-shot burned the ground by her feet; a warrior stood before her, a battle-axe in his hands. He cut at her – missed, and fell back with his throat slit. And then she was climbing up the low hill, her rage and the demonic strength and madness urging her on.

'Kill her,' Partholon said wearily.

The general brought his arm back and threw his sword like a spear. The point struck her in the chest and exited through her back, close to her spine – but Loat merely staggered and continued running.

'The blood ... the blood ...' the prince whispered, his shaking fingers pointing to the thick ichor that had seared the ground where Cichal One-Foot had fallen. Mercan stooped and dipped the point of his dagger into the thick leprous-green blood, and as Loat came over the brow of the hill, plunged the dagger into her throat.

The effect was immediate. Her face collapsed in upon itself and then her body folded, caved inwards, large grey flakes breaking away, whirling away on the wind like ash.

The withered husk of the old, old woman dried up into a crumbling powder and was swept away.

The Final Battle was over; the Fomorians were defeated.

But the Partholonians did not survive their victory over the demon horde. Partholon lingered awhile, but his wound grew infected and despite the attentions of Aeolas, Fos and Faud, he died seven days later.

And where the prince was buried became a barren spot, and as the years passed, the circle of desolation spread about his grave, for the infection survived him. And it was from this spot that the plague spread.

Its growth was insidious and it took several years to manifest itself, but eventually it raged throughout the country, wiping out whole settlements in a matter of days. And so, what remained of the Partholonians returned to Sen Mag, the spot where they had first landed, close to where they had defeated the demons.

And so on that feast day sacred to Bile, the God of Death, the remnants of the Partholonians succumbed to the plague. And they died where they fell and it was left to time and the elements to cover their bodies and make a mound over it.

A little while later, when naught but bones and scraps of cloth and rusted metal remained, a shrouded and hooded creature came to the spot and laid a small posy of flowers on the low mound that marked Partholon's grave, and whispered a name over the field of death: *'Tamlecht Muintre Partholain'* – the Plague Grave of Partholon's People.

And Delgrade wept as she walked away.

CHAPTER 2

DERMOT AND GRANNIA

'And Fionn and the Knights of the Fianna came to Tara for the wedding feast in Maecadre's Halls ...'

The young golden-haired woman rounded on the poet sitting by her side. 'You mean this is my wedding celebration?' she hissed in amazement.

Dara nodded dumbly.

'No-one told me!' the maiden snapped, her sea-green eyes flashing angrily.

'But Grannia,' he protested, keeping his voice low, 'you agreed ... you consented to this match.'

'I did not!' she said loudly, and then lowered her voice as heads were raised and turned in her direction. She smiled in their direction and then turned back to the poet. 'When did I agree?'

Dara drank deeply, trying to calm the panic that was rising within him. His dark eyes darted over the assembled knights and warriors now eating and drinking their fill about the long wooden tables. If Grannia were to spurn Fionn now, then the commander of the Fianna would more than likely loose his warriors upon the company.

He breathed deeply. He must remain calm now; he must convince this silly woman that it was in her best interests – and Cormac's, her father – that she agree to wed Fionn.

'When Oisin, Fionn's son, came here to ask for your hand,' he began, 'you said that if Fionn was good enough to be considered as a son-in-law by your father, then he was good enough to be considered as a husband for you.'

Grannia's slim fingers closed about the stem of the goblet she was holding and her knuckles whitened. 'But look at him,' she whispered, glaring past the poet and across the table. 'He is older than my father; even his son is older than me!'

'He is a renowned warrior, a veteran of many a campaign, the hero of many a song and ballad,' Dara explained patiently.

'He is old,' Grannia said, 'I would rather marry my grandfather, Art, than marry him.'

'Princess,' Dara pleaded, 'do not spurn him. He has a violent temper, and he has not been reconciled with your father for many years. Your marriage will unite the Fianna with Cormac's army.'

'I will not wed such a creature,' she snapped at the poet. 'And now,' she added, 'I do not wish to discuss the matter further.'

'Princess ...'

Grannia placed her hand on his arm and, still smiling sweetly, sank her long nails into the soft flesh. 'I have given you a command.'

She dismissed the subject and began to pick at the remains of her meal. Her gaze drifted down the long table, and her hard eyes softened. 'Tell me,' she said quietly, 'who is the young man sitting next to Oisin and the boy?'

'The boy is Oscar, Oisin's son,' Dara said, nursing his bruised arm. 'Sitting next to him is Dermot Mac Dyna ... by all accounts one of the noblest of the Fianna.'

Grannia smiled shyly. 'He is indeed handsome.'

'He is said to have a love spot on the centre of his forehead, and no woman who looks upon him can ignore his charms. He is called the "Bright Faced," for his looks.'

'I have seen him before,' Grannia said dreamily. 'It was during that hurling match between Mac Lugh and the Fianna against Carbi of the Liffee and Tara. The Fianna were losing and the match had not long left to run when he,' she nodded at Dermot, 'snatched up a hurley, hooked the ball from one of the Liffee-men and scored; he scored twice more before the match ended ...'

'Princess ...?' Dara ventured.

The young maiden rounded on him and her eyes were hard and cold, her sharp-featured face set in a smiling mask. 'You must have something more to do than just sit here,' she said meaningfully.

The poet nodded stiffly and, bowing slightly to the princess, quickly left the room, his agile mind already composing the lay he would sing of the Battle of Maecadre.

Grannia looked past Queen Aeta her mother, and down at Fionn again. In his bulky furs and polished armour, with long strands of silver-grey hair still clinging to his balding pate, and his scarred face, he looked like an old bear – a toothless old bear. But like all such creatures, she reminded herself, still capable of wounding and killing and quick to anger. If she were to refuse Fionn now, to insult him ...

She looked down the hall at the Fianna sitting at the tables. Most of them were huge men, made all the more so by their polished armour and gleaming leathers or furs. Most, if not all, still carried their weapons, having refused to leave them outside the great iron-studded doors, and she noticed that no matter how much they drank, their hands never strayed far from their sword or knife hilts. They were beasts ... gross beasts. Except Dermot. He was neither as tall nor as broad as some of the others, but he carried himself proudly and his shining silver armour and supple leathers only added to his dignity. His hair was long and thick, as black as night's darkest hour, matching the colour of his eyes. His almost boyishly smooth face was unscarred, his nose long and unbroken and his teeth perfectly white.

And he would be hers!

Grannia waited until the night was far advanced and many of the knights of the Fianna and her father's men lay in drunken slumber. Cormac and Fionn – although deep in their cups – were attempting to play chess, and her mother sat with her head back against the tall wooden chair, her eyes closed and her mouth half-open, snoring quietly. She signalled her maid and, when the olive-skinned young woman stood beside her, instructed her to go to her chambers and bring her the Drinking Cup.

It was a small vessel of beaten gold, the handles incised with flowing script and glyphs, with tiny semi-precious stones set about the rim; a common enough goblet in Banba at that time. The princess poured a single drop of red wine into the bottom of the cup and swirled it slowly about. She passed her left hand across the rim of the cup and touched each of the stones in turn, bringing them to sparkling life. And slowly the vessel began to fill of its own accord.

The princess handed the brimming goblet to her maid and then watched anxiously as it was passed to Fionn. His red-rimmed eyes looked up from the chessboard and caught her tense expression and he smiled and raised the cup in salute. He drained it in one swallow – or thought he did, but when he looked into the goblet there was still liquid within. Graciously he passed the goblet to Cormac. 'Drink with me. Share your daughter's bride-cup with her husband.'

Cormac nodded and drank deeply from the cup and then, nudging his wife into wakefulness, he passed it to her to finish off what should have been the dregs. But there was still wine left in the cup when she was finished. The queen passed the vessel back to her daughter who raised it to her lips and pretended to drink.

Minutes later Fionn, Cormac and Aeta were sound asleep.

Grannia rose and walked slowly down the length of the hall. Nearly all the knights were asleep, snoring in drunken slumber, some lying across the polished boards of the table whilst others grunted beneath the tables like the animals they so resembled.

Dermot rose as Grannia approached, and bowed. 'May I offer you my congratulations,' he said quietly.

'You may not. I will never marry that gross pig!' she said calmly.

Dermot looked up in amazement. *'Princess!'*

'I do not love him,' she continued in that same level tone. 'I love you!'

For a moment the words didn't register with Dermot, and when they did he imagined that the princess was drunk.

She reached over and ran her fingers down the side of his face. 'No,' she said, reading his thoughts, 'I'm neither drunk nor mad. I love you. Flee with me now,' she urged.

The young warrior drew back in alarm. 'You *are* mad,' he snapped.

Grannia smiled and Dermot shivered, for her smile was cold and pitiless. 'I am not mad,' she whispered, 'I love you.' She gripped the long hair on either side of his head and, pulling his face to her, kissed him savagely. 'And I will have you,' she swore.

'Princess!' He pulled away, his dark eyes darting about the great hall ... if anyone had seen. But everyone was asleep, except for three warriors sitting at the far end of the table playing chess.

'Can you swear on your oath that you do not desire me?' she asked quietly, spreading her arms wide. 'Does my body not inflame you?'

'Princess, you are the most beautiful woman I have ever seen. In other circumstances perhaps ... but you are to be the bride of Fionn, my commander. My first loyalty is to him . . .'

'Listen to me warrior,' she said coldly, 'no such loyalty binds me, I feel nothing for your commander – nothing that is, except disgust. But if you hold your honour so highly, then let me impose on it. Let me bind you. I now place you under a *gaesa* to follow and attend me to the end of your days; I do so in the name of the Dagda and Danu, the Father and Mother of All.' She stepped closer to Dermot and smiled up into his troubled eyes. 'You are bound to me,' she said triumphantly, and then her eyes darkened as they looked over his shoulder. 'What do you want?' she snapped.

Dermot turned. 'Oisin ...?'

Fionn's son nodded grimly. 'Do you realise what you have done?' he asked Grannia.

Grannia stood beside Dermot. 'I love him,' she said defiantly, 'I must have him.'

'But at what cost?' Oisin asked, his voice chill with anger. 'Your love will kill him.'

'Oisin, what shall I do? She has placed me under a *gaesa*.'

'For your honour's sake, you must go with her – there is little else you can do.' He sighed and shook his head. 'I will see what I can do with my father; I will explain what has happened,' he said, glaring at the princess. 'But I fear he will want your head, for this will shame him greatly.'

'Go now, before he wakes, and may the gods watch over and keep you.'

Grannia's maid was waiting for them beyond the huge doors, a bundle of clothes and a small parcel of food hidden beneath her cloak. The young woman kissed the princess briefly, smiled piteously at Dermot and then fled down the echoing hall in tears.

The princess led him down through the palace corridors and out into a small walled area at the back of the huge rambling fort. It was a tiny herb garden, and the chill night air was redolent with the scents of herbs and spices. Grannia led the way through the garden to a small postern gate. But a short length of bronze-bound wood barred the gate. Dermot laid his weapons on the soft earth and, with muscles straining and the cords standing out in his neck, he levered the heavy bar from its metal clasps.

Grannia pulled at the door, the metal strips screaming as they tore across the stone path, and then reached for Dermot's hand. 'Come ...'

He shook his head. 'No, not yet. Wait for me just beyond the wall. I want to bar this door from the inside and attempt to throw off pursuit.'

'But how will you get out?'

Dermot grinned. 'Oh, I will.'

The warrior closed the heavy door as quietly as possible and then struggled to lift the massive bar into place. It dropped into the thick clasps with a solid booming that echoed and re-echoed from the dripping walls. He walked back into the midst of the garden, carefully measuring off his distance from the wall. He then examined his two spears: the *Ga-Derg* and the *Ga-Buidhe*, the Red and Yellow Javelins. The former was too stiff and unyielding for his purpose, but the latter was light and flexible ...

Dermot strapped the *Ga-Derg* onto his back and then, with the *Ga-Buidhe* held in both hands, he ran straight for the wall. His booted feet crushed delicate herbs and trampled fragile night flowers, and the scents, sharp and strong, sweet and sickly, acrid and cloying rose into the quiet air. At the last possible moment, at the very base of the wall, he ground the butt of the spear into the soft earth and, clinging to the end, rode the recoil up and over the wall. He balanced momentarily on the top of the wall, pulled loose the spear and dropped down the far side, rolling to his feet beside Grannia.

He stood beside her and looked back at the rising mound of Tara. 'There is still time for you to return,' he said quietly, 'no-one would ever know.'

She shook her head.

And then he kissed her gently. 'I'm not sure I can live up to such a love – a love that compels you to throw away a life of ease and luxury for that of a fugitive.' He stared intently down into her wide sea-green eyes. 'For make no mistake princess, we have taken the first step on a long and dangerous road this night. Fionn is a good friend – but he is an implacable enemy. He will hunt us down like animals ... and we cannot hope to outrun him forever.'

'Well, when we die, let us die together,' Grannia said smiling.

Dermot grinned. 'I hope to put that day off for as long as possible.'

'They travelled far that night. Dermot stole a pair of horses and a chariot from Tara's stables and, sticking to the hard roads so as to leave no tracks, they made for Ath-Luan where they abandoned the chariot and continued on foot to the Wood of the Two Tents where, in the very centre of the wood, Dermot constructed a large hut of reeds and mud and surrounded it with a tall fence of freshly-hewn saplings. He left seven doors in the fence, explaining to Grannia that when Fionn came – and he undoubtedly would – he would be forced to divide his force up into seven different groups to guard each of the seven doors. And above each door he placed a woven circlet of alder and oak which threw the openings and everything within the circle into shadow, so

*those standing without could not look in; and the circlets
also prevented anyone from entering without his express
command.'*

'What do you mean you've lost their tracks?' Fionn
demanded, throwing the reins of the chariot to his
charioteer, and leaning out over the side.

Cuan, chief tracker of the Clann Navin, stood beside the
chariot and pointed down towards the river. 'The chariot
tracks are clear and distinct up to that point, but then they
suddenly veer northwards. However, they are not so deeply
indented as before which would seem to indicate that both
Dermot and Grannia were not in it.'

Fionn leaned over until he was staring directly into
Cuan's eyes. The early morning sun gave his face an
almost mask-like appearance and his eyes were flat and
uncompromising. 'Your analysis is brilliant . . . and now tell
me in which direction they are headed.'

Cuan shrugged. 'It could be north or south . . .'

'Or east or west,' Fionn snapped. 'Are there tracks on the
far side of the river?'

'Aed is checking now,' the tracker said quietly.

'Well then,' Fionn hissed, 'report back to me when you
have something to report – and stop wasting my time!'

Oisin rode up beside his father. 'You were a little harsh on
him,' he said, dismounting.

'I do not suffer fools gladly,' Fionn said almost absently,
his head tilted slightly to one side, his eyes half-closed.

'We need the Clann Navin,' Oisin reminded him.

Fionn straightened suddenly and glared at his son. 'I am
Fionn, son of Cumhal . . . I need no-one.'

'Without Clann Navin we will never find Dermot and
Grannia,' Oisin said.

'They could be anywhere,' Oscar, Oisin's son said, riding
up alongside his father and grandfather.

The grey-haired commander of the Fianna shook his
head and pointed down towards the river. 'No, they are not
anywhere; they are there in the Wood of the Two Tents.' He

glanced back at Oisin. 'They are there.'

He tapped the charioteer on the shoulder and pointed down towards the river bank where the Clann Navin still sought signs of the fleeing couple. The chariot lurched and the iron-shod wheels spun and sank into the soft earth before taking hold.

Oscar turned to his father as the swaying chariot began to slide down the muddy incline to the river. 'Are they there?'

Oisin shrugged. 'If my father says they are, then they are there; you know he has the Sight.'

'What can we do?'

Oisin pulled himself up into the saddle. 'We will have to try and warn Dermot,' he said quietly. He turned and looked back down the ranks of the marching knights. 'Find Kylte and Dering, and get Bran, your grandfather's dog. Meet me in yonder clump of trees.'

Dermot awoke suddenly. The morning sun was slanting in through the woven branches that served as a roof for the crude hut, bathing the interior in a gentle emerald light. He sat up wondering what had roused him, his hands reaching for his sword. He rose quietly, careful not to wake the still-sleeping princess, and went and stood by the door of the hut and listened. But there was no sound, and then he realised that the wood, which should have been alive with birdsong at this hour, was strangely silent.

And then he heard it.

It was the whine of a dog, and it came from beyond the fence that bounded the small clearing and the hut. He slipped a cloak about his shoulders and padded on naked feet over to the fence. He could hear the creature moving restlessly through the fallen leaves, could hear its soft breathing. He peered through the closely-woven branches, but he could only make out the vague shape of a large hunting dog.

The beast whined again.

Dermot frowned – the sound was familiar. He reached up and pulled off the circlet of alder and oak above the door and

44

then stood with his sword held in readiness whilst the shadow which had darkened the doorway faded. The huge dog came to its feet, lunged towards the warrior – and rolled over, its tongue lolling.

Dermot fell to his knees beside the dog, laughing. 'Bran!' And suddenly he understood; Fionn was never far behind the dog, and he knew that Oisin or one of his few friends in the Fianna must have sent the dog as a warning. He nodded to himself, running his fingers through the animal's long coat. 'Go home Bran,' he whispered, 'go back to Oisin, let him know I understand.' The dog watched him, its ears twitching as Dermot spoke, and then it rose smoothly to its feet, turned and disappeared back into the wood, its russet coat blending perfectly with the autumnal foliage.

Some time later that morning Dermot and Grannia heard a distant voice shouting in the east. Dermot stood and listened. 'That was Fergor Loud-Voiced, Kylte's servant.'

'Why was he shouting?' Grannia asked.

'It was a warning,' Dermot said quietly, 'Fionn and the Fianna are nearby.'

'What are we going to do?'

'Do? We are going to do nothing . . . there is nothing we can do.'

It was close to evening when the Clann Navin found the hut surrounded by the wicket fence in the centre of the wood. One of the trackers, Aed – called the Smaller – climbed a tree and looked down into the enclosure. Grannia, looking up caught the sudden flash of sunlight on metal. She smiled secretively. The princess rose slowly and walked over to Dermot and knelt by his side. She took his head in her hands and kissed him passionately, turning his face slightly so the hidden watcher could see clearly.

What would Fionn say to that?

Fionn's wrath – when he heard – was frightening to behold. He almost beheaded Aed on the spot as he gleefully recounted his tale – for there was no love lost between the Clann Navin and Dermot. The old warrior raged and swore retribution upon Dermot, and promised on his oath that he would not grant him a warrior's death.

And as the last light of day was fading, Fionn sent his knights into the wood with orders to surround the palisade – and wait.

That night, Dermot and Grannia lay on their bed of moss and grasses and watched the campfires dance and flicker through the gaps in the walls of the woven fence.

The morning broke sharp and chill and the sky was pale and metallic, full of the promise of approaching winter. Dermot rose before the dawn however, and busied himself honing his two swords, *Morallach,* the Great Fury and *Beagallach,* the Little Fury, and sharpening the points of his two spears, the Red and Yellow javelins.

He had strapped Morallach across his back with the hilt by his left shoulder and was slipping Beagallach into the sheath on his right thigh when a shadow blotted out the wan sun. He threw himself to one side and rolled to his feet, both swords in his hands, ready to launch himself at the intruder.

'Angus!' The swords dropped from his hands as he embraced his foster-father, Angus, the God of Love and Lord of the Birds.

The young-seeming man smiled fondly at his foster-son, and although he was older than Dermot by several thousand years, he looked like his younger brother. 'You have changed Dermot. There are lines about your eyes, your brow is furrowed, and is that grey I see in your hair?'

Dermot grinned. 'It is called ageing, father. Something you will never have to worry about.'

The god gestured to the fence. 'Might it not be worry also? And you have worries enough, have you not? If you wish to live to age a little more, I think you and the princess should come with me back to Brugh na Boine.'

Dermot shook his head slowly. 'Thank you, but I cannot go. Take Grannia and I'll join you later ... perhaps in the Wood of the Two Swallows.'

'If you're still alive.'

'If I'm still alive,' Dermot agreed.

46

'Well, I am going nowhere,' Grannia said angrily, stepping from the hut.

Dermot rounded on her, his dark eyes flashing angrily. 'You will do as I say,' he snapped. He turned back to Angus. 'Take her!'

Grannia screamed as the god enveloped her within his feathered cloak and disappeared. Beyond the fence, the princess's scream drove Fionn into a fit of fury. 'He is abusing her!' He spat at his son. 'I told you he took her by force.'

'And I tell you he did not. She coerced him ...'

'Liar!' Fionn screamed. He drew his sword and waved it aloft. 'Take them,' he cried.

The Fianna surrounding the palisade divided up into seven groups, each company taking up position before the doors. The charm that Dermot had placed above the doors prevented them from entering; the woven branches were like iron, and their weapons rung hollowly and struck sparks as they attempted to cut their way through.

Dermot walked slowly around the enclosure, stopping by each door in turn, and before each his question was the same: 'Who stands without?'

'Oisin with Oscar and the Clann Bashure. You can come forth under our protection; Fionn dares not set the Fianna against itself.'

'I thank you Oisin, but I dare not.' He moved on to the next gate. This was guarded by Kylte Mac Ronan and his clan, and they too offered him protection. Conan of the Grey Rushes and the Clann Morna guarded the third gate; they were old friends of his, but still he refused their offers of protection. Cuan and a company of the Munster Fianna held the next gate, and Fionn, son of Glore of the Loud Voice with some of the Ulster Fianna held the gate after that, and again Dermot refused them.

The sixth gate was held by the Clann Navin, Fionn's trackers. Aed the Lesser, his twin Aed the Greater, Gonna the Wounder and Gathan of the Loud Voice with Cuan the Tracker stood in a semi-circle outside the darkened doorway, waiting for Dermot to step out.

'Who stands without?' he called.

'Friends of yours,' Cuan replied quietly.

The young warrior laughed. 'No friends of mine I'll wager; I recognise that voice. So the Clann Navin have found me at last. I am amazed at their abilities,' he said mockingly.

'Step outside and we'll wipe that laugh off your face,' Gonna growled.

'I would like to,' Dermot said, 'but I have promised myself only to leave by that gate held by Fionn.'

'Then you will never leave here alive,' the huge bear of a man said loudly.

Dermot moved to the last gate. 'Fionn?'

'I am here, come forth.' Fionn waved his men back, drew his sword and took up position directly in front of the gate. The early morning fell silent, and even the breeze dropped as if the very elements awaited the outcome of the confrontation between the aged commander and the young knight.

'Fionn, I have no quarrel with you,' Dermot called out, 'let me pass.'

'You have stolen my bride,' Fionn snarled. 'I will kill you.'

'I did not steal her – she came willingly. More than willingly. Fionn,' he pleaded, 'she does not love you, and she loves me enough to place a *gaesa* on me to go with her. Let her go.'

'I will never let her go,' Fionn said quietly 'she is mine – whether she wants it or not.'

Dermot pulled the ward from above the door and tossed it at Fionn's feet, and then he stepped out to face his commander. Both his swords were sheathed and he held his two spears point upwards. Fionn saluted him briefly – and then lunged with his sword. Dermot turned the blow aside with the shaft of one of his spears and, as Fionn leaned into the blow, deftly hooked his feet from under him with the butt of his spear. He leaped over the fallen warrior and ran – straight for the massed knights.

Gonna the Wounder of the Clann Navin unslung his battle-axe and prepared to meet Dermot's charge, swinging

48

the great double-bladed axe in wide sweeping strokes. Dermot stepped inside the arc of the swing and struck the giant on the side of the head with the shaft of his spear. Gonna groaned and his eyes rolled in his head. Without breaking stride, Dermot leaped over the fallen giant and vaulted over the heads of the advancing warriors into the trees. He ran lightly from branch to branch, knocking aside the spears that came too close with his short sword. The wood seemed to close in and envelope him within its leafy vastness. The wan morning sunlight, slanting in through the branches created shadows that danced and quivered with a semblance of life ... and suddenly Dermot was everywhere, every limb, every branch seemed to have assumed his shape, and the Fianna spent themselves chasing shadows and hacking at branches whilst Dermot made good his escape.

'What did you do to the trees?'

Angus smiled and spread his hands. 'A little magic ...'

'I didn't really need a little magic,' Dermot said quietly.

'I know that,' the god said, 'but who is to know what the outcome might have been if you had not had a little magic to aid you.'

'I don't need magic to defeat Fionn,' Dermot protested.

'Perhaps not,' Angus said, and then he added, 'What will you do now, where will you go?'

Dermot threw dirt over the last glowing embers in the fire and shrugged. 'There is nothing we can do – keep running, I suppose. Perhaps one day Fionn will find someone else, and Grannia will no longer be as important to him ...'

'Fionn will never forgive you,' the young god said quietly, 'and it's not that Grannia is that important to him; he had never met her until the wedding-feast. But what has infuriated him is that you have taken – yes, I know she oath-bound you – his bride. You have made him look a fool; he will never forget, nor forgive that. He will hunt you to the end of your days.'

'Well then, we run and keep on running ...' Dermot repeated.

Angus leaned back against the smooth bark of a tree-trunk and only his eyes were visible in the light, reflecting back the glittering stars. 'Then let me advise you: do not dwell near a tree having only one trunk; do not go into a cave with only one entrance, and do not land on an island with only one channel of approach.' He leaned forward, a rustle of silken cloth in the darkness. 'And do not eat your food where you have cooked it; do not sleep where you have eaten, and do not sleep in the same place twice.'

'You are advising me to keep moving?'

'Never stop.'

'It will be hard on Grannia,' Dermot said, looking over at the small figure wrapped in furs and curled in sleep beside the remains of the fire.

'It is a life she has chosen for herself. She loves you Dermot, and for that love she has renounced her family, her friends, her position and her honour. That same love will make her strong and enable her to endure the hardships'. The god paused and added quietly, 'I do not know if you love her, my son. But whatever you do, you must not betray her trust in you.'

The young man shook his head wearily. 'At first I hated her', he confessed, 'she trapped me, took me away from my friends, made me an outlaw with a price on my head. I hated her ... but it is hard to hate someone as lovely as Grannia for long. I don't think I love her ... but I do like her.'

Angus laughed quietly. 'Well, it's a start.'

Dermot and Grannia travelled west at first light. They stopped briefly at the Rough Stream of the Champions and then continued onto the Grey Moor of Finnlia. It was in the grey wastes of the marshland that they came across the last of the Fomorians, Modhan, who had been birthed of a human woman who had had congress with one of the demons. He was almost human in every respect but for a single eye set in the centre of his forehead. He stood almost twice as tall as Dermot and was proportionally muscled. But for all his huge size, he was gentle and unassuming, and shunned the company of men, preferring to keep to the lonely places where his great size and deformity would not attract attention.

He travelled part of the way with Dermot and Grannia and listened to their story, and when they came to the River Connagh in the south, he carried them both across on his broad shoulders – and thus was their friendship forged.

Modhan accompanied them south and west, across the River Behan and up into the hills where the giant used his great strength to enlarge an existing cave and fashion a crude dwelling place for them. And whilst the giant pounded the rock to powder with his massive fists and Grannia dragged away the dirt and grit on her cloak, Dermot hunted and fished.

And thus, in a single night, they broke nearly all Angus' warnings: not to sleep where they had eaten, not to eat where they had cooked their food, not to cook where they had caught it – and not to enter a cave with only one entrance.'

Dermot arose with the first grey light of dawn and found the giant sitting in the mouth of the cave, his broad back to the cold stone and his great studded mace lying across his knees. He was staring out into the west, watching the last remnants of night slip across the waves of the endless Western Ocean.

Dermot knelt by his side. 'What do you see?' he asked quietly.

Modhan pointed with his mace, like a monarch with a mighty sceptre surveying his kingdom. 'I sometimes pity you, son of Man, for even with your two eyes you do not truly see. Tell me what you see?'

'I see the ocean, I see the waves rising and falling ...'

'Aah, but you cannot see *beyond* ...' The giant turned to Dermot and the warrior was surprised to find his single eye glimmering with unshed tears. 'There is an empire beyond

51

the horizon,' Modhan said, 'a vast land of richness and beauty; it is still young, but it will soon be great.'

'Why do you weep?'

'I see its destruction and downfall,' the giant whispered. 'I see men in strange garments coming from the west in mighty vessels bringing with them death and destruction. I see the invaders stripping the land bare of its precious metals and jewels; I see the small brown-skinned-men – and they are not unlike Picts – in chains, sick and dying with the diseases the invaders have carried with them. And I see the great stones of the huge stepped mounds – even the smallest dwarfing Tara – tumbling in smoke and fire.' The giant stood suddenly, towering over Dermot. 'I will sleep now, awaken me at noon.'

The warrior watched silently as the giant made his way into the back of the cave, where he lay down and began to snore almost immediately.

Dermot looked into the west, curiously disturbed by the giant's vision, and he wondered if Modhan had looked into their future, and knew what lay in store for Grannia and himself. And decided that he didn't want to know.

He stood and stretched, feeling the muscles in his back twinge and protest after a night spent on a damp rock floor. He leaned against the cool stone and stared down onto the beach that lay far below the cave – and stiffened suddenly. He knelt slowly, careful not to make any sudden movements that might draw attention, and then sprawled flat out in the mouth of the cave and peered over the ledge.

There was a small boat coming in to beach on the rocky shore, with tiny ant-like figures moving about, hauling the craft up the beach. Dermot squinted out across the waves, mirror-bright and blinding in the morning sunrise, and there, black against the waves were the three silhouettes of tall masted ships.

Dermot armed himself with his swords and spears and crept from the cave and stealthily approached the small group of heavily armed warriors moving restlessly on the beach. They were small swarthy men with jet-black hair and sallow skins. Their features were crude, with lowering brows and protruding jaws. There was something familiar about them ... but although he knew them – they were either Picts or Gauls – he couldn't put a name to this particular group. The warriors were dressed in different shades of green: emerald, olive and sea-green, but three stood apart, and these were clad in richer garments, although of the same colours, except that they wore high boots of black, white and grey fur.

And then Dermot knew them: they were the Sea Champions of the Iccian Sea, pirates and mercenaries, and were commanded by three brothers, Duncoss, Fionncoss and Threnncoss – Blackfoot, Whitefoot and Strongfoot.

He had no doubt that they were looking for him, for the brothers had occasionally been employed by Fionn in the past. Their price was high, but they had never been known to fail. And they controlled a most formidable weapon: the Hell Hounds, three great wolfhounds that were immune to fire and water, sword and spear.

Dermot shouldered his spears, rose from the tall grass atop the dune and walked across the beach to the warriors. He smiled pleasantly and saluted them, 'A good day to you.'

Duncross nodded politely.

'You are far from the road,' Dermot said innocently, 'are you lost?'

'We are not lost,' Duncoss said, slowly drawing closer to Dermot, whilst Fionncoss and Threnncoss began to edge around to either side.

'Can I help you,' he asked, edging backwards almost imperceptibly.

'Perhaps,' Threnncoss said, and while Dermot looked over at him, his two brothers edged closer.

'We are looking for someone,' Fionncoss said from Dermot's left.

'A warrior,' Threnncoss added from the right.

'Have you see anyone strange around here lately?' Duncoss asked.

Dermot leaned on his spears. 'Describe him.'

'Oh, surely you have heard of Dermot Mac Dyna?' Fionncoss asked.

'One of the greatest warriors in all Banba,' Dermot said, fighting hard to keep his face expressionless.

'We are looking for him,' Threnncoss said, coming closer.

'Have you seen him?' Fionncoss asked.

'What are you doing here?' Duncoss suddenly asked, closing on Dermot.

The point of Dermot's spear snapped up and rested against Duncoss' throat. 'You are crowding me,' he said coldly. 'Now why don't you two just move back, and perhaps then we can continue this conversation like civilised beings.'

Fionncoss' right hand edged slowly towards his knife. The point of the spear pressed deeper into Duncoss' throat, drawing blood, the cold metal seeming to burn. 'Tell your companion to leave the knife alone,' Dermot said, almost casually, never taking his eyes off the warrior standing before him. Duncoss turned his head – the spear point scored a long cut across his throat – and brusquely ordered his brother to drop the knife.

The three Sea Champions backed away slowly, Duncoss wiping the blood from the puncture and cut on his throat.

Dermot smiled. 'I know you, I know your reputation, but I do not think you can catch Dermot Mac Dyna. He is no ordinary warrior, he has never been defeated in battle or single combat.'

'He is a man,' Duncoss said grimly, 'and no man can stand against us.'

Dermot shrugged. 'That may be so; but let me show you a feat I saw Dermot Mac Dyna himself perform some time ago,' he suggested, 'and then perhaps you will see what you are up against.'

'Any feat he can perform,' Threnncoss said arrogantly, 'we can perform.'

'Let us see if that is so. First I need a tun of wine ...'

The barrel of wine was brought over from the ship, and more of the mercenaries gathered around to watch, until eventually nearly the full complement of the three ship's crews were present. Dermot lifted the barrel in both hands, tilted back his head and began to drink. And he didn't lower the barrel until it was empty.

Threnncoss laughed scornfully. 'That was no feat.'

'It wasn't meant to be,' the warrior said quietly, 'I only needed the empty barrel!' He turned and walked back up the beach. 'Stay here and watch,' he called back.

Dermot carried the barrel up the dunes and climbed up the side of the hill. When he reached the crest, he set it on its side and pushed it down. He raced after it, leapt onto the rolling barrel and rode it downwards to the beach without stumbling or losing his balance.

The mercenaries laughed and mocked, saying that it was nothing but a mere balancing trick, but the first to try it missed the barrel completely and slid down the cliff face, breaking both arms and his neck. The second broke both legs, the third cracked his skull, the fourth shattered his spine ...

Nearly fifty mercenaries tried to ride the barrel down the cliff – none succeeded. By nightfall, the base of the cliff looked as if a battle had been fought about it, and the stones were slick with blood. Dermot departed at sundown, promising to return with the dawn with some news of Dermot Mac Dyna.

The three Sea Captains were waiting for him on the beach the following morning. 'What news of Dermot?' Threnncoss demanded.

'He is said to be heading in this direction, and was seen just to the north of here practising his spear-standing.'

'What is his spear-standing?' Duncoss asked.

Dermot shrugged. 'I would find it difficult to describe ...'

Duncoss laughed harshly. 'Then show us.'

Dermot took one of his spears – the *Ga-Buidhe* – and set it point upwards in the soft sand. The razor-sharp point glittered in the early morning sunlight and the yellow wood of the shaft glowed a deep bronze. Dermot stepped back a few paces, ran at the spear, somersaulted – and landed feet first on the point. He then somersaulted off and landed beside the three Sea Champions.

Duncoss shook his head doubtfully. 'It looks simple – it is, after all, only a matter of balance ...'

The first mercenary to try and copy the feat mis-timed his

jump and spitted himself upon the spear, the second actually landed on the spear point – and the point passed up through his foot and impaled him through the groin, the third lost a leg, the fourth his head ...

Again, nearly fifty of the mercenaries died or were severly wounded attempting to copy the feat, and by mid-afternoon the golden sands and polished stones about the spear were thick with the reeking gore of the mercenaries.

On the morning of the third day, Dermot again reported that he had heard nothing of the Mac Dyna, except that he was approaching the area, and once again he offered to show them one of the feats he had seen the warrior perform.

He took his sword Morallach – Great Fury – and set it between two forked sticks set upright into the sand. The sword was almost chest high off the ground, with the glittering edge pointing upwards, so sharp that it was almost invisible. Dermot leaped up onto the edge of the blade and quickly walked from hilt to point and back again. From his position atop the sword hilt he grinned down at Duncoss, 'Again, it's nothing more than a matter of balance.'

The first mercenary to try the feat fell before he reached the blade and, putting out both hands to save himself, lost them. The second landed on the edge of the blade – and lost both legs, the third slipped and lost his manhood, the fourth landed on the sword, tripped and fell forward – neatly severing himself into two halves ...

By noon the blade was so covered with blood and gore that it was almost invisible, and the Sea Champions were counting the cost of fifty dead and severely wounded men.

'And Dermot Mac Dyna can do all this?' Fionncoss asked in amazement.

'And more,' Dermot said quietly.

Threnncoss looked over at his brother. 'If even his simple feats are beyond us – what then of the man himself? Will we be able to take him?'

'He will run from us,' Duncoss said confidently.

'I don't think so,' Dermot said in amusement, 'I have heard that he is looking for you.'

'For us?'

'For the three Sea Champions of the Iccian Sea,' Dermot agreed. 'He should be here on the morrow!'

What remained of the mercenaries and pirates were waiting on the blood-encrusted beach the following morning when Dermot arrived. The sun had barely cleared the horizon and the beach was still shadowed, whilst above, the last remnants of the night still lingered as the tiny points of starlight faded before the coming of the day.

'What news of Dermot?' Threnncoss asked.

'He comes.'

'When?' Duncoss demanded.

'*Now!*' Dermot cried, drawing both swords and cutting down the mercenaries nearest to him. For a moment confusion reigned and in that short time he managed to slay many of them. In the heat of battle a curious change overtook the warrior; it was almost a beserker rage – but without the beserker's callous disregard for his own safety. He threw himself into the midst of the milling warriors, using both swords with equal proficiency, and pushed them back, using their own numbers against them. He could attack at will, but they were restrained and hampered by their companions. His attack lasted barely a hundred heartbeats before the terrified men broke and ran, leaving him alone on the bloody beach with the butchered remains of the green-clad warriors ... and the three Sea Champions.

They circled about him warily, keeping their distance, jabbing with spear and sword and then leaping back out of range again. Dermot easily parried the blows, turning slowly to face each of the brothers in turn, until it seemed as if he suddenly wearied of the game and dropped his swords to the sands. Threnncoss shouted and jabbed with his barbed spear. Dermot side-stepped the blow and caught the spear behind the head and yanked it – and the warrior – forward. He fell sprawling at Dermot's feet and the knight, still holding the spear, reversed it and struck him across the back of the head. Duncoss, seeing his brother fall, came in fast and low – and the shaft of the spear caught him across the side of the head, sending him reeling backwards. Fionncoss pulled a long throwing knife from his belt and flung it at Dermot. He shifted his head slightly, his hand snapped up and caught the knife as it flew by, reversed it, and flipped it back towards the mercenary. The leather and bone handle struck him full between the eyes, bringing him slowly to his knees, the look of absolute amazement frozen onto his broad face even as his eyes rolled in his head.

Dermot gathered the three senseless warriors into a circle and fettered them with chains of wood and iron he had fashioned the previous night; frail-secming things, but blessed with the old magic, and unbreakable.

Dermot was half way up the cliff when he met Modhan and Grannia on their way down, having heard the noise of battle and fearing for his life.

'And so they fled the Cave on the Cliff. They travelled on to Slieve Lougher but were overtaken by the three dogs of the defeated champions: the Hell Hounds.'

They heard the baying of the hounds from afar, echoing over the hills and marshes, growing louder and wilder, with the unmistakable howling of bloodlust in their cries. The giant lifted Grannia in his strong arms and together, he and Dermot raced across the fields fleeing the hounds.

About mid-morning however, it became apparent that they would have to stop and fight, and it would be far better to do so in a place of their own choosing rather than be overtaken by the dogs on open ground. They marched on until they reached a barren, rocky incline which rose sharply and was broken only by a narrow defile, barely wide enough for three men to pass abreast. In this spot, only one, or at most two of the dogs could approach together.

Modhan lifted the princess and set her on the pinnacle of

a tall pillar of stone called Dobar's Stone that rose like an accusing finger into the darkening skies. Then he and Dermot retreated down the defile to await the dogs.

They appeared suddenly, breaking out from the cover of the trees and racing across the field towards the human and Fomor. They were huge beasts, standing almost fifteen hands high and with heads larger than any horses'. As they ran their coats rattled and sang metallically, and their paws struck sparks from the stones. Their eyes were wide and slit-pupilled like a cat's, and burned with an unholy intelligence. One of the beasts pulled away from the others and, although he was almost twenty paces from the warrior, leaped for his throat.

Dermot threw himself to the hard ground and rammed the *Ga-Buidhe* into the cleft in the rocks with the point tilted upwards. The huge dog came down onto the spear point, its massive jaws snapping the shaft, swallowing the bronze head and jagged lump of wood: it coughed and choked; blood-flecked foam spattered the front of Dermot's jerkin. The dog howled – the piteous cry shut off suddenly and the heavy carcass fell on him, pinning him to the ground ...

Modhan stepped forward and kicked the second dog as it raced for the fallen warrior, sending it rolling back down the rocky defile into the grassy glen. His gnarled hand slipped inside his rough woollen jerkin and pulled out a small black pouch. He carefully undid the drawstring ... and a tiny green and gold lizard scuttled out onto the palm of his hand. And he threw it into the face of the third animal.

The Hell Hound snapped and swallowed the lizard, never faltering as it raced towards the giant. Suddenly it stopped and howled. It stood twitching, its massive head thrashing from side to side, snapping at itself. It rolled over and its iron shod paws began to tear at its skin, striking sparks from the heavy fur. The animal screamed and screamed again, its cries almost human. The giant raised his mace ... and the second dog leaped across the body of the fallen dog and threw itself at the giant's throat, its long yellow fangs glistening with acid saliva. Modhan realised that, with both arms raised and both hands clutching the mace above his head, his throat was exposed ...

The beast's jaws clicked shut barely a blade's thickness away from his throat. Dermot stood, still holding the snapping dog's hind legs in both hands and swung it against the stone walls again and again, pulping its head.

Meanwhile, the third hound now lay still, and only the occasional rippling of its legs or stomach muscles indicated that it still lived. A thin red smear appeared on its throat. It grew and spread, and then its whole throat folded back like some obscene flower opening, and the tiny green and gold lizard crawled out, its hard eyes glittering blackly. Modhan carefully lifted the creature from the hound's carcass and thoroughly cleaned it with a corner of his jerkin, urged it back into the black pouch and tucked it back into his inner pocket.

Dermot and Modhan had defeated the invincible Hell Hounds.

And on the beach where Dermot had left them bound and fettered, the three Sea Champions of the Iccian Sea slumped in exhaustion and drifted into that long final sleep ...

'And so Dermot and Grannia wandered the length and breadth of Banba pursued by Fionn and his warriors. Many were their adventures in the woods and hills, the fields and dales of the Green Land.

Modhan, his term of service to the two lovers now completed, left them at the Wood of the Two Swallow Trees, and they continued north to the Forest of Doros where they settled in the shade of the magic quicken tree guarded by the giant Shavran the Surly, kin to Modhan. And Dermot made a pact with the giant to protect the tree and its fruit from all thieves.

And so the years passed. But Dermot and Grannia aged not, for the fruit of the quicken tree was blessed and sacred to the De Danann, who had left it behind when they retreated to the secret and lonely places. There were others like them in the silent groves in the Isle of the Ever Young, and the quicken tree garnered something of their magic and power.

Many tried to steal the fruit of the tree – but none succeeded, for none could prevail against Dermot, and the heads of those he had slain hung like grisly fruit from the branches of the trees in the Forest of Doros.

But in time, Grannia longed for the older, more mature fruit – of which it was said that man could be made immortal. But Shavran refused to share it with the lovers, he quarrelled with Dermot, and in a battle that lasted a day and a night, the knight slew him.

As time passed, Angus interceded with Fionn and Cormac begging forgiveness for Dermot and his wife – for they had been wed in the midst of the forest by the god. Reluctantly, both king and captain agreed.

And so Dermot and Grannia returned in triumph to Kesh Corran where they lived in peace and happiness for many years.'

Grannia sat in the streaming sunlight brushing back her golden hair with a small ornate comb of elk's horn. 'I'm lonely,' she said plaintively.

Dermot looked up in surprise. 'Lonely?' He stood and dropped the knife he had been sharpening onto the polished wooden table. He put his arm around his wife and buried his face in her fragrant hair. 'How can you be lonely; you have four boisterous young sons and an equally boisterous daughter to cope with?'

Grannia nodded slowly. 'I know, I know, but ...'

'But ...?' Dermot prompted.

'But I miss my father, my mother, my sisters ... my family,' she said defiantly, and Dermot could see the spoiled petulant look in her face, a look that reminded him suddenly of that night so many years ago now, when she had placed him under a *gaesa* to flee with her.

61

'Your father does not wish to see you,' he reminded her gently.

'He will see me.' She threw down the comb and turned in the low backed chair to face her husband. 'He *will* see me; I know he will.'

'How do you know?' he asked, humouring her.

'Angus told me.'

'*Angus!*' he roared. 'What have you been doing?'

'I asked Angus to find out if my father ...'

'You mean, you asked my foster-father to intercede with your father for you?' Dermot demanded angrily. 'You asked him to do that once before, but I still had to go crawling back to your father and Fionn for forgiveness; I lost a lot of face then, I am not about to do so again.'

Grannia stood, and the morning sunlight outlined her in gold. 'You won't have to lose face. No-one knows – only Cormac and Fionn.'

'Fionn!'

'I have asked both Fionn and my father to feast with us.'

Dermot bit back his reply and shook his head slowly. 'You shamed me once before, Grannia; you dragged me away from my friends and family, and now you're about to drag my name through the muck again ...' He breathed deeply, calming his rising anger. 'I am not about to argue with you, nor am I about to cancel your invitation. But let me tell you this ...' and his voice turned chill and deadly, 'you have overstepped yourself this time, and I hope – and pray – that you will not regret it.' He turned away, leaving Grannia standing by the window and paused by the door. Only his eyes showed the pain and betrayal he felt. 'Remember this: Fionn never forgets, never forgives.'

Cormac and Fionn were received at Kesh Corran with all due ceremony and honour and they spent much of the first day feasting and making merry. Dermot renewed many of his old friendships with the Fianna and Grannia was received by her mother and sister – who had married Fionn in her place.

It was late into the night by the time the revels drew to a

close, but although he was exhausted Dermot couldn't sleep. He was filled with a foreboding of doom and twice he started from a light doze hearing the agonised cry of a hound. The third time he sat up and would have gone out to investigate had Grannia not awoken and bade him return to bed. And what little sleep the warrior did catch in what remained of the night was troubled with strange dreams that left him cold and shivering in the chill light of dawn.

Grannia watched her husband dress. 'If you're going hunting,' she said, as he pulled on his leather jerkin, 'take the Red Spear and Morallach.'

Dermot laughed. 'I'm only going hunting; I doubt if I'll come across anything that might call for Great Fury. Not unless, of course, I'm about to be savaged by a wild quail.' He lifted the Ga-Buidhe from the wall and belted on Beagallach, and then, catching sight of Grannia's face tight with fear, he relented and added, 'I'll take Morcolle, the wolfhound.'

Grannia rose from the bed and kissed him gently. 'Be careful,' she whispered softly, 'come back to me.'

And her words raced along his spine, touching it with ice.

The morning was bright and chill with a wind whipping in from the north and west, carrying with it the tang of the broad Western Ocean. Dermot's breath plumed before him and his eyes smarted in the wind. He found Fionn and several of the Fianna in the stables at the back of the fort. The commander greeted him civilly enough and then nodded into the north and east. 'My men flushed a massive boar sometime late last night,' he said, 'we're about to go after it now.'

'I'll ride with you then,' Dermot said quietly, and added, 'I heard the cries of hounds last night ...'

'Aye ... we lost three of my best dogs. The beast is huge and cunning, but we'll have it by noon.'

Dermot rode with Fionn out through the gates of Kesh Corran, their dogs Bran and Morcolle racing on ahead, their keen senses seeking the spoor of the boar. They rode on into the morning until they came to a small hillock on

Benbulbin, a huge flat-topped mountain. They had become separated from the rest of the hunters, although they could still hear their cries echoing across the mountain side, carried on the morning air. Fionn and Dermot dismounted, tied their horses to a low stump, and continued climbing. The view from the top of Benbulbin was astounding: the entire countryside lay spread out below them like a mulicoloured tapestry, whilst behind them, the mountain sloped downwards to the sea.

Dermot was so absorbed in the view that he didn't hear the stealthy rustlings in the underbush ... Suddenly the boar came crashing out of the undergrowth and raced towards them, its wickedly curved tusks already stained with the blood of men and beasts.

Fionn began to back away slowly.

Dermot looked at him in surprise. 'Where are you going?'

'I am under under a *gaesa* never to hunt boar,' he shouted.

The warrior swore, and then called out to the commander of the Fianna. 'Then leave me your dog, Bran; Morcolle stands no chance against the beast alone.'

Fionn smiled strangely and shook his head. 'No ... no, I cannot leave you my dog. He ... he has chased this animal before and barely escaped with his life. And I doubt in any case, if either he or your dog could stand against the boar.'

Dermot pulled his short sword from its sheath, suddenly remembering his wife's advice to bring Morallach. He looked over at Fionn. 'I have never known Bran to flee from anything; the dog knows no fear.'

'Be that as it may, Dermot Mac Dyna, he will not stand with you against the boar of Benbulbin.'

Dermot caught the note of triumph in the old man's voice and sudden comprehension dawned. 'You've planned this; you've led me here ...' He looked over his shoulder at the charging boar. 'You've led me to my death.'

And the boar was upon him.

Dermot's javelin glanced off the beast's armoured hide without drawing blood. The warrior threw himself to one side as the animal thundered past. He rolled to his feet and, with both hands clasped about the hilt of Beagallach, struck it down between the boar's shoulder blades. It squealed and reared up on its two hind legs – something he had never seen a boar do before – and the sword, tangled in its long bristles, flew from his hand and shattered against a stone. The boar turned abruptly and raced back towards Dermot. It was a truly enormous animal, standing almost as tall as a horse and twice as broad. The sharp bristles on its back were as long as Dermot's fingers and its tusks were as long as his forearm. Dermot waited until the last possible moment, until he could feel the boar's stinking breath on his face, and then he launched himself forward and over the animal's back. He fell as he landed and slid in the dew damp grass. His fingers touched cold metal and he found the hilt of his shattered sword with a jagged lump of metal still remaining in it. He pushed himself to his feet and called for Morcolle – but the dog was nowhere in sight, and even Fionn had disappeared ... but his mocking laughter remained on the chill air.

The boar turned in a surprisingly short space and was upon Dermot before he knew it. He twisted desperately to one side, but too late, and the boar's razor sharp tusks ripped into his stomach and chest. He screamed and fell on grass that was suddenly sodden with his blood. The boar turned and struck again, tearing open the existing wound ... and Dermot rammed the shattered sword down the beast's gaping mouth with the last of his strength. The crazed animal convulsed and attempted to swallow the obstruction, its squeals rose in pitch and intensity, and then stopped. The boar fell dead, its life blood welling from its torn mouth and throat.

When Fionn and the hunting party returned, they found Dermot lying in a widening pool of his own blood beside the already stiffening body of the huge boar. The warrior smiled wanly, his lips reddened with blood-flecked spittle. 'So ... so you finally achieved what ... you failed to do ... all those years ago,' he whispered slowly.

Fionn stood over the fallen warrior and shook his head

sadly. 'I never meant for this to happen,' he said quietly, but although his voice and face showed pity, his eyes were bright with laughter.

'I am close to death,' Dermot whispered, 'do not lie to me now.'

'You knew the boar would kill him,' Oisin accused his father. 'With your gift of foreknowledge, you knew he would not survive this day.'

Fionn smiled and let all pretence of sorrow and pity fall away. 'Aye, I knew, and my only regret is that all the people of Banba are not here to see their hero fall and perish, slain by a wild boar.'

'You shame me,' Oisin said, turning away. And slowly, one by one, the Fianna turned away from their commander.

Fionn knelt beside Dermot. 'And so, even in death you bring me nothing but ill luck. When you fled with Grannia –'

'No,' Dermot interrupted, 'I did not flee with her; she placed me under a *gaesa* – you know that. You know also that your own son advised me not to break my oath.'

'No woman is worth a man's oath,' Fionn snapped, 'a man should be strong enough to resist a woman's charms.'

Dermot smiled grimly. 'There will come a time – and shortly too – when your own son will ride away from you on the back of a woman's horse.'

'If you think to frighten me with your prophecies, then you are sadly mistaken. Your time has come.'

'Fionn, if you allow me to die you will have compromised your honour beyond redemption.'

'What honour had I left when you stole my bride-to-be?'

'Can you not see that your own actions compromised your honour ... you made too much of it. If you had forgiven her, you would have emerged as the victor ...'

'I chose not to forgive her – or you.'

'Well, make up for that now,' Oisin said, coming up and standing over his father and Dermot.

'I do not think I want to.'

'I think you should,' his son said tightly, 'because if you refuse to help him now, you will lose the respect of the men.'

'Is that a threat?'

Oisin shrugged.

Fionn rose from the ground slowly, his face tight with anger. 'What would you have me do?' he asked icily.

'Aid him.'

'How?'

'Let me drink from your hands,' Dermot said weakly, 'I know that when you were granted the gift of foreknowledge, you also received the gift of healing.'

'It is not a gift I have often used,' Fionn protested.

'That is nothing to be proud of,' Oisin snapped.

Fionn looked about the flat mountain-top. 'There is no water here; I must have fresh spring water . . .'

'Beneath the bush that lies at my feet,' Dermot said, 'there is a spring. I can feel its trembling through the ground.'

Oisin grasped the bush close to its roots and pulled it up in a shower of earth. Immediately fresh spring water gurgled up and ran down the hill in a quick sparkling brook. 'There is your water.'

Fionn went slowly to the brook and caught a little of the fountaining water in his cupped hands. He straightened – and dropped the water.

'Fionn . . .?' Dermot said gently.

'Father!'

The old commander pointed to the fallen warrior. 'For years he has made me the laughing stock of all the Forts and Raths in Banba. He has become a hero, and I the villain, and now he expects me to heal him.'

'It will show your generous spirit,' Oisin snapped, kneeling beside Dermot and cradling the warrior's head in his arms.

Again Fionn stooped and lifted a little of the chill sparkling water in his hands. He walked over to Dermot and knelt by his side. He lifted his hand and brought the liquid close to his lips whilst Oisin helped him sit up . . . and as Dermot's lips touched it, Fionn opened his fingers and let the water fall onto his blood-soaked jerkin.

'Father,' Oisin said coldly, 'unless you bring Dermot the water now, I swear that two bodies will lie on this hill.'

'You will never defeat me,' Fionn said.

'Perhaps not. But you cannot afford to destroy the Fianna if you choose to fight. For when you slay me, each and every one of the knights will challenge you in turn; how long do you think you can stand against the greatest army in the history of Banba?'

But even as Fionn brought the third handful of water to Dermot's bloodstained lips, the wounded warrior shuddered once – and died.

Fionn looked at the water cupped in his hand and said softly, 'I tried.'

Oisin stood and pulled off his cloak. He straightened Dermot's limbs and then covered him with his cloak. 'No father,' he said, without looking at him, 'you did not try. You have what you always wanted: Dermot dead ... and I will never forgive you.'

He stood whilst the remainder of the hunting party slowly filed past and laid their cloaks over the still body.

'For here lies one of the noblest of the Fianna.'

'And when Grannia heard of her husband's death – and there were some that whispered murder – she wept bitterly and blamed herself. She went immediately to Benbulbin, but when she arrived there she found Angus standing over the cold body with a host of the De Danann. And the god sorrowed with her, and he took the body of Dermot with him into the Shadowland where he instilled a flicker of life into it – but only a flicker, for it was beyond his power to bring the body back to full life.

And each evening, as the amber sunlight fades across the god's gardens, he walks with Dermot amidst the groves and magical arbors.

And until the day she died, Dermot would pass through the Veil of Sleep and walk and make love to Grannia in the Land of Dreams.

And death re-united them.'

CHAPTER 3

THE RETURN OF OISIN

The young man slowly climbed the innumerable steps leading up to the tower's summit. Standing on the small stone-enclosed platform he could see the storm far out on the horizon. The sky was grey and leaden, almost indistinguishable from the sea which boiled and seethed beneath the storm's onslaught. Sheets of white and silver lightning ripped through the lowering clouds, and he could almost imagine that he could hear the crack as the heavens were torn apart by the levin bolts.

But above his head the sun shone from a flawlessly blue sky and the sea, far below at the base of the crystal walls of the palace and as far out as the irregular circle of reefs that bounded the isle, was flat and undisturbed. He looked down, and could see the gleaming towers and glittering palaces of Tir na nOg reflected in a watery mirror.

For a single moment his clear grey eyes clouded as he looked out across the enchanted sea towards the storm beyond the reefs on the horizon. And for a single moment he longed to be standing on the shores of his distant homeland, feeling the rain and salt spray on his face, the wind plucking at his hair and the pounding of the storm-maddened sea on the sands by his feet. For a single moment ...

'You still long for home after all this time?' He turned as a shadow fell across the crystal stones. A soft small hand enfolded his, the smooth fingers gently caressing the stiffened muscles, loosening the locked joints. 'Why?' The voice was as soft and gentle as the hand, lyrical, concerned.

'It is my home,' he said simply.

'Oisin – this is your home now,' she stated flatly.

An errant gust of wind touched his face and whipped strands of his dark hair across his eyes. He looked out across the sea once again, and emotion flickered behind his eyes, and was gone.

But Niamh Golden-Hair had seen his look, had seen the pain and loss that lurked behind them. She held his hand tightly feeling the hard muscles bunch and ripple beneath the smooth skin. She rested her head against his broad chest, feeling his strong heart pound against her cheek. He had lost none of his youth, he was exactly as he had been on that fateful day when she had taken him from his father and the Fianna almost ... how long had it been now?

But then, time meant little in the Land of the Ever Young, one of the strongholds of the Faery Folk. In ten years, a hundred years, even a thousand years hence, Oisin would still be as young and as handsome as he had been on that day when he had ridden away over the waves on her foam-flecked horse to the magical isle. His skin would remain smooth and unwrinkled, no grey or silver would touch his raven locks, neither his sight nor his hearing would dim. There would be no difference in him.

Or would there?

Already, after perhaps only thirty years in the Crystal Palaces of Tir na nOg, she could see the first signs of loneliness that had begun to grow within him – a loneliness that would quickly grow to an all consuming passion that would gnaw away at him, a passion that could so easily turn to a hatred of her and what she had done to him.

'Go back then, if you must,' she whispered gently, blinking away the tears. 'Go back, spend a little time in your own land and return to me refreshed.' She sighed and bit her lip, but there was nothing else she could do; she loved him, she could do nothing to hurt or harm him.

Oisin kissed the top of her head, breathing in the delicate perfume of her golden tresses, and then he tilted up her small oval face and kissed her long and deeply. And once again, for the thousandth time, the princess of Tir na nOg longed to belong to the world of Man once more so that she

70

might fully experience the love of Oisin. But that was impossible; everything had its price, and the price of eternal life was sterility.

The white steed pawed at the golden sands as if it were eager to be off across the waves. Oisin stood beside the horse and held Niamh in his arms. 'I will return shortly,' he promised.

But Niamh shook her head. 'I fear I will never see you again. You were born in the world of Man and you will die in that same world.' Salt tears gathered at the corners of her large green eyes. Oisin brushed them gently away and kissed her.

'No. I will return to you some day, some way.'

She watched him mount, swinging easily into the high saddle, his burnished mail glinting golden in the sunlight, the horse's coat glistening like satin. She laid her hand on his leg and looked up into his eyes. 'Remember Oisin, remember; do not dismount from the horse. It is from this world, it is part of this world and it carries a little of this world with it always. Whilst you remain astride it you remain partly in the Otherworld, and are still subject to the Shadow Realm's laws. Dismount, and you will once again belong to your old world.'

The young man smiled and shook his head. 'I will not dismount.'

'And remember,' she concluded, 'time has no hold over Tir na nOg, but it rests heavily over your homeland. Do not expect to find everything as it was.'

He nodded. 'The years will have wrought changes,' he mused, 'but surely not that many.' He laughed, the first time she had seen him laugh in a long time. 'I will not lose my way.' He bent down and kissed her tenderly on the cheek, and then he urged the horse forward, out over the waves. The horse's golden hooves struck the water, sank slightly and then bit, as if it were galloping over soft earth.

Niamh stood on the warm sands watching her lover gallop across the seas of Faery back into the world of Man, and she wept for she knew she would never see him again.

Once Oisin passed beyond the magical reef that bounded the isle he was almost back into the world of Man, but some of the magic still lingered, and he once again saw the hart pursued by the red-eared dog, and the young maiden pursued by the warrior with the golden sword. He remembered he had first seen them – how long ago? – when he had first come to the Land of the Ever Young. He had asked Niamh about them then, but she had dismissed them, saying they were but the shadows of what had been, what would be, but what never was. He watched the dark warrior pursuing the maiden; her brown steed never seemed to gain any headway, and his white steed never gained on her mount, and he wondered if they were forever doomed to chase one another across the seas, and he resolved to question Niamh upon his return.

He passed the Land of Virtues where he had rescued a young maiden from the Fomorian king, and he smiled in fond remembrance of that battle: it had lasted three days and three nights. His father, Fionn, would have been proud of him, for his opponent had been a monster, standing almost twice his height and three times his girth and with the strength of a dozen men. And his blood had been black.

He urged his horse onwards; by the gods, what would it be like to fight again, to feel the blood-lust rising ... rising ... rising? The exhilaration of battle, the heady wine of victory, the spoils, the acclaim – what more did a man want?

The barren black Cliffs of Moher rose out of the sea in a solid line stretching from horizon to horizon. The sea foamed about their base, roared and howled through the countless caves and caverns, sending foam leaping skywards. He smiled triumphantly. He was home.

But somehow the cliffs seemed smaller, less majestic than he remembered them.

The horse's gold-shod hooves struck sparks from the pebbled beach as he came ashore. Oisin stood in the saddle, easing the muscles in his thighs and buttocks – it had been a long time since he had ridden such a distance. He eagerly scanned the land before him for any sign of habitation or movement. But there was nothing, and no-one. The beach sloped gently upwards, flanked on either side by the worn cliffs, and rolled back into flat green fields crossed with irregular stone walls. His brow furrowed in puzzlement as he urged his mount up the beach and across the withered grasses towards the open fields.

When he had left Banba there had been a Fort off towards the north, but now there was nothing but a smooth mound where it had stood. A broad highway had run down along by the cliffs and dipped down towards the beach, and now there was nothing but a thick track, overgrown and disused, and it was much nearer to the cliff edge than it should have been.

The warrior loosed his sword in its sheath – clearly some evil was abroad in the land – and rode on.

Oisin rode across Banba's green fields that day of his return from the magical isle. His amazement and wonder soon turned to something akin to fear, for nothing was as he remembered it. The Duns and Raths of his friends were gone, the roads had vanished and the great Forts were no more. Even the forests seemed to have shrunk. His wife's words echoed within his head, pounding with ever increasing intensity: *'Time holds no sway over Tir na nOg ... it rests heavily over your homeland ... heavily over your homeland ... heavily ... heavily.'*

He saw no-one as he rode across country – although he sometimes thought he saw someone disappearing into the stunted bushes that lined the small and rutted tracks, but they might have been animals fleeing his approach.

And the day wore on.

About evening he rode down into Glen na Moile in the east. He cleared the trees that lined the side of the glen – and stopped in amazement. For a group of children were attempting to lift a fallen dolmen off their companions. They must have been playing about the sacred relic when it had fallen over, trapping some beneath. But as Oisin rode forward, he suddenly realised that these were no children but rather full grown men and women. But they were so small, so puny . . . hardly men at all.

They scattered at his approach, their eyes and mouths wide with fear, but he sat there unmoving until they crept from the bushes and approached him warily.

'I am Oisin,' he said slowly, 'son of Fionn, Knight of the Fianna. Tell me of my father and of the Company, and tell me what evil has fallen over this land.'

One of the men, a tiny man in a rough brown garment with a silver cross about his neck, stepped up to the warrior and spoke to him in a voice trembling with fear. 'We know nothing of Fionn and the Fianna save what is told in the legends ...' He pointed at the dolmen. 'There are people trapped beneath, will you use your great strength to lift it off them?'

Oisin gazed down at the little man in horror. Legend? Had Fionn and the Fianna passed into legend? By all the gods, how many years had he wasted in the Land of Eternal Youth?

'And what of Oisin?' he asked hoarsely, his eyes hard and flat, gazing unseeing into the distance, knowing yet dreading the answer.

'There was one,' said the man in brown, 'a son – I think – of Fionn who was taken by a *bean-sidhe* – a fairy woman – off to the Isles of the West, and he is said to be living still.'

Oisin smiled gently, and then he rose up in the ornate saddle, spread his arms wide and shouted, 'I am Oisin, son of Fionn; I have returned from Tir na nOg!'

And only the echoes answered him.

He manoeuvred his horse over to the toppled dolmen and leaned down. His calloused hand caught the edge of the huge slab of stone, the muscles in his shoulder and arm tensed, and then he heaved. The huge slab was torn out of the soft earth and sent whirling across the field to shatter against the ground.

And in the same instant, Oisin's saddle girth snapped with the strain, and he fell to the ground. A cry of horror caught in his throat as his voice seemed to catch and rattle. His hand reached for the reins, but the white horse shied away as his hand shrivelled into a withered claw before his eyes. The horse grew ... and grew ... and grew until it was enormous, and then it turned and was gone.

Oisin writhed on the ground as all the years he had passed in the magical isle claimed him now. His thick raven locks turned grey, then silver and then fell from a scalp suddenly scabrous. His sight – his perfect sight that could count the individual feathers on a sparrow's wing at five hundred paces – dimmed and faded and shadows raced in and gathered about him. The noon faded to a thick twilight and his hearing – that could hear a worm moving through the earth – died to a muted roaring. His smooth skin wrinkled, cracked and hung in loose wattles from his chin, arms and legs. The weight of his armour dragged him to the ground and as he fell he could hear his suddenly brittle bones grind together and he knew that any sudden movement might shatter them completely.

A shadow moved across his dim sight and a face – no longer tiny – swam in his vision. It was the small man in the brown cloth. The silver chain and cross about his scrawny neck glinted blindingly. Oisin could barely make out his words, but they sounded reassuring and he could feel the man working on the buckles and straps that held his armour. The last words he heard before he drifted into unconsciousness were blurred and muted and he could only make out part of the sentence . . . 'take you to Saint Patrick.'

And on the magical isle, Niamh bent her head and wept as she saw the riderless horse galloping across the waves towards her.

Oisin survived for several months after his return. He and Patrick struck up a curious friendship and they often spent the long evenings arguing the Old Celtic Faith against the New Christian Religion. And in the end Patrick prevailed and Oisin, last of the Fianna, last of the Heroic Age, was baptised a follower of the Christ.

CHAPTER 4

FIRE ON THE MOUNTAIN
(A Legend of Saint Patrick)

The grey-haired warrior leaned across the young man in the long woollen robe and pointed with the charred end of a twig. 'Tara is here ...' he scratched in the dirt, 'and Slane is here on the north bank of the Boyne.'

'So Slane is visible from Tara?' the young man asked.

'On a clear day, yes.'

'And if I can convert Tara?'

'If you can convert Tara, you can take all Eriu.' Dichu stood and dusted off his hard hands. He looked down at the young man. 'But first you must convert Laoighre – and that,' he added, 'is impossible.'

Patrick stood and rubbed his sandle-shod foot over the rough map drawn in the dirt. 'Will he listen to me?' he asked, looking up at the grizzled warrior. He was not a tall man, standing almost a head smaller than Dichu, but the older man felt dwarfed by his presence.

'He will listen to you – but you will never bring him into the New Religion. His father was Niall of the Nine Hostages, and Laoighre follows his father's ways and is firmly entrenched in the Old Faith.' Dichu pulled his dyed woollen cloak across his shoulders, shivering as a chill breeze whistled through the almost bare trees. 'However, his queen Angras might listen to your words – and she has great influence with the poets and bards. If you could convert her, and she them, then half your task would be completed.'

The small Roman nodded, his grey eyes lost in thought.

76

He ran his fingers through his prematurely greying hair and sighed wearily. 'And the Druids?' he asked.

Dichu turned to face the holy man. 'You will never convert the Druids. They will oppose you every step of the way. They will call upon their gods and their Powers to strike you down and if that fails then they are not above hiring men to do their work for them.'

Patrick shrugged. 'My God will protect me,' he said with absolute confidence.

'And your followers also,' Dichu waved a bare arm at the small group of men and women huddled beneath a stand of trees, 'they too will do their utmost to protect you.' He patted the knife that hung by his side significantly.

The Roman's eyes flashed in sudden anger and his high-boned, hollow-eyed face flushed. 'I will renounce the first man who uses violence in my name,' he snapped. Clouds scudded across the night sky and the hard points of starlight sparkled in his eyes. 'I have taught you of the One God, the True God, and I have read to you from the Holy Books – and you told me you understood and would follow the teachings and honour His Name. But do you not understand that He teaches peace, not violence?'

Dichu rested his heavy hands on Patrick's thin shoulders. 'Listen to me holy man. I was amongst your first converts to the New God; you built your first church in my Dun. I honour you, I honour your . . . *our* god. But you must remember Patrick that what you are teaching is totally opposed to the codes we have lived by since the time when the Ancients took Eriu from the demons. You must be patient,' he said gently, 'give us time.'

The land was dark. No lights burned in the Duns or Raths; no fires glowed in the Forts and even the shepherds' fires on the hills were extinguished.

For this was the time of waiting. It was the time sacred to the God of Fire, a time *between*. The winter had passed, the spring and summer were yet to come. All across the land the people waited for the first sign of the coming season: the

Druid fire that would rise before Tara's walls. The fire that would signify light and life, growth and heat.

But now, 433 years since the birth of the Christ, the Festival of Fire and the Christian Feast of Resurrection fell on consecutive days.

Lucetmale the Arch-Druid watched his priests carefully weave the wands of oak and green yew into the Circle of Life and place it like a crown about the smooth circular stone. The old man bent and lifted the heavy stone in his strong arms and carried it to the small platform surrounded by bundles of green and freshly-cut wood. He bowed to the four cardinal points, then turned and faced the east where the sun would shortly rise. He pushed back a lock of greying hair under the thin gold fillet that encircled his head and his dark brown eyes raked the skies for the first sign of the approaching dawn, eager to light the fire of the new season.

He half-turned as Laoighre the High King and Angras his queen came up behind him.

'It is almost time,' he said, his cracked voice breaking harshly on the still pre-dawn air.

The High King nodded, his dark eyes moving ceaselessly over the almost flat plain spread out before him. He stiffened suddenly. Angras felt his tension and laid her small hand on his arm.

'What is it?' she whispered.

Laoighre pointed and the queen gasped in amazement.

For on the north-eastern horizon a thin tendril of fire rose into the night skies!

'Blasphemy!' Lucetmale screamed, his right arm rigid and pointing. A low moan rippled through the assembly as all heads turned towards the tiny spot of fire which flared and grew, casting its yellow light far out into the night.

The Arch-Druid screamed like an animal in mortal pain. His gaunt frame shook in rage and spittle frothed his lips. He mouthed incoherently at the light burning against all tradition and law on Slane Hill.

Laoighre instructed one of the Druids to take Lucetmale away and calm him down and then he called for his warriors and chariots, and took the north road towards Slane.

Dichu wiped the sweat from his brow and moved away from the roaring fire. He coughed and spat ash and cinders from his dry throat. The old warrior was surprised to find himself trembling like a raw recruit on the morning of his first battle. But then, wasn't that what he was: a recruit in the first battle between the New Religion and the Old Faith? He squinted back into the glowing heart of the huge fire, and while a part of him still cowered in terror at what he had done, another part rejoiced and almost welcomed the coming conflict.

The small Roman joined him as he walked away from the fire. Patrick's clothes were singed by the flames and his hair and beard still smouldered. His sallow cheeks were glowing and ruddy and his white teeth glinted in the shimmering light. 'Will they come?'

Dichu smiled at the holy man's almost youthful enthusiasm. 'Oh aye, they'll come, you may rest assured of that. You have sent them a war arrow...' He pointed south and west. 'And I'll wager that even now they are preparing for war in Tara.' He shook his head. 'I don't think you know what you've started.'

Patrick nodded seriously. 'Oh, I know sure enough.' He pointed back up the hill at the raging fire still being fed by his followers. 'That fire symbolises the light of the New Religion shining out into the night of ignorance that still shrouds this land.'

Dichu laughed briefly. 'But let us hope that it is not a fire that will quickly burn itself out.'

Patrick smiled. 'It is a light that will burn forever,' he stated firmly.

'I think,' Dichu said slowly, 'it is a fire that will consume us all.'

*

The rattle of the chariots echoed out into the stillness of the dawn air and the horses' hooves struck sparks from the hard packed earth. The watchers on Slane Hill heard the company approaching before they saw them through the thin mist that rose from the soft ground.

Patrick sat by the roadside toying with a blade of grass. His rough woollen cloak was damp with dew and he was shivering with the chill, but his face was impassive as he watched the war chariots draw nearer. They stopped and fell into a box formation, with the king's ornate chariot in the centre. Armoured guards darted into the bushes, wary of an ambush. Only when they were sure that it was safe did Laoighre, Angras, the Arch-Druid and Ochru, a Druid, approach.

Patrick stood before the High King. Laoighre was almost a head taller than the Roman and broader, but even he could sense the power that radiated from the small man.

'You lit the fire?' Laoighre asked quietly, his breath pluming on the damp morning air.

'I did.' Patrick's accent sounded strange to the High King's ears, harsh and guttural, and with just a trace of the north in it.

'Why?'

'There were several reasons,' the small man said softly. 'It was a dark night and I sought to bring light into it. It is the season of my God and I wished to honour Him with a Paschal Fire.' He paused and added, 'And I was cold.'

Angras laughed. 'You are bold enough,' she said loudly. 'Tell me, what are you called and why do you flaunt the ancient laws of this land?'

The Arch-Druid frowned at the queen and snapped. 'Kill the blasphemer now!'

'I am called Patrick,' the Roman said, ignoring the Arch-Druid's outburst, 'and I have been sent to this land by Germanus of Auxerre to spread the Word of Christ.'

'I have heard of this Christ,' Laoighre said, 'there was one before you ... ' he looked towards the Druid and raised his eyebrows.

'Palladius,' he snapped.

The High King nodded. 'Aye, Palladius, but he failed to convince me with his arguments about a God that promised nothing but peace.' He shook his head. 'No, it is not a man's religion.'

Patrick smiled. 'I am the son of a Roman, Calpornius; I am descended from a race of warriors that once conquered nearly half the known world. And yet even now, the followers of Christ grow and multiply amongst my own race.'

'But your empire is in decline,' Ochru the Druid said grimly. 'The Christian faith has weakened them.' His hand slipped under his robe and touched the hard cold metal of a sacrificial knife. Slowly his lean fingers curled about the carved hilt.

'My race declines because of its excesses,' Patrick said patiently. And then his dark eyes flashed in amusement. 'Tell me Druid, when was the last time you used that knife?' He laughed at Ochru's expression and added, 'There is a thin crack in the metal where the blade meets the hilt. One solid blow and it will surely crack.'

Laoighre's hand shot out and pulled the Druid's arm from beneath his cloak. The dagger gleamed bronze in the wan morning sunlight as the High King plucked it from the Druid's tingling fingers and held it close to his eyes. He nodded slowly and then dropped the knife point first onto the hard road. The blade cracked and snapped off just below the hilt.

'What do you want holy man?' Laoighre asked quietly, his eyes still on the shattered knife. He was a warrior who followed the old ways; he believed in omens and portents, and he knew with an icy certainty that the broken blade was such.

'I only want to talk to you,' Patrick said, brushing water droplets from his cloak ...

Ochru cried aloud in rage and launched himself at the Roman, his fingers hooked into claws, reaching for the smaller man's eyes.

And then he stopped as if he had been struck.

A sudden gust of wind howled about the small group, plucking the Druid from his feet and hurling him backwards. The wind screamed and tore at him – but left everyone else untouched – sending him rolling across the ground. There was a sickening crack – and the Druid's skull shattered against a jagged lump of stone. The wind died as suddenly as it had arisen.

There was a long silence broken only by the murmurs of fear and wonder from the warriors about the chariots. The High King nudged the still body with his foot and looked across at Patrick. 'You will attend me in Tara on the morrow,' he said and turned away, but not before the holy man had seen the queen flash him a brilliant smile and the Arch-Druid shoot him a look of venom.

Dichu laid his hand on Patrick's arm and stopped him. The warrior's hard grey eyes narrowed as he stared towards a small copse of trees that stood just off the road.

'What is it?'

Dichu shook his head. 'I thought I ... Yes.' He bent his head and spoke quietly to the holy man. 'There is someone or something in those trees.'

'How do you know?'

The warrior glanced upwards and Patrick followed his eyes. A lone black bird was winging into the west.

'That's the second bird that landed and immediately took off again from those trees. Something must have startled it.'

Patrick ran his long slim hands through his greying hair. 'What do you suggest we do?'

'Pray?'

Conn parted the bushes and peered down the road at the small group standing there, apparently deep in conversation. He could recognise the holy man and the warrior, Patrick and Dichu standing out in front. He eased his sword from its sheath and stepped back into the shadow of a tree joining the score of warriors waiting in ambush.

The spot they had chosen for the ambush was less than an hour's march from Tara's walls. The road narrowed and wound down into a little valley and was surrounded on either side by trees and bushes, and the saint's company would have to march in single file to pass through.

The bushes rustled as the warriors moved closer to the road.

Patrick led his followers off the road and tersely explained Dichu's fears. He gathered the two score men and women into a small circle and bade them bend their heads and pray. The saint raised his hands over the group and called aloud for his God, and then he prayed silently for a long while.

He could feel the power gathering about him; he could feel the strength and conviction of his faith solidify and harden into a solid force. He gathered the force into his inner being – and cast it forth.

Conn ran his thumb along the edge of his sword nervously. The holy man and his followers had disappeared into the trees and had not reappeared. He looked around at his men, seeing his own nervousness mirrored in their drawn faces.

The trees suddenly parted and Conn squinted into the sunlight trying to make out the shape that had stepped out onto the road. But the sun was in his eyes blurring his vision. The shape moved and then another stood beside it and another ...

And then he recognised the shapes. It was a herd of deer. Patrick and his followers must have startled them, driving them out of the shelter of the trees.

The deer ran past the trees where the warriors lay in ambush. They were sleek wild-eyed beasts and they galloped by as fleet as the wind and accompanied by a strange whispering breeze.

And Conn and his warriors remained in the trees awaiting the saint and his followers.

And later generations would call the prayer the saint had composed to protect them from the ambush the Breastplate of Saint Patrick.

The road into Tara was lined with silent waiting people. Already rumours of the small Roman's powers and deeds had begun to circulate and they were curious to see the man who had defied the laws and traditions of the land, the wrath of both the High King and the Arch-Druid and lit the fire that had blazed out over the land. Many shivered as he passed, for they felt the aura of power that emanated from the small dark man and others called upon their wild and savage gods to protect them from the holy man who was bringing demons back to Eriu.

As Patrick approached the main hall, he ordered his followers to remain outside and pray for his success. Dichu protested, but Patrick was adamant; he knew this would be the Arch-Druid's last chance to strike back and slay him, and he didn't want any of his friends killed on his behalf.

Maecadre, the Great Hall of Tara, was silent. The rows of princes and nobles stood in silent ranks, their robes of richly woven cloth and highly polished and decorated armour contrasting sharply with the stark simplicity of the Druid's white robes. All heads turned towards the door and the holy man was suddenly conscious of his travel-stained and dusty robes; he grinned in embarrassment and then smoothed his features into an unreadable mask.

As he entered the great hall an old man stepped out from the crowd and saluted him gravely.

'I am Dubhthach, Chief Poet of Eriu,' he said in a deep mellow voice, 'and I bid you welcome.'

'I thank you sir for your courtesy,' Patrick replied.

'And I too welcome you,' a younger man, also wearing a poet's robes, said quietly. 'I am Fiacca.'

Patrick bowed deeply to the young man, remembering

something Dichu had said; ' ... *and the word of a poet or bard is feared by both king and commoner, and in many cases their word is law. If you can convert them* ... '

Patrick walked forward and stopped a little way from the long table at the top of the room before the huge open fire. He leaned upon his tall battered walking stick and bowed to the king. 'I have come,' he said simply.

'You are welcome here,' Laoighre said.

'He is not!' The voice was cold and rasping, filled with hate and malice. Lucetmale stepped from the ranks of the Druids dressed in his ceremonial robes of white and silver and carrying a short sickle of rank. 'He has transgressed and blasphemed one of our most ancient rituals, slain one of our company with his magic – and yet you welcome him here!' The Arch-Druid spat. 'Your father would denounce you.' He pointed at the holy man. 'Your father would have tossed his carcass to the carrion crows,' he sneered.

'Druid,' Laoighre said quietly, but with a note of ice in his voice, 'take care what you say now, for you will never have a chance to take back your hastily chosen words.'

But the Druid's rage had passed beyond all the bounds of caution. 'My words are not hasty, king. They have been carefully chosen. You have shamed your father before the assembly of the princes of Eriu; he would disown you, cast you out for not upholding the faith.'

A low angry murmur ran through the crowd and whilst some looked scornfully at the king, others glared at the Arch-Druid.

'Druid,' Patrick said in his strange accent, 'your argument is with me, do not try to strike at a king who is too honourable to strike back. Why do you fear me?' he asked suddenly.

Lucetmale laughed, and his laughter climbed dangerously close to hysteria. 'You do not frighten me,' he howled, 'you are nothing, less than nothing.'

The saint smiled enigmatically. 'Then why did you don your robes of office and carry in your symbol of authority if you did not feel threatened? Is it perhaps because you think

– or even know? – that my powers are greater than yours?'

The Druid's mouth opened and closed soundlessly and spittle frothed on his lips. 'Call upon your gods,' he snarled, 'let them protect you. But behold the power of the gods that are old beyond reckoning ... '

His left hand traced a glowing arc in the air with the golden sickle and his voice deepened as he began to chant in the ancient tongue of the Druids. Over Tara the skies abruptly darkened and heavy storm clouds rolled in from the north. Icy winds carrying swirling flakes of snow and ice moaned through the draughty hall and outside Maecadre the terrified cries of the people rose above the howling wind.

And then it began to snow. Great silent flakes fell from the leaden clouds, quickly covering the spring fields beneath a thick mantle of white. Servants attempted to build up the roaring fire, but the wind that whipped through the chill hall extinguished the flickering flames and the princes and nobles shivered in the unseasonal cold.

Patrick tapped his walking stick on the stone flags, the sharp report catching the company's attention. 'It is a fine trick – but now remove it.'

Lucetmale laughed. 'There is no way it can be removed. It is a product of the Elementals; I can call them only once in every cycle, but they will return on the morrow.'

'What!' Angras snapped. 'Are you saying that having brought this snow and ice down upon us there is no way to remove it? The people freeze and the summer crops will be ruined.'

'It is doubtful whether the summer crops would have grown in any case since this holy man,' – he spat – 'disregarded the law and lit his fire before the Holy Flame.'

Patrick raised his walking stick and immediately the hall fell silent. His cold eyes bored into the Arch-Druid's and Lucetmale felt the fear that had seethed within him, since that first thin tendril of fire had risen into the night sky, begin to harden and solidify. And he knew then with a chilling certainty that there was no possible way he could defeat this small Roman.

'Your magic is useless – it is worse than useless for it brings nothing but ill. It is like your faith: you have forgotten the side of Light and Life, and only the Dark remains. Behold the Light of the New Religion!' Patrick slowly traced the symbol of the cross in the chill air with his long stick. The end of the stick began to glow with a gentle green light which left the image of the cross burning on the air. And suddenly a warm gust of wind blew in through the open window and almost as one the assembly moved to the windows and doors and stared out over the snow covered fields. The heavy storm clouds were visibly disappearing. The sun broke through and burned from a flawlessly blue sky, but the snow, instead of melting and flooding the fields, dried into tiny white flakes which the warm breeze scattered and carried out across the sea.

The Arch-Druid then called upon the Powers of Darkness to cover the land, and abysmal night covered Tara in a thick clinging blanket. And the Arch-Druid's laughter hung mockingly on the stinking air, for the Night had wafted from the very pits of Hell and was heavy with the fetor of the damned.

But the saint's wand cut through the night with a golden-green light, sending it howling back to its infernal pit.

Lucetmale then called upon swarms of flies and directed them towards Patrick, but they refused to land upon his person and settled back upon the Arch-Druid in a filthy shroud. He then sent glowing balls of fire floating towards Patrick, but he merely touched them with his wand and they dissolved into glittering motes of dust.

And finally the Arch-Druid threw his sickle onto the ground where it shifted and writhed and assumed the form of a huge crimson-and-gold serpent which slithered swiftly towards the holy man. But Patrick stooped and gently placed his stick on the cold stones where it assumed the form of a small brown skinned serpent – which overwhelmed and destroyed the larger crimson-and-gold snake.

In the silence that followed, Patrick bent and retrieved his stick and handed Lucetmale back his sickle. Tendrils still clung to the golden semi-circle and the Arch-Druid drew back his hand with a cry of pain as the power arced from the blade to his hand. The air in the hall was rank and bitter, metallic-tasting and blue fox-fire raced along the warrior's weapons and gathered in glowing balls in the darkened corners of the room.

Patrick dropped the sickle onto the floor at Lucetmale's feet and turned to the High King. 'Is this enough?' he asked wearily.

Laoighre nodded. 'It is enough. You have shown that your gods are greater than ours ... '

He paused as the saint shook his head. 'Not gods – but God, one God only.'

'But I thought there were three gods?' the king protested.

The holy man shook his head and reached inside his tunic. He pulled out a tiny sprig of shamrock and held up the weed. 'Look; see how the three parts grow from the one stem and yet form part of the greater leaf, the three coming from the one and the one being part of the three. It can be likened to the God of Peace: the Three Who are One, and the One that is All.'

The king raised his hand. 'You have convinced me Roman – but you will never convert me; I follow the path laid down for me by my father and his father before him. But you have my oath that you shall travel this land unmolested, preaching your New Religion in peace and dignity. Let us drink on it.'

The king and queen stood as slaves carried in tall goblets of gold filled with a pale white mead. Laoighre and Angras raised their cups to their lips and drank deeply, but Patrick paused with the rim of the goblet at his lips. He frowned and breathed in the heady fumes and then he carefully made the sign of the cross over the liquid. The mead foamed briefly and then the saint drank it ...

Lucetmale's scream of triumph turned to a howl of rage when Patrick remained standing. He snatched the vessel from his hands and stared into its half-empty bowl. He raised haunted eyes and stared at the saint. 'You should be dead,' he screamed.

'My God protects me,' Patrick said.

'And mine will protect me,' the Arch-Druid shouted and drained the goblet. He coughed as the fiery liquid burned its way down his throat and into his stomach . . . and continued burning. His throat, mouth and lips seared and blackened as the acid ate through them and he screamed in agony as the fluid ate through him. His lean body convulsed and writhed on the stones as the poison, meant for Patrick, destroyed him.

'Yours is a powerful god,' Angras said quietly.

'Mine is the only God!'

CHAPTER 5

BANSHEE

The scream cut through the brittle silence of the December night like a knife. It hung trembling on the sharp air, lost and desolate – the cry of a soul in the very depths of despair.

And those who heard it knelt and prayed for themselves and their families and made the Sign of the Cross above their doors and across their windows. For it was the wail of the banshee, the cry of death.

Maeve sat up suddenly. 'What was that?' she whispered. Her mother and brother raised their heads and listened. 'It's probably the wind coming in over the marsh,' Kieran said, and edged the candle closer to his book so that its light washed the pages in yellow.

A spark cracked in the fire and Maeve jumped, her heart pounding. Her mother smiled over her knitting, 'My, but you're jumpy tonight, dear,' she said quietly, the long needles clicking softly, her eyes never leaving her daughter's face.

'I thought I heard something,' Maeve said, shaking back her long red hair, now burnished copper in the firelight, 'a cry ... or a scream.'

The clicking of the needles stopped and Nora Slattery crossed herself quickly. 'Don't say such a thing child.'

'I heard nothing,' Kieran insisted, 'but it could have been the ice settling on the roof or a branch breaking beneath the weight of snow,' he said quickly, trying to calm the fear he saw in his mother's eyes.

He stood and stretched, the candle on the table lending

his lean face deep shadows and hollows, giving it an almost skull-like appearance. He flipped the book shut with his index finger and waved his hand across the candle extinguishing the flame. The corner of the two-roomed cottage plunged into darkness. 'Well, I'm for bed ... '

And then they heard it.

It was a scream, a wail of anguish that rose and fell like the howling of a moon-struck dog. It seemed to rise above human hearing, grating along bone and nerves, setting the teeth on edge. It struck raw nerves in the listeners, plumbing deep into their unconscious, drawing forth the primeval fear of the night, the dead and the undead, and the creatures that howled in the darkness.

'Banshee!' Nora Slattery moaned and fell to her knees on the hard earthen floor and began to pray, her thin lips moving silently. Maeve, who had risen to her feet, knelt beside her mother, the blood draining from her face, leaving her freckled cheeks ghastly in the wavering firelight.

The death-wail came again, only this time it was nearer, and there seemed to be an undertone of sobbing in the heart-broken cry. It faded and was lost on the wind.

Snow slid off the roof and thumped into the drifts piled up against the walls, making them jump, and the fire hissed as stray flakes found their way down the chimney.

'It's the banshee,' Nora whispered, 'she's calling someone this night; kneel Kieran and pray for their soul.' Her eyes, when she looked up at her son, were wide with fear and glistened with unshed tears.

'It's probably just a lost dog, Mother,' Kieran said gently, although he knew that no dog could make such a sound.

'Kieran, it's the banshee,' Nora insisted.

The cry drifted across the night again; Kieran turned his head trying to catch the direction of the sound. 'It's coming from the west, from the direction of the marshes,' he said. He knelt beside his mother and sister. 'It's just a farm animal caught in the marsh,' he reassured them, 'it's probably freezing to death or slowly drowning in the bog ... there is no such thing as a banshee, *a bean chaointe*, it's only a superstition.'

'You're better educated than I ever was,' Nora said quietly, 'but you've still a lot to learn. You won't find everything in your books, my boy.'

'Perhaps not,' he agreed, 'but there is still no such creature as a banshee, a fairy woman, a portent of death. Mother, we are almost into the twentieth century and banshees and leprechauns do not exist!'

'Your father saw a leprechaun once,' she said softly.

'Aye, in the end of a bottle, no doubt,' Kieran snapped, and instantly regretted it. He leaned across to his mother and patted her shoulder. 'I'll go outside and see what it is,' he sighed.

'No!' Nora Slattery turned and caught her son's arm in both of her frail hands. 'No, you mustn't go outside, you can't.'

He shook off her hands. 'Yes mother, I can!'

She saw the hard look come into his eyes, the same look his late father used to have when he returned home from a drinking bout and began to accuse her of some terrible things. There were times like this, times when she saw that look in her son's eyes, when she would grow cold and the old fear would begin to gnaw inside her.

Kieran pulled on an extra jumper and wound his scarf about his neck and then he took the shotgun down from above the fire. He broke it open, loaded both barrels and slipped a handful of additional rounds into his jacket pocket. He paused by the door. 'Lock this after me.' He smiled briefly and pulling back the bolt, jerked open the door and slipped out into the night. Maeve waited until she was sure that he wasn't about to return and then stood and crossed to the door and slammed the bolt home. Returning to her mother's side, she knelt and prayed.

Kieran swore as he floundered into yet another deep drift and cold wet snow drifted in over his boot-tops. He was going to catch a chill, he knew it, and then his mother would have the great pleasure of telling him, 'I told you so.'

He shook his hands and breathed on his fingers, trying to restore feeling to them. If, by any chance, he had to use the shotgun, he doubted he would be able to feel the trigger never mind pull it.

He stood beside the listing gate and looked around. Behind him, almost completely obliterated in white was the cottage with the long snaking line of footprints sunk deep in the snow leading away from it. To the left lay the flat expanse of the marsh, the murk now covered beneath a mantle of white. Before him, standing barren and leafless was a little copse of trees, the bare branches stark and skeletal against the ground.

Kieran stiffened suddenly. Something had moved through the trees. Something white – whiter than the snow, if that was possible, and he had only seen the movement because it had passed before the black branches. He brought the shotgun up and across his chest, wincing as the cold metal burned his fingers, and closed the breech with a click that echoed in the absolute silence. He thumbed back the hammers and slowly crunched his way towards the trees. Something flickered at the corner of his vision and he spun, bringing the shotgun up to his shoulder – but there was nothing there.

He almost laughed aloud when he realised he was shaking – and not from the cold either. He shook his head; here he was, jumping at shadows. There was nothing out this night – and no-one but an *amadán*, and that included himself, would be crazy enough to go wandering the fields on a bitter December night with a loaded shotgun looking for banshees! He moved closer to the trees, and then almost shouted as a white mass moved before him ... and then he laughed aloud: it was only snow falling from heavily laden branches.

He was turning back when he heard the cry. And although he was cold, the sound chilled him to the marrow. It hung almost tangibly on the night air, as fragile as glass – and as sharp. The young man stood knee-deep in the cold wet snow torn between turning back to the cottage, with its warmth and human companionship or pursuing the cry which promised nothing but loneliness and despair.

He followed the cry.

It led him to the edge of the marshes and taunted him from its depths. He knew that to attempt to cross the frozen wasteland was suicidal. Even in the height of summer he would only cross the shifting marshes in broad daylight – and only then with a very good reason.

Kieran stood on the lip of the slight depression that led downwards into the marshland and tried to identify the sound. He stood, oblivious to the cold, his head cocked to one side, listening.

It was the voice of a young woman or child; but then surely a child's voice would be shriller, and that voice seemed to hold a wealth of maturity in it: it was the voice of a young woman. And then, was it a cry of despair or anger, pain or fear? He listened again as the wailing drifted out from the marsh: it was a cry of absolute despair and sorrow. He squinted out across the marsh; did something move there or did his eyes deceive him? With this white lunar landscape it was hard to say, but he thought he had seen something – was it grey or white? – drift through the low snow-covered bushes. He was almost tempted to set out across the marsh in search of the sound. It was strange, but he felt as if he should know what cried out in such despair. He should know! He ground the butt of the shotgun into the rock-hard earth in frustration – and then he suddenly realised that it was loaded and the barrels were pointing at his head! He laughed self-consciously and, trying to ignore the hammering of his heart and the icy sweat that chilled on his brow, broke open the gun and pulled the cartridges out with numb fingers. With a last lingering look out across the frozen waste, he turned back and set out for home.

'The banshee cries for certain families,' Nora Slattery said to her daughter.

'But will it cry again tonight?' Maeve asked.

'I don't know,' Nora said, 'it usually haunts a certain family or clan until a death occurs. But whether it forewarns a death or brings death is something we will never know.'

'What are they like Mother?' Kieran asked, turning from his book.

Nora shrugged. 'No-one knows. Very few people have actually seen them and lived. Oh, legend says that they are sometimes old hags, lost souls condemned to wander between this life and the next as heralds of death. And then again, they are sometimes said to be beautiful, for banshee means *bean-sidhe*, a fairy woman, and fairy women are supposed to be either very ugly or frighteningly beautiful.' The old woman shook her head slowly and added a sod of turf to the fire. 'But they are only supposed to follow either families of the "O's" or "Mac's", or else families that have distinguished themselves in Ireland's history, and they rarely come to ordinary folk – unless there is a terrible death in store for them ... She turned to her son. 'And was it the wind you heard last night?' she asked, her voice heavy with sarcasm, 'or are you now prepared to accept our superstitious beliefs?'

Kieran shook his head. 'Oh, well it certainly wasn't the wind, but it wasn't a banshee either. I still think it was an animal trapped in the marsh.'

'You'll catch your death,' his mother said sharply, 'wandering about at that hour.'

'Aye, perhaps,' Kieran said, and then he raised his hand. 'Listen ... !'

The cry was closer now, closer and sharper. It was the sound of a young woman sobbing and then wailing aloud, her keening rising and falling in something akin to a melody.

Nora screamed and fell to her knees, pulling her rosary from her apron pocket; Maeve fell to her knees beside her mother and prayed also, tears springing to her eyes – although she could not have said why. But Kieran, moving like one possessed, shrugged on his worn coat and wound his woollen scarf about his neck. He slipped his thin hands into a worn pair of gloves, tucked the shotgun under his arm and went out into the night.

And the chill blast that whipped in through the open door was like the wind from the grave.

Kieran followed the ebb and flow of sound across the fields out towards the marsh. Tonight he would trace that cry to its source – even if he had to cross the marsh to do so. The metal of the shotgun felt warm in his gloved hands, the metal so cold that it burned, but he welcomed the throbbing pain, for it helped to blow away the cobwebs that had smothered his brain all day, making him dull and stupid.

He found himself crying, and his tears were for the woman who was weeping; he cried for her anguish. If only he could share the pain, if only he could understand it, then perhaps he could help, perhaps he could ease her pain. If . . . if . . . if . . .

She was waiting for him by the low wall which bounded the fields from the road. A young woman, her grey garments covered in snow, ice glittering in her hair and eyes. She was terrifyingly beautiful. Her face was small and oval, her eyes huge and slightly slanted and her lips were peeled back from unnaturally long teeth. She raised her arm and beckoned to him. Kieran stopped, confused, shaking his head. Slowly, very slowly, he raised the shotgun and sighted along the length of the barrels, but the pain, the terrible pain and loss in the young woman's eyes stopped him, and he felt his own tears freeze on his face. He let the gun fall into the snow and slowly approached her.

He felt the warmth as he approached. A gradual warmth that spread upwards from his feet and engulfed him in its heat. He was warm, so warm. His fingers were slick with sweat as they fumbled with his glove and pulled the scarf from about his throat. The woman opened both arms and her eyes blazed with sudden fire . . . and the heat was all about him, engulfing him, unbearable, unendurable. He closed his eyes, feeling it sear his face, burn into his outstretched hands, strip the skin from his bones, eat into his brain, burning . . . burning . . . burning . . .

Sergeant Lochran touched the brim of his helmet in salute and spoke quietly to the hollow-eyed woman. 'The doctor said he must have fallen and perhaps struck his head and lain there unconscious. He was very badly frost-bitten ... the cold, the cold took him, ma'am.'

The old woman turned her glassy stare on the uncomfortable policeman. 'No,' she whispered in a thin thread of a voice, 'it wasn't the cold and frostbite that took my Kieran. Not the cold.' And then her voice rose to a shriek. 'The banshee took him! The banshee!'

The sergeant shook his head and turned away. Aye, he had heard the rumours, and he had heard the strange wailing in the night, but banshees indeed! Wasn't it curious though the way young Slattery's skin had been stripped from him in great charred lumps? Almost as if he had been burned.

Almost.

CHAPTER 6

CREATURES OF THE WERE: THE WOLVES

Andrew Connelly groaned wearily as he sank up to his ankle in thick marsh water. He pulled his foot free and attempted to shake off the clinging mud. The old man swore as he glanced up at the darkening skies: it was almost sunset and he was still no nearer to finding those damned cows than he had been earlier that morning. He leaned on his stick and attempted to catch his breath; he was no longer as young as he used to be and he was too old to go tramping the hills and marshes.

And by God, he could use a drink!

He straightened his thin frame and pressed the calloused palms of his hands to his aching back, groaning aloud as the muscles protested. His sharp grey eyes squinted towards the sinking sun, gauging its distance to the horizon: he had at most an hour or so of daylight left. He shrugged; well there was little he could do, he would look beyond the next hill – and then those blasted animals could go hang!

The sun was close to the horizon by the time Andrew crested the low hill. He was breathing heavily and his heart was pounding in his chest. He drew a soiled handkerchief from his pocket and wiped the beads of cold sweat that had gathered on his lined forehead. He shivered as a cold gust of wind blew in off the Atlantic, bringing with it the fresh promise of rain.

Andrew shaded his eyes from the sun's crimson light and stared down into the valley below him. Dusk had already gathered in the hollow and only the very tips of the trees were still touched with light. He shook his head and squeezed his eyes shut: there were tiny red and yellow spots swimming lazily behind his closed eyelids, a sure sign that he had already overtaxed himself and further exertion might bring on an attack.

The old man suddenly breathed deeply, turning his head to catch an elusive odour that had drifted past. He breathed in again and this time he was sure: he could smell smoke on the twilight air. He squinted down into the valley, his sharp eyes seeking any sign of human habitation – but there was nothing ... well, almost nothing. There was a low weed-covered mound beneath a small stand of trees which might once have been a cottage, but now? He blinked: a thin white wisp of smoke climbed upwards, winding through the branches until it reached the red and gold touched tips of the trees and was shredded by the wind.

He prodded the slope with his stick and began the slow and laborious walk down into the hollow.

And behind him the tall grasses parted and cold, black eyes regarded him hungrily.

Andrew had almost reached the cottage – he could see that it was a cottage now, although it was almost lost beneath a covering of weeds and earth, making it seem as if it had been built into the ground or grown from the soil – when a door opened. An old, old man stood in the opening beckoning to him.

Andrew stopped suddenly, his heart beginning to pound painfully again. 'Good evening to you,' he called from where he stood.

The old man nodded pleasantly and spoke in a surprisingly strong and vibrant voice. 'A good even to you. Are you lost?' He spoke slowly, carefully and his voice was almost accentless. 'We can offer you a little food if you hunger and something to assuage your thirst.'

Andrew shivered – there was something about the old man that chilled him to the marrow, but he did seem pleasant and the very thought of food had set his stomach rumbling and his mouth felt dry and gritty. He nodded and approached the old man slowly, his joints beginning to stiffen now. 'I'll thank you kindly for that,' he said carefully, 'I've wandered most of the day in search of a pair of cows that didn't come in for milking this morning and I'm fair exhausted.'

The old man nodded sympathetically. 'You look tired,' he said and then held out his hand. 'James Squire.'

Andrew introduced himself and took the proffered hand and felt it hold his in a surprisingly strong grip for so frail a man. Squire stood nearly a head taller than Andrew – who wasn't small by any means – and he was as thin as a lath. The flesh clung to his body, outlining the muscles and bones beneath, and his head was almost skull-like in appearance with large dark eyes sunk deep into the flesh. His mouth was a thin lipless slit and when he smiled he revealed abnormally long yellowed teeth. His hair was nearly gone and clung in mangy tufts to his scabrous scalp.

He stood aside and allowed Andrew to enter before him, and as the door closed, cutting out the last remnants of the dying sun, the vague stirrings of unease he had previously felt congealed into a hard knot of fear that nestled in the pit of his stomach and gathered behind his throat.

'My wife Morgaine.' James Squire introduced the haggard old woman with skin like ancient parchment, dead and dry, her face a mask out of which her eyes sparkled intently. She pointed a long bony finger at Andrew. 'Who is this?' Her voice was like cracked leather.

'He is a traveller,' her husband said slowly, as if speaking to a child or simpleton. 'He is lost and he hungers. Bring him food and drink.' There was an unmistakable note of command in his voice. He indicated a place by the small fire, suggesting that Andrew should warm himself, for it was growing chill and the hovel was damp and cold and the streaked walls ran with moisture.

Andrew sat by the fire, feeling the heat soak into his face and outstretched hands. He looked about curiously; the large main room of the cottage was filthy, with piles of wood and straw gathered in the darkened corners. Rank water pooled on the hard-packed earthen floor which was rutted and scored. Andrew wrinkled his nose in disgust: the room stank and he wondered if they slept with their animals under the same roof.

Squire returned with a dusty bottle and two chipped cups. He handed Andrew one of the cups filled with an almost clear liquid. He breathed in the fumes, his eyes watering as they stung. He caught the old man looking at him, smiled and swallowed the liquid in one go. He knew what it was even as it burned its way down his throat and enflamed his stomach: poteen. Properly made, it was one of the most potent liquors known to man, but if it had spoiled in any way ... He shuddered and wiped his hand across his streaming eyes.

James Squire smiled, his long yellow teeth glistening wetly in the firelight. 'Brewed it myself,' he said quietly.

Andrew nodded dumbly, finding his throat and mouth still numb from the effects of the poteen. He could feel it in the pit of his stomach, spreading its warmth through his system.

'I dare say you have never tasted anything like it,' Squire said proudly.

Andrew nodded and coughed and when he spoke his voice was barely above a whisper. 'There's no denying that.'

'We will eat soon,' his host said – and then he paused, his head cocked to one side, listening.

'What is it?' Andrew asked, but the old man waved him to silence.

And then he heard it: a low soul-destroying howling that echoed down from the hills. It came again and again, coming nearer, growing in intensity. 'What is it?' he whispered. It sounded like the baying of dogs ... it sounded like the crying of the damned ... it sounded like the howling of wolves – but that of course, was impossible.

'It is the wolves,' Squire said slowly. He carefully refilled Andrew's cup and then went and stood by the door, his hand upon the latch. Connelly watched in growing alarm; just what had he got himself into? Squire was joined by his hideous wife and together they waited on either side of the door, a strange smile playing about their lips, their eyes glassy.

He almost screamed aloud when something scratched at the door. He rose, about to beg Squire not to open the door, when Morgaine turned and looked at him, her teeth bared ... and the look in her eyes chilled him to the marrow: for they were filled with a terrible hunger.

Squire opened the door and a huge grey wolf loped in. It stood almost waist high to the old man and the muscles in its back and calves rippled smoothly beneath its silken fur. It turned its huge head and regarded Andrew through yellow eyes and its cavernous mouth opened, exposing long, glistening yellow teeth.

Andrew felt his heart beginning to pound forcefully and his breath shorten, beginning to come now in harsh gasps. He moved away from the creature, towards the fire, seeking a weapon, anything to use against the wolf. He had left his walking stick down beside his chair, if he could reach that ...

And then the creature growled deep in its throat and the sound froze him in his tracks.

The grey wolf raised its head and howled and somewhere outside an answering cry drifted down across the valley. The grey wolf padded across the room, making no sound on the earthen floor, pushed open the door to the cottage's only other room and disappeared inside.

Andrew stooped as his foot touched the heavy walking stick and his questing fingers brushed the smooth wood. He clutched it in both hands, holding it across his chest and was about to move towards the door and if necessary, strike both Squire and his wife and flee, when another wolf stood in the doorway.

The beast was, if anything, even bigger than the first, a great black-maned wolf who regarded Andrew balefully for what seemed like an eternity before turning and disappearing into the other room.

Andrew gasped as an agonising pain shot through his chest and down into his arm. He could feel his heart pounding strongly as if seeking to burst through his chest. His breathing was shallow and harsh; black spots danced before his eyes in intricate patterns before finally coming together in a solid black tide that rose up and overwhelmed him …

The face was that of a young man … or a woman … or both. Andrew Connelly groaned and opened his eyes fully, attempting to focus on the face – or faces? – looming above him. A strong hand held his shoulders and lifted him forward whilst the chipped cup which he had drunk from earlier was pressed to his lips. He moaned and pulled his head away, but someone spoke softly and insistently to him, 'Drink, it is but water.'

The liquid was ice cold and tart and the shock of it made him gasp. He sat up carefully. He was lying on the ground where he had fallen – had he fallen or had Squire caught and held him as he fell? He seemed to recall …

There was a folded cloth beneath his head and a filthy rug had been thrown over his legs. Squire and his wife hovered in the background speaking in low tones, as if angrily debating a point. And beside Andrew knelt a young man and woman. He had to blink and look again when he saw them, for they were almost identical in every respect, except that the man – although he could not have been above one-and-twenty years – was totally grey and his twin sister was raven. Their eyes were huge and seemingly bottomless, but they regarded him kindly, and the only feature that marred their looks were their overlong teeth.

The young man helped Andrew to his feet. 'You are somewhat recovered?' he asked, his voice totally accentless and with the same slow deliberation of his father. Connelly nodded dumbly. He looked from the boy to the girl and then over to the door leading to the other room. The wolves … where were the wolves? And then he suddenly realised the significance of the boy's grey hair and the girl's night-black tresses.

The girl touched his arm and he flinched and pulled away. 'You have no need to fear us,' she said quietly.

The boy nodded to his sister and they both moved away

from the terrified man. 'You must try and remain calm,' he said quietly, 'lest you bring on another attack.'

Andrew nodded and attempted to regulate his ragged breathing and calm the pounding of his heart. Another attack would kill him.

'Who are you?' he asked, his voice surprisingly calm.

'I am Morgan,' said the young man, 'and this is my sister Morgaine.'

'And the wolves?' Connelly asked quietly.

'We are the wolves.'

Andrew nodded slowly, accepting it as one would accept a dream. He felt light-headed and dizzy and the twins' faces floated in and out of focus with every breath he took.

'We know you,' Morgan said slowly, his voice echoing within Andrew's pounding skull.

'We have met before,' Morgaine said, her eyes looming huge before his befogged vision.

Andrew shook his head, the effort almost exhausting him. 'No ... ' he whispered.

'Yes,' she persisted, 'many years ago ... '

'Do you recall aiding a young dog trapped in a bog ... ?' Morgan asked, his voice and sallow face beginning to fragment into wispy tendrils that scattered like wind-blown smoke.

And Andrew remembered.

It had been late summer with the day darkling towards twilight. The quiet of the evening had been shattered by the piteous howling of a dog and Andrew, returning home from the market, had cut across the fields towards the sound. He had found the animal sinking in an area of marshy ground, but strangely enough, it was not the trapped animal that was howling but another standing at the edge of the bog. Andrew had approached the dogs cautiously. They were a strange breed: large-boned, small headed, one grey, one black. He leaned in over the marsh and hauled the grey dog out by the scruff of its neck. It neither whimpered nor snapped and the black animal had stood silently by whilst he had freed her companion. And before they had run off the black bitch had licked his hand fleetingly.

'I remember,' he said slowly.

'And now we would repay that service,' Morgaine said.

'There is nothing ... ' he whispered.

'You have lost your animals – two cows, nearly a quarter of your herd.'

'We will return them,' her brother added.

'I do not need ... ' he began.

'You need rest,' Squire said. 'Rest.'

Andrew Connelly awoke with the sun on his face. He sat up with a start and then sneezed as wisps of straw fell out of his hair. He realised with a jolt that he was lying in his own barn.

He found the cows waiting outside the wooden shed, standing patiently in the damp morning air. They were not his own animals – in fact, they were like nothing he had ever seen before: they were large-bodied, long-horned cows, but with tiny eyes. And as he found out later that day, their milk yield was phenomenal. Andrew guessed that they were a gift from the werewolves and always ensured that a little offering of food was left on the window-ledge every evening. It was always gone by morning, but he never attempted to watch the takers. And strangely enough, when his neighbours were troubled with foxes and hares later on that year, Andrew's livestock was unscathed.

When he died two years later, the cows disappeared and for many weeks after his death the local people heard the mournful howling of dogs coming from the direction of the graveyard.

CHAPTER 7

CREATURES OF THE WERE: THE HARE

Cathal shivered in the chill pre-dawn air, his breath pluming whitely before his face. He stamped his feet on the hard ground and attempted to restore circulation to his numbed toes, but with little success. He had been standing up against a newly made haystack for most of the night and now he was cold – bitterly cold – angry and just a little bit frightened.

The young man glanced up at the heavens, where a full moon was still riding high even though the sky to the east was paling towards dawn. The stars still glittered as sharply as before, but now they seemed a little more distant and somehow smaller as if the dawn and the coming sunlight shrivelled them into tiny specks. He had watched them wheel across the heavens through the night and he felt a curious sense of loss as they disappeared one by one, taking the magic of the night with them.

He blinked, abruptly realising that it was possible to dream standing up and apparently wide awake, and shook his head; he had nodded off. A tiny sound – loud in the twilight silence – caught his attention and he shifted his grip on the heavy shotgun, his numb fingers curling about the trigger, his thumb resting on the hammers. He pressed in closer to the damp straw and parted a tuft, peering out across the field now glittering with frost. He could see his few cows standing huddled together in the far corner of the field beneath the bare branches of an old chestnut. One moved, her smooth hide scraping against the worn bark of the tree with the dry rasping sound that had alerted him. Cathal slowly released his breath and eased back the hammers on the heavy gun; there was no-one coming to steal his milk – yet! But this morning, he told himself grimly, he would get them, and then ... he patted the shotgun's polished stock.

He had first realised that someone was stealing his milk almost two weeks ago when, for no apparent reason, his cows began to go dry. His father had examined the cattle and pronounced them sound and his bride's father – eager to assist his new son-in-law – had travelled the fourteen miles down from Clonmel to see the animals and he was also of the opinion that they were healthy beasts.

But they continued to give no milk.

When Cathal took them in and kept them in the sheds overnight they gave milk first thing in the morning, but if they were left out in the fields, they were dry.

The evidence was unmistakable: someone was milking the cows in the mornings before Cathal.

Cathal started awake. The sky had brightened perceptibly in the east; it would soon be time for him to milk the animals. A disturbance rippled through the cows and they slowly ambled out from under the shade of the tree – all except one which remained, stifflegged, wide-eyed and shivering slightly. Cathal squinted into the twilight; he could see no-one near the beast, there was noth ... A flicker of movement about the cow's udder caught his attention. There was something there!

Bending almost double, he darted across the field and began to creep along the side of the rough stone wall that separated his land from the road. As he neared the animal, he could hear sucking and lapping sounds, much as a babe makes at its mother's breast. He dropped flat in the high grass that bordered the wall and – ignoring the icy dampness that soaked through his already sodden clothes – began to worm his way towards the cow.

And then he saw it.

It was a hare. A large grey hare sitting beneath the cow on its hind legs and pulling at the milk-swollen teat. Thick yellow milk dribbled from the hare's tiny mouth and ran down its matted chest, pooling at its broad feet. Cathal eased the shotgun forward along the ground and sighted the creature in the centre of both barrels, and then he waited. If he fired now he would disembowel the cow. And so he waited, grinding his teeth in frustration, while the hare drank the animal dry. Several times he was on the verge of pulling the trigger, but the thought of the cost of the cow made him stop and think again.

Then the hare, with an almost human sigh of contentment, hopped away from the empty cow. It paused in the centre of the field and began to groom the droplets of milk from its fur. Cathal fired. The heavy shotgun roared and the blast tore up a sod of earth just in front of the creature. It squealed with fright, leapt straight up into the air, and then it was off, bounding towards the gate. Cathal fired again and the pellets tore into the wooden gate, shattering the bottom bar. The hare twisted and fell heavily, but then it was up and out of the gate. Cathal swore, broke open the gun and, leaving the smouldering cartridges on the hard earth, he reloaded with almost numb fingers. He raced across the field and vaulted the gate, but the hare was gone. Swearing, he bent and examined the damage to the gate, and it was then he saw the blood: tiny reddish-brown spots that clung tackily to his fingertips. He grinned, his teeth a dull grey in the wan morning light and set off down the road following the spoor.

The tracks kept to the edge of the road, leading down into the village and this was strange, for usually these shy creatures avoided the places of man. But the quickly drying blood led down the main street, up past the church and down a lane. The young man grew alarmed – he knew this lane, knew it well. And he knew – somehow he knew – where the tracks would end. His heart was hammering wildly as he stopped before a low whitewashed door. He knocked hesitantly, but received no answer. He knocked again and then pushed the door open with the barrel of the gun.

She was sitting before a low fire, dressed only in her shift, washing blood from a shallow wound along the inside of her leg. She didn't even turn as she heard the door open, but said quietly: 'Come over here, Cathal and look what you've done to me.'

'Why, Aine,' he asked coldly, 'why?'

'Because you went and married that little slut,' she snapped. 'You loved me – you told me you did.'

'That was a long time ago,' the young man said gently.

'You remind me of my late husband,' she said, wincing as she pressed grit from the wound, 'he had a short memory also.'

'Aine,' he said slowly, 'surely you never imagined ... ?'

She turned and looked at him, her large grey eyes hard and accusing. 'What was I supposed to believe? I had just lost my husband, I needed comfort and you were there when I needed you. I never forced you to visit me; I know they may call me a witch in the village, but you came to me of your own free will. And you used me,' she said, her voice cold and deadly.

He leaned over and touched the hare's shrivelled foot hanging on a leather thong about her neck. 'What is this?'

'It is a good luck charm.' Her eyes challenged his, almost daring him to question her further.

'Do you deny that you have taken the form of a hare and suckled my cows dry?' he asked, his temper rising.

Aine's grey eyes flashed in amusement. 'Oh no, I'll not deny it. But no matter what these townspeople think of me, I think they will find that a little too hard to swallow – and just try proving it!' She stood, and the slanting rays of the morning sun touched her thin shift with blinding light, moulding the shadows to the contours of her body. 'And don't think I'll stop, Cathal Mac Thomas; I'll continue until I have ruined you, left you a broken man.' She smiled, a hard cruel smile that only touched her lips.

'I'll spread the word about the town ... ' he blustered.

'And you'll be laughed at,' she said silkily. 'The people here no longer cling to the old beliefs. There is nothing you can do.' She turned away and bent to the fire, ignoring him.

Cathal brought the shotgun up slowly and, holding it at waist level, pulled back both hammers. Aine spun round at the sharp sound and something like fear flashed through her eyes. And then she laughed. 'You don't have the courage to do it ... '

'But it's all I can do,' Cathal whispered. 'It's the only thing I can do.'

The noise of the shotgun blasts was incredible within the confines of the room, but the walls were thick and the cottage was situated a little apart from the other dwellings. There was no-one waiting for him when he left the bloody room, there were no shouts or cries and the only sound on the early morning air was the gentle twittering of a solitary bird.

Some time later on that morning, his wife asked him whether or not he had discovered who was draining their cows and he replied with a curiously glassy smile, 'Only a hare my love, only a hare.'

CHAPTER 8

THE FAIRY MIDWIFE

The child was early. The first spasms struck Roisin suddenly, the abrupt pain doubling her up. She gasped in shock and surprise; the child wasn't due for another three weeks. The young woman staggered as another contraction rippled through her, sending her reeling back against the heavy wooden table. Crockery slid across its polished surface and shattered on the hard earthen floor . . . but the noise was lost as the storm, which had threatened since early afternoon, broke overhead.

A long flash of lightning turned the twilight into noon and thunder rumbled down the valley almost immediately afterwards. The heavens opened, the rain sluicing down in an unbroken sheet. Roisin pushed away from the table as water began to pour in through the open window and sweep across the floor. A sudden gust of wind threw open the door, smashing it back against the stone wall, chips of wood stinging her face and hands. The young woman whimpered with fear as the door tore itself loose from her grasp, slammed back into its frame and tore loose from one of its hinges.

Roisin convulsed as a series of short contractions tore through her, leaving her pain-racked and gasping. She felt real fear then; fear not only for herself, but for the child also. If she were to give birth now, without any preparations or help and alone, then she would surely die.

Lightning flared again, a long jagged streak that came to earth in one of the lower fields, striking an already much charred oak.

Roisin straightened painfully and attempted to push the

window closed. Gusts of chill wind buffeted the glass and an icy rain, laced with chips of hail, hissed and rattled against the side of the cottage. The window flapped in the wind, struck the wall once and then shattered, sending jagged splinters of glass flying in all directions, lodging in her hair, burning her face and forehead. The rain and hail whipped in through the broken glass, soaking her blouse and skirt. She shivered with the cold and then screamed aloud as the pain lanced through her distended stomach. She fell to her hands and knees and hung her head in agony, her gorge rising. Blood dripped from her torn face, spattering on the cold, damp floor. She concentrated on breathing evenly, steadily, trying to calm her pounding heart. Thunder boomed overhead, making the very walls of the cottage vibrate, sending the dresser crashing to the floor, and her last thoughts before she slid into unconsciousness were of her husband, Mark, and their unborn child ...

Mark Farrell shivered beneath the spreading branches of a tree watching the pounding rain turn the already soft autumnal fields into quagmires. Lightning flared nearby, making him start with fright. He knew it was dangerous to stand beneath the tree, but he had no choice, he had been trapped beneath it when the storm had broken. And he had to be home: his wife was into her ninth month and he feared that the storm would frighten her.

Thunder rumbled in off the hills; he could feel it trembling on the air, coming up through the soles of his feet. Lightning cracked and the air was abruptly rank with the metallic taste of ozone. He watched a thin tendril of smoke thread its way skywards beyond the hill and guessed that the ancient shell of the oak tree had been struck once again.

Suddenly, every hair on his head rose and his bare arms itched and crackled. The odour and taste of ozone was strong now and he could feel the pressure building. He looked up into the tree ... and the lightning whoomped in blinding incandescence! The lightning bolt struck the tree directly,

112

charring its dark weathered wood to blackened cinders. The hammerblow struck Mark in the chest, throwing him away from the tree, sending him tumbling into the muck where he lay barely breathing, wisps of smoke rising from his charred and smouldering clothes.

Roisin awoke with a start, staring up at the smoke-blackened rafters in confusion, tiny spots of colour dancing before her eyes. She was cold, and her nightmare had left her covered in an icy perspiration. The last vestiges of that nightmare now drifted into the shadows of her mind leaving only fragmented images in their wake: the storm, the lightning painting the room in harsh white light, slivers of sparkling glass flying into her face; the face.

The face!

A long thin, high-boned face, stark white against the night-blackness of her long hair. The face of a young woman who had stared at Roisin through slitted grey-green eyes...

She closed her eyes and shook her head, attempting to dismiss the images, but when she opened her eyes the face – the face in her dream – swam back into her sight. The thin lips smiled, pulling back over a row of gleaming white teeth.

'Aaah, you are awake?'

Roisin sat bolt upright, the sudden effort making her head swim. It was no dream. But ... she was in her own bed, dressed in her best white cotton chemise, her skin freshly washed and tingling, her hair unbound and brushed. There was a peculiar odour in the room; the metallic harshness of blood mingled with the damp freshness of hot water and ... there was another odour, a scent of wild herbs and raw earth.

And then she realised: she was no longer heavy with her child!

The stranger leaned over and placed a cloth-wrapped bundle in Roisin's arms. The child screamed, its tiny face blotchy, screwed up in anger and fear. The young mother brushed away a tendril of blonde hair and kissed her child's forehead. Tears stung her eyes as she looked up at the stranger. 'Thank you,' she whispered.

The stranger smiled coldly. 'Do not thank me yet,' she said, in a curiously flat and exotic accent.

'Who are you?' Roisin asked.

The hard-eyed young woman smoothed the blankets and turned away. Her voice was hard and contemptuous. 'I am Maresch.'

'But, thank you – you have saved my life and the life of my child.' She looked up from the screaming babe. 'Are you a midwife?'

Maresch glanced over her shoulder at Roisin. 'I have had some experience,' she snapped.

The young woman was a little put off by Maresch's surly attitude, but persisted. 'Have you any children yourself?' she asked quietly.

The stranger rounded on her with blazing eyes. She stared through the young mother for long minutes before turning away and when she spoke her voice was cold and distant. 'No, I have no children.' She turned back to the fire and began to add more turf. The wet sods hissed and gave off a rank smoke which drifted about the room in a gritty haze. Roisin felt her eyes watering and she covered her child's eyes with a corner of the blanket. 'Could you open the door please?' she asked. 'It's very hot and the smoke ...'

The young woman turned and stared at her. In the dimness only her eyes were visible and they blazed with an unearthly emerald fire. 'The window has shattered and the door is still open ...' her voice was sharp, cutting through the haze of exhaustion which had suddenly claimed Roisin. She wiped the palm of her hand across her watering eyes and looked towards the door. It was indeed open, hanging crookedly to one side, but strangely, the smoke and fumes seemed to stay in the room and did not stream out into the evening air.

Maresch stepped closer to the young woman. She looked down at the small bundle clutched to Roisin's breast and held out her hand, the long thin nails catching the firelight and running red. 'Give me the child,' she said. 'It hungers, it needs feeding.'

114

Roisin shook her head slowly. 'No,' she whispered, 'I can feed the babe myself.' She raised her hand slowly, painfully, and attempted to undo the tiny buttons down the front of her chemise. Sweat beaded her brow and her arms trembled with the effort. Her fingers seemed thick and numb and she struggled futilely with the buttons. The haze in the room thickened before her eyes, biting at her throat, coating her mouth and lips with grit. She attempted to swallow, but found that her throat wouldn't work. 'Water,' she whispered.

Maresch leaned over the bed and stared down into her wide eyes. 'The babe; give me the babe. You must give me the babe of your own free will,' she insisted.

'Water,' Roisin begged, 'give me some water.'

'The babe,' the young woman hissed coldly, 'I will feed your child.' She pointed a crimson-tipped nail in the child's face. 'Like you, it thirsts.'

Roisin nodded, a barely perceptible movement of her head and tried to lift the small bundle in her arms. Maresch leaned over and snatched the child from its mother. Her eyes blazed and her smile was triumphant. She held the babe aloft, as if in offering, and then she lowered it and unpinned the neck of her curious dress. A flap of cloth fell away, exposing her smooth flawless breast. She pressed the child to it, stroking its cheek to make it open its mouth ... and the last sounds Roisin heard before she drifted off into unconsciousness were of her child eagerly pulling on the stranger's breast.

When Mark staggered in some hours later he found the cottage a shambles. A window gone, the door half-torn from its hinges, the dresser lying broken on the hard floor beside piles of shattered crockery. Water pooled along the floor and the air was thick and heavy with turf smoke. Strangely enough, his wife was lying in their bed, sleeping peacefully in the gown she had worn on their wedding night. But what terrified Mark was the fact that she was no longer pregnant and there was no sign of the child.

*

The old woman sat in front of the fire sipping raw poteen from a cracked cup and watching the young couple sitting across from her. The only light in the cottage came from the fire and the flames only highlighted their feverish eyes and deepened the shadows in the hollows under their eyes. The old woman shivered as the chill night wind whipped in through the boarded-up window and rattled the crooked door in its frame.

Mark shivered as the cold air traced the length of his backbone and he could feel Roisin trembling beside him. He leaned over and patted her hand, trying to calm her fears as best he could, but knowing that the loss he could see in her eyes was mirrored in his face. He reached for the bottle and handed it to the old woman.

'Nano Hayes,' he said shakily, 'you are our last hope.'

The wise woman smiled, her lined face dissolving into a mass of wrinkles in which her hard eyes glittered like stones. 'Ah sure, you have nothing to worry about,' she said, her voice surprisingly mild and youthful for such an old woman.

'But can you get our child back?' Roisin asked quietly.

Nano Hayes emptied the contents of the bottle into her cup and set the bottle down on the grate beside the fire. She stared thoughtfully into the almost clear liquid and when she looked up there was a strange expression in her eyes, one almost of pity. She nodded, her grey hair dancing with flecks of silver and gold. 'I can bring your child back – but are you sure you want the babe returned?' she added softly, looking at them both in turn. She raised her gnarled hand to still their protests and continued. 'Your babe has suckled the fairy woman, she has tasted the food of Faery, and she is therefore bound to the Otherworld.'

'My child was a girl?' Roisin cried.

'You did not know?' Nano Hayes asked. 'No, but of course you wouldn't have. Aye, she was a girl; a fine lass who would have grown tall like her father, but with her mother's light colouring.'

'How do you know our child was a girl?' Mark asked, holding his wife tightly.

The wise woman smiled enigmatically. 'Oh, I know, I know,' she said quietly. She sipped the raw spirit from her cup, grimacing as it burned its way down her throat and fired her tired blood. 'To continue,' she coughed, 'if I bring back your child, a part of her will forever remain in the Realm of Faery, she will be forever drawn to it, she will never feel at home in this world. And of course, there is no guarantee that the elven folk will not send an *iarlaisi*, a changeling, in her place ...'

'I'll know my own child!' Roisin said emphatically.

The wise woman laughed. 'Perhaps. But there would always be that little doubt that the child you were rearing was not your own. Every time it cried aloud in the night, you would start awake, wondering whether a *bean sidhe*, a fairy woman, would come and take her. Every time she started screaming as children often do, you would wonder if this were one of the signs of a changeling. You would be watching her constantly, wondering, waiting, waiting ...'

The old woman drank deeply, but her eyes never left the young couple.

The young man had come to her earlier that afternoon, sent there by the local parish priest. He was distraught, and his story of a storm, being struck by lightning and his wife's child being taken by a strange, cold woman with eyes of fire might have sounded like the ravings of a drunk or madman to any other listener. But not to Nano Hayes. She was a wise woman, a *mna allthacha*, aware of the country lore, learned about the various herbs and poultices that could be made from the seemingly innocent roadside weeds, one familiar with the ways of the *gentry*, the fairies. She was old; she could remember nearly sixty hot summers and an equal number of bad winters, and there were, she assured people, quite a few that she didn't bother remembering because they weren't worth remembering! But her knowledge, her lore, was traceable back almost to the dawn of time, back to when Banba had led the Caesir, the band of warrior women from the Isle of Meroe in the placid waters of the Nile, to

Ireland's wooded shore. And although many of the younger townspeople looked upon her with disdain, scorning her charms and advice, the older people still came to her when their cows wouldn't drop their calves or the hens stopped laying, or when they had a complaint the local doctor couldn't cure.

She had calmed the young man and, over a cup of tea, listened to his story, questioning him again and again about the storm and especially about the description of the young woman, Maresch.

When he had finished, she had leaned back on the hard wooden chair, her clawed hands clutching the scarred wooden table. 'Your child,' she said at last, her voice so low that Mark had to lean forward to hear it, 'has been taken by the fairies. The storm was brewed by them to keep you away from the cottage. Maresch was a fairy woman, a *bean sidhe*.'

'You must get our child back,' Mark had insisted and Nano Hayes had nodded silently and, gathering a collection of herbs and grasses and some curious knives together with a score of thin glass phials, had ridden with Mark out to the lonely cottage on the side of the pony and trap.

'Why did she take my child?' Roisin asked suddenly.

The old woman's head snapped up; the poteen was making her drowsy. She shrugged. 'I don't really know. No-one knows why the fairy folk take human children. Perhaps Maresch has just lost her own child – and that is a possibility since she was able to suckle your babe. And then again, perhaps she is unable to bear a child – many of the *sidhe* are barren, they are a dying race.'

'I don't care about the elven folk,' Mark snapped. 'I want my little girl back; I will not allow her to live in some Otherworld.'

The old woman laughed. 'That is excellent. Keep that anger, feed it, let it grow inside you and then go out and shout it at the foot of the fairy fort. If the fairies take your threats seriously, then they might just return your child to you.' She paused and then added, 'And then again, they may not; they are a curious folk,' she said wistfully, 'neither humans nor gods, feared by the former and without the latter.'

'I want my little girl back,' Roisin said suddenly, a ragged edge of hysteria coming into her voice.

'As you wish.' The old woman stood slowly, her stiff joints cracking as she stretched. 'I'll pass the night with you if I may. And in the morn, before the sunrise, we'll try and find your little girl. To your beds now, and be prepared for an early start.'

In the still pre-dawn silence the three figures moved quietly along the path and cut across the fields towards the low mound rising out of the earth like a great sea-creature basking in the waves. They sank slightly in the soft earth, the heavy bundles of withes and twigs tied to their backs slowing them down. The old woman walked in the lead, her hard eyes darting to and fro seeking any sign of the other folk who might still be abroad at this late hour, but the approach to the mound was clear and nothing moved except the wind in the grass.

Nano Hayes still carried the black-handled knife with which she had cut the fresh green branches from the trees lining their route. The grey light of dawn ran along the metal dulling the silver, making it glint like iron, catching the runes incised into the almost flat razor-sharp blade. She paused at a gap in the hedge that bounded the field in which the fairy fort rose. Her experienced eyes read the signs, seeking any disturbance in the side of the mound or on the dew-covered grass. But nothing was amiss: the Fairy Host had not ridden forth that night.

The old woman, followed by Mark and Roisin, walked across the field to the low, grass-covered mound. She paced around it, moving clockwise, her gnarled hands brushing at the grass, probing the soft soil. She encircled the mound once, twice and by the third time she was beginning to get desperate: the sky in the east had lightened to pink and salmon. Sunrise was fast approaching.

The sunrise had flamed the eastern horizon but the huge crimson orb had not yet risen by the time Nano Hayes discovered the concealed entrance to the fort. She called Mark over and instructed him to lay his bundle of sticks in the shape of a cross on the spot.

'But it looks no different from the rest of the ground, I can see no entrance,' he protested.

She patted his cheek and chuckled. 'You're not supposed to, you fool. They don't like visitors and they don't put out welcoming mats.'

The wise woman had then circumscribed the mound with a line of sticks placed end to end and had built small bundles at the four cardinal points. She then handed Mark a small bottle of oil and told him to dampen down the sticks, paying particular attention to the four small mounds. And, with a similar bottle of oil, she carefully traced the sign of the cross on the twigs above the entrance.

Then they waited.

Mark stood beside his wife. He could feel her heart pounding against his arm and although the morning was still chill, she was covered with a fine sheen of sweat. He could feel the tension building up inside him, gathering in a hard knot in the pit of his stomach, pounding in his temples. He stared into the east, watching the sky slowly brighten and run with long streaks of liquid colour. And then the slanting rays of the morning sun lanced over the mountains and burnished the tops of the tallest trees with pale gold. It touched the very tip of the fairy mound with a tiny spot of colour – and Nano Hayes struck fire from a flint and set the wooden cross alight.

The flames leaped along the length of the oil-soaked wood, the green bark and sap-laden branches sputtering and hissing, giving off dense clouds of smoke. The fire burned the sign of the cross into the dew-damp earth and then danced outwards around the mound, leaping like a wild creature, consuming all it touched. The lines of wood around the base of the hill sparked and crisped and the mounds at the four cardinal points blazed furiously and then died down

120

to little more than glowing cinders which smouldered intermittently. Thick grey smoke began to drift across the field towards Nano Hayes and the young couple, rolling and tumbling like tangles of wind-blown weed. The fresh morning air was now fouled with the bitter stench of freshly burned wood and boiled sap.

Roisin coughed and buried her face in her husband's arms and he felt his eyes watering as the smoke bit and stung. He looked across at the old woman, but she seemed unaffected by the billowing smoke. She was leaning slightly forward, her hard eyes shining, her head tilted to one side as if she were listening. Once she nodded and Mark could have sworn that he had heard something moving through the grass at the foot of the mound ... but the smoke was too thick and it might just have been the burned wood crackling.

And then he suddenly realised that there was far too much smoke for the small amount of wood they had burned!

Nano Hayes spoke in her curiously youthful voice. But the words did not come easily to her, for her throat struggled to shape a language that was never meant to be spoken by man. It was higher, thinner, sweeter than the speech of man. It vaguely resembled Irish, but a far, far older version of the language Mark spoke; in fact, it was closer in texture and sound to the speech the priests used during the Mass. But it was not Latin.

The old woman's tone changed; it was now demanding, angry. Something moved within the twisting wreaths of smoke – a tall attenuated figure – and was gone. Nano Hayes cried aloud, raised her hands high and seemed to be invoking a god or gods. Slowly, she brought her hands down, palms upwards, her fingers slightly cupped. She crossed her wrists before her face and slowly turned her hands so that the palms now faced the mound. A sharp metallic clang echoed across the field, followed by a slow booming and Mark thought he could make out an oblong area of blackness through the smoke. A light flashed blindingly, like the sun off polished metal and horse's hooves struck sparks from a stone before him. He held his wife tightly to his chest, his eyes widening in horror as a huge shadow loomed up before him ... a shape that might have been a horse and rider.

Nano Hayes dropped her hands to her side and pulled the black-hafted knife from her belt. She sketched a sign in the air before the shadow figure which had now reared up before her and the symbol etched itself into the smoky air in thin lines of silver-white fire. The shadow reared up, terrifyingly huge, monstrously shaped, and retreated back into the shifting smoke, its scream almost too high to register on human ears. Nano Hayes dropped to her knees and plunged the knife deeply into the earth. In the wan morning light she no longer looked like an old country woman slowly killing herself on raw poteen, but rather a creature out of Ireland's misty past, a sorceress with the power of the gods, a warrior-maid about to go into battle. Her face seemed younger, her body thinner, taller, her hair thicker and her eyes ... her eyes wide and compelling.

The silver-bladed knife sliced through the soft earth in a long rectangle. Mark breathed in the fresh odour of wet earth and it suddenly jolted him back to reality. He blinked and blinked again. The warrior-maid no longer stood before him, just an old, wrinkled wise woman, desperately calling upon a power that was never meant to be used by a person of this era, for it was the magic of an earlier age. He could see the dancing blue-white nimbus around her hands and hair, could feel it crackling along the ground, writhing like serpents. It reminded him of lightning, but it was a different power; whereas the lightning had been a raw elemental force, this was a stronger, harsher power – and it was under control. But whether it was controlled by Nano Hayes or the *sidhe*, he could not tell.

The old woman lifted the sod of earth high as if in offering, turning to the four cardinal points in turn, calling aloud in the strange musical tongue. She turned back to the fairy fort and stepped forward. Immediately, the smoke retreated, flowing inwards as if sucked. It clung briefly to her and for a moment it looked as if she were slowly drifting apart as the grey tendrils broke away from her clothes and

122

hair and flowed on into the mound. She took another step forward, another, another ...

The mound loomed out of the retreating fog like an island out of the mists and for a moment Mark thought he saw a huge gaping hole in the side of the fort, illuminated from within with tiny points of glittering light – but then it was gone, leaving only a shimmering imprint on his retina. But faint, faint in the distance and retreating downwards, he imagined he could hear the sound of a horse's hooves striking on stone.

Nano Hayes stepped up to the crisped shape of a cross over the blackened grass. She placed the sod of earth over the centre of the cross and stepped back. She turned and smiled at Mark and Roisin. 'Look,' she said, her voice strained and raw and her eyes weary.

Roisin broke away from her husband and ran past the old woman to the mound, her cry of delight hanging on the reeking air like the sound of a startled bird. She stood, picked something up and turned to her husband, her tears leaving long trails down her smudged face. She held a bundle in her arms. Mark walked across to his wife, doubt immediately forming. He paused by the old woman and searched her red-rimmed eyes. 'Is that our child?' he asked quietly.

Nano Hayes nodded. 'It is the child of your loins, the child of your wife's womb ... but it will never be your child.'

The years passed and the babe grew into a lovely young girl. They had named her Brigid, after Mark's mother, and although he loved his daughter dearly, there was always that little doubt that still niggled. Roisin bore him another daughter some years after the first, but she herself died giving birth, and Mark was forced to bring up the two girls himself.

The small family seemed forever dogged by ill-luck and it was whispered that they had been cursed by the fairies. Mark fell under the hooves of a horse soon after his wife's death and walked afterwards with a limp – and it was that which drove him to drink. His younger daughter, although a beautiful child, was blind in one eye and prone to sickness. And tragedy struck again some eighteen years after Brigid's birth when she was found dead one cold November morning at the foot of the fairy fort ...*

*see: 'Into the Shadowland ...' Irish Folk and Fairy Tales volume one.

CHAPTER 9

THE HAMMER MAN

Frazer brought his gun up as the birds broke from the low scrub and fired off both barrels. One of the long-tailed grouse fluttered and fell spiralling to the wet ground and he could see the dogs splash through the shallows towards the bird. He broke open the gun and let the smoking cartridges fall to the ground, his gloved hands fumbling in his belt for fresh rounds even though he knew it was almost too late in the day for any more shooting. The light was fading fast and low storm clouds, which had been gathering all afternoon, were now massed above the lowering bulk of the Mourne Mountains and the wind from the north was chill and damp. He left the gun open, tucked it under his arm and sloshed through the soggy ground towards his host, Sir Malcome Fitzgerald. He heard a single report of a shotgun down by the trees, followed by a ripple of gunfire as the birds rose again. Another smattering of shots disturbed the late evening and then he heard shouting: the shoot was finished. It had been a good day though; he had bagged a score – perhaps more – of grouse and perhaps a dozen duck.

Sir Malcome Fitzgerald turned as the tall Englishman in tweeds clambered over a fallen tree-trunk and strode across the field towards him. The old warrior noted the younger man's military stride and bearing with approval: it was a damned pity there were not a few more young men like him in the forces now. He handed his gleaming gun to his servant and smiled as Frazer joined him. 'Good shooting John; you caught a couple of tricky ones there.'

John Frazer pushed back his deerstalker with the back of his hand and carefully eased the cartridges from his Purdy shotgun and slipped them back into his belt. 'I missed a couple of easy ones also,' he said quietly, 'and you bagged a couple I never even saw.' He smiled, his teeth startlingly white against the dark tan of his skin.

Sir Malcome laughed. 'Now that, I just don't believe. I think you let a few by deliberately so that an old soldier like myself could try his hand.'

Frazer shook his head. 'Oh, I doubt if I would do that.' He tilted his head as a bracket of shots echoed into the evening air.

The older man shook his head, took off his cap and mopped his bald head with a large white handkerchief. 'Damned fools,' he grunted, 'I doubt if they can even see anything in this light.' He nodded at the lowering clouds. 'We had better be getting back,' he said, 'I know the signs, there is going to be a downpour soon.' He took his walking stick from his servant and marched briskly across the field towards the road.

'Must remind you of India,' he said pleasantly, 'come evening, come rain.'

John shook his head and laughed. 'There is nothing here that even remotely resembles India,' he said, 'the sounds, the colours, the freshness of the rain, the scents on the wind, they are all unique, unlike India where everything is stale, heavy with sweat and heat.' He nodded at the lush fields which bordered the road. 'I can see why you chose to settle here; I might do so myself in a couple of years' time.'

'Take it from me, my boy, don't be in any rush to settle down. Make the most of your youth – see the world whilst you're still young and fit. And remember, when you get to my age, you begin to slow down,' he patted his rotund stomach, 'and you begin to regret all the things you should have done.'

'Do the locals give you any trouble?' Frazer asked, his sharp eyes catching the glint of metal as the other shooters marched across the lower fields towards the road.

'Not me, no. I've always treated the local people with all due courtesy and they respect me for it. Further south though ...' he shrugged. 'Well, there are two sides to every story and I'm not about to go picking sides. It's true that some landlords are overly harsh, but it's also true that some local groups retaliate with equal harshness and brutality. Aah,' the old warrior waved and increased his pace, 'here are the others; let's go look at the day's bag.'

John Frazer stood at his bedroom window watching the full moon paint the wet ground with silver, listening to the water drip from the eaves and trickle down the gutters. It was almost two o'clock in the morning and the house was silent, the tired shooters already abed and the servants just retired. He struck a match and applied it to his pipe, the amber light touching his lean features with shadow, burnishing his blond hair in bronze. He puffed contentedly, leaning against the window frame allowing his tired body to relax, letting his mind wander out over the storm-drenched fields. He breathed deeply, inhaling the pungent odours of tobacco mingled with the damp freshness of the night.

It had been a good day and a good start to his leave. He had arrived in Dublin some two days earlier on leave from India; he had friends in the city and intended passing some time with them before going on to London. However, he had met Sir Malcome Fitzgerald, an old friend of his father's and he and his wife had invited him up to their country estate, away from the busy bustle of Dublin's social scene for a week of fishing and shooting. He found the countryside relaxing and, contrary to what he had heard, the people were friendly, unlike the native Dubliners who were surly and aggressive.

The Fitzgerald estate stood in the shadow of the Mourne Mountains, set in almost a hundred acres of lush grassland, woodland and marshes and it had the reputation for some of the finest fishing and shooting in all Ireland.

John pulled on his pipe, the bowl glowing warmly in the palm of his hand. He relished the silence of the night; there were no tropical birds or insects, beasts or humans crying and mewling outside his window in the stifling darkness;

127

there was no need to sleep beneath a net or else one would wake up in the morning with a mottled blood-flecked skin. And there was no need to sleep with a loaded revolver beneath the pillow or a naked sabre under the bed. He sighed, absorbing the calmness, the peacefulness of the Irish countryside. And whilst he stood by the window, staring out into the moonlit night, the pipe in his hand slowly went out and the tendrils of fragrant smoke died ...

John jerked awake suddenly. He realised that he had fallen asleep standing up, a trick he had learned during his patrols on the wild north Indian border. He twitched uneasily, all his instincts tingling: something had awoken him. He squinted out into the night looking for any unnatural shape or shadow on the light-dappled ground, his ears alert to any unusual sound and his nose seeking strange odours. But nothing moved in the grounds below his window and the air was sweet and clean with just the trace of his tobacco lingering. And the night was silent ... or was it?

He tilted his head to one side, listening. He thought he had heard a ringing ... but that might have been within his head. The young soldier shook his head and massaged his ears – and then he heard it again, and he knew what he was hearing was not inside his head. It was a sharp metallic ringing, as of metal on metal, distinct and musical. He closed his eyes and tried to trace the direction of the sound with his hearing alone. It was ... there!

His clear eyes snapped open and he found himself looking towards the dark, silver-tipped bulk of the Mourne Mountains. He stood by the window for almost an hour listening to the short musical notes tingling on the damp night air. At one stage he went to his bags and brought out his folding telescope and attempted to scan the slopes of the mountains, but the moonlight – even though it was quite brilliant – was too weak for his purposes, and he could see only blurs.

But the sound intrigued him. It awoke echoes deep within him, there was something about it ... something which called ... and called ... and called.

Frazer awoke with first light the following morn. He ate a hurried breakfast alone in the kitchen – much to the servant's discomfiture – and, leaving his apologies for Sir Malcome, set out across the fields towards the mountains, his kitbag on his back, a shotgun tucked under his arm and a loaded revolver in his belt.

As he tramped down the winding country road he puzzled over the conversation he had had with the cook – a small Irishwoman with tiny eyes lost in a huge round face that seemed continually creased in a smile. He had asked her whether there was any industry in the mountains, a quarry or foundry perhaps. She had looked at him strangely and then slowly shook her head.

'Ah sure, there's nothing this side of the Mournes except rock.'

'I heard something last night,' he said, sipping the scalding tea, his eyes never leaving her face. The old cook had stiffened and a mask had come down behind her eyes.

'And what sort of a sound would that have been now,' she had asked casually.

'Sharp and metallic,' he had said quietly, 'do you know of it?'

'Only what the auld folk tell me,' she had said and sat down in the chair facing him. 'And if you're thinking of following it, well then I wouldn't sir, for 'tis the Hammer Man, and many's the one that has followed that sound into the mountains and never been seen again.'

Frazer noted that she was wringing her apron in her strong hands and there had been a note almost of fear in her voice.

'Tell me about the Hammer Man?' he had asked quietly, stirring his tea.

The old cook had shaken her head. 'I know nothing sir, only that it's not safe to go climbing in the mountains. *They* are often to be found in the rocky places.'

'Who are *they*?' he had asked, although he already had some idea. In India he had heard tales of the creatures that lived in the mountains or the secret valleys. 'Demons? Devils?'

129

'The dark ones of the *sidhe*, sir, the dark fairies.'

He had nodded seriously. He had heard similar tales and had travelled far enough to know that there was still a lot that modern science could not explain. In India he had met with an Irish priest who had told him tales of the Dark Continent and the Far Orient that were hard to believe and he would have discounted except that the priest himself truly believed them.

The cook had impulsively reached out and held his hand. 'Don't go sir, don't heed the call of the Hammer Man.'

Frazer had gently extracted his hands and smiled at the old woman. 'Perhaps not then.'

She had returned his smile and then stood uncertainly. 'I used to have a son like you sir, and he used to humour me also, but when he was set in his mind then there was nothing that would shift him. Go then if you must. I'll pray for you.'

'Well I'll thank you for that,' he had said quietly, and then stood and left the kitchen. He didn't see the old woman wiping the tears from her eyes.

The day was warm and dry and his long measured stride covered the ground easily. By noon he was more than half-way to the foothills and he broke his march for a rough and ready lunch on the banks of a lake curiously entitled Silent Valley. By mid-afternoon he was climbing steadily. He scanned the rock face above him with his telescope occasionally, but could see no sign of habitation or even caves that might prove to be the source of the sound – although he guessed he must be close to where it had originated from. He searched the rock face and through the foothills for most of the afternoon seeking any clue – but there was nothing.

Then, as the light began to fade and the shadows lengthen, and he was beginning to contemplate returning, he heard the sound. It struck him like a bullet and rooted him to the spot. It *was* the sharp metallic sound of metal on metal, a steady, almost heart-like beat. It echoed and bounced off the rocks, reverberating, trembling . . . calling.

John Frazer turned and followed the sound of the Hammer Man up into the mountains.

The sound called yet lulled him and he followed it through the evening twilight and on into the night. A part of him knew that what he was doing was foolhardy; in India he had seen men follow voices only they could hear and fall to their deaths, or chase the marsh lights out into the bogs and sink in the mire. But this was different. This was real. It was not a figment of his imagination, neither a delusion nor a dream. Someone was hammering metal above him and he was determined to find them.

The moon slipped out from behind the clouds and spilled its silver-white light across the mountain face and the tiny figure that struggled up the worn and almost non-existent track. But Frazer recognised that he was following a pathway of some sort and he would follow it to the end. He had left his kitbag behind him on the rough track and now only carried the shotgun and pistol – and although the weapons were heavy, he welcomed their comforting weight.

He had been climbing for nearly two hours when the sound stopped.

He had been hearing it for most of the evening and on into the night and it took a few moments for it to sink in that it was gone. Echoes still belled within his head and his pulse now pounded to the same beat. With the sound gone he felt a sense of loss.

He looked around; far below him – he hadn't realised he had climbed so high! – the foothills disappeared into the moon-touched night, whilst above him the mountain still reared up into the purple, star-studded skies. However, the track he had been following led into a cleft in the mountain-side before him and from within the moonlight spilled blindingly on something. Frazer approached the crack in the rocks cautiously. The cleft itself was in shadow and the only sound was the persistent dripping of water and as he moved to one side the brilliant light disappeared. He stood by the entrance for almost five minutes listening and then, satisfied that there was no-one waiting within, he broke open the shotgun and loaded it. Frazer squeezed through the crack and found it suddenly opened out into a smooth pathway that led on downwards. On either side, the dark walls of the cliff rose upwards, whilst overhead the thin purple thread of sky was almost blotted out. Smooth stones rolled beneath his boots, the cliff walls were slimed and damp and he guessed that water had once cut through this crack in the mountain. He occasionally caught sight of the brilliance that had blinded him before, but it wasn't until he had forced his way out of the cleft that he saw the lake.

It was surprisingly large for a mountain-top lake. It stretched as far as he could see, but it was difficult to determine where the lake ended and the land began, for its still surface was dappled with ebon shadows and silver light, and the night hung heavily over the little valley.

A single musical note suddenly rang out from the depths of the shadowed valley. Frazer fell to his knees and thumbed the hammers back on the shotgun. He knelt in the mouth of the cleft, in the shade of a wild gorse and listened. He could still hear ringing, but this time he wasn't sure whether it was within his head or whether there was an actual sound.

A definite bell-like tone rang out again and in the shadows by the lake something flashed briefly and was gone. The silver point of light burned its way across Frazer's retina and even when he blinked he could still make out the vibrating spark. Silence fell again.

He rose cautiously and began to make his way towards the lake. Low clouds scudded in from the west, blotting out the moonlight, leaving him in total darkness – without the moon the night was absolute. In the darkness he splashed into the shallows – and froze, his senses flaring. He crouched in the cold water and listened. And then he suddenly realised that there was no sound: no night-birds called, no insects rustled, nothing moved in the earth or through the bushes. He felt the icy chill of fear along the back of his neck and his heart began to pound in his chest.

The shattering sound broke from almost in front of him, sending the young Englishman reeling backwards. The solid, bitter-sweet cadence was taken up again and the night was rent by the sound of metal ringing on metal.

Frazer pushed himself to his feet and peered through the bushes. For a moment he could see nothing and then the edge of the sinking moon cut loose from a heavy cloud, spilling liquid silver across the lake – and the small figure that stood on its banks. It was a man of medium stature, but muscular with incredibly broad shoulders which somehow made him seem smaller than he actually was. His long hair – silver-white in the light – fell across his shoulders and was held back from his forehead by a thin fillet of metal. His only clothing was a short leather kilt and Frazer could see the muscles in his arms and shoulders bunch and ripple as he lifted the heavy hammer and brought it down on the flat piece of metal he was shaping. He worked solidly, his muscular body covered with a fine sheen of silvered sweat and he seemed unaware of the chill breeze that had sprung up and now whispered through the tree-tops.

The young man looked up suddenly, his dark eyes mirror-bright and glassy in the moonlight. The hammer paused in mid-air and Frazer felt the sudden build-up of tension, an almost tangible force that sent ripples of fear along his spine. He brought his gun up and sighted the young man between both barrels. The hammer came down and pointed – straight towards the bushes! The Hammer Man spoke, the language guttural and rapidly interrogative. The question was repeated more urgently and now the figure took a step nearer the bushes. In his right hand he held the heavy hammer and in his left the long length of beaten metal he had been working, flat and slightly pointed at one end, resembling a sword blade.

Frazer stood, the gun pointing at the young man's chest. His heart was pounding and he felt terribly afraid even though he was facing a naked man armed only with a hammer.

The Hammer Man spoke again, this time in a different language, one that seemed vaguely familiar to the Englishman. Frazer shook his head. 'I do not understand you,' he said slowly and distinctly in English and then he repeated it in French and Hindustani.

The young man stepped closer and Frazer brought the gun up to his shoulder, his fingers tightening on the trigger. The Hammer Man stopped.

'There is no need to fear him, Mister Frazer.'

The Englishman spun around at the sound of the strangely echoing voice and in that moment the Hammer Man stepped in and struck the gun away with his hammer. The shock numbed Frazer's arm and shoulder and the gun discharged with a sound that echoed over the mountains like thunder. He fell to his knees, throwing himself to one side, his right hand groping frantically for his pistol, but the young man followed him down and laid the sharp point of his crude sword against his cheek.

'Do not resist, Mister Frazer.' The voice was high and thin, trembling on the air like a distant echo. 'Togha will not harm you.'

John turned towards the sound of the voice – and found himself looking up at one of the most beautiful women he had ever seen.

She stood, framed in the moonlight under the silver-tipped leaves of an ancient oak and although she was not tall, she exuded a presence, an aura, of absolute power and confidence. She stepped out from the shade of the tree and her long, low-cut gown flashed and scintillated in the light, almost the same shade as her white-gold hair. She smiled, white teeth showing through thin red lips, but her eyes remained hard. And when she spoke again, Frazer realised that she did so without using her lips.

'Why have you come here?'

He sat up, nursing his numbed arm. 'I followed the sound,' he said slowly.

'But surely you were warned not to,' she said, and he realised that her voice had the same slightly ringing tone similar to that of metal on metal.

'I was curious,' he said, slowly rising to his feet. 'The sound called me.' He was conscious of the young man standing behind him, the sword still resting on his shoulder with the point against his cheek. He could feel the roughness of the metal against his skin and whilst the blade had not yet been honed, the point was quite sharp.

'Who are you?' he asked the woman.

She smiled and stepped closer to him, her delicate perfume engulfing him, making his senses tingle. 'I am Delgrade,' she said, her voice echoing in his head, 'queen of the Partholonians, once of Scythia.'*

'Scythia?' he said dumbly, 'but ...'

'Do not tell me it is gone and do not think me mad. I was once the wife of Partholon, who led his people to this land three hundred years after the Great Flood cleansed this world of all life!'

Frazer forced a laugh, but a slow, cold terror was gradually taking hold of him. 'But that would make you ... thousands of years old.'

'Would it?' she said wistfully. 'I do not measure time as you do. But yes, I am old ... and weary.' She smiled up at him and her hard blue eyes were like polished stones.

Frazer breathed deeply, trying to calm the terror that threatened to send him screaming out into the glassy waters of the lake. 'What happened to the rest of your people?' he asked.

'We were of their race, but they were not our people!' she snapped, her voice crashing through the innermost recesses of his mind like the sound of the sea on a rocky shore. 'They cast us out, they renounced us ...' And then she screamed and Frazer cringed with the sound. 'But they are dead now and we remain! The plague took them, the plague that grew from my husband's body. We could see the fires burning in the south, sending up thick black smoke by day and brightening the night with the flames of the pyres and often the wind would carry the stink of roasting flesh ...' Her voice was harsh and broken now and her eyes danced with madness. The Englishman stepped back away from her until he felt the pressure of the blade begin to cut against his cheek.

'Why do you remain?' he asked, playing for time, trying to keep this wild madwoman talking.

*see 'The Dawn' - Chapter 1 Irish Folk and Fairy Tales - volume II.

Delgrade stepped away from him, turned and stared out over the lake. 'We remain,' she said, her voice now nothing more than a wind-carried whisper that trickled through his brain, 'because we are the children of the gods, and like our fathers, we are both immortal and vulnerable.'

'Vulnerable; how?' he wondered. 'I thought the gods were invincible.'

'The gods need the worship of men to survive, they feed off that worship, like the harpies off the souls of men or the vampire from the blood of virgins. We remain here because time has no meaning in this valley; here it is still the dawn of the world, within this valley our gods still live; here we are nurtured and protected. Were we to venture beyond the valley we would surely die – or else our minds would crack beneath the strangeness of the new world that has arisen. ...' Her voice faded and drifted off into fragments and Frazer knew that she was weeping silently.

'And the Hammer Man ... Togha?'

She glanced over her shoulder, her eyes silver discs in the moonlight. 'He was my lover once – a whim, a brief whim, but it was because of him I was cast out of the Partholonian camp – and it is because of him that I still survive today. I owe him much: my disgrace and my life.'

'Why does he hammer metal?'

'He was – is – a smith; it is all he knows and there is nothing else for him to do.'

'And you?' John asked, 'what do you do?'

Delgrade laughed aloud and the Englishman could hear the bitterness, the sadness, the loneliness in her voice. 'You could say that this valley is my garden, I tend it,' she said. And then her voice cracked and took on a new note. 'And like all good gardeners, I must weed it out.'

Frazer felt the fear congeal along his spine and settle into his stomach.

'Togha's work often brings people to me; oh, not so many as before of course, but enough.' She turned and faced him, her eyes blazing with a cold inner fire. Her tongue darted out and wet her lips and he was suddenly reminded of a snake about to strike. 'You see,' she continued, 'no-one must know of us. They would come to look and stare and their very presence would contaminate and eventually slay us. Even you, with your woven clothes, your weapon of steel and fire, your boots of leather, your device that measures time, even you have brought a little of your time into our valley, even you have aged us a little, even now, you are killing us!'

'But you cannot remain this way for ever,' Frazer said quickly, 'this is a small country, you will be found sooner or later. The world will find you.'

'But there is a time coming when the world will return to its former beauty, a time when the machines and artifacts of man will no longer dominate, a time when the old gods will arise again, a time when we can go forth into the world. A time of killing!' She stopped suddenly, her breathing harsh and ragged and then she spoke quite casually to Togha in their own tongue, but her meaning was clear.

Frazer kicked backwards with his foot, felt it connect with the young man's shin and threw himself forward. The crude sword whistled over his head, parting his hair. Frazer rolled as he fell, his right hand tugging the pistol from its holster. He jerked aside, almost losing his grip on the pistol, as the sword flashed out of the night and spun by his side, embedding itself into the soft earth. Frazer fired. His first shot went wild, but both Togha and Delgrade fell to the ground and melted into the night. He fired twice into a clump of bushes where he had last seen Togha, heard the first shot ricochet off stone and then the gasp of pain as the second shot struck home. He began to ease his way backwards, intending to make for the cleft in the cliffs. Something cracked behind him and he rolled over and fired instinctively. Both shots took Togha high in the chest spinning him around, sending him crashing back into the undergrowth.

A sudden lance of pain ripped through him, squeezing his head in a vice. He dropped the gun and held his pounding head in both hands attempting to relieve the pain. He was aware that it was intensifying, threatening to rip his skull apart. Through pain-filled eyes he saw Delgrade approaching slowly. Crimson bursts of agony rippled across his bulging eyes, blinding him and when he could see again, Delgrade was kneeling by Togha, cradling his head in her arms.

And for a fraction the pain disappeared. The Englishman rocked backwards with the cessation of the pain and his hand touched the cold metal of his pistol. And suddenly Delgrade was upon him, Togha's hammer clutched in both hands. Frazer tried to roll aside and fire at the same time. The hammer came down and he heard his shoulder bones crack with sickening pain. His hooked fingers tore into the soft earth as he waited for the killing blow to descend.

But it never came.

When Frazer awoke some hours later, the morning sun was striking fire from the easternmost peaks of the valley. The air was damp and chill, but he was bathed in a burning fever. He tried to move, but black waves of pain rose up and threatened to overwhelm him. He wondered why the madwoman hadn't killed him. Some time later, when he did manage to move without blacking out, he discovered the small body of Delgrade, queen of the Partholonians, lying in the long grass, stiffening in the crisp morning air, a small hole beneath her breast, Togha's hammer still clutched in her long-nailed fingers.

'Here! He's here!' A lantern was held above his head and a pale face, framed by the distant stars, peered down at him. And then Sir Malcome's broad face swam into view. The old soldier knelt down beside him, his eyes wide with concern and his face tight with worry. 'My God man, what happened to you.'

Frazer coughed and spat blood, images of his nightmarish descent down the mountain still flashing behind his eyes. He had had plenty of time to think of his answer. He coughed again and swallowed a little of the brandy from the flask Sir Malcome pressed to his lips. 'I was climbing,' he whispered and attempted a smile, 'I fell.'

CHAPTER 10

THE LOVERS' REWARD ... I

They lay in the long lush grass, feeling the gentle breeze caress their naked bodies with silken fingers and dry the sweat of their lovemaking. It was late afternoon and the sun was beginning to sink down behind the trees, throwing long shadows across the little pool and the tumbled stones that encircled it, calling forth the mystery of the place. In the distance a bell began to toll.

'Peter ...?' She ran gentle fingers down the side of his throat and ruffled the hair on his chest. He stirred lazily, opening his eyes slightly, his lips curving in a slight smile.

'Mmme?'

'It's late,' she whispered, 'I must go. No!' She pulled away from him as he reached for her again. 'I must go; Donal will be home soon.' She leaned over and kissed him swiftly, her full breasts brushing his chest, and then she stood, the slanting rays of the sinking sun touching her smooth skin in shades of crimson and bronze.

Peter Casside lay back and watched her dress, admiring the way she moved, the ripple of muscles across her back and along the length of her thighs, the pout of her breasts. She caught him looking and smiled gently. 'Tell me,' she said, almost absently, 'has Michael been asking any more questions?'

Peter rose on his elbows and stared across the quiet waters of the little pool. 'I think my brother is jealous of you ... me ... us,' he said and shrugged. 'He even warned me to stay away from you – said you were dangerous.' Peter looked up and smiled wickedly, 'Oh, and I could have told him just how dangerous!'

He pushed himself to his feet and pulled the young long-haired woman to him. He could feel his body responding to her nearness, feel the tingle of her fingertips as she traced his backbone. 'Sorcha,' he said quietly, 'what did you do to frighten him? There was a time when he wouldn't allow a word to be said against you ...'

She pressed her nails into his back and nestled against his chest. 'I did nothing – except choose you,' she added.

'But you married MacIntee,' he reminded her.

Sorcha pulled away from the young man and allowed a hard note to creep into her voice. 'I told you before; Donal is a very rich man. When he dies which, with his heart, should be very soon now, all that will be mine ...' She stepped closer to him and breathed gently, '... ours!'

Peter shook his head and turned away, looking for his clothes in the long grass. 'It's been almost two years Sorcha, and he is still as strong as ever.' He found his trousers and stepped into them. 'He sickens me: he is an animal, a gross pig, and the very thought of him ... and you ...'

Sorcha laughed quietly. 'You fool; didn't you know that he's been impotent since the first night of our wedding?' She continued mockingly. 'Mother gave me a little recipe which ensures that he is as potent as a gelding.' Her eyes locked with his and her full lips curled back from startlingly white teeth. 'Why do you think I need you so much, eh?' She pulled her shawl about her shoulders and, without a backward glance, followed the winding path around the pool that led down towards the village.

Peter Casside stood and watched her go, his damp shirt clutched in his large hands. A cloud obscured the sun and a shadow raced down the path after her and wrapped her in its embrace. He was suddenly conscious that it was very cold.

'And what then ...?' Michael Casside leaned back on the hard wooden chair and brought his paper and pencil around so that the wavering firelight could send dancing fingers of light across the page.

The old woman sitting across from him was almost lost in the shadows and only the pale oval of her face and her glittering eyes were visible. She shifted on the stool and spat into the fire. 'And so the Tuatha De Danann retreated into the hidden places, the shadowed isles, the deep barrows, for their time was past and the Age of Man had come ...' her hoarse voice faded to a rough whisper.

'Do they live there still?' Michael scribbled rapidly and looked up from the page, pencil poised.

The old woman laughed, a rough bark more animal-like than human. 'Oh, there are some that claim they do. They say the elven folk live apart from man except on those occasions when they sally forth in search of a wife or child. I have never seen one of the Shining Ones myself,' she added, 'but I have witnessed some of their servants, the creatures men call the *leprechaun* and the *Fir Dearg*.'

'Then they exist,' Michael insisted.

'Oh, they exist. They are not as you would imagine them – they are mis-shapen and ugly – but aye, they exist ...' The old woman broke off as the door opened and a stray gust of wind sent smoke and cinders wheeling about the small dark room. 'Who is it?' she called querulously.

'It's me, mother.' Sorcha dropped a bundle of wood by the door, crossed the room and kissed her mother. She gasped in surprise when she saw Michael and forced a smile to her lips. It was eerily frightening how alike Peter and Michael were; they were identical twins and the only way she could tell them apart was by the colour of their eyes, for whilst Peter's were dark, almost black in certain lights, Michael's eyes were colourless, mere alabaster ovals with just the faintest, faintest trace of pupil. But he was not blind.

Michael nodded stiffly. 'Sorcha,' he said quietly. 'How are you, how's Donal?' he added maliciously.

'I am very well and my husband also,' she said, stiffly formal. Then she added with a thin smile, 'How's that brother of yours?'

'Well, thank you.'

'Is he working?'

'He keeps busy.' Michael stood and nodded to the old woman. 'It's late now, I must be going – I'll see you tomorrow.'

Mother Cleirigh cackled. 'Tomorrow then ... and bring something with you; it's thirsty work all this talking.'

'I'll bring something.' Michael Casside promised.

Sorcha waited until she heard the sharp ringing sound of his footsteps on the path before turning to her mother. 'He is dangerous.'

The old woman stood and, leaning on her walking stick, hobbled over to the window to watch the tall thin figure disappear down the long winding road towards the town. 'We need him,' she said softly, 'the affinity between him and his brother is very strong.' She glanced over her shoulder. 'And what of Peter?'

The young woman smiled broadly. 'He's mine – he will do anything I tell him.'

Mother Cleirigh nodded. 'We are now nearly into October; I think it's time to remove Donal MacIntee – your loving husband.'

'Good; when?'

The old woman returned to the fire and eased herself onto the stool. 'Soon, soon. There remain some herbs to be gathered. On Samhain Eve then. And Sorcha,' she added, 'use Peter; it will be the ultimate test of his devotion to you.'

'And what of Michael?'

'As long as I can keep him here and supplied with titbits of folklore and legend, he is perfectly happy.'

Sorcha still looked undecided. 'Does he suspect?'

'About you and his brother? I think so. But as long as you and Peter remain discreet, he will say nothing.'

'We will,' Sorcha assured her mother.

'Good. Will you be seeing him tomorrow?'

'Of course. His appetite is insatiable,' she smiled.

'Start working on him tomorrow then, but gently, gently. You have nearly a month to bring him around to our way of thinking.'

Sorcha grinned. 'I know what to do.'

Her mother glanced across at her. 'I'm sure you do,' she said sharply. 'I'm sure you do.'

The candle had almost burned down to a stub by the time Michael pushed back the chair and rubbed his aching eyes. It was the small hours of the morning and he had spent several hours transcribing the material old Mother Cleirigh had given him. He patted the small bundle of paper covered with his neat precise hand, experiencing a sense of satisfaction. He picked up a blank sheet of paper and dipped his pen in the thick black ink. In the centre of the page he wrote: *'The Tale of Nuada Silver Hand',* and under that *'The Tuatha De Danann'.* He placed the page on top of the bundle and stood up, rubbing his stiffened back and neck.

Glancing outside, he was startled to see how high the moon was, and he suddenly realised that Peter wasn't home yet. He smiled self-consciously. Peter was almost a grown man now; he wasn't a child that needed constant looking after. Undoubtedly, he was out drinking with some of his friends or ...

He shrugged. Well, it was none of his business. He pushed open the door of the cottage and stepped out into the night, breathing in the chill air. The wind was blowing in from the sea, carrying with it the heavy tang of salt and he could see the silver thread of the Atlantic far in the distance. He leaned back against the door jamb and allowed the tension to seep from his body.

Strange images flashed before his fatigued eyes, images born of the tales old Mother Cleirigh had told him through the long afternoon. He saw the Tuatha De Danann as they once must have been: godlike creatures, proud and commanding. He saw their heroes and heroines sally forth to do battle with the demons from the north, saw them return triumphant. He saw their king Nuada, his silver hand fashioned by Goibniu the Smith and fitted by the magic of Diancecht the Physician, leading his forces out against the Fomorians in the Last Battle of Mag Turiad. He

saw the king's head shorn from his body by Balor, the one-eyed king of the demons, saw it tumble bloodily through the air ... but when it rolled to a stop, Michael found himself looking at the severed head of his brother.

He jerked back to reality with a startled gasp. He was soaked in a chill sweat that was already drying on his body, making his teeth chatter and sending shivers down along his spine. With a last glance down the deserted path into the village, he turned and entered the cottage.

When he awoke in the morning he found Peter's bed empty and although the sheets had been disturbed there was little evidence that his brother had slept in it. He pressed his hand against the straw mattress, but it was cold and dry.

He made a leisurely breakfast whilst re-reading his notes from the night before and then he moved about the small two-roomed cottage, generally tidying and cleaning up. His mother, who was spending a few days with her sister in Cork, would be arriving home sometime later that day. He moved stiffly, slowly working the exhaustion from his bones. He had slept badly the night before and his dreams had been troubled by the image of his brother's severed head. However, a new element had been added: above the head a huge crow had flapped – one of the Morrigan's creatures, the Goddess of Death ... – and the crow had Sorcha's face.

It was almost noon when he made his way down through the town towards the Cleirighs. Summer had come and drifted into autumn, but the summer weather lingered and the air was still warm and balmy, and although some withered leaves whispered along the ground, many of the trees were still in leaf. He breathed deeply, savouring the almost spring-like air; there was a name for this type of weather, Indian something ... some of the townspeople said that it forewarned a harsh winter – and an equal number said it promised a mild winter! So much for weather lore.

He bought a bottle of cheap whiskey in the local pub and

144

stuck it in his pocket beside his notebook and pencils. He walked down the main street and out of the town, past the cross-roads – reputed to be haunted – and cut across the fields towards the mean cottage tucked away behind a thin copse of spindly trees.

The old woman was bending over the fire when he entered, stirring a large fire-blackened cauldron. Michael smiled slightly; she looks like an old witch, he thought as he breathed in the sharp, but not unpleasant odour emanating from the pot.

'What are you cooking?' he asked suddenly.

Old Mother Cleirigh screamed and spun about, her long ladle raised threateningly. The young man stepped back from her, the look on her lined face chilling him to the bone.

For in that instant, he had glimpsed raw power and hate burning in her eyes, such that he thought was impossible in a human being.

And then she relaxed and the light died from her eyes. She looked at the ladle in her hand and chuckled self-consciously.

'Now look what you've gone and done – you've frightened the life out of me.' Shaking her head, she turned back to the fire and resumed stirring the pot.

Michael composed himself and repeated the question.

The old woman cackled. 'I'm brewing a little something for Sorcha – or rather, for her man.'

Michael felt an icy chill touch his heart. 'What is it?' he wondered aloud.

'Oh, a little something to help him ...' She paused and saw his look of incomprehension and continued. 'The man's impotent!' she snapped. 'And what use is that sort of man to a woman, eh? Well I'll cure him.'

Michael bent over the pot and breathed in the thick vapour. 'What's in it?'

'What does it smell like?' Mother Cleirigh asked.

'Liquor of some sort.'

'It's brandy,' she said, 'with orange peel, wormwood, snakeroot, cochineal, saffron and gentian root added.'

'Will it work?'

'Of course; provided it is prepared properly, it never fails.'

Michael stepped back from the pot, rubbing his watering eyes. 'Where did you learn all this?' he asked.

'My mother instructed me, as her mother instructed her; the charms and cures are part of our heritage going back generations.'

'Do you know any more?' he asked, pulling his notebook and pencil from his pocket.

'There is a cure for every disease, a herb for every ill. They grew from the body of Miach, son of Diancecht, sorcerer-physician to Nuada of the Silver Hand ...' She glanced over her shoulder at him. 'Do you know the tale?'

'Of Nuada, yes, but not of Miach and the herbs.' He reached into his pocket and passed the bottle of whiskey over to her. 'Here; drink and tell me.'

The old woman knocked the top off the bottle by tapping it against the stone mantel and then poured the clear and deceptively innocent-looking liquid into a dirty cup. She sipped the fiery liquor and gasped and, as she continued stirring she began to speak in a sing-song fashion, and strangely, her voice lost its aged harshness and dry cackle and became smooth and rounded, her phrases polished and well modulated ...

'Now some time after Diancecht had fitted the silver hand to Nuada's arm, the physician's son came to the king and told him that he could fashion a hand that would far surpass the creation of metal and silver wire that the king wore.

But the king was wary of the youth and questioned him further. 'Tell me,' he said, 'what you have done that your father cannot do.'

And Miach replied. 'There was a young man I knew who had lost his eye in a hurling match and had been forced to wear a patch to cover the gaping hole in his face. So I took the eye of a cat and fixed it in place of the lost eye and

146

breathed life into it and henceforth that man could see from that eye.'

'And what he does not tell you,' said Diancecht, coming up behind his son, 'is that the young man never had a night's peace again and was eventually driven insane. For, although my son had taken the eye from the cat, he had not taken the cat from the eye. It still retained its hunting instinct and at dead of night it would always snap open at the sound of the scurry of a mouse or the rustle of the wind through the long grass. It would follow the passage of a flight of birds more readily than the flight of an arrow.'

'But I had given him what you could not: sight,' said his son.

And Nuada remained silent until at length, he said, 'But if it were possible to have a hand of flesh and blood again . . .'

'It is impossible,' Diancecht protested, 'and if you remove the silver hand I have fitted you with, then it will be impossible to replace it again.'

'Trust in me,' Miach said, 'I can replace your hand.'

'Then I want nothing to do with this,' the physician said and turned on his heel and walked out.

And Nuada leaned forward and grasped the young man's jaw in his metal fingers and squeezed slightly. 'You are gambling with your life on this,' he said.

And so Miach took Nuada's severed hand which had been preserved in alcohol, and boiled it until every shred of flesh had dropped away and it was naught but bare bones. He then covered the bones with the blood of a virgin maid and the first seed of a young man and set it in a box wherein spiders lurked. The following day, the spiders had woven a web about the hand and the blood and seed had dried and hardened into something that resembled flesh. And then the young man had taken the hand and placed it against his breast so that his heartbeat might echo into it. This done, he coated the hardened hand with a mixture of wet ash and soot and left it to dry. A day later he brought it forth into the fresh morning air and washed the dirt off in the dew and dried the hand in the first rays of the morning sun.

And then he joined it to the king's arm.

It was perfect in every way: the skin soft and pliant, without blemishes, the nails long and rounded and the veins thick and alive, pulsating and throbbing. Nuada held his arm aloft, flexing and unflexing his fingers, watching the wrinkles and creases appear and the whorls and circles etch themselves into his fingertips.

'It's alive,' he cried.

But Diancecht was jealous of his son's success and, drawing his sword, struck his son across the forehead. But Miach healed the wound with his powers. Again his father struck his son and once again Miach healed the wound. And then Diancecht, grasping the sword in both hands, brought the weapon down on his son's head, almost severing the skull into two parts. And this wound Miach could not cure and he died.

And when they laid him in the earth a strange thing happened. For out of the barren ground, 365 herbs and healing plants grew, one for each joint and sinew of his body and each one with the power to cure the ills of that part of the body.

And then Aermaid, Miach's sister, carefully plucked each one and labelled it according to its nature, but Diancecht came and tore the labels from them and tossed the herbs about until they were hopelessly mixed and confused and there was no telling them apart ...'

The old woman's voice faltered and the familiar harshness crept back into it. She drank again from the cup and added, 'Oh, over the years, the druids and later the wise women, re-discovered some of the herbs and their uses, like elder for the shivers, daisy for the eyes, a gooseberry thorn for styes, the bark of an elder tree for a burn or hemlock to cause love ...' She shrugged, 'There are many such.'

'Didn't Diancecht prepare a special cauldron of herbs before the Battle of Mag Turiad?' Michael asked.

'He did; and all those who suffered wounds were bathed

in the cauldron and came out of it whole, their wounds healed.'

'Surely he could have healed Nuada's hand that way also?'

'Aaah, but the king had had his hand struck away. Had it only been wounded then it might have been healed. But whereas the cauldron could heal what was there, it could not replace what had already been lost.'

The young man scribbled frantically, the scrape of his pencil across the paper the only sound in the cottage beside the crackling of the fire. 'Are there special times for picking herbs?' he asked when he was finished.

'Herbs should be picked on Beltine Eve in the name of the New God if they are intended to be used for good and on Samhain Eve if they will be used in ... other work. Some are best picked at the dead of night, whilst others must be plucked with the first light of dawn or at midday ... *Sorcha*!'

Michael shifted in his seat, surprised to see the young woman standing in the doorway. The light was behind her, so he could not see the expression on her face, but he had the impression that she was angry.

'Mother!' She crossed the room in long strides, tore the bottle from her mother's hand and tossed it into the fire where it exploded in a roar of flames. She rounded on the young man. 'How dare you bring alcohol into this house.' Her voice cracked in the silence and her eyes, illuminated by the leaping flames, were chill and hard. 'I think you had better leave.'

'I don't understand ...' Michael muttered.

'I would not expect you to,' she snapped.

Michael breathed deeply, trying to calm his rising anger. 'I meant no harm – and your mother does not seem adversely affected by the drink.'

Sorcha placed her hands on her hips and her eyes locked with his. For a moment the tension between the two was almost palpable, an almost physical entity that threatened to engulf them both. And then Michael lowered his eyes, breaking the contact that had seemed almost too intimate. Sorcha laughed maliciously and turned away.

'Drink loosens my mother's tongue,' she said, without turning around.

'But your mother has told me nothing untoward. All I'm interested in is the folklore of our country ...'

She turned and took a step closer to him. 'And why, may I ask? What do you hope to gain by it; what use is it to you?'

'I will gain nothing by it,' he protested, surprised by the venom in her voice. 'It is interesting ... and it should not be lost.'

'I don't believe you,' Sorcha said coldly. 'There must be another reason. Now go!'

Michael looked over her shoulder at the older woman for support of some kind, but she had turned her back on him and was slowly stirring the contents of the bubbling pot.

He nodded slowly. 'I see,' he said, not sure that he did. 'I'm sure you do.'

He stuck his pencil in his pocket and crossed to the door, conscious of the young woman's mocking gaze on his back. As he stepped out into the early afternoon, he heard a low laugh behind him and Sorcha called after him, 'Give my regards to your brother.'

All-Hallows Eve.

The time of year when the boundaries between this world and the next weaken and the dead rise and walk amongst men. A time of year hallowed back into the distant past, honoured as Samhain, the new year. A time of year hallowed by both the followers of the Christ and those who still kept faith with the older, wilder gods.

A time of power. A time of death.

When Peter opened his eyes, he found Sorcha already awake, sitting up in bed, staring at him with a strange look in her eyes. He smiled sleepily and, pushing himself closer to her, rested his head against her midriff, beneath her breasts. Her long slender fingers gently stroked his sweat-curled hair and traced the curve of his neck, sending electric tingles racing down his spine. Beneath the blankets, his free hand moved slowly up the length of her leg, fingertips circling and encircling her warm flesh. He could feel his desire rising as his heartbeat quickened. He reached for her and pulled her down across him ... and then his breath caught as he noticed the long weal that ran down her left side beneath her breasts.

He traced its length with his fingertips. 'Who did this?' he whispered.

'Who do you think,' she said bitterly.

'I didn't notice it last night; when did he do it?'

She pushed herself off him and folded her arms across her breasts, her fingers clutching her sides as if she were cold.

'Oh, it was there, you were just too busy to notice it,' she said. 'He did it yesterday morning. I angered him, so he hit me – with the edge of his belt.'

Peter felt the slow bubble of anger begin to seep through him. He sat up and examined the mark carefully. It was a long weal, nearly four inches long and about an inch wide, the skin red and angry, slightly puffed around the edges. 'Bastard! Why did he hit you for God's sake?'

Sorcha laughed bitterly. 'Why? Does he need a reason? Oh, it was because although we've been married nearly two years now, he's never been able to consummate our marriage. Oh, he's tried ...' she smiled coldly, 'but as I've already explained, one of mother's little cures ensures that he never will.' She shrugged, the movement rippling the muscles in her torso. 'But yesterday he insisted – and he tried and he failed. He just wanted someone to take his anger out on; so he took it out on me.'

'I'll kill him,' Peter swore. 'I swear it – I'll kill him.'

'Brave words,' she mocked him gently, 'but you can do nothing for me.'

His hands tightened on her forearms. 'I swear it, I will do anything for you – even if it means killing him. I will not allow him to mistreat you.'

'Will you?' she breathed.

'I will.'

Sorcha leaned over and kissed him gently and then she

151

pulled a small bottle from beneath the pillow. The morning shafts of sunlight caught the bottle and held it, turning the dark liquid within ochre, sparkling from tiny flecks that circled slowly within the liquid.

'What is it?' he asked.

'It is a cure for potency!' She laughed at his shocked expression and then she laid a finger across his lips and her voice turned cold and urgent. 'Now listen to me, my love, and if you truly love me, then you will do as I say. Will you listen?'

She waited until he nodded slowly and then continued. 'This night is Samhain Eve – All-Hallows Eve, one of the Four Great Sabbats of the Old Faith, and the night when the dead walk.

'Now Donal is intensely superstitious and he will spend the night securely locked indoors, drowning his fears in a bottle, starting at every little scratch and knocking in the rafters and generally trying to drink himself into a stupor by early evening.

'But what I intend to do tonight is add a little of this,' she raised the small bottle, 'to his food.'

'But why?' Peter protested, 'what good will that do?'

'It will arouse in him an intense desire and, coupled with his long abstinence, a desire that should prove overwhelming.'

'But he will take you.'

'No. He will not take me. As soon as his lust is aroused – and I will do my best to aid him in that – he will come for me ... and I will flee into the night.'

'And ...?' Peter prompted.

'And he will follow,' she said quickly. 'Now, the drug will only last a short time and soon his old fears will take over ... and all we have to do is make sure those fears claim him. All we have to do is frighten him to death!'

Peter caught his breath. Oh, he had often thought of killing the old man. He was an animal, a beast; he deserved death. But certainly nothing so clever as frightening him to death – shooting him in an "accident", pushing him into the pond or sprinkling some of the poisonous mushrooms on his food. Somehow, actually terrifying the old man to death was ... different and to hear it spoken of in the cold light of dawn was somehow cruel ... and terribly frightening.

'And with him dead,' Sorcha continued, 'it will be just you and me and his money. We will be rich; we can move from here, go to Dublin or London or even Paris. Just you and me. Will you do it?'

Peter stared at the small glass bottle as if mesmerised ... for in the morning sunlight, the liquid was slowly taking on a blood-red hue, but then Sorcha tucked it back beneath the pillow and gripped both his shoulders, staring deep into his eyes.

'Will you do it for me?' she whispered gently.

He nodded slowly, the decision forming somewhere deep within him, but although he nodded, he could not dispel the idea that he was merely acting out a part and that the decision had never really been his to make in the first place.

Sorcha breathed her thanks and then gently pulled him across her body. Her legs opened in invitation as he settled between them and took his pleasure from her body.

But had he seen her a few moments later as the height of his passion swept him aloft to a shattering culmination, he would have seen such a look of disgust and triumph mingled on her face that perhaps his decision would have been different.

Donal MacIntee huddled over the fire, a plate on his knees, shovelling the food into his mouth. A bottle of whiskey stood on the floor beside him, already one-third empty. He was a short, squat man running to fat. His head seemed tiny on his wide shoulders and was totally hairless. Tiny eyes and a small mouth were almost lost beneath rolls of fat, and his face was lined with scores of broken veins.

Sorcha stood in the shadows at the other side of the room, watching her husband eat and drink, disgust and repulsion on her face. She had laced both the food and drink with the liquid 'cure' and it would start to act soon. She had slipped into the bedroom while he ate – the bedroom she had shared only a few hours earlier with Peter Casside – and when she emerged, she was dressed only in a flimsy garment of black lace. It was completely transparent, falling to just below her knees and open from her throat down to her deep navel. She had touched her temples, throat and wrists with a delicate perfume and unbound her hair, allowing it to fall down her back in a long shimmering wave.

Donal dropped the plate to the floor with a crash and, snatching the bottle from the floor, drank long and deeply, as if he sought to assuage a raging thirst. With his free hand he loosened his collar and looked around the shadowed room for his wife.

'Sorcha ...?' His voice was harsh and raw, both from the liquor and the hot food. Damn her, where was she?

'Yes?' The single word hung on the air for a long moment whilst Donal tried to absorb the image before his eyes. It was his wife Sorcha ... but it couldn't be. His eyes floated down her body, lingering at her breasts with the hard nipples showing through the black lace and down to where the shadows fell across her long legs.

'You called me?' she asked quietly, her voice a husky whisper.

He stood and took a step nearer to her, suddenly conscious of the pain in his groin, the pounding of his blood in his head and his sharp breathing. He wanted her – he needed her! And tonight he would have her!

He lunged across the room, reaching for her, but she slipped to one side, eluding him. Again Donal reached for her; one of his hands brushed the long shining length of her hair and he held on and came away with a thick tuft. Sorcha squealed in pain and stumbled to the door. She waited until he was almost on top of her and then she flung the door open and fled out into the night, her long black gown floating out behind her like a huge pair of wings.

Donal paused by the door, all his old fears coming back to haunt him and then the sight of Sorcha's almost naked body racing down along the path inflamed him further and he took off in pursuit.

And as he disappeared down the path, a single figure

dressed in black and carrying a large bundle stepped out from the shadows and silently padded after him.

Sorcha paused before entering the wood and pulled her gown over her head and hung it on a low branch. She revelled in the caress of the wind across her body; felt her breasts tighten as they would when her lover touched them, felt the long muscles in her thighs and abdomen tighten. She shuddered in pleasure and then turned and fled into the wood like some elder sprite or nymph from a dim and distant legend.

Donal was breathing hard by the time he reached the wood. His heart was pounding in his chest and his temples throbbed. He leaned against the bole of a fallen tree and felt the wind dry the sweat on his face. He shivered and was abruptly conscious of the silence of the night, the only noise the whispering insinuation of sound made by the wind soughing through the branches all around him. Something flickered before his face and he almost cried aloud, his hand striking out at the object only to become entangled in something soft and clinging. With his free hand he tore the cloth from his arm and held it to his face and inhaled Sorcha's delicate perfume. The scent inflamed him and he turned and followed the path into the fastness of the wood.

And behind him, the shadowed figure knelt on the ground and unwrapped his bundle and when he arose the outline of his head was somehow different, almost unnatural. And then he set off at a loping run into the wood.

By day the wood was a place of peace and solitude; it was small and familiar, almost friendly. The trees provided shade from the sun and shelter from the wind and rain. It had once been part of the great forests that covered Ireland in the far distant past when the land had been called *Inis na bhFodhbhuidhe* – the Woody Isle. But time, the elements and man – the worst offender – had gradually eaten away the great forests, leaving only a few small, almost pathetic looking woods in their place.

And if by day the woods seemed to sleep, by night they came alive with malign memories.

Donal MacIntee raced down the rough track between the

155

trees, the long branches lashing at his face and hands, clutching at him with taloned fingers. He stumbled through bushes and the thorns tore through the cloth of his trousers and flayed his skin bloody. Unseen roots sent him sprawling and as he lay panting on the ground, the huge trees crept closer, towered over him, leered down, prepared to rend and destroy ...

With a muffled sob, he pushed himself to his feet and continued on, running deeper and deeper into the forest, taunted by a mocking laughter and pursued now by someone moving through the wood.

He was almost mad with fear by the time he broke out from the forest and into a small clearing. He stopped suddenly, his heart hammering and his lungs labouring.

A low, throaty laugh came out of the shadows behind him. Donal whirled around and Sorcha stepped out into the light. Donal caught his breath and stepped backwards, out into the centre of the clearing. Here, in this wild and lonely place, on this night, with his wife standing naked before him, he was suddenly terribly frightened, even more so than he had been in the wood.

Sorcha took a step closer to her husband, the wan light from the heavens touching her skin with grey, lending her an almost ghostly appearance.

'S-S-Sorcha...?' His voice was hoarse, only a little above a whisper.

The young woman reached out with her left hand, the fingers splayed, palm downwards and then she slowly contracted her hand into a claw. 'I have called Him for you,' she whispered sibilantly.

'What!' Donal yelped.

'I have given you to my Master,' she whispered. 'He is coming for you!'

'Your Master?'

'My Lord Satan!' she cried aloud. 'Listen, even now he comes.' She suddenly jabbed a finger at Donal. 'And he is coming for you!'

And from the shadows behind Donal a terrifying laugh suddenly issued, low and obscene. He whirled around as the bushes trembled and shook and then something stepped out from the trees that sent Donal reeling back in absolute terror. It was a creature, taller than a man, with eyes of burning fire. And from its head rose antlered horns.

Donal turned to flee, but stumbled and fell and before he could rise a heavy clawed hand fell on his shoulder and the hideous face closed with his. *'You are mine!'*

Donal felt the pain lance through his left arm and shoulder and then blossom in his chest. His head exploded in fire as one hand tore at his breast, seeking to ease the pain, the unmerciful, unremitting pain. And he wondered, as the darkness exploded into fire, why he did not feel his heart pounding ...?

Sorcha walked across the clearing and stood above the corpse, staring down at the sightless eyes and the gaping mouth and then she turned to the antlered figure and nodded. 'You did well.'

Peter struggled with the heavy mask, pulling it from his head, drying the sweat on his face with the back of his hand. He was gasping for breath with the heat of the mask and the exertion. He ran his fingers through his sweat-dampened hair. 'Is he dead?' he asked.

Sorcha nudged the corpse with her bare foot. 'He is.'

'What do we do now?' Peter asked. Reaction was setting in and he began to shiver.

'We do nothing,' Sorcha said. 'We leave him. I'll report him missing around noon tomorrow ... he will be found sooner or later.'

'And what about us; what will we do?'

Sorcha stepped over the body and pressed herself against Peter. 'Oh, I'm sure we can think of something,' she said, feeling his body beginning to respond to her closeness. She pulled him down into the dew damp grass and with practised fingers pulled the clothes from him and there, beside the stiffening body of her husband, they made love.

November quickly gave way to December, bringing with it snow and ice. The scandal surrounding Donal MacIntee's death soon passed only to be re-inflamed almost immedi-ately when she and Peter Casside announced their engagement and posted the banns. There was talk in the town and there were some, including the local doctor, who had seen the look of absolute terror on MacIntee's face, who believed that his death was not entirely natural.

Michael Casside kept to himself and avoided old Mother Cleirigh. He had his own suspicions about the death of Sorcha's husband and a terrible gnawing fear was growing about his brother's involvement in it. Their mother was shocked with her son's involvement with the young widow and especially so soon after the death without allowing a decent time for proper mourning.

But Peter merely laughed at his mother's disgust and his brother's fears, and ignored them both.

As the year drew quickly towards its turning, a small party of strangers, who were passing through the town were forced to stay there by the bad weather. They took shelter with several of the villagers until such time as the roads were opened again. However, they were friendly people and entered into the preparations for the coming Christmas with great enthusiasm. And Peter noticed that Sorcha also, became very involved with the preparations and seemed curiously excited at the prospect of the approaching festive season.

Michael's eyes snapped open and he lay still on the hard bed listening to the pounding of his heart, wondering what had awoken him. The sound of cloth on cloth brought him bolt upright ...

'Sssh, it's only me.' His twin moved closer to his bed. He leaned over, his face a pale oval in the darkness. 'I've got to go out,' he whispered.

'But mother ...'

'Mother is inside, snoring drunk, she'll never know.'

'But Peter, for God's sake, it's Christmas Eve ...'

'I know ... I know ... Look, I won't be long.' He shrugged

into his coat and pulled on a pair of woollen gloves. He gently eased open the frost encrusted window, allowing a chill blast to sweep through the room and then pulled himself up onto the sill and slipped out into the night. Wearily, Michael climbed from his warm bed and quickly closed the window, the cold metal stinging his fingers. He rubbed a circle on the glass and squinted out into the night, but there was no sign of his brother.

Peter hurried down the road, head down, hands tucked deep into his pockets. He walked by the side of the road on the stiffened grass, the only sound in the night the slight crunching of his footsteps.

Sorcha was waiting for him at the crossroads. She was enveloped in a long hooded cloak and her features were lost in the cowl's shadows. She started almost perceptibly as Peter crept up behind her and as she reached out to embrace him, he was surprised to find her arms were bare. She drew his head down close to hers and breathed gently into his ear. 'Follow me; tonight I need you so badly ...' She ran a long-nailed hand down the side of his face and traced the contours of his lips. 'Tonight,' she whispered, 'I will make you mine - forever.'

Sorcha led him into the wood - the same wood they had led her husband into a few weeks ago. Beneath the trees the ground was hard but unmarked by ice and the tiny brook that wound its way amongst the trees still trickled sluggishly. Sorcha stopped by the brook, stooped and touched it with her fingers and then brought them to her lips. She gasped with the chill and then huddled closer to Peter. 'Tell me,' she whispered, 'did anyone see you leave tonight?'

He shook his head in the darkness. 'No-one, no-one except Michael that is.'

She smiled suddenly, her teeth startlingly white in the darkness. 'He is of no consequence,' she murmured, and then asked, 'Does he still talk about me?'

159

Peter laughed grimly. 'Oh, he does occasionally; and now he warns me about you. He says you're an evil influence and ... other things.'

She smiled slightly. 'Tell me, what does he say about me?'

Peter shrugged uncomfortably. 'He says your mother is a witch and in all probability you are also.'

'Oh, and how does he make that out?'

'He said something about the stories your mother told him, something about charms and spells.'

Sorcha nodded. 'I told my mother to keep her mouth shut!'

Peter stopped suddenly. 'But ... it's not true is it: you're not a witch!'

The young woman laughed and in that desolate place, at that time of night, her laughter was hideous and obscene. 'You fool!' she said, her voice hard and chill. 'Of course I am a witch, as my mother was before me and her mother before her. I was dedicated to our Lord and Master whilst still in the womb.'

Peter dropped her arm and stepped back away from her, fear and confusion flickering across his face. 'But ...'

'But that shouldn't bother you now, should it? All you wanted was me ...' She suddenly opened the cloak, revealing her nakedness beneath. 'All you wanted was this!' she spat contemptuously.

Peter took a step backwards and would have turned and fled had Sorcha not called out in a hollow, commanding voice. 'Stay!'

His muscles abruptly locked and he was unable to move. He broke out in a cold sweat as shadows moved on either side of him and from the trees a small group of cowled and cloaked figures emerged. Sorcha gestured to him. 'He is ours!'

'A twin?' The voice was that of a man, and the accent was strange, definitely not from the town.

'They are almost identical,' Sorcha said, a deferential note creeping into her voice.

'You have done well; and the other?'

Sorcha smiled grimly. 'He will be mine,' she promised.

'We must have him.' There was a hint of a threat in the man's voice.

'We will,' Sorcha snapped, 'but first let us take this one.' She tapped Peter lightly on his shoulder, sending pain lancing down his body.

'Come!' she commanded in the same hollow, slightly echoing voice she had used before.

Obediently Peter turned and, surrounded by the cloaked figures, followed Sorcha into the depths of the wood.

And although it was warm beneath the blankets, Michael Casside shivered, tossed and turned, his dreams uneasy.

Peter immediately recognised the clearing into which Sorcha led them: it was where they had trapped and terrified Donal to death. Like some dumb animal, he was led to the centre of the clearing to where a huge slab of stone had been recently cleaned of its lichens and mosses. Tiny crystals sparkled in the rock in the wan light and the stone itself seemed too regular to be natural.

Sorcha turned and smiled coldly at Peter and a long black-hafted knife glittered in her hand as she raised it. Her eyes held his as she approached and he almost vomited as she slashed at him with the knife. A thin thread of fire blossomed across his chest and his coat and shirt hung in long tatters. Again and again Sorcha slashed at him, the razor sharp blade lacerating his flesh as it cut away his clothing. Soon, he stood naked, his clothes in an untidy bundle about his feet, hot blood trickling in thin lines from scores of cuts on his chest and arms. Sorcha laughed and wiped the blood from the knife on the edge of her cloak and then stood back as two of the hooded figures caught him by the arms and legs and laid him across the stone slab. Curiously enough, the stone was not as chill as he expected and it was as warm as if it had baked in the afternoon sun.

Peter felt absolute terror engulf him; his mind screamed aloud and he attempted to pray, but his gods seemed so very

161

distant on that cold December night and he felt so alone.

Michael came awake suddenly. He glanced over at his brother's bed, but it was empty. Silence pervaded the cottage and he could tell from the position of the stars through the window that the night was far advanced. He settled himself back; the uneasiness that had troubled him earlier had returned, but now it was something more, for now it was something approaching fear.

The figures had shed their long cloaks and now moved widdershins about the naked figure lying on the slab. And although they too were naked, they seemed unaffected by the December chill. Peter strained to make out their features, but from his horizontal position it was almost impossible. No-one looked familiar ... and then he suddenly realised that these were the strangers who had been 'forced' to stop over in the town by the harsh weather.

They were chanting aloud in a strange tongue, a language that sounded not unlike Irish, but a far older version of the language. And although he could not understand their words, even he knew they were calling someone ... or something. He squirmed on the stone, but the invisible bonds that held him were immovable, unbreakable.

Suddenly a figure loomed up out of the night and stood over him. It was Sorcha, her breasts heaving as if she were in the throes of passion. There was something wild and free about her, something primeval. And then the realisation struck home, perhaps fully for the first time; she was a witch and she was about to sacrifice him to her pagan gods!

To his amazement, she leaned over and kissed him, and he found then that he could speak once again. 'Why Sorcha, for God's sake, why?'

'Whose gods?' she murmured softly, almost intimately. 'Yours or mine – and remember, mine are far older, far stronger. They were ancient when your Christ was butchered on a tree; they were strong then and time has only

162

made them stronger, whilst your faith is still growing.' She ran her fingertips down the length of his body, from collar-bone to groin and then down again, tracing a long V on his flesh. 'Your faith may have driven us underground, but as your own church should know, a faith is at its strongest when it is being persecuted.'

'What are you going to do with me?' Peter asked calmly.

'We are going to sacrifice you to our Master,' she said simply.

'Is your god so weak that he needs the sacrifice of men to sustain him?'

Sorcha laughed gently. 'You sound like your brother,' she said, almost absently. 'But no, our Master does not need the sacrifice – but we do. You see,' she said slowly, 'twins are linked in a very special way, there is a bond between them, an unbreakable bond. And although they are complete in themselves, yet they are like two parts of the one person.'

'What are you trying to say?' Peter snapped.

'Oh, gently, gently,' Sorcha chided. 'What I am trying to say,' she whispered, climbing astride Peter, 'is that we are going to sacrifice you at a critical moment, thus ensuring that your powers, your abilities – undeveloped as yet – will be passed on to your brother. We will give him part of your soul as it were; we will make him something more than a man – and I will control that man!'

'Never!'

'Oh yes,' she whispered, 'oh yes.' She slid her body down his, arousing and exciting him against his will, for although he felt revulsion, his body betrayed him and responded to hers.

The feeling of oppression had become stronger and Michael Casside shivered in a cold sweat. There was a terrible feeling of foreboding within him . . . and there was nothing he could do about it.

Sorcha clinically observed Peter's reaction. When he

became too excited, she drew back and allowed his excitement to lessen, for the timing must be right, and it would be soon, for the dawn was almost upon them.

The small clearing was now enveloped in a glowing nimbus of raw power; it cracked and sparked like summer lightning, writhed along the cold hard ground like a serpent. The tiny crystals in the stone glowed with a blue fire bathing both Sorcha's and Peter's bodies in a ghastly hue. The stone was now warm, almost repuslively so, for it resembled human flesh.

And as the first rays of the Christmas morning sun broke over the trees and touched the stone with golden fire, Sorcha brought Peter to a shattering climax – and plunged her dagger into his labouring heart!

Michael awoke screaming.

He felt as if something had been torn from within him. There was a void, a terrible aching void ... and then something seeped into that void, something which trembled and shivered like a new-born babe. It was both strange and familiar; it was and at the same time was not, his brother. But it *was* part of him.

Michael knew then what Sorcha had done to his brother. She had slain him in a mid-winter sacrifice and now the power that had been his brother's, his essence, his soul, had passed on to him. And soon, he knew, she would come for him.

But she would never get him. He would flee now, hide away where they would never find him. And in that instant he swore an oath; an oath to cleanse Ireland from the scourge of witchcraft.

And in that moment, Morand the Witchfinder was born.

CHAPTER 11

THE BLACK BOOK ... II

'Burn it. Burn all of it!' Tom Kennedy spat into the hay rick and turned away in disgust. He walked the length of the field, pausing at each rick in turn and at each one breathing in the heavy sweet odour of mouldering hay. He turned as he reached the low stone wall that bounded his fields and watched his men systematically torch the ricks, sending plumes of grey-white smoke curling up into the early morning sky. He shut his eyes to the destruction and shook his head; unless he bought expensive feed for his cattle during the winter, they – and his family – would go hungry.

'Tom ... Tom, get over here.' He turned and ran across the field to where his foreman was stamping out the flames that licked hungrily about the base of a small stack.

'What is it Pat?'

The wizened old man pointed silently into the rick with his pitchfork.

Tom Kennedy stared into the heart of the haystack, covering his nose and mouth with the sleeve of his coat. The stench was revolting – and it was not just the odour of burning wet straw. It was stronger, nauseous and cloying. His eyes watered and he drew back shaking his head. 'What is it?'

The old man prodded the stack with his pitchfork, dislodging a sizeable amount of hay, revealing the interior. Tom took a step forward and swore. 'Jesus preserve us; what is it?'

'It's a side of meat,' Pat Coonan said, 'and I dare say you'll find a couple of eggs in there also, aye, and in each and every one of the spoiled ricks.'

Why?' Tom prodded the mouldering, maggot-infested slab of meat with his stick, knocking it to the ground.

'Why? Well to ruin the stored hay of course. I told you before this lad, someone doesn't like you and they're doing their damnedest to ruin you.'

Tom shook his head stubbornly. 'I don't believe it,' he said.

Pat Coonan looked up at the young man standing before him, the early morning light bringing out the grey streaks in his black hair, although he was no more than eight-and-twenty, and softening the hard lines of his cheekbones and jaw. He was the spit of his father – and as stubborn.

'Now listen to me,' he snapped. He held up a gnarled hand and began ticking off points. 'Your wells have gone dry and if they haven't gone dry then they have been poisoned. The cows have slung their calves – there's not one that has carried her calf full term this season. No hen has laid a fresh egg for a month and we had to destroy the abominations the sow birthed. And now, someone has gone and ruined a year's growth – and ensured that you'll either starve this winter or enter the new year without a penny to your name!' He laughed and spat at Tom's feet. 'And you tell me no-one has done this to you!'

The younger man suddenly slashed at the hay rick with his stick, sending tufts flying into the still air, where it hung momentarily and then drifted down in silent wisps. 'What in God's name am I to do then?' he demanded. 'Who is going to believe that someone has put a curse on me ... is trying to destroy me?'

The old man shifted some dry straw onto a smouldering patch of grass and watched it smoke and suddenly burst into flame. With the end of his pitchfork he hoisted the burning grass onto the piled straw and watched the flames rapidly regain their hold over the rick. 'Oh, there's plenty would believe you,' he said quietly. 'Some already have,' he added. He looked up and caught the spark of anger in Tom Kennedy's eyes and raised his hand placatingly. 'Now before you get all hot and bothered, I've only done it for your own good.'

'Done what?' Kennedy snapped.

'I've spoken with some of the old folk, people who have some experience with this ... sort of thing, and I've also spoken with Father Horgan ... '

'And when they were finished laughing what did they say – beside the fact that my foreman has gone just a little out of his head?'

Pat Coonan ignored the jibe and continued quietly. 'Oh, there was no laughing I can assure you; they believed what I told them and treated it very seriously indeed.' He paused and prodded the burning rick with his pitchfork, sending sparks spiralling upwards. 'And they advised me to find the Witchfinder!'

Ireland never experienced the witch hunts that plagued England and the continent, and there was never a witchfinder to equal the status of Matthew Hopkins who carried on his reign of terror through the length and breadth of England during the 1640's. There were however, certain people, mainly clerics or those wise in the ways of the country people and the country lore, who took it upon themselves to seek out those who practised the darker side of witchcraft, and foremost amongst them was the priest men called Father Morand, the Witchfinder.

Father Michael Morand strode down the length of the field past the still smouldering hayricks. Tom Kennedy hurried to keep up with the priest's long-legged gait.

'We checked all the ricks Father and it was as Pat said, there was rotten meat and eggs buried in every one of them.'

The tall dark-haired priest nodded impassively as he reached the loose stone wall at the south end of the field. The sun reflected off his eyes, turning them into mirrors, the effect sending shivers along Tom's spine, for the priest's eyes were the most frightening he had ever seen. They were colourless, but with the texture of frozen water and they never seemed to look at a person, but rather through them to a point beyond.

And if the truth were known, Father Michael Morand terrified Tom Kennedy.

'Your foreman said you had been experiencing other ... difficulties,' the priest said softly.

'Coincidence only, Father,' Tom said in embarrassment.

'Tell me,' Father Morand commanded.

'I'm sure you have already been told,' Tom snapped and walked away from the priest.

'Indeed, I have.' The priest's voice drifted across the still morning air, 'But I want you to tell me. Now come back!' The tone of command stopped the younger man in his tracks and he turned, almost unconsciously, and walked back to the priest.

Father Morand placed his hand on Tom's shoulder and spoke in a quieter, gentler tone. 'I'm only trying to help you; if you resist me, you are only aiding those who are trying to destroy you.'

'Father,' Tom said, almost desperately, 'I have no enemies; no-one has any cause to hate me.'

'Ah, but my son, someone has cause enough – aye, and reason enough – to use the Dark Lore to ruin you.' He stretched to his full height and with his stick pointed out across Kennedy's fields. 'Tell me; who owns the lands that border on yours?'

'I own the land as far as the stream.' He pointed south. 'Beyond that it belongs to my brother Seamus.'

'Is your holding greater than his?'

'Considerably. There is also a great difference in age between us – around ten years or so.'

'That would make him about eighteen,' the priest said.

'It would.'

'Is he married?'

Tom laughed. 'Oh no, he lives with our mother. He is very devoted to her – and she to him. I can't see him marrying whilst she still lives.'

Father Morand nodded and then pointed across to the west. 'And over there?'

'The land beyond the road has been held by the Dilane

family for generations – although when Paddy Dilane dies it will have to pass into other hands,' he added.

'There are no children?'

'None.'

Father Morand turned and squinted into the morning sun. 'And here, how far does your land extend?'

'Well most of the land this far east is infertile. I'm treating it of course and allowing it to lie fallow. In a couple of years ... ' he shrugged, 'well it might yield something then.' He pointed to a small copse of trees beside a broken down wall. 'The wall marks the boundary of my land. Beyond that it's more or less common ground.' He spun around and pointed back across the fields towards the north. 'My lands end just behind the white-washed house.'

The tall priest turned slowly and surveyed the land that bordered Kennedy's fields and then his strange colourless eyes fell on the younger man. 'Go home Tom,' he said gently, 'try and get some rest.'

'What will you do?'

The priest smiled curiously. 'I will do nothing,' he said quietly.

Father Horgan lowered his voice and spoke quietly to the tall priest standing by his side. 'You're attracting a lot of attention.'

Michael Morand nodded courteously to a small group of gossiping women who were staring openly in his direction. 'I know,' he said softly, 'I always do.'

'It doesn't seem to bother you,' the older priest remarked.

'No, not now. It did at the beginning; it was one of the many reasons I changed my name.'

'Morand is not your true name then?' Father Horgan said in surprise.

'It is not the name I was baptised with,' he said slowly, 'but Morand was the name of my own choosing – I've grown used to it.'

The two clerics turned off the main street and down a

169

winding lane that led to the side entrance of the church.

'Was there any official announcement made of my visit?' Father Morand asked.

Father Horgan pulled a long key from a pocket in his sleeve and laughed roughly. 'There was not! We wouldn't like it whispered about that the Witchfinder had come ... although,' he added ruefully, 'I dare say most of the town already know, or if they do not, then they will by nightfall.'

Father Morand nodded as he entered the gloom of the church. 'Good.'

'You want that?' the older priest said in surprise.

'I have a certain reputation,' Michael said quietly, lowering his voice to a whisper in this place of worship, 'it is a reputation I must admit to have fostered somewhat. Those who dabble in ... the Elder Faith and the Dark Lore and ... other beliefs, have cause to fear me. Often that same fear will cause them to make a mistake or attempt to complete a task before its appointed time. All I need is that tiny slip.'

'Is that what you're looking for now?'

Father Morand's colourless eyes took on the pale gold of the candles' glow. 'That is what I am waiting for,' he said quietly.

And beyond the town, in a decaying, weather-beaten cottage, two figures sat in the foul-smelling silence and listened to the first spatters of rain hiss off the mildewed straw on the roof.

'The Witchfinder is in town.'

'He does not frighten me.'

'Then you are a fool.' There was a pause and a rat squeaked in a corner and then the voice continued. 'We must hurry, we must finish it tonight.'

'It is too soon.'

'We have no choice.'

The storm had lessened somewhat by the time Father Morand reached the Kennedy house perched on the rise above the road. Although it was not yet seven o'clock, it was already dark. Low clouds, heavy with rain, rolled languorously across the heavens, propelled by an icy wind.

Father Morand rapped on the heavy wooden door with the iron ferrule of his stout walking stick. The door was opened almost immediately by Pat Coonan, Tom's foreman. He stepped back from the door with a gasp and brought up a long-barrelled shotgun and levelled it at the priest's chest.

Michael Morand chuckled. 'It would surely be embarrassing if you were to shoot me now,' he said gently.

The foreman stepped back and, with his free hand, reached for the candle burning on a small side table in the hall. He lifted it above his head, shedding its wan light onto the priest's hard features. He sighed and lowered the shotgun. 'It's yourself, Father.' He laughed shakily. 'You put the heart crossways in me,' he admitted, and added, 'when I opened the door and saw you standing there, I thought you were the Devil himself.'

'What has happened Pat?' the priest said urgently, stepping into the hallway.

The foreman closed the door and shot the bolts, and then led the way down the short hall and into the main room. It was large, taking up almost the entire ground floor of the two-storied building, but it seemed smaller with the number of people gathered in it. All conversation stopped as Pat led the priest into the room.

'This is Father Michael Morand,' he said unnecessarily.

The group of men nodded respectfully and a low murmur ran around the room ... '*Witchfinder ...*'

The priest stepped up to the fire and stood with his back to it, soaking up the heat, letting it take the chill from his damp clothes. He looked around the room. There were almost twenty men present, most of them armed with shotguns or long-barrelled fowling pieces, some with knives or pitchforks. He was about to demand an explanation when the door opened and Tom Kennedy entered. He looked tired and drawn and there were dark circles under his eyes. He accepted a drink from a hip flask and his hand was visibly trembling as he raised it to his lips.

'How is she?' Pat Coonan asked quietly.

Tom coughed as the raw spirit burned its way down his throat, but when he looked up his fingers were still and his voice was steady. 'The doctor is still with her,' he said, 'and the midwife said she will stay the night.' He shrugged. 'She is sleeping now ... she'll be alright.'

The priest stepped away from the fire. 'I think you had better tell me what happened ... and the reason for this gathering.'

The young farmer started, noting the tall priest's presence for the first time. He smiled wearily. 'I'm glad you're here Father, truly I am.' He waved to a chair. 'Sit down please, all of you, sit down. Pat ... ' he turned to his foreman, 'some drinks for my friends.'

'What happened Tom; tell me.'

The young farmer poked the fire to a blaze and then placed a log in the centre of the flames. He sat back on a low stool, his eyes never leaving the flames licking hungrily about the dry wood.

The room grew silent as he spoke, the men drawing closer together, occasionally raising their heads to listen to the sounds of the night and the rain dripping from the trees outside the windows.

'I returned home when I left you this morning, Father. I delayed only a few minutes to talk with my brother Seamus whom I met on the road. He was heading into town and couldn't delay. As I crossed the yard however, I noticed that it was unusually quiet, and there were no hens running about. I had a look around, but couldn't find them.' He paused and breathed deeply. 'Just before I went in, I checked the barn. And I found them ... Someone ... someone had torn their heads off and then ... tied the carcasses about the rafters with their entrails ... ' He shuddered and drank deeply, allowing the liquid to sear the foul taste from his mouth.

'On the back door I found a frog crucified head downwards, and some words drawn onto the wood in the frog's blood.'

172

'What words?' Father Morand snapped, leaning forward in his chair.

Tom shook his head. 'I don't know; Sab ... sab-something.'

'"Saboath?"'

'Something like that. And then,' he continued, 'in the kitchen ... in the kitchen I found ... ' he broke off and swallowed, and when he continued, his voice was barely above a whisper. 'I found the hens' heads sitting in the tea cups on the dresser. And I found Berni unconscious on the floor ... '

'How is she now?' the priest asked.

'She awoke briefly, but she was very distressed and the doctor gave her a powder. She is sleeping now, but her dreams must be disturbing, for she is speaking and mumbling.'

Father Morand stood. 'Is she speaking now?'

Tom Kennedy nodded.

Without a word, the priest pushed his way through the crowd and made his way up the stairs to the bedroom where Bernadette Kennedy lay in her troubled sleep.

The doctor was packing his small black bag when the priest entered. He looked up, a hand raised to prevent whomever it was from entering, but stopped when he saw the priest's collar. The midwife, a stout young woman from the next town, rose from her seat by the fire and curtsied to the tall figure in black.

Father Morand turned to the doctor. 'Will the shock have any adverse affect on the child?' he asked directly.

Doctor Johnson shook his head. 'I don't think so. The child is due this month, it should be fully grown, and there is little likelihood of any deformity forming now. However, the shock may bring the child on prematurely,' he added.

The priest walked across the room and stood by the bed, and his colourless eyes softened as he looked down at the young woman tossing and turning in her sleep. He turned to the doctor. 'Is there nothing you can do to ease her sleep?'

Johnson shrugged. 'She sleeps, I can do nothing more for

173

her. I have no control over her dreams.'

Father Morand nodded slightly and then leaned over the bed, listening to the rasping whispers that came from the young woman's slack mouth.

'Raum...Shax...Vine...Gaap...Andras...Flauros...'

The tall priest blanched, and with trembling fingers traced the Sign of the Cross on her fevered brow. The young woman shuddered once and then sighed. Father Morand turned to the doctor. 'She will sleep peacefully now.'

'What was she saying?' the doctor asked quietly, glancing across at the young midwife who was regarding them curiously.

The priest ran his fingers through his thick black hair and shook his head. 'She was calling upon the demons of destruction, hate and revenge,' he said slowly.

'The time approaches; is everything prepared?'

'It is.'

A shadowy figure moved across the floor of the cottage, careful not to disturb the circle drawn onto the hard floor with tiny flecks of powdered lamb's bones. 'Tonight, we will destroy the mother and unborn child – and ultimately the father!'

The night drifted on towards midnight, and the storm which had blown most of the afternoon and intermittently through the night now died down leaving a chill silence in its wake. The room was quiet, men speaking in whispers, drinking carefully or tending to their weapons. They had come of their own accord when they heard of the afternoon's happening, drawn together by the common country bond. Tom Kennedy was one of theirs, his family had lived in the county for generations, he was well liked and respected. And, much as they would gather together to hunt down a fox that was attacking their coops, they gathered now to do what they could to help him fight the force that was threatening his family.

The clock on the wall struck midnight, its hollow chimes

making everyone jump, but helping to break the morose spell that had fallen over the room. Pat Coonan, who was more than a little drunk, suddenly turned to the priest. 'Father, is it the witches?'

Michael Morand spoke into the deathly silence that now claimed the room. 'It is possible. There is some evidence of witchcraft,' he said carefully.

'Ah, I knew,' Pat said, 'I was in Clonmel in '94 when there was that witch burning.'

The priest nodded. 'I was there also; it was a shocking affair,' he said.

'What happened?' one of the men asked.

Father Morand poked the fire and tossed a length of wood onto it. 'It must have been around March 1894 or thereabouts, when I was called in to investigate what was later called the Clonmel Burning.'

'Did they ever hang that madman, Father?' Pat Coonan asked suddenly.

'They did not; they gave him twenty years hard labour.'

'It was no more than he deserved,' the foreman said.

'Yes,' the priest continued, 'it was in March '94 when I was asked to assist an Inspector Wansborough in the investigation of a brutal murder which had taken place in Ballyvadlea, which is some ways to the north of Clonmel, between Cloneen and Mullinahone.

'A young woman, Brigid Cleary, had disappeared, and her husband, Michael, her father Patrick Boland, along with an aunt, cousins and a local herb-doctor, stood accused of her murder. But what made this affair unusual – and the reason I was called in – was the fact that Michael Cleary claimed that his wife had been taken by the fairies and a changeling, who was also a witch, had replaced her.

'Michael Cleary, with the aid of his relatives, forced Brigid to drink potions prepared by Denis Ganey, the herb-doctor, and when these did not have the desired effect of driving out the changeling's assumed form, one of the group, her cousin, John Dunne, suggested that they hold her over a fire, so that the flames – which she was accustomed to in hell – might shake off her form.

'They tortured her in this fashion for several hours, and then calmly retired for the evening.

'In the morning however, Michael Cleary went completely beserk, and after repeatedly burning his wife with a red-hot piece of metal, emptied the contents of an oil lamp over her and set her alight.

'But this time there was a witness – a neighbour, a Mrs Burke, who had called upon Brigid Cleary, and was a horrified witness to the morning's events. She alerted the police ...' the priest's voice trailed off and he drank quickly from a glass of water. 'I found the body several days later with my ... craft. She had been buried in a shallow grave just a little ways from her home.' He shuddered and breathed deeply. 'Her injuries were terrible; her legs were but charred stumps, and the skin of her back and abdomen was burnt almost beyond recognition, and her left hand was but a withered claw.

'Michael Cleary was insane of course, and the others ... well, some were definitely evil and took some delight in the poor woman's sufferings, but the rest I would say truly believed in what they were doing.

'But they confused the fairy and the witch-lore; they believed Brigid was a changeling who was also a witch ...' Father Morand shook his head, 'and that of course, is impossible.'

'And was the woman of the *sidhe*, Father?' someone asked in a hushed voice.

The priest shook his head. 'I doubt it, although her husband claimed that she was some two inches taller than his wife, and that he had seen her astride a smoke-grey horse riding out of Kylegranagh, a local fairy fort. However,' Michael Morand added, 'while I was in town, I discovered that Michael Cleary's mother has something of a reputation for being wise in the ways of the fairies and that she would often go to the fairy fort.' The priest drank again. 'Undoubtedly, the son knew of these rumours, and perhaps his own fear that his wife might do the same drove him over the brink of madness.'

'And I thought such things were long since past,' Tom

Kennedy murmured, almost to himself.

The priest smiled. 'Unfortunately not. I know for example that you Tom, spent some time both in Cork and Dublin, away from the land and the elements; you have forgotten your country lore – otherwise, you would have called me in much sooner.'

'But witchcraft, Father!' the young man protested.

'Yes my son, witchcraft. Whilst there is good, there must also be evil: one cannot exist without the other. And there will always be those who are attracted to the mystique that surrounds witch-lore, they are attracted to the power and secrecy that clings to the occult. For such people, its lure is unbreakable.'

'But does it work?' Tom asked.

The priest nodded grimly. 'It works, because they believe that it works.'

The storm which had died down briefly, now blew up again, venting its fury in a maelstrom of destruction about the house. Gale force winds ripped the leaded tiles from the roof and sent them winging into the night like obscene birds. The rending and tearing brought the group in the sitting-room to their feet, and then Morand, followed closely by Tom Kennedy went out into the hall and up the stairs, taking them two at a time. They burst into the bedroom to find the doctor lying on the floor beneath a pile of shattered tiles, an angry cut welling blood from the side of his face, and the midwife cowering in a corner. Father Morand pointed to the sleeping woman, and screamed above the howling of the storm that was now tearing in through the open roof. Even though Tom couldn't hear him, his meaning was clear. As Tom bundled his wife up in the blankets, the priest pulled the shivering midwife from the corner. She struggled and struck at him, seeing only a tall figure in black that reached for her with long talons. Her hooked fingers caught his face and one long nail caught and tore the skin of his face, just below his eye. The priest grunted, and then struck the girl a glancing blow on the point of her chin. Her eyes rolled in her head and she slumped unconscious. With surprising ease, the tall priest caught the heavy girl in his arms and ran for the door. He dragged the doctor to his feet and pushed him out onto the landing and slammed the door shut just as the chimney, which had been swaying wildly in the wind, tore free and came crashing down through the roof into the bedroom below.

The priest tucked the unconscious woman under one arm, and hauled the stunned doctor to his feet, and then, pushing Tom in front of him, headed for the stairs. They were half-way down, when they met Pat Coonan coming up fast. He swore briefly at the sight of the priest holding the two still bodies and Tom carrying his still sleeping wife.

'What's happening?' he shouted above the howling of the wind.

'Witch-storm!' Morand shouted.

The storm howled around the house, ripping shutters from the windows, tearing up fences and rails. The barns and outbuildings were battered into matchwood; all standing crops were flattened and the fields turned into muddy quagmires.

In the sitting-room, the assembled men were numbed with fear, the weapons they had handled so confidently earlier that evening, now useless against the outraged forces of nature.

As Father Morand, Tom Kennedy and Pat Coonan pushed their way into the room with their charges, the fire in the grate suddenly blazed azure and emerald and then exploded in a shower of flaming cinders and sparks. The men scattered, stamping on the scores of tiny fires that started in the room. The priest ducked as a lump of wood came through the window and shattered on the wall above his head. He handed the groaning midwife to Pat and then walked to the centre of the room. He stretched to his full height and, seemingly oblivious to the storm that now whipped in through the open window, crossed himself and his lips began to move in silent prayer.

The storm grew in strength and force immediately. The

room's three other windows shattered beneath an on-slaught of fist-sized lumps of hail. The temperature in the room plummeted. The oil lamps shattered and the flames burned blue-green before dying. A foul odour pervaded the room, an odour of rotten meat and burned flesh, of putrefying fish and ozone.

Tom Kennedy gagged and covered his wife's mouth and nose ... and then he felt the child kicking. Bernadette moaned and her face spasmed in pain. Tom felt the muscles in her back ripple and flow, and he could feel the sudden increase in her heartbeat. A small cry escaped her lips, and then she cried aloud in pain. She was going into labour.

The priest bowed his head and crossed himself once again. And then he raised his hands high and, with splayed fingers began to gather the force of the storm to him, reeling it in as an angler a catch ... He could feel the abrupt upsurge of power as the force was concentrated about his body, could see the writhing blue nimbus gathering about his head, could hear the sharp crackling along his body. Tendrils of fire ran along his pointing fingers and gathered in small pulsating blue globes about his nails. Tiny silver and black dust motes danced about his head, twisting and turning like flies, suddenly flaring into incandescent spots of white-hot heat that threatened to blind the priest.

Every hair on his head rose and crackled with the raw power that now encircled his body. His head became a ball of livid metallic colours as the forces sparked from his hair, and Tom Kennedy watched in horror as the colour was slowly leeched from the priest's hair, leaving it silver-white.

Father Morand began to cry aloud in a strange language, the words seeming to echo slightly in the room. He then turned to the four cardinal points and spoke in a different tongue – and suddenly the electrical tension in the room increased, forcing everyone onto the floor or up against the walls leaving the Witchfinder the only one standing. And then he faced the East and cried aloud in what everyone recognised as a variant of English.

'And we abjure and abhor thee, and command thee depart in the Name of the Living God and of the True One, of the

Three that are One, and the One that is All. I command thee depart in the All-Powerful Names of the Most High God: On, Alpha and Omega, Eloy, Eloym, Ya, Saday, Lux, Mugiens, Rex, Salus, Adonay, Emmanuel, Messias!

'I command and compel thee depart with all thy infernal legions by the Names which are Unutterable save by the sigils, V, C, and X, and by the Names which are Holy: Jehova, Sol, Agla, Riffasoris, Oriston, Ophitne, Phaton, Ipretu, Ogia, Speraton, Imagon, Amul, Penaton, Soter, Tetragrammaton, Eloy, Premoton, Sitmon, Perigaron, Irataton, Plegaton, On, Perchiram, Tiros, Rubiphaton, Simulaton, Perpi, Klarimun, Tremendum, Meray!

'By the Names of Power, I command thee depart: Gali, Enga, El, Habdanum, Ingodum, Obu, Englabis ... DEPART!'

The priest brought his hands together. A blue-green light abruptly detonated in blinding incandescence which seared the flesh and blinded. A demonic howling filled the room, and then a voice, like that of brittle glass, spoke, '*You can never defeat me priest; whilst your god remains, so do I!*'

And then ... nothing.

The silence was almost as terrifying as the howling. It hung, heavy and cloying over the shattered room and the numbed figures. Michael Morand had a momentary vision of floating above the house, looking down at the devastation that had turned the building and the fields around it into an almost circular spot of utter destruction. And then he was falling, plunging down and down, through the shattered wood of the stripped roof and the destroyed bedroom, and into the sitting-room, where one lone figure still stood in the centre of the room, surrounded by the destruction and the cowering bodies.

The priest shuddered as he felt the presence of his dead brother sink back into quiescence, and with the withdrawal of his occult and spiritual strength, he slumped, exhaustion washing over him in a long grey tide, and he fell to the floor unconscious.

*

'He has defeated us!'

'But we have called the Master forth – He will demand payment!'

'Then let us ensure that it is not us He takes.' A pause, and a small naked figure broke the circle with a word, and crossed over the thin white lines on the damp floor. An aged hand reached for a large red bound book and pulled it from its shelf above the fire. 'We must try again – and this time we must not fail.'

Father Morand awoke to the sound of a child's cry. The plaintive wail brought him bolt upright, and then he staggered as blackness washed over him and set his head spinning. He sat on the edge of the couch, feeling the morning sun warm on his face, before pushing himself to his feet with a groan. The door opened and Pat Coonan entered. His old face looked even more lined and exhausted and his eyes were red-rimmed and hollow. He forced a smile when he saw the priest on his feet.

'It's good to see you up, Father. For a while there ... ' he let the sentence hang.

The priest patted him on the shoulder. 'Thank you,' he said simply, and then he smiled wanly. 'If I look half as bad as I feel, then I need a good strong drink.'

The foreman laughed slyly. 'Father,' he said, pulling out a hip flash, 'if I looked half as bad as you, then I'd need a drink.'

'Join me?' The priest lifted the metal flask and swallowed some of the raw liquor. He coughed and handed the flask back to the foreman.

'My pleasure!' Pat drained the remainder of the flask in one long swallow.

'And now,' the priest's expression turned serious, 'the mother ... ?'

The foreman grinned. 'The mother and child are doing fine.' He smiled at the priest's expression.

'And Tom?'

'Shaken, but otherwise all right. He's outside now, having

a look at the damage.' The foreman shook his head in amazement. 'I was here – and even I don't believe it.' His voice changed, taking on a more serious note. 'We're ruined, you know?'

Father Morand nodded slowly. 'I know that. And you know it's not finished yet.'

'Aaah, I thought that,' the foreman grimaced in disgust.

'However, there might be something I can do about that,' Father Morand said. 'I might be able to stop them.'

'You specialise in miracles also?' Pat asked.

'Only sometimes.'

Father Michael Morand spent the remainder of the day in the church, searching through the old parish records, reading through the diaries of past parish priests. He was unsure what he was looking for, he was merely following an instinct he had followed many times before, instincts which had never failed him.

And towards evening, as the golden light of afternoon faded from the dim attic through which he had crawled unearthing the records, he found it. In the dim light, he couldn't even read the title of the dusty manuscript, but he knew, he *knew*, that this was what he sought.

He dusted off his hands and, tucking the manuscript into his shirt, climbed down from the attic and lit a candle. In the wavering light the thick paper turned parchment yellow and the ink inscription on the first page seemed to fade before his eyes. '*A Historie of ye Local Churches and ye Holie Places of Worshippe.*' The date at the bottom of the page was faded, but Father Morand thought he could make out the numerals, one, seven, one, one ... 1711. It was written in a scrawling hand that tended to diminish almost into illegibility as it neared the right hand margin of the page. The priest took the manuscript downstairs, cut across the church and out the side door, and slipped into the parochial house he was sharing with Father Horgan. He sat down by the log fire that blazed in the grate and began to read.

He was still reading some hours later when Father Horgan came back after saying evening mass and all his attempts at conversation were rewarded by monosyllables. The parish priest retired around midnight, but Father Morand remained deep in the manuscript until early morning when he suddenly found the answer.

He knew how to discover the identity of the witches who were attacking Tom Kennedy and his family. For he knew the location of one of the infamous Black Books.

The character of Saint Mochta's Abbey changed as evening drew on. It was something to do with the way the light seemed to retreat from the aged stones, making it one with the gathering night. By day, it was a place of worship, sacred to the teachings of Christ and his followers, but by night it re-assumed the mystery and majesty it had held as one of the Old Places, places that had been sanctified to gods that were old before the New God walked this world.

Tom Kennedy winced as the tall priest let the heavy brass knocker fall to the metal stud set into the dark aged wood of the huge double doors. The sharp metallic sound hung on the still night air like a clarion call, sending birds in the forest below the Abbey wheeling and cawing into the sky.

The priest stepped out of the shadow of the door and looked down the winding road, noting the almost obscured signs of defensive earthworks. From the low hill, the Abbey commanded a view of the four roads that met beyond the forest at Dead Man's Crossroads, where the locals, with a certain degree of morbid humour, maintained the gallows that gave the spot its grisly name. Father Morand breathed deeply, savouring the slightly scented fresh night air, and he could almost imagine himself dressed in skins and leathers with torcs and rings of gold or bronze about his forearms, guarding the hill-fort in some ancient time of legend. He smiled fondly at the image, and then the shuffled sound of footsteps brought him back to the present.

The huge door opened silently, revealing a yawning cavernous interior. A shadow moved across the opening and a small figure stepped out into the night. The balding monk bowed slowly and addressed the pair in Irish.

'Good evening brothers; how may I be of assistance?' He spoke slowly and in a voice barely above a whisper.

Father Morand greeted him in Irish and then switched to rapid Latin. The monk listened intently, his round face expressionless, his eyes flat and unemotional. He nodded once when Father Morand had finished and then stepped aside and allowed the priest and the young man to enter before him. The old monk then leaned against the door and slowly pushed it closed, until it shut with a curiously final hollow booming. The Witchfinder clutched the young man's arm above the elbow, making him jump, and whispered quietly in his ear. 'Follow me; say nothing unless you are spoken to.'

Tom nodded, and thought bitterly that there was little else he could do.

The monk led them down through high-ceilinged corridors, with huge vaulted windows, stark and plain, but with a simple beauty in their austerity. They saw movement in the distance, shadowed figures intent on their own private tasks, and once a door opened and a cowled monk stepped out into the hallway. He stopped when he saw the young man and the priest, bowed slightly and crossed himself, remaining in the doorway until they had passed.

The hall was badly lit, only smouldering torches set into verdigris-stained holders, set high on the smoke-stained walls brightened the gloom, the wan pools of light only serving to make the corridors seem darker.

The monk eventually led them down a side corridor and out into a small enclosed garden surrounding a miniature pool, where he bowed and left them without a word. Father Morand waited until the monk's shuffled steps had faded, then looked at Tom and silently pointed to a stone bench that ran along one wall. The priest walked around the pool, admiring the sudden flashes of gold and bronze that danced within its night-blackened waters. He breathed in the heavy bitter-sweet odours of the herb garden, briefly recalling his youth and the herbs that used to shed their comforting scents beneath his window at night.

'There are many ways to God, are there not?'

Father Morand turned at the voice, and found himself looking into the broad smiling features of a bulky man clad in the simple brown sackcloth of the monks.. The priest nodded. 'God is found in many places,' he agreed. 'You are the Abbot?'

'I am. Diglach, I am called in this holy place.' He spoke in calmly measured tones, his voice smooth and cultured. He gestured. 'Tell me; what do you see? We do not have many visitors here and it is always interesting to have the opinions of outsiders,' he explained.

'I see a place of great beauty, of peace and calm. A place where nature has been fashioned for the greater glory of God.'

The Abbot smiled. 'For the glory of God,' he repeated, shaking his head. 'It is an Eastern idea,' he said, 'to set aside a garden, a place to feel God's hand touch the earth, and to be one with Him again. Stone walls are not enough.'

'Has the idea found favour with the brothers?' the priest asked curiously.

'We have always been workers of the soil,' Diglach said quietly. 'Our Order has cultivated seeds and crops, trees and shrubs since the time of the Norsemen. And whilst such natural things all possess a certain beauty, they are still functional. The brothers find it comforting to come here and meditate amidst that which is grown for beauty's sake.'

Father Morand nodded silently.

'But you must excuse me,' the Abbot said, 'I fear I tend to ramble on about my garden; I will do penance for my sin of pride.' He shook his head sorrowfully and crossed himself.

The priest couldn't resist a smile at the huge man's woeful expression. 'It is something to be proud of,' he remarked, looking around at the carefully tended shrubs and ornamental bushes.

Diglach smiled. 'Well perhaps it is at that. And now Father,' he said, his small eyes darting across to Tom Kennedy and back to the priest. 'How may I help you?'

Michael Morand glanced over at the young man sitting on

the cold stone bench and then looked back to the Abbot. Diglach caught his look and deliberately turned away, nodding with a barely perceptible movement of his head. The priest dusted off his hands and moved away into the shadows, followed by the huge Abbot, leaving Tom Kennedy alone with his troubled thoughts.

It was almost an hour later when Father Morand returned with the Abbot. Diglach looked troubled and there was a slight sheen of sweat on his bald head. The priest's face was set in grim lines, and his eyes were hard and pitiless. He gently roused the younger man, who had dozed briefly and, without a word or a backward glance at the Abbot, led him back into the echoing halls of the monastery.

Tom Kennedy struggled to clear his muzzy head of the ragged remnants of his dream. He had been standing in the middle of his sitting-room whilst everything around him slowly melted into a sticky putrefying mass. As he watched the walls ran like liquid and disappeared and he could make out two figures through the gaping holes. Their faces had been in shadow, but there had been something terribly familiar about them ...

The priest stopped before an arched doorway. The door had not been opened in a long time, and a delicate tracery of silver cobwebs clung to the door and lintel. Michael Morand gently brushed aside the spiderweb and left the tattered strands against the wall. He took a rusted key from a bent nail above the door. In the light of a distant torch the key glittered blood red and screamed like a soul in torment as it turned in the lock. The door cracked and groaned as it opened before swinging silently inwards. Father Morand paused before entering the windowless room and, taking the stub of a candle from a ledge just inside the door, handed it to Tom. 'Light it,' he commanded.

And the young farmer was not surprised to find his fingers trembling and his palm wet with perspiration as he held the wick to the wavering flame of the torch in the corridor.

*

The room was dark and chill, the flickering candlelight sending monstrous shadows scuttling into the corners. It was almost completely circular, but where there had once been a window was now only a wall. Along one wall stood a low wooden chest and in the centre of the room stood a high reading desk - and there was nothing else.

Father Morand took the candle from Tom and knelt by the chest. He ran his fingers along the heavy dark wood which gleamed wetly in the wan light. A section of the wood clicked and the lid cracked open. The priest crossed himself before opening the chest and then he stood and looked down into the interior.

Tom Kennedy edged forward and looked around the priest. The chest was lined in white silk, which gleamed as whitely as if it had been freshly washed, and it was empty except for a large cloth-wrapped bundle. The priest pointed. 'Pick it up - but carefully.'

The young man bent and lifted out the bundle, clutching it to his chest. It was surprisingly heavy, and it was wrapped in a thick, parchment-like cloth which made it difficult to hold. He carried it over to the reading stand and put it down, looking to the priest for instructions.

'Untie the ribbon.'

Tom unpicked the wide black ribbon that bound the bundle and let it fall to one side.

'Now, unwrap the ... covering.'

The thick cloth cracked and snapped as he carefully eased it away from what was revealed as a book. Tiny flakes of white material fell in a powdered snow to the dusty floor, and even when it had been removed, the heavy cloth still retained the impression of the book.

The young man drew back slightly when the volume was finally uncovered. It must, he thought, be almost ten inches thick, and it was bound in a thick black leather which gleamed with purple highlights. The wan candlelight ran like oil from its tooled surface, lingering briefly on the metal rims and clasps that held the book. Tom reached out and traced the design of a five-pointed star etched deeply into the leather, and then he drew his hand away with a gasp.

187

The leather felt warm, almost like ... human flesh.

Father Morand intoned briefly in Latin, and then he turned to the young man. 'Undo the clasps carefully and allow the book to fall open.'

'But it's lying flat and it's too thick,' Tom protested.

'Do it!'

The young man carefully unhooked the two clasps and let them fall back onto the wooden reading desk. There was no possible way a book that size would – could – fall open of its own accord.

An icy wind rippled through the room, making the two men shiver and sending dust motes circling into the dry air. The heavy black binding flapped like a stranded fish and then fell back, striking the wood of the reading desk with a solid thump. The thick white pages fluttered in the wind, whispering sibilantly together.

And as suddenly as it had started, the ghost-wind died, leaving an almost echoing silence in its wake. The Witchfinder pointed to the book. Tom Kennedy looked at the pages in confusion.

They were blank.

The priest abruptly gripped his arm and pulled it taut, forcing it out over the blank pages, twisting the hand until his palm faced upwards. The younger man struggled, but the priest's grip was unbreakable. Father Morand shifted his hold, bringing Tom up onto his toes as his elbow threatened to crack. With his free hand, the priest took the small silver crucifix from around his neck and with the sharpened edge, cut a small cross into Tom's index finger. The young man gasped in pain and surprise, but the priest ignored him. Father Morand squeezed blood from the tiny cut and then turned the hand downwards so that the blood dripped onto the virgin sheets. The crimson spots spattered and then haloed, like ink on blotting paper, until there were four red circles on the page in the shape of a cross. The priest then released Tom's arm and closed the book.

The young man stumbled away from the priest, rubbing his aching elbow. 'Are you mad?' he screamed.

And Father Morand's eyes caught and held his. The

priest's strangely colourless eyes swirled with colour which rapidly changed until they took on a predominantly amber hue. The priest held out his hand. 'Come!'

As if in a trance, Tom Kennedy returned to the reading desk and the Black Book.

'Place your right hand upon the book and repeat after me ...'

The young man placed his hand on the flesh-warm cover, feeling the arcane design etch itself into the palm of his hand, and repeated the priest's formula.

'*In the Name of God the Father and of His Son Who is of the One, and of the Spirit Who is of the One, I call upon Ye now in the cause of Truth and Righteousness, to show unto me my malefactor. I ask this in the Name of the Three Who are One and the One Who is All. Amen.*'

Tom staggered as he finished repeating the prayer and the priest caught and held him. 'Easy now,' he whispered gently, 'we are almost done.'

'Father ... ?' He raised a trembling hand to his forehead and looked around with a blank confused stare.

Father Morand placed his hand on the young man's head and, calling upon his strength, poured it out. The farmer shuddered and then immediately straightened. His eyes had cleared and the tremor had left his hands. 'What remains to be done, Father?' he asked calmly.

'Perhaps the hardest part of all,' the priest said wearily. 'When you open the book, you will find ... something. A name, a face ... or perhaps just a hint of the identity of whomever wishes you evil. But as soon as you see and understand what is on the page, you will cry out in a loud voice, "*In Name of the God Who is One and the One that is All, I cast thee forth from this world, never to work thine evil again.*" And then you will sprinkle the page with holy water.' The priest held up a small crystal vial. 'But Tom,' he added solemnly, 'you must act immediately when you open the book, if you delay it will mean your death ... or worse. For you will have forged a link with the witch and yourself, and whereas they will have been drawn here and will therefore be confused, you will have the advantage – but

189

only for a moment. On your life you must not delay – no matter who you see!' The urgency in the priest's voice was unmistakable and the young man thought he could detect a hint of fear in his colourless eyes. He nodded quickly and took the bottle of blessed water from the priest's hands and then, breathing deeply, prepared to open the Black Book.

He felt the raw power surge through his fingertips and up through his hands and into his arm as soon as he touched the cover. The thick black binding was warmer now, and seemed to writhe beneath his fingers, and it felt like sweat-slickened skin. The air in the small chamber was heavy and rank with the taste and odour of something resembling ozone mingled with a scent of wild herbs. The atmosphere was oppressive and ... waiting.

With the fingers of his right hand he pushed the cork from the small bottle and held it over the book, ready to use. And then he opened it.

The pages sparked and cracked as he opened them, leaving sharp gleaming after-images imprinted on his retina. The pages seemed to flicker and what had once been blank was now misted over with script and characters in a score of tongues. And almost of its own accord the book fell open to the page tinged with red. It took Tom Kennedy a few seconds to interpret the red design on the page. The blood had run and twisted, forming a design that at first glance seemed abstract, but on closer examination ...

He blinked ... and the image seemed to leap off the page and sear itself into his brain.

It was the image of his mother!

He stared in horror at the crimson picture, slowly shaking his head. 'No ... no ... no...' From a great distance he heard the priest shouting at him to act now ... now ... *now* ... And then the lines on the page twisted and the image opened its eyes and its thin lips moved in a grim parody of a smile. Tom Kennedy screamed – and dashed the page with the blessed water. He could hear a voice inside his head, a cold mocking voice, the voice of his mother. It was laughing at him, a chilling evil laugh – that abruptly changed to a hideous scream as the holy water struck the page. '*In ... In the N-Name of the God ...*' he intoned in a shaking voice.

The image on the page mouthed silently and the aged face contorted and grimaced in rage or fear or agony, or perhaps all three. Where the water had struck, the crimson mark began to run down the page, leaving a dark brown scorch mark in the paper.

'*... cast thee forth from this world never to work thine evil again.*'

The fireball ripped through the tiny cottage, leaving little more than a crumbling stone husk in its wake. The roof caved in and one of the walls collapsed. Perhaps old Mrs Kennedy had been storing liquor as some of the local people thought, or maybe Seamus, that crazy son of hers, was brewing poteen.

Wasn't it curious though, the way the spell of bad luck that had hit her other son, Tom, died with her. Of course, she never liked Tom - always preferred Seamus, her pet. And wasn't it strange that they only found one body - that of a young man, presumably Seamus - in the ruin; of course, the destruction was such that it was perfectly conceivable that the old woman's body was completely destroyed.

CHAPTER 12

THE HAND ... III

The pre-dawn air was raw and the animals' breath plumed whitely as Sorcha walked out across the field towards them. Ice cracked underfoot, and she clutched the worn shawl tightly about her thin shoulders, but it was poor protection against the chill.

Sorcha ran her hands along the flanks of the two milch cows, feeling the wasted muscles beneath the cold skin. With numb fingers, she examined the udders of both animals; they were thin and shrunken and there seemed little likelihood of milk from either. Nevertheless, she set her pail down beneath the smaller of the two cows and, with expert hands, grasped the teats and squeezed a few pitiful drops of thin, yellow milk from them.

The second cow was dry.

Sorcha set the pail down on the scarred wooden table with a bang. There was barely enough milk to cover the bottom of the container. She tugged the woollen scarf from her head and flung it onto the room's only chair as she crossed to the smoking fire. With a short length of metal, she coaxed the fire to a blaze and then fed it with lumps of wet turf. She sat back on her heels absorbing the heat, allowing it to soak into her chill bones. The wavering flames painted her lined face in warm bronze, gilding it with the appearance of youth, hiding the years, and turning her eyes to points of amber light. She ran a broken-nailed hand through her greying hair and massaged the muscles at the base of her neck.

Sorcha eased herself to her feet and crossed to the table. She poured the contents of the pail into a chipped cup, and then tasted it with her finger. She grimaced with the taste; it was thin and bitter, with a hint of musk about it. She glanced out the window. There was still a little while to go before sun-up, although the sky had paled considerably to the east. But whilst the night still lingered, she could work.

Swiftly, she brushed the table clean, sweeping crumbs of stale bread onto the floor and then, crossing to a low cupboard under the window, took a small, ornately carved box and a dark folded cloth from it. Carefully, almost reverently, she spread the cloth over the table. It was of heavy, dark silk, with a curious design picked out in silver thread on it. Sorcha positioned the cloth precisely on the table, making sure that the centre of the star design was exactly in the centre of the table. She then placed the cup with the milk in the centre of the star.

Sorcha stepped back to the sink, and poured icy water from a bucket over her hands and scrubbed them thoroughly, scraping away the grime and encrusted filth. Returning to the table, she bowed thrice to each of the four Cardinal Points, and invoked the four elements of Earth, Air, Fire and Water. She then walked widdershins around the table, tossing salt over her left shoulder and murmuring an incantation in a tongue that was older than man.

Sorcha sensed the gathering forces. She felt the eerie trickle of power along her forearms, raising the hair, sending painful tingles through her fingertips. The fire in the grate – which had died to little more than glowing embers – suddenly blazed into a roaring furnace, the flames tinged with blue and green, before abruptly dying completely.

In the silence, she could hear the pounding of her heart, and her breathing was as laboured as if she had run a great distance. Mastering her trembling hands, she undid the metal catch on the dark wooden box and threw back the lid. Inside, the box was lined with crimson silk, tiny points of what might have been jewels, picking out an arcane design. Sorcha reached in and carefully withdrew a withered hand!

193

She held the mummified claw aloft as if in offering and swiftly kissed the palm. And then, with infinite care, she placed the hand above the cup and began to stir the milk with the stiffened forefinger. The long talon scraped along the bottom of the enamel with an almost animal-like screech.

And even as the claw continued its circular motion, the cup began to fill. The clear white liquid rose slowly, until it threatened to overflow the cup. Sorcha grinned triumphantly, and held the claw aloft once more. And what had once been a shrivelled, withered claw, was now young and fleshily-plump, resembling the hand Sorcha had hacked from her lover's corpse so many years ago. Once more she kissed it, and this time her lips lingered on the warm flesh before she replaced it in its ornate box.

She was replacing the box and cloth in the cupboard when the first rays of the morning sun turned the window molten with light.

Sorcha took the cup and, careful not to spill anything, emptied it back into the pail. The liquid hit the bottom with an almost musical drumming, which was quickly replaced by a thick viscous gurgling as the pail continued to fill ... and fill ... and fill ...

By the time the sun had risen above the trees, Sorcha had two pails full of fresh, warm milk, and the enamel cup was still not empty. The old witch ran her hand across the top of the cup and nullified the spell with a phrase, and then drained what remained with a swallow. She felt the fluid course through her, invigorating and refreshing her, and she knew she would feel neither hunger nor thirst that day.

She glanced at the window again, gauging the time from the position of the sun: it was almost time to leave for the market.

Sorcha hurried down the rutted track carrying the heavy pails on her shoulders. She walked upright, even though the heavy length of wood that held the pails bit deeply into her flesh. The early morning air was sharp and bracing, and the late November sun touched the hard, barren earth with its wan light. Sorcha's shadow danced along the track before her; a long thin wraith, with the bar of the pails across her shoulders, resembling a cross.

There was a small crowd gathered at the cross-roads, the women gossiping animatedly together, and the men sharing a pipe, leaning against the hedge. Sorcha smiled inwardly as all conversation stopped as she approached. She was fully aware of her own reputation, and at times revelled in it. It gave her a curious sense of power to know that she instilled fear into the townspeople and local farmers.

She walked through the group without a word, glancing neither left nor right, and as she walked on towards the town, she could feel the hostile stares directed towards her back and the low buzz of conversation. A sod of earth struck the ground beside her and another sailed over her head – but she also knew that they were almost afraid to hit her because of her reputation.

Dunogh was typical of many small Irish country towns; a row of low houses built along both sides of the main street, a post office, a few small family run shops and a church. The church – with its new steeple – dominated the west end of the town, and in front of it, a few small children played on the green.

Sorcha began to peddle her milk at the first house she reached. She would then work her way down one side of the street, up the other side, and then head off home.

She stuck her head in the open door and, forcing a smile to her thin lips, called out 'Hallo ... Mrs O'Brien are you in ...?' She heard muffled footsteps approaching from the other room, and a short stout woman appeared from the shadows.

'Aaah Sorcha, it's yourself. I was just thinking of you: I need some milk for the childer ... '

The young priest sat in the back of the church, attempting to absorb the peace and calm of the ancient building. But the peace would not come and he found it difficult to pray, to concentrate on the well-polished phrases of his faith. He looked up with such despair on his thin face that the older man sitting by his side was forced to smile. He leaned over and patted the young priest's shoulder. 'Come now Father, compose yourself and tell me the full story.'

Father Fintan nodded slowly and sat back on the hard wooden pew. 'I don't know what to do,' he said quietly.

The older man clasped his hands about the hawthorn walking stick and smiled gently. 'If you knew what to do, you would not have brought the matter before your superiors, and they would not have passed the matter on to me.'

The young man looked up. 'Is it true what they say about you Father Morand?'

The old priest smiled. 'And what do they say about me?'

'They say you are an expert on the ways of the fairy folk and witches – a Witchfinder.'

Father Morand tapped the metal ferrule of his stick on the polished floor, the sudden sound echoing like gunshot. 'Aaah, but you mustn't confuse the two. The fairy folk, that is, the descendants of the Tuatha De Danann, the People of the Goddess, who once ruled this land, are not always evil. They can be capricious, and even by our standards wicked. But their wickedness is like that of a child – and it can usually be traced to a cause.' He waved a gnarled hand expansively. 'This church, for example, is built on a fairy fort. Was there any trouble during its construction?'

Father Fintan shrugged. 'It was before my time, but I could check for you ... '

'It might prove interesting.'

The young priest sat upright suddenly. 'There is something,' he said, almost apologetically.

'And that is?'

'We've recently had a new spire installed. The old one had been severely damaged during a series of thunderstorms over the past few years, and had been struck by lightning on numerous occasions. But while the new construction was going up there were several strange instances: tools missing, cement hardening too quickly, wood warping and cracking overnight ...'

Father Morand laughed quietly. 'That's it exactly. The fairy folk at work. And I dare say,' he added, 'that once you sprinkled the work area with holy water, said a few *pater nosters* and *ave marias*, the trouble stopped?'

Father Fintan swallowed audibly. 'How did you know?'

The old priest laughed again. 'Oh, I've seen the same pattern repeated over and over.' He dismissed the subject with a wave of his hand. 'But to continue. Whilst the fairy folk are not by nature evil, witches, be they male or female, make a conscious decision to follow either the Right- or Left-Hand Paths, the Roads of Light and Darkness. But it is their own choice, made with their own free will, although,' he added ruefully, 'the Left-Hand Path is often the more attractive, with its immediate rewards and power.'

'Are there many witches in Ireland?' The young priest's voice had fallen to a whisper, and he glanced uneasily at the altar.

Father Morand shook his head. 'We are lucky in that respect. There are but four organised covens throughout the country, but they are slowly dying out and one is almost finished. Of course, there are many wise women, called witches, wise in the country-lore, conversant with the *Sidhe* folk, the fairies, and their ways. But these are not true witches.'

'Is Sorcha a witch?' Fintan asked.

Father Morand shook his head, his colourless eyes gazing into the distance. 'I do not know; I've only read a second-hand report. Tell me what you know of the woman.' He stood suddenly. 'Let us walk; I'm not as young as I used to be and I feel my bones stiffening.'

The two priests walked down the side of the church, turned and genuflected towards the altar, and then made their way out the door. Michael Morand breathed deeply, savouring the country air, whilst the young priest examined his companion covertly. It was the first time he had seen him in the full light of day. The older man had come late the previous evening and had been shown straight to bed by

Fintan's housekeeper, and in the morning he had been gone, and the young priest had found him praying on his knees at the back of the church.

Father Morand stood a head taller than the younger man, and the shock of snow white hair and colourless eyes gave him the appearance of a blind biblical prophet.

The older man repeated his question. 'Tell me what you know of this woman.'

Father Fintan muttered an apology and, tucking his hands into his wide sleeves, began. 'She is a strange woman in many respects,' he said, 'she lives alone in a tiny run-down – even by country standards – cottage on the outskirts of town. She owns two cows, a few hens and a cat ... '

'Nothing else?' Father Morand interrupted.

'Nothing. The only name I have ever heard her called in the town is Sorcha,' he continued. 'However, I went back through the parish records and came across a marriage between a Donal MacIntee, a local farmer, and a young girl by name Sorcha Ni Cleirigh. This was back in the '40's, some sixty years ago. Now, two years later, in November 1844, there is a note of a burial of the same Donal MacIntee. In December of the same year, a record has been made of the banns being posted for a Peter Casside and Sorcha MacIntee!'

'One month later,' Morand whispered. 'How did MacIntee die?'

'It didn't say in the records, so I went to the home of the local doctor. He is the son of Doctor O'Connell, who practised in this neighbourhood around that time. And in one of his old journals, I found a note of the death.'

Father Morand rubbed the iron ferrule of his stick against his boot as he listened; he didn't need to be told any more, the story was terribly familiar. 'Go on,' he murmured.

'Apparently the husband died of a heart attack ... at least that was the medical finding. But Doctor O'Connell had added a footnote in his own hand to the effect that, in his opinion, the man had died of fright, for there was a look of absolute terror frozen onto his face.'

The old priest nodded slowly, his hard face set in grim

lines. 'Would I be correct in thinking that he was found in a clearing in the wood?' He pointed south towards the trees.

'Yes!' Fintan looked around, startled. 'But how did you know?'

'The case is not unfamiliar to me. I was ... passing through this town about that time.' Father Morand gripped the handle of his walking stick until his knuckles showed white. The younger man drew back from his fellow priest, for the light in his colourless eyes was dreadful.

'And what of her lover?' he asked suddenly, his voice harsh and grating.

'I checked the records,' the young priest said quietly. 'She never married him, for his death is recorded on Christmas Day of that same year. Apparently, he died on Christmas night – although his burial did not take place until the end of January.'

'The Winter Solstice,' Father Morand said. He caught the young man's look of incomprehension. 'The festival of Christ-tide is not a Christian one,' he explained, 'it is an arbitrary date chosen by the Church in all its wisdom to disguise the old pagan festival.'

'It is the birth of Our Lord,' Fintan protested.

Father Morand shook his head. 'It symbolises the birth of Christ on earth; but do not think that it is an exact date. Read your Testaments man,' he snapped. 'It is a pagan feast – take my word for that, and I will wager my eternal soul that young Peter Casside was sacrificed to the Great God Pan on that date all those years ago.'

'Father!'

'The body; was it ever found?'

'Not all of it. It was washed ashore some weeks later – the fishes had been at it, it was recognised by the clothing.'

The old man tapped his stick against the stone steps. 'Aye, that would disguise the mutilation, sure enough.'

'I don't understand.'

Father Morand ignored the question. 'And just why did you contact your superiors about this woman?'

'Some of the townspeople came to me accusing her of witchcraft.'

'Indeed; and what makes them suspect her?'

Father Fintan shivered slightly in his thin coat. The whole subject was disturbing enough, without having this old man taking it so seriously. 'Apparently, she has two cows, Father. Now, according to what I have been told, her land is neither rich enough, nor does she spend enough on feed for her animals to produce either the quantity or quality of milk she sells.'

The old priest smiled suddenly, and his smile was almost as terrible as his anger.

'Have you ever heard the like?' Fintan said despairingly. 'Here we are, into the twentieth century, and people still believing in magic and witches ... ' he trailed off and coloured.

'Including old priests who believe in fairies, eh?' Father Morand smiled. 'You have a lot to learn, my son. I travelled in my youth with a friend of mine who later became a priest, a missionary. He opened my eyes to some of the evidence of the Otherworld that still lingers in Ireland. And when he went away we kept up a regular correspondence over the years. And the stories he wrote concerning the beliefs and rites of the pagan lands he was preaching in, convinced me that there is still magic abroad in this world. Oh, perhaps the word magic offends you? Call it a force then, a power. A power that may be tapped for either good or evil. Some of the great saints could touch this force and work their miracles through it, but there were others who perverted it to their own evil ends ... ' He reached out and patted the young man on the shoulder. 'You are young, wait; do not form any hard and fast judgements on such matters yet.' He looked back down the street and continued in a different tone. 'But to answer your question; then the answer is yes, I have heard of similar spells. And the belief that a witch can draw off a neighbour's milk is not uncommon across the water in Britain and Wales.'

'Do you believe it?' asked Fintan slowly.

'Perhaps.'

'That is not an answer.'

'Father, when you asked for help and guidance from your

200

superiors, they did not send me just because I was handy or close-by. I joined the priesthood later than most, and in my youth I had made a special study of the Otherworld, the Shadowland of Fairy and the Realm of Witchcraft. And when I took holy orders, rather than lose all that knowledge and experience, I was given the brief to seek out and study the occurrence of the Otherworld and the *Sidhe*.'

'You *are* a witchfinder!'

The old priest laughed, tears starting into his eyes. 'So I'm called, but dear me, nothing so dramatic. I am a folklorist certainly, a collector and recorder of the rapidly vanishing country lore. Occasionally, I perform an exorcism – in many cases the mere fact that the exorcism had been performed provided all the patient needs, and they are "cured". And then, in a tiny fraction of cases . . .' he smiled. 'Tell me,' he said suddenly, 'do you know what my name means?'

Father Fintan shook his head.

The old priest smiled slightly. 'Aaah, few do. It is an ancient name – an honourable one also. It was borne by the Abbot of Clogher and the Bishop of Nemdrum in the Middle Ages and later, but it goes back further, for Morand was one of the Judges of Banba and, like Solomon, his judgements were always fair and honest.' He turned and held the young priest's eyes with his hard stare. 'You see, I too am sometimes a judge,' he paused and added softly, 'a judge, a jury and sometimes . . . an executioner!'

It was mid-afternoon by the time Sorcha returned home. The sun was already beginning to sink down behind the low mountains in the west and the chill wind that had blown through the day had taken on a sharper, keener note. Low clouds gathered in the north and west, promising rain or sleet.

Sorcha kicked open the scarred wooden door and entered the dark interior of the single-roomed cottage. The fire she had kindled that morning had sunk to low embers and bathed a small circle before the fire in warm amber light, but otherwise the room was in darkness.

201

The old witch stopped just inside the door, her senses tingling; something was awry. Her hard eyes darted about the room, noting the dark shape of the table in the centre of the room, and the black oblong of her straw-filled bed in one corner. Everything seemed in place ... but she couldn't shake the impression that she wasn't alone in the room.

Water dripped somewhere from the roof, the sound curiously muffled in the silence, but it broke the spell that held her by the doorway. She dropped her two empty pails in the corner by the door and slowly crossed to the fire, still clutching her shoulder brace. She knelt before the grate, her questing fingers seeking the candles tucked into a niche beside the fire. Normally, she didn't use them, but tonight was different and the darkness, usually her companion, now threatened.

The wick sputtered and then flared, shedding a warm opalescent light around her, dusting her grey hair with silver and turning her skin to wax. Sorcha held the candle over her head and looked about – and screamed!

There was someone sitting at the table.

A light flared in the centre of the room and a small stub of a candle blossomed light, lending the tall figure sitting behind it a demonic cast to his features. 'Hello Sorcha.'

The witch gasped and held the wooden shoulder brace tightly in both hands. 'Who ... who are you?' she whispered.

The figure in the shadows chuckled. 'What, don't tell me you're surprised? Surely you knew I would come for you one day?'

'Who are you?' she suddenly screamed, feeling a dread chill envelop her heart.

The figure moved the candle away from his face, so that the light illuminated it more fully. He smiled regretfully. 'You do not remember me, Sorcha – although,' he added, 'I think for a moment there you confused me with ... something else. I am Father Morand,' he said suddenly.

With an almost physical effort, Sorcha composed herself. For one single moment, she had thought ... She caught the look of amusement in the old priest's eyes: he had planned it that way.

202

'Who are you?' she repeated, her voice chill with fury.

'I have already told you: I am Morand.'

'What are you doing in my home?' She stepped closer to the table and raised the length of wood threateningly.

'I have come for you Sorcha – as I swore I would so long ago.'

'But I've never met you before ... '

'Never?' The old priest smiled curiously. 'Never?'

Sorcha brought the shoulder brace crashing down onto the table, sending the candle toppling onto the floor. 'Get out of my house.' Her voice was hard and flat – tinged with anger and something approaching fear.

'You know me, don't you Sorcha.' Father Morand stood, a huge hulking figure in the semi-darkness. His eyes caught the spark of light from the last embers of the fire and glowed with tiny pinpoints of red light. 'You remember Peter Casside?' He caught her sudden intake of breath. 'Yes, I see that you do. He was your lover ... your sacrifice ... and my brother!'

The witch drew back suddenly. The anger and hate in the old priest's voice was almost palpable. His words struck her like a blow. 'You are Michael Casside?'

'I am Father Morand,' he said icily.

'Morand the Witchfinder!'

'Only occasionally,' he said laconically. 'A priest, a researcher, a folklorist – but yes, witch hunting is part of my profession.'

'Why have you come back?' she asked quietly.

'I've been drawn here by chance – if you believe in such a thing called chance.' He smiled grimly. 'I always swore to come back for you someday.'

'I looked for you,' she continued in that same quiet reflective tone. 'But you just disappeared. You didn't even attend your brother's funeral. You were always different, always special ... it was one of the reasons we chose you. You have a strange aura, do you know that? You would have made a fine warlock.'

'I prefer to use my powers in the cause of good,' he said wearily. 'It was not a difficult choice to make when I learned what you had done to my brother.'

'He was to be the sacrifice – you were to be my husband.'

The old priest smiled, his teeth showing white in the semi-darkness. 'I know. You needed the affinity of twins, didn't you? Sacrifice one, and send the power released through that death into the soul of the twin, and then, once the twin is kept under control, you would have access to almost unlimited occult power.'

'And it so nearly worked,' Sorcha said, her voice lost in distant memories. 'With that power, we could have called forth Our Master into this world.' And suddenly hate and anger blazed in her voice. 'And you destroyed all that!' She struck out with the heavy shoulder brace, but Father Morand turned the blow aside with his stick, and rapped her across the knuckles. She dropped the length of wood with a curse and sucked her bruised fingers.

Father Morand shook his head slowly. 'Listen to me; my faith teaches forgiveness and, although it's hard, a lot of time has passed between us, and if you're willing to forswear your witchcraft then I am prepared to forgive you.'

'And if not?'

The old priest made his way to the door and opened it. He stood, outlined against the gathering storm and shook his head slowly. 'If you do not ... ' he murmured softly. And then he continued in a different tone. 'Well then, I shall be forced to pray for you.' He nodded briefly, turned and disappeared into the night.

Long after he was gone, Sorcha crossed to the open door and carefully closed it. She leaned back against the rough wood, feeling the boards through her thin clothing and looked around the room. Night had fallen fully and, with the heavy clouds obscuring the stars, the room was in complete darkness with only two burning embers, that reminded her of eyes, glowing in the hearth.

Feeling all her years, she went to the fire and lit one of the candles from the embers, and then she sat on the hard wooden chair, placed the candle on the table before her and gazed deep into its wavering flame.

She knew, somewhere deep inside her she knew, that

what was happening now had been ordained long ago, even before she had sacrificed Peter to the Old One on that hard cold night so long ago. She stared into the flame and watched the years roll by, rising with the thin tendril of black smoke and disappearing into the shadows. She saw herself as a young woman, drunk with the power of sacrifice, feeling the force slide through her body and engulf her. That had been a time when she could have had anything she wanted. The coven had been powerful then, for it had achieved the ultimate offering: the sacrifice of a baptised follower of the Christ to the Master.

But the power they had gained was but a fraction of the total. The force released by Peter's death passed on to his twin – and had she been able to find and keep that twin then nothing would have stood in their way of absolute power. Sorcha ground her teeth in rage; but Michael Casside had disappeared that night. She had spent years searching for him, and over those years her powers had wasted away, and the coven had broken up and gone their separate ways. And so she had returned to her native village, practically with nothing, and so poor that she was forced to draw off her neighbour's milk with a dead hand.

Until now.

For now Michael Casside had come back. She found it curiously ironic that he should have entered the priesthood, but on reflection it did not seem so strange, for the power that she would have utilised to her own ends, he now shaped in the Church's work.

She passed her hand over the candle flame, dousing it. The sweet smell of candle grease enveloped her, making her think of the church, bringing with it old, old memories of her childhood when her father used to bring her there every Sunday morning. She smiled at the thought; how could she have explained to him then that she was already one of the Old Faith; how could she have explained to him that she had been promised to the Horned God while still in her mother's womb?

She pressed her nail into the soft wax around the top of the candle; there had been a time when she had shaped with more than wax. She thought of the tiny dolls made from mud and blood, with flecks of hair or nail parings or blood woven into them, and how she had manipulated men with them. And then she wondered whether it might be possible to create a doll of the priest ... ? But she shook her head. His faith alone would protect him.

The witch stood and went to her low pallet of straw in the corner of the room and prepared for bed. She wondered why she had never connected Michael Casside with the priest, Morand. She had known that Michael would have the power that his twin's death would have given him, and she knew that the priest had a reputation for having a frightening and powerful presence. On reflection, the connection seemed simple. But she had been looking for a frightened young man, possibly crazed with the sudden unleashing of strange powers upon him, she had never connected him with the ice-cold Witchfinder.

She unrolled her long hair and let it flow down her back. Once it had been as black as a raven's wing and as soft, but now it was streaked with long strands of grey and silver, and was hard and brittle under her fingers. She lay back on the rough pillow, feeling her heart beating in her breast. The sound was loud and strangely solemn; it seemed more like the tolling of a distant bell.

'And you spoke to her?' Father Fintan pushed aside the remains of his supper and leaned across the table.

Father Morand patted his lips with a napkin and nodded briefly.

'Does she admit her witchcraft?' the young priest pressed.

Father Morand sat back in his chair, toying absently with the silver crucifix about his neck. 'She did not deny it,' he said quietly, 'but then, she hardly could with me.'

'I don't understand, Father.'

Father Morand smiled. 'You see, my son, I knew her once, oh, many years ago, before I took Holy Orders. In fact, you might say she was one of the reasons I joined the priesthood.' He laughed suddenly. 'Who would have thought it: a witch driving a young man into the church?'

Father Fintan smiled uncertainly, unsure of the joke.

The old priest leaned over and patted his hand. 'Oh, don't look so worried – I've not lost what little sense I've left.' He leaned back in the chair and continued, his voice soft and wistful.

'But first, a confession. I lied to you when I said I was passing through this town when MacIntee and later Peter Casside died. I was born in this town, I was living here at the time.

'I first met Sorcha many years ago, when I was a young man. I was deeply interested in the fairy lore of this part of the country then, and I had been recommended to speak with Sorcha's mother, who had something of a reputation as a witch. But of course, the dividing line between witchcraft and fairy lore is very faint and in some cases almost indistinguishable.

'The old woman was very helpful, and her knowledge was phenomenal. I visited her over several years making notes from her fund of stories about the superstitions and beliefs, cures and herbs. Some of it I've never forgotten. And it was then I met her daughter, Sorcha. She was a stunning beauty, but a wild, untamed – and dangerous – beauty. I fell in love with her immediately.' Father Morand laughed. 'Oh, let me tell you, I made a fool of myself over her. At first she ignored me, but later, she did accept my advances. And then one day, my brother Peter accompanied me to the Ui Cleirighs. And suddenly everything changed.' The old man closed his eyes, and his face tightened in pain. 'You see, my brother and I were twins, he being older than me by a few minutes. In looks we were identical, the only difference being that whereas my eyes are almost colourless, his were dark, almost black.

'Sorcha took an immediate interest in Peter, and they soon became very close. But you know,' he opened his eyes and looked at the younger man, 'the more I came to know of the family, the more I came to distrust – and eventually fear – them. The old mother's lore, whilst being true in every sense of the word, was always dark and forbidding, and although she often talked of the Dark Elves and the Hidden Ones, she knew very little about the Shining Ones, the last of the De Danann, the *Sidhe*.' He shook his head slowly. 'Oh, it's so easy to say now that I should have known, and I did warn my brother, but he laughed off my fears and eventually came to believe that I was jealous of him and his involvement with Sorcha ... and who knows, perhaps I was.' He was silent then for a long time, and when he continued, there was a new note to his voice, a harder, harsher note, one of anger and rage ... one of power.

'And then it was suddenly announced that Sorcha was to be married to old MacIntee. He was rich – even by English standards – and almost twenty years her senior and, strangely Peter wasn't unusually heartbroken by the whole affair. Two years later the old man was dead, and one month after that my brother became engaged to her. A few weeks later, he was dead.' The old priest sat forward, resting his elbows on the table and cupped his face in his hands. 'And I can tell you the exact night and the precise moment he died.' He looked across at Father Fintan, and the younger priest winced at the look of anguish in the older man's eyes. 'I felt him die!'

There was silence in the small dining room after that, and the crackling of the fire seemed unusually loud. Father Fintan was the first to move, carefully unclasping his hands, which he had unconsciously squeezed together. He winced as the circulation returned. 'What happened?' he whispered hoarsely.

The old priest's eyes glazed as he gazed into a different time. 'It was Christmas night; a hard, cold, bitter night, the sky cloudless, bright with stars. I lay awake in my bed watching them wheel across the heavens, waiting for my brother to come home. He had crept out earlier that evening, gone off to see Sorcha, but now most of the night was gone and the dawn was almost upon us.

'I dozed, but even so, I began to feel his distress just as the sky was brightening; just a tingling at the base of my spine, but that quickly grew into an all-pervading panic, a soul-consuming fear. And as the first rays of the morning sun touched the eastern sky, he died. And I felt it. It was as if a part of me had been torn out, ripped asunder.' Father Morand shook his head slowly, as if in wonderment. 'I lay there helpless, sobbing like a child; I had never felt so alone in my entire life. But as I lay there, I felt the first tendrils of a strange power creep into me. It was part of my brother, a ... a force, an inner strength if you will, and in that moment I knew what had happened to him, and I knew what I must do ... '

'Yes ... ?' Fintan prompted.

The old priest's eyes lit on the younger priest's. They blazed with an inner fire, and Fintan was suddenly terrified. 'I decided I would seek out and destroy witchcraft at its very roots, and I would do so with the full authority and backing of the church!'

'The church has never condoned killing,' Fintan said. 'It teaches love and kindness; it teaches forgiveness.'

'There are some who are beyond forgiveness.'

'No-one is beyond Our Lord's mercy.'

'Why should those who have renounced God's mercy and love on this earth hope to find it in the next?' Morand brought his hand down on the table, making the plates and cutlery jump. 'They have lived by a sword of their own choosing, let them die by it.'

'Your hate will destroy you, Father,' Fintan said quietly. He stood and bowed to the older man. 'I will bid you a good night; I will pray for you.'

Father Morand smiled apologetically. 'My son, you cannot tell me anything about myself that I do not already know. But I will thank you for your prayers.'

Fintan nodded. 'I will, Father.' He paused by the door, and then added impulsively. 'Perhaps it would be best if you left ... ?'

Morand nodded. 'Perhaps it would,' he agreed. 'To-morrow then; I have a little business to finish in the morning, but afterwards I will go.'

*

209

Stray wisps of chill mist seeped through the door as Sorcha prepared for the ritual. The cottage was cold and damp and even the turf fire blazing in the grate did little to dispel the dampness or take the bite from the air.

Sorcha shivered in her worn clothing, but it was something more than the weather that sent icy shivers up along her spine. For some reason, she felt extremely reluctant to use the Hand this morning, and there was an almost physical revulsion at the thought of touching the withered member.

And then she looked at the pitifully few drops of almost colourless milk that barely covered the bottom of the pail, and knew that she had little choice.

'Ah, here they are now!' Martin O'Leary pushed open the door and held it whilst his two young daughters struggled in with the pails of milk clutched in each hand. 'The best there is.' O'Leary dipped a finger in one of the pails and sucked the thick white liquid from it.

Father Michael Morand nodded sharply. 'Where is it stored?'

'Here Father.' The farmer patted a series of large wooden churns. 'And they are leakproof,' he added, anticipating the priest's next question.

'But you have been losing milk?' Morand insisted.

O'Leary nodded. 'Someone has been drawing off my milk. I know the signs,' he continued. 'It happened when I was a boy and my father warned me about it.' He sniffed the cold air. 'Can you smell it?' he asked. 'Like lightning ... '

Morand nodded. 'I know,' he said quietly, 'it has begun, and it will get stronger presently as she draws upon the spell.' He paused and looked around the shed. 'Did you do as I requested?'

'We have.' O'Leary pointed. 'We've poured the milk into one pail only, and we've had a fire burning since late last night with a poker heating in it; it should be white-hot by now.'

'Good; then all is in readiness.' Father Morand glanced

out the grime encrusted window and noted the first grey tinge of dawn lightening the eastern sky. 'Then there is nothing more for us to do but wait.'

The old witch ran her fingers across the wrinkled palm of the withered hand. She could feel the residue of power still lingering in the leathery flesh, could feel it race through her fingertips, setting her nerves afire. It was a powerful talisman, she knew – but it could have been so much more powerful. Stifling her regrets, she hurried on with the incantation.

The spell was almost complete. The cup sat in the centre of the table on the dark, heavily worked arcane cloth, like a chalice in some blasphemous offering; salt had been sprinkled and the words said. All that remained to be done was the Drawing with the Hand.

The air in the shed had grown even colder and taken on a definite metallic taste and odour, and a barely audible crackling pervaded the room.

Morand tensed and then breathed deeply. 'Soon,' he whispered, 'soon.'

Sorcha kissed the palm of the hand and then dipped the index finger into the small cup and began to stir the milk. She could feel the power growing, could feel the tenseness in the air as the hair on her arms and head rose in wavering strands. She felt the hand begin to pulse in her palm and the flesh softening and swelling. She felt her own hand grow numb as the tingling made its way up her arm, into her shoulders and down into her breasts and then on into her stomach. She felt the feeling growing, rising to engulf her.

And as she stirred, the level of the milk began to rise ...

O'Leary swore briefly. 'Look!' He pointed into the open

211

churn. And before their eyes, they could see that the level of the milk was slowly but surely sinking.

Morand wrapped a thick cloth about his hand and pulled the white-hot poker from the glowing coals. With the red firelight beneath his face, he looked truly godlike ... or demonic. He called aloud in a language O'Leary didn't understand, crossed himself – and plunged the hot poker into the slowly disappearing milk!

The mummified hand exploded into flames. Sorcha screamed in agony and dropped it onto the ornate cloth, which immediately sizzled and burst into flame. She fell back nursing her badly burned hand. The flames quickly took hold of the old wooden table and ate through the dry wood, filling the cottage with thick black smoke – and the foul odour of badly burned meat as the hand was consumed.

Sorcha attempted to crawl to the door, but had to throw herself to one side as the blazing table fell to the floor, sending sparks and hot cinders around the room. One fell on her straw pallet, and a single wisp of smoke rose steadily, and then it too, burst into flames. The heat was intense, and Sorcha felt the skin on her face and bare arms sear and blister. She could barely see and her breath came in pain-wracked sobs. As she reached the smoking wooden door, the windows blew out and the ornamental plates on the dresser shattered with the heat. She burned her fingers on the metal latch as she lifted it and pushed. But the door wouldn't move – it had swollen with the heat.

The milk boiled and discoloured as Morand twisted the sizzling poker in a clockwise fashion. A thick – almost human-like – skin formed about the metal, quickly darkening until it assumed a leathery consistency. It suddenly became more and more difficult to turn the poker and the skin was becoming harder and harder, until now it even looked like leather. It assumed strange shapes and patterns, some suggestively obscene and others ... even

212

more disturbing. And sudden a hand formed in the dark skin, a severed, long nailed claw ...

Morand shouted and attempted to withdraw the poker – but it was stuck fast, and he couldn't remove his hand! The metal grew uncomfortably warm, warmer, and then unbearably hot. The metal glowed red and then white hot. The priest screamed as the poker ate into his hand, searing and crisping the flesh, peeling it back from the bones. A thick stench of burning meat filled the shed and O'Leary, gazing in horror, gagged, before turning to run for help. Morand fell to the floor and writhed in agony, the poker still clutched between his smoking fingers.

And then in his pain, he whispered, 'I forgive her ... ' And the poker fell from his hand.

And the door snapped open.

'How is she?' Morand asked the doctor as he changed the dressing on the priest's hand.

Doctor O'Connell shook his head in amazement. 'Oh, she is much the same as you are – in fact, her wounds are almost exactly the same as yours.'

'Will I ever use it again?' Father Morand nodded at his left hand, now swathed in thick bandages.

The young doctor shook his head. 'Never, I fear.'

'Will she have the use of hers?'

Again the doctor shook his head. 'Never.'

Later, when the doctor had gone, Father Fintan came in and sat with the older priest. The young priest thought the older man looked tired and ... aged. He had lost a lot of weight in the last three days, and he was no longer the avenging biblical prophet he had first seemed.

'Sorcha's confessed,' he said quietly.

Morand nodded. 'Good; I'm glad.'

'She wants to see you.'

'When I can get up again, I'll go and see her,' the old priest promised.

'Father,' Fintan said slowly, 'what happened?'

Morand was silent for a moment and then he said softly, 'We were linked, my brother and I. It was a link that had been strengthened by my brother's death, a link that had been forged by Sorcha. I struck at her through him – or that physical part of him which still survived. It struck back at me.' He turned and looked at the younger man with his strange unwavering stare. 'I sought revenge,' he said softly, 'where I should have offered forgiveness.'

There are not many people in Ireland now who remember the Witchfinder; indeed, many will deny his existence altogether. But in some of the lonelier country towns and villages, the older folk will occasionally tell of Father Michael Morand, the Witchfinder.

VOLUME III

For Anna,
hoc opus, hic labor est.

Contents

Contents

Chapter One

ARRIVAL

The sorceress held up the goat's steaming entrails in the fresh morning air; drops of thick dark blood spattered her face and breasts and ran down her slender arms, but she ignored them as she sought to decipher the signs.

The morning sun broke through the greying clouds behind her and ran slickly along the glistening ropes, tingeing them with pink, making them faintly translucent. And in the intricate whorls and creases the small, sallow-skinned woman read the future, divining the trends, the possibilities and the probabilities.

The sorceress nodded slowly and carefully dropped the entrails into the brazier before her. The flesh hissed and spat and tainted the fresh salt air with the smell of burning meat. Sinde then bowed to the four cardinal points and silently offered the remains of the animal to her own dark gods. She then stepped back and indicated that her servants might toss the carcass into the purifying flames. The small woman accepted a cloth from an acolyte and wiped away most of the blood before walking across the smooth sandy beach to where her mistress sat on a low flat stone at the foot of the cliffs with Cipine, Trayim and Ain her principal advisors. The four women looked up as the sorceress joined them.

'Well?' Caesir asked quietly, her huge dark eyes wide and concerned.

'It is as I predicted,' Sinde whispered, 'the waters rise slowly but surely; the goddess approaches with each passing day...'

Unconsciously the four women glanced skywards, where the huge disc of the moon hung low in the sky, its broken irregular features clearly visible even though the sun now rode high in the sky. For the past few seasons, the great white goddess had been steadily approaching the domain of man, as if the goddess herself wished to walk his world.

And for the past few seasons – especially at the turn of the year – the tides had been getting higher and higher and much of the lowlands along the banks of the Nile had been submerged with great loss of life and crops. Even Caesir's own island, Meroe, was now much reduced in size, and it was no longer possible to walk across to the mainland at low tide.

'What will happen?' Cipine, a huge woman clad only in a loin cloth and gold bangles, asked.

Sinde shrugged. 'If the waters continue to rise as the goddess nears, then I fear she will soon be ruling a land of waves only.'

The red-haired northerner grimaced. She was used to fighting tangible foes; the elements were something beyond her control – and for the first time in her long and bloody career she was frightened. 'What can we do?' she asked quietly.

Before Sinde could answer, Caesir held up her slim hand, her pointed nails glistening in the sunlight. 'If the goddess comes to earth,' she asked the sorceress, 'where will she rest?'

Sinde considered, and then she pointed to the south and west. 'In the waves, many days hence.'

'Are we not safe then?' Ain, the tall dark-skinned, curly-haired warrior from the lush rainforests to the far south, asked.

'Nowhere will be safe,' Sinde said quietly. 'When the

2

goddess lands, she will create a wave that will sweep all before it; those in the valleys and,' – she smiled bitterly – 'on the islands, will be called to their gods.'

Ain frowned, and then her startlingly white teeth flashed in a smile. 'If the wave is coming in from the west, could we not flee into the east?' She glanced across at the princess. 'There is no dishonour in fleeing before a stronger enemy. There is a saying in my homeland: "Flee before a hungry beast, for he is easily taken when he has eaten his fill." '

Caesir nodded, sunlight gliding down her sleek black hair. 'No, there is no dishonour in fleeing; but is there anywhere to flee to?' She leaned forward and stared intently at the sorceress. 'What land is there to the west? What is the last land before the Emptiness?'

Sinde laughed gently, the sound no louder than the sighing of the wind. 'I have told you before,' she whispered, 'there is no emptiness; this world is like a fruit, a ball, it is round.'

Cipine laughed good-naturedly. 'Aye, so you've said, and some day we'll sail to the very edge of the world and you can tell me again as we stand and watch the waters boil over into the Nothingness.'

The tiny easterner smiled and bowed. 'Yes, some day we will.'

Caesir turned back to the sorceress. 'But is there land to the west?' she persisted.

Sinde knelt on the warm golden sands and drove her hands deep into the smooth grains. Her dark eyes closed and she spoke aloud in the sibilant, whispering language of her race. The air began to tingle and the fresh salt odour was replaced with a harsh metallic taste. And slowly the sand began to shift and flow. Strange arcane patterns etched themselves into the sand at the women's feet; images formed, some reminiscent of beasts, some of men and, even more disturbing, some that were a mixture of both, like Caesir's animal-headed, man-bodied gods.

3

And then an abstract pattern formed, a strange irregular circle, cut almost in half by a large depression. The sand continued to flow and suddenly Cipine leaned forward and pointed with her short blunt fingers.

'It is a map!'

Caesir fell to her knees in the sand. 'Yes, a map; I have seen my father use something similar ... and we are here!' She pointed to the lower right-hand corner of the design.

The sorceress nodded. 'And now let us see what will happen when the waters come,' she said. She bent her head and murmured again in her own tongue, and once again the sand shifted and flowed. This time, however, the movement began on the right-hand side, and swept slowly across the design, obliterating most of it, leaving only tiny sections untouched; only in the far left-hand corner did any semblance of the original design remain. Sinde sighed and sat back on her heels.

Caesir stood, her long gown whispering as it settled about her tall, slim figure. 'We must flee into the west then,' she said quietly, almost to herself. She stared down the beach to where the muddy waters of the Nile lapped at the brazier and the smoking remains of the sacrifice. Her eyes traced the shoreline, noticing where the waters had risen over the past few seasons, and reclaimed the land to itself. Once the island had been longer ... twice as long as it was broad ... but not now. The princess glanced up into the heavens; soon the goddess would descend, and then the waves would sweep in from the west ... She shuddered. Few would survive the goddess" coming.

Caesir turned back to the women. 'You must gather your forces; Cipine, choose sixteen of your bravest warriors; Ain, the same number of your best trackers and hunters; Trayim, fifteen of your craftswomen. They must be ready to leave within the five-day, they must be prepared to leave their families, friends and possessions ... and above all, they must be sworn to secrecy.'

4

Cipine stood, towering over the princess by more than a head, and almost twice as broad. 'Just over fifty of us and yourself then... is that all?'

Caesir paused and then smiled. 'Fintane will come with me...'

Cipine laughed gruffly. 'I thought he might.'

'My father, Bith, will accompany us also,' the princess added.

'We will need a pilot,' Trayim suggested quietly, 'even just to navigate us up the river.'

Caesir nodded. 'Any suggestions?'

'A countryman of mine, Landra,' Ain said. 'His skill with crafts and vessels of all descriptions is second to none.'

'I have heard of him,' Cipine agreed, 'he is good.'

'Approach him then,' Caesir said absently, looking down the beach, 'swear him to secrecy and then tell him a little... but only as much as he needs to know.'

'And if he refuses to come?' Ain asked with a slight smile.

Caesir looked around, her eyes wide with surprise. 'Then kill him, of course.'

Caesir stood beside Sinde in the prow of the long low ship. White water washed in over the jutting prow and darkened their heavy sealskin cloaks. The princess shivered as the chill soaked through to her bones. 'And where are we now?' she asked the sorceress. 'Surely we have neared the end of our journey?'

The small easterner nodded briefly, the movement lost as the frail craft rocked in the treacherous cross-currents that struck amidships. 'Soon,' she shouted above the crash of the waves, 'soon.'

They had been at sea for nearly forty days now, and, curiously, it had taken them far longer to travel the winding length of the rising waters of the Nile than it had to sail across the tideless Middle Sea, out through the Gates onto

5

the endless Western Ocean. They had struck north then, and the weather had quickly turned colder and wetter and the seas rougher.

The princess glanced across to her right. For the past few days they had been following the coast, but this had now disappeared beneath a covering of low grey cloud. 'What of the lands to the far east?' she asked Sinde.

The sorceress shook her head. 'Lost beneath the waves. Most of the lowlands are even now awash; the mountains and hilly areas remain untouched as yet ... but the water is still rising. It will soon reach your land.'

Caesir stared back into the east, her mind's eye seeing past the grey clouds and slate coloured sea, seeing her homeland once again, trying to imagine the ancient civilisation, the palaces, the cities and their teeming inhabitants of many colours. And then she saw the wall of water crashing down and racing inwards sweeping all before it ...

The Nile folk were used to floods, they probably wouldn't even take any special precautions; would disregard the rumours that were trotted out every season about huge walls of water sweeping up the Nile; would carry on regardless; would live and laugh and love; would die ...

'Land,' Sinde said quietly.

The island rose out from the water like a heavy cloud, almost indistinguishable from the sea and sky. From a distance all they could see was barren grey rock, with no sign of either vegetation or wildlife. Even as they neared, and the island took on shape and definition, they could see that nothing moved on the rocky beach, no seabirds called in the air above the island or nested in the cliffs, and no greenery broke the drab greyness.

'That's all?' the princess asked quietly, her voice almost lost in the roar of the waves. 'Are you sure this is the island?'

'Beyond this point there is nothing but water; it would take a season or more to reach the Land Across the Waves.'

Caesir shook her head, disappointment evident in her face and eyes. 'But to have come so far... for this!'

'It is not overlarge,' Sinde agreed, 'but then, we shall not be using it for long,' she added cryptically, and turned away before Caesir could question her further.

The sea around the island was treacherous with shifting cross-currents and Landra struggled with the much battered reed and wattle vessel, bringing it through the jagged rocks and reefs that seemed almost to guard the isle. A spearlike splinter of rock rose up through the current, threatening to split the vessel in two, but a sudden wave carried them up and over the stone, dropping them down into a watery hollow. The abrupt blow sent Caesir tumbling backwards and she slid across the smooth deck towards the edge, her fingernails catching and breaking in the woven reeds.

Cipine shouted in alarm and threw herself forward, but the boat tipped, spilling her to one side, throwing her away from the princess. And then Fintane caught at Caesir's flailing hand. The boat lurched, climbing upwards, knocking him to the deck. His fingers scrabbled along the reeds before catching and he hung there as the craft angled upwards, clinging desperately to the deck with one hand and the princess with the other. Cipine released her grip on the deck and allowed the angle of the craft to send her rolling across to the couple. She grabbed Fintane's foot and held on while the craft righted itself. Ain also threw herself forward and caught a handful of Caesir's cloak, hauling her back from the foaming waves.

Landra the pilot shouted a warning and there were screams of terror as a huge wall of water bore down on them. The massive southerner leaned against the tiller, his muscles bulging as he attempted to wrench the craft to one side.

The boat rose up and seemed to hang momentarily before plunging into the trough. Ain crawled across Caesir and Fintane, covering them with her body, and Cipine anchored herself as best she could to the deck and held on to the southerner. The craft rose and fell again – and this time a rock wall flashed by on the right-hand side, sheering off the oars, scraping the side of the craft. Luckily the oarswomen knew by now when to leave the oars and tie themselves to their benches, and the splintering wood did little damage. The craft was thrown forward, stone scraped briefly along the underside and then the rocks ripped up through it, disembowelling the frail craft . . . but the momentum of the waves carried it forward and up onto the beach.

The morning dawned bright but chill. Caesir gently disentangled herself from Fintane's arms and crawled out from under the thick wool and hide blanket. She could hear the crackle of burning wood and the aromatic odour perfumed the salt-rich air. She passed two of Cipine's warrior women standing guard in the mouth of the large cave. She had to admire them for their courage and stamina: they had gone through what she had – and more probably – and had then been forced to stand duty for what remained of the evening and through the night.

She found Cipine and Ain standing around a huge fire built amongst the rocks. Wood crackled and sparks spiralled skywards as the northerner added more wood . . . which, Caesir suddenly realised, was part of their craft. The two women seemed almost unnaturally cheerful considering that they were now marooned on a tiny island at the very edge of the world.

Sinde and Trayim glided silently out from one of the smaller caves and daintily picked their way down the rough beach to the fire. Caesir watched them; from the distance they were almost indistinguishable, they were country-women of the same height and build, with the same racial characteristics: high thin features, slanting eyes, fine hair.

They were friends, close friends ... and possibly more than that.

Caesir turned to the sorceress. 'Are we safe here?'

The easterner considered before answering. 'This is the most distant western island from the mainland,' she said slowly, her voice almost lost against the hiss of the surf on the shore. 'Here we will be safe, the rising waters will spend themselves on the continent and be swallowed in the vastness of the ocean. However,' she added with a slight smile, 'it might be wiser to move to the high ground for the next few days...'

Cipine laughed. 'I've not yet met a magic man or witch who didn't cover themselves in every way.'

'But can we get off this island?' Ain asked.

The sorceress shook her head. 'No.'

'*Ssso*...' Caesir looked down the beach to where a small group of women were scouring amongst the stones for driftwood and other sea wreckage, 'here we remain. This is our new home; what is it like, I wonder?' She looked across the leaping flames at Cipine.

The northern mercenary nodded. 'The island is oblong as far as I can see. From up there' – she pointed up towards the cliffs – 'I can see a few rivers, at least one small lake, young trees, grasses.'

Caesir nodded and looked at Ain.

The southerner shivered slightly with the cold and shook her head. 'I can see no signs of habitation ... there are some beast marks, small creatures, and not many at that.'

Trayim the Craftswoman added. 'It would be difficult – if not impossible – to build dwellings of any kind from the trees or grasses. The soil is hard, not suitable for growing, and it is neither rich enough nor of the proper quality to fashion pots and other vessels.'

Caesir turned back to the sorceress.

'What you have been told is true enough. But this island is

9

rich enough to support us all. Some creatures, little better than beasts, live in the caves on the eastern shores. Further north, livestock is plentiful and the seas about these shores are rich and swarming. I can ... induce the trees to grow and the grasses to thicken.'

Caesir nodded.

'And now I think we should discuss the problem of breeding,' Trayim said quietly. 'If we are to remain on this island for the rest of our days, surely we should see to it that our children inherit it?'

'There are some fifty women,' Caesir said slowly, 'and three men.'

'And one of them is an old man,' Ain added.

'He is still virile,' Caesir said.

'But for how long?' Trayim asked. 'He is an old man, near the end of his days.'

'Surely it is too soon to be thinking of children?' Caesir asked.

Sinde shook her head. 'Death will soon walk amongst us.'

Caesir turned back to the craftswoman. 'What would you suggest?'

'If we divide the women into three groups,' Trayim said slowly, 'one group to each man. Put some of Cipine's warriors, Ain's hunters and my craftswomen into each group; hopefully, by the end of the season most of the women will be with child. In twelve or fifteen years we can start breeding between the three groups. In our lifetime we could see a strong community growing up.'

'But we need land,' Ain protested. 'At the moment the island can feed us ... but when children start coming along, that will both decrease the number of hunters and farmers and at the same time increase the number of mouths to feed.'

Sinde looked up from the flames of the fire. 'I can push back the sea and increase the land,' she said.

Caesir sighed. 'Then it only remains for us to divide the

10

women. I will go with Fintane, of course; Ain, will you take your countryman, Landra? And that leaves my father to you, Cipine.' She paused and added, 'Try not to kill him, will you?'

The mercenary grimaced. 'I'll do my best.'

'I understand you need to remain apart from men,' the princess said to the sorceress.

'My magic depends on it,' Sinde said.

'And for that reason also I have excluded you, Trayim. You will remain with Sinde, and ensure that she wants for nothing. We need her powers now as never before.'

The craftswoman bowed silently.

Caesir turned back to Cipine and Ain. 'If you could send out hunting parties today, perhaps we could sort out the groups and set off within the next few days?'

Ain grimaced, her teeth startlingly white against the blackness of her face. 'It's already been done.'

Stones and pebbles clattered down the beach as Fintane stumbled out from the cave, blinking in the morning sunlight. Caesir looked up at him, and then turned back to the group gathered around the fire. 'Until the hunting parties return then?'

The four women nodded and slowly drifted away from the fire. Cipine and Ain wandered down the beach, lost in conversation; for two women from wildly differing cultures and climates they found much in common. Sinde and Trayim turned and climbed back up the beach towards one of the smaller caves, their arms slowly encircling each other's waist. Caesir remained by the fire waiting for Fintane to join her, watching the remains of their vessel turn to black ash.

And above them on the cliffs, flat, yellow eyes regarded them unblinkingly.

Sinde awoke suddenly, shivering violently, her heart

11

pumping in her breast. She lay staring up into the blackness, aware of the distant pounding of the sea and the slow regular breathing of Trayim beside her.

Something had awoken her; something had nudged her subconscious into wakefulness.

The sorceress caught and held her breath and then slipped into a slow regular rhythm. One by one her senses shut down; sight first, although she did not notice it in the blackness of the cave, then hearing – the whisper of the sea and Trayim's breathing faded and were replaced by a low ceaseless hum. Touch went next – the warm feather touch of her companion's skin, the roughness of the blanket and the stone floor beneath... and then she was floating in a featureless grey void. She waited a moment and then sank deeper into herself – and a semblance of sight returned. Pastel hues formed and quickly deepened into vivid colours; Trayim's sleeping body was outlined in an aura of brilliant crimson, whilst the cave growths glowed amber and warm bronze.

Sinde willed herself forward and outside the cave. The cloudy black night came alive with colour and light. She could distinguish the auras of the remainder of the group, the brighter and starker auras of those that were awake and alert, and in the next cave, the blinding aura of a couple in the throes of passion.

She floated higher and began to tone out the usual auras, and gradually the night drifted back into shade. The sorceress expanded her perception, and then she felt the first malevolent tendrils of an alien presence. Her shields flared as she caught sight of the bone-white light and then she was falling... falling... falling. She stopped above the harsh pulsating glow and allowed the night to come alive again with colour and light. She attempted to make sense of the colours below her: a blood-red aura tinged with black and surrounding a hard knot of cold white light. It was human – but only vaguely so; smaller, broader, the arms unnaturally long, the head abnormally large. She probed, attempting to read any signs of intelligence – but there was nothing, only a cold terrible hatred and a ravenous hunger.

The creature moved, and Sinde was suddenly aware that it was creeping towards a bright human aura. She fled back to her own body, the night dissolving into flame around her and then bursting into pain as circulation abruptly returned to her numb limbs. She cried out – and then Trayim was beside her, her small hands cradling her head.

'Outside... outside...' she gasped, 'alarm...'

Trayim pulled the dagger from beneath her pillow and darted out into the night. 'Leos, Inde,' she called. She heard the scuff of bare feet on stone as the two guards came running. 'There is something out here,' she said urgently, 'waken the others.'

Leos, one of Ain's hunters, nodded, only her eyes and teeth visible in the darkness, and slipped off towards the other caves. Inde, one of Trayim's countrywomen, stayed by her side, a long shaft of fire-hardened wood held across her body.

A pebble rattled off the stones and Trayim spun around, her knife hand coming up, her eyes probing the darkness. She sensed something moving and then she caught a rank beast odour. She opened her mouth to cry out and then the creature was upon her. The knife was struck from her hand and went spinning down amongst the rocks. Inde screamed and struck down with her spear, but the shaft snapped against a stone, and then she suddenly realised that she dare not strike again for fear of hitting her mistress.

Trayim struggled beneath the beast's weight, its foul fur against her mouth and in her eyes. She felt its short blunt fingers tearing at her flesh, and its snapping fangs were dangerously near her throat. She drove her straightened fingertips into the creature's side, and at the same time drove her knee upwards into its groin. The beast grunted and then howled as the knee rammed home. It shifted its

13

grip on her arms and its wide hands found her throat; its fingers locked and it began to squeeze.

Trayim gasped and choked, struggling for breath. Her lungs laboured and her head began to pound. Tiny spots of colour danced before her eyes and there was a roaring in her ears. Her feebly waving arms attempted to break the beast's hold, to plunge her fingers into its eyes, but it kept snapping at her, its teeth clicking alongside the palm of her hand. The spots of colour before her eyes intensified ... And then the sky exploded with light.

Trayim had a momentary glimpse of a broad sloping brow and tiny eyes and then it was gone. Hands grabbed her and dragged her away, scraping her already torn flesh on the rough sand and stone, but she pushed them away and sat up.

Overhead the night sky was aflame with a brilliant red globe that hovered just above head height, crackling and spitting. In the crimson light she could see the huge figure of Cipine outlined against the darkness, the muscles in her arms and torso rippling as she held the squirming beast high above her head, laughing as she evaded the flailing paws.

A shadow moved out of the night and Ain the Huntress joined the northerner. She gazed up at the creature for a moment and then slipped her green stone knife from its sheath along her forearm. The huntress stood back and nodded to Cipine. The mercenary grinned and threw the creature at Ain's feet; she stooped, the blood-lust running liquid through her ebony body, and the stone knife glittered before it came away dripping.

Abruptly the globe of fire sputtered and shrank in upon itself and for a moment the witch-light danced around Sinde before it disappeared.

In the silence that followed the pounding of the waves seemed unnaturally loud, and the hiss of the surf on the shore seemed almost menacing, but then someone called for torches and the shouts broke the spell.

14

Caesir appeared in the cave mouth with Fintane, and hurried down the beach, a naked short-sword in her hand. She glanced back at her betrothed, and snarled in disgust as she noted that he held back, making sure that the danger was past. By the time she reached the beast's carcass Sinde was kneeling beside Trayim, her delicate hands running down her lover's body, checking for broken bones or cracked ribs. The Mistress of Craftswomen was badly bruised, scratched and torn, but none of her wounds was serious. The sorceress helped her to her feet and half carried her up to their cave where she had a small supply of salves and ointments which would help heal the wounds.

Caesir joined Cipine and Ain standing over the body of the creature. She nudged it with the flat of her sword, but it didn't move: its throat had been expertly cut from ear to ear.

'What is it?' she asked flatly.

'Beast-man,' Cipine said without hesitation. 'In the forests of my homeland they are sometimes found in small colonies. Perhaps they were once men that had lived wild and degenerated into beasts,' she suggested.

Ain knelt and, in the light of the flickering torches, turned the creature over. She shook her head. 'No, I've seen this type before in my homeland,' she said slowly. She glanced up at the princess. 'Surely you recognise the beast?'

Caesir frowned. 'It is not unfamiliar; but this is less brutish than the animals I once saw in the floating menagerie.'

The huntress prised open the protruding jaws and examined the broad teeth. 'There are two types,' she said in her deep, mellow voice, 'the man-beast and the beast-man. The first is a creature that although outwardly manlike is a wild beast, both shy and gentle; the second is not a beast, but not yet a man – it is something caught in between.' She looked up at Caesir and Cipine. 'This is a beast-man, and look at these teeth . . . it is a meat eater,' she added quietly.

Cipine laughed humourlessly. 'We must have seemed like

a gift from the gods to this creature.'

Caesir nodded. 'A gift indeed – and I dare say it was not alone. They will be back.' She glanced up at the sky which was already lightening in the east. 'The night is almost done. Call in your sentries Cipine, double the guards around the caves and keep the fires burning.' She looked over at Ain. 'Will they be back tonight?'

'I doubt it, not tonight – but tomorrow perhaps, or the day after, but they will be back.'

The princess tapped the palm of her hand with the flat of her sword. 'Well, there is little we can do for the remainder of this night, but in the morning...' She looked at both Ain and Cipine.

The huntress nodded. 'We'll scout this creature's trail back to its lair...'

'And then what?' the mercenary asked, a grin already beginning to spread across her face.

Ain laughed. 'And then you'll get a chance to quench that battle-thirst you have.'

Caesir made her way up the beach to the sorceress' cave. She found Trayim sleeping peacefully on a thick blanket with Sinde kneeling over her, gently rubbing a malodorous salve onto her naked body. She looked up as the princess entered.

'Is it dead?' And then she nodded and answered her own question. 'Yes, it is dead.' She turned her attention back to her companion and resumed smearing the salve over a dark ugly bruise beneath Trayim's left breast.

'How bad is she?'

Sinde shook her head. 'Not bad. Bruised, cut, a cracked rib. She was lucky...' The sorceress moved aside and allowed Caesir to see the dark, regularly spaced bruisemarks around Trayim's throat.

The princess nodded. 'She was lucky,' she said softly. 'She saved our lives... but it was you who gave the warning?'

Sinde nodded. 'I felt it; it was cold, so cold, filled with nothing but the desire to kill... and kill... and kill... and feed!' She shuddered.

'We will destroy them,' Caesir promised.

The sorceress turned her head and the flickering torchlight touched her red-rimmed eyes. 'If you do not then they will surely destroy us all.'

The princess nodded silently. She stood in the mouth of the cave for a few moments watching the sorceress work and then turned back into the night.

Sinde meticulously covered Trayim's entire body with the healing salve and then, with herb-scented water, washed her hands. She then slipped off her robe and lay down beside her companion. Trayim moved in her sleep and her arm snaked across Sinde's shoulders. The sorceress adjusted the thick blanket over them both and then held her tight.

'... And so,' Caesir concluded, 'if we are to survive in this strange land, we must bear children.' She paused and looked at each one of the faces of the women gathered below the mouth of the cave. Many of them had been taken as slaves to her father's palace, torn from their tribes and nations. Some had been born slaves and others, like Cipine's viragos, were escaped slaves and runaway freewomen. This island had represented a chance for them to experience true freedom... but now they were being forced to submit themselves to a man.

'We will divide into three groups; one group to each man: Fintane, Bith and Landra.' She hurried on, aware of the growing murmur of indignation. 'The three groups will then settle in different parts of the island...'

'And do what?' one of the women demanded savagely.

Caesir leaned forward, her eyes and voice chill. 'We will survive!' She allowed her gaze to roam over the group again. 'There is no choice in this matter – anyone who does not

17

consent will be slain out of hand.' Her voice hardened. 'Is that understood?'

And this time there was no reply.

Ain carefully parted the long grass and peered down into the small valley that bordered the sheltered beach.

Cipine, lying on the hard ground beside her, swore quietly.

'By the gods, I didn't realise there were so many.'

Ain's dark eyes probed the hillside, seeking signs of habitation. She stiffened and nudged the mercenary in the ribs; Cipine edged forward and grunted. Almost directly below them the hillside was riddled with caves and the slopes below them were rank with excrement and the remains of birds and small animals. Lower down the slopes were the beast-men – scores of them. At first glance Cipine reckoned that there must be close on three times their own number – and that wasn't counting the females or young, who could probably be counted on to fight in any case.

'We'll never take them,' she said quietly.

'Look,' Ain said suddenly, moving back and allowing the mercenary to slide across to her position. Cipine followed her arm. 'There is only one entrance,' Ain said slowly, 'only one way in...'

'...Only one way out.' Cipine stared at the cleft, a ragged knife-slit in the mountainside, barely wide enough for two to stand abreast. She looked across at the huntress. 'If we can hold the cleft...'

Ain nodded. 'The beast-men are meat eaters, but do you see any game down there?'

'Nothing.'

'Then they must hunt abroad for it. And if we can take and hold that entrance, we can contain the creatures within the valley... hunger will soon turn them upon themselves.'

'What about the trees, the bushes?' Cipine argued.

18

'Burn them. And the fire should terrorise the beast-men.'

The mercenary nodded slowly. 'It could be done ... and it might just work. But instead of trying to hold the entrance, why not just block it with a landslide, and post guards up along here to discourage any climbers.'

'Yes! Although the cliff-face may be just a little too steep even for them.'

'And what about the sea?'

'The beast-men fear the water, they will not venture out into the waves.'

Cipine nodded again. 'It might just work.'

In the light of a tiny fire just inside the mouth of a cave Ain and Cipine carefully outlined their plan to Caesir, Sinde and Trayim. The princess listened intently, elbows resting on her knees, her chin cupped in her palms. When they were finished she sat back against the rough cold wall and knuckled her tired eyes. 'Is there no other way?' she asked at last. 'Must we begin our rule of this land with slaughter ... or would it be genocide?' She turned to Sinde. 'You said that they have the capability to become true men in time?'

The sorceress nodded. 'In time, yes. But we will not see it, nor our children, nor our children's children.'

'They are animals,' Ain gently reminded her, 'intelligent, dangerous animals, and like all animals they are governed by instincts ... but they are not human!'

'Is there no other way to kill them then; something swifter, less lingering ...?'

'What's got into you, girl?' Cipine snapped, 'you've never had scruples before. I've seen you order a slave slain for dropping your comb; I've watched you wager on the man-fights; I've hunted the devil-fish with you and watched you kill without compunction or pity ... and now you're cribbing over the death of a pack of wild animals.'

'This afternoon,' Caesir said quietly, staring deep into the fire, 'I divided the women up amongst the three men. I did it by lot but, as I've already said, you Ain will go with Landra, you Cipine with my father...' She raised a slim elegant hand as the mercenary opened her mouth to protest. 'I know your tastes do not run to men – but there is nothing else to be done; besides, he is an old man with fifteen other women to contend with, and you may be just a little too big and a little too mean for him.'

The mercenary nodded glumly.

'But first we must take care of the beasts,' the princess continued. 'Your plan is sound, and if there is no other way, then put it into effect as quickly as possible. And that valley sounds very enticing,' she added.

Ain nodded. 'It's good land, but it's been hunted out. The bay however is sheltered, the fishing would be good.'

'Excellent. When the beasts are gone we can settle one of the groups in it. Will the beast-men come tonight?' she then asked Sinde, changing the subject.

The sorceress shook her head. 'I don't know. I can only sense their rage and hunger once they near me.'

Ain nudged the fire with her calloused foot, sending sparks spiralling upwards against the ceiling. 'It's possible – no, probable, but this,' she nodded at the fire, 'is our greatest protection. If we build a vast fire in the cave mouths and then double the guards we should be safe.'

Cipine stood. 'I'll set a few traps with stones, sticks and some jars; at least they'll give us some warning when the beasts come.'

The beast-men came that night. Caesir, lying near the back of the largest cave in Fintane's arms, heard the sudden clatter of stones and then a jar breaking, and knew immediately that something prowled outside the cave, skulking in the darkness beyond the fires. She shook Fintane, but he only moaned and rolled over. The princess

20

spat in disgust; in the past few moons she had learned much about her betrothed. She slipped from beneath the furs and, pulling one across her naked shoulders, padded on bare feet down to the mouth of the cave and the leaping flames. She found both Cipine and Ain already there, fully armed and in their leather kirtles, breastplates and helms. Sinde and Trayim, who had moved from their own smaller cave, joined them a moment later.

Caesir turned to the sorceress. 'How many?'

'Many. A score, perhaps more. They can smell us; we are fresh meat.' She smiled. 'In these confined caves our odours must be appetising.'

Cipine growled like a wild bear. 'The first one to stick its head in here will feed on my sword,' she swore.

'If it doesn't run from your ugly face first,' Ain added.

'Well, you're all right – it won't even see you,' Cipine retorted, 'unless you open your eyes or smile at it... and then you'll more than likely blind it.'

Landra joined them, a curved sickle in one hand and a long flat-bladed knife in the other. The pilot was as tall as Ain and blacker, but his eyes had a yellowish tinge and his teeth were stained and blackened. 'Are they there?' he asked slowly, his accent thickening his words.

A stone rattled down the beach and then another jar shattered, answering him.

Something moved in the night beyond the fire and flat yellow eyes glinted briefly in the light and then something sailed in through the flames and bounced off the walls. The small group fell back as more stones rattled off the walls and ceiling.

Ain knelt and gathered up a few of the large round stones. She waited until she caught a glimpse of movement and then flung a stone out through the flames. A howl of pain testified to the accuracy of her aim. A spate of missiles clattered about the cave, and was then followed by silence. Ain tossed a few more stones out into the darkness, but they only rattled harmlessly down the beach. Cipine edged closer to the mouth of the cave, her broad double-edged sword naked in her hand. She squeezed her eyes almost shut against the fire's glare and squinted out into the night. Something moved at the corner of her eye and she turned – just as the first of the beast-men came flying in over the flames. She reacted unthinkingly, throwing herself forward and down, bringing her sword up: disembowelling the creature. It thrashed about in a pool of its own blood and innards until the huge mercenary stooped and, catching it at groin and neck, hoisted it up over her head and tossed it out over the flames back onto the beach. The savage screams which had risen during the sudden attack died again, and silence once more fell on the beach – to be replaced by a hideous snarling, such as dogs make over a bone.

The remainder of the night passed quietly. A few stones were thrown into the cave, but nothing else attempted to brave the fire. As the sky paled towards dawn the small group broke up, leaving Cipine and Landra standing by the greying ashes. The ebony pilot stood in the mouth of the cave, staring out wistfully at the sea breaking on the rough beach.

Cipine glanced across at him. 'Why don't you come back from there,' she growled, 'they may still be out there.'

Landra shook his head. 'They are creatures of the night,' he replied, 'they've already returned to their lairs.'

'How do you know?'

'We have them in my homeland,' he said turning around to face her. 'They are not true animals; in my country the wise men say that they are the spirits of men condemned to walk this world for their crimes.'

Cipine laughed at the belief. 'My gods may be harsh but they are fair.'

'You are of the north,' the pilot said, a statement rather than a question, 'a mercenary, pirate and worse,' – Cipine grinned broadly – 'leader of a band of wild warrior women...' he paused and added softly, 'and you have been given to me.'

The mercenary went suddenly chill. 'I have been given to no one. I understood that I had been allotted to the old man to try and bear at least one child, and since I would not ask my troops to do anything that I myself would not try, I will do that. Where do you come in?' she demanded loudly.

Landra grinned broadly. 'I won you in a fair wager – and I rather think the old man was pleased to lose you.'

Cipine's knuckles whitened about the pommel of her sword. 'Well, I am honour bound to accept that,' she said coldly, 'but,' she added warningly, 'do not expect me to take any pleasure from the act, and I've heard also that you find inflicting pain to your liking. Try that with me – and I'll break you in two!' Cipine turned on her heel and walked away, leaving Landra staring after her, a curious smile playing about his thick lips.

Trayim's delicate long-fingered hands touched the huge slab of stone. 'It is weak here ... and here,' she said softly. 'Strike it – *hard* – and the whole wall will come down.'

Cipine ran her hard calloused hand down the seemingly smooth surface of the rock face. 'How do you know?'

The easterner smiled shyly. 'I am a craftswoman; I have worked with many materials, including stones, semi-precious and otherwise. This rock is flawed, take my word for it.'

The mercenary grunted and then glanced over her broad shoulder at Ain. 'What do you think?'

Ain looked up at the sheer walls of the ravine rising on either side. The narrow band of sky high above them was startlingly blue against the blackness of the stone. 'If Trayim says it will come down...' she said doubtfully.

'And how are you going to knock it down?' Cipine asked.

Trayim smiled and shook her head. 'I'm not – you are!'

'Me?'

'You,' the craftswoman insisted, 'you alone have the strength.' She pointed at the stone. 'You will strike the rock here!'

'And then?' the mercenary demanded.

'You run.'

One of Cipine's warriors came back down the ravine towards them. She stopped and bowed briefly. 'The creatures are sleeping; most of them down by the shore, but a few on the slopes. However there is nothing moving up this end.'

Trayim looked at Cipine and Ain. 'Is all in readiness?'

'My warriors are in position along the cliff tops,' Cipine said. 'As soon as this wall comes down those beast-men are going to try scrambling up – and we'll be waiting for them.'

'We'll then send a few fire-arrows in,' Ain added, 'just to help things along.'

Trayim nodded and turned away, followed by Ain and the warrior, and slipped quickly down the ravine into the shadows. Cipine walked slowly down the defile towards the opening that led out into the enclosed valley. She stood concealed in the shadows and stared down towards the golden beach. The sun was slanting in across the mountains, dappling the greenery, reminding her of the great forests of her homeland, and the small picket-enclosed village amidst the thick dark trunks that was the abiding memory of her youth. Angrily she shook the memory aside.

The beast-men were lying across the lush grass in small groups of three or four. Some tossed and turned restlessly in the warm afternoon heat, whilst others moved listlessly along the shore, but keeping well clear of the sparkling waves. She made a rough count; Ain's scouts had reported that all the beast-men had returned from their night's hunting – but even if only one escaped, it might endanger their own small foothold on the tiny isle. They had to kill

24

them all in one go. It wasn't a clean death – but the women were outnumbered.

The huge mercenary returned to the stone Trayim had marked. She found Mila, one of her guards, already there, holding Cipine's huge mace in both hands. Cipine nodded her thanks and, instructing her to wait, began to unbuckle her heavy armour. She stripped off everything: greaves, breastplate, helmet, knife and sword. Mila bundled the weapons and armour in her arms and staggered down the ravine, leaving Cipine alone, clad only in a light shift and sandals before the marked stone.

She spat into her cupped palms, bent over and lifted the mace easily, although Mila had had to struggle to carry it to her. It was a huge stone ball with a natural hole running directly through the centre. Into the hole Cipine had fitted a short handle: a highly polished branch from an ancient oak tree wound around with strips of seasoned leather. Leather bands also encircled the ball, and these had been fitted with shards of metal. The northerner could swing the mace one-handed – and the results were devastating.

She now stood directly in front of the marked stone, her broad feet set firmly into the soft ground, her columnar thighs tensed. She slipped her right hand into the leather thong and began to swing the mace gently to and fro. Her left hand gripped the haft just above her right and her knuckles began to whiten. Her breathing deepened and regulated as it always did before a battle, and she could feel the pulse pounding at her throat, temples and breast.

And then she swung at the stone.

The mace struck the spot Trayim had marked – and shattered. Both of Cipine's arms went numb and she could feel every bone in her body shake with the blow. Chips of the shattered ball flew back and stung her face and neck like angry insects. She staggered backwards, turned and started to run – and fell. For a moment she lay there, trembling...

25

and then she suddenly realised that it wasn't her trembling – it was the entire ravine. The mercenary heaved herself to her feet; her arms were still numb and tingling, her wrists and shoulders ached, and even her ribs hurt, and she wondered whether she had cracked some with the force of her blow. She glanced back over her shoulder: there was a visible dent in the stone where she had struck it and radiating out from the depression was a series of ever widening cracks. Even as she watched they raced up the slab and large chips of stone dropped down. The air was suddenly filled with whirling dust motes which stung the eyes and caught at the throat. Cipine threw herself forward and rolled to one side as a flurry of rocks and large stones tumbled down from the heights just behind her. She pushed herself to her feet and raced for the end of the ravine, dodging the larger stones that were falling now. And then there was a loud crack as the entire side of the cliff-face fell inwards behind her. The concussion threw her forward again and she covered her head with her hands as jagged lumps of stone hurtled past. A score or more bit deeply into her back and thighs, and a larger piece struck her a glancing blow just above the ear that left her dazed and sickened. She grew aware of voices, and then hands gripping her under the arms, dragging her to her feet, supporting her down the length of the defile, while the walls collapsed in behind them. She looked up and glimpsed a long bar of light, and then the whirling dust blotted it out, and then there was nothing.

Two white staring eyes in a black-skinned face swam into view; she blinked and they divided into two. Cipine blinked again and Ain and Landra's faces separated and solidified. The mercenary attempted to sit up, but Ain pushed her firmly down.

'What happened?' she whispered eventually, surprised at how weak her voice sounded.

'The rock face fell in,' Ain said, 'just as Trayim said it

would. Unfortunately, you were struck several times by falling rocks.'

'And the ravine?' Cipine croaked, her throat raw with dust.

'Is blocked,' Landra supplied. He was kneeling by her side, looking intently at her ... and Cipine suddenly realised that she was naked, the ragged and bloody remains of her shift lying balled at her feet. For some reason his smile disturbed her and she felt a sudden surge of anger. She glared up at him. He saw her look and smiled insolently and allowed his gaze to drift slowly down her body, lingering briefly on her huge breasts before drifting lower.

Cipine pushed herself into a sitting position, closing her eyes as the world swam around her and pulsed blackly in time to her pounding head. When she opened her eyes, Landra was gone and Caesir now knelt beside her. The princess smiled and nodded. 'It is done. The beast-men are trapped; some have attempted to scale the cliff-face, but your warriors have forced them back.' The princess leaned forward, gave Cipine her hand and helped her to her feet. 'We have a lot to thank you for.'

The mercenary shrugged, and then winced as her head renewed its pounding. 'I'm not pleased with what I've done,' she said quietly, 'it will be a terrible death for them.'

Caesir nodded. 'I know; that is how I feel, but it is necessary; there was no choice – as you yourself pointed out.'

'And now?'

Caesir smiled. 'We wait; time and hunger will do our work for us.'

Landra came for Cipine that night. The mercenary awoke with the sound of ragged breathing above her. Her nostrils dilated as she caught the rank animal odour of stale sweat on the heavy atmosphere, and she immediately knew who was standing there. Her hand closed about the dagger beneath the rolled cloak that doubled as a pillow.

A foot nudged her side. 'Wake up.'

She lay unmoving for a moment and then slowly rolled over on her side with a groan. 'What... what is it?'

There was a rustle by her side and then a sweat-slick hand brushed her thigh. 'It's me,' the pilot said hoarsely.

Cipine sat up slowly, still feigning drowsiness. 'What do you want?' she mumbled.

The warm damp hand moved slowly upwards. 'I have come for you; we will lie together this night.' The pilot's breath was raw and foul against her face. He moved closer and then lay down beside her, and Cipine, who had fought her way from one end of a barbaric continent to the other, braving unimaginable horrors and terrors, shrank from the southerner's touch. Landra laughed. 'Why so shy, surely you do not fear me?'

'I fear no man,' Cipine said coldly.

'Well then, I think it's time you learned!' The pilot gripped her flesh and twisted, while his other hand found her shoulder and pushed her back to the cold stone. He lowered his body over hers and she felt his sour breath warm on her cheek. Cipine struck inwards with the edge of her hand, catching Landra just beneath the ribs, pushing him off her. He growled like an animal as he came to his feet, and Cipine heard the dry rasp of a blade being withdrawn. The mercenary smiled grimly and moved into a fighting stance: she was going to cut this bastard into fish bait.

Landra moved and Cipine dodged instinctively, turning her body to one side and stabbing inwards with her knife hand where she imagined the southerner to be. Her blade caught flesh briefly and then pulled free, and then she threw herself backwards as she felt the other change direction. In the total darkness she felt the whip of a knife blade above her head, and she knew that for that instant Landra was off balance. Cipine kicked upwards with the flat of her foot,

28

catching him full in the groin. He screamed like an animal and fell to the ground retching. Following the sounds, Cipine kicked him again, and his teeth clicked together like two stones striking, and his head bounced off the ground.

The mercenary realised that she would have to finish it quickly now; Landra's screams had attracted attention and already she could hear shouts. She moved in until her foot touched his quivering leg. Sure of herself now, she stepped forward and then brought her foot down full force between the pilots legs. He howled like a gutted stallion and continued screaming until the mercenary drove her knife up through his jaw into the brain.

The morning was sharp and chill and the waves sweeping in from the south were grey and sombre. Caesir shivered and pulled her heavy woollen cloak tighter about her slim shoulders. She looked at Sinde walking by her side and shook her head in wonderment, for the sorceress was clad in nothing more than a thin white shift that was moulded to her tiny figure by the wind.

'Are you not cold?'

Sinde shook her head. 'I learned as a very young girl how to control and regulate my body.' She reached over and touched Caesir's hand. The princess started: the easterner's hand was warm and dry.

They continued walking in silence and then Caesir suddenly asked, 'What are we going to do now?'

'He was a brutal, violent man; all the women he lay with bore the bruises and cuts of his lust; he took pleasure in pain.'

'But Cipine didn't have to kill him!' Caesir protested.

'They were fighting in the dark,' Sinde reminded her.

The princess nodded. 'I know that. I also know that Cipine is one of the deadliest fighters either in or outside the arena. I once watched her fight three men – criminals – at the one time... and she was blindfolded. She dispatched them without even being touched.'

The sorceress shrugged. 'He was of little use in any case; of the eight or ten women he bedded – even though at least half were fertile at the time – none have conceived.' The sorceress continued gazing out across the white-capped waves, and her eyes glazed. After a moment she blinked slowly and then turned away from the sea and looked up the beach towards the caves. 'He has left us nothing but his blood.' Her voice changed, becoming distant and gentle. 'When we are gone,' she said softly, 'and our names have all but been forgotten, he will be remembered: Landra, the first dead man in the land of Caesir Banba.' She turned away and walked quickly up the beach, leaving the princess standing by the hissing waves, strangely troubled.

Later that morning Caesir climbed the cliffs to stand beside Ain and Cipine, and stare down into the valley. The slopes directly below them were covered with thick dark blood where the guards had forced back the beast-men. At the foot of the cliffs, a broken-limbed corpse was being dragged away by two of the creatures.

'What will they do with it?' Caesir asked.

'Eat it,' Ain said without turning around. 'They will feed off their own dead for a while.'

'And then?'

'Then the stronger will start killing the smaller and weaker... and then the survivors will start killing off each other.'

Caesir turned to Cipine. 'What did you do with Landra's body?'

The mercenary smiled, and continued smiling as Caesir's gaze snapped downwards and then back to the mercenary's face. She shivered and turned away, suddenly terrified. Her dream, which had grown during the long voyage, of starting afresh in this new land, was rapidly crumbling into dust.

The beast-men were vermin, lower than slaves or animals: they had to be wiped out. But now one of their own number was dead, his carcass tossed to the animals to be devoured, and no matter what he was or what he had done his corpse deserved a little more respect, and Caesir came from a race that welcomed death and the new beginning it brought and had a horror of the desecrated corpse. And for the first time the princess realised that she was no longer in control; Ain, Cipine, Tayim and Sinde held the reins of power, for while they each controlled one facet of life on this tiny island, she had nothing.

And she wondered then what would become of her... indeed, what would become of them all?

The beast-men died surprisingly quickly, and in the end it was their own viciousness that killed them off. In the confined space of the valley tempers quickly grew short and violent, and bloody arguments ensued... with the victor eating the tastier morsels of the loser and leaving the corpse to rot beneath the sun. The rotting corpses soon attracted swarms of black insects that had plagued the Caesirians around their fires, and then the vermin arrived.

They never did discover how the rats arrived on the island; perhaps they had been there all along, living in warrens underground. Two days after Cipine had slain Landra, the guards on the cliff tops reported that black shadows were drifting across the ground and engulfing the corpses. It was Ain with her sharp eyes who made out the countless small furry bodies.

And four days after that the plague struck.

The symptoms were terrifyingly familiar to the women who had lived along the banks of the Nile, and who had lived with the constant threat of plague. It manifested itself with swellings in the armpits and groin, followed by fever, bleeding, muscle tremors... and death.

31

Even Sinde's magic couldn't combat the invisible killer, and in a matter of days it had devastated the small group. Ironically Cipine, for all her great strength and stamina, was one of the first to fall, swiftly followed by Ain and Trayim. Bith, Caesir's father, was one of the last to die, but Fintane drank a concoction of his own devising, and died swiftly and easily.

In the latter days the few women who remained gathered all the bodies together in a great pile, and for a day and a night the cleansing flames leapt and raged, reddening the night sky and darkening the day with heavy clouds. Caesir lingered a few days after the last of the women had died, struggling vainly to the end. And Sinde buried her by the seashore where, generations later, the Partholonians would discover and puzzle over the bones.'*

The sorceress walked the cliffs in the evening of that final day. Smouldering embers still glowed in the heart of the great funeral pyre, and sparks and cinders drifted across the beach and draped the low grave-mound with wreaths of fire. The eastern sorceress shivered in the evening breeze and smiled grimly, remembering her last conversation with the princess.

Caesir had been close to death, her once proud beauty gone forever, her fine features bloated and her body wasted. Speech was difficult and the sorceress had to strain to hear her.

'Is this ... retribution?'

Sinde shook her head.

'But if we had not killed the beast-men and Landra, surely the rats wouldn't have come?' she whispered brokenly.

Again Sinde shook her head. 'No, they were here all the time, they would have come out sooner or later.'

* see 'The Dawn' *Irish Folk And Fairy Tales* vol. II. chap. 1

'The blood... the blood attracted them.'

Reluctantly the sorceress nodded.

'In your homeland, does the land itself have a soul?' the princess asked, her eyes bright and glistening.

Sinde nodded. 'We call it the *anima*, the spirit of life.'

'This is a young land,' Caesir whispered sadly, 'I fear we have let it taste blood too soon; I fear it may develop a taste for it.' She shuddered. 'May the gods forgive us for what we have done.'

Sinde blinked. The wind was cold on the cliff-top. The fever had her, she knew, and soon she would drift off into that final sleep and the rats would have her bones. She looked down into the valley, but already night's shadows had claimed it, and there was nothing moving, and no sound from it save the stunted trees rustling in the breeze. She walked on. Coloured spots danced before her eyes and then she doubled up as pain lanced through her. Images – like smoke-dreams – flashed behind her eyes; curiously garbed and armoured armies marched across mist enshrouded fields ... war chariots cut through tall waving grass ... stately processions wound along polished gleaming roads ... a golden-haired warrior lay slumped against a pillar, a raven perched on his shoulder ... white-robed priests chanted in the midst of dark forests ... long-prowed ships rode the waves ... dark-cowled monks fell beneath their axes ... gold and bronze banners flapped in the wind ... gold and bronze ... gold ... bronze ...

Sinde blinked. She found herself standing on the cold stones of the cliff-top staring out across the waves towards the west into the sunset. Gold and bronze burned across the sky. She blinked again and for a single instant it turned red like freshly spilled blood. She staggered and looked down. Far, far below her the waves pounded against the cliffs in white-foamed fury. And then the foam too was touched with frothy pink. There was blood on this land, there was

33

death also ... its history would be a bloody one ... blood and bronze and gold ...

And blackness.

'From the east they came, the princess, the warrior, the huntress, the craftswoman, the sorceress, and their followers. They fled the waves and found the land, and death claimed them.'

Chapter Two

I – THRICE CURSED

Ebblue sat up suddenly, pushing the sleeping body off her, her head tilting to one side, listening. Beside her Necca rolled over and groaned and she immediately clamped a hand over his mouth. His dark brown eyes snapped open and he struggled for a moment to sit up. His stepmother looked down and shook her head silently, her right hand pointing towards the door. Necca's eyes registered understanding and he slipped from the bed furs and padded naked to the window ledge where he had left his knife and clothes.

There was a sudden clatter of metal off stone in the corridor outside and his knife snicked wetly as it slid from its oiled sheath. He jumped over the rumpled bed and stood with his broad back flat against the cold stones by the door, the knife in his right hand held flat against his thigh. Ebblue threw back the covers and crossed to the huge fireplace, smiling regretfully at Necca. He grinned as he watched her reach up and unhook the crossed hunting spears from above the mantel and hurry back to his side. Naked, carrying the two spears, she looked like the Morrigan – the Goddess of Death – in her human form. She pressed herself against him, her flesh warm against his, her breasts brushing his arm, and her breath on his neck. And together they waited for what they both realised would be her husband's and his father's guards.

There was a soft scratching at the door, and then a hoarse

voice whispered, 'Necca... Necca...'

Necca looked down at Ebblue; they both recognised the voice. It was Rian, his brother's. He raised his eyebrows in a silent question, and his stepmother nodded.

Necca eased the latch up with his free hand, and the door swung silently inwards. Rian stepped into the room – and stopped with the point of a spear pricking his throat.

'Slowly, brother, slowly,' Necca whispered, 'are you alone?'

Rian nodded, and then winced as the spear point tore his flesh. 'I'm alone, but by the Dagda and Danu, you've got to get out of here.' He pushed the spear down and swung around to face his brother and stepmother. His eyes widened momentarily at their nakedness and then he hurried on. 'Father knows! Someone – Bona I think – has told him, and he's on his way here now, with a company of guards...'

He stopped suddenly as Ebblue raised her hand. 'Someone's coming,' she snapped.

Rian went white. 'What are you going to do?' he demanded. 'You're trapped.'

Necca smiled coldly. 'There's not a lot we can do now, is there. But you brother, you can hide...' he gestured towards a huge ornate wooden chest.

Rian shook his head and drew his knife. 'We've grown and played together, we've learned and...' he glanced across at his stepmother, who was not in fact much older than himself, 'loved together. Let us now die together.'

Necca smiled and, pulling his brother close, embraced him. 'What more does a man need,' he said quietly, 'than the love of a woman and the loyalty of a brother?'

Rian smiled quietly. 'Shouldn't you both... put something on?' he suggested. 'Things are going to be bad enough as it is without you both inflaming the situation by father finding you naked and,' he glanced at the long furrows down his brother's back and the red bite marks on Ebblue's breasts, 'all the signs of a night's passion on you.'

The tall dark-haired warrior grinned. 'You were always wiser than me, little brother,' he said, 'you would have made a fine poet or a druid.'

Rian stood with his ear to the door while both Ebblue and Necca dressed hurriedly. The early morning sun, slanting in through the small high window, caught the whirling dust motes and touched them with gold and bronze. The glittering motes lingered briefly on the two lovers, uniting them in a band of sparkling light, and Rian, looking across at them, smiled bitterly. They were made for each other; they were perfectly matched, both in years and needs, and yet the quirk of fate that had brought them together would never allow them openly to proclaim their love.

Marid MacCairde, King of Munster, had married for the second time, nearly eight years after the death of his first wife. It was a surprise move, and even more surprising when he had chosen the daughter of one of the western seaboard chieftains, a small dark-haired, dark-eyed, full-bodied beauty who would, it was hoped, bear him fine sons, brothers for Necca and Rian, his sons and only children by his first wife.

However, almost from the first, Necca had found himself drawn to his stepmother, and although she had resisted his advances and attentions at first, she had gradually accepted her stepson first into her heart, and then into her bed. Rian had seen the signs early on and, on more than one occasion, spoken to his older brother about his growing involvement with their father's new bride. Necca had listened, and although he knew, deep down he knew, what he was doing was wrong, he was trapped: chained by shackles far stronger than iron.

And so Ebblue and Necca had become lovers, snatching stolen moments alone together whilst they hunted, or whenever Marid would fall into a drunken slumber early in the evening and it would be left for Rian to carry him to his bed – after first ensuring that his brother and stepmother had had time to themselves. Rian wouldn't have said that he approved, but, realising that there was nothing he could do about it, endeavoured to further the affair discreetly, and without allowing any hint of it to reach his father.

But he knew it couldn't last for long.

Soon the servants had begun to talk, and on more than one occasion a startled herdsman had come across them frantically coupling in the tall lush grasslands that bordered Marid's domain, or the huntsman would remark how they would both disappear after a hare or hart when even the dogs had lost the scent.

Whispers had trickled back to the king, but he ignored them; he knew his son and he trusted his wife. But the seed of doubt had been sown.

And that suspicion had finally flowered into absolute certainty.

A wandering druid had come to the king's court; a small wild-eyed, dark-skinned man whose northern and eastern ancestry were clearly written on his broad brutish features. But he was a druid and well versed in the laws and ancient spells for controlling the forces of nature. For shelter and food through the coming winter months which he promised would be a hard one, the druid – Bona – promised to work his magic over Marid's fields, bringing out the best in beasts and crops.

The druid had quickly worked his way into the king's confidence, and soon Marid was coming to rely more and more on the small twisted man. And that night in a drunken stupor he had asked the druid if it were true that his son and wife were lovers.

Bona had smiled through his misshapen teeth and whispered in his raw hoarse voice. 'I'll wager your son has shared your wife's bed more times than you have.'

Rian had entered the dining hall just in time to see his father strike the druid to the ground and call for his guards.

A spear butt struck the door, swinging it open, and Marid stormed into the circular bedchamber. He stopped just inside the door, colour rising to his face at the sight of his two sons, both armed and waiting, with his wife behind them.

'So... this is how I find my bride – and my sons! Well, have you been taking turns with her, or perhaps both together...' Marid trailed off into incoherence.

Rian took a step forward. 'Father, you don't understand...' he began.

'I understand that I have found my two sons in my wife's – *their stepmother's* – bedchamber. I understand that at least one,' he looked at Necca, 'is not long awake, and I understand that my two sons are armed, and have drawn weapons on their own father.' The king stepped forward and then he suddenly struck Rian, sending him sprawling back against his brother. Necca caught him, and then swung the spear around so that the point was tilted towards his father. 'Your argument is not with Rian,' he said quietly, 'he is innocent.'

'But he knew, he *knew*,' Marid raved. 'He knew his brother was lying with his stepmother; he knew his father was being cuckolded behind his very back – he *knew*!'

Bona the druid slipped in behind the king and touched his shoulder; Marid shuddered and began to breathe quietly. The livid colour left his face and his fists unclenched. He ran a trembling hand through his wiry grey hair and took a step backwards. When he spoke again, his voice was calm and controlled. 'However, what is done, is done, and there is no escaping it. You must go – both of you – and you,' the harshness crept back into his voice as he glared at his wife, 'you have shamed my name. Take your belongings, your lovers, and anyone else who will follow you and go. I will not soil my hands with your blood.' The druid touched his shoulder again and the anger left the king's voice to be replaced by an unnatural calm. He turned to his sons. 'I curse you both,' he said evenly. 'You have taken my wife – who was more precious to me than the very waters of life, and so I curse you: let the water that sustains all life be your bane. You took my life from me and so I take it from you!' Marid MacCairde bowed stiffly, pushed past the druid and the warriors crowding the doorway, and marched down the silent corridor.

Bona the druid lingered for a moment, his flat, fishlike eyes regarding the trio with malicious amusement, and then his gnarled hand rose and sketched a sign in the air which went abruptly chill, and then he too turned and glided silently down the corridor.

Ebblue, Necca and Rian rode away the following morning with close on a thousand of their followers. The early morning sun cast long shadows along the ground and Rian, glancing back at the fort, saw the double shadow of his father and the druid snaking across the dew-damp grass, and for a single instant both shadows mingled and took on the shape of a huge crow – a portent of death.

And then the small druid raised his arms and the air above the fort began to crackle with suppressed forces as he wove his curse about the brothers and their followers. Dark clouds swept in from the west and rapidly obscured the heavens, blotting out the sun. Thunder rumbled and a quick spasm of lightning rippled through the clouds, illuminating them from within, and then there was silence in which the wind dropped and it seemed as if the morning held its breath – waiting. The air was heavy and tart, full of the promise of rain – which never materialised.

And then the druid began to chant, using a tongue that had been old when man first climbed down from the trees, a language that was inhuman and never meant to be shaped by human throats, and Ebblue, Necca and Rian felt the chill hand of death caress them all.

The incantation completed, the druid leaned forward and pointed one long, sticklike arm at the company. 'The water which does not come now will one day find you,' he screamed, his voice thin and high on the heavy air.

Necca laughed. 'Eat your words, old man,' he called, plucking a tiny ornate dagger from his belt and throwing it with all his might at the druid. The distance was almost a hundred paces and no one, least of all Necca himself, expected it to come even close to the druid – it was merely an act of defiance. But Ebblue leaned forward across her mount and called upon Danu to avenge her, and then she gestured, a tiny movement of the fingers, and suddenly a chill wind swept across the plain, catching the tiny glittering point, carrying it up and up... A stray sunbeam touched the metal, making it blaze molten in the gloom, and then it fell...

Bona screamed and his hands touched his throat and came away red, and then he slowly toppled from the walls and fell, like a broken limbed doll, to the hard ground beneath.

Necca, looking pale and shaken, turned back to his brother and lover. 'It seems as if the gods themselves are on our side this day.'

But Rian, having watching Ebblue while she was calling upon the goddess, could only smile uncertainly and nod.

The brothers travelled northwards, spending the first night by the shores of a small lake. The moon was high when Necca and Rian walked the perimeter of their camp, moving quietly through the massed hide and cloth tents, checking on the guards, the horses and the warriors concealed in the trees and bushes against sudden attack. They climbed a small knoll and stood on its tip, and stared down into the little valley, the moonlight washing the lake with silver and shadow to one side, and the tiny spots of fire, crimson and gold in the night on the other. Wind rustled through the trees, stirring the nearly leafless branches, whispering through the piled leaves about the trunks and roots, and the long grass hissed like water-splashed fire.

'What will become of us?' Rian asked suddenly, unconsciously keeping his voice low, loath to break the night-woven spell.

Cloth rustled and Rian guessed his brother had shrugged. 'We'll go on, find ourselves a valley with fresh water and settle down. There are enough of us to make it work.'

'Will our father come after us?' Rian wondered.

'I doubt it. Most of the people down there have friends or family back at court. He won't come after us,' he repeated softly, 'not after what happened to his pet druid.' He laughed.

'You don't think you caused that, do you?' his younger brother asked.

Necca's eyes shone whitely in the paleness of his face, and he shook his head. 'Oh, I doubt it; coincidence . . . or maybe the gods *are* on our side.'

Rian turned and stared up into his brother's face. In the gloom he could barely make out the features, just an indistinct pale oval and the harsh glitter of his eyes as they roved across the small encampment. 'Necca,' he said quietly, 'you were watching your knife or the druid, I'm not sure which, but I was watching Ebblue when you made that throw. She was staring at the clouds and talking, whispering, chanting, I don't know,' he shook his head. 'But her lips were moving, and when you threw the knife, she leaned forward across the horse and spoke aloud, and I heard the name *Danu*, and then the fingers of her right hand gestured . . .'

'What are you trying to say?' Necca asked coldly.

'I'm not trying to say anything,' Rian said quickly, 'I'm telling you what I saw – you can draw your own conclusions.'

'And what are your conclusions?'

'I think . . . I think Ebblue may have some of the Power.'

He stepped back and continued quickly. 'It is the only conclusion I can come to – and before you do or say anything hasty, why don't you ask her?'

For a long time Necca stood rigid, staring down into the encampment, and then he turned away and began to run down the incline into the camp. Rian sighed and followed him.

The tent was set a little way back from the others, in the midst of a tiny copse of trees. Hides had been stretched from tree to tree, enclosing a rough square, and on a framework of more branches and poles, waterproof hides had been thrown. The guard stationed outside the tent, tending the smoking fire, came to his feet with spear levelled as the brothers crashed out of the shadows into the clearing. He opened his mouth to call out a challenge, when he recognised first Necca and then Rian. He grounded his spear and saluted as they both passed him without a word and entered the tent. In the shifting glow from the small fire, the sentry's eyebrows rose and a smile touched his lips. So, it was true about the two of them sharing her ... and at the same time too ...

Within the tent all was in darkness, although the bitter stench of resin still lingered on the air where a torch had been lately extinguished. Necca stopped so suddenly that his brother stumbled into him. 'Get us some light,' he commanded. Rian grunted and, turning back, pushed through the leather flap. Without a word he pulled a burning branch from the fire, waved it through the air to bring it to a blaze and carried it back into the tent.

Inside, he found Necca standing over Ebblue who was lying bundled up in the sleeping furs. In the flickering torchlight, with the furs bundled up to her chin, and her raven hair loose and unbound, she looked curiously childlike and innocent. Necca knelt and kissed her on the forehead and her eyes snapped open: old, worldly eyes, and the illusion of innocence was shattered. She sat up and the furs slipped away, revealing her full breasts, forever wiping away any lingering thoughts Rian might have had that she was childlike in any way.

'What is it? What's wrong?'

'Nothing... nothing,' Necca soothed her. He glanced across at Rian. 'My brother has something he wishes to discuss with you... with us.'

'Now? But... what time is it?' Ebblue demanded.

'The moon has reached its zenith and is beginning to sink,' Rian said quietly.

Ebblue looked from Rian to Necca. 'Can this not wait?' she asked quietly.

'I'm afraid not.' Rian put the torch to the tiny brazier and blew the kindling alight. It spat and sparked, sending tiny points of light wheeling upwards to die against the thick hide. He then ground the torch out against the earth and tossed it into a corner. 'Tell me,' he said quietly, 'what did you do when Necca threw his knife at the druid today?' The red firelight danced across his face, lending his eyes a maturity and depth they lacked in the full light of day, and for one moment Necca could see his father in him.

'What did you do?' he demanded.

'Do? I prayed,' Ebblue said softly. 'I prayed that Danu might hear my prayers for revenge.'

'If you were praying for revenge, then surely you should have prayed to the Morrigan?' Rian snapped. 'And tell me, what were your fingers doing when you were praying to the goddess, and before that, what were you doing looking into the heavens and muttering?'

'I... I...' She turned to Necca. 'What is this? What is he trying to say?'

Necca shook his head. 'I don't know – but answer him, tell him what you were doing.'

There was silence then in the tent for a long time, the trio frozen in a tableau of their own thoughts, with the same emotions: fear, anger, concern, flickering across all three faces, but for different reasons. At last Ebblue sighed and, suddenly realising that her breasts were bare, pulled the bed furs up to her chin, drew her knees up and encircled them with her arms, and then rested her chin on her covered knees. 'I have the Power,' she admitted tightly, 'but I have never used it for anything but good.' She looked up at Rian. 'When you saw me looking up into the clouds, I was trying to draw down the rain, to break the druid's spell, but he was the stronger and beat me in that. However, the effort left him exhausted and it was a simple matter to call up the wind and carry the knife to his throat. He could have brushed it aside with a similar wind, but to have done so would have meant that he would have had to relinquish control of the pent up storm, and his spell would have come to naught. He was caught in a single moment of indecision – a final moment of indecision.' She smiled and the shadows danced across her face, wiping away the harshness that had touched it while she talked. But then the smile slowly faded and the hard look came back into her eyes. 'But the spell, the curse, still remains. I'm doing the best I can to hold it in check – but sooner or later it will strike.'

'What curse?' Rian demanded.

'The curse of water – your father and the druid both cursed you to die by water.'

'When will it strike?' Necca asked slowly.

Ebblue shrugged. 'I have no way of knowing. Today, tomorrow, a season's time, a generation...'

'Can you not use your power to divine the future?' Rian asked.

Ebblue smiled. 'My power in that direction is very limited.'

'But you could tell us something?' Rian persisted.

'A little.'

Rian turned to his brother. 'Surely that is better than nothing?'

Necca stood. 'Perhaps. But do we want to know a fraction

45

of the future?' he wondered aloud. 'Is the anxiety of knowing better than the fear of not knowing?' He looked down at Ebblue. 'Read it for us then,' he said at last.

Ebblue nodded and, pushing down the furs, slipped from the bed. The warm firelight gilded her smooth skin, tanning it a light bronze. She pulled one of the furs off the bed and draped it across her shoulders before sitting down crosslegged on the cold ground. She looked up at Rian. 'Bring me a piece of coal and a knife,' she said.

When he brought the coal and handed her his knife, Ebblue drew a circle on the ground with the coal and then, taking both Necca's and Rian's hands, nicked their forefingers with the knife. The blood spattered onto the ground inside the circle and immediately darkened. Then, with the knife again, she divided the circle into four quarters, ensuring that there was one drop of blood in each quarter. Reverently she placed the knife to one side, the tip of the blade just touching the edge of the circle and pointing northwards. And then, placing both hands on her knees she closed her eyes and leaned back, her head tilted up towards the heavens, brow furrowed, and slowly, slowly, she began to call upon her Power.

Her hands clenched into fists and then the fingers splayed. Slowly they began to move up her thighs and in towards her groin where they lingered briefly before continuing on up across her flat stomach and then over her breasts where they crossed, her right hand going over her left shoulder, and her left hand to her right shoulder. She was breathing heavily now, her breasts rising and falling rapidly, the muscles in her stomach rippling and her knees trembling. She began to pant loudly and then her breath came in ragged gasps which quickly turned into groans that ended in a short shrill scream. Her head slumped forward and her hair tumbled into her lap.

Necca made a move to go to her, but Rian touched his shoulder and shook his head, and when they both looked back they found she was staring coldly at them, her eyes black and glittering like lumps of coal. They looked *old*, ancient beyond reckoning; it was as if she had touched some primal core deep within herself, dragging it to the surface. But even as they looked her expression changed, her eyes softened, the tense muscles in her head and neck relaxed and she assumed her more normal expression. A shadow of a smile touched her face, which now looked tired and worn.

'I'm sorry,' Necca said quickly, 'I didn't realise it would be so difficult for you.'

Ebblue shook her head. 'It was not that difficult... no, that's not quite true,' she quickly corrected herself. 'In a way it gets easier every time, but the reaction gets proportionally worse. However,' she shook her head, 'I reached the state of meditation necessary to draw upon the future memories...'

'*Future memories?*' Rian asked.

'Much as we remember the past, so too do we know – *remember* – the future, if only we know how to look and where to look.'

'Did you see our future?' Necca asked.

'Not one – there is never one immutable future, there are always a few, but some of course have a greater probability than others. In your – *our* – case there are many, many futures... but all with the one outcome,' she added in a whisper.

'And that is?' Rian asked, although he knew what her answer would be.

'They all end in death,' Ebblue said quietly, her voice sounding unnaturally loud in the silence.

Rian shivered suddenly in the cold night air. He had a feeling he had just been given his own death sentence, a feeling that, no matter what he did or where he went, there was no escape... a feeling of absolute hopelessness.

'And is that all?' Necca asked, 'death – just death? Is there nothing else you can tell us?'

'There is perhaps one thing,' Ebblue said doubtfully, 'I

saw a mountain pass, a long thin defile cut between two high cliffs, and on either side of the pass were two tall pillars of dark green stone. When we came to the pass we divided into two groups – one group going around the mountain, and the other through the pass. And then I felt a great disturbance, the sudden shock of mass death cut across the dream plain I inhabited... One group had been wiped out ... but I don't know which group... I don't know,' she screamed, and then she buried her head in her hands and wept bitterly. Necca nodded to his brother, dismissing him, and then he went and knelt by the young woman.

The brothers and their followers continued northwards. But now they were continually harried by bandits and a sudden spell of bad weather which further slowed them down. The attacks on their camps became more and more frequent and, since they were moving through mostly open countryside with little shelter, losses, particularly among the beasts, were high.

Ten days after they had ridden away from Marid MacCairde's fort they reached the Pass of the Two Pillars. Over the previous day the character of the land had changed; from lush grassy plains it had steepened into a rock-strewn wilderness that gradually inclined upwards. And then it had levelled out and led towards the mountains of the north – and the only way through the mountains was through the pass. The alternative route was an extra ten day journey through the foothills.

The brothers led their followers along the banks of a dried-up river bed, with outriders on either tall bank and ranging far ahead and to the rear. But the countryside seemed deserted with no signs of life. Just before they reached the pass they came upon two rotting skeletons slumped beneath the branches of a spreading oak tree. Time, the elements and scavengers had dealt harshly with them, and now they were little more than white sticks poking through the rank tall grass that had sprouted from the richly fertilised earth. It was a dire omen whose significance was lost on no one in the company.

The pass was guarded by two tall pillars, remnants of the architecture of the ancient Tuatha De Danann who had once walked Erin's green fields. The pillars were carved from a heavy dark green stone and worked with tiny glyphs and pictograms. There was some evidence that a third stone had once topped the two pillar stones, much in the manner of the great stone circles in the land across the water to the east, making it a kind of gateway, but the lintel stone had long since disappeared. Down one side of the left-hand pillar was a vertical line of script in *ogham*, the incised writing form of the druids. For those with the education or training to read the lines and slashes it was a warning of *'Bane and misfortune on an evil heart or unclean spirit to pass beyond the threshold ...'* Time had cleansed the latter half of the message.

And it was here the brothers parted company, for they had both recognised the location in Ebblue's warning vision, and had decided that one group should go north through the pass and the other would go around the mountain ... and the gods themselves could look with favour on what group they willed.

Rian and his followers turned west and followed the foothills. The path was rough and broken, obviously ill-used, and quickly began to lead down into a small, almost bowl-shaped valley. Night was drawing in, with shadows racing in from the east, blotting out the last lingering light from the west, forcing them to camp in the valley. The night was cold, made all the more so by the ancient trees that crowded in on them. The tiny winking camp fires did little to lighten the gloom or dispel the chill and even the wind seemed to whisper portents just beyond the edge of intelligibility.

Around midnight Rian was awakened by shouts and cries to find that some of his company had come across an old woman living in a construction of branches and grasses beneath the trees. She was old, that Rian could tell immediately, a genuine oldness, not the artificial ageing that hunger and hard times touched many with. He looked into her eyes and started – for they were no longer human, and regarded him balefully and with all the intelligence of an animal.

'Why have you brought this woman here?' he asked quietly, his voice pluming whitely on the chill air.

'She was caught stealing water,' Doran, Rian's servant, answered quickly.

Rian pulled a torch from its holder and went to stand over the old woman. In the flickering light her face seemed even more frightening, with every muscle and nerve twitching and leaping. 'If you had asked, you would have been given water,' he said gently.

The old woman spat at his feet. 'My people have never asked for anything – we have always taken what we wanted. *You*!' she jabbed a bony finger in his direction, 'you did not ask my leave to enter here; this is my land, and you have trespassed.'

Rian smiled. 'We did not know this valley belonged to anyone ...'

'Do not humour me boy; I was old when your grandparents were but drooling babes. My people have held this land since time out of mind.'

'Then you must be of the De Danann,' Rian said with a smile. A ripple of laughter passed around the small group.

The old woman spun around. 'Oh, laugh if you will, but my mother was one of the People of the Goddess ... and I possess their powers!'

Rian turned away. 'Give her some water,' he said,

suddenly weary of her chatter. 'Send her on her way.'

'*Send her away, send her away*,' the old woman screeched. 'I am not your servant or hunting dog to be sent away. I am of the House of the Goddess; you will pay me all due respect and honour,' she demanded.

Rian spun around. 'Old woman this has been a long day. I have parted company with my brother and friends – and I'm not even sure if I'll ever see either him or them again. I'm tired – and you're irritating me!'

The old woman's laughter shrilled on the cold air. 'You will never see your brother again, Rian, son of Marid; neither you, nor your people will live to see the sun sink again!' She pulled away from the hands holding her. 'You have been cursed by water by one of the white-robed ones – it is fitting, aye, fitting! I too curse you, but I curse you in the name of a far older Power, for I curse you with the very soul of the land itself. Water you have kept from me – water shall be your bane!'

And she was gone. She dashed past and disappeared into the shadows behind Rian and fled into the night. Doran would have gone after her, but Rian stopped him. 'What's the point? A crazy old woman; what will you do with her?'

'But she cursed us . . . she cursed us,' Doran stuttered, 'and she was of the Old Folk.' Fear had turned his face ashen in the torchlight.

'She *said* she was of the De Danann,' Rian reminded his servant, 'there is a difference.'

'But she still cursed us,' Doran repeated sullenly. 'We should go after her, make her lift the curse.'

'You will stay here,' Rian snapped, 'or I will curse you – and with more than words. Return to your duties; we will break camp with the dawn.'

Rian turned away and re-entered his tent. He lay awake for the remainder of the night however, the old woman's words echoing through his head. There was no need to send the servants after her; there was nothing either they, or indeed she, could do: it was fated that he would die.

The morning was bright but cold, and with a touch of the fast approaching cold months in the fresh breeze. Rian and his followers set out with the first light of dawn, following the winding track that led through the thick undergrowth and tall trees. The guards were nervous and the animals skittish, and the entire valley seemed to be unusually silent: no morning birds sang, no animals scuttled through the undergrowth, and there was an air – a thick brooding sensation which hung over the little valley like a blanket – which plucked at the nerves and set the senses on edge. Shadows flickered just at the edge of their vision, and the horses shied from pools of darker shadow that edged closer to the track. Some of the more ancient trees seemed to shed a chill miasma, an aura of cold and waiting evil, and Rian started again and again, hearing a cold mocking laughter from afar.

However, towards mid morning the character of the land changed as the track led up and out of the valley. The iciness and the feeling of being watched gradually disappeared, although Rian, standing to one side of the track and watching his people slowly file past, noticed that the entire valley seemed unnaturally shadowed.

They rode westwards, and towards late afternoon left the foothills and entered a broad flat plain bounded on three sides by mountains and the fourth by a dark forest of short stunted trees. As the sun sank into the mountains in the west, Rian and his followers camped in a small natural hollow in the centre of the plain; easily defended and protection of sorts from the ice-tipped breeze that had blown up with evening.

They set their camp for the night in the hollow, with the elderly, the women and children down in the centre and the outer perimeter guarded by a strong force of warriors. This was a strange land – stranger still since they had seen no one throughout the day, and the only living things they had come across were a few solitary birds winging swiftly westwards in the latter half of the evening.

The day darkened swiftly, and storm clouds, which had massed in the north and west for most of the day, rolled across the night sky, obscuring the harshly glittering stars and making the air oppressive.

Rian, touched with a feeling of foreboding, walked to the edge of the hollow, watching, waiting. Occasionally the moon peeked through the clouds, its vacuous face made sinister with strands and wisps of cloud. He started when he imagined the racing clouds formed the face of the dead druid, Bona, and for a moment his last words rumbled across his brain like the sound of distant thunder: 'The water which does not come now will one day find you... find you... find you...' And then the cloud face dissolved and was gone – and was replaced by the leering face of the old woman in the forest: 'You will not live to see the sun sink again... water you have kept from me, water shall be your bane... water be your bane... your bane...'.

Rian grinned mirthlessly. Well, at least he had proved the old woman wrong; he had lived to see the sun sink again, and as for water being his bane...

Lightning and thunder cracked simultaneously, making him jump; he swore at his own fright and attempted to calm his pounding heart. He turned around and began to run down towards his own tent: soon the heavens would open and there would be a downpour... and the land needed the water, he decided, stumbling on the hard, dry earth.

By the time he reached the tent it was raining. It wasn't like a normal downpour: the rain fell straight down in a solid mass, striking the hard ground with almost physical force, turning what had been a dry, hard-packed earth only moments before into a wet clinging morass. The ground, dry as it was, swiftly absorbed the water, but it was eventually sated and slowly but surely the water level began to rise.

Rian lay in his tent listening to the drumming of the rain and watching the leather slowly bellying inwards with the weight of the water. Unable to sleep, he prowled the interior of the tent, before eventually pushing out into the rain. The force of the water struck him like a blow, plastering his hair to his head, blinding and deafening him. He stumbled back into the tent and wiped his face, and then crouched in the opening watching the deluge. And then to his right-hand side, one of the tents, unable to bear the weight of the water, collapsed, and then suddenly it seemed as if the whole camp was sinking down into the mud. The fires and torches were gone, doused by the water, and chaos reigned as people stumbled around in the darkness, sliding and falling in the slick earth, trying to find their families or friends. A row of tents collapsed and Rian himself barely escaped being trapped beneath his own as the weight of water folded it in upon itself. The screams of those trapped beneath the tents were drowned out by the frightened cries of the horses and the drumming of the rain. A shout rose briefly above the noise, a cry of warning which was quickly silenced, and then the stampeding horses raced through the hollow, trampling everything in their path in their efforts to reach the higher, drier ground. One struck Rian a glancing blow as it galloped past, sending him crashing backwards. He fell against another person – female by the sound of it – and they both sank into the muck. The woman struggled, kicking and scratching, terrified as liquid muck trickled into her open mouth. Her flailing arm caught Rian across the throat, making him choke. He rose to his knees, and then her knee caught him in the groin, sending him crashing to the ground, retching as the pit of his stomach blossomed fire. He fell face forward onto the ground – and the water and mud were almost over his head. He jerked backwards, pulling his face free of the mire, and then something large and heavy pounded through the mud, spraying him as it went past; there was a terrified scream followed by a sickening wet crunch as the horse trampled the young woman.

Rian attempted to push himself to his feet – and now the water and mud were almost up to his knees ... and still the rain fell unabated.

And then he felt the ground before him tremble, and was aware of a disturbance in the rising water. He heard the snorting and muffled breathing and smelt the terrified horse, and felt the forelegs crash into him ...

The rain continued for the remainder of the night. Out of Rian's five hundred followers barely a score survived – those who had been unlucky enough the night before not to find a space to pitch their tents close to the centre of the hollow and had been forced to camp on the higher ground around the edge. The hollow itself was gone, and there was a small placid lake in its place, its mud-dimmed waters hiding the bodies and artifacts that lay just a little below the surface.

And those few of Rian's followers that had survived rode away into the east and were forgotten, but thereafter the lake was known as Lough Rian ... which time and ignorance has changed to Lough Ree.

Necca awoke with a start. He lay still, his eyes probing the heavy darkness, wondering what had awoken him. He moved slightly, and then he suddenly realised: he was alone in the bed furs, there was no warm breathing body beside him.

'He's dead.' The voice from the darkness was soft, the mearest whisper, and tinged with sorrow. 'I'm sorry, there was nothing else I could do.'

'Ebblue? What's happened?'

A white blur moved before him, and then knelt by his side. He reached out, brushed her breast and then touched her shoulder. 'What has happened?' he repeated softly, aware of a cold chill settling into the pit of his stomach.

'Rian is dead, most of his followers also. The waters have claimed them.'

Necca's fingers tightened briefly on Ebblue's shoulder and then the pressure slackened. '*Sssso*,' he whispered, 'the druid's curse finally caught up with him.'

Strands of fine hair brushed his arm as Ebblue shook her head. 'Your brother was cursed, yes; but Bona never had the power to actually call down his curse. He laid it yes, but he could never call it down. Rian must have been cursed again – and thrice cursed is doomed.'

'Thrice cursed?'

'Your father cursed you both also,' his stepmother reminded him.

'So, I am twice cursed also?'

Ebblue nodded. 'We are all barely this side of destruction,' she said quietly.

'What can we do?' Necca demanded.

Teeth flashed white in the gloom. 'There is nothing you can do... nothing at all.'

Necca, Ebblue and their followers continued on through the pass and followed the track, and towards mid morning they entered the carefully cultivated fields and tended white-sanded roads that led to Brugh na Boine, the abode of Angus Og, the God of Love and the ever-living son of the Dagda.

They rode past strange, slant-eyed, slit-pupilled and deeply tanned creatures who tended the fields or raked the roads. Some raised their long double-jointed fingers in a curious salute or blessing, but others merely regarded them expressionlessly.

Necca reined in his mount and waited until Ebblue rode up beside him. 'What are they?' he asked.

'They are the servants of the De Danann, and some,' she nodded briefly towards a tall, slender figure standing over a dull, lifeless bush, 'have the De Danann blood in them: halflings.' Necca swore softly, for even as he watched the bush began to quiver and tremble, and the dull lifeless leaves changed colour perceptibly, assuming a rich and vibrant hue, and the drooping branches rose to face the sun.

There was a flash of white, startling them both, and then a snow-white dove swooped down from the skies and circled slowly about them, the gentle beat of its wings fanning their faces. It folded its wings and alighted on the head of Ebblue's mount and regarded them for a moment through hard black eyes before taking to the air again and winging south towards the simple white stone walls of Angus' Dun.

'Angus' messenger,' Ebblue explained. 'He is sometimes known as Angus of the Birds; the birds are said to be four kisses that the wind stole from him and transformed into living creatures.'

Necca reined his mount to a halt and watched a white-robed figure leave the dun and walked slowly down the shining road towards them. 'What is this Angus like?' he asked.

'In looks he is said to be very beautiful; a woman's features on a man's skull. But remember,' she warned, 'he is the son of a god – and a god himself in his own right – and he possesses terrible power. His other name is the Disrupter,' she added, and then she leaned across and touched her lover's arm. 'Fear him Necca, fear him, and do not anger him.'

'I fear no man,' Necca said quitely, his voice cold with anger.

'Then you are a fool, Necca MacMarid.' The voice was thin and high, like a pure musical note.

Necca dismounted and walked up to the god. Angus was

tall, a head and more taller than Necca, who was by no means small. His long white robe, somewhat similar to the garment worn by the druids, enveloped his body, but Necca got the impression of leanness, but combined with wiry strength. His face was youthful – almost boyish – beardless and unscarred, and his golden hair was curled close to his skull. But what caught and held Necca's attention were his eyes: they were large and oval, completely dominating his thin face. The pupils were black and flecked with tiny spots of gold that matched his hair and brows... and they were old. They betrayed his great age; his body might not age, the years would never touch it, but his eyes recorded and mirrored his experience. Necca shivered, and for one brief moment saw the image of an old, old man inhabiting the body of a youth through some foul sorcery.

'You should fear me,' Angus said softly, his voice barely above a whisper, yet carrying clearly to all present.

'You are the God of Love,' Necca said sarcastically, 'and why should I fear the God of Love?'

The god smiled. 'There is little love left in you; I see anger and much hate... and fear. And I am only acceptable to those who are at least willing to accept me.' The god paused and added, 'Are you?'

'I want nothing from you,' Necca said quietly, 'but my people are tired; we would wish to rest in these fields for the night, and we will be gone in the morning.'

'*No!*' Angus shook his head emphatically. 'You cannot stay here.'

Necca stepped closer to the god, and breathed in his raw wild perfume. He rested his hand on his dagger. 'We can go no further,' he said coldly, 'we will stay here.'

Angus turned away, and his words hung delicately on the still air. 'Then on your own head be it.'

Necca's followers camped as far from the white dun as possible, huddling around a few blazing fires, talking quietly, starting at every sound. Necca had doubled and then redoubled the guards around the camp before retiring for the night with Ebblue. But he found the sorceress cold and unresponsive beneath his touch, and when he attempted to hold her she turned away and wrapped her arms around herself. 'Not tonight,' she whispered, 'not here. Can you not feel the Power in the air? What would happen if I were to conceive – what would I bear?' She turned her head to face him and he caught the liquid glint of tears in her eyes. 'We should never have come here, Necca. Angus may be the God of Love, but he is also the Lord of the Birds – and some birds are harbingers of death and eaters of the dead.'

'We will be gone with the dawn,' he soothed her.

'It may be too late then,' she said finally, and turned her head away from him.

Necca was awakened close to dawn by a wild-eyed and terrified guard. The man was almost incoherent with fear and could only drag the half naked prince from his tent and across to the corral where they had left their mounts. Necca pushed his way through the group of silent men and then stood horrified before what remained of their horses. For the animals had been slain – and not only slain, but butchered, mutilated. He remembered what Ebblue had said about Angus being Lord of the Birds: it looked as if some great raven had torn out each animal's entrails and then picked at the flesh . . . and, significantly, all the animals' eyes had been plucked out.

He breathed deeply, quelling his rising gorge. 'Did anyone hear anything . . . see anything?' he demanded.

The guards shook their heads. 'It was sorcery, my lord,' one said.

'Aye, sorcery,' another agreed.

'What will we do now?' another asked.

Necca turned away from the carnage and pushed his way through the guards. 'There is nothing we can do – except talk to the god,' he spat.

Angus was waiting for him when he returned to his tent.

Ebblue was sitting up in a corner, the thick furs pulled up to her chin, shivering visibly, her eyes wide with fear. Necca could almost taste the strangeness in the air, and he assumed that this was the Power she had spoken of the night before. It was sharp and flat, like the air before a storm, and his skin began to tingle as if a host of insects were swarming over it.

'You killed my animals,' he accused, walking around the god and kneeling by Ebblue's side. 'Are you all right?' he asked her.

She nodded and clung to him.

'I warned you not to stay,' Angus said.

'And I told you we would.'

'This is a strange and dangerous land,' Angus said. 'It is not the land you know – you have passed beyond your own fields and partly into the Shadowland, and all manner of creatures stalk these lands at night,' he added quietly.

'You killed my animals,' Necca stated flatly, 'and unless we find fresh mounts, then I am afraid we must stay here.'

The god nodded and his old eyes hooded over in a smile. 'That is why I am here; I have come to offer you mounts, or at least,' he added slowly, 'a mount.'

Necca rose from Ebblue's side. 'A mount? You have come to offer us one miserable horse! Well, you can take your horse...'

'This is not an ordinary horse,' the god said calmly. 'It cannot be ridden; the man has not yet been born that can tame him, but it will act as a beast of burden.'

'God,' Necca snapped, 'we had twenty beasts carrying our belongings – your one horse is not likely to make much difference is it?'

'You must wait and see,' Angus said with a smile. He bowed shortly, turned and slipped through the tent flaps.

Necca sank down beside Ebblue. He found himself trembling with anger and frustration; he felt like a child struggling against a parent: there was nothing he could do –

and he knew it. His stepmother put her arms around him and pulled his head onto her breast, and then she held him while he wept.

It might have been a horse. At some time in the dim and distant past its ancestors might have been of the equine breed, but now ...

The creature stood about fifteen hands high – which was normal – but about four times the length of a normal horse! It was eight-legged, and at least two men could have sat side by side on its back. Its head was broad and flat, more reminiscent of a bull's than that of a horse, and just beneath its large rounded ears were tiny stub horns. Its eyes were flat and yellow, slit-pupilled like a cat's and its teeth were sharp and pointed ... and Necca wondered what meat this creature ate. Its coat was smooth and glossy and tinged with a metallic green, and its hooves were cloven, like a goat's.

The prince turned to the god. 'What abomination is this?'

The god smiled. 'It is a whim ... a minor indulgence,' he smiled again. 'But it will carry all your belongings without tiring. However, a warning: do not allow anyone to mount the beast, for to do so would be fatal ... and not only to the rider I fear. Secondly, once the creature begins to move, it must be kept moving, and on no account must it be allowed to stop.'

'Why?' Necca demanded.

The god smiled, the corners of his lips curving upwards, but his eyes remaining cold and hard. 'You disobeyed me and spent the night in my domain. You will never again spend any length of time in any one place; you are doomed to wander for the rest of your days. You see,' Angus said conversationally, 'I too have cursed you. Oh, I know you have been cursed twice, and now I am adding my curse to that. But to discover the curse, you must first allow the creature to stop.'

61

'And you are the God of Love?' Necca said slowly.

'I am what you make of me,' Angus said, turning away.

Necca and his followers departed close to mid morning, the strange beast loaded down with their belongings. The creature moved uncomplainingly in a plodding steady movement, and responded to blows on either shoulder to make it turn. With onset of evening they camped in a small stand of trees and Necca, mindful of Angus' warning, detailed a group of his men to walk the creature around the camp again and again until dawn, when they set out again, moving north and eastwards this time. They continued on for ten days, their pace necessarily slow, dictated by the plodding of the beast which was not much faster than a man's walk. Necca's warriors naturally fretted at this slow pace and some foraged ahead, seeking a suitable camping spot. Towards the afternoon of the tenth day, they returned with news of a broad flat plain ahead, dotted with stands of stunted trees.

They reached the plain towards late evening, when the shadows were beginning to lengthen into night, and even Necca had to admit it was perfect. The flat plain – although affording no natural protection – meant that no one could approach them undetected, and once the trees were cleared there would be enough wood to construct a large fort.

And so they made their way downwards onto the grasslands, and it was here that Necca made his first grievous mistake. The plain had possibilities; properly protected and with a fresh supply of water the land could be worked to produce at least one – and possibly two – good harvests. However, while the prince was taken up with his plans for the future, the creature was allowed to stop moving...

He had rotated the drivers regularly, but even so the task of guiding a slow moving beast, which at the same time both terrified and awed, quickly grew boring, and now, with the end of their journey in sight, the drivers grew lax, until for one moment they forgot to drive the creature.

It stopped.

Ebblue screamed a warning and, calling upon her powers, sent a bright needle-sharp jab of fire in its direction. The glittering point struck the animal in its hindquarters, jolting it into movement again. But the damage had already been done. The ground beneath where the beast had stopped had abruptly grown wet and marshy, and now a bubbling pool sprang forth. The gurgling water began to fountain upwards, growing higher and higher. Necca threw himself forward onto the water, trying to press it down with his body. He could feel the chill liquid immediately soaking through his jerkin; he could feel the pressure against his chest, pumping and pulsating like a heartbeat; he could feel it pushing upwards, could feel it growing stronger. And then in a sudden gush it carried him upwards, lifting him completely off his feet and tossing him to one side. The water rose in a long slender pillar, fountaining up into the darkening night sky, catching the last of the sun's rays, cresting into a fine rainbow-hued spray.

Necca scrambled to his feet – and immediately slipped and fell in the mud. The hard ground was sinking. And then Ebblue was by his side, her hands moving quickly, her slender fingers tracing intricate patterns in the damp evening air. She cried out in a strange wailing accent, the words rising and falling with the pulsating of the water. And then her words began to slow, and as they did so, so did the water. Soon she was only whispering – and the gushing water had fallen to the merest trickle. She knelt in the muddy earth and placed both hands flat across the puncture in the ground – a puncture in the shape of a cloven hoof – and the water stopped.

Necca helped Ebblue to her feet, and gently scraped most of the muck from her hands, and although his own hands were trembling, his stepmother's were as steady as a rock.

'The spell will last a day and a night,' she said, a little

breathlessly. 'You must have a wall built around it, and then I'll transfer the spell of containment to the stones of the wall, and that will hold it.'

'Was that Angus' curse?' Necca asked quietly, still shaken by the suddenness of it all.

The sorceress nodded.

And then the prince smiled. 'Then, we have beaten him – we've tricked him. His spell has been used – and yet we still live.'

'Unless we cover this water hole,' Ebblue said quickly, 'his spell may still claim us.'

By the afternoon of the following day the well hole had been covered in; smooth stones covering the actual hole, and then a low wall built around that, roofed and with a round wooden door bolted into the stone. Ebblue transferred her spell of containment into the stones of the wall and the ground it covered, but adjusted the wording of the spell so that the door might be lifted thrice in every day, but for no more than twenty-one heartbeats – so that water might be drawn off. Necca then had a small round beehive-shaped hut built around the wall and over the well, and installed an old woman, Marue, whose husband had been lost early on in the journey, as the well keeper, and it was her task to ensure that the well was kept locked and covered at all times, and only opened for the time specified.

And so Necca and his followers settled on the Plain of the Grey Copse around the magic well, and there they prospered, for even in times of drought the well never ran dry, nor during the hardest winter did it freeze over.

And the years passed.

Ebblue bore Necca two daughters: Aeru and Liban. She survived the birth of her second daughter by barely a month but, weakened by years of hardship and the constant use of her powers to renew the spell of containment, and having to call forth the crops from the land and turn aside the worst of the storms that might have shattered the small community,

64

she died and was laid to rest beside the well.

As they grew towards maturity the two girls began to resemble their parents: Aeru favouring her father and Liban bearing a startling resemblance to her mother, and also touched with her mother's powers and capable of small magics.

In time Aeru married Curan, a stranger who had wandered into their camp late one evening, wild-eyed and ranting of great *peist* – a serpent – that had pursued him. Aeru had nursed him back to health, but his wits had been addled, or perhaps the cold breath of ancient sorcery had touched him, for his eyes were thereafter wild and seeking, and in night's darkest hours he would often start from his bed, shouting and crying out, pointing at creatures only he could see. But Aeru came to love the strange, gentle and caring poet and married him – even though his nickname about the camp was 'the Simpleton'.

But it was the Simpleton who first predicted the well's overflowing.

It was a warm summer evening and the air was heavy and humid, seeming to press down on the hard dry earth. The evening was hushed with no birds singing or calling and no wind rustling the long grass. The sun had dipped down behind the trees to the west, but the rounded tops were still touched with bronze and ochre fire. The People of the Well – as Necca and his followers had come to be known – were gathered around Curan who sat easily on a low tree stump regaling them with a tale of Erin's ancient past, a tale of the coming of the first invaders to the tiny island: wild warrior women from the far and mysterious east. They sat enthralled as the Simpleton engaged them with words and images, calling forth the pictures of the savage beast-men as they attacked the caves of the Caesirians, and then drawing down the tragedy as the easterners succumbed to the final deadly plague, the ultimate fate of many of Erin's early invaders. He finished his tale in a whisper, and the only sound in the still night air was the sobbing of a young woman as she imagined the tiny eastern sorceress toppling into the waves as the huge funeral fire stained the sky behind her.

Curan smiled as he finished his tale and the light of madness began to burn in his eyes. 'And now that I have told you of the past, would you like me to tell you of the future?' He grinned broadly, and those nearest him drew back, for if touched he was capable of great violence during these fits. 'But what's this I see?' he asked in a hushed and wondering voice. 'Why, the end of the Caesirians is not that much different from the fate of the People of the Well.'

'What do you see, Curan?' Necca asked quietly, tiredly. The years had not been kind to him. The prince was greyed and bowed, and touched with a heaviness of spirit that nothing could ever lift, and only seemed to lighten in the presence of his daughters, and especially Liban.

'I see death, prince,' the Simpleton mocked. 'I see death . . . and in a fashion I can see life. Life and death . . . life and death,' he began to chant in a singsong voice.

'What sort of death?' the prince demanded, aware of the growing murmurs of unease behind him.

Curan looked across at the well hut with its tiny ever-lit torch flickering over the door. 'A wet death,' he said, and fell into a fit of giggling. Necca turned and searched the crowd, and then, catching sight of his daughter, nodded to her and then to her husband. Aeru came forward and gently lifted Curan from the tree stump. The crowd moved back as they passed, afraid to help her carry the drooling man, knowing that he could bear no touch but hers.

Necca stared after them, something like the old fear beginning to seep back into his bones and the cold knot beginning to form at the pit of his stomach. For he knew then, he knew with an absolute certainty, that the gods could never be cheated . . . and that thrice cursed was doomed.

*

For some weeks thereafter the well was guarded with extra vigilance, because, for all Curan's rantings, his prophecies in the past had proved uncannily accurate and it was generally accepted that he had the Sight. But as time passed the extra guards were drafted to other duties, for it was now harvesting time, and every hand was needed to bring in the crop before the raiders and bandits came. And so old Marue was left alone once more in the small dark hut, with no company but the gurgling and trickling of waters inside the round covered well. Sometimes it spoke to her.

It had begun as a whispering at first, the merest thread of imagined sound. She had doubted it of course; a woman alone day and night should expect to hear strange and unusual noises, and of course, she was no longer young, and age played strange tricks on the mind. But the sound continued, whispering her name, calling her, calling... calling...

And soon she began to lie across the flat well cover, her ear pressed against the cold damp wood, listening. She could hear the voice of her husband, and sometimes of her children: both the children she had and those she had thought she might have but which never came... they all lived within the waters of the well.

And the voices begged for release.

But the well could only be opened three times in any one day: at sunrise, when the first rays of the morning sun touched the tip of the round hut; at noon, when the hut cast no shadow; and at sunset when the hut's long shadow raced darkly across the ground.

The well cover could only be left off for the space of twenty-one heartbeats, and over the years Marue had grown expert at counting the beats. At first she had held her own wrist and counted the pulse, but then she realised that excitement might rob them of valuable time for drawing the much needed water if her pulse were speeded up, or sickness could cause a fatal error if her pulse were slow. And so now she usually counted steadily while three young girls drew the water up in large pails and poured it into the barrels that were kept in the hut for that purpose.

On the last fine day for harvesting the girls were early for the noon drawing, and they disturbed Marue who was deep in conversation with her long dead husband, Rael. He was pleading for release, begging her to free him from the cold, so cold water...

The old woman came to her feet quickly, hearing the girlish laughter just outside the closed door. One of the girls tapped loudly, and then pushed it open and stepped into the room. She stopped just inside the threshold, allowing her eyes to adjust to the darkness.

'Marue? Marue... Oh, there you are. How can you bear it so dark in here?'

'It's the light, my dear; when you get to my age the light burns your eyes. Is it time?'

'Almost.' One of the girls stood by the door watching the last vestiges of shadow disappear beneath the glare of the sun. 'Now!'

The two girls pulled away the cover and began to draw off the water as quickly as possible; Marue immediately began to keep count.

'*One... two... three...*'

Her husband wasn't in there, she knew that. Her husband had died on the road here, coughing out his lungs with a chill caught walking around the perimeter of the camp one damp night.

'*...four... five... six...*'

He had died, choking on his own blood, and you might say Necca killed him, and hadn't Necca been cursed in the first place? They were mad to have followed him. And what right did he have to bring them all this way –

'*...seven... eight... nine...*'

– if he had been cursed; and thrice cursed at that. By father, druid and god. He was doomed. He was a walking

68

dead man, and he had killed her husband as surely as if he had driven a dagger into his heart.

'...ten... eleven... twelve...'

And now her husband lay dead beneath the cold, dark water, trapped forever by Ebblue's spell. And what of her children? They too lay trapped beneath the waters.

'...ten... eleven... twelve...'

What about her two sons who had died when Necca's father had warred with the neighbouring tribes? And what about her daughter – the daughter that had cost her her womb – who had been stolen when Miridach, King of Ulster, had come raiding four – or was it five? – seasons ago? They had killed her, probably raped her also, but they had certainly killed her, for she now lived beneath the waters and whispered late at night to her mother about the cold, cold water.

'...thirteen... fourteen... fifteen... sixteen... seventeen... eighteen...'

One of the girls glanced across at the old woman in alarm. The old woman's lips were still moving silently in a count. But Gael had been drawing the water now for three seasons, and she knew – *she knew!* – something was wrong, for the old woman had only reached eighteen, and yet *she* had already counted twenty-one!

Her scream was lost as the pent-up water erupted upwards in a solid pillar that ripped through the roof, scattering the rounded stones and ragged bodies across the flat plain. The rest of the hut blew outwards, the stones scything through the men, women and children caught in their path. They were the lucky ones.

The ground opened out in a great V-shaped cut that spewed water upwards as it raced across the ground – and then the land abruptly sank. The two arms of the V swung around and joined, and the oval of land between them dropped downwards and was engulfed in the rising water, and over the shouts and cries rose the exultant wailing of the released water, crying out its release.

And in a matter of twenty heartbeats the entire Plain of the Grey Copse sank down beneath the water, the whole community wiped out in an instant, and when the dust and grit and water had settled, where there had once been a green and fertile plain was now only a broad flat lake. The poets and travellers called it Lough Necca, but time and ignorance has changed that to Lough Neagh, the largest lake in the islands of Britain and Ireland.

II – THE MERMAID

Liban, Necca's daughter first heard the screams, and then chunks of rock ploughed into the ground by her feet. She looked up and saw the seemingly solid pillar of water rising straight up into the noonday air, sunlight sparkling and glinting in rainbow hues making it a thing of beauty... until she saw the bodies and realised what had happened. For a single heartbeat the pillar faltered, and then Liban was thrown to the ground by a hammer blow. She attempted to climb to her feet, but the very ground itself was shaking, trembling violently... and then it shifted.

Liban saw the sheer cliffs rear up all around her, the sky was blotted out by shifting clouds of dust, and a grey wall of water rose up... and slowly it began to topple down towards her.

The young woman stared at it for a shocked moment, and then she plunged her hands deep into the soft earth, calling up what little she remembered of her mother's lore and her own natural talent. Her throat worked, shaping words and phrases that were already ancient when the world was young, drawing forth the very magic of the land itself.

And the crashing wall of water toppled and fell...

Liban flung up her hands – and the water stopped barely a hand's breadth from her face! The grey-black water

70

exploded in a frenzy against the invisible wall, and then flowed over and around the tiny bubble of force with which she had surrounded herself. And so she sat there, secure, while all around her the water rose and indistinct shapes, murky in the filth, brushed against the force wall; and sometimes they assumed definite shapes and peered inwards with staring eyes and cried out with open mouths. Liban trembled as the figures attempted to claw their way in; she knew they were the corpses of her people, but the water seemed to give them a strange life... and at times it seemed as if they *were* alive. But as the afternoon wore on, and the lighter coloured surface of the water disappeared upwards into the distance and darkness closed in, Liban, already exhausted with the effort of calling up the earth magic, fell into a troubled and fitful sleep.

When she awoke it was pitch black and she was cold. For a moment she stared around wildly, disorientated by the absolute darkness and the complete absence of sound: where were the muted shouts of the guards, and the crackling of the camp fires, and the children's shouts and cries...?

Memory returned, and with it terror. She was trapped here, and the Dagda only knew how far she was beneath the surface of the water. She couldn't drop the force wall, for the very pressure of the water would surely crush her, and yet she couldn't survive here for very much longer; already the air tasted sharp and caught at the back of her throat. Besides, she had no food and – she began to laugh hysterically – she had no water... *no water*...

She dug her long nails into the palm of her hand drawing blood, the pain shocking her back to reality. If she allowed the madness of fear to overcome her, then death would surely follow. If only she had some light.

The young woman raised her hands and touched her face.

71

She breathed onto the palms before bringing her long fingers together, and then she lowered her head and called upon her inner strength. Light blossomed at the tips of her fingers. It was faint and tenuous and pulsed in time with her heartbeat, but Liban poured more of her strength into the tiny glowing ball and it gradually grew and swelled until she could cup it in the palms of both hands. The glowing ball was pure and white, tinged with the merest trace of emerald since Liban had called upon the earth magic earlier. It shed its cold light all around her ... but there was nothing to see. No fish swam in the depths of the water, no creatures scuttled under the stones and even the whirling corpses had disappeared. The water was dead, and it would take many years for life to seed itself in its cold depths. Liban raised the globe of light above her head, but she could still see nothing, only the edges of the blackness as it retreated before the light.

And so she was trapped; there was no escape – at least in her own form.

The thought hit her like a physical blow, the shock numbing her. It was horrible, too horrible to even think about.

But as the day – or was it night? – wore on, the thought returned and began to whisper insidiously within her head. She was trapped ... trapped ... trapped ... The word beat inside her until she wanted to scream and scream and scream. She struggled against the madness that clustered around her, tainting her thoughts like the very tainted air she was now breathing. If she didn't make a decision soon, then she would be dead: the air couldn't last much longer and already she was breathing in her own poisons.

And of course there was no real answer. If she remained where she was, then she would die; if she dropped the force wall, then she was dead, but if she changed her shape? And if she survived, then what would be the price? To assume a form that could survive in the cold waters of the lake was possible, but to reassume her own form was another thing entirely, and she doubted if she did effect the first transformation whether she would have either the strength or power left to accomplish the second.

But there was no choice.

Liban stripped off her clothing, folding it in a neat bundle by her side, although she knew she would never use it again. She then lay down on the soft, damp ground and spread her legs to touch the force wall with either foot, and her hands stretched out to touch cold fingers against it on either side. She closed her eyes and allowed the darkness to close in and take her, and with the darkness came the fragments of dreams and old nightmares. Liban allowed the images to slip and flow across her closed lids ... until she caught at one and held it. She concentrated on the nightmare image, calling it forth from the very depths of her mind, adding in details, visualising it in its entirety. And then she began to add to it, gradually overlaying her own image onto the picture she had built up, until in her mind they became one and the same.

She opened her eyes. The small bubble of force was bright with silver ghost fire, the residue of her Power, illuminating her slim body in delicate metallic shades. Liban raised her head slightly and looked down at her body, past her small breasts and the swell of her stomach ... and then she began to draw upon the last of her waning strength.

What seemed like silver dust motes began to gather on her legs, reflecting and refracting the dim light, blinding her. Soon her legs from her groin downwards were bathed in a luminous sheet of darting light, and she felt the numbness creeping upwards from her toes, rising... rising... rising, slowly engulfing her.

When she awoke her head was pounding and throbbing, her throat was raw and coated and her eyes were streaming. She breathed in the foul air and choked, and then struggled to sit up. But her feet were dead and she couldn't feel her legs. It was dark within the bubble, the ghost light was gone, but she managed to throw a dim shadow-light along her fingers... and she saw.

The spell had worked: she was no longer fully human. She had successfully transferred her nightmare image to reality, and now she wore no legs; they were gone and in their place a gleaming scaled fish-tail flapped against the ground. There had been other changes also: her fingers had grown an extra flap of skin between them and a membrane had closed across her nose, and beneath her chin on her throat were two semi-circular serrated openings: primitive gills. A light scattering of scales dusted her body, and her soft breasts had firmed and hardened.

Liban held the light for a long time, examining the changes in her body through the tears which misted her eyes, and then she allowed the light to die, repulsed at what she had become. In the darkness she sat up and traced an arcane pattern against the invisible wall, allowing the earth's forces to slip back into the damp ground. Water seeped in from under the edges of the weakened wall, quickly covering the fish-tail and beginning to creep up her naked body. She didn't feel the chill, and could only feel the water's pressure as a gentle push. She breathed deeply and held her breath as the water rose up over her mouth and across her eyes. Her vision blurred and then cleared, and she was conscious that she was no longer holding her breath. She opened her mouth – and nothing happened, although she could feel a cold gentle susurration in the sides of her throat as the gills worked. The water took her then, lifting her buoyantly upwards, and she rode the still turbulent water, practising manipulating the fish-tail, but rising towards the lightening water at the same time.

Liban broke the surface, and felt the skin cease flapping on her throat; her mouth worked, and she was suddenly breathing normally again. Her vision blurred as something slipped across her eyes, and then she could see clearly. She saw the broad flat surface of the newly formed lake, black now in the night, but silver-touched with moonlight, speckled with the hard points of light from the stars. And then she wept; she wept for the beauty she now saw, and the beauty that was lost forever beneath it; she wept for her father and sister and her people. She wept for herself; what she had been and what she had now become.

Beoc sent the small round currach skimming across the flat waters of the lake, lost in thought, muscles working automatically. He was still slightly stunned by the Abbot's decision to send him – *him!* – to Rome to bear the missive that Congall, Abbot of Bangor, had drawn up, into the very hands of the Pope himself. It was ... it was an honour, and the young monk shouted for joy. And something answered him.

Beoc started and caught a crab, the oar cutting into the water, catching and then suddenly coming free, tumbling him back into the tiny wood and hide craft. It tilted dangerously, spinning around and shipping some water.

The young man sat up carefully in the small craft and listened intently, sweat beginning to glisten on his already balding head. Someone – something – had answered him; it wasn't an echo.

The boat rocked gently on the waters of the lake while the young monk bailed out the water with cupped hands. And then a long sharp *V* suddenly sliced through the water towards him. Beoc froze, and stared at the white water, entranced. Across the water in Scotland there were tales of great *peisti* – serpents – in some of the older lakes, but there were no snakes in Ireland, not since Saint Patrick had driven them out. But what then could it be? The young monk poked into the water with the oar ... and it was abruptly snatched from his grasp, almost pulling him in with it. He cried out, calling on God for protection... and then a head broke the surface of the water.

It was the head of a young woman, her black-green hair plastered wetly to her head, her small dark eyes blinking rapidly. Her mouth moved once and then she spoke in a curiously flat accent, using an archaic mode of speech. 'I am sorry, I did not mean to startle you.'

Beoc looked around. He was almost in the centre of the huge lake, many miles from either shore... and yet, where was this young woman's craft?

She came up out from the water, her shoulders and then her breasts breaking the surface, and she clung to the side of the currach for support, tilting it dangerously. Beoc glanced down at her hands – and he suddenly knew: they were webbed!

The young man crossed himself. 'You... you are a sea-maid?' he asked in a small voice.

'So I have been called,' she replied softly, her vowels clipped, her speech broken, as if she had not spoken for many years.

Beoc scooped a handful of water from the bottom of his craft, blessed it, and then threw it over the maid. She blinked and tossed her head, scattering fine droplets in every direction. However she did not scream or cry out when the water touched her: she was therefore no demon. 'Who are you?' Beoc asked quietly.

The young woman lay back in the water and Beoc caught a glimpse of a green-gold tail undulating gently beneath the surface of the water. 'I am Liban,' she said slowly, 'once daughter of Necca and Ebblue, who walked this land some three hundred and more of your years ago.'

'Necca and Ebblue! But they are myths; this lake is called after Necca... Lough Necca.'

'He was my father.' The mermaid smiled at the young monk's confusion. 'Oh, but do not think I always wore this

76

form; listen and I will tell you my tale…'

And as the currach drifted slowly across the broad lake, Liban swam alongside relating to Beoc the tale of the thrice cursed brothers, her witch-mother and the final enchantment that had rendered her into her present form.

It was close to evening when the small craft beached on the eastern side of the lake. Beoc shook his head attempting to clear his mind of the visions the young woman had woven, of a time when the One-God had still not come to Erin's shores, a time when the old gods held sway, a time of power and enchantment, a time of magic. 'Will I see you again?' he asked her suddenly.

'Do you wish to see me again?' she said shyly.

'I do.'

Liban smiled. 'I will meet you a year and a day from today on that stretch of water called Inver Ollamh in the east.'

Beoc laughed. 'You know no one is going to believe me,' he called out as the mermaid drifted slowly out into the darkening waters.

'Bring them with you,' she laughed, 'but promise me you'll be there,' she added.

'Oh, I'll be there,' the monk swore as the dark-haired head slipped without a sound beneath the flat black waters of the lake.

'Father Abbot, you cannot!' Beoc demanded.

'Brother, you forget yourself,' Congall reminded the younger man quietly. 'It seems your journey to the Holy City not only broadened your outlook, but also taught you some of their ill manners.'

Beoc looked wildly around the shores of the little inlet at the monks preparing thick nets and taking up positions with long pointed gaffs by the waterside. 'Father, a year ago she promised me she would come here of her own free will. She will come,' he said insistently, 'but she is not a … a …'

77

'A what, my son?' the abbot said gently. The older man took the young monk's arm and led him aside. 'My son, she is a sorry creature. If your story is true – and I must admit I have checked the facts and they seem to bear out her tale – then she is possibly the last of the followers of the Old Faith – and trapped in an unholy body that is neither beast nor man. But a body,' he continued, 'fashioned by the most foul sorcery. And while she might be able to survive in this unnatural form, her eternal soul is trapped, trapped in the body of one of the damned . . . and it is crying out for release. We have a calling – no, a duty – to try and carry the Word of the Risen Christ to her, to try and release her from her sentence and bring her into the bosom of the Church.'

'And if she doesn't want to be brought into the bosom of the Church?' Beoc asked quietly.

The abbot looked at the younger man in shocked amazement. 'Brother, it seems we must talk at some length when this sorry episode is finished. Such thoughts are heresy. Perhaps the sea-maid enchanted you . . .'

'Only her innocence enchanted me.'

'Aaah, you see! You may have renounced the lusts of the flesh, but they can still attempt to claim us. They are the sendings of the Evil One. Tell me my son, have you thought of this maid over the past year?'

'Often.'

The abbot smiled triumphantly, but said nothing.

About mid morning the smooth surface of the inlet was disturbed by a long foaming line of water that cut directly across the lake towards where Beoc waited, sitting on a low stone, his head buried in his hands. Some of the monks noticed the disturbance and brought it to the attention of the abbot, but he only nodded silently, and indicated that they should return to their positions.

The black-green-haired head broke the surface, and hard black eyes regarded Beoc for a moment. 'Why so silent, holy man?' she asked in her strange accent.

The young monk started and looked up. He quickly glanced to either side. 'Quickly, you must flee, you cannot stay here. Go...go!' He ran down into the shallows and attempted to push the mermaid away.

Liban resisted him. 'What is the matter; I thought...'

'It's the abbot,' Beoc explained in a rush, 'he wants to capture you, to set you up as an example of what will happen to those who follow the Old Faith, of how it will eventually pervert and destroy them. There are monks here to...'

The young monk yelped in surprise as he was roughly grabbed from behind and thrown to the ground. He had a brief glimpse of brown-robed bodies rushing past him and then he heard the shouts and screams...

The first monk to reach Liban paused momentarily at the sight of her bare breasts; he closed his eyes and crossed himself – and then something crashed into his legs, sending him toppling backwards into the arms of another monk. They both went down in a flurry of arms and legs, kicking and struggling in the chill water. But now other arms were reaching for the mermaid. Her fluked tail swept out catching one high in the chest, lifting him off his feet and throwing him backwards. The tail then flipped back and snapped across another's face, snapping teeth, jaw and nose in one fluid movement. One grabbed Liban's arm – and shouted in surprise as his grip slid along her scaled flesh. Her webbed fingers caught his hair and pulled him down, plunging his head beneath the water. His shout ended in a gurgle. Another leaped across the fallen monk with a net in his hands. Liban's tail swept up and caught him between the legs, doubling him up, and then her tail hit him again, striking upwards and into his face, propelling him back onto the beach. But now there were monks coming from all sides. Liban thrashed and struggled; her webbed fingers tipped with long, slightly curving nails tore flesh and gouged eyes before they were finally caught, and her tail broke limbs and ribs, cracked skulls and flattened faces before it was entangled in a lead-weighted net.

They carried her – still struggling – to the shore where Congall stood, a vial of holy water in one hand and a cross in the other. He blessed her, scattered some of the holy water over her and proceeded to intone the ritual for the dismissal of spirits. Liban gradually quietened and lay on the rough sand watching him intently. When he was finished she smiled and spoke in her flat and broken voice. 'Holy man, you remind me of a druid my father once told me about; he too was an arrogant, ignorant man.'

Congall smiled benevolently. 'I forgive you of course, my child.'

Liban spat. 'I do not want your forgiveness, all I want is my freedom.'

'But you will never be free while you are trapped in that ... body, and are ignorant of the One True God.' The abbot turned away. 'Take her to the abbey.'

'Hold!'

Congall turned slowly. 'What is it you want Fergus?' he asked, a hard note creeping into his voice.

The speaker was a huge man, standing a head and shoulders above the rest of the monks. He regarded the abbot from clear grey eyes, and when he spoke his speech was slow and measured. 'Am I to take it that you are claiming this maid?'

Congall looked surprised. 'But of course, why not? She has been taken in my domain.'

'Aaah, but I actually held her,' Fergus said. 'While your monks were being battered about like birds in a strong breeze, I alone held her.'

'That sounds suspiciously like pride in your voice,' the abbot snapped.

'And is that anger I hear in yours?' Fergus asked. 'And do you not want the maid so that you can go down in history as the first abbot since Patrick to convert one of the Old Folk to the Way? Is that not pride?'

'The mermaid belongs to no one,' Beoc said suddenly, 'she is free – and has been free for three hundred years. She came here of her own free will to see me – *me!* And now will you all leave her alone,' he shouted.

'Beoc, as your abbot I command you to be silent,' Congall said.

The young monk rounded on the older man. 'If you continue, then you will find that you are no longer my abbot. I once respected you – aye, honoured and even loved you – but I am quickly coming to loathe you,' he spat.

'Brothers... brothers... brothers...' Niall, one of the oldest monks came between them, his hands raised. 'What are you doing? What has happened to you? Can you not recognise the hand of Satan amongst you?' The old monk turned to the abbot. 'You have claimed the maid, you wish to convert her to the Way, and that is worthy... but are the reasons behind it worthy?'

The old man then turned to Fergus without waiting for an answer from the abbot. 'And you brother, why do you want the maid? What will you do with her, for look, she cannot be used in the manner of women even if we were not sworn to celibacy. Would you just keep her so that you could say, "*Look, I caught the mermaid of Lough Necca?*"' The old monk slowly shook his head and looked across at Beoc. 'And you my son, why do you want the maid?'

'I don't want her,' Beoc said quietly, 'she is not mine. I wished to talk with her, nothing more. But if I could have her now, then I would surely set her free.'

Niall smiled toothlessly and then turned back to the abbot. 'Let us not dispute the matter today. Let us rest and tend to our wounded. Tomorrow is the Sabbath, and surely we will have our answer then?'

'And what about me?' Liban asked quietly.

The old monk knelt painfully by the mermaid's side. 'You, I fear, must remain with us until the morn. But you must not fret,' he added gently, 'the night will bring many things: the cool air clears heads, the darkness aids thoughts, and the night brings dreams...'

The dream was the same for the three holy men. They were each standing alone by a lakeside on a moonlit night. The sky was clear and the surface of the water by their feet was smooth. Suddenly the water shifted and rippled, and the mermaid rose from the sea in a gilded chariot drawn by two snow-white oxen. The chariot then raced up the beach and cut across country. Each monk followed until he came to a crossroads. He could hear the chariot approaching in the distance... and he could also hear the approach of the other two monks. He cut down one of the roads and waited for the chariot...

In Congall's dream the ox-drawn chariot carried the girl to him.

And for Fergus the mermaid was brought to him.

And in Beoc's dream the oxen carried Liban to him.

Niall supervised the loading of the chariot, ensuring that the mermaid was comfortable, and that the oxen were securely yoked together. And then, followed by the rest of the monks from the monastery, he led the oxen to the nearest crossroads.

The three claimants to the mermaid had arrived earlier and taken up positions on the road. Straight down one arm of the crossroads Congall knelt by the side of the road, his hands clasped in prayer. To the right Fergus busied himself weeding a patch around a small roadside shrine, and to the left Beoc sat with his back against a stone, reading a precious handwritten copy of the Book.

Niall walked the beasts around in a circle and then he moved away. The oxen continued to circle aimlessly for a while and then they broke out of the rut and moved off...

82

down the left hand path, towards Beoc.

The young monk looked up at the sound of hooves. The mermaid smiled down at him. 'I never doubted,' he said quietly.

'Neither did I,' Liban said, as he gently lifted her down from the chariot and then carried her across the fields and down onto the beach towards the waves.

And there they talked long into the morning, whilst back at the crossroads Congall and Fergus argued with Niall. And when they finally reached the young monk and the mermaid, they found Beoc reading to her from the Book, and Liban silently weeping.

The monks gathered around in a circle and sat listening to Beoc. Fergus turned to Congall with awe in his voice. 'It is a long time since I heard anyone weep to hear the word of the Lord.'

The abbot nodded. 'There is a lesson here for all of us.'

And when Beoc had finished, and the sun was sinking into the west, Liban turned to him and said, 'You must baptise me into your faith.'

'But... are you sure? You know so little about it...'

'But you believe in it?' Liban persisted.

Beoc nodded.

'You believe in it strongly enough to foreswear your family, a wife and children of your own?'

Again Beoc nodded. 'My faith is my family, the church my love.'

'It must be a fine faith to attract devotion such as yours.'

'It is,' Beoc whispered, and all around him the monks nodded silently.

'Then baptise me,' Liban insisted.

'But listen to me,' Beoc said desperately. 'If I baptise you then your spell will be broken, you will regain your own form and age will once again claim you; you will die.'

Liban nodded. 'I know.' And then she added, 'All I ask is that when I die I will be laid to rest in your own grave.'

Beoc nodded, blinking back the sudden sting of tears.
The mermaid smiled. 'Then begin...'
'Are you sure?' Beoc whispered.
'Begin!' Liban commanded.
'I baptise you in the Name of the Father... and of the
Son... and of the Holy Ghost...'

Chapter Three

THE WOLF MAIDS

The sunlight lingered briefly in the mouth of the cave, gradually turning from a pale bronze to a deep purple, briefly flaring red before sinking into the Western Ocean. The night stars – which had already claimed the sky to the east – began to glitter in the salmon and rose coloured sky above the sunset, their harsh brilliance still dull and muted. A few seabirds called plaintively before settling down on the white-streaked cliffs, and soon the only sound was the hissing of the sea on the sands far, far below and the whisper of the breeze through the tough razor-edged grass.

And in the mouth of the cave a shadow moved, and large oval points of light glittered briefly amber before blinking out.

Giolla awoke suddenly when he heard the panic-stricken bleatings of the newly born lambs. Remaining in the shadow of the standing stones, he knuckled the sleep from his eyes and peered down the valley. He could see the white moving shapes of the sheep milling about, but nothing else: there were no horses, no sounds of metal on metal, no shouts, no flaring torches. The young man fitted an egg-shaped stone into his sling and, swinging it slowly, moved as quietly as possible down into the valley. A long low dark shape moved across the whiteness of the sheep and Giolla instinctively loosed his slingshot. The hard stone struck something soft and he heard a muted yelp. Dogs!

And then the night was split asunder by a bone-chilling howl, freezing the young man in his tracks. It was immediately answered by another, and yet another. Not dogs – *wolves!*

Giolla's fingers trembled as he attempted to fit another stone into the leather sling, and he dropped it. He could hear the creatures moving now, could hear their hoarse panting, and then the sudden scream of a slaughtered lamb cut through him. He had another stone fitted and the sling was buzzing around his head. He followed the sickening crunching, and then a pair of eyes reflected the silver of the moonlight as they moved towards him. He stepped back and loosed the shot with a snap of his wrist. There was a solid crack followed by a short snarl, and then there was something moving in from his right-hand side, the grass rustling in its wake. He dropped the sling and managed to pull the short knife from his belt before the wolf tore his throat out.

Barra picked up a lance and tested the sharpened point before taking up his stance. He glanced across at Ide, winked and then turned back to the target: a flat stone with an almost circular hole through the middle strung from the branch of a tree.

Barra pushed strands of flaming red hair from his eyes and looked over at Finan standing between him and the target. 'It's too close,' he complained, 'I can't get a proper throw at it.'

The smaller, darker man laughed. 'And what will you do if the Fomor come riding south one of these fine days, eh? Ask them to wait while you work out the range?'

Barra laughed, and then, drawing back his arm, loosed the spear. The slim javelin flew high and its underside scraped along the upper edge of the stone.

Barra swore and, in one smooth movement, pulled up

another javelin from the ground and threw. The polished length of wood went neatly through the centre of the hole.

Ide laughed and clapped her hands, and Barra, glancing across at her was momentarily startled, for with the setting sun on her red hair it looked as if it were aflame.

Finan came over to him and handed back the two spears. 'My turn,' he said, flexing one of the spears slightly, testing its balance.

'Of course, if the Fomor come, you'll make sure you have a spear of the proper weight and the correct balance.'

Finan grinned and assumed his throwing stance, one foot behind and at right angles to the other, the weight on his right foot. He drew his arm back, breathing in and out slowly; his muscles tensed...

And then the wolves howled.

Finan looked at Barra and immediately all thoughts of the contest were forgotten. Moving quickly they gathered up the spears, pulled the stone from the branch and threw it in the back of the chariot. Barra hitched up the horses while Finan stood watch, a spear in his hand and another close by his side, its point stuck into the soft earth. Ide too caught something of their urgency and quickly gathered up the combs and pins with which she had been adorning her hair whilst the men contested the game. She too had heard the stories of the past few weeks about the pack of killer wolves that were roaming the district.

It was impossible to tell how many animals were involved, and although some reports said only one, the destruction was so great that more than one animal had to be involved. Entire fields of sheep had been wiped out, the shepherds and their dogs butchered also. Lonely farmhouses had been attacked and the occupants slaughtered, with the livestock then killed or scattered out into the fields to trample the crops.

And there was evidence of wolves everywhere, but with tracks three times larger than even the largest wolfhound in all Erin. Several parties had gone in search of the animal or animals; all but one hadn't returned, and of the last group there were only three survivors – out of more than twenty men and horses and ten large hunting dogs.

And now most of the fields lay untended, the farmers and country folk having pulled in to the local forts, seeking shelter in the shadow of their walls. A messenger had been sent to Tara to beg help from the king, but neither he nor any word had returned. The roads of western Erin were deserted, with only the occasional heavily armed party of horsemen or company of fast-drawn chariots venturing forth.

Finan brought the chariot around in a tight circle and began the long climb up and out of the small sheltered valley. Barra stood by his left side, a spear clenched in both hands, his sharp green eyes reading the ground ahead and to either side of them. Ide stood between the two men, one hand clutching the side of the bucking chariot, the other holding a bundle of spears.

It was generally accepted that the wolf or wolves were not natural, and it was whispered that they were were-creatures. They were possessed at any rate with unnatural strength and cunning, and certainly did not fear man, as most of the wild creatures did.

Finan was sweating heavily by the time they reached the crest of the hill, and he swung the whip out over the horses' heads, snapping them into a gallop. He knew they would not be able to sustain the pace for long, but once they were out of the low scrubland and stunted trees and onto the flat moorland then he could ease up.

The chariot rattled over the rough track, jolting them to either side. Ide clung to Barra now, who stood with splayed legs watching a movement in the bushes behind and to their left. When he was sure the trembling leaves were moving contrary to the wind, he turned and shouted to Finan above the crack of the breeze, 'We're being followed.'

The small dark man nodded and snapped the whip again, urging greater speed from the already tiring animals. The chariot slewed sideways around a sharp downward bend, spraying the bushes on their left-hand side with grit and small stones, sending crows wheeling skywards. Finan grimaced; crows were the creatures of Morrigan and portents of death. But they were now on the level and racing down across a flat wasteland of stone dotted with tiny clumps of scrub and bush. They could see for miles across the lichen-green and heather-purple stones... and there was nothing moving.

Finan began to breathe more easily. 'Maybe it was just...' he began, and then Ide screamed. Three huge wolves had come out from behind the rocks on their left-hand side. They stood at the foot of the slight decline, unmoving, watching the bucking chariot intently. And then as one they moved, cutting away across country, moving diagonally to their left, until they dropped out of sight behind some rocks.

'By the Gods,' Barra swore, 'did you see the size of those animals?'

'They're going to cut us off,' Finan said, pointing with the whip. 'They'll probably be waiting for us where the road narrows.'

'Can we beat them to it?' Barra asked.

'We'll try,' Finan said, beginning to whip up the horses again, calling up the last of their strength for one final mad gallop.

'What are we going to do?' Ide asked quietly, her panic held tightly under control.

Barra looked at Finan and then back to Ide. He smiled with a confidence he did not feel. 'We'll think of something,' he said.

It was said that Cascarach could charm the birds from the trees, and bring even the most maddened boar to his feet.

It was said that Cascarach was elven, half-elven, a god, a demon...

It was said... but then, many things were said about Cascarach – and most of them were true.

That he was elven – or half-elven – there was little doubt. He stood taller than most other men and was unnaturally thin; his features too were thin and pointed, his eyes slanted, and although he was a man into his eight and twentieth year, he wore no beard and the hair on his head hung loose and shining to his shoulders, unbanded and unbraided. And as a harper he was unsurpassed; generations would come and go before Erin saw even a shadow of his like again in the blind harper, Carolan.*

He was Sighted also.

There was about a fingerspan of wine left in the goblet, and Cascarach was drunk enough to wonder idly whether he should drink it or toss it into the dying fire and watch the flickering flames turn blue and green. He gently ran his long delicate forefinger around the rim of the goblet and allowed the images to form in the blood-red liquid. It was an amusement, nothing more: his Sight would read moments of intense emotion and render them into images for him in any available liquid.

The Harper blinked at what he now saw, and sat up straight, nudging the goblet and shattering the image. He swore and activated the spell again and then fought to make sense of the still swirling image. He curbed his impatience while it settled. His frown deepened, and then slowly turned to fear... and then anger...

The three huge wolves had pulled down the horses, leaving

* see Chapter Five.

the smoking carcasses where they had fallen, and attacked the humans. Barra had managed to place a javelin through the side of one of the creatures, but even as he looked one of the other wolves had gripped the shaft of the spear in its huge jaws and pulled it from the other's flesh. The wound had spurted once and then congealed into a solid crust. Finan swung a spear and rapped another beast across the snout with it, jabbing for the eyes. The wolf snapped, its yellowed teeth closing with an audible click as it covered its stinging nose with its forepaws. The three wolves now paced slowly around the felled chariot, darting in, snapping, darting back out again, slowly wearing the humans down.

Seen close up the wolves were huge creatures, standing as tall, if not taller than the fallen horses, their coats long and seemingly metallic, glinting in the rapidly disappearing light. When night fell, so would the humans.

Ide, Finan and Barra stood back to back, spears in their hands, jabbing when the creatures came too close. Their only great fears were night and exhaustion... and both were rapidly approaching.

Cascarach began drumming his fingers on the table as he watched the three wolves beginning to circle the fallen chariot and take up positions around it; their next move, he knew, would be to attack simultaneously at the weak link, and the weak link was the woman. He shifted his Sight and, sure enough, the largest of the wolves was now opposite her. He saw the animal's muscles begin to quiver, saw it prepare to jump...

The sheet of lightning ripped open the sky almost above their heads. Ide screamed and stumbled back against the two men, who also staggered with fright. But the three wolves, instead of attacking, also leapt backwards, the whites of their eyes showing. Again and again the lightning tore across the sky, turning the gloom into the brightest semblance of day, etching abstract images into their minds and eyes: *a bush ... a tilted stone ... the harness of the dead horses ... the blood burned black in the light ...*

And then a series of forked lightning came to ground around them, pounding the earth with its force, befouling the air with a sharp bitter stench that caught at the throat and eyes. A bush exploded into flames, and a wolf, its coat singed, darted yelping into the night, followed by the second and then the third as a patch of earth was gouged out and a stone shattered with the force of the levin bolts.

Cascarach slumped back exhausted and drained the remainder of the wine in one swallow.

The Harper made his way westwards the following day. His journey took him through the heart of Erin, into the ancient spreading forests and the broad fertile grasslands and out into the rocky wasteland that was Connaught. It wasn't entirely barren – it just seemed that way. But compared with the rest of the island it looked like a cursed place, and indeed, in a future that would have been unimaginable to the Harper and the people of his day, the invader that history would call Cromwell would banish the Irish to Hell or to Connaught, there being little to choose between the two.

But it had its own natural beauty that appealed to the Harper's non-human blood, and he found it stirring feelings inside him that had lain dormant for a long time. Cascarach made his way to the fort of Calte, the local lord, and inquired after the two men and the woman who had recently escaped the wolves. Barra, Finan and Ide were brought before the tall stranger, who told them, in his high, almost musical voice, of the attack of the wolves and the intervention of the lightning.

'How do you know all this?' Barra had demanded, and in reply the Harper had gestured and tiny threads of flame had danced along the warrior's wristlets and down his sword sheath. 'How do I know? Why, because I sent the lightning.'

'Then you know of these creatures?' Calte intervened. He was an old man now, but he had once held his place as one of the foremost warriors in all Erin. 'And if you know of them, what are they... and more to the point, can you rid us of them?' He sat back against the wall in the large gloomy room, the firelight highlighting the wrinkles in his face, and especially the new ones around his eyes and mouth that had formed in the past few weeks since the wolves arrived.

Cascarach smiled, his teeth unnaturally long and somewhat pointed in the light. 'I made... enquiries along the way,' he said quietly. 'The wolves are, in fact, the three daughters of the Lord of the White Fort...' He gestured vaguely to the west. 'You will find no reference to this lord, his lineage or his domain; his title and name were struck from the records and the bards foresworn even to mention his name again.'

'Why?' Finan wondered.

Cascarach smiled and shook his head. 'That, even I do not know. But to continue: these are evil creatures, and they were bound in the form of wolves on account of their crimes generations ago in the Dawn of Man. But it now seems as if they have found some way to break free of their bondage and hunt abroad.'

'But can they be stopped?' Calte demanded.

Cascarach nodded, his pale gold hair shimmering like silk. 'They can... but it is not easy. And, since the three women were born of the one birth, they must be slain together, with one blow.'

'One blow?'

'One blow!'

Calte smiled in the darkness, one half of his face moving, the other side lost in the shadows. 'If you can bring these three creatures together,' he said softly, 'then I can slay them for you.'

Cascarach nodded. 'Well said, but how?'

'In my youth,' the old lord said, 'I found a spear on the beach just below,' he jerked his thumb back over his shoulder. 'It was longer than any spear I'd ever had, and so I kept and used it.' He paused and sipped from a heavy earthen goblet, and then indicated that Barra and Finan could sit. They squatted down beside the fire whilst Ide remained standing, her hand on Barra's shoulder, her fingers idly toying with a lock of his fire-bronzed hair.

'There were still Fomor abroad in those days,' Calte continued, 'and they would occasionally raid us – and we them. And it was then that I discovered a curious thing about my spear: it never struck just one person, but always two or three, and on one memorable occasion, three warriors and two mounts.' The old man shook his head in fond remembrance and drank again. 'And I remember a time when I went hunting. There was a huge serpent in one of the lakes up north. It had killed many people and destroyed crops and so we – my brothers and I – set out to destroy it. Well my brothers tried, and two of them died attempting it, but when I loosed my spear it struck the creature beneath the mouth, passed through it and continued on through four of the serpent's coils before ending up in its barbed tail. Aye,' he nodded decisively, 'if you can bring the wolves together, I can get the three of them at once for you.'

Bres leaped from the currach and hauled it up the beach, sand scraping along its bottom, but the hide covering, although flexible, was tough. The old man pulled the craft above the high-water mark and then, taking a long reed-woven pot from the wood and hide boat, set off down the beach collecting the finer pieces of sea wreckage. There had been a high tide the previous night and the higher reaches of the beach were strewn with weed and curiously shaped pieces of wood. The old man wandered about the base of the cliffs, slowly and carefully filling the basket strung to his back. Seabirds mewled on the cliffs above his head where they had their nests, and he reflected that if he were ten years younger and if his bones hadn't started to stiffen, he would be up those cliffs in an instant and lifting himself a few eggs. The old man shook his head sadly and stepped back, still looking up, but the nests were well back on a ledge and invisible from the ground. Bres was about to move off when he caught sight of something glinting in the cool mid morning air, something long and fine and metallic. It was probably just a stone, but the more the old man looked at it, the more he was convinced that it was a piece of metal or cloth. He pulled his sling from his belt and looked around for a suitable stone; he had a score or more of almost smooth round stones in the pouch on the left-hand side of his belt, but it would be wasteful to use them...

The first stone struck below the gleaming strand and clattered back down onto the beach. The second was high, but it loosened a small pile of grit and stones which succeeded in sweeping the metallic strand down onto the beach. Bres stooped painfully and brushed aside the grit to pull out the strands. There were about six of them, entwined together; they looked like hair, but felt like bronze...

The old man felt his heart begin to pound painfully as he carefully folded the metallic strands and slipped them into his pouch. Moving as quietly as possible he pulled the basket onto his shoulder and stepped down the beach, sticking to the sandy patches, avoiding the stones. He gently eased the basket into the currach and then began to push it down the beach, wincing as the scraping of sand along its bottom seemed hideously loud on the morning air. As he pushed it into the waves with a sigh of relief, he turned back and looked up the beach towards the cliffs, and from where he stood he could just make out the irregular opening of a cave high on the cliff-face.

At first the notes were inaudible, but they swelled with the sunrise, until it seemed as if the delicate music was part of the dawning of the day. Cascarach the Harper sat crosslegged on a broad flat stone above the cliffs, his head bent, seemingly lost in thought, strumming his whitewood harp absently.

It was two days since Bres had brought the metallic hair to Calte's fort. The lord had immediately mounted an expedition to the sheltered bay, but of the twenty men who had set out, only two survived to tell the tale of the three huge wolves that had attacked them in a long defile that led out onto the beach, slaughtering the men and mounts.

So now Cascarach sat alone; if the wolves came, he would attempt to lull them with his music, subtly suggesting that they might appreciate it more fully if they assumed their human forms.

The Harper played long into the morning, and the sun rode through the heavens, lengthening and then gradually shortening the shadows along the ground, and then slowly beginning to lengthen them again as the afternoon wore on. But the music flowed tirelessly, ceaselessly, testament to Cascarach's inhuman strength and endurance. And then, just as the sun was beginning to dip below the lip of the cliffs and into the chill western ocean, the wolves came. One moment there was nothing, and then the grasses parted, and the three huge creatures were standing before and on either side of him. Cascarach made no sign that he had noticed their presence but merely continued playing, his fingers barely seeming to move, and yet drawing the full power from the ancient instrument.

And the wolves slowly approached, their jaws wide and slavering.

The Harper played then as he had never played before, his music weaving a spell, lulling, soothing and calming the beasts. He knew that if they attacked now, he would have no chance; he could not play and draw upon his other magical powers at the same time. And so he played for his life.

And one by one the great wolves sat down before the solitary figure in the lonely landscape and listened to him play.

Cascarach played long into the night. The stars rose and danced sedately across the heavens before sinking again, and the sky to the east brightened greyly in the false dawn, but still the Harper played. And then, as the first tentative rays of a copper sun sent his shadow wavering long into the dew-damp grass, he stopped.

The wolves' heads came up and their eyes snapped open. 'I need rest, but I will play again this evening,' he said softly. He carefully wiped down his instrument and slipped it back into its ornate case. He stood slowly and massaged the small of his back. 'It is true that dogs – and especially wolves,' he added hastily, 'have a far greater range of hearing than man, but man's hearing is far more subtle.' He smiled. 'And it is impossible to appreciate the full depth and beauty of my music in your present form.' He nodded briefly and, turning his back on the savage animals, walked away from them.

The Harper slept through the day, but by evening, rested and refreshed, he was back on the broad flat stone, his harp on his knee, and this time Calte was lying flat in the long grass off to his left-hand side. They both knew it was a gamble; if the wolves came that way neither Calte nor Cascarach would stand a chance.

The sky in the west came alive with fire-streaked wisps of

cloud against which the tiny black specks of seabirds wheeled and circled. The Harper sat facing the sunset so that the sunrise would be on his back, and then he eased his harp from its case and began to play.

The melody was different this time, it was softer, slower, soothing. It seemed to take on the mood of the evening and magnify it, intensify it – until it seemed as if the very night itself took voice and sang. The birds themselves, saluting the close of the day with a bright flurry of song, grew silent and listened, and soon the trees and bushes around the Harper were bright with tiny burning eyes as the night creatures gathered.

The Harper played into the night allowing nature to dictate his music, weaving the whisper of the grasses and the muttering of the trees into it. The night absorbed his music, enfolding it within its darkness, taking it to itself, becoming part of it.

Suddenly all the fire-bright eyes blinked out and were gone, and the three wolves stood before the Harper. He nodded a greeting and continued playing, but said softly, 'If you were to assume your human forms you would appreciate my music better.'

The wolves took no notice but merely continued staring at the Harper. Cascarach continued playing and the night rode on for midnight, and slowly he began to lower the tone of his nightsong, dropping it down and down until even Calte lying stiff and prone in the wet grass could barely hear it.

There was a sudden movement and the chill air about the wolves shimmered and then something like a skin fell away and the three daughters of the Lord of the White Fort were revealed. They must have been beautiful once, for they still retained a shadow of their former loveliness. That they were of the same stock as the Harper was plain: the high cheekbones, the slanted eyes and pointed chin indicated that, but where they differed was in their eyes. Whereas the

Harper's were bright and alive, the women's were lifeless, resembling large flat stones, seemingly without pupil or white, and their faces were totally devoid of expression.

They swayed in time to the now quickening music, and Calte too could feel its lure; it pulled them in, drawing them closer to the Harper, bringing them together ... and slowly Cascarach bound them in chains of music and held them through the night.

The sky brightened, its greyness spilling across the eastern sky like turgid water, and then out from the greyness light the colour of freshly spilled blood tinged the sky, and the sun rose in the east.

The three women cringed in the bright light; creatures of darkness, twilight or cloudy days, the harsh light of day was painful to them. They attempted to pull away from Cascarach and reach the discarded wolf pelts, but the spell still held. And then as one they turned and lunged for him, their hands clawed, their long nails ready to rend and tear ... and Calte pushed himself to his feet and threw his spear before collapsing back onto the ground.

The weapon hummed as it spun through the air, the pyramidal head revolving rapidly. The razor sharp point struck the nearest woman just above the right breast, passed partially through her body, struck through her sister's chest, and lodged itself in the third woman's throat, locking them together like three gaffed fish. The bodies swayed on their feet, the same expression now irrevocably etched on their faces, and then slowly they began to crumple. The feet went first, turning to a grey and bone-white dust that quickly ate its way up their legs and consumed their bodies, until soon the spear was lying in a pile of dust on the blackened earth.

Cascarach, his harp tucked under one arm, helped Calte to his feet. The old man groaned aloud with the agony of returning circulation and he was shivering with the chill. He limped across to the three mingled piles of dust and nudged them with his foot. 'And that is it?' he asked quietly.

'The werewolves are gone?'

Cascarach nodded and looked out across the sea. 'You know,' he said softly, 'it is the end of an era; for generations creatures like these, werewolves, ghouls, serpents, *peisti*, blood-suckers have come out of the Cave of Crucha.' He looked down at the pile of dust by his feet which was already beginning to be scattered on the wind. 'These were the last of the Dolours Company, the outcasts of this world, banished by the gods and the Tuatha De Danann into the Shadowland. We will not see their like again.'

'Thank the gods for that then,' Calte said, and then looked curiously at the Harper. 'You sound almost sorrowful.'

'I can see my own race going the way they went; shunned, feared, hunted.' He shook his head and walked away from the old lord, taking the path that led down to the beach. 'And each day,' he said quietly, but clearly, 'a little more magic goes from this world.'

Chapter Four

THE NINE

The diver emerged spluttering from the icy waves. He hawked, spat a mouthful of salt water and shouted up at the vessel rocking beside him. 'There's no reef, no weed...' He coughed as a wave slapped across his mouth, and then reached up as the captain leaned over the edge of the low craft and stretched down his arm. Cathal hauled the young man in easily and then called for a blanket. 'There's nothing but clear water as far down as I can see,' the diver continued through chattering teeth.

Cathal nodded his thanks and then turned to the young man in the long white robes of the priests standing beside him. 'Well, what do you think?'

Sesnan shrugged. 'If there is no weed and no reefs – and I don't see how there could be,' he added, indicating the flat expanse of grey water with the smudge of the Pictish coastline to the south and east, 'then the only conclusion I can come to is that we have been trapped by magic.'

The young king nodded. 'It's what I feared. There's not that many reasons for a boat to stop in mid sea without any cause, is there?' he added with a smile. He looked across at the druid, not many years older than himself. 'What would you recommend?'

Sesnan smiled and shrugged again, the bones of his shoulders showing through the thin woollen robe. 'An enchantment of this sort is very localised, and we must therefore assume that whatever is holding us is directly below. Someone will have to go down ... oh, I can give them some protection,' he added hastily, seeing the look of shock on the king's face.

'I'll go,' Cathal said quickly, recovering from the shock of discovering that someone – or something – beneath the waves was holding them motionless.

'*No!*' The druid's normally calm voice had risen slightly, and he was suddenly conscious that the crew of the becalmed craft were looking at him curiously. 'No,' he repeated in a lower tone, 'you cannot.' He held up his hand to forestall the king's protests. 'I know I said I could give you some protection, but look ... look all around you; what do you see?'

'Water; Pictland to the south ...'

The druid nodded, wisps of his thinning white hair falling over his intense eyes. He was an Outlander, a foreigner from the lands far to the east of Banba, beyond the dividing waters, from distant Gaul, and he looked conspicuously out of place amongst the swarthier, smaller Gaels, his blond hair and blue eyes contrasting sharply with the brighter, reddish-bronze, gold or black hair, and the green, black or brown eyes of the islanders. But they respected him because of his Faith and because of his powers, and at four-and-twenty he was one of the youngest men ever to have risen so high in the strict hierarchy of the druids.

He touched the king's arm and led him away from the listening ears of the bewildered and frightened crew. They had set out four days ago to negotiate a treaty with the flaxen-haired northerners, who had recently taken to raiding the coastal towns. Cathal had decided to take three boatloads of men with him, more as a show of strength than as a measure of protection. They had set out along the north-western coast of Banba heading northwards, hugging the relatively sheltered coastal waters – but with the broad Western Ocean beating in incessantly there was little enough shelter anywhere on that bleak coast. Having rounded the tip of Banba they then crossed the icy stretch of water that separated the island from its nearest neighbour. They continued northwards, weaving in and through the countless tiny islands of Pictland and avoiding the many tempting sheltered bays and inlets; many an unwary ship had come to grief in those sheltered inlets at the hands of the barbaric Picts.

That morning they had rounded the tip of Pictland and, although the water was still chill and speckled with tiny clumps of ice, the day was bright and warm – but the wind from the north and west was razor sharp.

And then they had suddenly stopped.

The three craft, moving in a roughly triangular formation, had abruptly ground to a halt as if they had struck a reef, tumbling men to the decks, flinging some into the icy waters. The sails billowed and flapped in the wind, and the waves washed over the sides of the crafts, but they remained unmoving.

Cathal sent teams of divers down, but one by one they had all returned with the same report: nothing, there was nothing down there, no weed, no reefs...

Which left... sorcery!

Cathal and Sesnan stood near the bow of the ship, staring down into the dark, grey-green waters. The king's smooth unbearded face was set in grim determined lines, and he had that same set to his mouth that his father had when he had made up his mind about something – and would not be budged.

'Now, why can I not go down?' he demanded. 'You said you could give me some protection.'

'And as I said to you, what do you see all around you?'

'Water!'

'Yes,' Sesnan nodded, 'water... and I am a druid. I work

103

with the soil, with growth and life and green things. I draw my magic, my power, from the earth itself. Water is not my element. Here, my powers are weakened and diminished. If I give you protection I cannot guarantee that I can keep it.' He smiled briefly. 'And I will not allow you to risk your life.'

The young king smiled. 'I know that – and I thank you for it. But I must go down; I cannot afford to send anyone else down . . . the gods alone know what they might find. In any case, if we have been stopped by some magical power I hardly think it likely that whomever – or *whatever* – has stopped us will allow me to drown. If they wanted me dead and they possess this power they could just as easily have struck me with a thunderbolt or swept me overboard with a gust of wind.'

The druid shook his head and sighed. 'You have the glib tongue of a poet or bard,' he said.

He didn't feel the cold: his limbs were still tingling from the unguent Sesnan had rubbed into them, and although no light seeped in through the grey water he found he could see – not well, but enough to make out vague shapes in the water. He fell, quickly at first, but then more slowly, sinking into the depths of the grim Northern Sea. He kept his arms pressed to his sides and his feet together, his body rigid, allowing the currents to carry him. When the light above him went he twisted his head and, remembering to keep his mouth tightly shut and ensuring that the plugs remained in his nostrils, looked upwards. But the oblong shadows of the ships were gone, and he could see nothing but the blurry twisting of some sea creature against the shifting grey-black waters.

Something darted close to his face and his head snapped back. The urge to cry out was almost overwhelming, and then he saw it was just a tiny shoal of minute fish moving together as one. He found it difficult not to breathe through his mouth and he had to constantly fight against the impulse. He could hear his heart pounding in his head and the druid's last words pounding along with them. 'You are now, in effect, breathing through your skin; the salve will allow it to filter and extract the breath of life. But if you open your mouth the water will destroy you, crushing your lungs, destroying your brain.'

But it was a far easier thing to say than to do when it went against the habit of a lifetime, Cathal decided ironically.

Cathal drifted downwards, whilst all around him the life of this chill sea swarmed. Shoals of fish he vaguely recognised twisted and moved together like a single organism to follow his progress, and other, more recognisable fish, but the size of which he had never imagined, observed him through eyes that seemed alive and alert – and intelligent. Yet other, more sinister creatures coiled smoothly past him, neither fish nor serpent, but something of both. Hideously monstrous sea creatures came forth from the long trailing lengths of weed that now rose from the blackness below him. He must be nearing the bottom. And then he suddenly realised there was nothing below him. His sorcery-enhanced sight enabled him to pierce the utter night of the sea and bring it to a ghastly semblance of daylight, but strain as he might he could see nothing.

The young king loosened his sword in his sheath, the only piece of clothing he wore, and prepared to meet whatever had trapped his ships. His ghost-sight blurred and then something sparkled brightly once and disappeared. For the first time since he had entered the water – how long ago had that been? – he felt cold... an intense and paradoxically burning cold. Sensation disappeared from his hands and feet almost immediately, and then slowly and painfully claimed his arms and legs. He fell into blackness and he knew his sight had gone then, and next his hearing, until the only sound in his universe was the frail beating of his own heart – and even that was slowing.

He was dying.

Perhaps he drifted into unconsciousness or perhaps he continued to fall through the blackness – in the absolute darkness it was impossible to tell, but suddenly there was light: harsh, blinding, painful – and warm – light. He was conscious that he was still and unmoving with something solid beneath his back. Carefully he explored his senses; feeling had returned, and it had been the agonising tingle of returning circulation which had brought him alert. Cathal gritted his teeth and tried not to cry out with the pain...but he welcomed it also, for it meant he was alive and feeling. And he was sure the dead did not feel.

He was sure he could see: the orange and speckled blackness of his own eyes was clearly visible through his closed eyelids, and he could hear a low sibilant whisper, much as the wind makes through long grass.

Something warm and gentle touched his bare leg and the shock made him sit up suddenly, clutching for his sword – but that was gone, and the sudden effort sent waves of blackness washing over him, and his first – and last – image was of a startlingly beautiful young woman before he lapsed into unconsciousness.

When he awoke again it was night – or what passed for night in this strange kingdom. Although the sky was clear there were no stars strewn across the heavens and no moon rode the skies like some great bird; instead, long trailing wisps of speckled white light drifted lazily overhead like strewn gauze, and although it lacked the hard brilliant beauty of the night stars it had a beauty peculiar to itself.

'It is very beautiful, is it not?' The voice came from behind and Cathal, who had been leaning up on one elbow to stare at the sky, started and swivelled around to face the voice. It belonged to the young woman he had seen briefly before passing out. At first sight she seemed very small, but in effect she was nearly as tall as the young king. She was very beautiful – that was the first fact that impressed itself upon him, and she possessed a strangely exotic beauty. But, by the same token, her looks were not of faerie: her features lacked the angularity of the elven folk, and her breasts – for she was naked – were full and large nippled, unlike the *mna-shee* who were always small breasted like children. Her eyes were large and round, slightly protruding he discovered later, and seemed to blink very slowly and deliberately. Her nose was small, slightly tilted, her lips thin and she spoke through a tiny gap in her mouth, without moving her lips or showing her teeth. Her neck was perhaps longer than the women of Banba, and although her breasts were full, her waist was incredibly slim, and her thighs and legs ended in the tiniest feet Cathal had ever seen.

She smiled, again without opening her mouth, and spoke in a lilting accent. 'You are Cathal, son of a king and king in your own right of the westernmost province of Banba.' It was a statement rather than a question.

The young man came slowly to his feet, wincing as his stiffened muscles protested. 'I am; and who are you?'

'I am Samde,' the young woman said quietly. She walked past him and began to make her way down through a field of tall grass. Cathal lurched to his feet and staggered after her. He looked back over his shoulder and found he had been lying on a small flat-topped knoll that rose from the field like a great basking whale.

Samde cut diagonally through the waist-high emerald-green grass, making for a stand of stunted trees that clustered at one side of the field. As the young king neared them he could see that they resembled stunted, incredibly old oaks, and time had etched human-like masks into the gnarled trunks. The branches – the topmost of which was no higher than his head – began to rustle and quiver as he followed the young woman through the trees, and soon the entire copse was trembling as if in a stiff breeze. The rustling branches cast shadows on the trunks below, and the twisted faces twitched and gibbered with a shadow-life. But Samde strode unafraid through the trees, occasionally brushing one aside with the flat of her hand if it came too close to the track, and where she touched it the wood darkened and scorched. She led the young king out from the copse and into another field. It was smaller than the first, and made even more so by the large circle of standing stones that dominated the centre of the field.

The stones were taller than the king, fashioned of a smooth green stone through which white and silver veins ran like wrinkles. Cathal counted seven and twenty of them standing in a perfect circle. And before every third opening sat a young woman. As he neared Cathal thought they were Samde's sisters, but as he entered the circle and looked around he realised that they were identical to her. He turned slowly, looking at each of the nine in turn – and as he completed a full circle he discovered that Samde had disappeared and he couldn't pick her out from the other women.

The nine women regarded him coldly, their eyes sharp and appraising, and Cathal began to grow uncomfortable beneath their direct gaze. 'What do you want?' he demanded, fear and anger raising his voice to a shout. 'By what right do you hold my ships in thrall?'

'Right? We recognise no right.' The voice, identical to Samde's, came from his right.

'We heed no rights,' a second voice added from behind him.

'Save our own.' And this from off to his left.

Cathal spun around to face each woman in turn. It was like looking at nine polished shields, each one reflecting the same warrior. He stopped and held his pounding head in his hands and concentrated on breathing evenly and deeply. When he looked up the fear and anger were gone from his eyes and his voice was calm. He faced the woman directly across from him. 'Why have you stopped my ships?' he asked quietly.

The woman nodded and a smile touched her thin lips. 'Because we want you,' she said simply.

'Me?' He laughed. 'You will get little ransom for me.'

The woman smiled, the corners of her mouth twisting upwards without showing her teeth. 'What use would we have for your baubles?' She shook her head. 'No, king, it is you we want.'

'What for?' Cathal demanded angrily, attempting to quell the rising fear that threatened to send him grovelling to the ground.

'You will perform a single service for each one of us,' she continued in the same flat monotone. 'If, at the end of nine nights, that service has been completed successfully, then you and your ships are free to leave.'

Cathal nodded grimly. 'And what is this service?'

'You will lie with each one of us for one night,' she said quietly, 'and if on the morning of the tenth day one – just one – of us has conceived, then you may go.'

It was physically and mentally impossible to tell the women apart; they looked identical, felt the same and even reacted the same way. It was as if they were copies or parts of the same person. None of the women seemed to take any pleasure from the physical act, and they regarded it as a necessary duty.

However, over the next nine nights Cathal did piece together enough to recreate part of the women's history.

They were the children – the spawn – of Sinde, the sorceress who had come to the island in the dawn of the world with the princess Caesir Banba, fleeing the rising floodwaters in the east. Then the plague had come and decimated the princess' followers, and Sinde alone survived

– but briefly. She had fallen or jumped – accounts differed – into the sea from a cliff, and had been dashed to pieces on the rocks below – nine distinct pieces in fact. And the magic and power which had been part of her life now followed her into death. Her body regenerated, and the nine parts assumed the original's shape, appearance, memories and abilities... but the emotions, which were part of the soul, were lost with the sorceress' death.

And the Nine were one and yet individual, and their powers – either singly or as a unit – were incredible. For generations they had worked beneath the waves creating a timeless pocket of magic-spawned land, imbuing it with what they imagined, or remembered, of the world above. But it was a precious illusion – and the nine knew it. And knew also that they were weakening and the illusion was dying.

The magic was fading from the world of men, and its effects were slowly seeping through into the depths of the ocean, gradually eroding the pocket of timelessness of its vitality, and beginning to touch the women with age. They realised then that they needed new life if they were to survive; they would have to bring forth children... children in their own image.

And Cathal had been chosen to be the father of this new generation.

And the children, being born of the sea and surrounded by it, would be able to draw their magic and strength from the ceaseless waves.

And having a human sire would allow them to cull the vitality of the land... and they would rule the land and the seas.

The Nine had first constructed a series of Gates through which they could look out onto the world of man. Generations passed while they scanned the times and places of the world alien to them, seeking the one who would be the father of their children. They had watched the launch of the three craft from the west coast of Banba and followed its progress carefully. Something about them attracted the Nine, and they had eventually narrowed it down to two people: Cathal and Sesnan the Druid, but they had chosen the king over the druid for his looks, youth and royal blood.

The nights passed slowly for the king, and what had at first seemed a novelty soon grew boring and then agonising. The women were completely unresponsive and were loath to even touch him, and yet were always extremely careful and gentle. They never kissed.

Eventually the nine nights passed and in the cool light of morning Cathal once again stood in the centre of the stone-enclosed circle and waited as the women passed judgement upon themselves. And one by one they slowly shook their heads and said quietly, 'I have not conceived...' until all but one, the women directly before Cathal, had spoken.

The king stared at her desperately, his eyes sunken and feverish. 'And you,' he demanded harshly, 'have you conceived?'

For a long moment there was silence, and then the corners of her mouth twitched and turned up, and for the first time since he had encountered the Nine Cathal saw something like life sparkle in their eyes. She nodded once. 'Yes, I have conceived.'

When Cathal awoke he was lying on his back on the rough boards of his ship staring up into the concerned face of Sesnan the Druid. 'We thought you drowned,' he said simply.

The druid helped the king into a sitting position, and Cathal clung to him and squeezed his eyes shut as the world spun around him and black spots sparked before his eyes. 'Where are we...?' he whispered, his voice raw and hoarse.

111

'Still in the same position... we haven't moved.'

'But... but how did you maintain the position for so long?' he croaked.

Sesnan looked puzzled. 'You have been gone barely an hour,' he said quietly, and then he nodded in understanding. 'Aaah, but you forget that time in the Shadowlands marches to a different beat than in our own world. How long were you gone?'

'Nine days,' the king whispered in wonder.

'And but an hour has passed here,' Sesnan said, helping the king to his feet and holding him while he found his legs.

Cathal braced himself and waited until the druid dropped his supporting hand. He breathed deeply, savouring the fresh salt air. 'Give the order,' he said loudly, 'we are free to go.'

Cathal's mission to the east was not successful; captured and imprisoned upon landing, he and Sesnan spent several years in captivity while the rest of his crew were sold into slavery. However, after several desperate bids for freedom, they eventually escaped with the aid of the druid's magic and the king's wits. They freed a score or more slaves who in turn liberated more and then, with a captured ship, they set out for Banba.

They came south this time, avoiding the spot where they had been captured and held the last time, and sailed around the coast of the Britons, over the spires of sunken Lyonesse, and then swung north again, passing Mona, but now keeping the coast of Banba in sight at all times on their port side. Some of the crew of freed slaves had been part of Cathal's original crew, and they wept openly at the sight of their homeland. It had been seven years – almost to the day – since they had first set out from the wild western shores of the island. It felt good to be coming home.

*

112

The morning was like a flawless gem; crystal clear and bright, with even the most distant landmarks and islands clearly visible. No clouds marred the heavens and there was little or no breeze.

Cathal and Sesnan stood in the prow of their stolen craft just behind the carven figurehead and watched the coast of Banba rise up from the sea. Behind them the men rowed strongly, a low rumbling sea-shanty helping to maintain the beat; for some it was a homecoming, for others a chance to start again as free men.

The years spent in captivity had changed both men; Cathal had lost the boyish flesh of his youth and had hardened into a warrior. His flesh had tanned and darkened and although not yet thirty summers his reddish hair was now flecked with silver. And the only remaining vestige of his youth was the occasionally innocent look in his eyes.

Time had dealt a little more harshly with the druid. He had never been fleshy but he was now thin, his hair gone except for tufts above his ears, giving his face a skull-like appearance. His intense eyes had sunk deep into his face, like coals burning through cloth, and his pale complexion had turned sallow. But his power was undiminished.

Sesnan looked up suddenly, his head tilted back, his nose questing like a hunting dog's. He moved his head from side to side in an attitude of listening.

'What is it?' Cathal asked.

'Something...'

'What?'

'A... disturbance; something... something powerful is approaching.'

The metal craft came up from beneath the waves in an explosion of foaming water. The rhythm of the oarsmen was broken and several men were struck by the flailing lengths of wood. Shrieks of fear mingled with the moans of those with broken bones or cracked ribs, and as the craft lost momentum it began to wallow in the flat sea.

The strange craft bobbed on the waves nearly two lengths away from them. It was a small arrow-shaped vessel, high both fore and aft, and with a single mast set amidships. It was constructed – or perhaps sheathed – of metal, a shade something between copper and gold. In the early morning sunshine it was afire with reflected light, and the figures moving about the deck were little more than shadows.

The metallic craft began to move towards them, drifting contrary to the waves. It turned out of the light, the fire died, and the figures on the deck leapt into stark relief. And although they were dressed in long flowing black robes, Cathal immediately recognised them as the Nine.

The strange craft edged closer, until it was barely a length away from the ship. The women lined the rail: nine identical, motionless figures in black, only the ovals of their faces visible, their eyes startlingly bright. There was a sudden shifting movement and the woman nearest Cathal held up a small black-swathed bundle. 'Behold your son,' she called, her voice echoing slightly across the waves, and then she twitched the cloth aside. In her strong, bone-white hands she held a young boy high out over the water. The resemblance between him and the king was unmistakable: the same startling red hair, the same high bone structure and jutting jaw. But he also carried the other-worldly strangeness of his mother, the same flat expressionless eyes, the same tight-lipped grimace. The child reached out with long-fingered groping hands.

'My son?' Cathal whispered.

'No,' the druid said quietly, 'the seed may have been yours, but the womb that carried it and the woman that bore it are not human; there is nothing of you in that child.'

'My son...' The king stared entranced at the child. To return to Banba with a boy-child – a son – would make up for all those missing years. A son, and something his father, Ridonn, King of Munster would appreciate. He looked across at the child again; handsome aye, and well formed.

He would grow up to be a fine young man. A son any father might be proud of. Impulsively he reached across for the child.

Sesnan struck down his outstretched hands. 'It is not your child,' he insisted fiercely. 'Take it and you are taking your own destruction, aye, and the destruction of Banba unto yourself. That... that child has more power than the greatest druids ever dreamed of. The child is master of the sea! Take it, accept it, invite it into your fort and remember, by inviting evil in you grant it leave to work. You will enable it to consolidate its power with the magic of the soil and stones. In effect you will have enabled it to become the most powerful creature in this world, both on land and sea...' The druid trailed off, realising the king was not listening to him. He was clearly entranced.

Cathal looked across at the young boy, still dangling from his mother's hands. His son.

'Father... take me... I am yours... take me...'

Cathal ignored the tiny voice whispering insistently inside his head and looked up at the mother. 'How is he called?' he asked.

'NO!' Sesnan shouted, drowning out her reply. He grabbed Cathal's arms and swung him around. He stared deep into his eyes... and drew back suddenly, for there was no recognition there. 'Do not ask his name,' the druid said forcefully, 'do not take any part of him to yourself.'

The king pushed the older man aside almost casually, sending him sprawling to the deck, leaving him there while he turned back to the woman and repeated his question.

'He is unnamed; his naming is yours, he is your son.'

'I am your son... take me... take me...'

The druid pushed himself to a sitting position and threw up his hands, calling down his magic. A huge wave rose up between the two ships and crashed down on the metallic craft, sending it spinning away from them. And now a wind began to blow from the south and west, filling the huge cloth sail, sending it cracking taut on the mast. The longship leaped forward, tumbling many of the unprepared crew to the decks. Cathal fell beside the druid and when he looked up there was murder in his eyes. Sesnan gestured again as the king reached for his knife, and Cathal felt his muscles lock and freeze into rigid bands. The druid held up one long forefinger. 'Trust me and wait,' he said gently.

Now the crew had found their positions and were pulling strongly towards the west, and the craft fairly skimmed across the waves, foaming white-water spraying up on either side. The rocky coastline of Banba quickly solidified and took on both shape and definition, a strip of golden beach highlighting the solid blackness of the jagged cliffs.

But now the metallic craft was turning about, and slowly and inexorably it gained on them.

Sesnan made his way to the prow and continued working his magic. The closer they came to shore the stronger he became... but he needed something more, and he needed it now. He leaned against the smooth polished wood of the figurehead, his damp palms staining the wood – and then something like a spark leaped from it to his skin. And suddenly he knew. His ancestors, the forebears of the current invaders, had known the magic of imprisoning some of the lesser spirits – usually the spirit or sprite of the material, be it wood, stone or leather, in which they were working. When they constructed a craft such as this they usually imprisoned the elemental in the snarling figurehead, and then, in times of greatest danger, they would call it up, using its raw energy to come to their aid. The current generation didn't know the craft – but they were shipbuilders and they followed the old ways, and perhaps a little of the old magic might yet remain.

The druid stood behind the figurehead and placed both hands flat against the sides. His head tilted back and his eyes rolled shut. He allowed the force to gather within him and then he slowly and reluctantly allowed it to trickle out

116

through his fingers and into the wood. He felt the rush of energy leave him and he felt the cool wood begin to heat up and the wooden side of the snarling figurehead assume a warm fleshy texture. Slowly he ran his hands down the dragon-shape ... and slowly the ship came alive beneath his hands.

Raw power pulsated through the boards, lifting the craft clear of the waves and the oarsmen were thrown back on their benches, watching stupidly as their oars rattled uselessly in their locks. The cloth sail filled and stretched on the mast until it threatened to burst asunder.

But the vessel of the Nine continued to approach.

And then the boards began to smoulder and burn with the power that now ran through them. Wisps of smoke rose only to be shredded on the wind – but it was the same wind which now fanned the fires. The decks and rails went first, the wood darkening, the grain blackening in abstract patterns, and then, when the decks grew too hot to stand upon, the blackened wood began to flake away in stinging cinders. And then the mast went. There was a sudden explosion as the wood burst into a pillar of flame and almost instantly collapsed, draping the deck with thick sailcloth which immediately began to burn, spreading fire every-where. The crew worked frantically to toss the burning cloth overboard, but the damage had been done: small fires now dotted the deck, the rowers' benches were burning and even the oars were crisped and blackened.

But the shore was very close now.

The burning sailcloth which had been thrown overboard lay directly in the path of the Nine's vessel, and the metallic hull cut partially through the thick hide before sticking fast, bringing the craft to a lurching halt.

Sesnan slumped against the figurehead exhausted. Perhaps the spell had been incorrectly set, perhaps he had invoked the elemental incorrectly, but the ship should never have burned. He winced as he felt the heat through the thin soles of his boots ... and he suddenly remembered the king: he had left Cathal lying spellbound on the deck ...

The king's leather jerkin and breeches had absorbed much of the heat, but his face, arms and legs were raw and blistered, and there was a look of madness in his eyes.

The bottom of the longship scraped sand, and then ripped along a hidden rock; water boiled and hissed as it splashed over onto the blistering decks. The craft lurched, recovered, and lurched again, rending itself against a sandbar before finally shuddering to a halt. And now with no wind and flying water to dampen the fire, the flames leapt forth while the men threw themselves into the shallow sea, more frightened now of the flames than of the metallic craft closing in fast behind them.

Sesnan helped the king to his feet and, half carrying, half pulling, brought him to the ground. The king could barely stand and was forced to lean against the druid for support. His hand, which had been twisted clawlike by the heat, gripped Sesnan's arm through the soiled white cloth of his robe with painful intensity. Sesnan drew the king from the burning ship and through the shallows to a small crag of rock that rose out from the water just behind the stricken vessel. He made to turn away and return to the ship, but Cathal caught his robe and pulled him back.

'I will have my son,' he gasped, his breath coming hard and fast.

Sesnan shook his head. 'I am truly sorry, my friend; sorry for the injuries I have caused you, and sorry because I cannot allow you to take that child.'

'*Don't listen to him father ... take me ... take me ... I am your son ... your son ...*'

'My son,' Cathal said slowly.

'He is inhuman,' Sesnan insisted.

'My son.'

'No!'

'*Yes!*' And Cathal plunged his dagger into the druid's

chest, driving upwards into the heart. There was an instant before death claimed him in which the druid's eyes registered something more than pain and surprise, something that was perhaps close to fear, and then the light of life died in them and he slumped into his friend's arms. Cathal stepped back and allowed the corpse to slide to the rocks, where the waves were quickly tinged with crimson.

'Your son.'

'Father...'

'My son!' Cathal held out his hands for the boy, and the mother lifted him high once as if in offering, before throwing him across the space that separated the metallic craft from the king.

And then there was perhaps a moment, a moment when time itself stood still, and Cathal saw several things at once. He saw the mother smile, saw four tusklike fangs glisten in the light, saw the same light glisten off countless shimmering scales on her skin, saw the child flying through the air arms outstretched, saw himself reaching out, felt the weight in his hands, felt the pain – the agonising, searing pain of his crippled hands – saw the child slipping, saw the robe falling away, saw its body and the interlocking scales and the misshapen feet, saw him strike the blood-stained rock, his head bursting asunder like rotten fruit, heard him scream, saw the tusks again, saw a black forked tongue...

'My son,' Cathal whispered, blackness overwhelming him, sending him tumbling forward into the bloody waves.

Chapter Five

THE HARPER

He was a small, round-faced man, his balding head fringed with tufts of iron-grey hair. His clothes, now shabby and patched, had once been of good quality and he wore them as if they still retained their former finery. His only possessions seemed to be a knobbed walking stick and a wood and decorated leather harp case. He was blind and called Carolan... and the finest harper in all Ireland, if not the world.

The funeral procession made its way slowly along the winding country road, the wailing of the women and the professional keeners mingling with the creaking of the cart and the dull plodding of the horses' hooves. On the cart a plain wooden coffin rattled against the boards, the new nails sparkling in the morning light. A large group of people followed the cart, led by the deceased's young wife, her family and the local priest. She was weeping uncontrollably, damning both god and man in her grief, whilst the neighbours looked on and whispered amongst themselves, puzzled at young Ian's sudden and inexplicable death.

The young man – married not eight weeks previously – had been out in the fields, helping with the haymaking. It was one of those long hot and dry days that seem to linger on long after they should, holding a memory of the summer past. Ian had stripped to the waist and had climbed atop a hay rick and was tying down a large sheet over the top of the rick when the wind blew up out of nowhere and swept across the field. Warm at first, it had rapidly chilled and intensified almost to gale force; chaff and stubble were lifted and spun through the air, tiny stones hissed and buzzed through the still standing grains, and the grass was flattened in a broad swath as the wind moved across the field in a solid – but contained – mass. Most of the field hands were thrown to the ground and lay there while the wind passed over them ... but some were caught in it. With most it was just a case of grit or dust in their eyes, but others were not so lucky. One young man running across the field when the wind struck was caught with one foot in the air. He was spun around with the force of the wind and fell hard on his arm, and the sound of breaking bone was clearly audible above the wind's passing. Another had just placed a ladder up against a rick and had started to climb when it struck. The frail wooden steps were jerked from under him, throwing him headfirst into the rick, lacerating his skin and cracking nearly a dozen ribs.

But for some reason the cold wind seemed to vent its full fury upon the rick on which Ian was standing and, curiously, he was seen to strike out with his pitchfork – which was later found with its head snapped off. The leather sheet was ripped from his grasp, striking him roughly across the chest and shoulders, sending him rearing upwards. He balanced precariously, his arms windmilling ... and then the top of the hay rick dissolved beneath his feet, carefully stretched and tied straw flying in all directions. Ian's scream was lost as he fell downwards into the heart of the rick, which was immediately torn asunder by the wind's icy fury.

And when they pulled him out from the remains of the rick he was dead, and with not a mark on his body.

The Harper's blind white eyes blinked and his head turned

in the direction of the wailing. He recognised the sound immediately; the ritual keening for the soul of the recently deceased, mingled with the genuine cries of grief by the relatives and friends. He turned his head slightly, listening. His sensitive hearing caught the steady beat of the horses' hooves, the creak of the harness and the rattle of the iron-shod wheels over the rough ground. Gripping his gnarled walking stick tightly he pulled himself to his feet, facing the direction of the sound. Behind, and above his head, a four-armed signpost shifted slightly in the wind and the dust of the crossroads was whipped up into his face. He turned his face away as grit clogged his nostrils and battered against his useless eyes; there were times, he mused, when having no sight was an advantage: you would never be troubled with grit in your eyes for a start!

He had lost his sight at the age of fourteen from smallpox. It should have killed him – and there had been times when he wished it had – but it had taken his sight and departed, like a thief in the night. There had been times also when he had been tempted to take his own life, but ... and there was always that *but*; the *'but'* that was composed of fear, determination and religion.

And then he had gradually become aware of new sensations and the sensitivity of his other senses: hearing, smell, taste and touch. Especially hearing and touch. He was apprenticed to a harper, and he found a strange fascination for this, the most difficult of instruments, and the speed at which he mastered it was almost frightening. He would often spend hours just tracing over and over again the intricate spiralling design on the smooth polished wood of the soundbox of the harp his teacher had given him, and his rounded fingernails would caress the myriad strings, drawing just a ghost of a sound from them.

When he was twenty-one – and had far surpassed the old teacher – he had set out along the lonely hedge-lined roads, feeling the breath of the wind on his face, hearing the whispered rustling of the leaves and tasting the freshness of the air. He would often spend days in one place, learning from the old harpers, building up his repertoire, creating his own compositions before taking to the road again.

He had been on the road for over a year before he came to the tiny village in the west, in sight of the broad Atlantic and close enough to the sea to hear the hollow booming of the waves against the towering Cliffs of Moher. There was no harper in the village, and the local piper was an old, old man, blind and almost deaf, his fingers stiffened by age and hard work. The old man played occasionally, his fingers moving automatically, for he could no longer hear himself play, and he played only dirges because he was incapable of playing quickly with his crippled hands. There was nothing there for Carolan – and yet he stayed. There was something about the district, something that appealed to him. By day he would wander the roads and tracks about the village, allowing his acute senses to lead and guide him, and invariably he found himself drawn to one particular field where he would sit on the crest of a small hillock and listen to the wind, taste its salt freshness and feel its touch on his blind eyes.

And he would hear the music.

It was faint at first, the merest tendril of brittle sound, but he found that if he lay against the ground the music swelled in volume and took on a fragile clarity. And he would often spend the night there, huddled beneath a thin blanket, listening to the ethereal music – and unable to tell whether it came from the ground or from inside his own head.

And it wasn't until he was leaving the village that the old piper told him that he had been sleeping atop a faerie rath.

'Of your charity, sir, if you would play a dirge for us.' The voice, although young, was tinged with an infinite weariness, as if he had seen so much pain and suffering that nothing more could surprise him.

'You would be the priest?' the Harper asked and looked up, and the priest gasped in surprise at the sightless white ovals. And he knew of only one blind harper...

'You are Turlough Carolan?' he asked quietly.

The Harper nodded silently.

The priest glanced back down the road to where the procession could just be seen rounding the bend, the heads of the people visible over the hedges. He had gone on ahead after the short service in the home of the deceased to prepare the grave. He had been surprised to find the small man standing beneath the signpost, a harp case in his arms, his head bent as if lost in thought.

'What ails you father?' the Harper asked suddenly.

Startled, the priest hesitated before answering. 'What...?'

'I may have lost my sight, but God recompensed me in other ways. You are troubled, that much is obvious. Something worries you; what I wonder?' he mused. 'The funeral... the deceased...? Aye, the deceased,' he nodded decisively. 'And why should you worry about the dead? Perhaps because the death was not natural?' He nodded briefly. 'Not natural, but not murder,' he continued shrewdly, reading more from the priest's silence, the quickened heartbeat and breathing than a sighted man could ever possibly have done. 'So, you are not happy about the death – but it was not murder, and yet it was not natural... there was therefore another agency involved; a supernatural agency perhaps?' He turned his blind eyes up towards the priest. 'How did the death occur, father?'

There was silence for a long time after that, and then the Harper heard a sound that was partway between a sob and a gasp. 'I don't know,' the priest confessed, 'but, God forgive me, I think the faeries took him.'

*

124

Carolan was standing beside the priest when the funeral procession stopped at the crossroads. The mourners had grown silent and only the broken sobbing of the dead man's wife was audible above the whistling of the wind. The Harper waited until everyone was still and he had their positions fixed in his mind's eye before moving forward. With his every sense alert, he reached out with his long delicate fingers and touched the crude wooden box: there *was* something... His fingers tingled as they did when he brought a new song to life, birthed from the murmurings of the wind and rain. He breathed deeply, inhaling the cold damp air that tugged at his lungs. He tasted it like a liquid, mentally removing the odours of horse, man, raw wood, heather and damp grass... and *yes*, there was a tinge of exotic spices on the air: the tell-tale touch of faerie. Slowly he turned his head from side to side. He cut out the anxious whispers of the people, the impatient stamping of the horse, the creak of the harness; he could hear something, the merest whisper on the wind, the shadow of...? He moved closer to the coffin. Above the corpse a ghost of the elven call still lingered.

The Harper moved back to the priest. He was sweating and there was a flush to his skin. When he spoke his voice trembled slightly. 'Quickly, give me my harp; he is not dead – not yet!'

The priest pressed the heavy leather case into the Harper's hands. Carefully, and with something approaching reverence, the Harper undid the laces and slipped the harp from its case. The morning light ran like liquid along its polished surface, nestled in the runic scrollwork, giving it depth and striking fire from the strings.

The Harper sat down on a milestone by the side of the road, rested his long delicate fingers on the strings and began to play. His fingers moved and yet there was a long moment's silence as if he hadn't touched them. And then it

125

seemed as if the wind itself took voice. It began as a low, barely felt trembling in the air, like the humming of a branch in the wind, and then it grew and swelled, the sound growing, strengthening. Tiny minor notes spun and darted, gone before they could be truly identified, but adding to the music's intensifying spell. The Harper's fingers seemed to barely move and yet the incredibly delicate music grew and took on body, enveloping the silent procession in its spell. It called to them, plucked at some deeply hidden and forgotten part of them; and the mourners felt an incredible longing... but for what, they could not say, except that they felt a *loss*.

And then the tenor of the music changed as Carolan called the faerie folk to himself. Although it was still soft and entrancing, it now had a stronger commanding core to it. It compelled, for it was the song of the untameable elements. And it drew the faerie folk.

The mourners could see nothing, hear nothing save the music, and yet they knew with an absolute certainty that the *gentry* had come. The very taste of the air had changed, from fresh and chill to hard and metallic and touched with the flavour of exotic spices. Many felt the tell-tale icy chill along their spines or at the base of their necks, and those who were fey actually saw the sudden thickening of shadows about the Harper and above the coffin.

Carolan looked up from his harp, a tiny smile on his lips. 'Ah, so you came.'

'*You knew we would; you knew we had no choice.*' The voice was like that of a child's, thin, high and pure but, unlike a child's, tinged with absolute weariness. '*What do you want, harper?*'

'The soul of this young man.'

'*We do not have his soul; that belongs to his god.*'

'I want that part of him which you have stolen.'

To the silent watchers it seemed as if the Harper were holding a conversation with the empty air, and yet the horse

126

was terrified, rolling its eyes and trembling all over, too frightened even to run.

'*What is this man to you?*' the voice demanded. '*He is nothing.*'

'He is human… and he has a wife who grieves for a husband lost before his time.' The Harper's fingers brushed the strings and the ethereal music spun out once again. The shadows wavered and solidified slightly, assuming a definite man-like form, although taller and thinner than anyone present.

Carolan smiled. 'At the moment I have only called forth a tiny part of you, but take care lest I call you into the full light of day.'

'*You have not the power,*' the voice stated flatly.

'You forget, creature, that I learned my craft on the barrows of your people. The birds and beasts are mine to control, aye, and even the very elements should I so wish.' The Harper's rich voice rose, taking on a commanding note. 'So have a care lest I drag you forth from your duns and raths and hidden places and let the pure light of the sun shrivel you.'

The shadows about the coffin moved in agitation and slowly began to shred and fragment, like wind-blown smoke. The creature's words drifted back to the Harper as if from a great distance. '*So be it, harper. You may have that part we have of him – but we did not take his heart, he gave that of his own free will, and that will always be ours!*'

There was a sudden scream, followed by the sound of pounding. The lid of the coffin moved and then abruptly splintered and fell off. Ian sat up.

There was a stunned silence, during which the priest and the mourners stared incredulously at the 'corpse'. And then the priest slowly crossed himself and dropped to his knees on the road and began to pray aloud. Slowly the entire funeral procession followed his example.

And then Ian began to scream, a long drawn-out soul destroying scream, a scream of terrible loss or absolute insanity. Again and again he screamed like a demon, until the Harper fingered his harp and the young man fell back into the coffin, unconscious.

They carried him back to his own small house where, with the attentions of the local doctor and a drop of whiskey, he regained his senses. When he opened his eyes he looked curiously about the small dark bedroom as if seeing it for the first time, and then he smiled tentatively and reached for his wife's hand. 'Ah Mary . . . I've had such a terrible dream . . .'

The young man drifted in and out of unconsciousness for the next few days, and occasionally when he awoke the light of madness burned bright in his eyes. But the Harper was always there, and his music soothed and calmed him. However, in his sleep, he ranted and raved and, coupled with what he told them during his lucid moments, Carolan and Mary were able to piece together his tale.

He had been atop the hay rick tying down the sheet when he had heard the galloping. It sounded as if a troop of well-shod horses were rapidly approaching, which was strange because there were few troops in the district, and certainly none mounted. He had stood on the hay rick and looked about and sure enough, out from the woods to the south – or rather out from *above* the woods to the south – came a troop of mounted . . . *men*?

They were taller than mortal men and even their steeds seemed unnaturally tall and thin. The riders were dressed in strange shining armour that shimmered and sparkled as if it reflected sunlight – even though the sun was in the wrong position. Long colourful cloaks streamed behind and they carried glittering swords and delicately wrought spears.

The faerie host – for he knew what it was – raced past him, almost six feet above the level of the ground – and yet

128

he could see the sparks struck by the horses' hooves. He felt the wind of their passage as the host rode by, felt it pluck and tug at him, saw the men in the field below falling, buffeted by the wind, saw others cowering, saw the thin, sharp-boned faces of the riders laughing. He was seized by an almost uncontrollable anger: how dare they do this; by what right did they terrify men, and then laugh at their fear? The last man was galloping towards him. Ian pulled the long pitchfork from the hay beside him and faced the creature. He saw the look of surprise on the elven lord's face, and then a cruel smile touched his lips, and beneath his ornate plumed helm his face hardened into a mask of absolute inhumanity. His sword seemed to leap from its scabbard and come alive in his hand, darting, twisting, moving of its own accord. Ian lunged, and the elven warrior easily parried the clumsy blow, and the slightly curved sword sliced through the wooden handle of the fork as if it were no more than butter.

And Ian had one last glimpse of the elven mount's wild yellow eyes before the gleaming length of the sword swung down... and he had awoken after a series of terrifying dreams in a coffin.

Turlough Carolan went his way some days later, convinced that there was nothing more he could do for the young man. Ian McGee was healthy and fit and already showed signs of throwing off the effects of the strange bout of living death he had undergone.

But as the years passed, however, a hint of the old madness returned, and whenever a cold wind blew he would cower in a corner, screaming.

He took to walking the moors calling for them, and he would often race from hilltop to hilltop, trying to catch any vagrant scrap of wind. And it was said that he had left part of his soul behind in the Shadowland, or perhaps he had given his heart to one of the *mna-shee*, and it was well known that once one had been taken by the faeries one was never truly normal again.

On the twenty-fifth of March, 1738, Turlough Carolan died in Aldford, in the country of Roscommon. His funeral and wake was a huge affair, for the Harper, in his travels around Ireland, had made many friends and was much loved. Mary McGee travelled the hundred or so miles to the wake to pay her last respects to the man who had brought her husband back to life. But when she returned her husband was dead. It seemed he had climbed atop a hay rick and stood there as he had once before. Perhaps he lost his balance and fell... perhaps. He was found with a broken neck at the base of the wind-blown rick.

There had been no wind that day.

Chapter Six

FAMINE

The harvest had failed – again. For the second year running the potato crop had been struck with blight, leaving the fields sodden masses of rotting vegetables. The spectre of famine and its companion, Death, stalked the land. Entire families were wiped out as sickness and disease decimated the weakened people. Many attempted to flee, urged on by the tales of richness and plenty in the Americas, Canada and Australia – and many died on the rotting coffin-ships that had no chance of surviving the wild Atlantic.

And the unlucky – or lucky, depending on the point of view – also embarked on a journey: the final one into Eternal Night. Those families blessed, or cursed, with a *banshee* grew accustomed to her bitter-sweet wailing, and the doors between this and the Otherworld remained open far longer than they should. The ghosts of the recently dead clung stubbornly to this world, and indeed, in some areas entire villages carried on a shadow-life in the twilight hours.

But wraiths of a different kind also walked the land as the suffering of a nation called forth the spirits of the past. Tall dragon-prowed, many-oared ships were sighted off the coasts; wild-haired warriors gave battle on lonely moors with misshapen beast-men; and tall, ethereally beautiful creatures walked the roads.

One other creature too went abroad, a creature from the Shadowland, a creature of the terrible times, the *Fear Ghorta*, the Man of Hunger.

Towards early afternoon the rain, which had been threatening all morning, finally fell, turning the already sodden fields into stinking pits. Eamonn stood there dumbly, watching the clay about his bare feet turn to almost liquid muck. Wearily he dragged his feet free of the mass and trudged on, his eyes glued to the ground, looking for anything – *anything* – edible. So far he had been lucky – very lucky; he had managed to find three fairly large potatoes, none of which showed any sign of blight. At the time he could scarcely believe his luck; the field had been scoured many times by others before him, but he guessed that the recent rains had brought them to the surface.

Twice that morning he had been forced to hide while packs of men and women roamed the fields, searching everyone's bag, and once he had struck out and knocked a younger and fitter looking man to the ground. The stranger had stopped him and demanded to know what he had found that morning and, without even stopping to think, Eamonn had hit him hard and with the last of his strength, leaving him retching on the cold ground, doubled up and clutching himself.

Eamonn looked up into the leaden sky, and allowed the cool water to run down his face, cooling his fever. He was twenty-two; he looked ten or more years older than that. Skeletal thin, the flesh tight to the bones on his face, giving it a skull-like appearance, and with only patches of hair clinging to his head, he looked like one of the walking dead. Only his eyes were bright and alive – and they burned with fever.

Then, having decided that the rain was down for the day and, keeping an eye out for the gangs of parasites, he set out for home.

There had been a partial failure of the potato crop – the

staple diet of the Irish peasantry in the nineteenth century – in the autumn of 1845. The result was that, in the following year, 1846, since much of the seed which should have been sown had been eaten through the hard winter, there was a smaller crop than usual, and much of what had been sown failed. All through that winter and on into '47, the famine was at its height, and what the hunger or cold didn't kill, the fever did.

Deirdre was waiting for him, huddled up against the wall hugging a tiny, almost rock-like crust of bread. The small one-roomed construction was cold, cold and damp Eamonn realised, as the stale earthen smell caught at his throat and lungs making him cough. Tiny flecks of blood spotted his hands.

Deirdre carefully handed over the bread, holding it like delicate glass, anxious not to let so much as a crumb drop. 'I got it today in the *toighthe-brochain*, the soup kitchen,' she whispered, her once musical voice now raw and hoarse. 'I saved it for you.'

Eamonn smiled his thanks and, soaking the bread in water, thoroughly chewed and swallowed the crust; it was like swallowing gravel. He opened his small bag. 'I was lucky today,' he said slowly, careful not to aggravate the coughing again. He pulled out some long grasses, nettles, a score of mushrooms and the three potatoes. 'We'll not go hungry tonight.'

'We must thank God for that then,' Deirdre muttered.

'What about the rent?' Eamonn asked. The rent was due, and although in some cases the landlords – usually absentee and living in either Dublin or Britain – had waived the rent, others were still demanding their due . . . and the rents were, more often than not, paid in kind: crops, potatoes, maize, turnips.

'I've heard nothing; but there was some talk in the

toighthe that they may be held over until next year.'

'That would be something,' Eamonn said quietly, 'but let's wait and see – we can only live each day as it comes.'

The night wore on and it began to rain again. The heavy drumming on the worn thatch above their heads kept them both awake, and they huddled together around the glowing embers of their tiny fire. Somewhere in the darkness of the room water was dripping, a dull monotonous sound that grated on the nerves and soon took on the likeness of a heartbeat.

They ate before dawn, using what little food they had sparingly, carefully hiding away one of the potatoes and a handful of mushrooms. They ate the potatoes raw, knowing it would give them a feeling of fullness, but their meagre rations did little for their hunger and only gave them cramps which left them both doubled up for almost an hour afterwards.

As the sky paled in the east Deirdre and Eamonn stood in the doorway of their pitiful dwelling and watched the sun come up over the tops of the trees. The sky flamed purple and grey and the colours gradually burned themselves into light, giving the day a delicate beauty.

They had been standing in the doorway for some time before they realised that there was someone watching them. Deirdre saw him first; she started and gripped Eamonn's arm, nodding to her right.

Eamonn eased his wife back into the room behind him and waited in the doorway until she brought him a long length of wood. He watched the figure carefully, squinting through the wisps of mist rising from the damp ground, trying to make out whether it was alone.

'What do you want?' he demanded eventually, when the figure made no move or sound. He winced as the shout tore his throat, and his voice sounded raw and harsh in his own ears.

The figure came forward. It was a man, although at first

sight that wasn't immediately obvious. He was almost naked and skeletal; his ribs were completely visible through the stretched skin, and his arms and legs were stick-like. The skin had fallen away from his face, leaving it skull-like, his eyes deep-sunken and shadowed, and his head was balanced on a thin scrawny neck. He took a step forward.

Eamonn brandished the stick. 'What do you want?' he repeated.

The creature's mouth worked silently, and then he croaked, 'Water.'

'Be off with you, we have none.' Clean water was as difficult to find as food.

'Water,' the stranger repeated.

'Eamonn,' whispered his wife, 'give him some.'

'We've barely enough for ourselves,' he hissed. 'And look at him,' he gestured with the stick, 'he's almost gone; giving it to him would be like throwing it away.'

'Give him some.'

Eamonn began to shake his head, and then he shrugged. He dropped the stick to his side and gestured to the stranger. 'All right then, but we don't have much mind ...' And then he smiled and sighed. 'But what we have I'm sure you're welcome to.'

The man came forward slowly, hesitantly, like a dog that has been beaten once too often and is wary of any offers of kindness. He smiled tentatively as he slipped past Eamonn into the room behind him, his eyes button-bright and shining in his corpse-like face.

Deirdre handed him a pitcher of water, instructing him to drink slowly, and then passed him the last potato. The stranger looked at it curiously, moving it round and round in his frail hands. He made two efforts to speak before any sound came out.

'You cannot spare this,' he whispered, his voice soft and gentle, like a lost child's.

'Eat it,' Deirdre commanded.

135

'But it is all you have.' The stranger's eyes began to burn brighter, feverishly darting around the room. 'You have nothing else; what will you eat ... and you don't even know me,' he said in a rush.

'We know that you are hungry,' Eamonn said quietly, 'and I doubt if one potato is going to make the difference between life and death for us.' He slipped his hand through his wife's and squeezed. 'Anyway, I don't expect we'll last through this winter.'

Deirdre said nothing, but squeezed Eamonn's hand and blinked back the sudden sting of tears.

The old man bit into the raw potato. The skin was hard and yellow, and the flesh bitter and foul, but he chewed his tiny mouthfuls thoroughly before audibly swallowing. 'You've lasted this long,' he said, 'surely you will last the rest of the winter?'

Eamonn smiled grimly. 'We have no food ...' he gestured at the empty pitcher, 'no water, no firewood, no turf, no crops. So even if we do live through this winter, we'll have no seeds to grow for next year, so we'll go hungry again and again the following year and again ...' Abruptly he stopped and began to cough, bright red blood spattering against the sleeve of his shirt. 'Like you,' he gasped, 'we are the walking dead.'

'Perhaps not.'

Eamonn looked up, and Deirdre gasped in surprise. The stranger's voice had changed, deepened, strengthened. And although the same half-naked skeletal figure was still standing before them, his posture had straightened and his expression had changed from totally abject to one of absolute confidence. He gestured with one long-fingered hand, and both Eamonn and Deirdre felt something ripple and flow through the room, immediately followed by a cold sharp gust of wind. The fire blazed in the hearth and when Eamonn turned around he found it was burning prime-cut turf, and he blinked against the pleasantly acrid odour of turf smoke which quickly filled the room.

'Who are you ... what are you?' Deirdre whispered, clinging to Eamonn.

The stranger smiled, his face no longer looking so skull-like now, but merely menacing and totally different. 'I am the *Fear Ghorta*, the Man of Hunger,' he said gently, his voice echoing and ringing inside their heads.

'What ... why are you here?' Eamonn asked, his voice a little above a whisper.

The *Fear Ghorta* shrugged, his bony shoulders moving visibly beneath the thin covering of skin. 'The time of famine is my time, for it is only then that I can walk in the world of men unnoticed.' He paused and continued in a different tone. 'I am of the Tuatha De Danann, and yet not of them. In their latter days, the People brought many creatures into existence, some pleasant and beautiful to look upon, but others ...' He shrugged again.

'We are the Guardians of this land,' he continued, 'and we are not without our powers. I have walked the length and breadth of Ireland these last two years, watching, waiting and occasionally interfering in the affairs of men. It is said that I bring famine, but that is not true; famine brings me, calling me forth from the ancient barrows of the Tuatha. My duties in these times are many, but my main task is justice. I have come across others like you: people willing to share their last crust with a total stranger, giving completely of their charity.

'But I have also come across others; people with plenty, hoarders, thieves and the like who will not even give the crumbs from their tables. And some are wealthy men, not needing the money or food, wanting nothing, but greed, greed rules aye, and will eventually destroy them.' The *Fear Ghorta* smiled again, showing his teeth, which were short and even except for the two incisors which were longer and pointed. 'And these I have been forced to deal with: a blight taking their crops of grain, a fire destroying their valuables or homes and, in one or two cases, leading them astray, making them cross a patch of "hungry grass". And you know, unless you eat immediately upon crossing the grass, you will remain forever hungry and could even die of hunger within that yellowed circle.'

The *Fear Ghorta* put the half-eaten potato on the table beside him and his long-fingered hand passed over it, and immediately it was whole again. 'No matter how often you cut this,' he said to Deirdre, 'keep a little back, and in a little while it will be whole again.' He pointed across at the empty pitcher. 'And that will never be empty.'

The *Fear Ghorta* turned quickly and slipped out into the morning, and was gone.

Deirdre and Eamonn survived the Great Famine. 1847 slipped into '48 and that moved inexorably towards '49 and '50. The young couple, by keeping a low profile, and using their magical gifts sparingly and carefully, rode out the worst of the hunger.

Eamonn stopped coughing blood, and when he eventually did get to plant seeds two years later they sprouted quickly and strongly, and he managed to reap two harvests.

They never saw the *Fear Ghorta* again, although they occasionally heard whispers of the skeletal stranger who roamed the countryside repaying kindness with kindness and pettiness in kind.

And in time the Man of Hunger returned to the barrows of the Tuatha De Danann and slept, and sleeps still ...

Chapter Seven

THE SEAL WOMAN

Declan Fitzpatrick climbed back up the rough beach, carefully picking his way through the stones, the sea-water on his bare feet already beginning to turn chill. The young man paused briefly on a smooth boulder before leaping across a deep pool onto the broad stretch of sand that ran up almost to the foot of the cliffs. He sat on the warm dry sand and dropped the heavy bag of cockles and crabs beside him and began to dry his feet with a scrap of cloth. He swore as he patted dry the rolled ends of his trousers – they would stiffen and stain. The sackcloth bag by his side suddenly twitched and a large crab scuttled out from it; it paused in the sunlight and then darted down to the beach, instinct directing it towards the water. Declan shouted and kicked some sand over the orange and bronze creature; it stopped and then darted away at a tangent. Declan scooped it up and, wary of the snapping pincers, carried it back to the bag. He knelt in the sand and shook the bag open before dropping the crab into it where it struck with a sharp click, which immediately excited another dozen or more snapping claws. The grey-eyed young man carefully appraised the day's catch – a couple of pence certainly, maybe even sixpence – before pulling the neck of the bag tight. He glanced up at the sun: it was nowhere near its zenith, and therefore still too early to head into town for the market.

Declan carried the bag to the nearest pool and slowly immersed it, and then he placed a heavy stone over the mouth of the sack to prevent it from opening. The salt water would keep his catch fresh until it was time to go. He then climbed up to his usual place: a small hollow in the cliffs, enclosed on three sides and open to the skies. Within, the ground dipped slightly and the sand was pure and clean, still warm from the early morning sun and sheltered from the tendrils of breeze that blew in off the broad expanse of Blacksod Bay. From where he lay he could just make out the seal caves that pitted the cliff-face across the bay, and he knew that behind him and to his right lay the small fishing village of Doogort at the foot of Slievemore. He made himself comfortable in the soft sand and, resting his head on his crossed arms, closed his eyes and slept.

The morning wore on and the sun turned the sea into a vast panorama of molten silver rolling against the warmer bronze of the beach. The wind dropped and the heat rose in shimmering waves from the sands, and one by one all the sounds of the seashore died: no gulls called or mewled from the cliffs, nothing crawled or scuttled clacking down the beach and even the barking of the seals was silent. Time stood still.

And then the smooth reflective water of the bay was disturbed by a series of ripples that moved steadily in towards the beach. Something small and sleek broke the surface for a moment, disappeared, and then almost immediately reappeared again. The water foamed and fell in molten droplets from the creature that rose up out from the water, a dozen more following in its wake. The thirteen creatures moved up towards the beach, the sun clothing them in silver and gold, and the heat haze distorting their shapes.

Declan knew it was late when he awoke. The sand beneath

his body was cold and hard and his little nook was in deep shadow. He lay still wondering how long he had slept – it must be sometime after noon by now – but perhaps if he hurried he might still make the market. He eased himself to his feet, feeling his stiffened muscles protest and his bones creak like an old man's. He rubbed the base of his neck and twisted his head to and fro; he could hear ringing in his ears ... and then he realised that it wasn't in his ears!

Declan dropped to the sand again and pressed himself back against the cold wall; he could hear singing – or was it singing? It sounded like voices raised in conversation or laughter, but musical, so musical, and coming from the direction of the beach.

The young man lay flat on his stomach and edged his way towards the small cave mouth; this portion of the cliff was in shadow and he was reasonably certain that he could not be seen from below. He peered over the lip of stone and down onto the beach – and caught his breath in astonishment.

Twelve stately figures – men and women – moved slowly and fluidly around the central figure of a tall elderly man. The men were short and broad with dark glistening skin and short, tightly curled hair, while the women were taller and slimmer, their colouring lighter than that of the men and their hair longer and gleaming wetly in the sunlight. The old man standing in the centre of the slowly moving circle was almost as tall as the women, but his skin was cracked and seamed with a network of tiny wrinkles, and his short hair was silver-white.

Their mouths were moving and Declan strained to make out their words – and then he realised that the music he was hearing *was* their speech. It was low and gentle, almost like the sound of water over rounded pebbles, chattering, whispering, rich with the music of the sea.

He watched the circle break up into six couples, who continued to walk clockwise around the old man for a couple

141

of turns, and then each couple paused before him and bowed briefly before breaking out of the circle and disappearing in amongst the rocks.

Declan watched a couple lie down on the sand almost directly below him. Their movements were slow and stately, and they came free of their long cloaks with fluid ease. And then they began to make love in an unhurried, almost dance-like ritual.

The old man moved through the rocks and up the beach, his right hand moving in something akin to a blessing as he passed each couple and lifted up their shimmering cloaks. When he reached the last couple, just below Declan, the old man bent and murmured something to them; their laughter was light and studied, the sound like the foaming of the waves across weed. The grey-haired man walked past them and, almost at the mouth of the cave, stooped and arranged the bundle of cloaks on a broad flat stone; he then turned and retraced his steps down the beach.

A cloud slipped across the sun and shadow raced after him, leeching the colour from the sea, robbing the sand of its heat. Declan watched it coming and shivered with the chill, but he waited until the area directly below him was darkened by the swiftly moving cloud before making his move. His arm snaked out, groped amongst the rocks until it touched something cold and smooth, and then quickly withdrew it.

He sat back in the small cave and examined the cloth carefully. It was a large rectangle of brown-black; almost silk-like cloth with two tiny whalebone buttons at the throat. He ran his fingers through the short hair-like tendrils and felt its sensuous touch send ripples up along his arm. He held it up and what little light remained in the small cave ran like liquid along its surface and it was as smooth and supple as a length of rope.

It would fetch a pretty penny in Doogort.

He folded the cloak and slipped it inside the front of his shirt.

The stylised ritual lovemaking came to an end, and one by one the couples broke up and, first the men, and then the women, came and picked up their strange cloaks. They moved down the beach in a silent line and as they reached the water's edge they swung the cloaks up onto their shoulders and then threw themselves forward into the water. The mirror-bright waves foamed and splashed, hiding them completely and all that was visible was a triangular *V* cutting through the water towards the south.

But one remained; a dark-haired, dark-eyed young woman, clad in a long shift of almost translucent cloth. She stood silently over the spot where her cloak had lain, her eyes half-closed, her head tilted back and her broad nostrils dilated.

The young man shivered suddenly; there was something wild and elemental about her ... something terrifying. The woman's eyes snapped open, her head lowered and then she slowly turned towards the opening in the cliff. Her mouth moved and the strange liquid speech hung on the salt air between them. He didn't understand the words but the meaning was clear.

Declan stood, drawn out against his will. His hands trembled as they fumbled to pull out the gutting-knife from his belt.

The young woman smiled, exposing small pointed teeth and her dark eyes caught and mirrored the sunlight. Her arm came up, the green-tinged white cloth of her shift whispering as it slid along her bare skin, and she opened her hand. She spoke again, and this time the music seemed to blur and buzz within Declan's head, and he suddenly found he could understand what she was saying.

' ... *my cloak.*'

She took a step closer and Declan could smell her perfume; rich and sharp with the tang of the sea.

He took a step back and shook his head slowly. 'I ... I have no cloak,' he mumbled through thickened lips.

'Do not lie to me.' The music which underlay her words was sharp and discordant.

'What ... who are you?' he asked slowly, suddenly barely able to formulate simple sentences. He shook his head, attempting to clear the muzziness which clouded his thoughts.

The music shrilled discordantly, and then lapsed back into words. *'Give me back my cloak foolish mortal.'*

Declan took another step backwards. His foot slipped on a smooth stone and his ankle struck against another. The sudden pain brought him back to his senses. His hand found his knife and he dragged it free and waved it in front of the woman's face.

She smiled. *'Your puny weapon does not frighten me. We have faced the spears and thunder-sticks of your people for generations; we have no fear left in us. All we feel for you is loathing.'*

'What are you?' Declan demanded. 'Where have you come from?'

'I have come from a past age, a forgotten era.' She blinked slowly and deliberately, and her eyes lost their metallic glint. She gestured back down the beach towards the waves. *'You saw?'* She nodded without waiting for an answer. *'You saw. Know then that we are the last of the Rón, the Seal Folk, banished to the waves when the last of the People of the Goddess fled the fields of man. I am Eán; give me back my cloak.'*

The young man slowly pulled the cloak out from beneath his shirt. The cloth, now shining rich and translucent in the warm sunlight, was warm and sensuous to his touch. He ran the back of his hand along it, and shivered involuntarily; it

144

was softer than the finest calfskin.

Eán's short, slightly webbed fingers reached for the cloak. Declan jerked it back out of her reach and menaced her with the knife.

'Why do you need it?' he asked, his voice surprisingly calm.

'Once in every century we come forth from the seal caves to perform the Rite of Life, and consummate the sharing of life. Children born of the union will be like ourselves – creatures of both worlds, able to assume the form of man – but those conceived in the sea will be wholly of the sea. The cloak is our passport to this world of yours – without it, we would remain forever in the sea.'

'It is very beautiful,' Declan said quietly.

'It is.' Once again Eán reached for the cloak.

Declan drew back and his eyes half closed calculatingly. 'There is supposed to be treasure in the sea,' he mused. 'Didn't some of the ships from the Spanish Fleet that sailed against Elizabeth sink in these waters? And were they not supposed to be carrying gold and precious stones? Well, young woman, if you want your cloak back you must be prepared to pay for it.'

'It is beyond price,' Eán said quietly.

'Nothing is beyond price,' Declan grinned. 'Bring me a gold bar or a handful of jewels and I will give you back your cloak.'

'And if I do not?'

Declan held up the cloak and almost gently brought the point of the knife against the material. He pressed and the cloth seemed to melt under the tip of the blade. 'Well then, I would be forced to cut your lovely cloak up into ribbons and sell them to the farmers and fishermen's wives.'

'You are a cruel man, Declan Fitzpatrick,' the young woman said quietly.

The young man started. 'How do you know my name?' he demanded.

145

'*You are known. You hunt the little creatures of the rocks and pools; you are known.*' She turned away. '*Come with me then if you desire your treasure.*' She walked down the beach, the slight offshore breeze moulding her flimsy gown to her slight figure. Declan, walking behind her, watched the muscles bunch and ripple beneath her tanned flesh and he felt his desire rising: he would have one other treasure he decided ...

Eán stopped almost at the water's edge. White froth foamed about her bare feet and across her slightly webbed toes. She turned to Declan and held out her hand. '*Give me the cloak now.*'

'What?' he demanded, 'and have you swim off and leave me standing here like an *amadan*. One of the first lessons we learned at our mother's knee was never to take our eyes off the leprechaun when you caught him; as soon as you looked away he would be gone.'

'*We are not the Earth Folk,*' Eán said stiffly. '*The Rón keep their word.*'

'There are very few who keep their word nowadays,' Declan said grimly. 'But before you go, at least give me a kiss to remember you by.'

Eán backed away, her eyes wide in fear or horror. '*I will be back,*' she insisted.

'Oh, I don't think so,' Declan said. 'As soon as I give you this cloak you'll be gone, and I'll never see you again. And since I won't be getting any treasure, you can at least leave me something ...' His large hands reached for her, but she pulled away and his fingers caught the flimsy material of her shift and it came away in his hands. He dropped the torn cloth and the cloak and lunged for her; she stumbled backwards and together they fell into the shallows. Eán gasped and the breath was forced from her body as Fitzpatrick forced himself on top of her. A wave washed in over them and the salt stung her eyes and bit at her throat. Fear and desperation lent her strength and she sank her sharp teeth into his arm and pulled, drawing blood. He grunted in pain and struck out at her, but she twisted to one side and his blow only splashed the soft sand. Another wave washed in over them and Eán retched as she swallowed some of the salt water. In her present form she could drown.

The music was wild and disharmonious now, high, shrill and desperate. Declan was aware of it only as a mild discomfort at the base of his skull and along his teeth; he was far too intent upon satisfying his own lust.

And then the water boiled about them and Declan looked up into the face of a huge bull seal. It struck at him with large flippers, the blow rattling his teeth, almost cracking his jaw. Pain lanced through his leg as sharp teeth ripped through cloth and flesh. Another blow made his head ring and bloodied his nose, and then something struck him a massive blow across the chest sending him reeling backwards off the body of the Rón. He saw her scrambling up as he fumbled in the water for his knife ... and then a broad tail came up out of the water towards his head ...

It was almost sunset when he awoke, shivering and bloody. His face was puffed and both his nose and several of his teeth were broken. There was a sharp pain in his side whenever he breathed deeply, and there were two nasty open wounds on his thigh and shin.

Declan eased himself gently to his feet and stared across the darkening waters towards the seal caves dotted in the cliffs ... and counted himself lucky.

But in the end of course, the sea – or the Rón – claimed revenge. The following summer, during a particularly low tide, Declan Fitzpatrick wandered far out amongst the rocks in search of large crabs and other shellfish. And there he must have slipped on the weed-covered rocks, fallen and broken his ankle.

The tide washed his broken body ashore two days later.

Chapter Eight

THE CLURICAUN'S TALE

Will Slater stumbled over the cluricaun – literally! He was drunk again, and had somehow managed to wander off the road, but like most drunkards he had an innate sense of direction and he knew, somewhere deep within his pickled brain he knew, that if he kept his face to the sea breeze he would, sooner or later, arrive home.

It was a warm night, one of those September nights when the heat of the day clings to the ground, rendering sleep impossible and only dissipating close to dawn. Will had taken off his patched coat and carried it over his arm, the tails trailing in the dirt, the bottles in the deep pockets clinking pleasantly together.

He stopped in the middle of a field and pulled a squat, thin-necked bottle from his waistband, and attempted to guide it to his mouth. But he was swaying slowly from side to side and most of the whiskey snaked its way down his stubbled cheeks and onto his soiled shirt and waistcoat. The fat, middle-aged man gasped for breath as the alcohol burned his throat, staggered on – and fell. The bottle in his hand shattered and he cursed fluently in both Irish and English, but his fat had protected him from any real hurt and the only actual bruising had been to his pride. He sat up and dusted off his hands, and looked back over his shoulder to see what had thrown him ...

He was drunk. He knew he was drunk. He had set out that evening to get drunk; and he had succeeded gloriously. His

148

calloused hands dug frantically in the pockets of his coat for another bottle, but his thick fingers only touched wet cloth and glass fragments. Almost absently he withdrew his fingers and licked the drops of alcohol from them. He blinked slowly and deliberately, closed his eyes, squeezed them tightly, and blinked again. And again.

His father had died from drink: he had seen purple and green snakes writhing up the walls and bloated spiders with human faces crawling across the bedspread before he had eventually passed on. But he had never seen one of the Little People, or more particularly a cluricaun. Will blinked again. But the cluricaun was still there; lying either drunk or asleep beneath a bush.

A cluricaun – sometime called a leprechaun. No bigger than his arm, dressed in a red waistcoat, green jacket, long green hose and wearing a pair of huge black brogues with enormous silver buckles. A black three-cornered hat covered the creature's face, slowly rising and falling with its breathing. A pair of tiny wrinkled hands were crossed over its breast, and a white corn-cob pipe had fallen from its fingers.

Will Slater's first thought was of gold. Cluricauns were reputed to have a secret store of gold, and all one had to do was capture and hold the creature and make it tell where the hoard was hidden.

He slowly heaved his great bulk off the ground and then crept towards the tiny creature. He was inclined to think that the mannikin was drunk; else why hadn't it woken up when he had fallen over it? He opened his coat, the odour of raw whiskey assailing his nostrils, and crept closer to the creature.

The cluricaun stirred.

Will threw himself forward and wrapped the sopping coat about the tiny man. He hit the ground hard and rolled over, holding the squirming bundle to his broad chest. He heard tiny cries of anger and rage which quickly became

149

slurred as the whiskey-soaked cloth enveloped the creature in an alcoholic haze. And by the time Will – now completely sober – reached his mean two-roomed cottage, the cluricaun was singing at the top of its surprisingly strong voice, and its ribald song even made *him* blush.

Sean Og awoke in darkness with the mother-and-father of all hangovers; he hadn't felt this bad since the last Shoemaker's Ball, and then of course someone else had been buying the drink, but last night now . . . He frowned, his face dissolving into a mass of wrinkles; last night? Well, but he'd be dammed if he could remember last night; if it had been a party it must have been a good one, for he couldn't remember a thing about it.

The cluricaun groaned aloud and sat up – and struck his throbbing skull against something hard and wooden. He groaned again, and tried blinking away the dancing coloured lights that swam before his eyes. He stretched out his foot, and the hard leather sole of his shoe struck wood, and when he reached out on either side his calloused fingers once again touched smooth wood.

He sat up again, more cautiously this time, until he felt the top of his balding head touch the top of the box – for that, he reasoned, was what he was in. He hammered on the walls, the sound booming inside the box, making his head ring. 'Oy, let me out,' he shouted, or rather, attempted to shout, but his throat felt as if it had been scrubbed down with soapstone, and it came out as little above a whisper. He tried again. 'Let me out.'

Will Slater awoke feeling sick, his head pounding in long slow waves. He had passed a restless night, dreams of wealth and riches drifting across his subconscious, bringing him awake every hour or so. He would be rich; he would have everything he had ever wanted, everything he had ever dreamed about ... and yet he still felt curiously dissatisfied.

He broke his fast hastily on milk and eggs, his red-rimmed eyes never leaving the small oaken chest into which he had thrown the cluricaun. He heard it awake and noisily explore its surroundings, and had listened to its tiny cries with a thin smile on his lips. He had ignored them.

It was almost midday when he returned to the cottage. Outside the sun was at its zenith and slowly peeling back the surface of the earth, exposing it like a gaping wound, and then bleaching it dry, discarding it and going onto another layer. Will stopped by the door, allowing his eyes to adjust to the dimness of the interior, feeling the sweat dry on his corpulent body. He waited, listening, and when he was sure that there was no sound from the box, crept across the hard earthen floor and knelt beside it. He was tempted to crack open the lid and peer within, but that he knew was what the cluricaun wanted. He rapped on the side of the box with his knuckles.

Sean Og came awake with a start, cracking his head once again against the lid of the box. He swore and rubbed the swelling atop the swelling on the crown of his head. 'Let me out,' he demanded.

'Never – at least, not until you give me your crock of gold,' the rasping voice amended.

'Never, at least, not until you let me out.' Sean Og smiled in the darkness. If the box were only opened for a second he would be gone, and then God help the Big Fellow who had captured him: he wouldn't have another day's peace for the rest of his life.

'Tell me where you keep your treasure,' the voice demanded.

'Let me out and I'll show you,' Sean Og wheedled.

'No!'

The cluricaun shrugged; that wasn't really playing the game. 'If you don't let me out now, I'll never speak to you again,' he said petulantly.

'Tell me where your treasure is and I'll let you out; otherwise you'll stay where you are!'

The cluricaun then made a suggestion as to where the Big Fellow could go look for his treasure and Slater, in turn, hammered on the box with all his might, making the creature's head ring.

And that was that.

Every morning thereafter Will would ask the cluricaun the whereabouts of his treasure, and every morning he would receive no reply. He knew the creature was alive; often he would hear the metallic tapping of a cobbler's hammer – although what the creature was working on was beyond him. Once he awoke to find the cottage dark with a thick pall of malodorous smoke; he panicked and jumped from his bed, and was half way out the door before he realised that it was coming from the box: the cluricaun was smoking.

It was about three years later that Will found the small stack of driftwood down by the shore. It was bright yellow wood, and the sea and weather had worked it into a variety of unusual shapes. He had carefully polished it with an oily rag and then taken it into town where he sold it to a visitor for a few pence. That evening the cluricaun laughed in his deep base voice, and continued laughing far into the night.

Will lost weight, and the excess skin hung in flaps on his face and body, and what little hair he had had fell out, leaving his head totally bald and skull-like. His watery eyes retreated into shadows, and he took to talking to himself. He still drank, but now he wasn't so particular what he drank, and took to buying a couple of bottles of locally brewed poteen from the hill farmers. It was deceptively clear – almost like water – but it would take the varnish off a table or scour rust from a piece of metal.

And then one day his brother came to visit, having heard rumours of Will's increasing ill health and haggard appearance. They had argued – which was usual – and Tomas fled from the house without even waiting for a cup of tea. Half-way down the path he slipped and broke his leg in two places. The cluricaun was laughing when Will returned from the doctor's late that evening and was still laughing when the sun rose in the morning.

As the years passed Will grew increasingly eccentric. He would often spend hours wandering the hills and marshes talking aloud, planning how he would spend his fortune. The townspeople took to avoiding him, for he had a violent temper, which was apt to flare up if he thought someone was even looking curiously at him. But when he was in his cups he would often talk of his treasure, his secret hoard, and although most people just laughed at the idea, there were a few who took the trouble to wander out to his cottage to investigate. And then the stories that Will Slater's cottage was haunted began to circulate. Voices were heard in the cottage, and sometimes a short ringing sound accompanied a bass singing, and occasionally puffs of curling black smoke would drift across the empty room.

And the townspeople shook their heads and some prayed for the lonely drunkard who had obviously been driven out of his wits by the spirit that was haunting him.

In the twelve years that Will Slater kept the cluricaun prisoner – after that first brief conversation – the only sound it made (except for the hammering, of course) was to laugh three times.

It was winter; one of the hardest winters Ireland had experienced in a long time. What crops remained in the fields were destroyed and the rivers and streams froze into solid blocks of ice. Food and fuel quickly ran short, and there were whispers of famine abroad ...

Will quickly used up what little fuel he had about the house and, with no drink left, he was forced to make the long journey into town. He was also forced to use a little of his savings. Some years previously, when he had realised in one of his sober moments that his drinking was becoming serious, he had buried some money in a small cask at the bottom of the field that abutted onto his cottage, and at the same time had made the resolve never to touch it except in the direst emergency. He had often been tempted, but somehow had always managed to resist that temptation – until now. Digging up the cask was back-breaking work, for the ground was like iron and the wood and metal of the spade and pick were so cold that they burned his hands. It took him nearly two hours to dig down the three feet to the money. There was nearly twelve pounds in the little cask – a sizeable amount for the time – but he only removed three and reburied the rest.

When he returned from town with his fuel, food and drink, the cluricaun was laughing again.

Slater was three-parts drunk and, tossing the wood and turf to one side, putting the bottles and parcel of food on the table, he crossed to the box and wrenched open the lid. His calloused hands closed on the surprised mannikin, threatening to snap him in half, and brought him back out into the cold light of day.

The cluricaun looked much as he had done almost twelve years ago when Will Slater had first stumbled over him. Perhaps his clothes looked slightly shabbier, and his hair and beard were somewhat longer, but his shoes still sparkled as if they had been made that morning – and perhaps they had, for the cobbler had little else to do

Will held the struggling creature up before his face. 'In twelve years you've done nothing but laugh twice – and for no apparent reason – and I demand to know why you're laughing now!'

Sean Og smiled innocently and stuck his pipe in his mouth. Will grabbed the pipe and ground it into splinters in his hand. 'Tell me!' he roared, 'or by Christ I'll do the same to you.'

The cluricaun looked at the Big Fellow before him and sighed resignedly. 'Well,' he began conversationally, 'do you remember the first time I found something to laugh about?'

Will frowned and slowly shook his head; it had been so many years ago now.

'Ach, you remember,' the cluricaun said, 'it was that time you found that unusual yellow wood down on the beach ...'

He nodded, suddenly remembering.

'Well, that was part of the wreckage of a ship that went down off this coast a little over three hundred years ago. You probably don't remember, but there was a storm the night before: it carried the wreckage to the surface ...'

'I don't see ...' Will said doubtfully.

'One of the pieces you sold for a pittance was hollow,' the cluricaun paused and added in a slightly malicious voice, 'and it was filled with gold coins.'

Will felt his heart miss a beat and the blood rush to his face.

'The second time I laughed ... do you remember that?' Sean Og asked.

'When my brother fell,' Will muttered.

'Aye, when your brother fell and broke his leg. Now, if you and he hadn't fought, and he had stayed just a little while longer, he would never have fallen.' The cluricaun cocked an eyebrow at the Big Fellow. 'It's funny, don't you think?' He shrugged at Will's expression. 'Well, perhaps not then.'

'And now,' Slater said through gritted teeth, 'why were you laughing just now?' He was in a towering rage, the cords standing out in his neck and the veins in his temples throbbing furiously.

'You dug up some money this morning,' the cluricaun said. 'But you left quite a bit behind – and while you were in

155

town a knacker wandering by, wondered why someone had gone to all the trouble of digging a hole in this weather and then filling it in, and so he investigated. Well, you can imagine his surprise in finding quite a little hoard ...' The cluricaun began to laugh again ... 'It's funny, it really is ...'

Slater screamed aloud, a red haze falling down over his vision. He flung the cluricaun to one side and raced from the cottage, down into the field. Half-way across the icy field he could see the disturbed earth, the black hole in the whitened earth. He was screaming aloud, although he didn't realise it; his heart was pounding furiously, and his head was threatening to burst with its throbbing. He stood over the hole and his clenched fists pounded against his sides again and again ...

Something flickered at the corner of his eye. He looked up to see the cluricaun casually walking past him, his three-cornered hat at a jaunty angle, a new pipe in his mouth. He paused and winked slyly at the Big Fellow. Slater felt the anger boil up and overflow within him; he threw himself forward after the creature, but his foot slipped on the ice-slick grass and he fell. He scrabbled to his feet, slipped and fell again ... His red tinged sight was now turning black at the edges. He slipped again and felt the pain ...

There is a local legend which relates how, on a winter's night, in the local churchyard, a cluricaun will come and sit on one of the headstones, and hammer incessantly on an already perfect shoe. But then, Will Slater was a 'character' in life, and it's not unusual to find that he still has something of the same reputation even after his death – which in itself is noteworthy. It seems he went wandering out into the fields without a coat on a bitterly cold day. He then fell into a hole and, although there is evidence to suggest that he attempted to rise to his feet, it seems he never succeeded. The cause of death was put down as exposure, but the doctor's own report hints at something more, for in it he states that there was a look of absolute ferocity frozen onto Will Slater's face ... and what about the tiny footprints found in the snow beside him?

Chapter Nine

POTEEN

'Christ!' John Joe spat the clear liquid onto the ground.
'Tastes like piss.'

'Let me,' his brother, Paddy Joe said, leaning in over the
rusted barrel and dipping a battered tin can into the
bubbling mixture. He carefully brushed off the evil-looking
froth and breathed in the vapour: his eyes immediately
watered and his nose began to run. He sipped cautiously,
and then copied his brother and spat the liquid onto the
ground. 'By God, but that's a powerful batch you've brewed
up for us now.'

John Joe nodded glumly. 'Aye, but we'll never sell it.' He
ran his short stubby fingers through his greying hair. 'No
one will drink the stuff.'

His younger brother chewed thoughtfully on a ragged
thumb nail. 'Is there nothing you can do to it,' he asked
eventually, 'add more sugar or something?'

'I suppose we can try.'

'Or ... maybe we could water it down,' his brother added
diffidently.

John Joe glared at him; no one was adding water to his
poteen!

The brothers were in the process of adding more sugar to
the bubbling poteen when they heard the short shrill
whistle from the field below the cottage: excise men
coming!

They had about five minutes. The bags, bottles and cans

were tucked away into their respective hiding places, and by the time their youngest brother ran up, red-faced and out of breath, only the large bubbling vat remained. 'They're on their way up,' Micky Joe panted. 'Two of them; a couple more in the village. What'll we do?'

John Joe swore. They had a couple of gallons of almost drinkable poteen ready, and now to lose it all to a couple of nosy excise men ...

'We can't dump it,' Paddy Joe said suddenly. 'Micky, you hook up the tube and we'll drain it off ...'

'But there's no time,' Micky Joe said frantically, 'they're too close.'

'Then there's only one thing for it,' John Joe snapped and, putting his shoulder to the large drum, tipped it over. The clear liquid disappeared into the already damp ground and the bitter-sweet odour was blown away on the breeze. Micky Joe scuffed his foot on the sodden ground, rubbing away the ugly scum that had been bubbling on the top of the liquor.

And when the two excise men arrived five minutes later they found the three brothers industriously attending to the worn thatch on the cottage.

'Well, well, what do we have here,' John Miller said loudly to his companion. 'If it isn't John, Paddy and Micky Joe – and all working too ... probably for the first time in their lives I shouldn't wonder,' he added with a grin.

'A good day to you, sir,' John Joe said, climbing down off the roof. 'What can we do for you today, eh?' He looked at each man in turn. 'Could we offer you a little something, perhaps?' And then he added with a sly grin, 'There's tea freshly made, and there's some ice cold milk.'

John Miller turned to his companion, an older man with florid cheeks and a thick beard, smoking a pipe. 'As you can see, the MacCarthys are a hospitable lot.' He turned back to John Joe. 'But are you sure now you wouldn't have anything stronger about the house, eh?' He sniffed the air. 'Is that sugar I smell?' he asked innocently.

'That's God's own breeze,' Paddy Joe said quickly, 'blessed with the smell of turf and heather.'

'It smells like sugar to me,' the older man said quietly.

'The air always smells sweet up here,' John Joe said.

'This is Mr Ferguson, my superior,' Miller said to the three brothers. 'He is on a tour of inspection of this region. Can we go in?' he asked and, without waiting for an answer, entered the small evil-smelling cottage. John Joe hurried in after them, while the two younger brothers remained outside, frantically checking for anything that might give them away and implicate them in poteen making. But the only evidence that they could see was the soaking ground that squelched with every step and oozed clear 'water'.

Miller and Ferguson reappeared some moments later; Ferguson holding a large handkerchief to his face and even Miller, who should have been used to it, was looking slightly green. Behind them John Joe winked at his two brothers. 'Will that be all gentlemen,' he asked, smiling at their discomfort.

Ferguson nodded dumbly and concentrated on lighting up his pipe, attempting to dispel the foul odour that still clung to him with the fragrant tobacco.

'Have you been keeping animals in there?' Miller demanded.

'Aw sure, we're only poor country folk, we don't have room for cow barns and the like,' John Joe said slowly. Behind the two men, Paddy Joe began to choke with laughter, and his older brother glared at him. The cottage John Joe had shown the two excise men was now only used for keeping sheep in winter!

'It reeks,' Ferguson rumbled, puffing on his pipe, the glow from the bowl lighting up the waxed tips of his moustache. He struck another long match and pulled strongly on the flame.

'Aye, well ...' Miller said thoughtfully, 'I know you've been up to something, and I'll be back,' he warned.

'Oh, we'll look forward to that,' Paddy Joe promised.

'A good day to you then,' Miller snapped and turned away.

Ferguson allowed his gaze to drift over the three brothers in what he thought was a stern and warning manner, but which only succeeded in making him look like a short-sighted goat. 'Good day, then,' he rumbled and, turning away, tossed the match on the damp ground ...

Eight miles away in Aughacasala the townspeople heard what sounded like the distant rumble of thunder, but thought nothing of it; there was a storm due anyway.

Chapter Ten

THE CATSPELL

'You know he'll never marry you,' Grannia said to Sinead as they crossed the field towards the house. The dark-haired, dark-eyed young woman smiled secretly and whispered, almost to herself. 'Oh, we'll see about that.'

'But he does not love you,' Grannia protested.

Sinead glanced across at her companion. 'But I love him,' she stated flatly.

The older girl shook her head in exasperation, the fading sun catching highlights in her reddish-bronze hair, burnishing it to gold. 'He'll ruin you – take my word for it. He'll end up marrying one of those fancy women in Dublin or London; you're just a bit of a diversion for him on his holidays.'

Sinead gazed dreamily up at the orange and black-tipped clouds riding in from the west. 'Oh, but he's handsome and kind ... and wealthy,' she added.

Grannia laughed. 'And why shouldn't he be; his father owns most of the land hereabouts.'

'He'd make a fine catch.'

'But you won't catch him,' the older girl said finally.

Sinead's dark eyes snapped open, and Grannia felt a chill wash over her, for they were flat and cold and merciless. 'He will marry me,' she persisted, her voice low and hoarse, 'and you can help me.'

'Me?' Grannia whispered.

'You can meet me tonight outside Leary's Pub, an hour or so after closing time.'

'I can't; I won't be able to sneak out,' Grannia protested weakly.

'Of course you will,' her friend insisted, 'you've done it before – and you'll do it for me, won't you?'

'What are you going to do?'

'Oh, you'll have to wait and see. But come along tonight – and you'll dance at my wedding, I promise you.'

Giles Blackburn vaulted the low stone wall and strode across the hard, dry ground towards the cottage, whistling tunelessly between his slightly prominent teeth. He wasn't half-way across the yard when the cottage door opened suddenly and Sinead darted out, raced towards him and threw herself into his arms.

Giles staggered back and attempted to disengage the young woman. 'Steady ... steady on now,' he said pleasantly. He moved resolutely towards the open door, only too conscious that anyone could come along the road at any moment and, whatever his own reputation, he would do nothing that could anger his father – and threaten his allowance.

Once amidst the darkness of the tiny cottage however he kicked the door shut with his heel and, wrinkling his nose against the sharp, acrid turf smoke that permeated the entire room and clung to everything, he kissed Sinead deeply. His soft hands moved slowly up and down the young woman's back, feeling the smooth ripple of muscles beneath her thin cotton blouse. He held her close to his chest and he could feel the pounding of her heart against his ribs ...

With a gasp Sinead pulled away. In the semi-darkness he could see that her face was flushed and that she was breathing deeply. 'Why, I'm quite out of breath,' she panted, both hands going to her cheeks, feeling their heat.

'So am I,' Giles said, staring intently at her. 'You do that to me.'

She smiled, and for an instant Giles loathed himself for what he was doing. The girl was beautiful, very beautiful: a small, heart-shaped face surrounded by a mane of thick black hair, which matched the colour of her large, wide eyes. Her lips were full and red and her cheeks were glowing with health – and not the artificial colouring that city women were forced in many cases to use. She would make some farmer a fine wife . . . and in a few years she would be old and fat, aged beyond her time with the bearing of too many children . . .

The young man smiled sardonically; that was, of course, if she could find herself a husband once it became known that she had been friendly with the landlord's son.

'What are you smiling at?' Sinead asked quietly.

'At you.'

'At me? Why?'

'Oh, because I love you,' he said softly.

She stepped closer to him, and he could smell the corn sweetness of her hair and the freshness of her recently washed skin. 'Do you Giles, do you really?'

'You know I do.' He reached out and his fingertips touched her shoulder and began a slow descent onto the curve of her breast.

'And will you marry me, Giles?' she asked, a note of pleading in her voice.

His hand stopped. 'I've said that I will,' he said carefully, not liking the way the conversation was turning.

'When?' she demanded, a hard note coming into her voice. They had had this conversation before, and the answers were always the same.

'When we're ready,' he said cautiously. His hand moved fractionally lower.

Sinead pulled away. 'You've told me that before,' she accused. '"When we're ready . . . when we're ready."' She swung around and faced him. 'Will we ever be ready?' she demanded.

Giles stepped back at the fierce light in her eyes. He forced a smile. 'Of course we will; time ... all we need is time.'

Sinead smiled bitterly. 'All you want is this!' Her hands rose and touched her small breasts through the cloth of her blouse. 'And what happens then? You'll no longer need me, nor want me. If you ruin me my father will throw me out, and I'll end up selling myself in the pubs or on the streets for the price of a meal – is that what you want?' she suddenly screamed.

The young man took her into his arms, and pressed her face to his chest, more to stifle her shouts than anything else. He stroked her long hair, murmuring softly as if to a child, and wondering frantically if anyone had heard her.

'Hush now, hush; I've said I'll marry you – and I will, in a while, in a month perhaps. I can't just now; I've got to work my way around my father, convince him that we really love one another. Look,' he said desperately, 'I'll take you up to Dublin in the next few days, and we'll pick out a fine dress and some shoes ... How does that sound?'

Sinead nodded dumbly. She slowly pushed away from him and wiped her eyes with the back of her hand. 'That sounds nice ... very nice,' she said quietly. He reached out for her but she pushed his hand away. 'No! I'm ... I'm not feeling well ...' And then she smiled through her tears. 'You can go now, but come to me tomorrow night. My father's going to town in the morning – and he usually stops in for a few drinks with his cronies; he won't be home till late. It'll be just you and me.' She smiled again and ran her fingernails down his stubbled cheek. 'Until tomorrow night then ...' And then she turned away and disappeared into the other room.

Giles waited a few moments to see if she would reappear, but then turned away and wrenched open the cottage door. He paused blinking on the threshold for a moment and then pulled the door closed behind him.

The young man strode jauntily down the dirt road towards the town. He would never understand women – and especially Irish women. One moment she was going on about her ruined reputation and the next she was telling him that her father would be away which would give them time together; he shook his head in wonderment.

He glanced back at the cottage. There was a small figure standing in the doorway and a white arm rose and waved him goodbye. He waved back and blew a kiss, smiling broadly in anticipation of the following night.

But if he had been able to see Sinead's expression, or the cold look in her dark eyes, then perhaps he might not have gone on his way so merrily.

Sinead touched Grannia on the shoulder and pointed. The red-haired woman started, and then squinted into the darkness in the direction of her friend's pointing finger. The moon slipped free of its covering cloud and illuminated the long row of mean cottages and tiny shops in silver and shadow. In the sharp light the young woman could see the low sleek shape of a cat slinking through the laneway opposite. There was a rustle of cloth by her side and then Sinead darted across the street towards the darkened lane. Grannia hesitated for a moment, and then gathered up her skirts and followed.

She found Sinead on her knees in the mouth of the alley, whispering sibilantly, an evil-smelling fish-head in her hand. For a moment nothing happened, and then the shadows moved and the cat came forward slowly, its back arched, treading carefully on its claws, the fur on its neck and spine rigid. It stopped before Sinead and spat, before darting forward to snap at the fish-head. Her hand closed about the creature's neck, catching the mangy fur and twisting it, pulling it up off the ground. The cat screamed and spat, its claws catching and raking her hand. Grannia

166

fumbled with the rough sack Sinead had given her earlier, and held it open while her friend dropped the struggling creature within. Sinead then snatched the sack and, holding the mouth tightly in both hands, swung it hard against the wall of the alley. There was a sickening crunch and the sack went limp.

There was silence for a long time after that, and then Sinead turned back to Grannia, who was crouching back against the cold stone wall, her eyes wide with fear and her hands to her mouth. 'Go home now,' she said gently. 'It is done ...' The moon slipped free from the clouds and turned her eyes to flat silver discs. 'Forget what you have seen ...'

The red-haired woman nodded briefly, turned and slipped from the alley and down the moonlit street. She held her arms across her chest, holding herself, and she was shivering violently; for the killing of the cat had touched something deep within her, some primeval memory that whispered of magic!

'You're a fine cook, Sinead, I'll say that for you.' Giles leaned back on the hard wooden chair and loosened the buttons on his waistcoat. 'You'll make someone a grand wife ...' He coloured and stopped, realising what he was saying. But Sinead only smiled and turned away to the open fire.

'Would you like some more tea?' she asked quietly.

'Tea? Tea, yes, that would be nice.' The young man leaned forward and rested his elbows on the table as he watched her bend over the heavy black kettle, noting how her breasts strained against the thin cotton of her blouse and the glimpse of ankle beneath her heavy woollen skirt. He shook his head slowly and sat back, tilting the chair on its two rear legs, and stared up at the smoke and time-stained beams.

Sinead risked a glance over her shoulder, and then quickly pulled the small cloth bag from the niche beside the fire. Still rattling the kettle with one hand, she deftly pulled the drawstrings open with her teeth and poured the reddish-brown powder into the steaming water, which immediately took on a faint pinkish tinge. She poured the boiling water into the teapot and the coloration was lost as the tea darkened the water.

'I hope you like it strong,' she said, handing him a chipped china cup.

Giles nodded. 'The stronger the better,' he grinned, and then grimaced as the scalding tea burned his mouth – and the tea *was* strong with a brackish saline taste that was reminiscent of the sea.

Sinead moved slowly around the table and stood behind the seated man. She placed both hands on his shoulders and began to work her small hard fingers into the muscles. Giles tilted his head back and smiled up at her, feeling a sudden, almost overwhelming wave of desire rise up inside him. She leaned forward and kissed him, her lips briefly brushing his, sending shivers down along his spine. Sinead smiled and watched as his eyes began to glaze, and then she whispered a *word* into his open mouth ...

The young man convulsed, his muscles spasming and locking. The hair on his neck and the back on his hands rose stiffly, and the light of intelligence in his eyes died completely to be replaced by a blank glassy stare. Sinead smiled triumphantly down into his upturned face and waited until the last of the muscle tremors had ceased. She then bent forward and began to hiss insistently into his face. '*You love me ... you love me ... you love me ... you will marry me ... you will marry me ... you will marry me ...*'

'I love you,' Giles Blackburn repeated numbly, 'I will marry you.'

'I don't mind telling you that I think you're a charlatan, and that I'm wasting my time here,' Henry Blackburn snapped, his usually florid complexion now crimson and glowing.

168

'Then why are you here?' the old woman asked, smiling slightly at the other's discomfort in the tiny cottage.

'Because ... because ...'

'Because you're desperate,' the old woman said. She turned away from the large man and looked across at the woman sitting across from her on a low stool. 'Why have you brought Mister Blackburn here, Nora?'

The woman smiled shyly. 'Well, I'm the cook for the squire as you know, and he's in trouble, but being English he doesn't see it for what it is.'

The old woman slowly shook her head, her hard eyes darting from the large woman to the tweed-clad landlord. 'Start at the beginning, Nora,' she said gently, 'tell me what you mean.'

'You are Nano Hayes,' Blackburn interrupted, 'the local wise woman or witch or whatever you're called around here. My son – usually a sensible enough lad – has been acting very strangely recently, and has even gone so far as to propose marriage to one of my tenant's daughters ... a pleasant enough lass,' he added hastily.

'But not a suitable match for your son,' Nano Hayes finished.

'No,' the landlord said roughly, 'not a suitable match. I know something is wrong; Giles is a fine lad – high-spirited I know, but not foolish, and certainly not stupid enough to propose marriage to a country girl.'

'And especially not an Irish country girl,' the old woman added with a sly smile.

'That's not the point,' the Englishman said slowly. 'It's ... it's that he's not well ... he's not been acting himself recently.' He shook his head and spread his hands. 'I've tried everything, but the doctors say he's fit and well, and I know no one in the town is selling him drink.'

'You're not suggesting that because I have a certain reputation that I might have ... cast a spell on him?'

'What? Of course not!' Blackburn snapped, but the old

woman detected a note of doubt in his voice.

'And then again, he might just be in love with her,' she suggested quietly.

'What! Nonsense; he's already engaged to a very respectable young woman in London.'

Nano Hayes turned back to Nora. 'Why have you brought Mister Blackburn here; this doesn't seem like something for me.'

The fat cook wrung her hands and looked across at the old woman through eyes that were suddenly brimming with tears. In the dancing flames of the fire Nano Hayes looked thin and insubstantial, almost wraithlike. She had been old when Nora had been a girl – indeed, she had arranged Nora's match, and now she had three fine grown-up daughters, with two of them already married – and how old would the old woman be now? It was said that she had some of the *gentry*'s blood in her, and they were reputedly long-lived, but all she herself knew was that in her lifetime Nano Hayes had not aged one whit.

'You know Grannia?' she began quietly.

'Your youngest?'

'Aye, that's the one. Well she has been having terrible nightmares lately, and screaming about eyes and cats, bags and potions and weddings. I called in the priest, but he only blessed her and said it was tiredness and not getting the right food, and that there was nothing to be worrying about. And the doctor said the same.

'But a few nights ago I sat up all night with her. She was talking and crying in her sleep, and going on as if she were wide awake, and then I started to ask her a question or two – and, Mother of Divine God, but didn't she answer me!'

Nano Hayes nodded. 'That can happen,' she said quietly.

Nora leaned forward on the stool and her voice dropped to little more than a whisper. 'Nano, she spoke of her friend Sinead O'Dwyre catching a black cat and killing it by beating it to death ...' The woman's voice trailed off in horror.

The old woman sat back, her breath hissing through her yellowed and worn teeth. '*Aaah,* it becomes clear.'

'What becomes clear, what are you talking about?' The landlord pushed himself to his feet. 'Talking rubbish, absolute rubbish ...'

'Sit down!' Nano Hayes snapped, her voice cracking in the dim, shadowy room, and almost unconsciously Henry Blackburn subsided into his chair. The old woman turned her head and stared at him, her grey eyes large and glittering in the firelight. 'You are ignorant – and that excuses you somewhat, but do not let your ignorance blind you to the facts. However, persist in your stupid attitude and you will surely lose your son.' The old woman leaned forward and tapped him on the knee. 'You are lucky that Nora here is wise in the ways of the country; there are not many alive now that would recognise the catspell.'

'The catspell?' Blackburn said quietly.

Nano Hayes sat back in her chair and the shadows raced in and enfolded her, until only the pale oval of her face and her bird-bright eyes were visible. 'The catspell is one of the most ancient love charms known to man,' she said quietly.

'But ... but a cat!' Blackburn protested.

The old woman smiled briefly. 'Since the earliest times cats have always been associated with mystery and magic, and the ancients even had a cat-headed goddess. It is said that cats are not truly of this world; that is one of the reasons witches used them as familiars – the spirits from the Otherworld easily inhabited the body of the feline rather than something wholly from this world.

'It is possible to kill and cure with the body of a cat,' the old woman continued, 'and cats can bring both sickness and death and, under the proper conditions, carry it away with them. And if a woman wishes to bind a man to her,' she said, her voice barely above a whisper, 'then she will find a cat, a black cat, and slay it with violence but without touching it and in the name of the Evil One. The very life essence of the creature is then dedicated to *him*, and in return the body and organs may be used in *his* name to work *his* will. The cat's liver or brain is then cut out and dried, and ground into a powder in the light of a full moon. Added to food or drink the powder renders the man open to suggestion, and then the woman works her will upon the man, holding and binding his soul and senses to hers.'

'Superstitious nonsense!' the landlord snapped, but there was a note of doubt in his voice and his eyes looked troubled.

The wise woman smiled. 'And yet you tell me that your son has been acting strangely recently, has professed undying love for this girl and, I shouldn't wonder, even threatened to take his own life if he is not allowed to wed her?'

The landlord nodded.

'And yet you claim he is a sensible lad!'

Henry Blackburn stared into the glowing coals for a long time before turning back to the old woman. 'Tell me what I must do,' he said quietly.

Giles Blackburn leaned back against the cold, damp wall sipping the scalding hot tea, watching Sinead dress. She smiled across the bed at him and then provocatively turned her back as she buttoned up her cotton blouse. She walked slowly around the rumpled bed and brushed past him, out into the cottage's only other room. Giles followed her, placed the chipped cup on the table and, wrapping his arms around her waist, laid his head on her shoulder. 'I love you,' he whispered, his breath warm and moist against her ear. She giggled and struggled around to face him, staring deep into his eyes, watching the light beginning to fade as the potion began to take effect again, dulling his senses, inflaming his lust. 'Marry me!' he breathed heavily.

'Yesss,' she hissed and pulled his face down on a level with hers.

The door of the cottage suddenly slammed inwards, crashing off the wall and coming loose from one of its hinges. The room filled with men, some of whom Sinead vaguely recognised. One grabbed her arm, dragged her away from Giles and sent her spinning against the wall, where she slumped down, dazed. Giles went for the knife in his back pocket, and then a short stick rapped him across the elbow, numbing his arm; another blow caught him in the pit of his stomach, doubling him up; and then another blow across the back of the head sent him crashing to the floor.

Henry Blackburn preceded Nano Hayes into the cottage. The landlord knelt by his unconscious son, and touched blunt fingers to the lump on the back of his head. He looked up at the man standing over his son. 'If you've harmed him ...' he warned.

'I've broken more heads than you've seen rents,' the man grinned, slapping the stick into the palm of his hand, 'and I know how hard to hit,' he added cheerfully. 'He'll wake up in an hour or so with a head the size of today and tomorrow.'

Blackburn looked up towards Nano Hayes. 'I can only hope you know what you're doing.'

The old woman came forward and looked down at the unconscious man. 'He'll be all right presently; lift him up now and take him back to his room. I'll follow along shortly.'

Four men came forward to lift the young man, when suddenly there was a scream from the other side of the room and Sinead threw herself forward, a heavy earthen pot in her left hand. She swung the pot at Nano Hayes, but she, with an agility surprising in such an old woman, stepped away from the blow, and one of the men struck the girl across the knuckles with his stick, and the pot flew from her hand and shattered against the wall. The girl then threw herself forward onto the man, but he casually backhanded her away from him, knocking her to the floor where she lay in a sobbing heap while the still unconscious Giles was carried out.

Back at the Manor Nano Hayes watched while Giles was undressed and laid on his bed. Under the watchful eye of both Henry Blackburn and his wife, she pressed a cold compress to the lump on the back of his head and then, opening her small bag, she removed a tiny glass bottle from a thick wad of wool. Henry Blackburn took a step forward and reached for the bottle, but Nano Hayes held it away from him.

'What is it?' he demanded.

'A ... cure,' the old woman said carefully. She held up the bottle and the liquid within sparkled emerald green in the late afternoon sunlight.

'Is it the antidote?'

Nano Hayes shook her head. 'There is no antidote to what he has been poisoned with. The drug he was given only dulled his mind, leaving it open to suggestion ... and there is nothing we can do to counteract that – except wait: time will heal him. This,' she held up the bottle, 'will only help him sleep and rest easy tonight and for the next few nights, until the actual potion has passed through his system. Like all drugs it must be renewed regularly, and from what you tell me Giles has been under its influence for some weeks now – he should be strongly addicted to it. He will need something to help him combat its effects.'

'But I thought you said that hitting him with the hazel sticks would help drive out the ... the ... the ...'

'Hitting him with the hazel sticks only nullified the spell briefly,' Nano Hayes explained, carefully measuring some of the green liquid into a half glass of water. 'As well as the potion, Sinead used an ancient spell to bind him to her. I used an equally ancient spell to counteract that part of it: the two opposites cancelling out each other.'

'What must we do now to keep Giles from that dreadful woman?' Mrs Blackburn asked quietly.

'He must be kept here, he must not be allowed to leave the room, and he must only eat and drink food and liquid that has been prepared in this house. He must have no alcohol and no fruit that is not from your own orchards. You must ensure that nothing he eats has been tampered with.' She bent over the bed and, lifting Giles' head, tipped a little of the green-tinged water down his throat.

'Is there anything else we can do?' Henry Blackburn asked.

The old woman glanced across at the couple standing by the door. She nodded briefly. 'Aye, there is one other thing you might do,' she said quietly. 'Pray.'

The first night Giles Blackburn ranted and raved, calling out Sinead's name over and over again, begging her to marry him. But he had been securely tied to the bed, and two of the landlord's men stood watching through the night. Nano Hayes came the following morning to administer the emerald liquid to the young man, who had by then fallen into an exhausted sleep, and that night he rested a little easier, although he still cried out Sinead's name. The third morning Giles was awake when Nano Hayes arrived, and he refused to drink the green-tinged water. The old woman smiled gently and shook her head, and then suddenly cracked her calloused hand across his face. While he was still shocked and dazed she held his jaws in iron fingers and poured the liquid down his throat.

And so it went on for four more days, but with Giles Blackburn becoming more lucid and clear-eyed with each passing day, until on the morning of the seventh day he actually swallowed the emerald liquid without a struggle. As Nano Hayes turned to leave, he said suddenly, 'I've been a fool, haven't I?'

The old woman turned back and smiled gently. 'Aye, you have, but we all make fools of ourselves at some time or another, and yours was not particularly of your own making.'

175

'The girl witched me, didn't she?'

Nano Hayes nodded. 'You could call it that,' she agreed.

'What will happen to me ... to her?' he asked quietly, looking down at his trembling hands.

'Nothing will happen to you, I should imagine. I should think however, that you will be sent back home or perhaps to the continent to recuperate. And in future,' she added with a sly smile, 'choose city-bred girls for your sport – or at least those with no knowledge of the country lore.'

'And Sinead; what will happen to her?' Giles asked.

'Justice is a mystery,' Nano Hayes said enigmatically, nodded briefly and left the room.

In a small country town it is almost impossible to keep anything secret for long, and the story of Sinead's attempted bewitching of the landlord's son was soon common knowledge. The local people, brought up in a staunchly Catholic country and with a horror of witchcraft, shunned the young woman, and in desperation she fled the town. Rumour placed her in Cork, and later in Waterford, but she never returned to her native town.

And some years later a small article appeared in the Freeman's Journal which, had Giles Blackburn read it, might have stirred some twinges of memory:

The city coroner today passed a verdict of accidental death on Miss Sinead O'Dwyre. Miss O'Dwyre, of an address in Rutland Street, died from blood poisoning when she was bitten in the neck by her pet cat.

But had Nano Hayes seen the article she might not have been surprised.

Chapter Eleven

THE BLACK CLOUD

It was back.

Seamus O'Rourke blinked away the sudden tears that stung his eyes, laid down the heavy bow-saw, crossed himself and began to pray. And although he was a tall, robust man, he was trembling like a whipped pup.

It had started some three weeks earlier. He had been clearing away the little field of scrubby woodland that bordered his strip of land, when he felt the chill fingers begin to trace their way down his spine and nestle in the small of his back and at the base of his skull. He was country born and bred, well versed in the country lore, and he knew without doubt that what he had just felt was a faerie blast. He shivered, and not with the cold, and made a mental note to leave a little something out on the doorstep for the *gentry* that night.

And then he had glanced up.

From where he was standing he could see the small white-washed cottage across the fields, with the diminutive figure of his wife moving to and fro outside it. But it was not that which held his attention: for directly above the house floated a thick black cloud. Seamus blinked and rubbed his hard hands across his eyes, but the cloud remained. It circled slowly above the thatched roof of the cottage, rippling and flowing as if disturbed by a strong wind, gradually drifting lower.

He felt the numbness begin then; sensation disappeared from his feet and slowly crept upwards, painfully encasing his legs in icy blocks. His vision began to darken about the edges, and startling splashes of colour darted across his retina. He fell forward onto his face, his legs now nothing more than slabs of icy stone ... and then the cock crowed.

The raucous cry cut through the morning air like the sudden rasp of a saw through wood, shocking the birds in the trees into flight, their cries and calls splintering on the air. Seamus immediately felt the excruciating return of circulation and his sight began to clear. The cock crowed again, and it seemed as if the whirling black cloud shivered like a piece of hammer-struck metal. And then the cock crowed for the third time. The cloud began to fragment, its dark colour lightening to a pale – almost white – grey and disappearing on the slight breeze that blew in over the mountains from the sea. Once again the chill fingers touched the fallen man, but briefly, like a feather touch, and then they were gone.

Seamus lay on the ground, his legs jerking and trembling of their own accord, his face spasming as pain lanced through the taut muscles of his calves and thighs. As the pounding in his ears subsided, he gradually became aware once again of the sounds of the morning: the wind whispering through the trees, the bird calls and the sudden flutter of wings, the creaking of wood and the paper-dry whisper of leaves across the ground. He also heard an irregular splashing sound which he realised was blood dripping from a burning scrape across his face. The old man rolled over and onto his back and breathed in the fresh morning air tainted with the distant tang of salt and the more fragrant odour of freshly cut wood. And he relished all the sights and sounds of that early September morning, for he knew he had just been touched by death.

*

It had happened again, some three days later. Once again he had been touched by the chill wind and then the cloud had gathered above his cottage and leeched him of his strength, leaving him numb and shivering as darkness closed in on his sight. And once again the cock had crowed three times, banishing the cloud.

And it happened again three days after that ... and again ... and again ...

But each time the cock had crowed and the cloud had disappeared.

By now Seamus lived in terror of the cloud, and every third day he would refuse to go out, and he remained indoors, drinking heavily. He lost weight and his features became haggard, his eyes sunken and lost. He took to watching the cock intently, and soon even began talking to the bird. And every morning when it crowed he would start from his bed with a scream.

And then, for over a week, the cock didn't crow and the black cloud didn't appear over the cottage, and Seamus began to hope that it was over.

But now it was back.

Marie O'Rourke jumped with fright when the cock crowed. She glanced across at the shadow of the sun on the floor: it was close to noon, and that bird had already crowed several times that morning. And she was getting sick and tired of it crowing at all hours of the day. She held her pounding head in her hands and then shouted at the bird standing on the window-ledge. It fluttered its tiny wings and crowed again.

It was worse this time. Although the cock had crowed twice now, the numbness was still there, whereas before it would have been clearing. His vision though *was* clearing, and he

179

could see the oval shape slowly drifting away from the house.

Marie squeezed her eyes shut and concentrated on breathing evenly. She couldn't take much more of this. First there was Shea coming home every second day now, cut and bruised, and now he had taken to sitting inside all day and drinking, and when she spoke to him he either ignored her, or snapped back.

And then there were the headaches. The doctor in the nearby town had told her that they were caused by worrying about her husband ... that they were nothing to unduly concern herself about ... and how long had they been married now ... over ten years and still no signs of any little ones ... well that's probably it then, a man of Seamus' age gets to worrying about heirs ... it will soon pass and everything will be fine ...

But the headaches persisted, and the crowing of the cock made it seem as if her head were about to explode. And on the window-ledge the cock puffed itself up once again, making ready to crow ...

One more time, if the cock would crow just one more time, then the cloud would go and the numbness would leave him. Just one more time.

The long-bladed, wooden handled kitchen knife neatly severed the bird's head just as it opened its beak to crow again. The blade buried itself in the window frame, and Marie fell backwards as the fountaining blood splashed over her. The bird's wings fluttered and its nails tore into the woodwork before it tumbled over and fell into the room, where it was quickly surrounded by a thickening pool of blood.

The cold slammed into Seamus like a fist, driving the breath from his lungs. It hammered at the base of his skull and encased his spine in a leaden sheath. The cock, if the cock crowed ...

The cloud above the cottage solidified into a dark whirling oval, and then, as Seamus looked up, it began to fragment, like wind-blown smoke, but leaving wisps and tendrils still hovering over and about the cottage. Seamus blinked, blinked again as his vision darkened, and then he cried aloud, for the remaining pieces of the fast disappearing cloud were taking on a shape. He squeezed his eyes shut, but when he opened them again the images remained: images of his long dead parents and brothers.

'Dearest God ...' he breathed. The chill abated somewhat when he spoke the Name, and he staggered to his feet, and then, half walking, half crawling he staggered across the fields towards his cottage.

Inside he found his wife sitting on a straight-backed wooden chair, her head buried in her hands, her tears staining the wooden table. Seamus leaned against the door frame, watching the colours dance before his eyes in time to his pounding heartbeat. 'The cock ...' he gasped.

Marie gestured wanly towards the window.

Seamus fell across the room towards the window, clinging tightly onto the few pieces of furniture and the walls. He sank to his knees beside the headless cock, and then turned to stare up at his wife. 'Woman,' he whispered, 'you have killed me!'

It was some days before anyone from the nearby town

181

chanced to pass by the lonely cottage. As is usual with country folk they turned off the road and took the winding path that led up to the cottage, to pass a few words with Seamus and his wife.

They found Seamus O'Rourke lying dead beside a decapitated cock, and while there was plenty of blood, none of it seemed to be his. They also found Marie O'Rourke lying asleep in the bed in the next room. And when they woke her they found she was quite mad, and she talked incessantly of cocks crowing ... and a dark cloud ... and the cold ... the terrible cold.

And when the story went around the town, those wise in the country lore nodded their heads sagely, for hadn't they warned Seamus about clearing that patch of scrubland that touched on his fields, for wasn't it sacred to the *gentry*, and wasn't the Black Cloud of Torment one of *their* own special punishments?

Chapter Twelve

THE CARD PLAYER

The last of the late night revellers had gone and the fire burned down to smoking embers, but still the four men continued playing. Behind the wooden counter the barman dozed on a high chair, a half finished drink before him, an empty bottle by his feet. The pub was silent except for the occasional rattling snore from the barman and the greasy-slick pat of the cards as they fell onto the stained table. The four men hadn't spoken now for over an hour; the cards spoke for them, and tiny movements of their hands, or a nod conveyed whole sentences. There were a dozen empty glasses on the floor and half that number again on the table, some with drink still in them, but long since gone flat.

Three of the players were obviously brothers: dark-haired, dark-eyed, with the same bone structure to their faces. They were dressed in rough working clothes, patched and worn, and carried with them an odour of fresh clay and sweat. Their hands were calloused, the nails dirty and broken, but they handled the cards as if they were delicate crystal.

The fourth player was totally different. He was taller than the brothers and almost excessively thin. He was dressed in a shabby black suit with a soiled white shirt and stained tie. And yet his iron-grey hair was neatly combed and gleaming and his short square-cut beard was carefully trimmed. His hands were long and thin, the nails clean and rounded, and he handled the cards with practised ease.

The four men had been playing for nearly four hours now and what for Colm, Diarmuid and Padraig had started out as a bit of sport had by now turned deadly serious, and they were playing with an almost frightening intensity.

The three brothers had been playing quietly together at their usual table in the corner of the room, when the stranger had come over and asked if he might join them for a couple of hands. Glad of the company they had agreed, and drank his health in the beer he bought. The stranger had lost steadily at first, small amounts to each of the brothers, but enough to excite their interest in the game. And then he began to win; a hand here and then another, and then he would lose one, win one, and win again. And slowly, but surely, he was winning steadily.

The brothers lost back what they had won earlier from him, and then they began to lose their own money. Occasionally one or other of them would win a hand, but only to lose it again quickly.

And the stranger, unlike the brothers who would immediately pocket their winnings, left what he had won on the table: an enticement and lure.

The night wore slowly on into morning, and gradually the sky to the east began to lighten in anticipation of the dawn. And the brothers had little else to lose.

The stranger laid his cards face down on the table. His sharp eyes touched each of the brothers in turn, and then he smiled. 'Well?'

Reluctantly Colm fanned his cards and dropped them onto the table, followed by Diarmuid and Padraig. The stranger smiled again. 'My hand wins,' he said quietly.

'Again,' Padraig said ominously.

'Perhaps once too often,' Diarmuid added.

'You've just about cleaned us out,' Colm said quietly, 'we don't have much left to wager.'

The stranger smiled, the corners of his mouth twisting upwards, but his eyes remaining cold and hard. 'You have

184

your lands, your house ... your souls. You have not lost everything.'

'If you think we're going to wager our land or house well ... you've got another think coming,' Colm said quickly.

The stranger touched the pile of money before him. 'How much would you make in a week,' he asked suddenly, 'three pence, sixpence, a shilling, two shillings? There is – *what* – five pounds here. Well, let's make it double or nothing.'

'But we cannot,' Colm said, 'we can't afford it.'

'How much would you say your land is worth?' the stranger persisted. 'Five pounds ... ten pounds; let's say ten pounds. I'll advance you ten pounds against the price of your land.'

'No!' Colm snapped.

'Yes,' Diarmuid and Padraig said quickly. Padraig turned to his older brother. 'What if we win?'

'What if we lose?'

And so they played another hand – and lost.

The old man smiled again. 'Let us now say that there is fifteen pounds on the table: five of mine, ten of yours. What else can we wager on?'

'We have nothing else,' Colm said forcefully. 'You have taken our land; what else does that leave us?'

'Why, your cottage of course. And how much is that worth?' He waved the question aside with his hand. 'Well, let's say ... fifteen pounds shall we?' His eyes were flat, blank and unblinking, like a reptile's. 'Shall we play?'

There was something manic about the game now. Each of the brothers felt that the initiative had been taken away from them, that they were little more than puppets being manipulated. To gamble everything: money, lands, cottage, and for such huge sums was absolute craziness, pure madness, folly ... and yet they continued playing.

The old man dealt the cards with practised ease, his fingers seeming barely to move, yet sending the paste boards skimming across the table to land, face down, before each brother. The atmosphere was electric as they slowly examined the cards – and the game continued.

They played – and won!

One moment they had nothing, and the next everything again: house, lands, money. It took a moment for the truth to sink in, but before they could react the stranger said calmly, 'Double or nothing?'

Something inside Colm screamed, *No ... No ...* but he found himself carefully shuffling the slick cards and slowly dealing them around the table. Double or nothing.

And so they played and they lost.

The old man smiled, and this time his whole face lit up. 'You can pay me what you owe me now,' he said quietly.

'We cannot,' Colm said numbly, 'we don't have that sort of money.'

'Oh dear ... But you do of course acknowledge your debt. But naturally this man is a witness to it all ... is that not so?' He swivelled around in the chair and looked across at the barman, who was wide awake and staring in amazement at the small group. He glared at the brothers.

'You're mad; what in God's Holy Name have you done? By Christ, you've sacrificed your house, your land ... and to what? A vagabond, a worthless tinker ...'

'Have a care my man,' the stranger said coldly, 'you may regret what you say. And bear in mind that you were a witness to what happened here tonight.'

'You *amadans*,' the barman suddenly shouted, 'he might as well own you now.'

The old man nodded seriously. 'I do own them.'

Colm began trembling violently, the gambling fever beginning to fade and realisation setting in. What about their mother ... where would she go, what would happen to her ... what would happen to them? It was the workhouse for paupers. He bent down to pick up his drink. The floor beneath the table was littered with bottles and glasses, clumps of earth and turf. He saw his brothers' bare feet, one twisted around the legs of the chair, the other firmly on the floor, and ... something else!

'*Jesus God!*' He erupted upwards, sending the table toppling over the stranger, and pushing his two brothers backwards at the same time. Glasses shattered and then a line of bottles behind the barman exploded one by one. The embers in the grate flared and the gas lamp blazed as an icy wind whipped through the empty pub. The lamp swung wildly on its chain before exploding into a ball of flame, but luckily most of the flames died on the damp earthen floor and the barman quickly beat out the others. The windows – with their thick bubbled glass – cracked and the door was ripped off its hinges and cannoned through the small room, crushing tables and chairs beneath its weight. And then the wind died as suddenly as it had begun.

There was silence in the pub for a long time after that, the only sound the steady dripping of alcohol from the shattered bottles. When the barman eventually did light a candle, he found the three brothers lying huddled beneath the overturned tables and chairs. The stranger was gone, but there was a stench of burned wood. On the underside of one table that lay directly across the door they found two cloven hoof-marks burned into the wood.

Chapter Thirteen

THE LAST OUTPOST

Between the shadowland of night and dawn the old magic still lingered, touching the mound with the ancient mystery that had once claimed the entire island. And in a way it was now an island, a relic from the distant past drifting serenely into the present and an uncertain future.

'What do you mean, they refuse to flatten it?' The American accent was raw and harsh on the chill morning air.

Michael Hughes smiled tightly, mastering his growing anger. 'The workmen have refused to level the fort – *that* mound.' He pointed across the hedgerows towards the low mound rising out from the morning mist which clung to the damp fields.

'Is this a goddam strike or what?' the small, dark American demanded angrily, colour beginning to seep into his cheeks.

'No, Mr Weiss,' Michael Hughes said evenly, no longer smiling now. 'It is not a strike. That hill is an ancient burial mound, a faerie fort, and for starters the workmen – Irish workmen remember – are extremely reluctant to bulldoze part of their national heritage ...'

'National heritage crap!' Weiss snapped.

'And secondly,' Hughes continued in the same even tone, 'it has a certain reputation. It is a faerie fort and they believe it would be unlucky – if not downright dangerous – to attempt to interfere with it.'

188

'What is it?' Weiss demanded. 'More money? Do they want more money? Give it to them! We're already four weeks behind schedule, and in five days' time there's a quarter million dollars worth of prefabricated buildings and equipment coming in here. I want an empty – *flat* – field to put it in. Is that understood Mr Hughes?'

'It's not the money,' Michael said quietly, 'they really believe that if they bulldoze the fort then something bad will happen.'

'If they don't bulldoze that ... that fort, then something bad will happen!'

Michael looked down at the angry strutting man, ridiculous in a three-piece suit with the trousers tucked into a pair of high green boots. 'And what do you mean by that?' he asked quietly, his breath pluming on the cold air.

Weiss looked up slowly. He smiled at the younger man, his lips drawing back from his too perfect teeth and his eyes remaining cold. When he spoke his Brooklyn accent was more pronounced. 'Then I think that my company which, I might add, has invested a lot of money in this project which would undoubtedly benefit this underdeveloped region, would be forced to reconsider its investment.' He finished slightly breathlessly and smiled triumphantly.

Michael Hughes shook his head and smiled. 'Mr Weiss,' he said slowly, and with something like pity in his voice, 'you have neither the power nor the authority to make such grand sweeping statements.' His voice changed slightly and took on a touch of humour. 'Whatever you may like to think yourself, you are little more than a sites manager.'

The American's face turned livid. He raised nis hand and pointed his fingers at the younger man's ace. 'You ...'

'Your company,' Michael continued, 'stanas to make a sizeable profit from this site, and it will also benefit from the numerous concessions that the Irish Government offers companies like yours which decide to invest here.'

The American visibly mastered his anger. He stepped

closer to the Irishman, and Michael could smell the nauseous odour of stale beer on his breath. 'And all you have to do, boy, is to act as a go-between; I'll take no crap from you. Back in NY ...'

'But we are not in New York,' Michael said calmly, 'we are in Ireland, and we do things differently here.'

Weiss suddenly changed tactics. He had become conscious that many of the workmen had gathered around and were listening intently to the argument. 'Mr Hughes, I am making a formal request that you ask your men to bulldoze that hill,' he said icily.

'They have refused.'

'I will, of course, be forced to make a full report on this matter,' Weiss said stiffly. 'What reason shall I give for their refusal to work?'

'They have not refused to work; they have refused to flatten that mound ...'

'What reason, Mr Hughes,' Weiss persisted.

'Fear, Mr Weiss,' Michael said, turning away, 'fear.'

When the world was young and magic and mystery still abounded; when the lands themselves were not fully shaped; when the creatures of imagination walked the fields and monsters ruled the depths of the new oceans, then the gods walked this world and communed with the sons and daughters of man. And some came across the seas in their great glittering ships that were of metal and precious stones. These were the Tuatha De Danann, the People of the Goddess, and gods themselves in their own right, and their power and majesty held sway over the small emerald isle for generations.

The Tuatha defeated many enemies and scoured the land of evil, but in the end they fell to the slayer of all gods: time. And slowly the power of the Tuatha was eroded away. New gods rose and came to prominence on the island, and foremost amongst these was the One God, the Christ. The people gradually forgot the gods of their forebears and the People of the Goddess became as other lost gods: more than mortal, but less than divine.

And so they retreated to the Secret Places: the hidden valleys, the Lands Beneath the Waves, the Magical Isles and the Worlds Below. Their numbers dwindled, but they survived in myth and legend as the Shining Ones, the Sidhe, the *gentry*, and time and ignorance confused them with their servants, the Dark Folk, and they became collectively known as the Faerie Host.

But they lived on.

And some remained in the Worlds Below, which could only be entered through the Faerie Forts.

Michael held the telephone a few inches from his ear and allowed the irate voice to drone out into the empty room. When there was a pause he put the receiver back to his ear. 'All I know,' he said patiently, 'is that the workmen have refused to bulldoze the mound. It's an ancient artifact, a local attraction ... Yes sir, I know there's a lot of money at stake here...' He paused and listened again. 'Look,' he said finally, 'there is nothing I can do. I've spoken to the men and I've met with a point blank refusal ... They've refused offers of more money, and they laughed when I threatened to fire them. And at the moment,' he added, 'they are in touch with their local T.D. in an attempt to have this whole project stopped – or if not stopped then at least relocated, and yes, I do know how much that would cost.'

There was silence at the other end of the line and then it abruptly went dead. Michael slammed down the receiver. What a mess: it was blowing up out of all proportion.

He had known something was brewing for the past few days. The workmen – locals employed under the direct labour scheme – had been growing increasingly nervous as the fields on either side of the low mound had been cleared and levelled, and he had been asked on more than one occasion whether they were actually intending to flatten the mound. He had answered cautiously that it was in the plans, but the workmen had only smiled and said that they were sure that he was only joking, and sure why would he want them to do something like that ...?

But that morning, when he had instructed the foreman in the day's work schedule – which included the levelling of the fort – the men had refused to work.

The phone rang again, but it was probably Weiss, checking to see if he had received that call from Dublin. He let it ring.

Outside the sun had burned off most of the mist, leaving the ground fresh and sparkling as if it had been dusted with broken glass. Although the window had been painted shut a long time ago, he could still smell the morning freshness of the air. He could see the tops of the trees moving in the breeze blowing in from the west, and low clouds scudded across the clear sky. From where he stood he could see the top of the mound over the roofs of the cottages opposite the hotel and across the hedgerows. To the south of the mound the land looked curiously bare; no hedges bisected the fields, no trees clumped together in the corners of the same fields ... there was nothing. Nothing except the garish yellow of the diggers and the drabness of the trucks in the flattened fields.

What price progress, he asked himself.

It was some time after eleven, and the trucks and diggers should have been moving and the air above the fields filled with shouts, the roar of engines and a thick blanket of dust. But there was no movement, no sound, and the only dust in the air was that which had been raised by the wind.

Karl – Carl, since he had long since dropped his Polish

connections – Weiss walked slowly around the low mound, his green rubber boots squelching in the sodden ground. He had been around the mound twice now, and he still could see nothing special about it, but the locals believed it to be a faerie fort, a burial mound, a barrow and God knows what else ... and they refused to dig it up. His own parents had come from one of the most superstitious stock in Europe, and they had carried their superstitions with them into the New World, but at least time and exposure to the twentieth century had rounded off some of their peasant edges. These Irish ... Christ, but some of them were still living in the last century.

The city people were all right, they at least knew which side their bread was buttered. But these country people ... The small dark American smiled ruefully; the thing was he had dealt mainly with country people when he had been negotiating this deal, and by God, but they were sharp! It was a country of contrasts ... and complete unpredictability.

He scrambled up the low mound, bending almost double and using the long wet grass to help himself upwards. It was at times like this that he remembered that he was no longer a young man. He dug his heels in and paused, pulling out a white handkerchief and mopping his face, while he allowed his heart time to slow down somewhat; his doctor had warned him about overtaxing himself. His rubber boots slipped with a squeak on the wet grass. With a sigh he put away his handkerchief and heaved himself upwards, pulling on the tufts ... and then he swore as a thin line of fire ran across his palm. He pulled out his handkerchief again and wrapped it across the long grass cut: this was not going to be his day! But he persisted and climbed up to the crest of the mound and stood there for a while, staring out over the fields, flat and dark and ugly to the south, the raw earth showing through like an ugly festering wound, contrasting sharply with the lush greenness to the north and east, and with the splash of colour of the houses to the west. He breathed in the fresh, clear air – and coughed. He missed the city smog.

Unnoticed by him, the blood from his cut palm seeped through the cotton handkerchief and dripped onto the ground, soaking into the grass.

Michael Hughes paused by the hotel desk and handed in his key. Dave Conlon grinned sympathetically at Michael's expression. 'You've had a hard morning of it, I hear.'

'News travels fast,' Michael said quietly.

'Ah sure, I didn't need to be told; I knew the lads wouldn't touch the fort.'

'Well, I wish you'd told me,' Michael said ruefully.

Dave Conlon grinned. 'Sure I thought you knew.'

Michael shook his head. 'I thought the men were having a bit of sport at my expense; I didn't think they were serious when they said they wouldn't touch the fort.'

'But you should have known.'

'How could I ... born and bred in the city, remember?'

Dave shrugged. 'Aye, well I suppose you're not as well up in the country lore in the city.'

Michael leaned across the polished wooden counter. 'Tell me why they won't flatten the mound then?' he asked. 'What's the significance?'

The small balding man folded his newspaper and laid it to one side. He took off his glasses and polished them on a scrap of cloth. 'Well now, you see, that fort goes back a long way, it's one of the reasons this town is here; you see, the town – it was a village then – was built beside the fort, so that the villagers would always be under the protection of the faerie folk. Down through the years many stories have grown up around that fort. I don't know the half of them, but old Matt, who drinks in Nelligan's, the pub next door, would be able to tell you quite a few if you were interested. He's related to an old witch who used to live around here, a

194

Nano Hayes, and her name is always connected with the fort.

'It's said that the last of the faerie folk live beneath the mound, and once, in my grandfather's time I think, they even found the body of a young girl lying at the foot of it one bright November morning, just after Hallowe'en.* The story goes that she was taken by the Sidhe for spying on them.' He shrugged. 'It's just a story, but sometimes, when the moon is full, you can hear all the dogs in the town howling and baying out in the direction of the mound ...'

Michael caught the twinkle in the other's eye and laughed. 'Why you ... I may be from Dublin, but I am Irish, and I can smell a story like that a mile away.' He paused and added quietly. 'However, you might try it on our American friend.'

Conlon grinned. 'I already have. He wasn't too keen on it either. Ah, but he's a sour puss ...'

'Where is he now?' Michael asked, suddenly interested.

'Oh, he's out. He left here some fifteen minutes ago, cursing and swearing like a trooper.'

'Where did he go?'

'He headed off down the street. He's probably going to the workings; he had his boots on.'

'Thanks.' Michael ran from the small hotel and darted across the street, squinting against the hard morning sunlight that reflected back from the whitewashed cottages and colourfully painted shops. He cut down a side street between two thatched cottages and then across a second, smaller street and down a lane between the newer shop buildings and out into the fields. He swore as he sank up to his ankles in the soft mire, the liquid muck seeping in over the tops of his shoes and staining the ends of his trousers. He kept to the edge of the fields and skirted the worst of the desolation, remembering the fields – clean, fresh and green

* see 'Into the Shadowland' *Irish Folk and Fairy Tales vol. 1*

– as they had been barely three weeks previously. The new project had certainly brought prosperity to the small country town, but the price had been high.

He met Weiss close to the foot of the mound. The small American was red-faced and covered in a light sheen of sweat. Strands of hair, which were usually trained across his balding head, hung down by the side of his face, giving him a curiously decrepit appearance. His pin-striped three-piece suit was stained and rumpled and there were dark patches of thick mud on the knees. He was holding his left arm awkwardly and there was a blood-soaked handkerchief wrapped around his hand.

He walked right past Michael without saying a word, and then he stopped abruptly. Without turning around he snapped. 'You get that mound levelled Mr Hughes, or I'll bring in my own men and do the job myself.'

Michael stood in silence watching him make his way across the field. He didn't doubt that the American would carry out his threat and bring in outsiders. How would the townspeople react then, he wondered? He shivered, suddenly realising how cold it had become, and turned up the collar of his light jacket, tucked his hands into the pockets and followed the American back across the fields towards the town.

Time had passed the mound by. It had been old when the followers of the New God had come in their frail crafts to the island's shore, and later, when the yellow-haired and pale-eyed Northerners devastated much of the surrounding countryside, they had left the mound alone.

Armies had camped in the fields around the mound, time and custom changing their clothing and weaponry, although in many cases the cause remained the same, but curiously enough they never actually camped on the slopes of the fort, nor posted lookouts on its crest, although it commanded an excellent view of the surrounding fields. For although the De Danann were gone, their magic and mystery remained, and time had enhanced the legends.

A blast of cold air whipped in around him as Michael pushed open the door to the pub. He stepped inside quickly and brushed off the worst of the rain onto a large rush mat before shrugging off his coat. Although he had only run in from the hotel next door he was soaked through.

The change in the weather had come on quickly, with a cold front moving in from the north, bringing rain and sleet with it. A razor wind cut down through the town's broad main street and whistled through the alleyways, and the only creature moving outside was a bedraggled stray.

The pub was warm and close, a huge open fire burning at one end of the room; shaded, low-wattage bulbs giving everything a faintly dusky appearance. Heads turned in his direction, nodding briefly before turning back to their drink or conversation. Many were from the works, others were local farmers, shopkeepers or the townspeople. Conversation was low and muted with a sudden shout of laughter rising briefly before sinking back into the general murmur of the room. Michael made his way around the small circular tables to the crowded bar, nodding at people he knew. He ordered a pint, and leaned back against the polished wooden bar sipping the dark white-headed Guinness while he watched the people.

To one end of the room, grouped around the fire, were the workmen, drinking quietly together, their faces serious and anxious; they seemed to be listening to someone, probably Banim, the foreman. Along the walls of the pub were the townspeople; the professions – doctor, teacher, clergy – sitting together, sharing a private joke, although they kept glancing across at the workmen. And then there were the shopkeepers and the farmers, some of the latter still in their working clothes and boots, with the women sitting quietly at one table, heads close together.

In a town like this everyone had their place – and knew it. In the pub only he was the outsider.

Michael turned around and caught the barman's eye. 'Old Matt,' he asked, 'is he in tonight?'

The barman looked hard at him for a few minutes and then jerked his head towards the fire and the group of workmen before turning away.

Michael eased his way through the crowd towards the fireplace and, as he neared, he could hear a soft voice, cracked with age, droning on. 'And then of course there was that time in Galway when a local man, an O'Grady I think it was, uprooted one of *their* trees. Well, no sooner had he done so when a terrible wailing and crying started up, and the sap on the tree turned bright red and flowed like blood, and the branches twisted and formed themselves into limbs until the whole tree took on the likeness of a young woman. It may be there still.' The voice paused and then added in a different tone, 'Of course O'Grady isn't; it doesn't do to interfere with the faeries.'

'What will happen then if the mound is flattened?' Michael asked suddenly.

There was a long moment's silence in which all heads turned in his direction. Old Matt settled back into his chair by the fire and lifted his half-finished pint from the table. He sipped from it and then shrugged his bony shoulders. 'I don't know,' he confessed. 'I believe however, that the Faerie Host might come out,' he added with a wry smile.

'And then again, they might not,' Michael said quietly.

The old man shrugged again. 'They might not,' he agreed, 'but I would certainly not like to put it to the test.'

Heads nodded in agreement as Michael looked around the group. 'Do you know that Weiss has threatened to bring in his own men to finish the job,' he said into the silence.

'It's their funeral,' someone said from near the bar.

Michael spun around. 'No, it's *your* funeral. This plant can put the town on the map, and bring in a lot of money ... *if* you cooperate. But if word gets out that you were not willing to honour your contracts and finish the construction ...' He trailed off, looking at the blank, shut faces; he just wasn't getting through to them.

'The Faerie Host rode out in my grandmother's time,' Matt said quietly. 'One of them claimed a human bride but was then forced to return her when the girl's husband came looking for her. Not long after that a young girl was found dead at the foot of the mound on the morning after All Hallows' Eve, and there was another time when my grandmother told me that she had been blessed by the faerie folk for a great service that she had done them.'* The pub had gone deathly silent, the only sound the hissing of the fire and the distant sound of wind and rain. 'And although my grandmother was a poor woman and had lived here nearly all her life,' Matt continued, 'she died wealthy ... a very wealthy woman indeed.' The old man finished his drink and continued quickly. 'They *are* there, the faerie folk, charming and delightful when they want to be, dangerous and capricious at will. They have slept for a generation, let them sleep in peace,' he begged.

Michael shook his head. 'There's nothing I can do. If it was my decision ...' he shrugged, 'but it's not.'

'But you can talk to your office, explain the situation ...'

'I already have; the project is to go ahead.'

A short burly man stood up from his seat beside the fire. 'If the American brings in his own men they'll get no cooperation from anyone in the town: there'll be no lodgings, no shop will sell them food and no pub will serve them drink. We can make it hard for them.'

'Mr Banim,' Michael said quietly, 'you're a small country

---

*see 'The Magic Lingers On' ... 'Into the Shadowland' ... 'Into Eternity' ... *Irish Folk & Fairy Tales vol. 1* town; you cannot go against the Irish Government and a large American corporation. They have both invested a lot of money in this project, and they are not going to stand by and see it wasted.'

'If they flatten the mound,' Matt said in a voice that was little more than a whisper, 'they may not have any choice.'

From the window of his hotel room Weiss could see the fields and the rusting machinery over the roofs of the cottages. A thin moon slipped from between the racing clouds, touching the metal with silver and coating the crest of the low mound in harsh reflective light.

Rain patterned against the window, and the small American absently rubbed his hand across the misted glass and squinted down into the rain-washed street. For a brief moment he found himself wondering what this town must have looked like a hundred years ago; similar to countless small country towns all across Europe, he should imagine; similar to the town from which his grandparents would have emigrated to the States.

He wiped down the glass again and looked across at the mound. He had spent the day in Dublin, checking through the countless volumes of folklore, myth and legend in the libraries and bookshops ... and he had come away more than a little disturbed.

He had come away with the knowledge that in no other country in Europe was the faerie tradition so strongly maintained and believed in by the country people. He had read some of the folklore collected by people like Hyde, Yeats, Lady Gregory, O'Sullivan and many, many more. And if one single fact stood out in the vast wealth of material that was available, it was the belief – the firmly held belief – that the faeries, the *gentry*, the leprechaun, the Shining Ones, the *ban* and *mna shee* existed.

Clouds closed in and the moonlight abruptly vanished,

plunging the countryside into darkness ... and that terrified Weiss. Born and reared in the heart of the city that never sleeps, he had never really known total darkness until this trip to Ireland. Beyond the town there was nothing, no lights – except the dim and distant beams of a car's headlights, and they only served somehow to intensify the darkness – no sound, except the soughing of the wind – the loneliest sound in the world.

With the light gone, there was only his own reflection in the glass, and he turned away. On the table beside his bed a couple of empty bottles lay side by side with those which had yet to be drunk. Weiss used a bottle-opener and prised the top off one and began to drink straight from the bottle. He flopped down on the hard bed and continued drinking; there was precious little else to do in this God-forsaken hole of a town.

He awoke much later that night, lying flat out across the bed, still fully dressed. The air in the room was close and heavy with the odours of stale sweat, spilled drink ... and something else. Weiss lay there, slowly becoming aware of the sudden chill in the room and the brightness outside his window. He sat up slowly, his heart beginning to pound and cold perspiration slowly trickling down his neck. His hand was trembling as he reached for the bedside light, but when he flicked the switch nothing happened.

A shadow moved across the window: tall and thin, with two hard points of green-gold light where the eyes should be. Weiss froze, the pounding of his heart increasing rapidly and painfully. He pushed his way up on the bed until his back touched the headboard and he drew his knees up to his chin. He tried to speak, but no sound came out.

The shadow-figure glided closer to the bed, the moonlight streaming through the window giving it both shape and definition. It was a man, excessively tall and thin as he had already noticed, and the moonlight touched his long, slightly Asiatic face with silver, with the shadows accentuating the high cheekbones, the pointed chin, the sharply tipped ears. And his eyes were like polished emeralds. They bored through the crouching American, stripping bare his soul, seeking the undersized Brooklyn urchin that still hid beneath the bluster.

Weiss didn't know how long the tableau lasted, but then the figure smiled, his teeth startlingly white against the shadow of his face, and the American buried his head in his arms and prayed, for the first time in over three decades, to a God he thought he had forgotten.

When he awoke the sun was streaming in through the window, a long bar of harsh light lying warmly across his face. He groaned and rolled over, allowing his senses time to reorientate themselves ... and came shockingly alert. His dream of the previous night returned vividly – or was it a dream? He could remember every detail with vivid clarity; surely it had been too real, too frightening to be a dream.

And all his dreams had died in his youth.

He examined the locks on the doors, but they were intact and didn't seem to have been tampered with. The window was painted shut, and the room adjoining his – a tiny bathroom – was windowless. Of course, it could have been one of the townspeople trying to frighten him, he reasoned. He checked the walls, tapping for any hollow spots, but they all seemed solid enough, and the ceiling was covered with squares of white tiling. Therefore no one could have entered the room, and it must have been a dream; there was no other reasonable explanation.

And Carl Weiss was not even prepared to consider any other explanations.

The new workers began arriving in the small town around noon. They were city men, mainly from Dublin and Belfast, with a few from Cork and Waterford, and their foreman was a short, stocky Londoner. The townspeople watched their arrival in silence, and waited until the buses departed, leaving the men standing in sullen silence, and then one by one they turned away, leaving the outsiders alone on the broad, windswept street.

Michael Hughes watched them from his bedroom window. He had just come from a long talk with Banim, in a last ditch attempt to try and have the work go ahead, but the foreman was adamant: his men would not touch the mound.

Weiss appeared below. He seemed more than a little drunk, his normally florid face was flushed and his eyes were protruding. He conversed with the new workers for a few moments, his arms moving wildly, and when he was finished the men raised a ragged cheer, before turning and tramping off towards the fields.

Shortly afterwards the sound of engines rent the quiet country air, and a cloud of dust rose up and quickly blanketed the fields. The noise and activity continued until darkness fell and then scores of camp fires blossomed up, studding the fields with shivering lights – and also answering one of Michael's questions: where was Weiss going to lodge the workers. Michael grinned slightly; it was a cold, damp field, and promised to be a wet and windy night, and he certainly wouldn't care to be spending a night under canvas.

Michael wandered down from his room close to midnight. He couldn't sleep, there was something in the air, something like a brewing storm, a tenseness ... an expectancy. He walked slowly down the cold, damp streets, his leather soled shoes echoing hollowly off the old stone walls. On more than one occasion he saw the curtains twitch or a shadow move behind the windows; it seemed he was not the only one who could not sleep that night. Almost unconsciously he found himself walking in the direction of the camp. There had been singing and shouting earlier on that evening, but the only sounds now on the night air were the crackled settlings of the many camp fires and the ghostly whistling of the wind ... and that too was strange, for they were the *only* sounds. He stood still and listened; no night birds called, nothing rustled through the grass ... silence.

He kept close to the hedges at the edge of the field and made his way towards the fort. There was a crescent-shaped moon high in the heavens, surrounded by a ghostly nimbus of cloud, shedding a delicate illumination over everything. Every now and again it would disappear behind a thick black cloud, but these were few and far between, and Michael had a torch tucked into his pocket. When he reached the edge of the field the moon disappeared briefly, and he stood quietly watching the silver move slowly behind the cloud, and then gracefully reappear again.

Although he had been expecting it, it was still something of a shock to discover the damage the diggers had done to the mound. Most of the field around it had been torn up and the side closest to him had been gouged out, and it gaped like a dark, open wound. At this rate they would have the entire fort flattened by noon tomorrow.

Michael took a step forward – and then something struck him across the base of the spine, sending him sprawling into the mire. A booted foot came down inches from his face and a hard hand gripped his hair and pulled his head back.

'Well, what have we got here?' The voice was flat and heavy with a Dublin accent.

Michael was yanked to his feet, his arm twisted painfully behind his back, forcing him up onto his toes. 'Put me down ... what 'n hell's going on?' he demanded.

'Well Mr Hughes, I must admit I never expected to find you here.' A torch snapped on, blinding him, and then flicked off again. When the orange spots on his retina disappeared, he found he could make out Carl Weiss and

204

another worker standing before him. The American nodded at the Dubliner holding Michael. 'Let him go ... but make sure Mr Hughes doesn't try to go anywhere,' he added. 'I must admit,' he continued thoughtfully, 'I had rather imagined that you would send some of your friends along to do your dirty work for you ...'

'What are you talking about?' Michael snapped. His spine was throbbing and the ribs in his lower back ached; he would bring charges for assault.

The small American smiled, his face bone-white in the moonlight, his teeth alabaster chips against the dark hollow of his mouth. 'Come now Mr Hughes, let's not play the innocent. Do you deny that you came here tonight with the intention of sabotaging some of our equipment, and then laying the blame on the ... faeries?' His voice was heavy with sarcasm, and tinged with something else which Michael couldn't identify.

'You forget, Mr Hughes,' he continued drily, 'I am American, and in the States we do things differently ... and that includes protecting our investment.' He nodded at the two burly guards. 'There are men staked out all around this camp,' he announced proudly, 'and as soon as any of your friends come near the machinery or the mound, well ...' He let the sentence hang.

'What will we do with him?' the Dubliner asked suddenly.

Weiss stared at Michael for a long time, and the young man suddenly felt his blood run cold, for the small, soft American, ridiculous in his three-piece suit and rubber boots was gone, and in his place stood a small and dangerous animal, with sharp, pitiless eyes and a scavenger's grin.

'I think Mr Hughes deserves to be taught a lesson,' the American whispered, his lips smiling, but his eyes remaining hard and cold. 'It will also show our village friends that we mean business ... and who knows, perhaps they'll reconsider their foolish decision to shun us.' Weiss turned away. 'He's all yours,' he said quietly to the two workers.

Michael managed to cry out once, and then an open hand cracked across his face, numbing him with shock rather than pain, and he was too stunned even to resist as his other arm was now hauled up behind his back and twisted savagely.

Time was a human measurement and the elven folk did not number the passing days and keep the fleeting years. If anything of theirs reckoned time, it was a subtle appreciation of nature, of spans of growth, decay and regrowth ... for there was no death in the elven fields.

And yet if they did measure time as humans did, it might be said that they had rested in their hidden world for many years without appearing and walking the fields of man. The last time they had sallied forth had been ... when? One human generation ago? Two? More?

But the humans did not bother them and they, in turn, did not interfere with the sons of man. Occasionally they felt the fleeting touches of human emotions: fear, wonder, awe and sometimes amusement as someone walked the mound.

But lately there had been a great disturbance, both mental and physical. Many, many humans walked the fields above their heads, and the very soil itself was racked with pain.

And now the fort itself was under attack.

The descendants of the Tuatha De Danann had felt with an almost personal and physical pain the huge mechanical diggers ripping into the sides of the mound. They knew that even if the entire mound was levelled to the ground they would still survive, but the mound was a link with the fields of man, one of the last links ...

The Faerie Host rode forth.

Michael's head exploded in pain, lights flaring behind his

eyes, and his ears began to throb painfully. He cried aloud, his mind shouting pain, before his senses registered that he had not, in fact, been struck. He heard a shout and then another, and then he was suddenly thrown to the ground, and he heard booted feet running across the soft earth.

Michael sat up stiffly, his eyes blinking wide in astonishment, for the night was bright with a soft glowing light. It was softer than moonlight and yet stronger, and flowed from the ripped-out side of the faerie fort, gathering into a pale glowing fog that drifted across the fields swathing everything within its folds. He cringed as the thick white blanket slowly enfolded him. It was surprisingly warm and dry, not cold and wet, and carried with it the odours of strange herbs and spices. Sounds became muffled, and the shouts of fear and anger were quickly dulled and then lost within it, and the air became leaden and still. There was silence for what seemed like a long time, and then haunting notes drifted through the night, snatches of old songs, whispers and tendrils of music hung on the air as if they could be touched.

Michael felt a longing well up deep inside him; a desire, an overpowering, overwhelming desire for ... what? He didn't know. He brushed away the sudden sting of tears with the back of his hand. He felt as if he had lost something ... something ... something ...

And he never realised that he wept for his youth, his lost innocence.

Shadows moved through the fog; tall, thin creatures that strode purposefully past him, metal clinking and jangling as they moved, and once he thought he heard a horse whinny.

Slowly, his back and spine throbbing painfully, Michael eased himself to his feet and began to walk towards the mound and the source of the light. He discovered then that there was a slight breeze blowing away from the mound, a warm, scented breeze that somehow reminded him of the long hot summers of his youth. The musical notes were more audible now; they hung sweet and clear like no other tune he had ever heard. And then there was a single note, a clarion call. He heard a rhythmic jangling and a steady throbbing beat coupled with a metallic tingling on the air. He stood indecisively, listening to it rapidly approaching him ... and then he abruptly realised what he was hearing.

Michael threw himself to one side as the Faerie Host rode back into the fields of man. A flailing hoof caught the sole of his shoe, and the blow jarred his leg all the way up to his hip: these were no ghosts, no shadows! He had a momentary glimpse of tall, thin proud figures clad in fantastic garb, riding mounts that were equally strange, before the glowing fog closed in again – and the screaming started.

He was lying on his back in the middle of the field when he awoke. He was shivering violently and his clothes were sodden with dew. He attempted to rise, and then groaned aloud as his stiff joints and muscles protested and the pain in the small of his back and twisted shoulders made itself felt.

The morning was silent; no birds sang, no creatures moved through the grass, no wind disturbed the trees ... and he experienced the same feeling he had the night before – one of expectancy about the place. He found he was alone in the field, there was no sign of the new workers, their camp or Weiss ... even the traces of the camp fires had vanished. Michael came slowly to his feet and limped painfully across the field towards the mound. Mist still clung to its sides, and it swirled and coiled about him as he moved into it, shifting and weaving like a nest of serpents.

And when he reached the side of the fort he found it was whole again!

There was no trace of the gaping hole where the mechanical diggers had torn out the side, no flattened grass,

208

scarred with heavy track and tyre marks.

There was a figure sitting atop the mound wrapped in a long silver-edged green cloak. He turned his head and gestured with one long thin hand, calling Michael up.

The young man hauled himself up the side of the fort, slipping and sliding on the dew-damp grass, while the stranger merely sat there, staring out across the fields, neither looking at him, nor making any effort to help. There was an air of complete detachment about him, and as Michael neared him, he began to make out the differences in the stranger.

Although he was sitting cross-legged and partially enveloped in the long cloak, Michael's first impression was of height coupled with extreme thinness. His head seemed almost misshapen; high cheekbones and a pronounced suborbital ridge gave his eyes a sunken appearance. His chin protruded and came to a point, and his ears were set close to his head and pointed also and tipped with tufts of fine black hair that matched the hair on his head.

'Who ... who are you?' Michael panted.

The young man's eyes flicked across at him and then turned back to his surveillance of the fields. Michael sat down beside him, drawing his legs up to his chin and resting his pounding head on them. A fit of shivering took him, leaving him exhausted.

'My name is Aran,' the stranger said suddenly, his voice – crystal clear and almost vibrant – startling Michael.

'Michael,' he introduced himself.

'I know.' Again that disquieting flick of the eyes before they turned back to the fields.

'What happened last night?' Michael asked eventually, when the youth made no move to say anything else.

'We rode.'

'We?'

The young man stood suddenly, unfolding himself with a

fluid grace; Michael eased himself to his feet, groaning aloud, and he found that Aran stood a head and more taller than him.

'Blood called us, and then we felt the disturbance,' the elven lord said, 'and the Host rode against the threat.'

Michael nodded. 'I see; what happened to the men?'

'They sleep in drunken slumber beyond the town; in the main they are unharmed, but they will never return to this place.'

'And the townsfolk?'

'They heard shouting and cries during the night, but they will assume it was a drunken brawl ... some of course will know, but they will say nothing.'

'And Weiss?' Michael asked finally.

But Aran only smiled and nodded towards the east. 'The sun rises, I cannot linger.' He started to walk down the side of the mound.

'Wait ... wait ...' Michael shook his head to clear it. He must be feverish, he had to be dreaming this. He slid down the side of the fort and came to a stop before the tall figure. 'Are you real?' he whispered.

Aran smiled, his teeth very pale and pointed. 'What do you think?'

'You look real ... but, faeries don't exist,' he finished in a rush.

'No, I suppose they don't,' Aran agreed.

'Then what are you?' Michael demanded.

'What do the country people call us?'

'The Shining Ones, the Sidhe, the Tuatha De Danann ...'

Aran nodded. 'And that is what we are. The last of the Tuatha De Danann, the People of the Goddess. We continue to exist because the people continue to believe in us. We are also tied to this land, and this is the last outpost of Faerie in this world. It will be a sadder, poorer place when we are gone – and that day is drawing ever closer.' The elven lord looked down on the young man. 'I am the last born of my race; born of a human mother and elven sire, mine was the first birth for many, many years. The elven race is dying, son of Man.'

'But ... but, what do you need to survive?'

'Faith!' And the elven lord walked down the side of the fort into the swirling mist, and was gone.

And Michael Hughes stood on the side of the mound and watched the sun rise over the last outpost of Faerie.

'Work on the Irish American project has been called off, it was announced last night. A re-evaluation of the costs involved, coupled with rising prices and spiralling inflation in Ireland, has caused the American backers to pull out and work on the project has stopped.

'Meanwhile, a verdict of accidental death has been returned in the case of Carl Weiss, the overseer of the project. Mr Weiss was found drowned in a river which runs close to the site of the projected plant. Mr Weiss, it is reported, suffered a massive heart attack.'